solutions@syngress.com

With more than 1,500,000 copies of our MCSE, MCSD, CompTIA, and Cisco study guides in print, we continue to look for ways we can better serve the information needs of our readers. One way we do that is by listening.

Readers like yourself have been telling us they want an Internet-based service that would extend and enhance the value of our books. Based on reader feedback and our own strategic plan, we have created a Web site that we hope will exceed your expectations.

Solutions@syngress.com is an interactive treasure trove of useful information focusing on our book topics and related technologies. The site offers the following features:

- One-year warranty against content obsolescence due to vendor product upgrades. You can access online updates for any affected chapters.

- "Ask the Author" customer query forms that enable you to post questions to our authors and editors.

- Exclusive monthly mailings in which our experts provide answers to reader queries and clear explanations of complex material.

- Regularly updated links to sites specially selected by our editors for readers desiring additional reliable information on key topics.

Best of all, the book you're now holding is your key to this amazing site. Just go to **www.syngress.com/solutions**, and keep this book handy when you register to verify your purchase.

Thank you for giving us the opportunity to serve your needs. And be sure to let us know if there's anything else we can do to help you get the maximum value from your investment. We're listening.

www.syngress.com/solutions

SYNGRESS®

1 YEAR UPGRADE

BUYER PROTECTION PLAN

CONFIGURING

Citrix MetaFrame XP

for Windows

Including Feature Release 1

Chris Broomes

Elias N. Khnaser

Ralph Crump

Melissa Craft Technical Editor

KEY	SERIAL NUMBER
001	KTY4T945T6
002	BTGRT4MPE3
003	SCHR63N56N
004	EVE34B32UN
005	97U8MU6CAR
006	NSC4RNTEM3
007	FRDVHTR47T
008	2BT9R564MR
009	73N5M4PNTS
010	ZX6YH23ZFC

PUBLISHED BY
Syngress Publishing, Inc.
800 Hingham Street
Rockland, MA 02370

Configuring Citrix MetaFrame XP for Windows

Printed in the United States of America

1 2 3 4 5 6 7 8 9 0

ISBN: 1-913836-53-1

Technical Editor: Melissa Craft
Technical Reviewers: Melissa Craft,
Thomas Eck, Elias Khnaser
Acquisitions Editor: Catherine B. Nolan
Developmental Editor: Kate Glennon

Cover Designer: Michael Kavish
Page Layout and Art by: Shannon Tozier
Copy Editor: Darlene Bordwell
Indexer: Robert Saigh

Distributed by Publishers Group West in the United States and Jaguar Book Group in Canada.

Acknowledgments

We would like to acknowledge the following people for their kindness and support in making this book possible.

Karen Cross, Lance Tilford, Meaghan Cunningham, Kim Wylie, Harry Kirchner, Kevin Votel, Kent Anderson, Frida Yara, Bill Getz, Jon Mayes, John Mesjak, Peg O'Donnell, Sandra Patterson, Betty Redmond, Roy Remer, Ron Shapiro, Patricia Kelly, Andrea Tetrick, Jennifer Pascal, Doug Reil, and David Dahl of Publishers Group West for sharing their incredible marketing experience and expertise.

Jacquie Shanahan, AnnHelen Lindeholm, David Burton, Febea Marinetti, and Rosie Moss of Elsevier Science for making certain that our vision remains worldwide in scope.

Annabel Dent and Paul Barry of Elsevier Science/Harcourt Australia for all their help.

David Buckland, Wendi Wong, Marie Chieng, Lucy Chong, Leslie Lim, Audrey Gan, and Joseph Chan of Transquest Publishers for the enthusiasm with which they receive our books.

Kwon Sung June at Acorn Publishing for his support.

Ethan Atkin at Cranbury International for his help in expanding the Syngress program.

Jackie Gross, Gayle Voycey, Alexia Penny, Anik Robitaille, Craig Siddall, Darlene Morrow, Iolanda Miller, Jane Mackay, and Marie Skelly at Jackie Gross & Associates for all their help and enthusiasm representing our product in Canada.

Lois Fraser, Connie McMenemy, Shannon Russell and the rest of the great folks at Jaguar Book Group for their help with distribution of Syngress books in Canada.

Contributors

Ralph "JJ" Crump (CCNP/CCDP, Citrix CCEA, MCSE, MCNE, Cisco Security Specialist, and Compaq ASE) is a Senior Consulting Engineer for an advanced solutions consulting firm in Atlanta, GA. He provides senior design and technical guidance for major clients focusing on enterprise deployments of thin-client, network, and security solutions. He has worked extensively in enterprise organizations designing and building infrastructure services and specializes in enterprise Citrix solutions, networking design and implementation, and security solutions. He has written several other books on similar topics including Microsoft Windows 2000, Network+, and Citrix CCA.

Craig Luchtefeld (MCSE, MCP+I, CCEA, CCNA) is a Senior Network Engineer for STL Technology Partners, a leading information technology systems provider in the Central Illinois region. Craig provides STL clients with network infrastructure planning, implementation, support, and troubleshooting. He specializes in server-based computing implementations and has played a key role in several Fortune 500 companies in the Midwest. Craig also contributed to the book *CCA Citrix MetaFrame XP for Windows Administrator Study Guide.*

Chris Broomes (MCSE, MCT, MCP+I, CCNA) is a Senior Network Analyst at Devon IT (www.devonitnet.com). Devon IT is a leading enterprise service provider specializing in voice and data network design, security, and VPN solutions based in King of Prussia, PA. Chris has worked in the IT industry for over nine years at large law firms, universities, and software manufacturers. He has a wide range of technical experience supporting and designing networks including Novell, DEC Pathworks, and AppleTalk, as well as Citrix WinFrame/MetaFrame and Windows NT/2000. Chris is also the President of Infinite Solutions Group, an IT consulting firm specializing in network design, integration and support, and training located in Lansdowne, PA. Chris is currently pursuing a M.S. in Information Science at Penn State University, as well as the CCDA, CCNP, and CISSP certifications. He is a member of the International Engineering Consortium. Chris has contributed to several study guides on Windows 2000, as well as to the *E-mail Virus*

Protection Handbook (Syngress Publishing, ISBN: 1-928994-23-7) and *Hack Proofing Your Web Applications* (Syngress Publishing, ISBN: 1-928994-31-8).

Connie Wilson (CAN, MSCE, CCA) is a Senior Network Engineer with GE Capital in a designated "Center of Excellence" technology site. Currently she has ultimate responsibility for design, implementation, and ongoing oversight of multiple Microsoft and MetaFrame servers supporting national and international GE divisions. Her specialties are troubleshooting, new product testing, thin client inter-company consulting, and systems optimization. Connie has a broad technology background with 15 years in progressively challenging IT work and a B.S. in Telecommunications. Before joining GE as an employee, Connie was an IT Consultant for GE, contracted primarily to bring a chronically problematic MetaFrame server farm to a high level of reliability.

Elias N. Khnaser (CCEA, MCSE, CCNA, CCA, MCP + I) is currently the Citrix Network Engineer for General Growth Properties. General Growth Properties is headquartered in Chicago, IL and is the second largest shopping mall owner and operator in the world, counting over 160 malls worldwide and growing. Elias provides senior-level network design, implementation, and troubleshooting of Citrix and Microsoft technologies for the company. Elias is also a contributing author at Techrepublic.com. Prior to working for General Growth Properties, Elias was a Senior Network Engineer at Solus in Skokie, IL, consulting for companies like Motorola, Prime Group Realty Trust, Black Entertainment Television (BET), Dominick's Corporate, and Total Living Network (TLN Channel 38).

Elias would like to acknowledge and thank the magnificent duo of Catherine Nolan and Kate Glennon of Syngress Publishing for their extraordinary patience and professionalism: thank you for making this a wonderful experience. Thanks also to Melissa Craft whose attention to the smallest detail was invaluable; to Steve Amidei and Chuck Tomczyk of General Growth Properties for their infinite support; to Stuart Gabel and Nial Keegan of Solus who opened the door of opportunity; to his friend Joseph K. Eshoo for all his help and encouragement, and to John Sheesley of Techrepublic.com for helping him write better articles. To his friends and family worldwide, this is for you! Finally, Elias would like to dedicate this work to his parents, especially his mother, and to the person that means everything in his life, Nadine Sawaya "Didi", for loving and supporting him.

Technical Editor

Melissa Craft Melissa Craft (CCNA, MCNE, MCSE, Network+, CNE-3, CNE-4, CNE-GW, CNE-5, CCA) is the Vice President and CIO for Dane Holdings, Inc., a financial services corporation in Phoenix, AZ, where she manages Web development, and the LAN and WAN for the company. During her career, Melissa has focused her expertise on developing enterprise-wide technology solutions and methodologies focused on client organizations. These technology solutions touch every part of a system's lifecycle, from assessing the need, determining the return on investment, network design, testing, and implementation to operational management and strategic planning.

In 1997, Melissa began writing magazine articles on networking and the information technology industry. In 1998, Syngress hired Melissa to contribute to an MCSE certification guide. Since then, Melissa has continued to write about various technology and certification subjects. She is the author of the best-selling *Configuring Windows 2000 Active Directory* (Syngress Publishing, ISBN: 1-928994-60-1), and *Configuring Citrix MetaFrame for Windows 2000 Terminal Services* (Syngress Publishing, ISBN: 1-928944-18-0).

Melissa holds a bachelor's degree from the University of Michigan and is a member of the IEEE, the Society of Women Engineers, and American MENSA, Ltd. Melissa currently resides in Glendale, AZ with her family, Dan, Justine, and Taylor.

Technical Reviewer

Thomas Eck (MCSE+I, MCSD, MCDBA, CCA, ASE, CNA, GCA) is a Senior Specialist with Perot Systems Corporation's Financial Services Industry Group. Currently, he is using his diverse background in development and system administration to manage an engineering/development team at a major global investment bank in the New York metropolitan area. His team develops tools to streamline and automate the bank's administrative and business processes on several Microsoft product platforms, and maintains particular focus on enterprise security, enforcement of business rules within administrative processes, and creating tools to empower users to securely manage their environment without engaging support staff. Thomas has written several books on system administration and development (including a best-selling title on Active Directory Service Interfaces) and writes regularly for *Windows & .NET Magazine*'s Solutions journals on the use of scripting for programmatic administration.

Contents

xi

**Advantages of
Distributed
Computing**

As many businesses have
discovered, the distributed
computing model carries
several advantages:

- Reduced hardware
  costs

- No single point of
  failure

- Flexibility

- Scalable architecture

Chapter 2 Farming MetaFrame XP Servers   55

Chapter 3 Routing and Remote Access   83

Direct Dial to Citrix MetaFrame XP

- Installing the Async ICA connection is done in Citrix Connection Configuration. A modem needs to be installed and configured before connections can be accepted.

- Using direct dial into Citrix servers is an extra burden on the servers and is not recommended unless the implementation is in a very small environment.

- In Citrix ICA Dial-In, encryption is limited to what ICA can offer. Encryption levels are 40-, 56-, and 128-bit.

Chapter 4 Designing the Thin Client Solution — 129

Data Storage

When designing a thin client solution, you need to consider two types of storage:

- **System storage** This is the location of the operating system files—the page file and the applications and system files.

- **User data storage** This is the storage of the user-specific configuration, user data, and system files.

**Basic Hard Disk
Configurations**

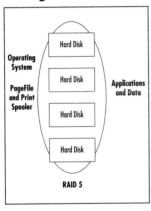

Chapter 6 Connecting Thin Clients 209

**Automating
Installation**

- Diskettes remain the simplest and easiest way to deal with small IT environments.

- Login scripts work very well; just make sure that you phase out your installation so as not to drastically increase network traffic and overflow your connection.

- Deployment servers such as Microsoft SMS, for example, should be used for large organizations with mixed IT environments.

Creating the ICA Sessions

ICA sessions are used in conjunction with MetaFrame XP servers. To create an ICA session, follow these steps:

1. Choose **Start | Programs | Citrix | MetaFrame XP | Citrix Connection Configuration**.

2. Click **Connection** and click **New**.

3. The New ICA Connection window appears. This time for **Type** we want to select **Citrix ICA 3.0** from the drop-down menu. Select the transport type you want to use from the **Transport** drop-down menu (for example, **async** for dial-in and modems, **TCP** for NIC cards). Use the tabs at the bottom of the screen to configure your protocol as we demonstrate later in the following section, then click **OK**.

Chapter 8 Citrix MetaFrame XP Management   **295**

Creating subfolders under the servers or applications folder in the CMC

1. Open the **CMC**.

2. Highlight either the applications folder or the servers folder.

3. Right-click the highlighted folder and click **New Folder** from the menu that pops up.

4. Once the subfolder has been created you can simply drag and drop servers or applications to it.

Deploying Applications to a Server Farm

Since a single server has limitations on the number of users it can handle before performance degradation becomes a noticeable issue for users, running the same application on multiple servers allows a server farm to combine the computing power of multiple single servers. To allow for this practice, Citrix has provided administrators two tools to help achieve this goal: Installation Manager and Load Manager.

**Encryption Strength
Options**

Citrix MetaFrame has five
encryption levels from
which to select:

■ Basic

■ 128-bit login only

■ 40-bit

■ 56-bit

■ 128-bit

Chapter 12 Printing   457

Web Server

The second component of NFuse is the Web server. Using a series of Java objects, extensions installed onto the Web server allow communication directly to the server farm to occur. The Java objects serve three functions:

- User authentication to the Citrix MetaFrame XP server farm

- Retrieving application sets based on user credentials

- Providing administrators the ability to modify the user experience without intervention

The Add Mappings Window

Business Drivers for Wireless Solutions

- Citrix solutions provide three main benefits: a consistent user experience; simplicity for IT workers who have to provide a consistent, powerful, effortless business access for business users; and a cost-effective transition to the Web-centric environment for organizations.

Chapter 14 Building a Portal   523

The Settings Window with Audio and Encryption Disabled

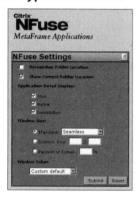

Configuring & Implementing…

Event Viewer Tips

The following points will help you in your work with Event Viewer:

- When configuring your server, be sure to set the Event Viewer's log size to one appropriate for your environment. If you opt to keep your logs for historical reference, do not forget to save and clear the logs on a regular basis.

- Citrix recommends setting the logs to 1024KB and to overwrite as needed.

- If disk space is an issue, move the logs to a location other than the default by editing the Registry.

- Be especially careful when security auditing is enabled, because logs tend to fill up quickly.

Foreword

Whenever I browse the computer section at a bookstore, I always look for the books with both the high-level overviews and the nitty-gritty details about the technology. These types of books are rare. Usually a book describes only what a newbie needs but fails to help that newbie get to the next level with the technology. Or a book will be mired in quirky minutiae that only an expert can understand. The ideal book, however, is the one that tells the reader about the technology, how to design for it, and to how to administer it. That is the type of book that we've put together here.

I've worked with Citrix products since I first installed a Citrix WinView box for 14 dialup users in the mid-1990s. I was impressed with the multiuser remote control capabilities at the time. I am even more impressed by the speed, graphics, and flexibility of the Citrix MetaFrame XP products today. I say "flexibility" because there are a whole host of problems that you can solve using Citrix MetaFrame XP. It is remarkable that one business needs a mobility solution, another business needs an Internet demonstration solution, and yet another requires a remote access solution, and that Citrix MetaFrame XP is the technology selected in each case.

Mobility is a growing field, and new ways of using technology are constantly being discovered. Today, you will find many business executives have cell phones, pagers, PDAs, and a laptop to help them port their office data anywhere they happen to need to work. People write presentations while on an airplane and even connect to their home offices and the Internet via the airplane phone to get their e-mail and run office applications. Engineers, research scientists, and property managers, among others, are required to be "in the field" to collect data using sophisticated technology.

In many years past, 3-by-5-inch cards and bound notepads were the only way that data could be collected in the field. Such data was later entered into a database, causing it to be "touched" twice and increasing the likelihood of errors. Even when technology to collect data electronically became available, many businesses found that the cost was prohibitive.

This situation is changing. The last few years have produced new mobile devices that are very cost effective, some priced at less than a hundred dollars per unit. Data can be gathered on a real-time basis, needing to be touched only once. Mobile devices have increased the demand for back-end support technologies so that those mobile devices can run high-end applications. But the very thing that makes a mobile device so cheap—the small size and capacity of the device itself—causes high-end applications to fail. Providing high-end applications to mobile devices is likely to be the next frontier for Citrix MetaFrame XP servers.

For network engineers and administrators, being able to design, deploy, and manage a Citrix MetaFrame XP server farm is the realm of the specialist. The product is one that is geared for businesses (and likely will not port to homes unless pervasive computing starts putting toasters and refrigerators on a home network), so it is unusual to find someone who has learned about the technology without having ever worked on a network with it. In addition, Citrix MetaFrame XP servers are usually a small percentage of what you might find on a network, so people with Citrix know-how are sought out for their skills.

For an engineer or administrator, Citrix is one of the top skills to have on your résumé. In fact, in 2002 CertCities.com rated the Citrix Certified Administrator (CCA) as number 8 out of 10 hottest certifications to get (http://certcities.com/editorial/features/story.asp?EditorialsID=37).

A new type of service provider has appeared on the horizon—the application service provider (ASP). The jury is still out on whether ASPs will become major players in the IT industry. There is an argument for them, though. ASPs function somewhat like the power company. Instead of providing your own generator and managing it through all its problems, the power company puts the equipment at your home and sends that power to you as you need it. You "rent" the power, depending on your usage.

In the ASP scenario, the application is provided by a Citrix MetaFrame XP server (or UNIX, or Microsoft Windows 2000 Terminal Services server) and delivered over the Internet to the client device. ASPs either charge a subscription rate for the application or require you to buy the license and charge a management fee for their overhead support costs; a few charge rent for hard drive space. The pricing is not even across the board, and most ASP companies are so brand-new that they don't have a history that people can count on. Most ASPs will not provide you your home equipment, either. Since computers are continually falling in price, the cost of owning your own computer and installing applications boils down mostly to support. So the world has yet to see whether ASPs will be the next Internet power generators. Even so, ASPs have boosted the status of Citrix MetaFrame XP on the market.

The inclusion of Terminal Services with all Windows 2000 Server versions is further making remote control technology more common. Riding on the tails of every standard Windows 2000 server, Terminal Services can be installed for remote server management. It won't be long before more administrators become familiar with the possibilities that this technology offers.

With Windows XP successfully making headway in the market (yes, Microsoft did meet its numbers!), more users at home and in the office will discover the Remote Desktop and Remote Assistance applications. Both Remote Desktop and Remote Assistance are based on the same protocol used for Terminal Services and provide similar remote control of Windows XP desktops. They even rely on the same Remote Desktop Protocol (RDP). Who knows where the technology will lead as people become more and more reliant on it.

Citrix MetaFrame XP with Feature Release 1 boasts a few new features. Because it is based on Windows 2000, you can share the latest Windows applications. Not only that, but all applications that you develop internally for the Windows 2000 platform can be shared to any type of client. This can significantly reduce business development costs, since an application needs to be developed for only one platform, even if multiple platforms are in use on the network.

The biggest feature that Citrix MetaFrame XP offers is its superior server farm management. A Citrix administrator can configure and manage servers, whether standalone or members of a server farm, from a console anywhere on the network. A bonus is that the Citrix management tools work with high-powered network management solutions, so you can truly manage the network from a single seat.

Enhancements make Citrix even easier to integrate into a network.

- Administrators on Novell-centric networks can deliver applications to their clients via Citrix MetaFrame XP, using native NDS authentication and printers.

- For networks that use 32-bit Windows clients, administrators can push application icons directly to the workstation's Start menu through the Program Neighborhood Agent.

- A Web interface called the Citrix Web Console lets administrators manage Citrix MetaFrame XP servers via intranets or the Internet.

- Even the individual CPUs on a server can be reserved for an application so that mission-critical tasks are kept at the top of the server's priorities.

Features like these, on top of the native ease of managing clients, make the latest version of Citrix MetaFrame XP an administrator's favorite tool.

We approached this book with two goals in mind. Not only did we want to provide the information that a person would need to administer a Citrix MetaFrame XP server and server farm, but we also wanted to provide some real-world, function-oriented information. To that end, you will find that earlier chapters are geared toward design, installation, and management of a server and server farm, whereas the later chapters provide the particulars surrounding specific solutions.

Chapter 1 gives a foundational discussion of the history of Citrix MetaFrame XP, the company, and the technologies MetaFrame comprises. By way of introduction, this chapter shows how Citrix MetaFrame XP and Windows 2000 Server with Terminal Services evolved as a cohesive product set. The chapter also discusses businesses' strategies and goals for the technology.

Chapter 2 explores the server farm management capabilities of Citrix MetaFrame XP. Not only is the concept of server farms introduced, but so are the methods for designing and managing them. This chapter initiates discussion of the Citrix Management Console (CMC), which is further described throughout the book. You'll find that the CMC is integral to all aspects of a Citrix MetaFrame XP server farm.

One of the first uses of Citrix products was remote access. Chapter 3 furnishes in-depth information about designing routing and remote access services (RRAS) for Windows 2000 Servers. It further discusses how to integrate a Citrix MetaFrame XP server with an RRAS installation. This chapter's material represents one of the essential skills for a Citrix administrator.

Chapter 4 is all about design. It can guide you through the complexities of sizing a server and making the decisions between scaling up a single server or scaling out into a server farm. It tells you where a Citrix MetaFrame XP server should be placed in relation to other servers and clients on the network as well as a variety of other design subjects. If you are just starting to put together a Citrix solution, this is where you should start.

The processes of installing and migrating to Citrix MetaFrame XP are the topics within Chapter 5. You can find the information you need for any type of Citrix MetaFrame XP deployment project. Not only is a new installation of a server covered, but also a migration from Citrix MetaFrame 1.8.

Making certain all your clients are licensed and properly installed is crucial to a Citrix MetaFrame XP deployment. Chapter 6 goes through all the essentials regarding licensing, the hardware and software requirements for the clients, installation procedures—even automation. You will learn how to deploy a thin client to multiple workstations and ensure that they have identical configurations.

Chapter 7 can get you to the point where the server is functional on the network. Simply installing a Citrix MetaFrame XP server will not immediately provide remote control sessions to your end users. You must also configure sessions so that clients can connect to the server. Configuring the server is a never-ending process because no network is ever static. You will always have new users or new ways to use the server and new applications that will force you to make some type of configuration change.

Chapter 8 goes further into server management, exploring the CMC and its various components. This chapter focuses on the tools needed to manage a server farm. One highly useful section looks at the SpeedScreen Latency Reduction capabilities of Citrix

MetaFrame XP. For networks with unpredictably slow links, being able to enhance performance for end users is a great achievement.

For an application server, the main ingredient for success is definitely the applications you install. In Chapter 9, you will learn what types of applications you should select (and a few to avoid), how to install them (yes, there are some special instructions), and how to optimize them. In addition, this chapter will show you how to publish applications and use the Program Neighborhood.

With a heightened focus on security in the IT industry, we've included a chapter for security strategies on Citrix MetaFrame XP. Not only does Chapter 10 cover some very sensible approaches to server and farm security, but it also discusses how to encrypt Independent Computing Architecture (ICA) traffic and use Secure Sockets Layer (SSL) when sharing applications across the Web to reduce the possibility of eavesdropping.

The final chapters of this book are solution-oriented. Chapter 11 teaches how to design and deploy an application server that supplies applications across the Internet. Printing, which is a sore subject whenever it doesn't work, is fully discussed in Chapter 12. Although wireless protocols are still emerging, Chapter 13 is dedicated to designing a mobile solution using Citrix MetaFrame XP on the back end. Chapter 14 will teach you how to develop a portal solution using Citrix MetaFrame XP with NFuse 1.6, which is freely downloadable from Citrix's Web site at www.citrix.com/download/bin/license.asp?client=nfusereg. Finally, Chapter 15 wraps up the entire book with monitoring and maintenance of the server.

I have found working with the authors on this book to be a delight. The authors each contributed his or her unique experiences with Citrix products to the chapters, filling the book with invaluable advice. I know from my own experience that the very thing that makes Citrix MetaFrame a great product—its flexibility as a solution to many different types of problems—is the one thing that requires an administrator to push the limit on his or her skills. I expect you'll find this book to be one of your favorite references, never far from where your servers sit.

> —*Melissa Craft, Technical Editor and Contributor*
> *CCA, MCSE, MCNE, CCNA, Network+, CNE-5, CNE-4, CNE-3, CNE-GW*
> *CIO, Dane Holdings, Inc.*

Chapter 1

Thin Clients and Digital Independence

Solutions in this chapter:

- **The Mainframe Model Meets Distributed Computing**
- **The Difference Between Remote Node and Remote Control**
- **The Evolution of the Thin Client**
- **Gaining Digital Independence with Thin Clients**
- **Achieving Bottom-Line Value with Thin Clients**

☑ **Summary**

☑ **Solutions Fast Track**

☑ **Frequently Asked Questions**

Introduction

Since computers were introduced, businesses have used them to simplify tasks so that their employees could be more productive and the businesses could realize cost reductions. Through acquisitions, mergers, and distributed IT administration, and sometimes merely because a mission-critical application is available on only a certain platform, businesses have accumulated different types of computer hardware, operating systems (OSs), and applications. In any business, it is not unusual to find users with multiple computing devices, whether a shared computer used for a specific application or a personal digital assistant (PDA) in every user's pocket.

The major challenge of a network with different types of computers is being able to deliver a mission-critical application to all users. This challenge is further exacerbated by the Internet because a business cannot predict the types of OS Internet users have or whether the business's application will work for them. In addition, Internet connections are notoriously inconsistent in regard to bandwidth availability. Applications delivered across the Internet must consume a fraction of the bandwidth that is available in corporate networks. In order to meet these needs, an application must be digitally independent from the OS and the infrastructure.

The thin client, such as that provided by Citrix MetaFrame XP, is the answer to these challenges. Since MetaFrame XP can deliver applications interactively via an Internet browser, it is virtually independent of a user's OS and hardware. Citrix MetaFrame's thin clients are termed "thin" because of the low bandwidth they consume. This, too, meets the need to provide applications independent of the digital infrastructure.

The Mainframe Model Meets Distributed Computing

It might seem a bit odd to begin a book about Citrix MetaFrame XP, a breakthrough product that can distribute an application to computers that don't natively support it, with a discussion about the history of the mainframe. You might wonder exactly how the mainframe and distributed computing models have anything to do with Citrix in the first place. The fact is that understanding both models is essential to being able to manage and troubleshoot Citrix MetaFrame XP in the long run. That's entirely due to the fact that Citrix MetaFrame XP and its previous versions are built on a model that mixes the mainframe model into the distributed computing model in order to gain the benefits of both.

Some of the advantages that you will see arising from this mixed model are:

- Running applications with transparent high performance over slow, unreliable connections

- Delivering applications to Internet users from within a browser
- Providing users with an application that is incompatible with their OSs without requiring them to change to a different machine or unfamiliar OS

A History of the Mainframe

A person who accessed a 100-megabyte (MB) hard drive weighing two and a quarter tons and costing more than $130,000 in the 1960s experiences a keen sense of wonder when tucking one of today's mobile multigigabyte (GB) drives, purchased for less than $1000 and weighing less than a pound, into a pocket. Computing during the 1960s and earlier was highlighted by exceptionally sizeable components. In fact, early computing was completely centralized, with dumb terminals surrounding an all-powerful main-frame. The earliest of these mainframes were large buildings filled with vacuum-tubed mammoths. Today's mainframes are contained in small boxes, some diminutive enough to fit under a desk. Regardless of the size or shape that these computers take, they serve an identical function: they act as a centralized brain used to compute multiple applications used by multiple, simultaneous end users through dumb terminal interfaces.

The original computer was the Harvard Mark I. Completed in 1943 with the collaboration of IBM engineers, the Harvard Mark I was so named because it occupied an entire Harvard University building. The Mark I was basically a huge calculator that had the ability to handle arithmetic functions and subroutines that could perform logarithms and trigonometry. Originally, IBM Selectric typewriters were used for Mark I input and output, but these were later replaced by IBM's punch-card technology. The Mark I was not the only computer at work in the early 1940s. In England, the Colossus Mark I was constructed and pressed into service during World War II to crack the German Enigma code.

On the heels of the Mark computers, the United States Army constructed the Electronic Numeral Integrator and Calculator (ENIAC) in 1946. Whereas the Harvard Mark I was a monstrously large calculator, ENIAC was an even larger computer capable of performing 100,000 calculations per second.

From the Harvard Mark I until nearly 1960, all computers used hundreds and thousands of vacuum tubes to execute calculations. It wasn't until 1958 that the first fully transistorized mainframe, the IBM 7000, was created by IBM. Considered the start of computing's Second Generation, this computer was first installed by the U.S. Air Force to provide an air traffic control system. In 1960, IBM introduced the first Basic Input/Output System (BIOS) in its 700 series of mainframes. This innovation enabled multiple processes to occur simultaneously. Another development was the ability to communicate with the mainframe over a telephone line.

Microchips, generally considered to constitute the Third Generation of computing, were the next innovation for the mainframe, arising out of the need for smaller computers. Until the arrival of the microchip, only governments and the largest businesses could afford computers due to their size and associated cost. The microchip replaced transistors, even being called a "flat transistor." Using microchips, new, smaller computers, called *minicomputers*, were created. Minicomputers, though smaller than mainframes, provided much the same features and functions as mainframes, and just as important, they used the same computing model as the mainframe. Today, minicomputers such as the IBM AS-400 are popular among small and midsize companies.

Computing's Fourth Generation was introduced in 1971 with the Intel 4004, the world's first microprocessor. Combining processing capability on a single chip with random access memory (RAM), the personal computer (PC) was born. Today's PCs, while far more powerful, with stunning graphic capabilities and vastly different applications from the original PCs, are still considered the fourth generation of computing.

Mainframes today offer a number of benefits. With the ability to run symmetric multiprocessing on more than a dozen reduced instruction set computer (RISC) processors, mainframes offer robust computing capabilities. Hardware advances have produced a highly fault-tolerant system for mainframes. Clusters, or groups of mainframes that act as a single environment, can keep mission-critical mainframe applications available even in the event of one mainframe's failure. Given the fact that a mainframe is a single point of failure for everyone using it, fault tolerance is of critical importance.

The Mainframe Model

Today's mainframes can support multiple simultaneous programs for multiple simultaneous users. The mainframe itself uses peripheral channels for input/output (I/O) processes in order to free up processing power. Because so many concurrent processes take place on a mainframe, it usually has an extremely fast bus speed and error-correcting hardware. The mainframe is considerably more powerful than minicomputers, even though the same computing model is used, and mainframes can support more simultaneous programs and users.

The mainframe model is centralized computing. The only processing power needed is that of the mainframe itself. The devices people use to access the programs on the mainframe are traditionally dumb terminals. Terminals are ASCII character-based devices. Figure 1.1 displays a typical mainframe model.

Also referred to as *green screens* due to their green text on a black background, these terminals are called "dumb" because they need no processing power whatsoever. Today newer "smart" terminals provide a built-in screen display instruction set. However, this does not change the location of processing within the model. Nowadays, most people use terminal emulation programs running on their networked PCs to access a mainframe.

This does not change the model in which all processing takes place on the mainframe. In this scenario, the client adds no processing power nor intelligence to the mainframe's applications. Figure 1.2 illustrates the use of clients with a mainframe and terminal server.

Figure 1.1 A Typical Mainframe Model

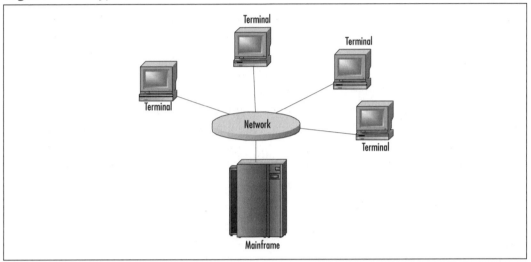

Figure 1.2 Terminal Emulation on PCs

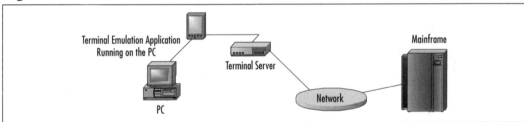

Centralized computing is organized into a single tier of processing. The application logic, located on the mainframe, is processed solely on that same machine. As a monolithic architecture for both applications and administration, the mainframe model provides many benefits and is used by organizations worldwide.

Advantages of the Mainframe Model

The mainframe model essentially uses the mainframe as a central repository for information as well as processing for every application. Terminals enable input/output into the applications. Nearly all administration takes place on the mainframe itself. This scheme provides multiple benefits:

- Hardware maintenance cost reductions

- Single point of administration

- One type of administrative skill set

- Simple architecture and low bandwidth requirements

Terminals and printers are the two most common components of the mainframe model. Terminals are relatively cheap. Since you can easily add or replace terminals without causing a major impact to the budget, and because they have minimal components, terminals carry very little maintenance or overhead administrative costs related to end-user hardware. Even though the mainframe itself has a high price tag, the ongoing maintenance costs are very reasonable.

A single point of administration is greatly valued in IT administration. Although it is true that a person could administer the entire mainframe from any terminal connected to the network, the single point of administration means that there is only one thing to administer—that is, the mainframe. The mainframe applications and data are all located in a single place. This makes it far easier to troubleshoot, change passwords, add users, change access rights, and manage applications than is the case in a distributed computing environment.

When a network is based solely on a mainframe and terminals, only a single administrative skill set is required. The only thing any administrator needs to know is how to run the mainframe. Programmers find that programming skills for mainframe programming languages are all they require. By contrast, a distributed computing model necessitates many different types of skill sets. The distributed computing model demands administrative knowledge of the network topology, client OSs, network OSs, protocols, and applications that are processed partially on the client and partially on the server. The complexity of distributed computing can drive up administrative costs merely in finding people with all the various skills or training them.

Designing a mainframe architecture is fairly straightforward. Because of the centralized nature of the model, the optimal placement of the mainframe is in a central location. Whereas originally terminals were hardwired to asynchronous communication ports on the mainframe itself, nowadays terminals are connected to a terminal server and can access multiple network resources. Due to the processing taking place only on the mainframe, the only information that travels between the mainframe and the terminals is keystrokes and display. This results in very low bandwidth demand on the network. Saturating a network with text and display traffic is difficult in today's high-capacity networks, which releases the network designer from a great deal of pressure.

Disadvantages of Centralized Computing

The mainframe itself has a major drawback. Mainframes are very expensive. That purchase price tag, which can run from several hundred thousand to millions of dollars, is followed by maintenance contract costs for both the mainframe hardware and mainframe applications. These costs are tolerable for companies that balance them against the benefits of office automation. The minicomputer, with a much lower price—in the tens of thousands to low hundreds of thousands of dollars—offers similar benefits and is often the choice for a small and midsize businesses.

A centralized computing model includes its own unwanted baggage, regardless of whether the central computer is a mainframe or minicomputer:

- **Single point of failure** The largest challenge with centralized computing is overcoming the fact that a mainframe is a single point of failure. Since most mainframes house a business's most critically important applications and are used by nearly every person in the company, mainframe failure can have a devastating impact on corporate productivity. Even though clustering can reduce the impact somewhat, a failure in connectivity between the mainframe cluster and terminals will render the same impact.

- **Character-based applications** Users who use dumb terminals often bemoan the fact that the mainframe applications are textual. Graphics applications on a mainframe are rare at best. Character-based applications are usually the only types available for mainframe users.

- **Potential bottlenecks due to time-sharing systems** Because all users access a mainframe simultaneously, there is a potential for bottlenecks. In times of heavy usage, the mainframe might not have the processing capabilities to respond to every user's session in a timely manner.

A History of Distributed Computing

The development of the microchip and smaller computers, along with the Transmission Control Protocol/Internet Protocol (TCP/IP) protocol stack, soon brought about networks with distributed computing capabilities. The keys to an effective network were interoperability and interconnectivity. The innovation of networking achieved communication between computers using dissimilar OSs. Networking also gave rise to client/server computing.

At first, connecting multiple computers to share files was beneficial. Then, with hard drives costing hundreds of dollars per megabyte, it became very desirable to share hard drive space. Organizations were soon able to save additional money by sharing printers through networking. It didn't take long for people to look for ways to harness and share the server processing power. This motivation developed into a *client/server architecture* model.

Xerox Corporation's Palo Alto Research Center (PARC) was the first to develop an Ethernet network coupled with Xerox Distributed File Server (XDFS) in order to duplicate the capabilities of a mainframe using smart workstations. The result was a tremendous decrease in cost to automate an organization. Apple Corporation borrowed these technologies and built them into its computer line. Graphical user interfaces (GUIs) added the ability for color pictures to be displayed. The mouse brought the now-familiar point-and-click methodology so that users can more easily manipulate graphics-based data. UNIX workstations, too, grew to incorporate graphical capabilities. Since then, Microsoft has come to dominate the personal computer market with its popular Windows OS.

Some centralization of duties became increasingly necessary. UNIX offered native server computing capabilities on every workstation. That is, any workstation could share resources, hold its own lists of users and passwords, and at the same time connect to other UNIX workstations and access those shared resources. Managing users on multiple machines added a tremendous amount of administrative overhead. This type of *peer-to-peer* networking, in which each PC acts as either a server or a client, is displayed in Figure 1.3.

Figure 1.3 The Peer-to-Peer Computing Model

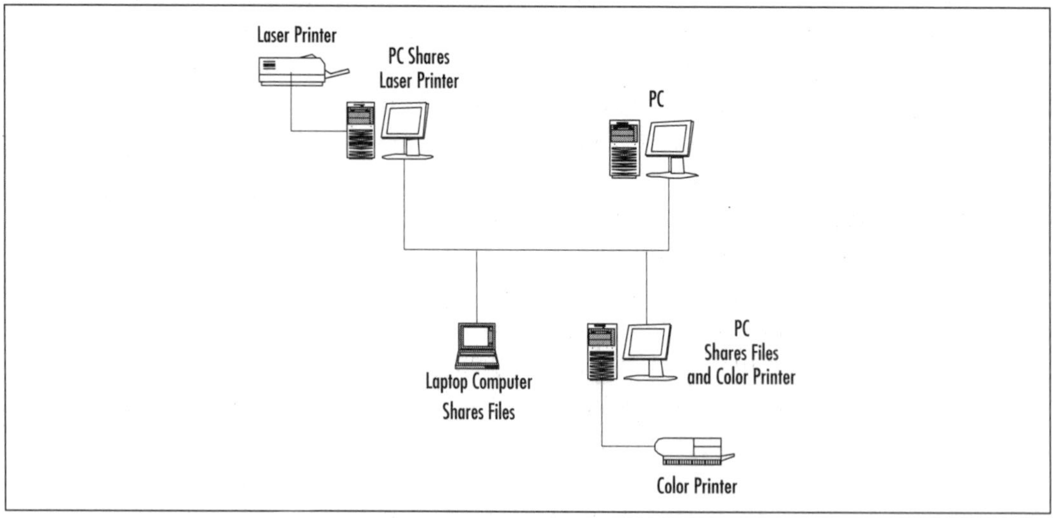

Novell's NetWare server OS moved in a more centralized direction. With a centralized server OS, it became much easier to administer users, passwords, printers, files, and other resources. This provided organizations with powerful applications, centralized management, and the low cost of PC computing. This client/server computing model is shown in Figure 1.4.

Figure 1.4 The Client/Server Computing Model

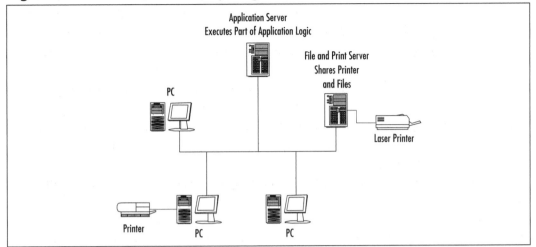

Even though the server offers a more centralized administrative model, it does not match the mainframe computing model. Applications do not run solely on a server and get delivered to a dumb terminal. Instead, depending on the application's individual architecture, application logic can be processed on the server, the client, or both. Because every computer in a PC network is capable of performing its own processing, applications vary based on the programmer's design. Whereas some applications use the server as merely the location from which files are shared, others divide their processing across both clients and servers.

When the application logic is processed on both the client and the server, it is considered a *two-tiered* architecture. In two-tiered architecture, the server runs a software application and processes information that does not need to be interactive. The client also runs a software application with logic that can access the server, perform edits, and do some business logic processing. This is a typical scenario for database computing, where the database is housed on a server and the server performs record searches and record generation, and where the application on the client accesses the database and performs edits.

Some database applications stretch this type of computing to a *third tier*. In this scenario, a database server houses the database, an application server performs business logic, and a client application performs input/output. Both of these models are shown in Figure 1.5.

Figure 1.5 Client/Server Architecture in Two- and Three-Tiered Structures

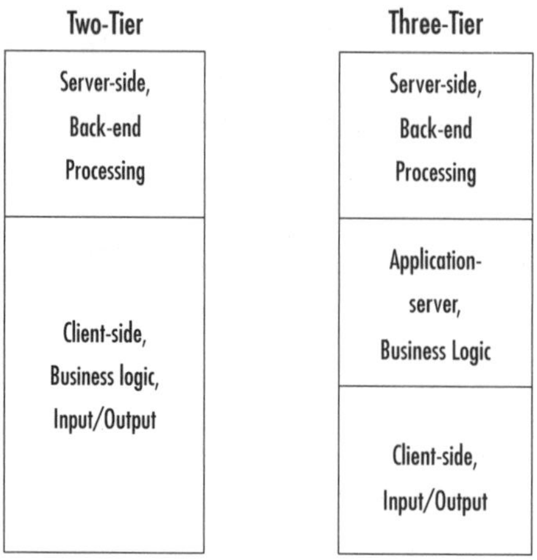

Two-Tier	Three-Tier
Server-side, Back-end Processing	Server-side, Back-end Processing
Client-side, Business logic, Input/Output	Application-server, Business Logic
	Client-side, Input/Output

Advantages of Distributed Computing

As many businesses have discovered, the distributed computing model carries several advantages:

- Reduced hardware costs
- No single point of failure
- Flexibility
- Scalable architecture

Mainframe hardware is extremely pricey. Servers, by comparison, are far less expensive. Even though individual PCs are much more expensive than terminals, the overall initial cost of implementing a distributed computing network is relatively small.

A truly distributed computing network has many servers running in multiple locations. If a single server fails, people are able to continue working using the resources of other servers. Even when connectivity to another location fails, users are able to work with local resources shared by local servers. When information is replicated across several servers, a server going offline does not prevent information access. This ensures that people can continue working. Furthermore, fault tolerance of redundant links further reduces the possibility of catastrophic failures.

In a distributed computing environment, a business is not dedicated to a single OS. Servers can run network OSs that include Microsoft Windows 2000, various flavors of UNIX, Novell NetWare, and others. At the same time, the business can select any number of OSs to run on the desktop. This provides for a very flexible environment.

With a distributed computing environment, a person can run an application remotely over phone lines, even those available on airplanes. Leveraging this flexibility, a company can truly maximize employee efficiency.

The very nature of distributed computing is to be scalable. Whenever growth of the business demands increased computing power, new servers can be added to the network. Server hardware manufacturers offer clustering, symmetric multiprocessing, and fault-tolerant components to scale up an individual server as well.

Disadvantages of Distributed Computing

The distributed computing model bears some undesirable aspects for organizations, which include:

- Heightened administrative costs

- Increased security risks

- Lack of centralized backup

The distributed computing model is rife with administrative costs. Because every server and client on the network is intelligent and has its own OS, each one requires administrative support for its hardware and OS. Though standardization is a best practice, it is not unusual to find multiple types of desktop and server hardware, multiple operating systems, even multiple versions of the same operating systems on a network. Applications add further complexity to the network, also requiring administration, upgrades, changes, and configuration. Even though you are avoiding the price of a mainframe, you must include the costs of the desktop devices to the distributed computing model's bottom line; they are at least five times more expensive than dumb terminals. When it comes down to brass tacks, if you use a distributed computing network as opposed to using a mainframe with dumb terminals, it simply costs more at the desktop, costs less at the server, and takes more people to manage the same number of end users.

Security risks increase with every server on the network. Although it isn't written in any manual, a network OS in its out-of-the-box configuration is not secure. The installer must configure security to match the policies of the business and seal off any server vulnerabilities. To top it off, the server administrator must apply any patches for newly discovered vulnerabilities of the server or any of its applications. Unfortunately, this process takes considerable vigilance, and even so, security holes do open up. Saboteurs have been known to exploit the weakness of one server in order to gain access to other, mission-critical servers. The physical security of a distributed computing network is also more susceptible to breaches because of the lack of centralized location for servers. Not every facility provides a locked, climate-controlled room in which to store its servers. Quite often, smaller offices place a server beneath a desk or in a closet.

A clear-cut set of security policies and procedures is required in order to conquer this shortcoming.

Backing up the data on a server is a crucial activity toward maintaining business continuity. In the event of a mainframe failure, the latest backup can be retrieved and restored, and business can continue. However, in the distributed computing model, many of the servers are located anywhere across the globe. Connectivity between those locations can be extremely slow and unreliable. It simply is not feasible to conduct a backup of data over such a link. An administrator must rely on people in each location to execute and manage backup procedures.

The MetaFrame XP Thin Client Model

It's now time to explain why we needed to review the mainframe and distributed computing models. You see, Citrix MetaFrame XP is built on a combination of these two models in such a way that it can maximize the benefits and minimize the disadvantages of both. Sound interesting? Let's look at the *thin client model*.

The thin client model uses some of the same concepts as the mainframe model. Rather than requiring the access devices to provide any intelligence, the thin client model treats them as terminals. However, these are not green screen terminals or terminal emulation programs used by the mainframe, since they must support graphical applications. Instead, these are Independent Computing Architecture (ICA) terminals and ICA client applications that enable emulation of a session running on a Citrix MetaFrame XP server.

NOTE

ICA terminals are also called *thin client terminals* and *Windows terminals*. If you are running Windows 2000 Server with Terminal Services but not using Citrix MetaFrame XP or previous versions, you will be running Remote Desktop Protocol (RDP) and will require RDP-compatible terminals and RDP client applications.

In the mainframe model, organizations are 100 percent dependent on a centralized computing power yet can easily administer it from a single seat. Because all the applications run on the mainframe, it is fairly easy to administer them with one place to go for installations, configuration changes, and rights access. The thin client model offers the same capabilities inasmuch as you are considering only the Citrix MetaFrame XP servers. It is likely that most organizations will combine a distributed computing model with the thin client model in order to leverage the benefits of both. It is also likely that some of those distributed computing servers will participate in the same domains as

Citrix MetaFrame XP servers and share in the user rights and privileges administration. It is also highly probable that end users will access the network from fully functional PCs with ICA client applications rather than using ICA terminals. So, when we say that the thin client model offers a centralized administration approach to applications, we refer to a network that implements *only* Citrix MetaFrame XP: When a network consists solely of a Citrix MetaFrame XP thin client model, the applications will be installed, configured, and administered only on the Citrix servers. No support is required at the deskside, since all sessions can be shadowed. (We discuss this hip little feature later in the book.)

So far in our discussion, the thin client model sounds a lot like a mainframe model. However, it shares some of the characteristics of distributed computing as well. The first and most obvious characteristic is that there is no mainframe in the thin client model. It uses servers—exactly the same types of servers as the ones being used for file and print services, application services, databases, and Web services.

Originally created to support remote users needing access to colorful Windows applications, the thin client model delivers a fully graphical experience to the user's desktop. Rather than inundating the user with fuzzy green characters on a black screen, an ICA client might appear no different from running Windows on the desktop.

Another important trait shared with distributed computing is the three-tiered architecture of application logic. The difference here is that most applications that Citrix MetaFrame XP can deliver in three tiers were not originally developed to be used that way. The thin client model actually extends two-tiered applications into previously unexplored territory. For administrators, this is an adventure just begun. Table 1.1 lists several of the characteristics of the various computing models.

Table 1.1 Computing Model Characteristics

Characteristic	Mainframe	Distributed Computing	Thin Client
Text-based mainframe or minicomputer	Yes	No	No
Terminals	Yes	No	Yes
Centralized administration of applications	Yes	No	Yes
Centralized installation of applications	Yes	No	Yes
Reduced costs for administrative overhead	Yes	No	Yes
Low bandwidth utilization	Yes	No	Yes

Continued

Table 1.1 Continued

Characteristic	Mainframe	Distributed Computing	Thin Client
Low-cost servers (relative to mainframe cost)	No	Yes	Yes
Graphical capabilities	No	Yes	Yes
Three-tiered architecture	No	Yes	Yes
32-bit applications delivered to any type of operating system or ICA terminal	No	No	Yes
Offline computing capabilities	No	Yes	No

Combined Advantages of the Two Models

As mentioned previously, the thin client model can maximize the advantages of both the mainframe model and the distributed computing model while minimizing both models' disadvantages. Looking at this statement in a little more depth, consider the advantages of the mainframe model:

- Hardware maintenance cost reductions

- Single point of administration

- One type of administrative skill set

- Simple architecture and low bandwidth requirements

The thin client model has many of the same advantages. Hardware maintenance cost reductions are easily realized in the thin client model. Unlike the mainframe model, the thin client model offers two ways in which it can reduce hardware maintenance costs. First, if a business decides to implement the thin client model, it can do so with ICA terminals that cost about a quarter of the price of a standard desktop PC. From that point forward, that business will not have much in the way of hardware maintenance costs due to the low maintenance requirements of terminal hardware.

The second way that a business can realize reduced hardware maintenance costs is unique to the thin client model: An organization can take an existing distributed computing network and migrate it to thin clients. To the end user, the thin client experience is no different than running a 32-bit Windows operating system on the desktop. But the hardware required to support an ICA client does not require Pentium processors, a large amount of RAM, or gigabytes of storage. Instead, an ancient 386 PC with minimal RAM (about 4MB) and storage (megabytes rather than gigabytes) can run an ICA client and appear to be a much more powerful machine running Windows 2000 locally. Not only does this extend the life of the machine, but because there is very little processing required of it, the machine is not overtaxed. Users can log on to any machine in the entire network and receive their own individual desktops, without worrying about leaving data on a local hard drive. This fact removes the need to move PCs around the network or reconfigure them individually. Therefore, a company can use thin clients to extend the life of their hardware, greatly decreasing their maintenance costs.

The thin client model provides a centralized approach to administration. Like a mainframe, all applications are located in a single place—on the thin client server. Applications need only be installed, configured, or deleted from a single location. Most, if not all of the rights, privileges, and administrative changes can take place in one server or through the domain management tools. The reason that this model does not necessarily use a 100-percent centralized administration is entirely related to the design and complexity of the environment. If it is a centralized design, more centralized benefits will be achieved.

It's a stretch to state that the thin client model requires only one type of administrative skill set. In a pure thin client model, using only Citrix MetaFrame XP servers and ICA terminal hardware, this statement is true. However, in most businesses that implement Citrix MetaFrame XP, the thin client model is mixed with the distributed computing model and can consist of multiple types of network and desktop operating systems and access devices, resulting in the need for multiple types of administrative skill sets.

Simple architecture, arguably, is not a characteristic of the thin client model. In fact, it can become quite complex to integrate a thin client model into a distributed computing model. The benefit in which the thin client model does succeed is low bandwidth requirements. An ICA client requires a minimum of a 14.4K modem link in order to function reasonably. Since most remote users connect via 28K or 56K modems, a thin client model performs extremely well.

The distributed computing model has other benefits that the thin client model can maximize:

- Reduced hardware costs
- No single point of failure
- Flexibility
- Scalable architecture

Earlier in the chapter, we mentioned that the distributed computing model avoided the huge price tag of hardware implementation that is suffered by the mainframe model. In the thin client model, this is also true. The thin client model uses network servers and does not require excessive investments in back-end hardware.

The mainframe model's biggest disadvantage is that it constructs a single point of failure for mission-critical applications. This is not true for distributed computing or the thin client model, which shares that ability to distribute thin client servers across a network and avoid a single point of failure. The benefits of distributed thin client servers are best realized using Citrix MetaFrame XP, due to its ability to distribute the load across a number of similar servers, which is discussed in Chapter 10.

Flexibility in computing enables companies to maximize employee effectiveness. The distributed computing model enjoys flexibility to a degree. The thin client model can take that flexibility to the next level. For example, one of the main benefits for businesses with a growing virtual workforce is to offer remote computing. Sometimes computing must be executed offline. At other times, it must be carefully controlled and run only online. A thin client model blended with a distributed computing model offers the optimal environment for these businesses. Online computing, of course, can be carefully controlled and centrally managed on a thin client server, whereas offline computing can take place using the device's operating system and local applications. It is up to the network administrator to decide which applications must be managed and which can be freely distributed. Furthermore, wireless public networks are adding new methods for remote computing. Because wireless networks have, up to this point, fairly low bandwidth capabilities, using a "thick" client application across one is next to impossible—that is, it's impossible without using a thin client.

An architecture that is scalable is yet another advantage shared by the thin client and distributed computing models. With the hardware available for clustering, storage area networks (SANs), symmetric multiprocessing (SMP), and redundant components, each server can scale up in size. The entire network can be scaled out through the addition of new servers. Furthermore, with Citrix MetaFrame XP, the servers can be load balanced so that sessions are spread evenly throughout the Citrix MetaFrame XP server farm.

NOTE

When you begin designing your thin client servers, you can throw out the rules that you follow for file and print servers. Because thin client servers have a much more intense usage of processors and memory, their design requires more of them. In addition, you have the options of scaling horizontally, by creating an application server farm, or scaling vertically, by beefing up a single server, to accommodate more simultaneous users. Make certain that your choices will meet your needs for user experience, power, performance, and availability of sessions.

New Thin Client Model Advantages

The popularity of today's personal computers has driven use of the distributed computing model. Even in businesses in which the mainframe model was fully implemented, distributed computing was adopted and meshed into the fabric of the network so that benefits of both could be realized. Doing so, however, also maximized the disadvantages of both models, since effectively, both models were still in use simultaneously. It is only with the thin client model that businesses can minimize the disadvantages.

One issue will continue to plague the thin client model: It relies heavily on administrative knowledge! The network administrator who walks in from a distributed computing or mainframe model background can easily become perplexed by the variety of options for designing, implementing, and managing a thin client network.

One of the benefits of the thin client model can become somewhat baffling to figure out. This is the ability to leverage the Internet to deploy applications. What you can do with Citrix MetaFrame XP is launch the ICA client from within a Web page and run an application. Doing so logically combines two different three-tiered architectures into the system, as shown in Figure 1.6.

Figure 1.6 Logical Processes in Launching an ICA Client from a Web Browser

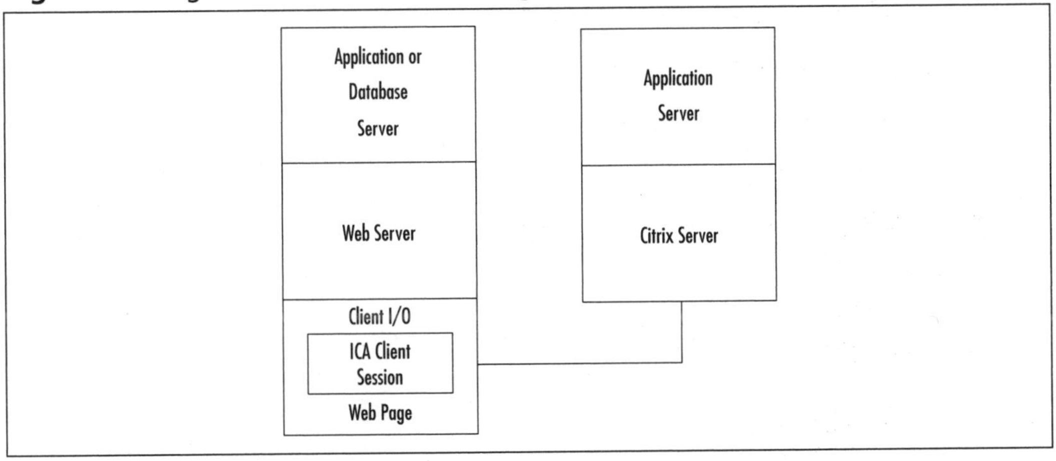

Overcoming the Disadvantages of Previous Versions of MetaFrame

Citrix MetaFrame XP is the latest version of the thin client solution offered by Citrix Systems, Inc. Each newer version introduced to market has surmounted many of the challenges found in earlier versions, a trend evidenced by the many improvements incorporated into Citrix MetaFrame XP.

How the Internet Figures into Client/Server Computing

The Internet is the world's largest network. Originally developed by the U.S. Department of Defense's (DoD) Advanced Research Projects Agency (ARPA) for the purpose of sharing radar data, the Internet, then called ARPANET, was turned on for the first time in 1971, with 19 hosts. After growing as a government and educational internetwork for over 20 years, the Internet was finally opened up as a global internetwork for commerce in the early 1990s.

Anyone with device and communication line access can access the Internet, surf Web pages, send e-mail, participate in chats and instant messages—even host their own Web sites for others to access. Businesses have begun to reevaluate and reprogram many back-end applications to fit the Internet, leveraging its global capabilities in order to reduce costs and execute business-to-business processes.

The challenge faced by many organizations is in overcoming low bandwidth. Even though cable modems, Integrated Services Digital Network (ISDN), and Digital Subscriber Line (DSL) lines can reach megabit-bandwidth rates, most people rely on telephone lines for Internet access. With typically 28K to 56K of bandwidth, these methods of downloading graphics and applications result in long waits that are increasingly intolerable to end users.

Citrix MetaFrame XP offers the ability to use thin client computing across the Internet in a variety of ways. By reorganizing applications to execute through a Citrix server, the barrier of low bandwidth is removed.

One of the more interesting changes is Citrix's recognition that people used Citrix MetaFrame's previous versions in different environments for different purposes. The product was flexible and had many features, but some were not necessary for certain types of implementations. As a result, Citrix MetaFrame XP has three different flavors: XPs, XPa, and XPe, scaling up from the small business implementation to a server farm management system. These versions are described in more detail later in this chapter.

Although prior versions could be installed on either a Windows NT or Windows 2000 server, a common theme for Citrix MetaFrame implementation was to deploy applications either over a virtual private network (VPN) or via a Web page. The latest Citrix MetaFrame XP is optimized to run on Windows 2000 and to deploy applications across the Internet. This is an improvement in performance for Windows 2000 servers as well as for businesses extending applications across the Web.

Taking the server farm concept to the next level, scalability of Citrix MetaFrame XP is unparalleled. Previous versions, although beginning to adopt the server farm concept, do not have the same manageability. In fact, Citrix MetaFrame XP removes the boundaries of geography from the server farm. An administrator can manage a Citrix MetaFrame XP server farm from anywhere around the globe.

One of the missions of the Citrix MetaFrame product series has been to deliver "any application to any device over any connection." Citrix MetaFrame XP provides the back-end delivery of these applications, while ICA clients work on PCs, Apple Macintoshes, UNIX, Linux, ICA terminals, and the latest in wireless devices. The infrastructure can vary from an Internetwork Packet Exchange/Sequenced Packet Exchange (IPX/SPX) network with native Novell NetWare servers to public wireless networks connected through the Internet to VPN solutions installed on corporate networks.

The Difference Between Remote Node and Remote Control

One of the very first reasons Citrix created its first WinView product was to help companies reduce the cost of providing remote control services to end users. WinView was a predecessor to Citrix MetaFrame XP based on OS/2. It allowed a user to dial in to the WinView server and use a DOS or Windows 3.1 version session running applications through remote control. By implementing WinView, a company could replace 15 dedicated remote control PCs with a single one. How times change!

Remote computing has grown up from two distinctly different methods:

- **Remote node** This is a form of computing that connects a PC or even a server to the network across a modem line. Often called *remote access*, remote nodes have grown to include VPN so that PCs can connect to a network across the Internet.

- **Remote control** This is the form of computing in which a remote PC takes control of the desktop of a PC that exists on the network. Originally, this type of computing was able to share a single session on a single network PC, and users had to dial up directly to that PC.

The unique thing about Citrix MetaFrame XP is that these two types of remote computing are combined and extended. Not only does it merge them, but a Citrix MetaFrame XP server can be implemented in conjunction with other vendors' solutions for remote node computing. In this section, we'll look at both types of remote computing and how they apply to Citrix MetaFrame XP.

Remote Node Computing

Remote node computing traditionally is handled via dialup modems. When the computer dials the network, the user is prompted to logon to the network, and from that point on the computer acts exactly the same as if it were locally connected to the network, barring any security limitations imposed by the remote access system. The user can usually send e-mail, transfer files, run network applications and communicate through instant messaging. The only difference is that, due to the low bandwidth capabilities usually demonstrated by dialup modems, network performance is typically very slow. For example, on the local area network (LAN), downloading a 3MB file can appear nearly instantaneous, whereas across a remote node connection through a 56Kbps modem, it can take more than 10 minutes to pull down the file.

Remote access today can be established through any of the following types of connectivity:

- Plain old telephone service (POTS)

- ISDN

- X.25

- VPN through the Internet using modems, wireless networks, cable, or DSL

The original method of remote access was performed using a dialup modem to connect to POTS, also known as the *public switched telephone network (PSTN),* which then connected to a remote access server's node. In doing so, the remote access client became transparently connected to the network. The remote-client-to-remote-server connection is referred to as *a point-to-point connection,* since only two nodes, or *points,* share a single connection. Figure 1.7 shows remote access via POTS.

ISDN offers a faster connectivity method compared to POTS. Developed as an upgrade to POTS, ISDN offers digital connectivity, typically at speeds of 128Kbps. The increased speed makes it very attractive as a remote node method. The point-to-point connection used is shown in Figure 1.7, but the modems are replaced by ISDN modems.

Remote access connectivity through X.25 is rarely used anymore. Even though it is an international standard for data transmission, X.25 is a legacy packet-based network that was used for wide area networks (WANs) and remote access in the early days of networking. Today, few X.25 networks are left; they have been replaced by networks with much faster connectivity capabilities.

VPNs are connected through the Internet using modems, wireless networks, cable, or DSL. A VPN enables the remote client to use the Internet to create a virtual point-to-point connection to a remote access server. Because the Internet is a public network, the virtual point-to-point link must be protected. This is done by *tunneling* the data within IP packets so that it cannot be decrypted by eavesdroppers. A typical VPN connection is shown in Figure 1.8.

Figure 1.7 A Remote Node Connected over POTS

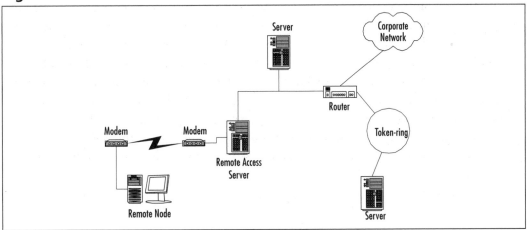

Figure 1.8 A Virtual Private Network Connection

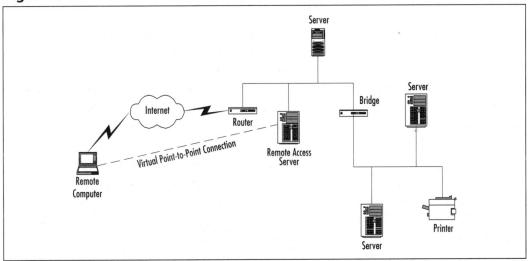

Remote access solutions offer many business benefits. It is rare to find a place where a phone line is not available. Being able to connect users to the local network from any location offers businesses the ability to extend their networks anywhere. Besides removing geographic limitations, telecommuting extends work hours to 24 hours a day, seven days a week. Remote node solutions have many advantages technically as well:

- Simple to configure

- Options for accessibility

- Security services to secure data

- Easy-to-manage hardware requirements

Remote node computing is fairly simple to configure. At the corporate network, the administrator installs a remote access server. The server is configured with either a set of modems or a link to the Internet, or both. The client needs remote access client software installed and configured to connect to the remote access server. Most desktop operating systems, such as Windows XP, include native remote access client software that is compatible with standard remote access servers.

A key benefit is to be able to connect over different types of media using a variety of networking protocols. As mentioned earlier, a remote node connection can be established across a phone line, an ISDN line, a legacy X.25 network, a cable network using a cable modem—in fact, across any Internet connection or dialup method. Remote node computing uses a set of standard protocols, such as Serial Line Interface Protocol (SLIP), Point to Point Protocol (PPP), and Asynchronous NetBEUI (AsyBEUI). These protocols can support multiple types of protocol stacks. For example, a PPP connection can transmit both TCP/IP and IPX/SPX traffic. For these reasons, remote access servers can be installed to work on any type of network.

Any aperture in the fabric of a network can expose sensitive information with potentially devastating consequences to a company. Since remote node services extend the network to any location, it is vitally important that the remote access servers and connections are secured from intruders and eavesdroppers. Many standard security protocols have been developed to help secure remote access. To ensure authentication, tunneling, and encryption, a network administrator can install Internet Protocol Security (IPSec), Challenge Authentication Protocol (CHAP), or Layer 2 Tunneling Protocol (L2TP), among others.

The hardware and management requirements for remote access computing are much easier to meet than those for remote control computing. To provide remote control computing, an administrator must place computers on the network to host remote control sessions in addition to providing computers as remote control clients. By contrast, remote node computing requires only the remote clients and one or a few remote access servers. Managing remote control hosts can be cumbersome compared with managing remote access servers.

Remote Control Computing

Remote control solutions enable a user to control a session running on a remote host. The keystrokes that the user types from the remote client are transmitted across the wire to the remote host, along with any mouse clicks. The graphics on the remote host's screen are transmitted back to the remote client. The applications are actually processed on the remote host. Most types of remote control solutions enable some form of file transfer between the remote host and the remote client. Unlike the rest of the remote session, file transfers are processed locally on the remote client.

One of the surprising benefits of remote control solutions is the ability for two people to view the same screen of information, even though those people are in two different locations. Some enterprising administrators used early remote control solutions to manage mission-critical workstations and servers on the network. They found that they could administer these servers from anywhere around the network, reducing the need to go directly to the servers to execute standard administrative tasks. Network management solutions today typically incorporate a remote control application for network workstations. Administrators use remote control sessions in response to help requests while the end user asking for help is still using the remote control host. This way, the administrator can diagnose and fix problems as well as demonstrate to the user how to carry out some function. Figure 1.9 exhibits how the remote control session functions.

Figure 1.9 A Remote Control Session

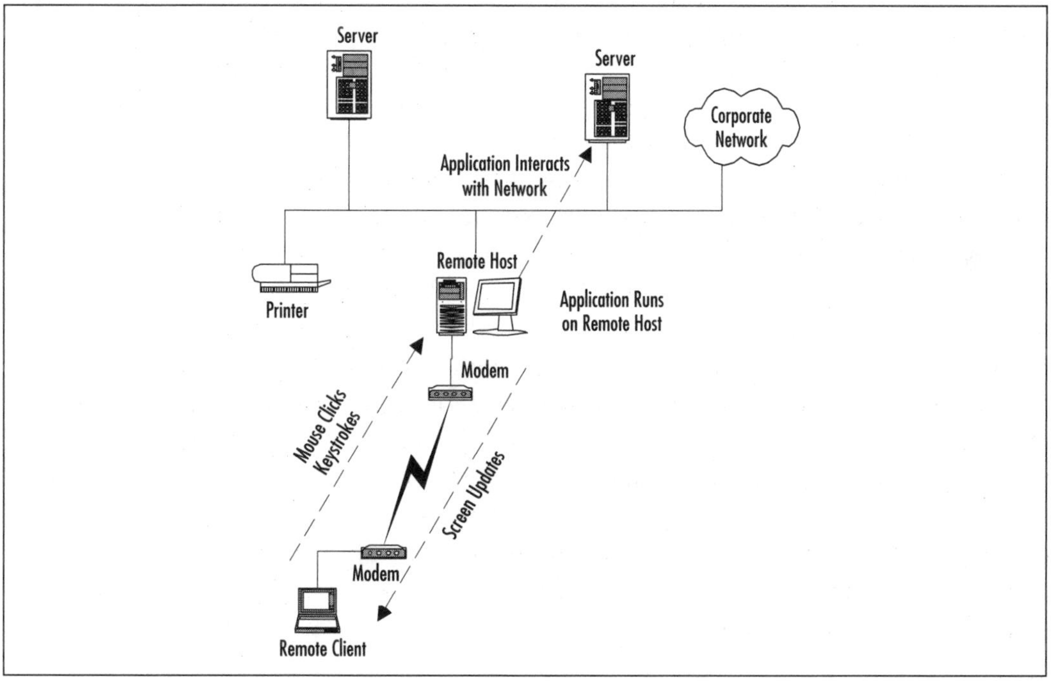

One of the main advantages to remote control software is the ability it offers support personnel to diagnose and troubleshoot remote systems without being physically at the system's location. Whether used to collect information for trending, license usage, or monitoring, this capability reduces support costs in terms of travel, time, and effort. It also improves support response times and results in higher end-user satisfaction.

Remote control software is useful for demonstrations, even as a teaching tool. A teacher can work on a remote control host while a student watches from a remote control client session. With either the teacher or the student able to control the session, the student can perform specific tasks under supervision.

For government and highly regulated industries, there are often rules regarding which PCs can store certain types of information. A remote control solution enables a company to maintain its security restrictions yet still enable key personnel to work with the data from their own workstations. Security for such a remote control solution should be configurable to prevent downloading of data from the remote control host to the remote control client.

There are some limitations to remote control. Like remote node, the bandwidth for dialup connections to a remote control host is very low. Unlike remote node, the type of data that transmits across the wire consists of graphics rather than file transfers. The higher the resolution of those graphics and the larger the number of colors used, the more bandwidth is consumed. Applications that heavily utilize graphics suffer degraded performance when executed via remote control.

A rather wasteful aspect of remote control is how many computers it uses. Since each remote control host supports a single session, it must wait, unused, until a remote client logs on. Then, during the session, both the remote control host and the remote control client are dedicated to a single session. When remote control software programs were introduced to the market, some businesses set up rooms with hundreds of PCs shelved and attached to modems simply to support telecommuting. Just one word describes this setup: *expensive*.

Both remote control and remote node have pros and cons. Citrix MetaFrame XP has the ability to combine the two types of remote computing in order to maximize the benefits and minimize the drawbacks. Table 1.2 demonstrates the characteristics of each type of remote computing.

Table 1.2 Remote Computing Characteristics

Characteristics	Remote Control	Remote Node	Citrix MetaFrame XP
Updates graphics on the remote client, receives keystrokes and mouse clicks	Yes	No	Yes
Many users can connect to a single server	No	Yes	Yes
Clients with older technology can run newer applications	Yes	No	Yes

Continued

Table 1.2 Continued

Characteristics	Remote Control	Remote Node	Citrix MetaFrame XP
Graphics-intensive applications hamper performance	Yes	No	Yes
Security options for encryption and authentication	Sometimes	Yes	Yes
Data can be accessible yet prevented from being copied to remote client	Yes	No	Yes
Full desktop is presented in a window to client	Yes	No	Yes
Applications can be launched transparently and appear to be locally launched	No	No	Yes
Can be used over any dialup or Internet connection	Yes	Yes	Yes

The Evolution of the Thin Client

The thin client model evolved from an idea developed originally in Citrix's WinView product in which multiple remote control sessions could run on a single server. Citrix was able to see the benefits and limitations of the mainframe and distributed computing models as well as remote control and remote node computing. Since these types of computing are merged into a single thin client model, their benefits increase.

Today's thin client model uses Citrix MetaFrame XP running on Windows 2000 Terminal Services. A remote client uses the ICA client software to connect to a server over any type of dialup or Internet link. Once connected, the remote client can open a virtual desktop or launch an individual application transparently. All application processing takes place on the Citrix MetaFrame XP server, with only screen updates being displayed on the remote client. With the thin client model, Windows terminal hardware can be used to connect to the thin client server.

In reviewing the thin client model, there are two key terms to understand:

> **Thin client** A thin client is the session that takes place between the server and its client. This session consists solely of the screen updates, keyboard strokes, and mouse clicks transferred between the two machines. The client is considered "thin" because it consumes very little bandwidth with its compressed traffic. Windows terminals are now available for use with thin client

servers. These thin client machines are similar to mainframe terminals, except for heightened graphics capabilities, occasional support for Web browsers, and some memory to increase performance. With such capabilities, they are considered "intelligent," even though they do not have the ability to process any applications locally.

Fat client A fat client is the session that takes place between a server and its client that transmits actual data between the two. A fat client is considered "fat" because of the relatively large amount of data transmitted and high consumption of bandwidth. A typical database application uses a fat client when client and server are on separate machines.

The History of Citrix MetaFrame

Citrix grew out of a concept developed by Ed Iacobucci, who headed the OS/2 program for IBM and Microsoft. Iacobucci conceived of a system whereby computers that were not designed to run OS/2 could start doing so. In 1989, Iacobucci formed Citrix Systems, Inc. (the name is derived from *citrus*, since the company is based in Florida) to take this concept forward. The name of the technology? MultiWin.

Product Evolution: From Citrix WinView to WinFrame to MetaFrame

MultiWin enables multiple users to simultaneously run multiple user sessions on a computer. In the process, the sessions share the system resources, including network interfaces, processor, memory, input/output, and other resources. After creating WinView on the OS/2 platform, the company soon realized that OS/2's days were numbered. In 1991, Citrix licensed the source code for Windows NT from Microsoft and began developing MultiWin on the Windows NT platform. Microsoft also invested in Citrix, buying 6 percent of the company. In 1995, Citrix unveiled its WinFrame product, the first one to combine MultiWin technology, the ICA protocol, and the Windows NT operating system.

The WinFrame product was extremely successful. Microsoft enjoyed an explosion in sales of Windows NT at the same time. Because of this success, Microsoft believed that it did not need Citrix's help to sell Windows NT and in February 1997 notified Citrix that it intended to develop its own multiuser technology. Citrix stockowners will remember the date: Citrix stock plummeted more than 60 percent in a single day. The public was not sure that Citrix would survive. Citrix and Microsoft, however, negotiated over the next few months until they struck a deal.

Microsoft had one objective: to become a player in the thin client market. Citrix had its own objective: to continue to be in the thin client market. The deal provided both. Microsoft licensed the MultiWin technology from Citrix. Citrix retained the right to continue development on the WinFrame product. Citrix also retained the ICA protocol and the ability to develop an add-on product for the Microsoft Windows NT Terminal Services products. The deal specified that Microsoft could develop its own thin clients, but only for Microsoft Windows operating systems. Citrix was free to develop ICA clients for any type of operating system. Citrix's stock revived immediately based on this news.

Under the new agreement, Microsoft quickly adapted MultiWin in Windows NT 4.0, Terminal Server Edition, with its own client using Remote Desktop Protocol (RDP). Although the surface of the Terminal Server Edition looked the same as the standard version, the inner workings were much different. The two required separate service packs, hot fixes, and special drivers. Microsoft asked vendors to certify its printer drivers to work with Terminal Server Edition.

Citrix quickly released the MetaFrame 1.0 for Windows NT 4.0 Terminal Server Edition. Later, it improved the product and released MetaFrame 1.8. These products offered several advantages over the "plain vanilla" Windows NT 4.0 with Terminal Services:

- Ability to deliver 32-bit applications to platforms other than Windows

- Low bandwidth consumption using ICA protocol

- Multiprotocol capabilities (RDP runs only over TCP/IP)

- Ability to launch the ICA client and applications from within a browser

- Ability to launch higher-resolution graphics yet retain low bandwidth consumption

Rather than release a separate edition of Windows 2000 for customers who wanted to run thin clients, Microsoft delivered Windows 2000 Server, Windows 2000 Advanced Server, and Windows 2000 DataCenter Server with the native ability to run Terminal Services. Microsoft had received a great deal of feedback about the ease of managing a server using the remote control features. Therefore, the company included a native license for two sessions to be running on each Windows 2000 server. When Terminal Services are activated, they can be activated for the two sessions in remote administration mode, or Terminal Services can be activated for multiple clients, each requiring a thin client license.

Citrix released MetaFrame 1.8 for Windows 2000 servers. Today, Citrix offers MetaFrame XP for Windows 2000 servers. Citrix continues to develop ICA clients that work with any version of MetaFrame. These clients can attach anything from a Linux box to an Epoch mobile device to a Citrix MetaFrame server and then launch a 32-bit Windows application.

MetaFrame XPs, XPa, and XPe

Citrix MetaFrame XP comes in three versions. Like Windows 2000, which scales from Windows 2000 Server to Windows 2000 Advanced Server to Windows 2000 DataCenter Server, the three versions of Citrix MetaFrame XP scale up in capabilities as well. The three versions are:

- Citrix MetaFrame XPs
- Citrix MetaFrame XPa
- Citrix MetaFrame XPe

Citrix MetaFrame XPs is the base version of the three. Created for a small deployment of thin client, it provides the application services across LANs, WANs, the Internet, intranets, and extranets. MetaFrame XPs offers many features. It uses the Citrix Management Console and Program Neighborhood. It has centralized printer management and license management. Not only does it support both Active Directory and Novell Directory Services, it can encrypt session data using the Secure Socket Layer (SSL). It also includes the NFuse version 1.6, described in the next section of this chapter.

Citrix MetaFrame XPa was designed with features that meet the needs of small and medium-size businesses. It contains all the features of XPs, but XPa also includes Advanced Load Management. Moving toward the server farm paradigm, Advanced Load Management enables the XPa version to dynamically manage the number of sessions assigned to any one of a group of XPa servers.

Citrix MetaFrame XPe builds on the features of XPa and adds management capabilities that are well suited for large organizations. In deploying a server farm, the XPe version should be selected due to its features. On top of all the other features, XPe includes the ability to package and deliver applications as well as system monitoring and analysis.

NFuse

NFuse 1.6 is best described as a portal product for publishing applications to the Web. The solution consists of three components:

- Citrix MetaFrame server
- Web server
- ICA client with a Web browser

Using NFuse, a Citrix MetaFrame XP administrator can publish any interactive 32-bit Windows applications or UNIX applications (when using Citrix MetaFrame 1.1 for UNIX) to the Internet so that they can be launched from within a standard browser.

With a little effort and organization, a portal with personalized information can be created for users so that they have Web-based access to all their tools and applications, without needing to install them locally. There is no need to reengineer a business application to fit the Web. Using NFuse, the Web can be leveraged with existing applications, reducing the time, effort, and costs involved in such a project.

Citrix MetaFrame 1.1 for UNIX

UNIX applications are used throughout businesses today. Since these applications can only be used on UNIX machines, in the past many organizations provided multiple machines per user so that the user could access both UNIX and Windows applications. With Citrix MetaFrame XP, a person who uses UNIX daily can also receive a Windows session on the same machine. However, with the prevalence of Windows on the desktop and the higher likelihood of finding users who are familiar with Windows, there is a need to deliver UNIX applications to people with non-UNIX platforms. This is the goal of Citrix MetaFrame 1.1 for UNIX. Besides offering remote access to applications, as do many other terminal emulation applications, Citrix MetaFrame for UNIX offers a high-performance graphical session using the same ICA client that can access Citrix MetaFrame XP servers.

   This product can provide UNIX and Java applications to any ICA client, whether Linux, UNIX, Epoch, Windows 32-bit, or DOS, over the same types of connections that Citrix MetaFrame XP can use. Improving the performance of graphical UNIX applications delivered across low-bandwidth connections and able to implement higher security, Citrix MetaFrame 1.1 for UNIX works with Sun Solaris, AIX, and HP-UX versions.

Windows 2000 Terminal Services

Windows 2000 with Terminal Services is the Microsoft thin client server that uses the MultiWin technology combined with Microsoft's RDP thin client. Windows 2000 Terminal Services uses RDP version 5.0. Previously, Windows NT 4.0, Terminal Server Edition, used RDP version 4.0.

   With Windows 2000 Terminal Services, a business has a complete multiuser thin client system. Users who connect to the server receive a traditional Windows 2000 desktop view. The client is presented in a window on the desktop. Figure 1.10 displays the standard Terminal Services desktop.

Special Mode for Installing Applications

Even though Windows 2000 Server has the Terminal Services capability built right into the code, you don't have to install it. You can choose to have a standard Windows 2000 file and print server. You can also choose to install Terminal Services in remote administration mode or in applications services mode. As stated earlier, remote administration mode enables two sessions for RDP clients to connect to the server. When Terminal Services is installed in applications services mode, many more clients can run sessions connected simultaneously.

Figure 1.10 The Terminal Services Client Desktop

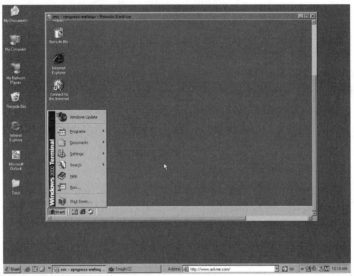

When Terminal Services have been installed, multiple interactive sessions can run on the server at the same time. Win32API calls have been reprogrammed so that they allow traditional Windows applications to use configuration files and registry information in a multiuser model. Some applications, such as Microsoft's Office suite, must be installed with a different template in order to function in a multiuser system. Other applications must be installed using *install mode*. There are three ways to put the server in install mode:

- You can use the Add/Remove icon in the Control Panel to invoke install mode.

- If an application's installation starts and you select the option to install the program for all users rather than just yourself, the server is automatically placed in install mode.

- You can also open a command prompt window and type **Change User /Install** to bring up install mode.

The normal mode for Terminal Services is *execute mode*. Whenever you are completing an installation, you should open a command prompt window and type **Change User /Execute**. More about installing applications appears in Chapter 9.

Overview of Terminal Services Licensing

Starting a new Windows 2000 server with Terminal Services, thin client services are immediately available. However, you must install them in order to use them. Furthermore, if you install the application services mode (as opposed to remote administration mode), you have 90 days to activate a license server to manage Terminal Services client licenses.

Terminal Services client licenses are different from standard client access licenses (CALs) for Windows 2000 Server. A standard CAL is required to access a file and print server. If you set up a Windows 2000 server with Terminal Services and never share files or printers from it, none of the users needs a standard CAL. They will need Terminal Services CALs (TS CALs), which are available as follows:

- You do not need to purchase a TS CAL for the most recent Microsoft Windows operating systems. Each Windows 2000 Professional, Windows NT 4.0 Workstation, or Windows XP machine has a built-in TS CAL.

- You may purchase from Microsoft a TS CAL for any other operating system installed on a network computer.

- You may purchase a Work-at-Home TS CAL from Microsoft. This is a discounted CAL that combines the standard CAL and the Terminal Services CAL and is intended for telecommuters.

- You may purchase an Internet Connection License. This is a special type of license for allowing up to 200 anonymous users to connect concurrently to Terminal Services over the Internet. This license is intended for users who are not employees of the company.

The Terminal Services licensing server is an option that can be installed on any Windows 2000 domain controller in Active Directory or on a Windows 2000 server in a Windows NT 4.0 domain. The licensing server tracks the available licenses and distributes them to client devices. When the licensing server is installed, it needs to receive a digital certificate from the Microsoft Clearinghouse in order to be activated. After activation, you can install licenses. You do not need a Terminal Services licensing server in order to run servers in remote administration mode. You can find more about Terminal Services licensing in Chapter 6.

Overview of Terminal Services Consoles

The native Windows 2000 management consoles will become a Terminal Services administrator's home turf for managing thin client connectivity. Other tool sets are available to help manage a Terminal Server from the Windows 2000 Resource Kit.

More in-depth discussions about these consoles and how to use them can be found throughout this book. All in all, you should become familiar with several different consoles, each handling a unique administrative task:

- Terminal Services Connection Configuration

- Active Directory Users and Computers

- Terminal Services Manager

- Terminal Services Licensing Manager

- Terminal Services Client Creator

- Terminal Services User Manager for Domains

- Application Security Registration

The Terminal Services Connection Configuration console, shown in Figure 1.11, is used for creating sessions and configuring the variables within them. You will use this console to establish the protocols that should be used by a session as well as the security for each session, including access and encryption for each individual connection.

Figure 1.11 The Terminal Services Connection Configuration Console

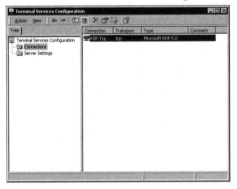

Each connection has multiple options for configuration. By double-clicking a connection name, the administrator can edit security options, remote control settings, the network adapter the connection is available to, and more. The properties for an RDP connection are shown in Figure 1.12.

The Active Directory Users and Computers Console is the primary method of managing users. In this console, an administrator can create new users, change user information, and delete users from the Active Directory domain. This is primarily a network administration tool for user information, it does include Terminal Services configuration options for users, as shown in Figure 1.12. The new Terminal Services information for users is distributed among four tabs:

Figure 1.12 Properties for a Connection

- **Terminal Services Profile** This tab allows the administrator to create a specific profile for thin client sessions. This profile can differ from a file-and-print profile. It is useful for administrators to be able to separate the thin client profile from standard profiles, especially when an administrator does not want to overwrite a telecommuter's or anonymous Internet user's home profile.

- **Sessions** This tab offers specific configuration information for a user's session. This information can customize how a session acts for a particular user, such as increasing or decreasing the disconnect time for a session rather than inheriting the standard session configuration.

- **Environment** This tab configures the way that a client device is handled when it is initially connected to the server.

- **Remote Control** This tab sets the security options for remote control sessions.

The Terminal Services Manager is the most interactive and useful of the administrative consoles. Using the Terminal Services Manager, you can view processes that are currently active on all Windows 2000 Terminal Services servers within the domain. The Terminal Services Manager is the optimal tool for monitoring and troubleshooting the sessions run by thin client users. Shown in Figure 1.13, this is the console that the administrator uses to view the processes users execute in their sessions.

A Terminal Services administrator is given only 90 days to activate a licensing server and add licenses for the sessions used on the server. During the 90-day period, the licensing server provides temporary TS CALs to machines that connect. These licenses are tracked. After the 90 days have completed for each temporary TS CAL, that machine can no longer access the server. However, once the licensing server has been activated and TS CALs have been installed, the machines connect to the server, and the temporary TS CAL is automatically upgraded to a standard TS CAL. To add licenses, you use the Terminal Services Licensing Manager. Figure 1.14 displays this console.

Figure 1.13 Terminal Services Manager

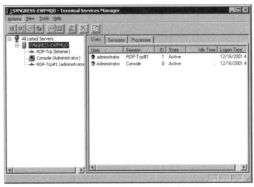

Figure 1.14 Terminal Services Licensing Manager

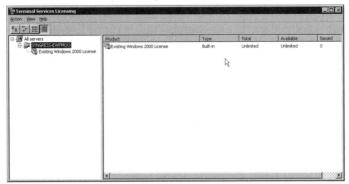

The client software for the RDP client can be generated from Windows 2000 Server with Terminal Services. This is performed through the Terminal Services Client Creator. Pictured in Figure 1.15, this console offers the ability to generate installation disks for either 16-bit Windows or 32-bit Windows RDP clients.

Figure 1.15 Terminal Services Client Creator

Although it is not installed as a default tool, you could find the Terminal Services User Manager for Domains an essential tool if you are using a Windows 2000 Terminal Services server within a Windows NT 4.0 domain. The standard User Manager for Domains in a Windows NT domain does not include the configuration options for users that you need for specific configurations. You should be careful not to use the Terminal Services User Manager for regular domain administration, since it will increase the record size for users due to the additional user parameter fields.

The Windows 2000 Server Resource Kit contains the Application Security Registration utility console. This is a tool that offers administrators tighter control over applications and who can use them. When this console is in use, a user cannot execute a listed application unless that user has Administrator privileges.

Remote Desktop Protocol

Remote Desktop Protocol (RDP) is to Windows 2000 Terminal Services as ICA is to Citrix MetaFrame XP. It is the protocol that carries the thin client session information, including transmission of graphical data and mouse/keyboard clicks, between the server and the access device.

The original version of RDP, version 4.0, was incorporated into the Windows NT 4.0 Terminal Services Edition. Windows 2000 Terminal Services and thin clients use RDP version 5.0. Based on the T.120 standards, RDP handles graphical transmission through an RDP display driver, which is run separately for each session. Each thin client session also runs its own Win32 kernel, with the display drivers contained in a session address of virtual memory. Receiving commands from the graphical display interface (GDI), the RDP display driver then passes them on to the Terminal Services device driver, which then encodes them in RDP format. The information is then sent to the Transport layer and through the protocol stack onto the wire to the client access device.

The new version of RDP, version 5.0, is packed with new features:

- **Bitmap caching** Storing graphics locally can enhance a client's performance. This is a new capability within RDP 5.0. During the session, graphics are stored locally and the client sends a list of keys corresponding to the bitmaps in cache. These keys are used to either call up locally stored graphics or to request new graphics from the server. Preset to 10MB, the bitmap cache storage size cannot be altered.

- **Client printer mapping** Without going into the difficulties of managing printers with RDP 4.0, the client printer-mapping capability adds a great benefit for administrators under RDP 5.0. When a client connects to a Windows 2000 Terminal Services session, the local printer (or printers) will be mapped to appear as network printer connections in the session. The client can print locally either from within the session or from applications running locally on the desktop. The prerequisite for this functionality is that the drivers for the printer exist on the server.

- **Local/remote clipboard copying** When launching a remote desktop, the clipboard in the remote desktop is separate from that of the local desktop. With RDP 5.0, information that is copied to the clipboard in the remote session can be pasted to the local clipboard.

- **Shadowing** One of the values that help desks and administrators have found in thin client computing is the ability to shadow a user's session and troubleshoot user problems. This capability is available with RDP 5.0. The administrator can connect to a user's session and "shadow" it, viewing the session on the administrator's desktop—even taking control of the session. Security settings must be established to enable shadowing, and rights must be granted to let a shadowed session take place. Prerequisites for shadowing are that video resolutions must be the same or better on the administrator's machine, and both the administrator and the shadowed user must be logged in to the same server.

The RDP client, which runs only on TCP/IP networks, is available for 16-bit Windows (Windows for Workgroups 3.11) or 32-bit Windows (Windows 95, Windows 98, Windows Me, Windows NT 3.51, Windows NT 4.0, and Windows 2000). Windows XP contains a Remote Desktop client in its native code. For any machine that will be connecting to a Windows 2000 Terminal Server, the RDP client must be installed. For any machine connecting to a Windows 2000 Terminal Server with Citrix MetaFrame XP, an ICA client must be installed, or applications can be launched from a compatible browser. You can read more about Terminal Services RDP clients and Citrix MetaFrame XP ICA clients in Chapter 6.

Citrix MetaFrame XP

Windows 2000 Terminal Services is the base operating system for Citrix MetaFrame XP. Extended by Citrix MetaFrame, the thin client server can support the ICA protocol clients in addition to RDP clients. The ICA protocol and Citrix MetaFrame's base features offer many advantages over standard Windows 2000 Terminal Services, one of the greatest advantages is the ability to treat large implementations of thin client servers as a single server farm.

Independent Computing Architecture

Independent Computing Architecture (ICA) clients are unique to Citrix MetaFrame XP. If you do not have Citrix MetaFrame XP installed, you cannot use the ICA protocol clients, even though the ICA client software is freely available for download from Citrix's Web site. The ICA client offers some advantages over the RDP client:

- Available for all Windows operating systems, DOS, UNIX, Linux, Macintosh, and OS/2

- Available for EPOCH and Pocket PC mobile devices

- Windows Based Terminals

- Full client device mapping, including audio, COM port, and printer mapping

- Local drive remapping

- SpeedScreen2 latency reduction

- Multiprotocol usage

- Seamless windows

Citrix offers software for ICA clients that operate on DOS and 16-bit Windows 3.1 as well as Windows for Workgroups 3.11, Windows 95, Windows 98, Windows Me, Windows NT 3.51, Windows NT 4.0, Windows 2000, and Windows XP. In addition to these, Citrix offers clients for a variety of UNIX operating systems, Linux, Macintosh, and OS/2.

Wireless and mobile devices offer a new opportunity for thin clients. Because these devices are so small, they cannot support extensive applications. They can, however, support thin clients and run full-featured applications in remote-controlled sessions. Being able to perform such computing over public wireless networks or using wireless modems, businesses can leverage wireless devices and thin client computing to increase productivity to new levels. Citrix offers ICA clients for EPOCH and Pocket PC mobile devices and will likely continue to release new clients for other mobile devices as this market develops.

ICA thin client terminal hardware is referred to as a *Windows Based Terminal (WBT)*. Each WBT runs an embedded ICA client that is immediately available to connect to the network. A WBT cannot run without a Citrix MetaFrame server on the network. Often used as a point-of-sale (POS) terminal or in kiosks, thin client machines do not contain complex hardware components. They mainly consist of a monitor, keyboard, and mouse along with the embedded ICA client.

An ICA client is able to run applications with sound by mapping remote audio to local audio. An ICA client can also map COM ports and LPT ports so that modems and other serial devices as well as all printers can be accessed. Keep in mind, however, that when audio mapping is used, it increases the bandwidth consumption of the session transmission.

Within a thin client session, the user sees the drives that are local to the server. This is not helpful if the user needs to save a file to the local computer. ICA clients can map a local drive to the remote session so that it appears as a drive letter within the remote session. In doing so, the user can save files and transfer files using standard drag-and-drop methods in the session's Explorer or simply save to the mapped drive letter through the application itself. There can be confusion, however, for users who assume that the C: drive in the remote session is the same drive as their local hard drive. Citrix has a solution to this problem. When you install Citrix MetaFrame XP, you are prompted to remap the local drives to different letters. The default is to remap the C: drive to M:. When you choose this option, a client connects to a session and sees the local C: drive as the session's C: drive, and the server's drives begin mapping from M: onward in the session. If you do *not* select the remapping function, when a client connects to a session, it sees the server's C: drive as the session's C: drive and the client's local C: drive as the session's V: drive (and any other local drives map backward alphabetically so that the D: drive is U: and so on.). Citrix MetaFrame XP allows the administrator to turn off client drive mapping altogether so that data cannot be saved to local drives at all. This option is helpful when you use thin client sessions in highly secure situations in which data should not be saved to other machines.

SpeedScreen2 is a feature that increases the performance of ICA. By cutting the average packet size 25 to 30 percent, the transmission rate is improved up to 60 percent. In remote locations, especially those that depend on unreliable satellite connections, SpeedScreen2 offers a tremendous advantage.

ICA is known for its high performance, even when transmitted to mobile and wireless devices. The reason it performs so well is that ICA consumes no more than 20Kbps. Because of its small size, a standard modem connection speed of 28.8Kbps appears to be running locally.

When you consider the Open Systems Interconnection (OSI) protocol reference model, which is shown in Figure 1.16, the ICA protocol typically sits at the Presentation and Session layers, just as RDP does. However, ICA was built to flexibly integrate with multiple protocols. It requires a Transport layer. If ICA is transmitted across a protocol that does not include a Transport layer, such as Internetwork Packet Exchange (IPX) or Internet Protocol (IP), ICA incorporates the services that are provided at the Transport layer. Figure 1.17 depicts how ICA works in conjunction with IPX running on an Ethernet segment.

In addition to all these functions, ICA clients have the same features as RDP clients, including:

- Bitmap caching
- Local/remote clipboard copying
- Shadowing

Figure 1.16 The OSI Protocol Model and RDP and ICA Protocols

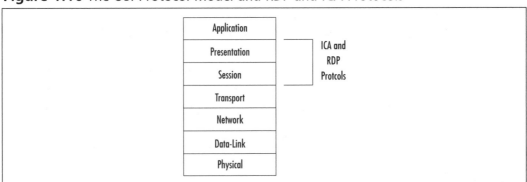

Figure 1.17 ICA with IPX over Ethernet

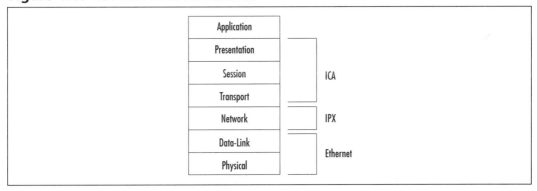

Many highly regulated industries, the government, and businesses that intend to use thin clients for confidential information require encryption to secure the transmission of data between the thin client and the Citrix MetaFrame XP server. Citrix offers SecureICA, which is available with 40-bit, 56-bit, and 128-bit capabilities, to encrypt session transmissions. This encryption uses the RC5 standard created by RSA.

ICA clients support seamless windows. An administrator can publish an application so that it launches from its own window without the remote desktop appearing behind it. This capability makes it appear as though the application has launched locally. Available only with 32-bit Windows ICA clients, the remote application appears in the taskbar and responds to **Alt + Tab** to switch between applications. Users will not know whether the application is remote or local. When using seamless windows, you should consider using license pooling, in which a client can open multiple remote applications and consume only a single ICA license. However, if you choose not to use license pooling, a client will consume an ICA license for each remote application executed.

Moving to the Server Farm

The key concept of the *server farm* has little to do with the ICA client. Server farms are centered around managing multiple servers on the network and preferably being able to treat them as a single resource for user access. Citrix MetaFrame XP offers enterprise-level scalability in its server management tools.

One advantage to Citrix MetaFrame XP is that it supports load balancing of published applications. Through application publishing, users connect to the name of an application rather than the name of a server. The back-end processes include load calculations to determine which server has the most available resources to support a new session. These back-end processes are shown in Figure 1.18.

Figure 1.18 Load Balancing of Published Applications

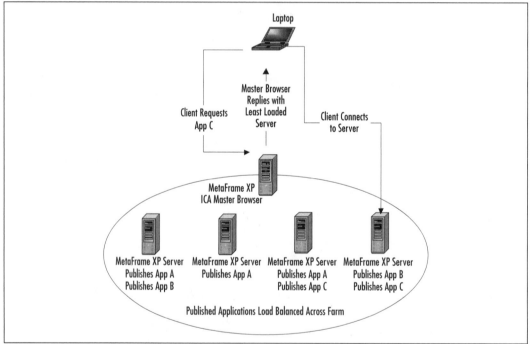

Load balancing for published applications is the first step. In a Citrix MetaFrame XP server farm, a group of servers that typically publish the same applications can be logically grouped together to facilitate application management. When using a server farm, users are not prompted for multiple logons. Instead, their credentials are passed to any server when a session request is made.

Citrix MetaFrame XP introduces a new concept called *Independent Management Architecture (IMA)*. IMA is a service that installs on each server. IMA services communicate with each other, supply data to a database, and update a local host cache in order for the server farm to be managed as a single unit. Citrix MetaFrame XP includes a number of management utilities:

- **Citrix Management Console** This is an IMA-based tool for managing the server farm. The administrator need only log on to a single Citrix Management Console to manage every Citrix MetaFrame XP server in the network. The administrator will be able to view and update all the servers within the enterprise, regardless of the farms to which they belong.

- **Citrix Web Console** This Web-based utility for managing the server farm is intended for installation on a Windows 2000 server with Internet Information Services (IIS). From the client perspective, you must also use Internet Explorer 4.0 or later. The Citrix Web Console does not support Netscape.

Because Citrix MetaFrame XPe is built for enterprise deployments, it includes additional management features that are not included in other versions, namely Installation Manager. Installation Manager helps an administrator deploy applications to predefined groups of servers. By creating groups and establishing this method of deployment, an administrator can save a great deal of time and effort in application deployment. Resource Manager is another feature included only in Citrix MetaFrame XPe. Resource Manager is a centralized location for settings, thresholds, and metrics and helps monitor the performance of servers in the farm. Network Manager is a third feature found only within Citrix MetaFrame XPe and helps integrate server farm management into enterprise network management.

Gaining Digital Independence with Thin Clients

The Internet brought about a certain sense of independence in computing. Using a common global internetwork, people could publish formatted text documents with graphics and reasonably expect that any operating system could access the information. Prior to the Internet and Hypertext Markup Language (HTML), the interoperability of various operating systems was limited because of the proprietary nature of document formats. Since then, browser capabilities have increased to include scripts, applications, and services. Digital independence, in the form of a person delivering an application to any device in any location over any connection, seemed to be the next step.

Mobile computing has brought a new element to the Internet. Mobile devices have limited capabilities because, although they are becoming smaller and more intelligent, they still do not have the screen resolution and storage capacity available in a desktop PC. This means that rendering Internet data to a data-enabled cell phone or Pocket PC must be adjusted for the smaller screen and storage of the mobile device. The transmission of the data through wireless networking is constrained due to the low-bandwidth capabilities of public wireless networks. Digital independence is not as easy to achieve as it might seem.

Citrix MetaFrame XP can be used to help break the bonds of proprietary networking. Using WBTs, a network administrator does not need to manage PCs in order to deliver 32-bit Windows desktops to the network.

For administrators with networks that include many different types of operating systems, whether UNIX, Windows, or others, being able to run the same application on any operating system can remove many headaches as well as reduce costs. In a business that has many different operating systems, when a mission-critical application is rolled out to all end users, some of the operating systems might be incompatible. An administrator is left with options that include developing special client applications for the incompatible operating systems, using a Web-based application that might not be fully featured, or not rolling out the application at all. This is a situation that calls for Citrix MetaFrame XP. Offering full digital independence, a 32-bit Windows application can be delivered to any ICA client, regardless of the operating system of the access device, even if it is a mobile one connected to a wireless network. In fact, an application can be delivered from within a browser on the Internet to anonymous users, if need be. Figure 1.19 displays how Citrix MetaFrame XP can be used to achieve digital independence.

Figure 1.19 Digital Independence with Citrix MetaFrame XP

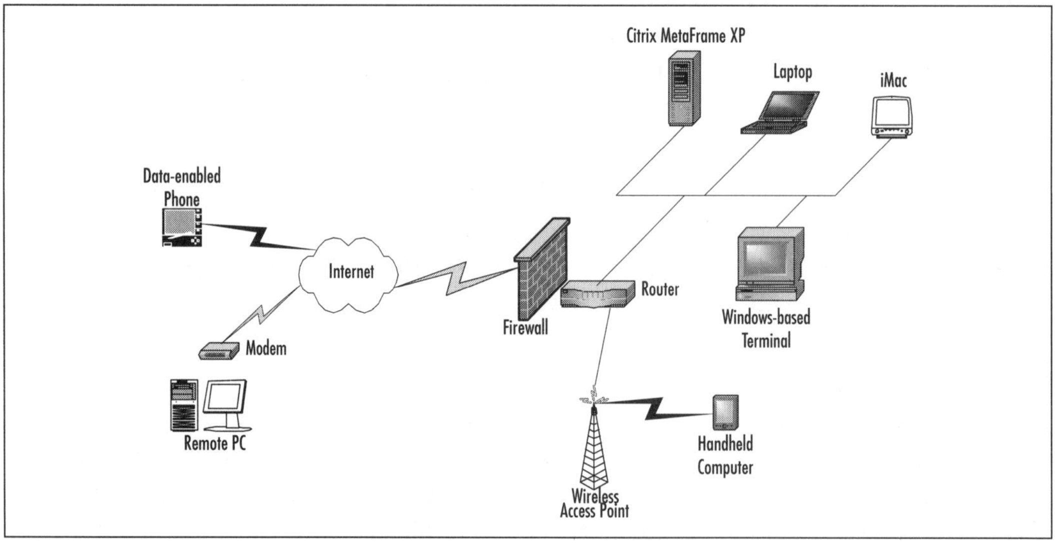

Achieving Bottom-Line Value with Thin Clients

When faced with a large deployment project for Citrix MetaFrame XP, most network administrators must justify the costs of the project. They need proof of corporate benefits in order to obtain budget dollars. A cost/benefit analysis might be necessary for making a decision between rolling out Citrix MetaFrame XP or selecting a different technology. Regardless of the impetus, looking at the financial impact of such a project is usually part of the decision-making process.

Usually two types of costs and benefits are reviewed: *hard dollars* and *soft dollars*. Hard-dollar costs are costs of items that are paid for with cash. Hard-dollar benefits involve items that can be accounted for as increased revenues. Hard-dollar benefits can also be costs that are removed, thereby increasing profits. For example, if you currently pay $100 per month for each PC's warranty, and by implementing Citrix MetaFrame XP with WBTs, you no longer pay $100 per month for any PCs, you will see a great improvement in profits.

Soft-dollar costs are items that cost time and effort but are not accounted for in a budget. For example, if 30 Sun Solaris users must walk 20 minutes to a different department daily to use a Windows 2000 PC in order to run a specific application, and their average hourly wage is $10, you are spending 600 minutes' worth of soft dollars a day, which equates to 10 hours of time, or $100, per day. Soft-dollar benefits are identical in nature. When you can save time or effort or increase productivity, you receive a soft-dollar benefit. The exact dollar value of any soft-dollar cost or benefit is not easy to figure out. Take our example of the $100-per-day soft-dollar cost. If you removed such a soft-dollar cost, you would receive a soft-dollar benefit. Given that an average person in that department had a productivity level of $100 per hour, you might think that the soft-dollar benefit would be an increase of 10 hours, or $1000, per day of productivity increase. But people are not that predictable. The likelihood that each person in that department would put all of the extra 20 minutes toward productive work is very low. In reality, you might expect a 50-percent productivity increase for those hours.

Calculating Costs

This section covers hard costs and then discusses how to calculate soft costs. When you calculate the hard costs of a Citrix MetaFrame XP project, you must list all the hardware and software to be purchased as well as the cost of any labor used in the execution of the project. When rolling out Citrix MetaFrame XP, you should consider the following costs:

- **Server hardware**

    1. Number of servers

    2. Type of servers

    3. Number of symmetric multiprocessors (SMP)

    4. Storage or Redundant Array of Inexpensive Disks (RAID)

    5. Amount of RAM

    6. Single or redundant network interface cards (NICs)

    7. Single or redundant power supplies

- **Peripheral equipment**

    1. Uninterruptible power supply (UPS)

    2. Number of keyboards

    3. Number of mice

    4. Number of monitors

    5. Number of keyboard/monitor/mouse switches

    6. Racks for storing server equipment

    7. Cables

- **Network connectivity** In most cases, you will likely leverage existing connections. However, if you will be installing new network or Internet connectivity, these costs may be incurred:

    1. Installation of new connections

    2. Monthly lease or periodic charges for connectivity

    3. Number of routers

    4. Number of hubs

    5. Number of switches

    6. Installation of cabling or wireless access points

    7. Number of wireless or standard NICs to replace existing

- **End-user equipment** Depending on your deployment, these costs might be incurred, regardless of whether or not you roll out Citrix MetaFrame XP. If so, you should not consider them in a cost comparison. If you are comparing a desktop rollout to a Citrix MetaFrame XP rollout, you will likely incur fewer costs in this area and therefore *must* include these costs for a true cost comparison:

1. Number of desktops

2. Number of WBTs

3. Number of mobile/handheld devices

4. Number of monitors

5. Number of keyboards

6. Number of mice

7. Number of NICs

8. Cables

- **Software**

1. Windows 2000 Server licenses

2. Windows 2000 Terminal Services clients

3. Citrix MetaFrame XP licenses

4. ICA client licenses

5. Number of application licenses

6. Number of new operating system licenses (only when rolling out new desktops with upgrades)

7. Utilities selected for use in deployment

- **Labor**

1. Design services

2. Assessment services

3. Configuration services

4. Installation services

5. Administrative and operational services

6. End-user training services

You will likely go back to your hard costs list and add or subtract items many times over. In the area of end-user equipment, you could find that you can use some old PCs currently stored in a closet or avoid rolling out PCs to a group of users because their equipment can be reused.

Soft costs are not as easy to quantify. You need to use a little imagination in order to determine the soft costs that will be incurred. You should consider how the project will be executed, delays that will be caused for end users, and how those delays will affect productivity. You should estimate any increase in needs for troubleshooting and help desk support, which generally increase immediately following a new technology deployment. The following list might help you:

- **Support costs**
  1. Increased help desk costs
  2. After hours support needs
  3. 24 x 7 management and monitoring costs
  4. Warranty support

- **Software costs**
  1. Software maintenance contracts
  2. Hardware maintenance costs
  3. Upgrade costs and frequency

Calculating Benefits

Businesses with thin client implementations derive benefits that affect the bottom line. Not only can a business implement a thin client solution to take advantage of new opportunities that can generate new revenue, but the business can reduce costs and avoid future costs. The situation depends on the project's business goals and how the technology is deployed to meet them. Some of the most common business objectives for thin client projects are:

- Reduce costs by extending the life of older equipment
- Reduce costs by avoiding implementation of higher-bandwidth links
- Reduce costs through use of remote control support methods

Extending the Life of Older Equipment

Avoiding the need to upgrade operating systems and desktop hardware can save millions of dollars in an enterprise network. The ability to deploy a thin client solution to every user in an enterprise is unlikely. Some users, through their heavy use of graphics-intensive applications or their need to work offline, cannot use a thin client 100 percent of the time. On the other hand, a business can deploy a thin client solution to users who never are expected to need offline computing. Reduced costs in this scenario consist of:

- Avoided costs of new equipment purchases

- Avoided costs of operating systems licenses

- Reduced administrative costs and increased productivity, since users can switch machines without loss of data

- Increased viability of data because data is stored to centralized servers

- Avoided costs of training for new equipment and operating systems

Reducing Bandwidth Consumption

In a telecommuting environment, the ability to execute mission-critical applications is increased. Running that mission-critical application across the wire can become frustrating due to performance across a low-bandwidth connection. Even if an individual connection could perform well, the corporate conduit to the Internet might not support multiple users running the application. If a client application is "fat," a modem connection might not be usable to support it. A company could be faced with installing cable modem connections, DSL, or ISDN links in order to support telecommuters. In the example shown in Figure 1.20, 10 users are running an application through the Internet. If the bandwidth consumption of these fat clients adds up to more than 1.544Mbps, the corporate Internet connection becomes a bottleneck for the users. Performance is affected, not only for the users on the Internet, but also for any users who are attempting to access the Internet from within the corporate network. The options are to either upgrade the Internet connection or to implement a thin client.

The benefits of implementing a thin client solution are:

- Avoiding the need for faster Internet links for telecommuters

- Avoiding the upgrade costs for Internet connectivity for the corporate connection

- Centralized management of the client application

Allowing the Help Desk to Shadow Users

The process of supporting end users can be fraught with visits to the deskside. If there is a problem with an application and the help desk staff cannot walk the user through the issue on the phone, a technician is sent to the desk to actually see the problem and troubleshoot from there. The ability to see firsthand what the user is doing or what errors are taking place is usually all it takes to fix the problem.

Figure 1.20 Running Applications Across the Internet

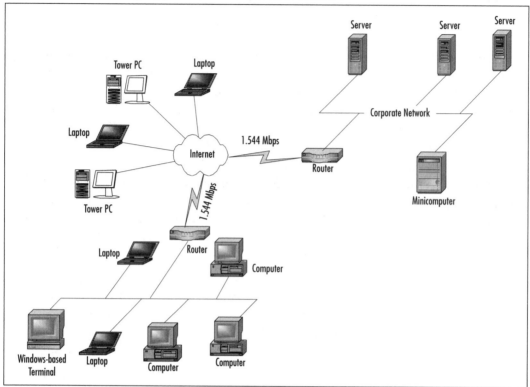

Shadowing a user's session can become a benefit by itself. Instead of a user calling the help desk and a technician being dispatched to the user's desk, sometimes many hours later, the help desk staff can shadow the user's session and view the problems directly, resulting in faster resolution. Since a deskside support visit costs as much as 10 times the cost of a help desk support call, shadowing can work out to be a tremendous benefit. The benefits for this type of situation consist of:

- Reduced numbers of deskside support calls
- Faster resolution for support calls
- Increased productivity for end users with support calls

Meeting Business Needs

Business needs fall into two categories. Some business needs are simply *musts*. Driven by regulatory compliance, relief from nuisance systems, or simply a requirement handed down from upper management, these types of projects are nearly always given top priority. The other category of business need is *growth*. Using technology as a means to grow the business makes for an exciting project.

Security

Technology security is a must. In regulated industries, data might not be allowed to be distributed across different machines, and users might not be allowed access to certain applications. Using Citrix MetaFrame XP, an administrator can easily meet these types of security needs. By installing an application on a Citrix MetaFrame XP server, the administrator can centrally manage it. The administrator can easily grant privileges or limit access to the application. Restricting the ability to print, map local drives, and copy to the local clipboard, the administrator can ensure that the data is retained solely on the Citrix MetaFrame XP server. The administrator can further encrypt the data transmissions and require authentication to either Active Directory or Novell Directory Services.

Internet Deployment to Unknown Clients

Using the Internet to deploy applications can be a cumbersome process. Many businesses have looked to application developers to reprogram their software to be Web-compatible and then have dealt with the process of securing, encrypting, and managing those applications and their data from an entirely new back-end infrastructure. This situation is complicated by the need to ensure compatibility with different browsers and desktop operating systems.

An administrator can easily install Citrix MetaFrame XP as the means to deploy applications across the Internet. This method includes a host of benefits:

- Avoiding the cost of application programming

- Avoiding the complications of integration

- Speeding up the deployment time

- Leveraging the existing investments in technology

Summary

Understanding the history of the mainframe and distributed computing models is the first step toward realizing the benefits that thin client computing can bring to an enterprise. The mainframe, built on a centralized system with heavy investment on the mainframe hardware and little investment in end-user devices, is easy to manage and monitor. Mainframe computing consumes very little bandwidth, which is beneficial to telecommuting. On the other hand, the mainframe is an inflexible model that does not allow users to have access to offline computing, and it does not have graphical capabilities.

Distributed computing, by contrast, is difficult to monitor and manage. It has a low investment in a central computing environment in comparison to mainframe costs, and it requires a much higher investment in end-user access devices. Although it is a flexible model, enables offline computing, and supports graphic-intensive applications, a distributed computing client can consume a great deal of bandwidth in telecommuting.

Thin client computing maximizes the benefits of both the mainframe model and the distributed computing model. By combining low bandwidth consumption, graphical applications, terminals, and centralized management, thin client computing offers the best of both models.

The history of Citrix MetaFrame XP is intertwined with that of Microsoft's Windows 2000 Terminal Services. Originally, Citrix developed a solution for OS/2 called WinView, which enabled multiple window sessions to run simultaneously to remote users running remote control solutions. This technology, named MultiWin, was ported to Microsoft's Windows NT Server, along with the Independent Computing Architecture (ICA) protocol. Microsoft realized the value of thin client computing and licensed the MultiWin technology from Citrix for their Windows NT 4.0 Server product as a Terminal Server Edition, then incorporated it into all Windows 2000 Server versions with Terminal Services. Microsoft did not license the ICA protocol and so developed the Remote Desktop Protocol (RDP) client for Windows desktops. Citrix retained ICA and incorporated it as well as the Independent Management Architecture (IMA) for server farms in the Citrix MetaFrame XP product, which installs as an add-on to Windows 2000 Terminal Services.

Employing thin client computing, users can work on sessions originating from a centralized server, similar to the mainframe model. The client requirements are very low, so businesses can extend the life of existing hardware or begin to incorporate mobile devices into their network infrastructure while still being able to deliver the latest applications. The bandwidth consumption of a thin client is much lower than a standard client for an application, making it an ideal solution for telecommuting.

Before implementing thin client computing, administrators need to consider the costs and benefits of the implementation. Using a cost-comparison method, it is easy to show how money can be saved by implementing Citrix MetaFrame XP rather than some other technology, such as a desktop upgrade project. When analyzing costs and benefits, both hard-dollar and soft-dollar costs and benefits must be taken into account. Hard-dollar costs are anything that must be paid for out of a budget. Hard-dollar benefits are found in avoided costs or increased revenues. Soft-dollar costs and benefits are not easy to determine, because they do not necessarily fall into a budget. These items can include increased productivity, reduced time consumption, and reduced effort.

This chapter has merely skimmed the surface of the concepts and technology within Windows 2000 Terminal Services and Citrix MetaFrame XP. As this book progresses, you will learn about starting a project for implementation of Citrix MetaFrame XP, the design process, installation, and ongoing administration. Solution-oriented chapters provide a holistic look at implementing Citrix MetaFrame XP with a single business goal in mind. Your adventure into thin client computing has just begun.

Solutions Fast Track

The Mainframe Model Meets Distributed Computing

- ☑ The mainframe model grew out of the original computing systems, dating back to the 1940s.

- ☑ Distributed computing gained in popularity when personal computers were put on the market.

- ☑ Mainframe computing has the advantages of reduced desktop hardware costs, single point of administration, single type of administrative skill set, and a simple architecture with low bandwidth consumption.

- ☑ Mainframe computing drawbacks include single point of failure, character-based-only applications, and potential bottlenecks due to time-sharing systems.

- ☑ Distributed computing has the advantages of reduced costs for centralized hardware (no mainframe), no single point of failure, flexibility, and a scalable architecture.

- ☑ The disadvantages of distributed computing are greater administrative costs, security risks, and lack of a centralized backup.

The Difference Between Remote Node and Remote Control

☑ Remote node is the ability to run a computer over a remote link and access network resources in the same way as though the devices were locally connected.

☑ Remote control is the ability to connect to a remote control host and view its screen locally on the desktop, taking control of that remote host in order to function on the network.

☑ Windows 2000 Terminal Services with Citrix MetaFrame XP offers the ability to connect as a remote node as well as run remote control sessions.

The Evolution of the Thin Client

☑ Citrix developed a technology called MultiWin that enabled multiple sessions to run on a single server for remote control computing.

☑ Citrix ported the MultiWin technology along with the Independent Computing Architecture (ICA) protocol to Windows NT in the Citrix WinFrame product.

☑ Microsoft licensed MultiWin in Windows NT 4.0, Terminal Services Edition, and developed a Remote Desktop Protocol (RDP) client for it.

☑ Today's Citrix MetaFrame XP runs as an add-on component to a Windows 2000 Terminal Services server, bringing the ICA protocol and Independent Management Architecture (IMA).

Gaining Digital Independence with Thin Clients

☑ Digital independence is the ability to run an application on any device over any connection.

☑ Mobile computing and wireless networks, being too small to store and run full-featured applications, are an ideal platform for thin client computing.

☑ Using thin client computing, an administrator can deliver a 32-bit Windows application to computers that run incompatible operating systems, to Windows Based Terminals (WBTs), or to handheld computers over networks running different protocols.

Achieving Bottom-Line Value with Thin Clients

- ☑ When weighing a thin client project, a cost/benefit analysis can help justify the project budget to a corporate sponsor.

- ☑ There are two types of costs and benefits to consider: hard-dollar costs and benefits that affect a budget directly, and soft-dollar costs and benefits that are more difficult to quantify.

- ☑ A business can implement a project with business goals of reducing costs, increasing revenues, and complying with regulatory requirements.

Frequently Asked Questions

The following Frequently Asked Questions, answered by the authors of this book, are designed to both measure your understanding of the concepts presented in this chapter and to assist you with real-life implementation of these concepts. To have your questions about this chapter answered by the author, browse to **www.syngress.com/solutions** and click on the **"Ask the Author"** form.

Q: How does Windows 2000 Terminal Services with Citrix MetaFrame XP supply both remote node and remote control computing?

A: Windows 2000 Server includes Remote Access Services (RAS). This is the server portion of a remote node computing solution. Terminal Services and Citrix MetaFrame XP add the ability to run many remote control sessions simultaneously from the server. A network administrator could install RAS and configure it to support both dialup and VPN clients. The network administrator could install Terminal Services and Citrix MetaFrame XP on the same server. A client could dial up or connect to the corporate network through the Internet and then execute a remote control session using a single server on the back end.

Q: How does thin client computing speed up performance?

A: A thin client uses very little bandwidth because it compresses the graphic instructions that are sent from the server to the client as well as the keyboard and mouse clicks that are sent from the client to the server. No actual data needs to be transferred, except when saving data to the local computer or when printing. The result is that an entire desktop appears to be running locally with excellent performance, even when the remote client is connected over a 28.8Kbps dialup link.

Q: We have users with Macintosh and UNIX workstations. Can we use Windows 2000 Terminal Services? Or must we install Citrix MetaFrame XP?

A: Windows 2000 Terminal Services supplies RDP clients for only Windows for Workgroups 3.11 and 32-bit Windows operating systems. You can look for a third-party vendor that develops RDP clients for Macintosh and UNIX workstations. Or you can deploy Citrix MetaFrame XP and use the ICA clients for them.

Q: We are concerned about security for our financial application. We don't want data copied to people's home computers, and we don't want people to shadow sessions. Our accounting department is proposing that they begin telecommuting. Can we use Terminal Services with Citrix MetaFrame XP to deploy the application and still maintain tight security?

A: Yes. You can restrict the security settings on the Citrix MetaFrame XP server to prevent all shadowing, or you can prevent shadowing on a user-by-user basis. You can encrypt the session and use directory services authentication. You can also prevent local drives from being mapped so that data can't be copied or saved to home computers; in addition, you can prevent printers from being mapped so that data can't be printed and used later on.

Q: We want to deploy an application over the Web without a lot of development effort. Should we use Citrix MetaFrame XP or Windows 2000 Terminal Services?

A: Windows 2000 Terminal Services, even though allowing a Web client, cannot publish an application individually through a Web browser, whereas Citrix MetaFrame XP can.

Chapter 2

Farming MetaFrame XP Servers

Solutions in this chapter:

- **Understanding Server Farms**

- **Designing a MetaFrame XP Server Farm**

- **Planning a Server Farm Project**

- **Introduction to XP Server Farm Management**

- ☑ **Summary**

- ☑ **Solutions Fast Track**

- ☑ **Frequently Asked Questions**

Introduction

Users and administrators alike quickly realize the value of a Citrix MetaFrame XP server in delivering applications for a variety of needs. However, it does not take long for one of these servers to reach its capacity. Administrators then bring other Citrix MetaFrame XP servers online to provide the needs for the new users. The problem seems to be solved, yet as new servers are added to the network, another issue arises: It becomes increasingly complex for users to determine which server to use. In addition, administrators are faced with having to install multiple servers with a variety of applications, configuring sessions and users, and managing them.

Server farms simplify these issues. When a server farm is constructed, administrators can manage the entire set of Citrix MetaFrame XP servers from a single point. Printer drivers and applications can be easily deployed to all the servers at once. Users can connect directly to applications without needing to know the location of an individual server.

Citrix MetaFrame—in particular, version XPe—was intended for a scalable server farm. Not only does it load balance user sessions across multiple servers and provide redundancy; it also provides easy administration capabilities. The first step toward installing a Citrix MetaFrame XP server farm involves understanding and designing one that will scale up with the network over time. Proper planning and project management can play a critical role in the success of your implementation. In addition, administrators must be capable of managing the farm after the installation to ensure that it remains reliable.

Understanding Server Farms

A server "farm" is typically a collection of servers that provide a similar service or function. The collection provides increased computing power over a single large system as well as a level of redundancy not usually available in any single PC-based server installation. The farm provides OS redundancy. Servers can provide processor, hard disk, power supply, and disk controller redundancy but very little in the operating system area. By farming like servers, even if the OS crashes, customers are still served. The customer might lose the current session when a server crashes, but he or she can immediately reconnect to another server and receive the same environment as before.

Citrix MetaFrame XP Server Farms

Windows 2000 Terminal Services can be placed into a physical farm and set to be accessed by methods such as Windows Load Balancing (WLB) or Domain Name Service (DNS) round robin. These methods are not truly load balanced, nor can the entire farm be managed as a single entity. WLB does not allow for all the metrics to be taken into consideration in determining the least busy server. DNS round robin will provide the address of a server that is offline, resulting in attempted connections to a server that is not available.

By adding Citrix MetaFrame XP to Windows 2000 Terminal Service, server farms can be managed from a single interface and provide redundancy and more robust load-balancing services to users. MetaFrame also allows administrators to take advantage of features such as published applications, seamless Windows, multiple-platform clients, the Citrix NFUSE Web portal, and local drive and printer access. A single server farm can span an entire enterprise or can be broken up into smaller farms for localized management. This flexibility allows administrators to choose to centralize licensing and management by creating a single corporate farm or to distribute licensing and management to regional or departmental administrators.

Designing a MetaFrame XP Server Farm

A well thought out design is key to a successful implementation. Before starting to build a new farm or upgrade an existing farm, take the time to document, evaluate, and design your new environment. Even though most deployments do not follow even the best plans to the letter, having a plan will ensure that your deployment does not stray too far from your intentions.

There are two basic approaches to designing your farm architecture. A single server farm centralizes functions and makes administration easier for a central IT group. Multiple farms can distribute the administrative load based on business or geographic needs. The next sections discuss the pros, cons, and concerns of each type of architecture.

A Single Server Farm

Creating a single farm carries many advantages, but it also presents some disadvantages. Based on your organization's needs, a single farm could be the best option. This architecture centralizes your management point and enables administrators to control the entire enterprise Citrix farm from a single console. An example of a Citrix MetaFrame XP server farm is displayed in Figure 2.1.

Advantages of a single Citrix MetaFrame XP server farm include the following:

- **Single point of administration** One Citrix management console can be used to administer the entire enterprise.

- **Pooled licenses** Your entire enterprise can use one pool of licenses. This is especially useful in "follow the sun" organizations in which, as users in one time zone log off, users in other time zones log on.

Disadvantages of a single Citrix MetaFrame XP server farm include:

- **Increased Independent Management Architecture (IMA) traffic** A single farm with multiple sites must be set up into zones. Each zone has a data collector, and each data collector communicates all user logon, logoff, published application changes, and server load information to every other data collector in the farm. These communications can create a significant amount of WAN traffic.

- **Replicated data stores** Citrix recommends having replicated data stores at each location to reduce latency and WAN traffic.

Figure 2.1 A Sample Citrix MetaFrame XP Server Farm

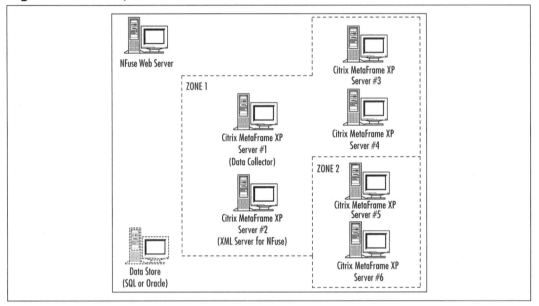

Multiple Server Farms

Multiple farms can be employed in both single- and multiple-site scenarios. Multiple farms can benefit, a single site by providing departmentalized licensing and administration. The use of multiple farms also diversifies the fault vulnerability in the event of an IMA issue or data store corruption that would otherwise cause an interruption in service.

Multiple farms can also solve problems related to numerous NT domains. Each domain could have its own Citrix MetaFrame XP farm, thus eliminating some of the trust issues associated with having a single farm span multiple domains. An example of multiple Citrix MetaFrame XP farms is displayed in Figure 2.2.

Figure 2.2 A Multiple Citrix MetaFrame XP Farms Design

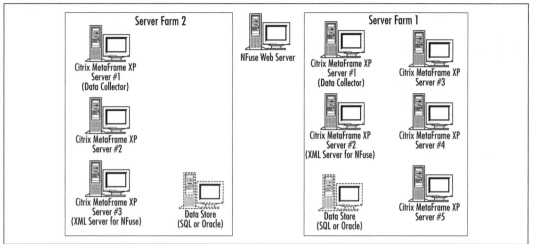

Mixing Citrix MetaFrame 1.8 and XP in a Farm

Many users of Citrix MetaFrame XP currently require the need for backward compatibility. This is a key component of any upgrade strategy. Citrix MetaFrame XP provides the capability to operate in a "mixed" environment consisting of both Citrix MetaFrame 1.8 and XP servers. Although little configuration is required to activate these functions, you must carefully consider use of this capability.

Citrix MetaFrame XP provides two modes of operation related to interoperability. First, *native mode* is used by default for farms consisting of only Citrix MetaFrame XP servers. This method of operation does not support older version of Citrix MetaFrame or WinFrame software. Operating in native mode, Citrix MetaFrame XP takes full advantage of the new features and scalability with the IMA.

The second mode of operation used with older versions of Citrix MetaFrame is *mixed mode*. Mixed mode, also known as *interoperability mode*, provides the backward compatibility needed to operate with Citrix MetaFrame 1.8 servers while migrating to Citrix MetaFrame XP. Mixed mode enables the older Independent Computing Architecture (ICA) Browser and Program Neighborhood services on the Citrix MetaFrame XP servers to support communications with Citrix MetaFrame 1.8 within the server farm. The next sections further explain the advantages and limitations of each mode of operation.

Citrix MetaFrame XP Native Mode

Citrix MetaFrame XP native mode is utilized within a server farm consisting of only Citrix MetaFrame XP 1.0 servers. A farm operating in native mode takes full advantage of new features available in Citrix MetaFrame XP in addition to several network enhancements. Characteristics associated with native mode include the following:

- The ICA browser server associated with Citrix MetaFrame 1.8 is no longer needed. A new service known as the *data collector* provides a more stable and scalable solution.

- Program Neighborhood services required with older versions of Citrix MetaFrame are no longer needed.

- Citrix MetaFrame XP servers cannot communicate with older versions of Citrix MetaFrame and Citrix WinFrame.

Citrix MetaFrame XP Mixed Mode

To allow compatibility with Citrix MetaFrame 1.8 servers within the same farm, mixed-mode operation must be enabled. Although Citrix recommends using this feature only when necessary, it does offer compatibility and a migration method for moving to Citrix MetaFrame XP without having to recreate your farm settings. However, mixed-mode operation carries several limitations that must be considered carefully. Features provided by mixed-mode operation include these:

- ICA browser compatibility with older version of Citrix MetaFrame is activated on each Citrix MetaFrame XP server in the farm.

- Program Neighborhood compatibility with older versions of Citrix MetaFrame is activated on each Citrix MetaFrame XP server in the farm.

- Citrix MetaFrame 1.8 and Citrix MetaFrame XP servers are integrated into a single farm for a seamless migration to Citrix ICA clients.

- Published applications can be load balanced across Citrix MetaFrame XP and Citrix MetaFrame 1.8 servers within the same farm.

- License pooling can be configured between Citrix MetaFrame XP and Citrix MetaFrame 1.8 servers located within the same TCP\IP subnet.

- The Citrix MetaFrame XP Citrix Management Console provides interoperability with Citrix MetaFrame XP and Citrix MetaFrame 1.8 servers.

- Citrix MetaFrame XP servers always act as the ICA Master Browser, providing more stable data storage.

Using Mixed Mode

In order to utilize mixed-mode functionality, you must activate the mixed mode configuration setting within your Citrix MetaFrame XP server farm. There are two methods by which to accomplish this task. In the first method, activating it *during* installation (the second method is to activate it *after* installation, which we'll discuss next), a prompt allows you to activate Interoperability mode. As shown in Figure 2.3, this option should be used only after careful consideration. Factors affecting the operation of Interoperability mode are shown in Table 2.1.

Figure 2.3 Activating Interoperability Mode During MetaFrame XP Installation

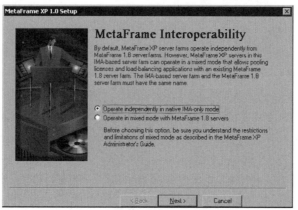

The second method is available after installation from within the Citrix Management Console. Once selected, several options become available in addition to services required for backward compatibility, such as the Published Application Manager and ICA Browser services. To activate mixed-mode operation, you must complete the following steps:

1. Start the Citrix Management Console by selecting **Start | Programs | Citrix | Citrix Management Console**.

2. Log in to the Citrix MetaFrame XP farm using an administrator ID.

3. Highlight the **farm name** and select **Properties**, as shown in Figure 2.4.

4. Next, select the **Interoperability** tab, located at the top of the window, as shown in Figure 2.5.

5. Check the **Work with MetaFrame 1.8 servers in the farm** option to activate mixed-mode operation.

6. As shown in Figure 2.6, a notification will appear, warning you of impending activity associated with this action. Select **OK** to continue.

7. Once completed, additional options will become available for managing licensing, as shown in Figure 2.7.

8. Select **OK** to complete the activation of Interoperability mode.

Figure 2.4 Selecting the Server Farm to Configure

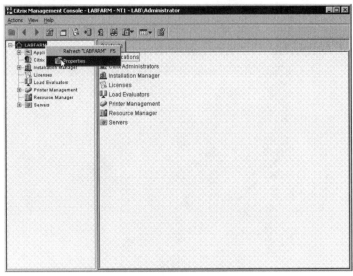

Figure 2.5 Selecting the Interoperability Window

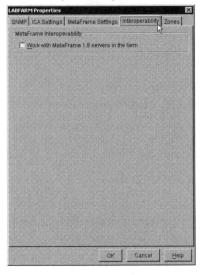

Figure 2.6 Warning Message for Interoperability Mode

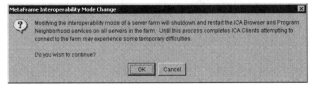

Figure 2.7 Additional Administrative Options Associated with Interoperability Mode

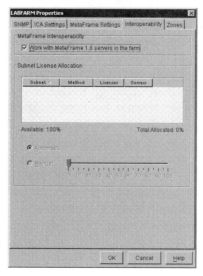

Due to the nature of the operation of interoperability mode, you must take several factors into consideration when you use it. Each of these items can impose a significant effect on the use of Citrix services if it's not carefully accounted for. Table 2.1 discusses each item and makes recommendations for usage.

Table 2.1 Interoperability Mode Issues

Issue	Description
Server farm name	The server farm names must be identical for Citrix MetaFrame XP and Citrix MetaFrame 1.8 servers for interoperability mode to operate correctly.
Application migration	Published applications can be migrated from Citrix MetaFrame 1.8 and Citrix MetaFrame XP. Special restrictions apply; for example, you can only use the Published Application Manager included with Citrix MetaFrame XP.
License pooling	Mixed servers with the server farm can share licenses.
Load balancing	Load balancing is supported between Citrix MetaFrame XP servers and Citrix MetaFrame 1.8 servers. There are several rules to follow, including one that states that a Citrix MetaFrame XP server must be the master browser.
ICA browser elections	Citrix MetaFrame XP supports ICA browser elections when running interoperability mode.

Continued

Table 2.1 Continued

Issue	Description
ICA gateways	ICA gateways are supported in Citrix MetaFrame XP only for backward compatibility. They should be used only to communicate with existing Citrix MetaFrame 1.8 servers on remote networks.
License migration	When using upgrades licenses, the existing Citrix MetaFrame 1.8 licenses must remain within the farm. Otherwise, the upgrade licenses will not function.
Server and farm management	When managing server and farm resources, you must utilize the updated utilities provided with Citrix MetaFrame XP. They are specially designed to handle interoperability issues.

Once Interoperability mode is activated, you can complete the migration from Citrix MetaFrame 1.8 to Citrix MetaFrame XP. After you have successfully upgraded your servers, Interoperability mode needs to be deactivated immediately. As shown in Figure 2.5, the farm's properties are used to activate Interoperability mode. The same option is used to deactivate this feature. Once you deselect this option and apply the change, Interoperability mode will be deactivated within your Citrix MetaFrame XP server farm.

NOTE

For more information about Interoperability mode, see the *Citrix Advanced Concepts Guide* found at www.citrix.com/support.

Configuring & Implementing...

Using Interoperability Mode

As described throughout this section, very careful consideration must be taken when you use Interoperability mode. This method of operation was provided as only a short-term solution while upgrading existing Citrix MetaFrame 1.8 servers. Once this mode is activated, all tasks and services that require this capability must be migrated to Citrix MetaFrame XP as quickly as possible. Serious issues can result from improper use of Interoperability mode. Citrix recommends that only experienced administrators use Interoperability mode.

Planning a Server Farm Project

The success of any Citrix MetaFrame XP farm depends heavily on a good project plan. Each step needs to be outlined, assigned, tracked, and refined throughout the life of the project. Be sure to include documentation in your project plan. Yes, most techies cringe at the thought of documentation, which is often out of date by the time it's printed and put in the binder, but it is a valuable tool to provide a baseline and insight into the thought processes of the planning and implementation teams. Most administrators do not fully appreciate the value of creating and maintaining good documentation until they inherit a legacy system containing a complicated setup with no documentation or even hand-scratched notes on how the system was installed, the application compatibility scripts that had to be written (much less what they do or why), or the system policies that were set or custom templates that were created. Now that we've described the nightmare, do everything possible to avoid passing this situation on to others.

Documentation doesn't take that long nor is it difficult to create. Simply sit down at the server with a laptop next to you and your favorite word processor open. Write down each step you take. Make screen shots of dialogs and insert them into the document. Copy and paste any scripts or policy templates that you modify or create, with a brief explanation of why the modifications were necessary.

Most technology projects follow the same process. First you have a business requirement that drives a vision. The vision gives rise to the method with which the company seeks to satisfy the business requirement with a process and/or technology change. This leads into the design stage. Design further leads to testing and development. Then you run a pilot and finally a full production deployment of the process and/or technology. At some point in the future, another business requirement could cause you to begin this process all over again, so it is somewhat circular in nature. The project cycle process is illustrated in Figure 2.8.

Figure 2.8 The Project Cycle

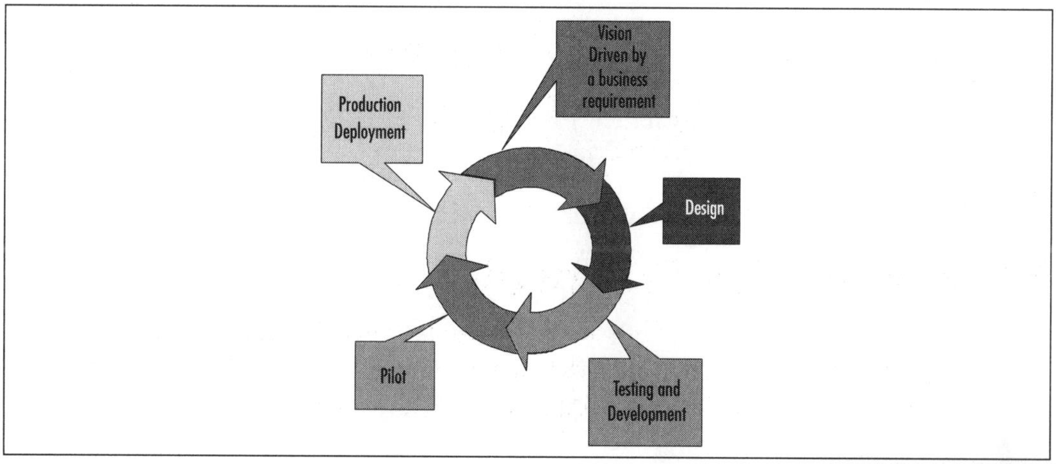

When you begin designing your Citrix MetaFrame environment—that is, the server and the network on which it will communicate—you should already have one or more business requirements and a vision that the Citrix MetaFrame XP server should satisfy. You should do your best to ensure that these business requirements are considered whenever you make a decision.

For example, if your business requirement is to eliminate viruses on the network and you discovered that they are being spread mainly through users bringing in diskettes from outside your network, you could deploy Citrix MetaFrame XP to control the spread of viruses—but that strategy would be successful *only if* you did not have diskette drives mapped to the Citrix MetaFrame XP sessions and/or if you replaced PCs with terminals that did not include diskette drives.

On the other hand, if your business requirement is to enable access to a SQL application on a global network on which slow, unreliable links are located in places such as Barrow, Alaska, and Moscow, Russia, you could deploy Citrix MetaFrame XP to provide a near-real-time access to the application. However, that would be successful *only if* you placed the Citrix MetaFrame XP server on the same subnet as the SQL server (or on a well-connected subnet in the same location, if the same subnet is not feasible) and if you provided dialup lines to back up those unreliable network links.

No matter what, you should always let the business requirement drive the technology vision. If you do, your project will be perceived as successful.

Gathering Business Goals

The object of most Citrix MetaFrame XP deployments is to satisfy a set of business goals. One of the first steps in creating your project plan is to identify the business goals you are trying to achieve. These goals are usually provided by your corporate managers, or they can be intrinsic goals that you identify. Some examples of generic business goals are:

- LAN-like remote access

- Thin client desktop replacement

- Easy deployment of applications to remote offices over the WAN

- Secure operating environment for outside vendors/contractors

These are just a few of the most common goals of organizations that consider Citrix as a solution. Every goal should be met for the project to be considered a success. However, the goals are tempered by technical limitations or application capabilities and must be mitigated with a well thought out and tested security policy.

To gather your business goals, you should make the rounds to all the user groups that plan to utilize the farm. Interview the group leaders, record their expectations, and ensure that they are realistic. Do not promise users functionality that you do not know that you can deliver. Users typically respond better to being told up front that a feature might not be available than finding out after the system is in production.

Document all the gathered goals for reference throughout the project as decisions are made and compromises are considered. At the end of the project, you can compare the list of goals to the production system to verify that all targets were met. The document can also serve to prevent members of any user group claiming that their goals were not met.

Identifying Existing Business Requirements

In addition to business goals, you might already have in place guidelines that you need to take into consideration. Guidelines such as the management model can impact the overall project in various ways, in addition to the actual design. For example, IT administrators managing the Citrix MetaFrame XP server farm must have access to the farm. Therefore, the servers need to be placed so that they allow efficient management and facilities to support the end product. Table 2.2 provides a few scenarios that illustrate how existing or planned business factors can impact a Citrix MetaFrame XP project.

Table 2.2 The Impact of Business Factors

Business Factor	Impact
Is the management model for IT resources such as Citrix MetaFrame XP servers centralized or distributed?	Centralized or distributed management dictates the placement of servers within your farm. Generally, Citrix MetaFrame XP implementations are more suitable to centralized management.
How are divisions defined within the organization?	Understanding how personnel are grouped within the organization helps determine application and resource use. Typically, some divisions need similar resources, but others do not. For example, individuals in accounting might require access to financial applications, whereas HR personnel may not.
What facilities are available to house the Citrix MetaFrame XP server farm?	Many organizations maintain data centers or specialized server rooms for housing server and network equipment. Depending on facility requirements, you might be limited to where servers can be placed within your network.
Are services such as Citrix MetaFrame XP charged to divisions within the organization?	Many organizations attempt to provide a profit center and thereby charge other divisions for the use of services. Based on how this works at your company, you could be required to separate servers and/or applications by division.

Determining the Gaps and Risks

Defining gaps and risks is the determination of shortcomings or weaknesses (gaps) and the possibilities of service interruption (risks) that a particular project presents to the user community. *Risk* as used in this context is generally defined as the potential for loss of critical components such as services or data. *Gaps* are represented as inaccurate data representing elements of a given project. Identifying gaps in your project helps to mitigate problems before they occur.

Larger organizations usually require a gap-and-risk assessment before any major project is undertaken. The assessment is customized to the unique environment of a particular firm, but some general questions present a basis for the type of information the assessment should cover:

- Do you believe it is appropriate to consider the potential for insider attacks, including attacks by insiders we need to trust (e.g., administrators)?

- Will use of the product help the firm generate significant revenues or reduce operating expenses?

- Will the product be used to process sensitive information?

- Would the firm potentially experience significant losses if the product temporarily stopped working?

- Would the firm potentially experience significant losses if an intruder obtained administrative control over the product?

- Has the product gone through a product security certification or a comparable formal security review?

- Is the product patched with all certified security-related patches?

- Are there known security defects in the product that cannot be corrected?

- Did *all* external connectivity required to operate the product receive approval from the appropriate review and authorization group?

- Does use of the product require granting a vendor unsupervised administrative access to a system on the production network?

Gaps based on these risks can include:

- How prepared for unauthorized intruders are the current and planned environments? Are appropriate countermeasures in place?

- Has proper planning been completed for the handling of sensitive data? Are planned safeguards sufficient in light of the level of confidentiality of the data?

- Does product security certification meet the level of security required for sensitive data?

Specifying the Return on Investment and Budgeting Considerations

One of the most elusive terms in technology is *return on investment (ROI)*. Most executives demand an ROI report to fully support a new project. ROI is defined as spending to improve yield or efficiency instead of using those funds for something else. This investment must then return by revenue or savings the original principal investment plus at least what the money would have earned or saved if applied elsewhere. There are three basic methods for evaluating ROI:

- The payback model
- Rate of return
- Discounted cash flow

ROI reports can get extremely complex. Table 2.3 illustrates a simplified report.

Table 2.3 Example of a Simplified ROI Report

Current Scenario	First-Year Costs	Ongoing Costs	Notes
Current desktop replacement cost	$899 x 1500 desktops = $1,348,500	$0	Current cost of the standard desktop PC
Current support per desktop per year	$347 x 1500 desktops = $520,500	$520,500	
Total	$1,869,000	$520,500	
Proposed Scenario			
Thin client desktop replacement	$499 x 1500 desktops = $748,500	$0	
Support cost per desktop per year	$216 x 1500 desktops = $324,000	$324,000	Based on each desktop support person supporting 300 users. Each support person makes $65,000 per year, including adjusted costs.
Citrix server investment	$120,000 hardware + $225,000 software	$0	
Total	$1,417,500	$324,000	

Continued

Table 2.3 Continued

Scenario	First-Year Costs	Ongoing Costs	Notes
Savings	$451,500	$196,500	Four-year savings: $1,041,000 Investment: –$451,500 ROI = (–$451,500 – $1,041,000)/ $1,041,000 x 100% = 143% ROI

Do not skimp when budgeting your project. Citrix MetaFrame XP is a very useful tool that has a tendency to attract increasing numbers of users and applications once a successful project is complete. More users and applications than your initial surveys identified will invariably turn up and vie for service from the farm. Make sure to budget for $N + 1$ servers so that no server is above 50-percent utilization, even at maximum user load. This planning will not only help redundancy—it will provide a respite from needing to add more servers right away.

Creating the Project Timelines and Establishing Milestones

Each project should be outlined using a project management tool to track project progress against the estimated timeline. The timeline should include milestones that indicate a project has definitely reached a particular point in the process. The function of the milestone is to establish a measure for quantifying project development progress. At each milestone, the project team should review the project's current status and determine what, if anything, needs to be done to adjust the timeline.

Use a project management program such as Microsoft Project to establish and track your progress. Although it could take a Ph.D. to fully utilize all the available features, any administrator who can click through a few dialogs can use Project well enough to manage even a complex Citrix deployment. Figure 2.9 shows a simple screen shot of a Gantt chart for an extended Citrix deployment.

Milestones for a typical Citrix MetaFrame XP deployment might include:

■ A document identifying all applications to be integrated

■ Documentation outlining the integration and testing results of each application

■ Server hardware installation

■ Pilot program completion document outlining issues to be addressed in the next phase

■ Complete documentation of every aspect of the project as the completion package

Figure 2.9 Sample Gantt Chart for a Four-Month Citrix Deployment Project

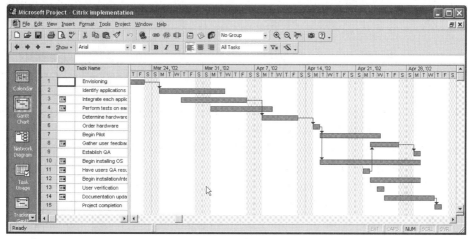

This is not a comprehensive list but should provide a basis on which to build a real project plan.

Planning for Training Needs

The most well-planned, perfectly implemented, most thoroughly tested, user-verified server farm will not be viewed as a success if the target audience does not know how to use it or the administration team can't properly support it. You should plan for training your users and administrators and have that training as a condition for project completion.

Administrator Training

As an add-on component to Windows 2000 Server, Citrix MetaFrame XP is very easy to administer for those with solid experience with NT/2000/XP. Sites such as www.thethin .net and www.thinplanet.com provide excellent newsgroups and downloads for collaborating with IT professionals and troubleshooting. Citrix offers several training courses for training on Citrix MetaFrame XP and its add-on components such as NFuse. The Citrix Certified Administrator (CCA) and Citrix Certified Enterprise Administrator (CCEA) certifications are fair assessments of an administrator's understanding of the key concepts of installing and administering a Citrix MetaFrame XP environment.

In addition to the implementation team, additional administrators could be required for day-to day support of the server farm. For example, you might need to train your help desk staff to provide basic administrative duties to the Citrix MetaFrame XP server farm for first-line support. To ensure that all administrators receive proper training, make certain that the resources you've identified to manage the server farm are included within your training plan for this project.

Note also that an implementation/project team will not necessarily include the administrator(s) who will manage the servers. Therefore, the project team should include one project task of training for administrators who will take over the new Citrix installation. This type of training should include describing the specifics of how to install apps, watching the baseline, and creating and maintaining any project documentation.

End-User Training

Citrix application linking and embedding features, combined with application publishing to Program Neighborhood, make the end-user experience very intuitive. Clients able to take advantage of seamless windows will find it difficult to discern between local and published applications on their desktops. Client drive and printer mapping makes running applications within a Citrix MetaFrame XP environment very easy for users trained to work in Windows-based environments who are familiar with navigating within a Web browser. Most users are able to begin using published applications with no training at all. With a reference card and brief training (conducted in small groups or using session shadowing), users can be trained to manipulate client settings to manage their experience with ease.

An Introduction to XP Server Farm Management

In order to properly implement and maintain a Citrix MetaFrame XP server farm, you must first understand the underlying architecture. Several key items weigh heavily on how your farm is designed. The IMA defines the underlying infrastructure that allows Citrix MetaFrame XP to operate. In addition, you must identify and account for bandwidth requirements when developing your implementation plan. Furthermore, listener ports directly impact client performance and availability. Each item plays a critical role in your server farm implementation and is therefore covered in detail in this section.

Independent Management Architecture

Arguably the most critical component of Citrix MetaFrame XP, the IMA defines the structural design. The IMA was designed to address the limitations of earlier releases of Citrix MetaFrame and WinFrame services. Several items, such as the dependency on broadcasting for services or the use of the ICA browser service, were defined as weaknesses in these older products suites. This led to scalability and reliability concerns that have been addressed with this new architecture.

For example, broadcast-based services, except for backward compatibility, have been removed to allow Citrix MetaFrame XP server farms to scale easily to large enterprise environments. The IMA represents the architecture and services that facilitate the operation of a Citrix MetaFrame XP server farm. IMA services such as the data store, the data collector, and zones are critical to the operation of any Citrix MetaFrame XP farm.

The IMA Data Store

The first component of the IMA is the data store. The data store is used to store information within the Citrix MetaFrame XP server farm that remains relatively static. Items such as installed licenses, published applications, and server listings are among a few found in the data store. In earlier releases, these items were typically stored in the registry of each Citrix MetaFrame 1.8 server. With the new IMA, the ability to centrally manage and maintain this information became critical.

Based on standard database formats, the data store can reside on a Citrix MetaFrame XP server or on a dedicated host. A single data store is used for each individual server farm. Currently, three databases are supported for use with Citrix MetaFrame XP: Microsoft Access, Microsoft SQL, and Oracle. Table 2.4 describes each database format and situations in which each should be utilized. Supported database formats for the Citrix MetaFrame XP data store include:

- Microsoft Access 4.x

- Microsoft SQL 7 SP2, 2000

- Oracle 7.3.4, 8.0.6, 8.1.5, 8.1.6

Table 2.4 Data Store Usage

Scale	Servers	Applications	Databases
Small	1–50	1–100	MS Access, MS SQL, Oracle
Medium to large	51–100	100–1000	MS SQL, Oracle
Large to enterprise	100+	1000+	MS SQL, Oracle

Another factor to consider about the data store is the access mode. Citrix MetaFrame XP offers two modes of access to connect to the central database managing the data store for a farm: direct mode and indirect mode. In direct-mode access, servers located within the farm talk directly to the database hosting the data store. For example, if you set up a dedicated Microsoft SQL server to act as the data store, all servers communicate to the database using direct mode. Direct mode can also be used when databases are stored on the same server as Citrix MetaFrame XP. Direct mode is used primarily when Microsoft SQL or Oracle is used as the database product.

NOTE

Disk space requirements for the data store are approximately 20MB for every 100 servers.

Indirect mode uses a Citrix MetaFrame XP server to communicate with the data store. This occurs when the IMA server requests access to the data store on behalf of another server. Indirect mode was designed to work around the limitations of Microsoft Access. When multiple users (or servers, in this case) try to access the same records, Microsoft Access has limited capability to prevent issues from arising. Indirect mode limits communication from multiple users by allowing a single server to communicate directly with the database on behalf of other servers. Indirect mode is most commonly used with data store implementations using Microsoft Access.

Designing & Planning...

Which Data Store to Use?

With the availability of three solutions for the data store, how do you tell which one best fits your environment? Microsoft Access was designed for very small server farms consisting of a few servers or very few published applications. Microsoft SQL and Oracle were designed for medium-sized to large enterprise server farms. SQL and Oracle are generally recommended, especially if you're using advanced tools such as Load Manager, Installation Manager, or Resource Manager.

When choosing between Microsoft SQL and Oracle, select the one your organization is most comfortable with. Both solutions provide scalability for large farms, but the staff at your organization might have no experience with one of the database formats. For example, if you primarily use Microsoft SQL within your organization, Oracle would probably not be the best choice.

During installation of MetaFrame XP, you select the access mode you want. The installation choice associated with selecting the access mode is shown in Figure 2.10.

IMA Zones

The next component associated with the IMA is a *zone*. Zones represent administrative boundaries for managing servers within a Citrix MetaFrame XP farm. Multiple zones are common in a single farm and are used to designate boundaries for servers within a farm. The most common boundary used with zones is geographic location. For example, you might have five servers in one location and three servers in another. The first location may participate in one zone while the other location is configured for another zone. Zones provide two primary functions:

- Efficiently manage data from all servers within a zone
- Distribute updates to servers in a timely manner

Figure 2.10 Selecting Data Store Access Mode

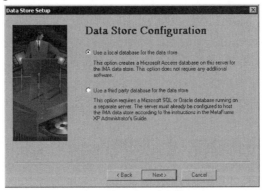

The IMA Data Collector

Data collectors are another component of the IMA. The data collector serves a function similar to that of the data store. They are used to manage information that changes frequently, such as current sessions, active licenses, and server and application load values within a zone. For example, when the server load values change for a Citrix MetaFrame XP server, it notifies the data collector of this change. Similar to the ICA browser in older versions of Citrix MetaFrame, the data collector acts as the central point of information when clients connect to your server farm.

Every zone with a server farm consists of one data collector. Although multiple Citrix MetaFrame XP servers can be configured to operate in this role, only one can be active within a zone at any time. To ensure this system operates correctly, an election process occurs. Based on a preset list of criteria, the election determines the most eligible server within the farm to take this role. An election starts if any of the following events occur:

■ Zone configuration is modified.

■ A server within the farm is started.

■ The current data collector becomes unavailable.

■ The QUERYDC utility is used to force an election.

If an election occurs, a set of criteria is used to determine which server will become the data collector. Any servers matching the first item are selected. If multiple servers match the first item, they are selected by the second item, and so forth. The criteria for selecting the data collector are:

1. What is the Citrix MetaFrame version? (Citrix MetaFrame XP always "beats" older versions.)

2. What is the current ranking as defined in the Citrix Management Console?

3. What host ID is randomly chosen at installation?

Although you cannot alter items 1 and 3, the preference can be modified to ensure that the designated servers win the election process. Figure 2.11 displays the option within the Citrix Management Console to designate the preference for data collectors. By default, the first server installed into the Citrix MetaFrame XP server farm is set to Most Preferred. All other servers are set to Default Preference.

Figure 2.11 Setting Preferences for Data Collector

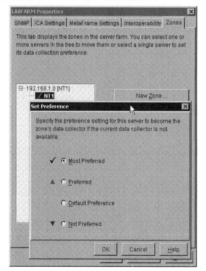

Bandwidth Requirements for a Server Farm

One of the key reasons for using zones is to manage the way that bandwidth is consumed within your Citrix MetaFrame XP server farm. The optimization of network bandwidth can be an ongoing effort. To manage the way in which your network links are affected by the use of Citrix MetaFrame XP, you must understand the normal bandwidth usage parameters.

In several scenarios, bandwidth utilization is key. For example, server-to-data-store communication must occur successfully for users to be able to locate resources throughout the farm. In addition, processes such as data collector elections must complete without latency, or your user base could be affected.

Server-to-Data-Store Communication

When a server starts and communicates with the server farm, it must query the data store to inquire about items such as published applications, other servers, and licenses. The amount of traffic generated by these updates is directly dependent on the amount of information included. As the number of servers or published applications increases within the farm, so does the traffic required to update a server. The following formula represents the amount of traffic associated with a server update at startup:

```
KB = 275 + (5 * Servers) + (0.5 * Apps) + (92 * Print Drivers)
```

For example, in a case in which you have a server farm with four servers, 12 published applications, and six print drivers, you would calculate the bandwidth used as follows:

KB = 275 + (5 * **4**) + (0.5 * **12**) + (92 * **6**)

KB = 275 + (20 + 6 + 552)

KB = 275 + 578

KB = 853

Data Collector Communication

Another item that can consume a fair bit of bandwidth for server farm communications is the data collector. Data collectors must manage updates between servers within a zone. Although they only send changes during a normal update process, at times complete updates are required. For example, if a new server comes online, a complete update must occur so that the server is aware of the information it requires. The following formula is used to calculate the bandwidth used for a complete data collector update to a server:

```
Bytes = 11000 + (1000 * Con) + (600 * Discon) + (350 * Aps)
```

In a case in which you have a server with 20 connected sessions, four disconnected sessions, and nine published applications, you would calculate the bandwidth used as shown here:

Bytes = 11,000 + (1,000 * **20**) + (600 * **4**) + (350 * **9**)

Bytes = 11,000 + (20,000 + 2400 + 3150)

Bytes = 11,000 + 25,550

Bytes = 36,550 or 35.69 KB

Listener Ports

One of the key components of terminal services and Citrix MetaFrame XP is the use of *listener ports*. Listener ports play a key role and must be carefully managed; without them, clients cannot access your terminal server. Listener ports work in cooperation with internal system components and client connections.

When a servers boots up, the terminal services components start the listener process. The listener service monitors for new client connections and manages the idle sessions. Once the listener service is operating, the session manager starts the idle ports to allow incoming connections.

Idle sessions start the core Windows process required for connecting clients. Once the process is completed, idle sessions wait for incoming connections. When a client connection is made, the idle session is turned over to the incoming client. The incoming client then continues the logon process and begins the session. Another idle process is then started and waits for new client connections. When each connection comes into the server, the server assigns it a session ID, and the connection is started. Figure 2.12 displays listener and idle ports within the Citrix Management Console.

NOTE

To add listener ports, you must modify the following registry key:
HKEY_LOCAL_MACHINE\System\CurrentControlSet\Control\Terminal Server\IdleWinStationPoolCount

Citrix recommends adding only what is necessary, because additional listener ports can degrade performance. Increase this counter from two to the number of listener ports needed.

Figure 2.12 An Example of Listener Ports

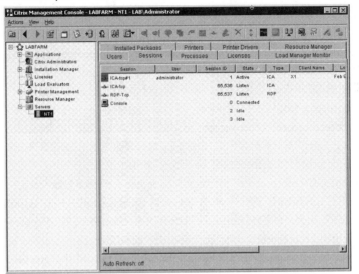

Summary

Citrix MetaFrame XP server farms work in cooperation with Microsoft Terminal Services to provide a complete thin client solution. In addition to the features already provided by Terminal Services, Citrix offers advanced management, load balancing, published applications, and Web-enabled technologies. The ability to provide access to users as one entity offers advanced fault tolerance, load balancing, and software management.

When designing a Citrix MetaFrame XP server farm, you must consider whether to place your servers in one farm or spread them across multiple farms. Multiple farms allow you more control with multiple domains; a single farm provides centralized management. Another factor to consider is interoperability with previous versions of Citrix MetaFrame. Interoperability mode provides access to Citrix MetaFrame 1.8 servers within your server farm but comes with several caveats. Items such as farm names, application migration, license pooling, ICA browser elections, ICA gateways, license pooling, and farm management must be carefully considered.

When planning a server farm migration, you must consider both technical and business variables. Using known methodologies, you can ensure that your project runs smoothly. First, you must consider the business objectives and goals of using Citrix MetaFrame XP. Next, you must identify the existing environment and enumerate the risks associated with this project. Doing so helps justify the project timeline and budget requirements. Specifying the return on investment provides some cause for supporting the specified budget. Training must also be considered to ensure minimal business impact for administrators and users.

In addition to business requirements, technical items that should be understood include the Independent Management Architecture, or IMA. The IMA provides the framework for the infrastructure of a Citrix MetaFrame XP server farm. Including items such as the data store, the data collector, and the zone, the IMA addresses the scalability and stability concerns for which previous versions were not known. Bandwidth requirements for server farm activity must also be calculated using formulas provided by Citrix. Listener ports are used to manage incoming client connections.

Solutions Fast Track

Understanding Server Farms

☑ Citrix MetaFrame XP server farms represent a collection of servers that provide a similar function.

☑ Citrix MetaFrame XP server farms take advantage of advanced features such as NFuse, published applications, load balancing, and centralized software management.

☑ Adding Citrix MetaFrame XP to Windows 2000 Terminal Services provides additional features such as client drive access, autocreated printers, and advanced management.

Designing a Citrix MetaFrame XP Server Farm

☑ Using a single Citrix MetaFrame XP server farm provides centralized management and software distribution capabilities.

☑ Using multiple Citrix MetaFrame XP server farms allows you to distribute the roles among multiple domains, geographic locations, or business divisions.

☑ There are several key factors to consider when you use Interoperability mode. These factors include the farm name, application migration, license pooling, ICA browser elections, ICA gateways, license pooling, and server and farm management.

Planning a Server Farm Project

☑ Using common and proven project methodologies ensures that your implementation goes smoothly.

☑ Understanding your business goals and objectives provides insight into how the business will use Citrix MetaFrame XP.

☑ A return on investment or ROI, study will help support budgeting requirements that have been defined for your initiative.

An Introduction to XP Server Farm Management

☑ The Independent Management Architecture, or IMA, provides the infrastructure for Citrix MetaFrame XP, including items such as the data store, zones, and the data collector.

☑ Bandwidth requirements can be measured using standard calculations.

☑ Listener ports are used to manage incoming client connections.

Frequently Asked Questions

The following Frequently Asked Questions, answered by the authors of this book, are designed to both measure your understanding of the concepts presented in this chapter and to assist you with real-life implementation of these concepts. To have your questions about this chapter answered by the author, browse to **www.syngress.com/solutions** and click on the **"Ask the Author"** form.

Q: Are multiple Citrix MetaFrame XP server farms common within an organization?

A: With older versions such as Citrix MetaFrame 1.8, multiple farms were more common. With the new features included in the IMA, the ability to consolidate your servers into a single farm has become much more practical.

Q: Does Microsoft Access provide a stable solution as a data store for a Citrix MetaFrame XP server farm?

A: Because of the use of indirect mode within a farm, Access can be a viable solution as a data store. It is recommended that you use Microsoft SQL or Oracle if you are planning to use any advanced features or grow into a medium-sized to large server farm.

Q: How many servers can exist in a zone?

A: By default, Citrix MetaFrame XP supports up to 256 servers within a zone. There is, however, a registry entry that can be modified to support a larger number. Further information is available at www.citrix.com/support.

Q: With all the limitations of Interoperability mode, is it better not to use it?

A: Citrix provides Interoperability mode to offer a short-term solution for migrating your current farm to Citrix MetaFrame XP. Citrix highly recommends that you run Interoperability mode only if necessary. If possible, avoid any changes, such as adding applications or modifying licenses.

Q: What will happen to applications published in Interoperability mode using the older Published Application Manager on Citrix MetaFrame 1.8 servers?

A: Applications published in this manner will not be available to Citrix MetaFrame XP users. In addition, the Manager might randomly appear and disappear within your farm and must be manually edited out of the registry to uninstall it.

Routing and Remote Access

Introduction

A majority of Citrix MetaFrame XP solutions are created for remote users, such as travelers, telecommuters, and Internet users. Due to their low-bandwidth consumption, thin client solutions are ideal when you need to provide an interactive application across a telephone line or Internet connection. Remote users can use a thin client to run an application from virtually anywhere in the world.

When designing a thin client solution for a business, you must take into consideration how users are going to gain access to the MetaFrame XP server. Will they be connecting via modems? Will they be connecting via a VPN? Will they be connecting to a branch office network and have traffic routed through? Will users need the flexibility to choose how to connect, depending on where they are located?

Even when a company has a VPN or remote access system in place, it should be examined when adding a thin client solution. The remote access servers need to have the capacity and accessibility that will meet anticipated usage. This could mean that an existing remote access server needs to be expanded, upgraded, or replaced. For a company without an existing VPN or remote access server, one needs to be designed from the ground up.

Windows 2000 Server includes a native service called *Routing and Remote Access Service (RRAS)*. RRAS supports VPN as well as dialup connections. A Windows 2000 Server can be installed with RRAS to work in conjunction with other remote access servers and is an ideal solution for expanding dialup and VPN services.

Designing and Placing RRAS Servers on the Network

The implementation of remote access on a Windows 2000 network can be very complex, depending on your specific needs and requirements. Often, a simple RAS solution fulfills the requirements of a small organization. As the organization's size and remote user base grows, much more consideration needs to be paid to the overall architecture of the RAS environment and the services it is designed to provide. In this section, we focus on the design and implementation of RAS servers in your environment and the methods for projecting both your current and your future needs.

Capacity Planning

The first piece to consider in discussing a RAS solution is the role it is being designed to fulfill. Careful analysis of your remote computing needs is required to make sure that you have taken all factors into account. Will your users work online or offline? Will they require applications to be served to them? Are they going to be moving large amounts of data? Will your RAS server need to provide services to both local and remote clients? Will there be any VPN technology involved? And what size will your user base be? Answers to these questions are all crucial to determining what hardware specifications will be required to meet the role the RAS servers will be expected to fill.

Another key factor is the type of RAS services you will be providing. Clients that will dial directly into a network using Dial-Up Networking (DUN) require different hardware and software than those utilizing a VPN solution. Windows 2000 RAS offers point-to-point, point-to-LAN, LAN-to-LAN, and LAN-to-WAN connections. Obviously, without knowing the type of service you are looking to provide, it will be difficult to know how you should scale your environment. That is why all of these factors must be taken into account when you are designing your RAS solution.

Considering Processor Power

Processor power is another key hardware consideration but not one that is typically a make-or-break component. Dedicated RAS servers use processor power mostly for operating system execution and packet routing. For this reason, having a cutting-edge processor is not essential for RAS server design. Most entry-level servers will function quite well in an RAS server role. A good processor speed is a Pentium III (PIII), 450 megahertz (MHz) or higher, although the server can function with much less. Keep Microsoft's Hardware Compatibility List (HCL) in mind when you are choosing server hardware.

Of course, if you are using your RAS server for other applications, the processor requirements will be much more important. RAS servers that run Terminal Services, for instance, will require quite a bit more processing power. For RAS servers that are mission critical, it might be a good idea to invest in a dual-processor system to provide some fault tolerance. Remember, processor power is always a good thing, but by itself it won't make a great deal of difference in an RAS environment. Symmetric multiprocessing (SMP) is seldom required for a simple RAS machine.

Monitoring RAM

RAM is perhaps the most crucial piece of existing system hardware that is used not only by RAS but also by the system as a whole. Without sufficient RAM, the entire RAS process can become bogged down in slow-moving system paging. *Paging* is the process whereby information is transferred from volatile, high-speed storage such as RAM to slower, nonvolatile memory on a hard disk. The problem with system paging is that is significantly slows the data retrieval process. If the operating system is forced to page out remote access information to the hard drive because of insufficient storage space in the RAM, it destroys the performance gains RAM can provide. For this reason, it is *strongly* recommended that RAM be your number-one consideration when you are pricing a system.

It's a tried-and-true saying that you can never have too much RAM. A minimum of 128MB is recommended; much more might be needed, depending on the total number of users and other functions the RAS server will perform. Remember, we're not just talking about RAM for remote access. You'll need a sufficient amount for your operating system, for any network routing the server performs, and for any other functions or roles it fulfills. Many organizations use the RAS server as a file-and-print server as well. This can work, as long as it is realized that inadequate hardware will hurt both roles the server is going to perform. For instance, using your RAS server as a database server would be high on the list of things *not* to do. The amount of RAM a database server typically eats would cripple the RAS performance.

RAM is relatively inexpensive in the grand scheme of computer hardware and can often be a solution to many problems involving slow remote access. Faster is always better, and any RAM is faster than hard drive access. Considering the impact RAM has on your overall system performance, carefully monitoring your memory usage can save you some headaches down the road.

NOTE

Use the Performance Monitor utility to keep track of *page faults per second*. If this number is more than a handful, you might need to think about upgrading your RAM. Also pay attention to *available bytes*. If this number is getting low, it's another key indicator that your RAS server is under-scaled. Page faults/sec can be found in the Memory object of Performance Monitor.

Choosing a Storage Solution

Storage considerations can be a tricky area where remote access is concerned. Often, storage is the furthest element from anyone's mind when they are putting together a RAS server. Careful choices with your storage options can have a big impact on the speed of your RAS service and make the difference between a successful and unsuccessful deployment. Storage on a dedicated RAS server needs to be sufficient to meet your needs for storing user profiles, connection data, and general operating system software.

The storage solution you choose should be fast and reliable because it will make a difference in your overall connection speeds. Slow disk speeds or a poor throughput speed can diminish the performance gains that faster RAM can provide. Inevitably, there will have to be some transfer between the disks and the RAM. The faster that transfer rate, the better your performance. Let's look at a few transfer technologies.

RAID

Redundant Array of Inexpensive Disks (RAID) is a disk subsystem often used to provide increased fault tolerance and data transfer speeds. Speed is improved because RAID systems stripe the data over multiple disks, which means that bytes or groups of bytes are written across each disk in the set. In this scheme, several disks can perform read/write operations simultaneously. Fault tolerance is achieved through the use of either *disk mirroring*, in which two disks contain an exact copy of each other, or *parity checking*, whereby a bit from Disk 1 is combined with a bit from Disk 2 using a Boolean XOR (a phrase that means *exclusive* in programming lingo) string, and the result is stored on Disk 3. If a disk should fail using either method, you either have a duplicate of the information can reconstruct it.

There are two flavors of RAID controller. *Hardware RAID* relies on special functionality built into the hard disk control. This is usually done with server-class machines and can come in all shapes and sizes. Some devices allow administrators to hot-swap a failed device, plugging the new drive in without having to take the server down. The information is then automatically rebuilt on the new drive. Hardware RAID is most commonly done with Small Computer System Interface (SCSI) drives because they usually spin much faster and provide better throughput than their Integrated Drive Electronics (IDE) counterparts. The second type of RAID is a software-controlled solution. This type is typically much slower than a hardware RAID controller and usually is used when a hardware RAID solution is too expensive. *Software RAID* erases many of the performance gains that hardware RAID provides and is best used only when fault tolerance is a must and software RAID is the only way to achieve it.

Fibre Channel

Fibre Channel is a special transmission technology that is designed to provide extremely fast communications between storage and communications networks. With Fibre Channel, hosts can communicate with a storage system (via SCSI) and each other (over IP) using the same network. Despite its name, Fibre Channel is designed to work over fiber, coaxial, or twisted-pair cabling. Each port with Fibre Channel uses two cables to transmit and receive data. A transmitter (TX) is connected to a receiver (RX) at the other end. The connection can be connection-oriented or connectionless using switched technology. In connection-oriented Fibre Channel, an arbitrary loop can contain 127 nodes. Nodes can be either a storage system or another computer. The biggest use of Fibre Channel technology is in storage area networks (SANs), which are discussed in the next sections. Figure 3.1 shows an example of Fibre Channel in both switched and loop environments.

Figure 3.1 Fibre Channel Environments

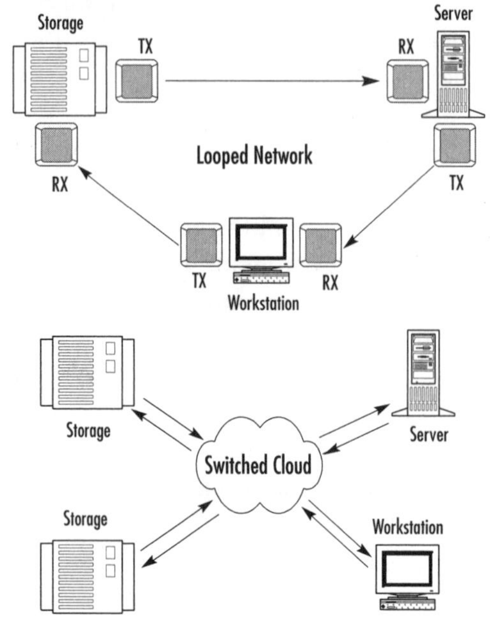

Storage Area Networks

With the increased capabilities of transmission technology, the demand for rapid retrieval of data from centrally located and dispersed data storage systems has become much more important. SANs typically utilize Fibre Channel technology to provide transmission capabilities up to 4.25Gbps each way. A centralized storage system is one in which a large storage device, typically a RAID cabinet with redundant drives and power arrays, is used by many separate hosts. It provides file redundancy, ease of management, and rapid retrieval of data over the Fibre Channel links. Centralized systems are also frequently used in server clustering to provide fault-tolerant solutions for critical applications.

Because Fibre Channel provides extremely fast communications capabilities, SAN nodes can be located centrally, campuswide, or even over a metropolitan area. With current technology, the Fibre Channel network can be extended over 20km. In addition, using a decentralized approach allows nodes to be connected to many different SANs. This means that multiple storage devices can be provided to a network, extending the capabilities of the individual nodes. Figure 3.2 shows a distributed SAN environment.

Figure 3.2 A Distributed SAN Environment

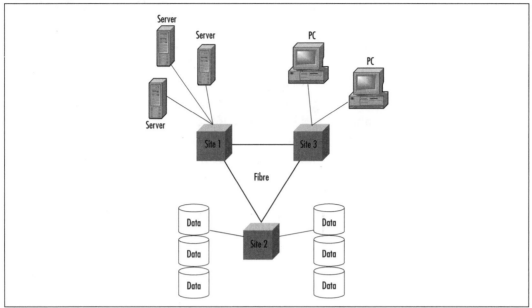

Choosing a NIC

Network interface cards (NICs) are the hardware used by the RAS server to communicate with the rest of the network. NICs can communicate over several different wiring solutions, depending on design. Common NICs are 10Mb Ethernet, 100Mb Ethernet, or Token Ring (4Mb or 16Mb). The NIC's communications speed has no direct impact on RAS performance, but it does affect the connection with the rest of the network. For a self-contained RAS server that hosts its own applications and data, this is meaningless. Few RAS servers are used in such a configuration, however. Most often, remote users need access to other network resources. At that point, the speed of the NIC becomes an issue.

Choosing a NIC is entirely dependent on the type of network infrastructure already in place. If you are running 10MB switched Ethernet, a 10/100Mb Ethernet card will do you little good beyond the initial 10MB Ethernet capability. In a 100Mb Ethernet network, that same card will (theoretically) provide you with 10 times the communication speeds. The NIC will always be based on the type of infrastructure you already have or plan to have.

Another consideration in choosing a NIC is whether or not to make a machine multihomed. A machine is multihomed when it contains two or more NICs that each connect to a network segment. These can be separate segments or the same segment in the case of multihoming a machine for redundancy or speed issues. Multihomed machines can act as routers if an actual router is not available, but this will eat up the central processor unit (CPU) to provide the routing service. Multihoming a RAS server should generally be restricted to machines that require redundant network access. Some NICs even contain dual network ports on the same card and allow for failover if the first port should go dead.

Choosing a Modem Standard

Choosing modems to fit your needs is the single most critical decision in designing a remote access solution. Earlier, we discussed the various roles that you might want your server to fulfill. Without the proper modem hardware, your RAS server is just a box in the corner that no one is using. There are thousands of different modem solutions out there, and picking one can truly be a challenge. First, you have to consider both the total number of users and the total number of simultaneous users you will have. If this is a RAS solution for two users, plugging a couple of PCI modem cards into the server will more than fit your needs. But what about those sites that need to provide thousands of available connections? Those need much more specialized hardware that we'll discuss in a minute.

You have some basic choices when trying to decide on a modem standard for your environment. First, what hardware do you feel comfortable with? There are plenty of brand name manufacturers for modems (although many modems that are packaged under different names are made by the same company), and picking between them can be a bit difficult. One way to choose is to look at the standards you want to implement. Will all your remote clients have the same modem type to dial in with? In that case, you might want to consider using the same manufacturer for your RAS solution. Do you need to support various modem protocols? Looking for a manufacturer with a good reputation for interconnectivity is important.

The big key in today's modem technology is 56K connections. The *56K* stands for 56,000 kilobytes, or 5.6K per second. This is the maximum connect speed that a traditional dialup method could support. Two main standards were initially developed for the 56K modem: X2 and Flex. Both were very popular, and a compromise had to be reached between them. As a result, the V.90 standard was developed. This standard allows both X2 and Flex modems to talk with each other and still negotiate the 56K speed. Most modems today are 28.8K, 33.6K, or 56K. Inexpensive 56K modems can cost as little as $20. Obviously, though, you don't want your users dialing in on a cheap modem.

If you are going to provide actual modems to dial into, such as a *modem bank* (a group of modems stacked together to save space and that typically roll over between each other when one is busy), be aware that for a user to achieve a 56K connection, you need to make sure that the modems on your end are capable of providing 56K dialup. Two users with 56K modems that dial each other will never be able to achieve better than a 33.6k connection speed. 56K dialup requires special modems on the provider's end and special lines between the provider and the telephone company. Otherwise, a 56K connection will not be initiated.

> **NOTE**
>
> You will never achieve a real 56K connection speed with dialup modems. Under U.S. FCC regulations, the maximum transmission rate for standard U.S. telephone lines is 53k. Regardless of what your connection speed indicator says, you will never really achieve more than a 5.3Kbps transfer.

Modem pools require special connections to the RAS server to allow the server to provide access via all the modems. Sometimes this is done through software management of the ports involved. Other times there is a serial solution provided. Regardless, the modem pool should not be located too far from the actual RAS server or network latency can develop.

Serial Cards

Obviously, you can plug only so many modem cards into a machine. There has to be some way of providing hundreds or even thousands of connections to a single server. In fact, several hardware solutions fulfill these needs. The first method is to use a dumb serial card solution. Unintelligent (i.e., "dumb") boards utilize the CPU to handle all processing requirements in sending data through the serial interface. This means that every port on the card interrupts the CPU every time it has data to send or receive. This method can really cut down on your RAS server's capabilities, but it is much more cost effective when the number of users can be small enough not to bog down the server.

The second option is to use an intelligent serial solution. Intelligent boards are capable of performing most of the serial data processing independent of the CPU. Intelligent boards can contain multiple CPUs to support the large number of serial ports they can contain. The system CPU must still be used when data is being transferred from the serial port to the system or for processing that information. Intelligent boards greatly expand the limit of serial ports that can be used by a RAS server. Without an intelligent board solution, a RAS server could easily be pegged at 100-percent usage by as few as 20 users. Unfortunately, without trial and error, there is no sure-fire method to determine which serial solution you should use. You could be pegging your processor with 50 users and a dumb board, only to buy a bigger server and still peg the processor. Either use trial and error to determine your load levels, or simply invest from in an intelligent solution from the outset.

Serial Port Hardware

Serial card solutions, whether intelligent or dumb, all have a general hardware scheme. A Peripheral Component Interconnect (PCI) or Industry Standard Architecture (ISA) card plugs into the RAS server and generally has a large interface port to which a group of cables, called an *octopus* or *fan,* is connected. Octopus cables are many 9-pin or 25-pin cables that end in a single interface that plugs into the back of the serial card. This device allows you to provide far more connections than would be able to exist on the back of a single card. At a certain point, this solution becomes unwieldy because of the large number of cables involved. When you're talking about 64 serial cables, that's a lot of weight to put on the back of a server. At that point, you need to consider a serial port concentrator.

A concentrator runs a proprietary cable from the back of the serial card to an external device that can sit a certain distance from the actual server. Concentrators can be daisy-chained with each other so that more ports can be provided. Daisy-chaining the concentrators does contribute to the total distance, however, and should be monitored carefully. Most concentrators have a limit as to the total distance they can be from the server. Traditional concentrators come in 16-port increments. Very often, concentrators are vendor-specific and require special serial cables to use. A wide variety of concentrators are available, each of which can provide a different kind of service, depending on the services you want to provide. For instance, some ports can be high-speed connections; others can provide standard service.

High-Speed Connections

More and more users are switching to high-speed connections in today's computing world. These connections can be everything from ISDN to Asymmetric Digital Subscriber Line (ADSL) and cable modems. ISDN users can connect with either true 64k or 128k connections; ADSL connections can go up to 9Mbps; and cable modems are capable of 2Mbps connections. All these connections require special hardware and wiring at the user's end. Deciding whether to allow these types of connections can be tricky. ISDN users can dial directly into your network (provided you are capable of receiving the ISDN call), but cable and ADSL users have to connect through the external network. This means that some type of hole must be opened in your firewall and might require a VPN connection for security. (We'll talk about VPNs and how they work a little later in this chapter.) All of this, plus the fact that these high-speed users will be eating up your bandwidth, leads to more costs for the network manager.

ISDN solutions are very popular for remote access. An ISDN connection consists of an ISDN line and a terminal adapter (TA) at the client end and some type of connection on the server side, such as a Primary Rate Interface (PRI) or separate ISDN lines to the ISDN card or router. ISDN runs over a special ISDN line called a Basic Rate

Interface (BRI), which provides two B channels and one D channel. The B channels are typically 64Kbps (although some phone lines only support 56Kbps) and can be used for either voice or data. This means that a user can talk over one channel and still maintain a 64Kbps connection on the other. When the user is done with the conversation, the second B channel can be automatically merged to provide 128Kbps speeds. The D channel is used for communications with the phone company. The TA and the phone company are always talking back and forth on the D channel, regardless of whether you are using any of the B channels.

Many large organizations use PRIs to provide ISDN connections to their users. In North America, an ISDN PRI is capable of providing 23 B channels and one D channel. This means that 23 users can connect to the ISDN device using one of their B channels, or that 12 can connect using both B channels. Connections for users can typically be limited to a single B channel to provide access to more users simultaneously. ISDN PRIs are typically carried over a T1 line, which, at 1.44Mbps, provides the necessary capacity for their 24 channels. Most of the control over the PRI and ISDN lines is done through the ISDN card or router management software you choose to employ.

Availability Planning

Planning the availability of your RRAS servers is an important step, especially in organizations that rely heavily on RRAS. If RRAS goes down, not only will your RRAS user be crippled and unable to get work done, but your organization will start losing money also. Thus the availability of RRAS is crucial. The number of users who need constant and uninterrupted access to RRAS will be a major factor in the planning process. Cost and the amount the organization is willing to budget and spend will be another factor to be considered. The larger the remote user base, the more complicated and costly redundancy solutions become. For organizations that have or expect to have a large remote user base utilizing RRAS and where RRAS is critical for getting work done, clustering and redundant components are a wise choice. In organizations that have a smaller remote user base and that need a cheaper method of providing fault tolerance, multiple RRAS servers should be considered. We discuss clustering, redundant components, and multiple RRAS servers in more detail later in this chapter.

Redundant Components

Redundant components are an ideal fault-tolerant method that provides redundancy down to the component level. Think of them as clustering for components such as modems or power supplies. These components can work together and support each other, and in the event that one fails, the other one takes over and ensures continuous uninterrupted availability. Redundant modems, for example, consist of two or more modems that back each other up in the event of a telephone line failure, a modem failure, or a serial port or cable failure. The other configured modems will automatically handle the connection, guaranteeing error-free delivery of data.

Redundant modems and power supplies are also *hot swappable*, a feature that enables you to install or remove a component without having to power down your server or interrupt service for the other modems. Power supplies can also be redundant; by associating a modem, for example, with dual power supplies, you ensure that the modem will continue to properly function, even if a power supply fails. Other redundant components —RAM, hard disks, controllers, and NIC cards—are available. (Earlier in this chapter, we reviewed RAM and NIC cards, the two most relevant to RRAS.)

Clustering Servers

Clustering servers is another excellent way to provide a fault-tolerant RAS solution. In a server cluster, machines are linked together (often by Fibre Channel) to provide constant availability of critical applications and services. If one member of the cluster fails, others will continue to provide the service for users, with no discernable difference. Clusters can typically be load balanced to provide good performance between them. Load balancing depends on the type of operating system you are using. With Windows 2000, load-balancing services are somewhat limited in the ways that they can balance network load among clusters. Typically, load in Windows 2000 is based on total number of users.

Another important consideration for Windows 2000 clustering is cost. The technology to implement a clustered solution can be expensive and should be considered only when it is absolutely critical that the service be constantly available. Clustering can be necessary and even cost effective when the remote user base is large enough to warrant it.

Using Multiple RRAS Servers

Multiple RRAS servers can be a cheaper alternative to clustering; in small to medium-sized environments where RRAS needs to constantly be online, RRAS is an ideal fault-tolerant solution. For example, instead of having a single point of failure via one RRAS server with 20 modems, you can have two RRAS servers with 10 modems each. This eliminates single points of failure and ensures that you always have at least one RRAS server online and ready to receive in the event that an unexpected system outage should occur (or even just maintenance work on one of the servers).

When you use RRAS, you usually make one telephone number publicly known, and then you use what is known as a *call rollover* to roll over to another telephone line when a busy signal or an unanswered call is detected. In the event that an RRAS server goes completely offline, the telephone lines that are connected to it will go unanswered and thereby trigger rollover. The call is then seamlessly and continuously rolled to another line that is available to pick up and make the connection. This method works well, especially when you have a small remote user base and need a cheap, redundant solution.

Placing the RRAS Servers on the Network

Now that you have all this great hardware, where do you put it? Some people make the mistake of thinking that you can just tuck your RAS server off in the corner of your network, and there it will hum away for years to come. In fact, if you don't carefully consider where you're putting that RAS server, you could completely congest a network segment and thus further limit your dialup users. They are already stuck at a maximum 56K connection. Putting them on a congested segment will further slow their transfer rates. When you consider RAS placement, you need to keep bandwidth considerations first and foremost in your mind.

It's a simple equation: More bandwidth equals more capacity for productivity. (Note we didn't say *more actual productivity*; that depends on the user!) If your remote user has to wait five minutes to download the updated file from the RAS server, that's five minutes lost to you. What if a portion of that five minutes' wait was not caused by the dialup connection but was instead caused by a poor choice of NIC? The fault is then on you as the network manager. As you look at RAS server placement, identify the resources your users will most often connect to. Is there a central file server that they will access regularly? Do they require access to certain print devices or maybe even CD servers? Knowing what devices they will need to access can help you identify where the bottlenecks in any plan will be.

For example, consider Figure 3.3. In this figure, the Acme Corporation has decided to implement a RAS solution for 30 users. They have decided to locate the RAS server near the network administrator's desk so that he can keep a close eye on it. Their typical user will need to access the central file share as well as a plotter device, also located centrally. Notice where the RAS server has been placed in relation to the commonly accessed devices.

For a user dialing in over the RAS server to connect to the backbone and the network devices located there, they must transverse Segment A (10Mb networks) to reach the backbone (100Mb). This means that any devices on Segments A and B will be using some of the available 10Mb, and the RAS users will be limited to whatever they can get. If there are too many other devices on those segments, the RAS performance could drop significantly. You might want to consider placing the RAS server on Segment A instead—or even better, on its own dedicated segment. This will allow the remote users to have the full benefit of the available bandwidth. Figure 3.4 shows this kind of RAS placement.

The placement in Figure 3.4 eliminates the congestion of other segments, and provides the full 10MB of bandwidth to the RAS users. If the resources were not located on the corporate backbone or not all located centrally, you would need to do some careful figuring to make sure that your bandwidth requirements will be met across all the segments that remote users will need to access. Good analysis, planning, and an in-depth knowledge of where your network stands and where it might be going will save you and your users time in the long run.

Figure 3.3 RAS Server Placement

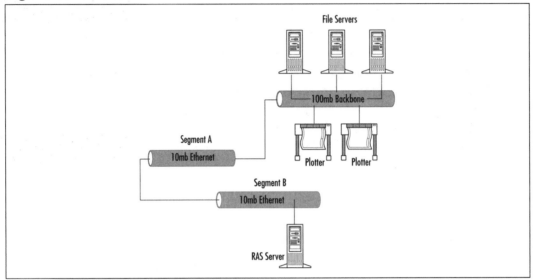

Figure 3.4 Improved RAS Placement

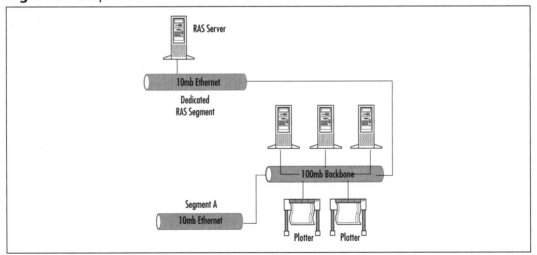

Remote Access Protocols

Remote access just seems to get more and more complicated. There are hundreds of different modems, at least five flavors of the major operating system (Win95, Win98, NT 4.0, Windows 2000, and Windows Millennium), and a multitude of ways to connect to a remote network. With all of these choices, sorting out your needs can be a difficult task. Once you have identified the type(s) of service you would like to provide, you have to figure out how you're going to do that. We've already discussed hardware considerations and placement. Now you need to look at the various software choices you will need to make. The first and most important is the protocol type you will use.

Dialup Clients

Dialup clients are remote users who access the network through a traditional RAS solution. Typically, this means they dial directly into the local network through a RAS server. Dialup clients are limited to the 56K connection speeds we discussed before and require no special hardware or software beyond the dialer and modem. Dialup supports two protocols: Point-to-Point Protocol (PPP) and Serial Line Internet Protocol (SLIP).

Serial Line Internet Protocol

PPP and SLIP are the two main dialup protocols in use today. SLIP is the older of the two. SLIP allows a remote user to make a serial link and transmit IP packets over it. SLIP was once very prevalent as a protocol, but it has since been replaced in most networks with PPP because it cannot provide the same security levels that PPP can. Today SLIP is seen mostly in older, unsecured network environments in which user security is not a consideration.

Point-to-Point Protocol

PPP has become the protocol of choice for remote access providers. Developed in 1991 by the Internet Engineering Task Force (IETF), PPP allows you to make a connection over any PSTN or high-speed line. PPP does this by encapsulating other protocols into special network control packets. Two examples are IP over PPP (IPCP) and Internet Package Exchange over PPP (IPXCP). PPP can also replace the network adapter driver. In that situation, the user is treated as a node on the network, and PPP can hang up and redial poor connections automatically.

Authentication Protocols

PPP has the added advantage of offering extra levels of security by offering two authentication protocols, Password Authentication Protocol (PAP) and Challenge Handshake Authentication Protocol (CHAP). PAP is the most popular and widely used of the two; it provides a simple method for a remote node to identify itself using what is known as a *two-way handshake*. CHAP, on the other hand, is a more secure protocol; it offers a three-way handshake that periodically checks the identity of the remote node.

Password Authentication Protocol

In PAP authentication, the server stores a list of usernames and passwords that it compares with the usernames and passwords sent by remote users. This information is not encrypted in any way; passwords are sent across the link in clear text, thereby classifying the use of this protocol as vulnerable. PAP is the most basic authentication protocol available to RAS administrators and should be used only when the need for password security is low.

Challenge Handshake Authentication Protocol

CHAP fully encrypts the username and password by getting from the remote server a key that is used for both encryption and decryption. CHAP encryption is called *dynamic* because a user receives a different key each time he or she connects. This secures sensitive exchange and can keep your network secure from attempts to snatch a password. Most RAS networks use a combination of PPP and CHAP for dialup and authentication.

VPN Clients

VPNs are relatively new to the remote access world. The purpose of a VPN is to allow users to make a secure connection to the internal network from outside the network perimeter, such as through a user's own personal Internet service provider (ISP). With the right software, network administrators can provide this capability to users to defray both telephone costs and hardware requirements. The primary benefit of a VPN connection is that as long as client software supports it, users can connect to the internal network from *any* external network connection. This means that high-speed devices such as cable modems and ADSL can make the connection to the internal network and still function at their full capacity (assuming you haven't throttled them in any way). This capability can be a real boon for people who consistently work from home.

There are basically two types of VPNs. The first VPN solution is hardware based and is managed internally. Usually it works via a server-side software package and a client-side software piece that are used to establish the secure connection. Two common solutions are Altiga (owned by Cisco) and RedCreek. The second type of solution is a managed VPN. In this scenario, a major ISP company such as CompuServe or AT&T allows users to dial into a local point of presence (POP) and then establish the secure connection to their internal network. The benefit of this method is that most of the VPN management is handled by the contracted company. The disadvantage is that these solutions are often limited to dialup only, which eliminates one of the major benefits of VPN technology.

VPNs work using a variety of secure packet technologies. The purpose of the VPN is to create a secure "tunnel" between the remote computer and the internal network. The tunnel passes the encoded traffic back and forth through the insecure world of the

Internet. Using the secure tunnel ensures that communications are as secure between the local and remote networks as they would be if the remote network were situated locally. This means that two corporate sites can also use a VPN connection to communicate with one another. The VPN operates logically as a WAN link between the sites.

The advantages to VPNs are clear. By providing remote users with the capability to connect through the Internet, the VPN allows easy management of scalability merely by increasing available bandwidth if the network becomes strained. VPNs save on telephony costs because users do not have to dial a local modem pool. Instead, they make whatever network connection they typically make (high-speed or dialup) and then use a client software piece to form the secure tunnel. Additionally, VPNs can give access to network resources that an administrator would never think of otherwise exposing to an outside connection. Security is the key behind VPNs.

When considering a VPN solution, you need to meet several requirements:

- **Support for multiple protocols** Any solution you choose must be able to handle the protocols commonly used on the public network (i.e., IP, IPX, etc.).

- **Authentication mechanism** There must be a way to verify each user and restrict access to users defined for VPN access. Typically, some type of auditing is also desired.

- **Encryption of data** It seems obvious, but the solution you choose must be able to encrypt the data to form the secure tunnel. Otherwise, the solution is worthless from a security point of view.

- **Management of client addresses** Solutions need to be able to assign the external client an internal address so that the network will treat it as a local node. The client's actual network address (usually supplied by the ISP) should be kept secret from the outside world to prevent certain types of hacking.

So under what circumstances would you want to provide a VPN solution? It all goes back to identifying your particular remote access needs. If you have users who constantly travel and who need access to the intranet no matter where they are or how they're dialed in, a VPN solution might be the right choice for you. If you want those benefits without the management overhead, you can consider a managed solution. Or maybe you simply need to provide both a RAS and a VPN solution to enable secure communications between campuses as well as give your users a dialup solution. Figure 3.5 shows a combination RAS/VPN solution.

In the next section, we'll talk about the various protocols available for a VPN connection, such as Point-to-Point Tunneling Protocol (PPTP) or Layer 2 Tunneling Protocol (L2TP). These protocols are the key to ensuring secure, efficient communications between remote systems.

Figure 3.5 RAS/VPN Combination

VPN Dialup
1. The remote user dials in to RAS server.
2. The RAS server authenticates the user.
3. The remote user requests file from campus B and that request is sent to the VPN server.
4. The VPN server sends the request through the firewall and across the Internet to the remote campus.
5. The VPN server on the remote campus receives the request and establishes a secure tunnel between Campus A and Campus B.
6. One the tunnel is established, the file is passed back from Campus B through the VPN server to Campus A, and then back to the remote user.

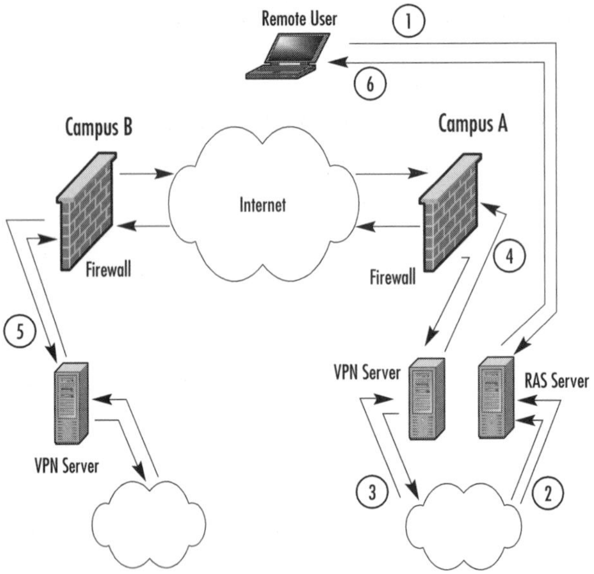

Point-to-Point Tunneling Protocol

PPTP is a Layer 2 Protocol that provides security by encapsulating the PPP frame in an IP datagram to be transmitted over an IP internetwork. PPTP can be used in LAN-to-LAN or even WAN-to-WAN networking. The original draft for PPTP was submitted to the IETF in June 1996; the current proposed specifications are contained in Request for Comment 2637 (RFC 2637) at the IETF Web site (www.ietf.org). PPTP uses a TCP connection to perform generic tunnel maintenance and a generic routing encapsulation (GRE, documented in RFCs 1701 and 1702) to encapsulate the PPP frames. The payload can be encrypted and compressed, depending on the requirements of the connection. PPTP assumes that the internetwork connection already exists.

PPTP uses the same authentication methods as traditional PPP. CHAP, Microsoft CHAP (MS-CHAP), PAP, Shiva PAP (SPAP), and Extensible Authentication Protocol

(EAP) are all available over PPTP. PPTP inherits the encryption and compression values of the PPP payload. Payload encryption is done using Microsoft Point-to-Point Encryption (MPPE). For MPPE to work in Windows 2000, the client must be using MS-CHAP or EAP as its authentication method. MPPE is a link encryption, not an end-to-end encryption solution. For an end-to-end solution, see the discussion of IPSec later in this chapter.

PPTP can encrypt IP, IPX, or NetBEUI traffic for transmission. Because it is a Layer 2 protocol, PPTP corresponds to the Data Link layer of the OSI standard. Tunnels are established when both endpoints agree to the tunnel and are able to negotiate the configuration variables required for communications. These typically encompass things such as address assignment, compression parameters, and encryption type. The tunnel itself is managed using a tunnel maintenance protocol. Once the tunnel is established, PPTP performs its encapsulation and the data is sent to the tunnel server. The server strips out the IP header and then forwards the payload up to the appropriate network.

PPTP, like all Layer 2 protocols, includes many useful features that it inherits from PPP. These include things like data compression, data encryption, support for token cards through the use of EAP, and a variety of user authentication methods. PPTP is available for all current Windows platforms and supports client-to-server and server-to-server communications. In addition, PPTP supports routed tunnels for both demand dialing and multilink routing.

Here is an example of PPTP packet generation in a Windows 2000 environment:

1. The client submits an IPX datagram to the virtual interface that represents the VPN connection. This datagram is typically submitted by the client's Network Driver Interface Specification (NDIS).

2. The data is passed by NDIS to the NDISWAN, where it is encrypted or compressed (or both) and provides the PPP header. This information is then passed to the PPTP protocol driver, which encapsulates it using GRE.

3. The packet is sent to the TCP/IP protocol driver, which encapsulates the packet yet again with an IP header. The packet is then submitted to the interface that represents the local connection using NDIS.

4. NDIS sends it to NDISWAN, which provides the PPP headers and trailers.

5. The final packet is submitted to the WAN miniport driver that corresponds to the connection hardware (i.e., the asynchronous port for a modem). It is then sent across the physical medium to the PPTP server, where the process is reversed.

Layer 2 Tunneling Protocol

PPTP was (and still is) a good idea, but it has been overtaken by other security technologies. Layer 2 Tunneling Protocol (L2TP) is a combination of PPTP and Layer 2 Forwarding (L2F), a proposal put forward by Cisco. The two protocols were very similar in design and function, so the IETF mandated that they be merged into a single protocol design. That design, L2TP, is documented in RFC 2661. L2TP utilizes the best features of both PPTP and L2F.

L2TP encapsulates frames as User Datagram Protocol (UDP) messages and sends them over an IP network. UDP messages are used for both tunnel maintenance and tunnel data. PPP payload can be encrypted, compressed, or both. L2TP differs from PPTP, however, in that it does not use MPPE to encrypt the packets. Instead, L2TP employs IPSec (which we discuss in the next section) for the encryption process. It is possible to create an L2TP packet without using IPSec, but it is not secure and is not considered a VPN. This is typically only done for troubleshooting purposes, to eliminate IPSec as a possible point of failure.

Like PPTP, L2TP utilizes the same authentication methods as PPP. L2TP also assumes the existence of an internetwork between the L2TP client and the L2TP server. Since L2TP tunnel maintenance is performed over the same UDP connection as the data transmission, the two types of packets have the same structure. The standard port for L2TP on both the client and the server in Windows 2000 is UDP port 1701. Windows 2000 L2TP servers support clients that default to a different port number.

Because L2TP does not use a TCP connection, it relies on message sequencing to ensure the proper delivery order of the packets. The Next-Received and Next-Sent fields within the L2TP control message are used to manage packet sequencing. Packets that are out of sequence are dropped. As you can see, L2TP is very similar to PPTP. So why would you choose one over the other?

For starters, PPTP requires that there is an IP internetwork, but L2TP requires only point-to-point, since the tunnel media establishes packet-oriented connections. This means that L2TP can be used over IP, Frame Relay, X.25 circuits, or asynchronous transfer mode (ATM) connections. L2TP also allows for multiple tunnels between two endpoints. PPTP is limited to only a single tunnel. This allows you to provide different qualities of service using multiple tunnels. L2TP also allows for Layer 2 tunnel authentication; PPTP does not. (This benefit is ignored if you are using IPSec, however, since it provides the tunnel authentication independent of Layer 2.) Finally, the overhead on an L2TP packet is 2 bytes smaller due to header compression.

We've mentioned IPSec a few times already, so now would be a good time to take a look at it.

IP Security Protocol

IPSec is a Layer 3 tunneling protocol and relies on packet technology at the Network layer of the OSI model. Tunneling in IPSec involves encrypting the IP payload and then encapsulating that encrypted payload in an IP header to be sent across any IP network (such as the Internet). This is an extremely beneficial method because it allows tunneling to be established across both intranets and the Internet. Any IP-compatible system can support IPSec traffic. However, Microsoft limits support for IPSec to its 2000 platform only. If you need to use IPSec with a Windows 95 client, you must get a third-party IPSec client program.

Layer 3 tunneling protocols assume that all the tunnel configuration issues have already been handled somewhere else. There is no tunnel maintenance phase for a Layer 3 protocol. IPSec functions at the bottom of the IP stack, which allows higher-level protocols to inherit its behavior. A security policy controls each IPSec session. This policy is used to establish the encryption method, tunneling method, authentication types available, and the order of preference for all of them. The IPSec client and server negotiate the tunnel based on that security policy, and all traffic is encrypted using the negotiated result.

Using IPSec in Windows 2000 requires that a computer certificate be installed on both the IPSec server and the client. This certificate can be obtained from the Certificates snap-in or the Windows 2000 Group Policy auto-enrollment. Once IPSec negotiation occurs, an IPSec security association (SA) is reached with the exchange of certificates. Encryption over an IPSec connection is either 56-bit Data Encryption Standard (DES) or Triple DES (3DES), where three different 56-bit keys are used for encryption and decryption. 3DES is an extremely secure encryption algorithm at this point and should be used for particularly sensitive communications.

IPSec is designed for IP networks, which means that packets can be lost or arrive out of order. Each packet is decoded individually of the other packets. The initial encryption keys are established as part of the authentication process, and new ones are generated every 5 minutes or 250MB of data transferred (for DES), and every hour or every 2GB transferred (for 3DES). This is more than enough to keep the keys from being decoded and packets decrypted in time to affect the system before it changes the key. Enough with the dry stuff, though; let's see about getting RAS installed.

Installing Routing and Remote Access Services

We've introduced you to all the basic concepts of Remote Access and VPN technologies earlier in this chapter. Now it's time to take a look at the actual installation and configuration of those technologies in a Windows 2000 environment. If you're already familiar with RAS installation and configuration in NT 4.0, make sure you pay careful attention to where the new tools are. Microsoft has made some serious changes to its interface with Windows 2000.

Configuring for Dialup Clients

When you talk about configuring a dialup RAS connection, you're talking about the server configuration. This involves the system design, installation, and activation. The client portion of a dialup configuration is not covered in this book due to the multitude of potential dialup clients that exist. See the individual operating system's documentation on how to configure that client for dialup networking.

Configuring Your RAS Server in Windows 2000

Before you purchase any new hardware or attempt to install any RAS devices, always check the latest copy of Microsoft's HCL for Windows 2000! This advice sounds simple, but all too often you can end up with a solution that simply won't work due to poor or missing drivers. Assuming you've checked the HCL and are ready to proceed with the installation, let's walk through the process of installing a modem on a Windows 2000 server.

Modem Installation

The following steps will guide you through installing a modem on a Windows 2000 server:

1. Click the **Start** button, then choose **Settings/Control Panel**.

2. Double-click the **Phone and Modem** options icon. You might be prompted for information about your area code, dialing system, and so on, if this is the first time you have used this option.

3. After you've entered all that information, Windows 2000 will launch the Phone and Modems Options applet. Click the **Modems** tab, then click the **Add** button to launch the installation wizard. Figure 3.6 shows the initial Modem Installation Wizard screen.

4. You can have Windows 2000 attempt to identify your modem for you, or you can define it manually from a list of supplied or manufacturer-provided drivers. If you leave the box labeled **Don't detect my modem; I will select it from a list** unchecked, Windows 2000 will attempt to identify and install the correct driver for it. If your modem is an older model (i.e., one not released after Windows 2000 came out), you are probably safe in letting Windows find it for you, in which case, move on to Step 8.

Figure 3.6 Modem Installation Wizard

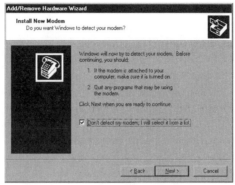

5. If the modem is more recent, you have better drivers for it, or you want to set all the options yourself, check the box and click **Next**. The next window you will be presented with gives you a long list of modem manufacturers and models. Search the list to see if your modem is listed there. If it is, you can highlight it and choose **Next**. (If it isn't, or you have more recent drivers, click the **Have Disk** button. You need to tell Windows the location of the driver files, usually either on the A: drive or a local hard drive. Highlight the modem driver and click **Next**.)

6. You will now be presented with a screen that asks you to choose the port on which you want to install the modem(s). You have the option of choosing any installed port (such as COM1 or COM2) to which your modem is attached. Alternatively, if you have multiple modems that are all identical and attached to multiple ports, you can select **All ports** and the modem drivers will be installed for all the ports. Figure 3.7 shows you the port selection screen. Make your selection and click **Next**.

Figure 3.7 Port Selection for Manually Installed Modems

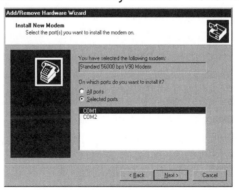

7. Finally you will get a screen telling you that your modem has been successfully set up. Click **Finish** to exit the wizard. See Figure 3.8.

Figure 3.8 Modem Successfully Installed

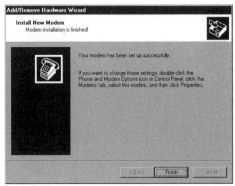

8. If you chose to let Windows find the modem for you, it will search all the available ports and present you with a list of modems that it found. Choose the modem that is correct, and click **Next**. Windows 2000 will automatically assign the port and install the correct drivers. You should receive a dialog box indicating that the modem has been successfully installed.

At this point, you can use this modem to make dialup connections. But this is your RAS server—you want *them* to call *you*!

RAS Installation

The goal of a RAS server is to accept incoming connections from remote computers and allow those users access to internal network resources. As we've discussed previously, this is typically done through a dial-in connection. Windows 2000 has built-in PPP that allows it to act as a universal gateway to provide remote access to your users. Any device that can establish a PPP connection can connect to a Windows 2000 RAS server. This list includes Macintosh systems, handheld devices—even UNIX hosts. The Windows 2000 server can route connections from those devices to any device internal to your network.

The following must be available for Windows 2000 to accept calls from remote clients:

■ Windows 2000 must be configured with remote access software to accept incoming calls.

■ Any client device that will attempt to connect to the server must be capable of establishing a PPP session.

■ Some type of connection device (modem, ISDN line, T1 line, etc.) must be connected to the RAS server.

- Some kind of connection device must be connected to the remote client, with the capability to establish a circuit between the two.

- A user account must exist on the Windows 2000 server for the remote user who will establish the connection.

As long as those conditions are met, you should be able to provide RAS services to your users. To start the installation of RAS on a Windows 2000 server or Advanced Server, complete the following steps:

1. Click the **Start** button, and choose **Programs | Administrative Tools | Routing and Remote Access**. This will take you to the Microsoft Management Console (MMC), and you should see your server listed in the left-hand pane of the MMC window.

2. Right-click your server, and select the option for **Configure and Enable Routing and Remote Access**. This will launch the Routing and Remote Access Server Setup Wizard.

3. Answer **Yes** to the first dialog box; you will be presented with a window like the one shown in Figure 3.9. Your first choice in the installation process is to determine what role your server will play. There are several predefined choices, such as a VPN server, RAS server, or network router.

Figure 3.9 The Routing and Remote Access Server Wizard

4. We want to choose the RAS server for now. Click the **Remote access server** radio button, and then click **Next**. You will be asked whether you want to configure this server as a *basic RAS server* (a standalone server with simplified control) or an *advanced RAS server* (capable of using remote access policies and being a member server of a domain).

5. If you choose to make this server a basic RAS server, Windows will give you a message stating that you must configure the incoming network connection in the Network and Dial-Up Connections folder. When you click **OK**, the wizard will end.

6. If you choose to configure the server as an advanced RAS server, you will be asked to verify that the protocols installed on your server are correct for what you are trying to provide your remote clients. Figure 3.10 shows the Remote Client Protocols window.

    As you'll note in Figure 3.10, it almost appears that you can select the protocols to use with RAS. Sadly, this is not the case. The RRAS Wizard assumes that you want to use *all* the available protocols with remote connections. If you want to remove protocols from your RRAS server, you must manually remove them after the setup is complete.

Figure 3.10 Remote Client Protocols

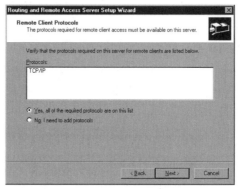

NOTE

Choosing **No, I need to add protocols** in the window shown in Figure 3.10 causes the wizard to stop at this step and the configuration process to be aborted. It is recommended that you continue the process and go back later to add the additional protocols you require. The one exception to this rule is TCP/IP. It is always recommended that you have TCP/IP installed before you attempt the RAS installation.

7. Assuming that you have TCP/IP installed, the next step in the wizard is to decide how you want to handle the assignment of IP addresses for dial-in clients. Because every device on your network requires a unique IP address, you must have a method of supplying them to your remote users as well. If you have a Dynamic Host Configuration Protocol (DHCP) server active on

your network (not necessarily on the same box as the RAS server, just somewhere visible to the network), you can use the DHCP service to automatically assign those IP addresses. This is the default option that the RRAS wizard will attempt to use. You must have an active DHCP server, and it must have enough available IP addresses, for this solution to work.

If for some reason you want to define the range of IP addresses that the DHCP server will use to assign addresses to remote users, choose the **From a specified range of addresses** radio button and then click **Next**. You will be presented with a window like the one shown in Figure 3.11, which allows you to define the IP address range. Typically this is done when you have scripts or other routines that are dependent on IP addresses. This would be one method of controlling the scripts and routines that run when remote users log in.

Figure 3.11 IP Address Range Assignment

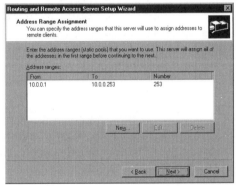

8. Once you have defined the IP address ranges you want to assign, click **Next**.

9. The next screen will ask you how you want to authenticate your users. The two choices you are given are **Yes, I want to use a RADIUS server** and **No, I don't want to set up this server to use RADIUS now**. If you don't know what RADIUS is, you're probably going to be very confused at this point. RADIUS, short for *Remote Authentication Dial-In User Service,* is used for authenticating and logging various kinds of remote access. RADIUS provides a security database in which users and devices can be defined for a variety of access levels. If you already have a RADIUS solution in place, you can configure the RRAS service to use it for user authentication. Here we'll assume you chose the **No...** button. Click **Next** to continue the installation.

10. Since you chose not to use RADIUS, you will be presented with a **Finish** button that will complete the installation of RRAS on this server.

Configuring & Implementing...

Using RADIUS

RADIUS is a very powerful tool when it's used in conjunction with remote access. Most VPN solutions support RADIUS as a protocol, and the accounting information that can be gained from a RADIUS accounting server is impressive. Still, a RADIUS implementation needs to be considered carefully before it is implemented.

RADIUS can be used to secure everything from Web pages to your local network. Many different RADIUS packages are available, but all of them share the basic protocol. Network devices such as routers can send accounting data as part of the RADIUS packet to an accounting server that can provide pages and pages of statistics. Basic RADIUS packages are relatively inexpensive, but the advanced accounting packages can really cost some bucks.

Windows 2000 includes its own RADIUS solution, called Internet Authentication Service (IAS). This is an optional component that can be installed through Add/Remove Programs. For more information on IAS, see the Windows 2000 help files or the Server Resource Kit.

At this point, your server is configured to accept the incoming connections, possibly assign them an IP address, verify them against some type of client database (Windows 2000 Active Directory or RADIUS), and let them access the network. But wait—we haven't defined who can use remote access yet! You don't want just anyone to have the ability to dial in whenever they want, do you?

The next step in granting your users remote access is to give them dial-in permissions in your Active Directory tree:

1. Click the **Start** button, choose **Programs | Administrative Tools | Active Directory Users and Computers**, and navigate to the user to whom you want to assign permissions. Right-click the user's name, and select **Edit** to get to the properties sheet for the user.

2. Select the **Dial-in** tab at the top of the properties sheet to configure this user for dial-in access. Figure 3.12 shows the **Dial-in** properties tab for a user. By default, the **Control access through Remote Access Policy** option will be selected. Click **Allow access** to grant this user dial-in permissions.

Other security options are available as well. If your modem and phone line support it, you can use Caller ID to verify that the user is calling from a certain phone line. If the user isn't calling from the defined line, he or she cannot make the connection. Of course, this precaution is useless if your users travel and access the RAS server from many locations. The second choice is to use the Callback options. When Callback is selected, the RAS server calls the user back at a predefined number to make the RAS connection. Again, this feature locks a remote user to one number. Another option is to assign this user a fixed IP every time he or she logs in. Typically, you would use this feature when you are trying to configure things such as firewall rules that are based on specific IP addresses.

Figure 3.12 User Dial-In Properties

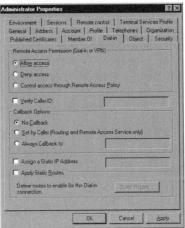

At this point, you should be ready to go! You have installed your hardware, set up the RRAS services, and defined your user's dial-in properties … so start those phones a-ringing! Well, not so fast—always make sure that you test your server to see if you are providing the level of service you want to make available. All too often, administrators rush to get a system in place and are suddenly confronted with the fact that it simply won't meet their needs. Think about having a test bed to run the server through its paces. The more testing you do, the better off you will be.

Altering Your RAS Installation

Sometimes you need to change the RRAS properties once you have them in place. The RRAS Wizard, although wonderful at helping you do the installation, makes a lot of assumptions behind the scenes that you might need to alter to better fit your environment.

To change these settings at a later date (or just to see what they are), do the following:

1. Select your server from the **Routing and Remote Access MMC**.

2. Right-click the server name, then select **Properties**. From here, you can alter the PPP controls, change authentication security, and remove protocols from

dialup networking, as we mentioned earlier. Figure 3.13 shows the RAS server configuration properties that can be modified.

Figure 3.13 RRAS Properties

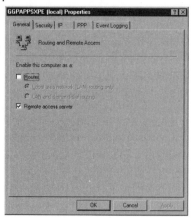

3.   The **General** tab is used merely to switch the RRAS server between pro-viding remote access services and acting as a router. A Windows 2000 machine that is multihomed (contains more than one NIC) can route traffic between subnets, just like any router would. The term Routing and Remote Access Services is called such because of the routing capabilities of Windows 2000.

4.   In the **Security** tab shown in Figure 3.14, you can see the security and accounting options for the RAS connections. As we discussed earlier, either Windows Authentication or RADIUS Authentication provides security. If you were to later install a RADIUS server in your environment, this is where you would enable it for RAS use. The Accounting drop-down menu allows you to choose **Windows Accounting**, **RADIUS Accounting**, or **None**. The default accounting provided by Windows for RAS connections is far less than what RADIUS can provide. Still, it will give you some basic communications statistics based on the parameters you set in the **Event Logging** tab.

5.   Clicking the **Authentication Methods** button will bring you to a list of authentication methods that you can use. The common ones are MS-CHAP and PAP, although there are many additional methods such as EAP or even Unauthenticated Access. Configuring this setting correctly is one of the major issues that remote access administrators run up against. Usually, it's just a matter of figuring out what your client uses. Sometimes that involves consid-ering what you will use in the future.

6.   Figure 3.15 shows the **IP** tab, where you are able to enable IP routing, define how clients receive their remote addressing, and add or remove IP ranges from

the address pool. This is also the window you would use to switch your RAS server from a statically defined pool to one provided by DHCP. IP routing must be enabled for remote access clients to be able to access the IP network to which this server is attached.

Figure 3.14 Security and Logging

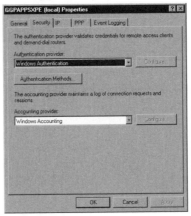

Figure 3.15 IP Configuration

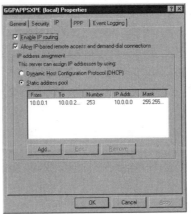

7. The **PPP** tab allows you to alter the properties that a PPP connection will try to negotiate with a remote client. You can define whether to allow multilink connections, use software compression, and the Link Control Protocol (LCP) extensions. Individual connection settings are done using the remote access policies. We'll discuss those a little later in this chapter.

8. The last tab is the **Event Logging** tab. From here, you can determine the types of events that will be logged using the method you chose earlier. Note the option shown in Figure 3.16 to **Enable Point-to-Point Protocol**

logging. This check box turns on a separate feature called *PPP tracing*. If this box is checked, events in the PPP connection establishment procedures are written to the Ppp.log file that is located in the systemroot\Tracing folder. You must restart the RRAS service for this setting to take effect.

Figure 3.16 Event Logging

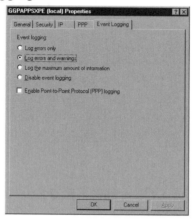

In addition to the configuration changes you might want to make in the RRAS server properties, it is a good idea to look at the ports configured for incoming RRAS calls. The RRAS Wizard assumes that all your modems are available for dial-in users. It also opens some ports that malicious people could use to try to bring down your server. It is a good idea to remove the ports that you won't be using. Figure 3.17 shows the Ports window in the Routing and Remote Access MMC.

Figure 3.17 Port Configuration

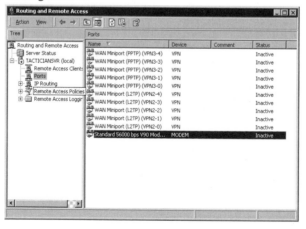

To configure a port for use with remote access, do the following:

1. Highlight the connection you want to enable and click the **Configure** button.

2. Check the box labeled **Remote access connections (inbound only)** and supply it with the connected phone number (if possible). You should supply the phone number only if you plan to support the Bandwidth Allocation Protocol (BAP), which allows you to initiate multiple connections to your server as long as multiple modems and lines are available at each location.

Remote Access Policies

There is one final piece to remote access configuration. In native mode, Windows 2000 allows you to define policies that are enforced strictly for remote access connections. Recall that as we saw in Figure 3.12, one of the options for a user is **Control access through Remote Access Policy**. These policies can be configured under the RRAS MMC. Remote access policies are important because they allow you to define sweeping policies for all the users who might access your RAS services. One of your policy options is to define remote access by *user groups*, which allows you to define remote access strictly by groups.

To create a new policy, follow these steps:

1. Select the **Remote Access Policies** folder, then right-click in the right-hand pane and choose **New Remote Access Policy**.

2. You will be asked to name the new policy, and will then be asked to configure the conditions for the policy. There are quite a few choices available, from Caller ID settings to specific login times and Windows user groups. These settings determine the policies that are applied to remote logins. Figure 3.18 shows the list of options available for policy conditions.

Figure 3.18 Remote Access Policies

We've now successfully configured the RAS server to provide remote access services to your users. Policies are established for the remote users, the hardware is configured, and the connections are all set. So bring on the users! Adding users to the equation brings up the next important topic: connection management.

Developing & Deploying…

Remote Access Policies

If you are running your Windows 2000 RAS server in a mixed-mode domain, the option to manage remote access by policies is not available. NT 4.0 RAS servers are incapable of receiving the remote access policy. For this reason, all users who need to access RAS services must be set to **Allow access** in their individual user properties, and the default remote access policy must be deleted.

There is one trick that you can use to allow or deny access on a per-group basis. If you create a policy using the Windows Groups condition that has a constraint that cannot be met, that group will not be allowed access. The common constraint is to use a fictitious number and enable the **Restrict Dial-in** option to that number only. Make sure that you test this solution before implementing it on a systemwide basis.

Managing Connected Users

Keeping tabs on users is something network administrators like to do. From troubleshooting problems to monitoring usage, the ability to monitor a user's session can be an invaluable tool in managing your remote access environment. Thankfully, Windows 2000 comes equipped with several built-in tools that allow you to at least begin to keep an eye on those users.

The first tool is, of course, the Routing and Remote Access MMC. Highlighting the **Remote Access Clients** subheading for your RAS server gives you a list of all the dial-in users currently connected. It also provides some statistics for each user, including length of connect time, current IP address, and even data transfer volume. Clicking an individual name brings up that person's property sheet on which this information can be found. Clicking the **Hang Up** button on the properties sheet can also break individual connections.

Another handy feature is the ability to message users who are currently connected to the system. This tool can warn users of impending shutdowns, inform them that they need to exit the system, or even tell them to get off the phone so you can give them a call! The message pops up like a basic Net Send command and identifies the originator. Users do not have the option to send messages back to you, however.

Another handy tool is Performance Monitor (PerfMon). Several RAS-related alerts can be set to allow you to gather information about the RAS service. These logs are stored with the normal Performance Monitor logs, and can be accessed through the PerfMon utility. Don't forget, RRAS supports its own logging system, which we talked about earlier. Those logs can give you a great look at how things are working with your RAS service.

Windows 2000 also includes a very useful command-line utility called *Netsh*. At a command prompt, type **netsh ras ?** to display a list of available Netsh commands that apply to your RAS service. Netsh is a query tool that basically checks the availability of services and their current status. This tool takes a little getting used to, but it can be a real boon to network administrators.

> **NOTE**
>
> The Netsh utility can be used for many different queries in Windows 2000. It's a good tool to become familiar with, not just for RAS but for server management in general. More information on Netsh can be found in the Windows 2000 Help documentation.

Configuring for VPN Clients

Installing the VPN software on a Windows 2000 server is very easy once you've gone through the steps to install the RRAS services. In fact, you've already done about 75 percent of the work! When you added Remote Access Service, Windows 2000 automatically added support for five L2TP and five PPP connections as part of the default installation. If you haven't already added RAS support, you need to go back to the section titled "RAS Installation" and start from there. We assume from this point forward that you've already completed those installation tasks.

The first step in the VPN installation process is to make sure that your ports are actually installed. Recall from the previous section that you can do this from the RRAS MMC as follows:

1. Click **Start | Programs | Administrative Tools | Routing and Remote Access**. When the RRAS MMC comes up, you should be able to find your server in the left-hand column.

2. Double-click your server to bring up the details for that server.

3. Right-click the **Ports** listing, then select **Properties** to see a list of available ports. Figure 3.19 shows the Ports Properties sheet.

From here, you can edit your ports and protocols according to the needs of your RAS environment. Remove ports that you will not need to use, because these can become security holes in your network.

Figure 3.19 Ports Properties

To configure a particular port of VPN use, highlight it and click the **Configure** button. Figure 3.20 shows you the configure screen for a port. Make sure that the **Remote access connections (inbound only)** box is checked, and for the phone number of the device, supply the public IP address of this server. Clients will connect to this IP address using the VPN client software.

Figure 3.20 Port Configuration

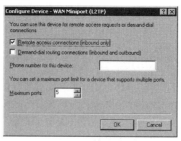

NOTE

The public IP address is used only when you attempt to connect to this server from outside the network perimeter. Usually, this connection is done through some type of Network Address Translation (NAT) so that your internal IP address scheme is not exposed to the outside world.

This window is also where you configure the maximum available ports for this service. This number should be scaled based on the maximum number of users your server can support in a VPN role. When you are considering this number, keep in mind performance issues such as Internet latency, the connection to your RAS server, and the typical connection your clients will make to their ISP (high-speed, dialup, and the like).

It is very important to note that due to the complex nature of a VPN packet, performance can be degraded from 10 to 50 percent! A great deal of this degradation occurs because of the encryption/decryption process that has to be handled at both ends, as well as the increased packet overhead involved with VPN networks. On a T1 connection at both ends, this might not be so noticeable. But for a dial-in client, a 50-percent reduction could be devastating. If it is at all possible, your users should always directly dial into your RAS server instead of making a VPN connection. The direct dial-in method provides the best connection speed and transfer rate.

PPTP

By default, the Windows 2000 RAS installation automatically enables five PPTP ports. These ports can be used to support older dialup networking clients who are not capable of making an L2TP connection. As we discussed earlier, PPTP encrypts the packet, sticks a PPP wrapper around it, and then shoots it off to the PPTP server. PPTP is based on the shared secret model of NT 4.0, which is far less secure than L2TP or IPSec.

The primary benefit to PPTP is that it's cheap and easy to implement. PPTP traffic is compatible with a NAT system, can support multiprotocol and multicast environments, and is much less expensive than public key systems that are used with L2TP and IPSec. And as we mentioned before, many older clients are not able to make an L2TP connection and rely on PPTP for VPN access. For all these reasons, PPTP is here to stay.

IPSec

IPSec is used to provide enhanced security for VPN traffic in IP unicast situations. It uses a public key infrastructure (PKI) to encrypt and decrypt VPN traffic and gives actual end-to-end security in the connection. There are two levels of IPSec tunneling. The first is a combination L2TP/IPSec tunnel, and the second is pure IPSec tunneling. IPSec tunneling is not recommended for VPN connections, because it fails to provide some basic services that remote users require.

IPSec utilizes the on-demand security negotiation and automatic key management services through the Internet Key Exchange (IKE) standard established by the IETF. Group Policy can be used in Active Directory to provide IPSec policy assignment and distribution to Windows 2000 domain members. Security can be established through public/private key signatures using certificates, passwords (but only to establish the trust), or the Kerberos 5.0 authentication that Windows 2000-based domains use. Kerberos is the easiest choice for deploying an IPSec solution.

Windows 2000 *only* supports L2TP over IPSec connections. IPSec is implemented in Windows 2000 through the use of policies. Several policies come predefined with Windows 2000, or you can create your own policy. To manage IPSec policies, use the Local Computer Policy snap-in for the MMC. Highlighting the **IP Security Policies**

on Local Machine subheading gives you the three existing security policies in the right-hand pane. These three default policies are:

- **Secure Server** A machine set as a secure server always tries to negotiate security with any client that sends it traffic. If security cannot be negotiated, the server ceases to respond to the client.

- **Client** A client policy makes the machine query the server to establish secure communications. If the server does not have a secure server policy, no data encryption is performed.

- **Server** A machine with a server policy attempts to establish secure communications, but if it cannot, it defaults back to sending packets in the clear.

IPSec does have some limitations, which is why it should always be implemented in combination with L2TP. The primary fault in IPSec is that it provides no user authentication. Instead, authentication is handled on a machine basis. This means that there is no way to identify who is using that machine. Another key limitation is that IPSec has no method of managing tunnel address assignment. Furthermore, it does not support NAT technology, multiple protocols, or multicast environments.

L2TP

Like PPTP, L2TP is automatically configured with five ports by the default Windows 2000 RAS installation. L2TP, as we discussed before, is a Layer 2 protocol that is a combination of the L2F and PPTP protocols developed by Cisco and Microsoft. Windows 2000 uses L2TP in conjunction with IPSec to provide the functions of VPN management that IPSec alone cannot provide. Since L2TP is a payload inside the IPSec packet, it can gain the benefits of IPSec (end-to-end secure communications, replay protection, and data integrity) without sacrificing the important features that PPTP can provide (user authentication, multiprotocol support, and tunnel address assignment).

L2TP management is performed in the same RAS MMC port configuration tool we discussed previously. Remember to set the number of L2TP ports to correspond with the correct number for your environment. L2TP is superior to traditional PPTP because it can support multiple tunnels between endpoints and works over any packet-oriented network. In addition, tunnel authentication is provided by the IPSec layer, which gives far better security than PPTP can provide for its tunnel. L2TP also operates with slightly less overhead than a PPTP packet. L2TP headers can be compressed to 4 bytes, compared with 6 bytes for PPTP. This might not seem like a lot, but remember the performance issues we discussed earlier for VPNs.

There are, of course, some drawbacks for L2TP/IPSec. As we mentioned before, IPSec cannot transverse a NAT solution. This still holds true when L2TP is added to the equation. Additionally, older clients will not support an L2TP solution. This means that many clients need to be able to utilize the PPTP connection type instead. In the end, L2TP over IPSec is the solution that Microsoft strongly recommends with Windows 2000. It is a bit more complicated to configure than plain old PPTP, but the enhanced security it provides is well worth it.

Upgrading and Migrating to RRAS

There are quite a few older RAS solutions in existence. Windows 2000 far surpasses all Microsoft's previous attempts at creating a RAS environment. With more and more RAS users flooding the marketplace, the systems themselves have become considerably more robust. One of the potential dilemmas you could run up against is whether to upgrade your existing RAS solution or simply do a clean install of Windows 2000. From an administration level, if it is at all possible to do a fresh installation of Windows 2000, that is always your best bet. Microsoft has improved its upgrade process, but it can still "hiccup."

If you must upgrade, Microsoft provides very little information on upgrading your RAS service. Whether this is an oversight on the company's part or is because Microsoft doesn't think anyone will upgrade those services, we're not sure. Regardless, since it is possible to do a direct upgrade from several previous versions of Windows, this might be an issue for you. Although most field-level administrators recommend a clean installation, Microsoft continues to insist that the upgrade process is fine. This section of the chapter covers the important considerations in choosing to upgrade from a previous Windows version.

A major consideration in looking at RAS migration is your hardware configuration. The hardware you are currently using must be compatible with Windows 2000. For older configurations, hardware will not be a problem. Microsoft supplies thousands of drivers in the Windows 2000 installation. However, some vendors might not have supplied Windows 2000-compliant drivers before the software shipped. Check your hardware vendors' Web sites to make sure that you have the most recent drivers for any hardware or software you plan to install on the RAS server.

Upgrading NT RAS

NT 4.0 RAS is very similar to the RAS service provided in NT 3.51. Both relied on Windows Dial-Up Networking to establish a connection from the client to the RAS server. Users were enabled for RAS connections using the Dial-Inn button under the individual Properties in User Manager for Domains. When you upgrade to a Windows 2000 server, all this information is theoretically moved to Active Directory. Users whose machines were configured for RAS access under NT 4.0 will also be configured for access under Windows 2000.

In reality, the upgrade process is not always that clean. Many administrators recommend removing Remote Access from the NT 4.0 installation before you attempt the upgrade. Then, once the Windows 2000 server is up and running, reconfigure the RAS service cleanly. This process requires a bit more work, but it can save you some potential trouble later. Even if you choose to let Windows automatically complete the RAS upgrade, you'll want to go back and check the assumptions that it made to bring them in line with your RAS expectations.

Upgrading from Windows NT 3.5x RAS

NT 3.51, like NT 4.0, can be directly upgraded to Windows 2000. And like NT 4.0, the user information should theoretically be migrated as well. Again, you're left to trusting the migration wizard to get it right. All too often, it won't. As with NT 4.0, the recommendation for upgrading the RAS server is to at least uninstall RAS before attempting the migration. Yes, it can work successfully. It can also screw up your Active Directory if it doesn't, and the last thing you want with a Windows 2000 server is a messed-up Active Directory.

NOTE

Although Citrix WinFrame is based on NT 3.51 technology, you *cannot* directly upgrade it to Windows 2000. You must perform a clean installation of Windows 2000. You could, in theory, upgrade the server to NT 4.0 Terminal Server Edition prior to upgrading it to Windows 2000. The odds of it working without anything breaking are probably about 50/50.

Migrating from a Third-party Remote Access Server

Quite a few third-party products provide RAS services to Windows NT administrators. Not surprisingly, many of these rely on the basic features of NT RAS. Some of them *might* migrate the data correctly into the Active Directory, but with a third-party solution, you are usually looking at starting over or getting the appropriate version for Windows 2000. It is not recommended to upgrade a RAS server with a third-party RAS solution in place.

Direct Dial to Citrix MetaFrame XP: The Alternative Method

Citrix MetaFrame XP can be configured to accept *direct dial-in* connections. Instead of using RRAS to allow your users access to your network and then access your Terminal Servers or Citrix MetaFrame servers through either RDP or ICA, you can allow them direct dialup access into the Citrix servers. This method, however, is not recommended except in very small implementations of Citrix MetaFrame due to the extra load it would put on the servers, thereby degrading performance. In the event that these servers will provide direct dial-in, they need to have modems installed and configured. Citrix servers need to configure the ICA protocol to accept asynchronous connections. All of this adds an extra unwanted load on the servers.

To enable direct dial-in for Citrix MetaFrame XP servers, make sure that all your modems are properly installed and configured and then complete the following steps to configure the asynchronous ICA connections:

1. Click **Start | Programs | Citrix | MetaFrame XP | Citrix Connection Configuration** (see Figure 3.21).

Figure 3.21 Citrix Connection Configuration

2. Click **Connection** in the **File** menu, and click **New** (see Figure 3.22).

Figure 3.22 New Asynchronous ICA Connection

3. In the **Name** field, enter a name for the connection you are creating.

4. In the **Transport** drop-down menu, make sure **async** is selected.

5. Select the device on which you want to create a connection.

6. Go through the **Advanced** button and the **Client Settings** button, config-
    uring the settings as you want them. When you are done, click **OK**.

At this point, the Async ICA connection has been set up on the server. Next, you
need to configure the client to access the newly created dialup service. To accomplish
this configuration on the client side, follow these steps:

1. Open **Citrix Program Neighborhood** and double-click **Custom ICA
    Connections**.

2. Double-click **Add ICA connection**.

3. In the **Add New ICA** connection window, select **ICA Dial-In** from the
    drop-down menu, and click **Next** (see Figure 3.23).

Figure 3.23 Citrix Dial-In Connection

4. Follow the prompts to configure the connection.

NOTE

When using ICA Dial-In, it is important to note that you lose the ability to use
any form of encryption except for that offered with ICA. You can't use IPSec,
because no network connection is running IP. This doesn't mean that your
Citrix Dial-In connection is not secure, but you lose the functionality and security offered by IPSec. SecureICA provides for 40-, 56- or 128-bit RC5 data
encryption.

Summary

Microsoft has paid a great deal of attention to remote access in Windows 2000: improved RAS configuration, native support for many VPN technologies, and a good help system. The company really seems to be taking RAS seriously as a technology, which is a good thing for anyone who must support remote users. In this chapter, we've discussed the design and placement of your RAS system, the various protocols associated with RAS and VPN technology, installing and configuring your RAS and VPN server in Windows 2000, and finally, some things to think about when considering whether or not to upgrade your RAS server from a previous version of Windows. Whew!

Design and placement of your RAS server is key to the success of your entire remote access offering. Poor placement or inadequate hardware considerations can cripple user productivity over your remote connections. Don't simply set down your RAS server in a dark corner and forget it's there! Make full use of your bandwidth and place the RAS server where it will do your users the most good. Usually, this isn't conveniently beside your desk!

Windows 2000 offers many more protocol choices for remote access. Trying to decide among PPTP, L2TP, or IPSec can be a real headache, but these protocols are the heart and soul of Windows 2000 remote access; choose them wisely. This chapter reviewed each protocol, what each does and how. We also discussed where protocols were appropriate to use and the way to find more information on each of them.

Installing Windows 2000 RAS services is made much simpler by the inclusion of an RRAS Wizard. This powerful tool is a real boon for quickly setting up your RAS environment, but it makes some assumptions you might not want it to make. Always make sure that you go back through the options after the wizard is done and make certain that its assumptions accurately reflect what you want. This chapter described the wizard and reviewed the process of setting up VPN technology, including configuring the IPSec policies for each machine.

We also looked at the upgrade considerations for your current RAS environment. The expert opinion is always that you should do a clean installation. If you can't do that, at the very least you should uninstall RAS services before attempting the upgrade. This will save you time down the road when you might otherwise be searching through Active Directory trying to figure out where it all went wrong. By now you're fast on your way to becoming an RAS and VPN expert.

Finally, we looked at the alternative method of direct dial into the Citrix servers and demonstrated how it is set up on the server side and on the client side. Direct dialup access into Citrix servers is not recommended except in very small implementations of Citrix MetaFrame.

Solutions Fast Track

Designing and Placing RRAS Servers on the Network

☑ Capacity planning is an imperative first step when you are planning your RRAS solution. This step determines the kind of hardware needed for the role you have chosen for this server.

☑ Hardware requirements such as RAM, CPU, NIC, and storage should be carefully chosen and should be able to comply with the capacity planning discussed earlier.

☑ Availability planning is another important consideration; solutions vary from redundant components such as modems to clustering RRAS servers or having multiple RRAS servers.

Remote Access Protocols

☑ SLIP is an older dialup protocol that has been replaced by PPP because of its weak security features. It is found in older implementations and in unsecured environments.

☑ PPTP can be used in LAN-to-LAN or even WAN-to-WAN networking. It offers advanced security features.

☑ L2TP is a merged version of PPTP and L2F that utilizes the best features of the two. The two protocols were so similar in design and functionality that the IETF decided to merge them into L2TP.

Installing Routing and Remote Access Services

☑ We strongly recommend that prior to buying any hardware to install in your server, you check the HCL to make sure that your products are supported. This can be a time saver in many situations.

☑ A RADIUS server is something worth looking at when you are installing or planning RRAS because of its impressive accounting information offerings and its ability to secure almost everything from Web pages to your local network.

☑ The use of remote access policies is a great way to control what your dial-in users can access and what they can do while they are connected.

Upgrading and Migrating to RRAS

☑ When you upgrade, we recommend removing the RRAS service, upgrading the server, then reinstalling the RRAS service fresh and reconfiguring it.

☑ Theoretically, you can rely on the wizard to upgrade Windows NT 3.5x or 4.0 to Windows 2000 RRAS, but experience has shown that this process is not entirely accurate.

☑ The best course of action for upgrading third-party RAS solutions is reinstalling the entire solution.

Direct Dial to Citrix MetaFrame XP: The Alternative Method

☑ Installing the Async ICA connection is done in Citrix Connection Configuration. A modem needs to be installed and configured before connections can be accepted.

☑ Using direct dial into Citrix servers is an extra burden on the servers and is not recommended unless the implementation is in a very small environment.

☑ In Citrix ICA Dial-In, encryption is limited to what ICA can offer. Encryption levels are 40-, 56-, and 128-bit.

Frequently Asked Questions

The following Frequently Asked Questions, answered by the authors of this book, are designed to both measure your understanding of the concepts presented in this chapter and to assist you with real-life implementation of these concepts. To have your questions about this chapter answered by the author, browse to **www.syngress.com/solutions** and click on the **"Ask the Author"** form.

Q: I'm trying to upgrade my Citrix WinFrame server to Windows 2000 and provide RAS services to my users. What's the easiest way to do this?

A: Unfortunately, there is no direct upgrade path from WinFrame to Windows 2000. To make the installation work, you'll need to do a fresh installation of Windows 2000 on the server, a fresh install of all your applications, and then migrate your user information. In addition, you might want to rethink your hardware because what was once sufficient for WinFrame might not be enough to run Windows 2000 robustly. Cheer up—it's the method we recommend anyway!

Q: I want to enable an IPSec policy that will challenge *all* my clients for secure communications and not make the connection unless they can negotiate a secure connection. How do I do that?

A: You can use the default IPSec policy Secure Server to provide that level of systems security. Be warned, however: Remote clients who cannot negotiate a connection will never be able to make a connection to your server.

Q: I want to send a message to all my currently connected users to warn them that I am about to boot the RAS server. How do I do that?

A: The RRAS MMC gives you the option to message all connected users. To do this, click **Start | Programs | Administrative Tools | Routing and Remote Access**. In the console tree, right-click **Remote Access Clients** and click **Send to all**. In the **Send Message** window, type your message and click **OK**. For users who don't get off the system in response to your message, you can highlight their names, right-click, and choose **Hang Up**. Off they go!

Chapter 4

Designing the Thin Client Solution

Solutions in this chapter:

Introduction

Typical client/server applications have two tiers: the client and the server. Each tier of a client/server solution provides some form of processing and management. Databases are an example of a client/server application. The database resides on the server and stores data. A client application retrieves data from the database and manipulates it, adds new data to the database, or deletes data from the database. The processing is shared.

Thin client solutions are built in three tiers: the thin client, the application server, and the data server. The thin client requires as little information as possible to travel across the wire, in order to be termed "thin." So, in this three-tier solution, processing is *not* evenly distributed. The application server takes on the role of processing, which a client would play in a standard client/server solution, and then transmits only the information necessary to the thin client. The data server tier remains the same as the server portion of a client/server solution.

The resulting logical design of a thin client solution becomes the basis for capacity planning, availability planning, and infrastructure design for a Citrix MetaFrame XP server. Because Citrix MetaFrame XP is installed on top of a Windows 2000 server with Terminal Services, its design is intertwined with that of the Windows 2000 Terminal Server. However, because Citrix MetaFrame XP uses the Independent Computing Architecture (ICA) protocol and has unique load-balancing capabilities, a Citrix MetaFrame XP design differs from that of a standard Windows 2000 Terminal Server.

Designing a Three-Tier Solution

When you implement a thin client solution in order to deliver an application to end users, your solution will likely involve three tiers. The thin client server provides a mid-tier architecture, since it sits between the client and the application server. When there are multiple Citrix MetaFrame XP servers in a farm, the farm collectively acts as a single service to any thin client access device. In addition, the farm acts collectively as a client to the network file, print, and database servers. This system is depicted in Figure 4.1.

Logical Design

If you followed the path of data as it traveled through a thin client solution, you would notice that the data is transformed in the middle. The data is changed from a logic function to a presentation format. Whereas the thin client server *physically* provides the mid-tier architecture, the server acts as the business *logic* layer.

Let's examine a typical client/server solution. Figure 4.2 shows a database server and a database client application running on a workstation. The database server provides a storage location for the database (or part of it, if it is a distributed database). The database server also conducts a variety of processes, such as sorting records and data backup. The application running on the workstation performs business logic, such as queries and reports. It also presents the data to the user in a usable format.

Figure 4.1 Three-Tier Architecture

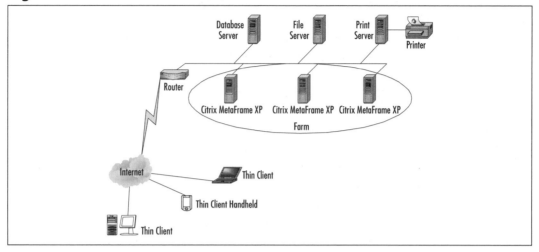

Figure 4.2 A Typical Two-Tiered Database Application

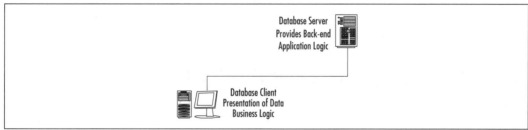

When you insert a thin client server into this scenario, it provides the business logic function and passes the presentation data to the workstation that runs the thin client software. The database client software runs on the server, not the workstation. This system is displayed in Figure 4.3.

Of course, the thin client architecture doesn't have to stop at three tiers. Depending on the type of system the thin client server is integrating with, the number of tiers can increase. Some client applications use multiple servers. Functions are distributed across application servers that provide business logic and back-end servers that store data and run underlying processes. The client application is generally limited to presentation of data in this type of architecture. When a thin client server is inserted into this system, the presentation of data is transformed from the database client presentation to the thin client presentation. Whether delivering the application across a different type of protocol or optimizing the traffic across slow links, a thin client server can greatly enhance an application's delivery.

Figure 4.3 Thin Client Architecture with Two-Tiered Database

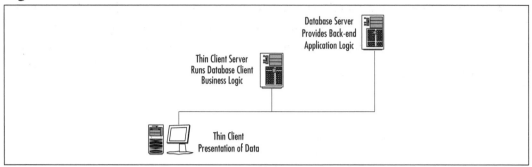

Data Storage

When designing a thin client solution, you need to consider two types of storage:

■ **System storage** This is the location of the operating system files—the page file and the applications and system files.

■ **User data storage** This is the storage of the user-specific configuration, user data, and system files.

These two types of data need to be stored in different ways. The first is fairly static in nature, rarely growing except for the paging file. The second is dynamic and can grow to a huge extent, requiring excess administration if not organized well from the start. It is best to separate these two storage types by creating two different drive letters. In doing so, you can protect system files from accidental corruption or deletion by a user running a session on the server.

Connectivity

The most important thing to remember in designing a thin client solution is that the Citrix MetaFrame XP servers need to be placed on a highly available connection to the application servers. This placement is contrary to most design strategies, which work in a tiered fashion:

■ Backbone layer

■ Access layer

■ Host layer

In this tiered fashion, client machines and workgroup servers are placed on the bottom, in the Host layer, which is usually well outside and away from backbone equipment and corporate servers. By keeping users next to the servers they access most, the amount of traffic is reduced from the backbone. The Access layer is then used for any authentication servers or hosts that act as a gate between the backbone and the end users. For example, firewalls and remote access servers fit into this category. The backbone is the highly available connectivity that runs between locations; it has a single purpose: to move traffic from one place to another. This type of design is shown in Figure 4.4.

Figure 4.4 Tiered Network Design

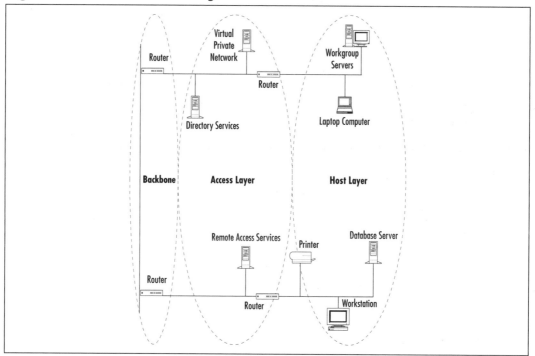

In a Citrix MetaFrame XP design, the size of the traffic between the Citrix MetaFrame XP server and its clients is negligible, or very nearly so. By contrast, the amount of traffic traveling between a Citrix MetaFrame XP server and the network servers to which it acts as a client can be huge. Therefore, the location of the end users is not a factor in determining where to place the server. In fact, the Citrix MetaFrame XP server should be directly connected to or near the backbone if it accesses servers in varying geographic locations, rather than in the Host layer. In Figure 4.5, the Citrix MetaFrame XP server must connect to Server A and Server B; therefore, it is placed near the backbone as near as possible to Server B rather than on the link that is closest to the client computers.

The next item is to ensure that the ports that carry ICA traffic are open and available between the client and the Citrix MetaFrame XP server. This can be tricky if you have clients accessing a Citrix MetaFrame XP server through a firewall or another host that filters traffic. In Figure 4.6, the client is using a public wireless network to access the Internet. The client uses a virtual private network (VPN) to reach the corporate network, which lets the user execute an ICA session to a corporate server. This cannot take place if there is any blockage of the ICA port (1494 is the default, but can be changed) on the firewall, any of the corporate routers, or on the VPN server.

Figure 4.5 Placing Citrix MetaFrame XP Servers Near a Backbone

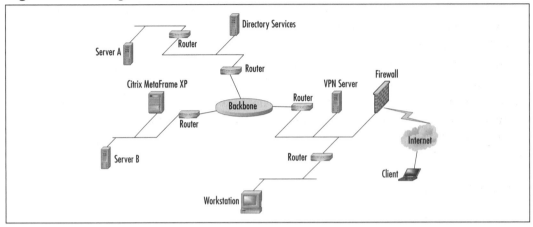

Figure 4.6 Do Not Block the TCP Port Used for ICA on Any Host Between Client and Server

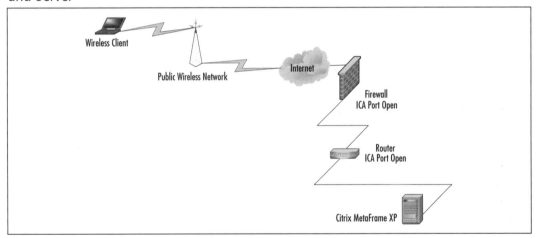

Designing and Placing Terminal Servers on the Network

If you're experienced with technology, you are already familiar with the way a technology project works. Most projects follow a similar process, although the names of the stages might be somewhat different and, occasionally, a stage might be split into two or combined into another.

Regardless of how the project is decided on, it usually starts with someone needing to get something done. For a project with Terminal Services and Citrix MetaFrame XP, the business requirement could be to deliver an application across an inhospitable network or to incompatible machines. The person who has that requirement might not know that you can achieve it through a Citrix MetaFrame XP server. In fact, the people who begin to put the project together could have several options that might not even include Citrix MetaFrame XP. The business requirement will drive a vision of what the best or optimal result should be. As soon as that vision is defined, the technology can be decided on. Once the technology is chosen, a design ensues, followed by testing and development, a pilot deployment, and eventually the final production deployment. The process repeats itself for all projects, taking some of what exists and building on it. This process is illustrated in Figure 4.7.

Figure 4.7 The Project Cycle

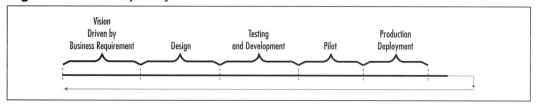

So, having said that, you should begin designing your Citrix MetaFrame XP server, farm, and the network on which they reside with one or more business requirements and a vision for your project to achieve. Every design decision you make should focus on those business requirements first. The business requirements are of primary importance to your design.

For example, if your business requirement is to prevent people from installing software on their local PCs, and you have selected Citrix MetaFrame XP as the solution, you can achieve the business requirement. But the only way you can do so is by deploying Citrix MetaFrame XP so that it is the only desktop that the users can access—either by using PCs that are scripted to automatically boot to an ICA session or by using Winterminals that do so automatically. Plus, you would have to establish group policies that prevent users from installing software onto the Citrix MetaFrame XP server(s).

On the other hand, if your business requirement is to enable access to a SQL application on a global network that includes satellite links with tremendous latency that causes the application to fail, you could deploy Citrix MetaFrame XP to provide access to the application. However, that would be successful *only if* you designed the Citrix

MetaFrame XP server to be connected to the same subnet as the SQL server (or on a well-connected subnet in the same location, if the same subnet is not feasible) and if you provided dialup lines to back up those unreliable network links.

No matter what, you should always let your business requirement drive your technology vision.

Identifying Hardware Requirements

The first thing you must do when undertaking a Citrix MetaFrame XP installation is ensure that the server you install contains hardware that is listed on the Windows 2000 Server HCL. Windows 2000 Server is just as intolerant of noncompliant hardware as Windows NT. If you are using older hardware, it might not be compliant. Most new hardware works just fine. You need to check all the internal components that you add to a server, including your network adapters and modem pools. The HCL is available online at the Microsoft Web site: www.microsoft.com/hcl/default.asp.

In order to achieve the best performance, your server should have the fastest processor and most RAM that is affordable. You will find that the server's performance is greatly enhanced if you make sure that these two components are maximized. The minimum values you should have are:

- **Processor** Minimum Pentium 166, recommended minimum Pentium II 300MHz

- **Memory** Minimum 64MB, recommended minimum 256MB

- **Hard drive space** Minimum 400MB, recommended minimum 2GB

So, starting from these minimum values, your next step is to determine how much *more* power, storage, or speed your server needs to provide your application to your end users.

Capacity Planning

The first part of your design involves specifying the size of one of your MetaFrame servers. This process is called *capacity planning*. Many Citrix MetaFrame projects begin with a single server. Then, as more users are acclimated to the system, they stay online longer, and the administrator ends up having to acquire more licenses and either add more power to the existing server or add more servers into a pool. Accounting for growth and usage patterns is easier if you simply start with a larger size than you need and plan to eventually have a pool of servers, *even if* you begin with a single server for your initial project.

The size of the server depends on two factors:

- The number of users who will be online concurrently
- The types of applications that will be used

These two factors are used to determine necessary size components—memory, processors, and storage—within your server.

To determine how many users will be online concurrently, you first need to know how many users will need access to the server at all. For example, if you have a Citrix MetaFrame server deployed so that the 40 people in your human resources (HR) department and the 30 people in information technology (IT) can access the PeopleSoft application from anywhere in the world, your total number of users is 70. If half those people are in London, England, and the other half are in Los Angeles, California, the mere time zone difference would drive the concurrent usage to a maximum of 35. You'll probably find that there will be closer to 20 concurrent users (about 60 percent of the maximum number of users) at any one point in time.

There is an easy way to manage the maximum concurrent users: Simply purchase that number of licenses, and no more will be able to logon! Users might not be happy about this limitation in crunch periods, though, so know the limits you want to impose and how those limits will affect the business.

Developing & Deploying...

Anticipating Server Growth

Expect the unexpected and double the planned size of your server. Growth and change in use of your MetaFrame server *will* happen. This story follows the typical pattern I've seen:

1. One business unit in the company needs the server to provide one application.
2. They start to use it and find that it would also be great to have their new MetaFrame server provide another application, too.
3. Somehow, some other business unit discovers that the MetaFrame server exists and decides that it would work well for their own application.
4. Then the server is maxed out on licenses, storage, memory, or processing power. So they augment the server and add another, larger server.
5. The next thing you know, there are multiple servers on the network, all with different applications.

Continued

6. After that, someone decides they should pool all the resources, and then all those servers need to be added to a MetaFrame server farm.

7. Around this time, someone discovers that MetaFrame can share applications over the Internet. This leads to new applications and possibly a second server farm on a demilitarized zone (DMZ) to service Web users.

8. The number of servers grows to multiple farms, with one farm serving the Internet, another serving a business unit, and so on.

Unexpected? To others, yes. To you—not anymore!

Applications drive the way that the MetaFrame server is used. If you are deploying the MetaFrame server to provide a PeopleSoft application, for example, you should take a moment to consider the other applications users will need available while they are using the PeopleSoft application. Do they need a calculator? Do they need a word processor? Do they need a spreadsheet? Do they need any other application that is utilized by this group? Each additional application for a user increases the stress on the server components.

Processors

The version of Windows 2000 Server that you use determines your maximum number of processors. Windows 2000 Server allows up to four processors using symmetric multiprocessing (SMP). Windows 2000 Advanced Server allows up to eight SMP processors. Windows 2000 DataCenter Server (from an OEM) supports up to 32 SMP processors.

NOTE

One of the methods for estimating your server's requirements is to characterize the resource usage of a typical user on a sample system. Then use Performance Monitor to scrutinize the processing, memory, paging file, storage, and network interface utilization characteristics of that user. Based on this information, you should be able to determine how many users can be supported simultaneously on a server.

You should determine the type of user who will be on the system before you determine the amount of server resources you need, whether those resources are memory, storage, or processors. There are two basic types of user:

- **Clerical users** These users mainly enter data into applications or run a set of basic tasks. Their main applications are word processing, e-mail, Web browsing, and spreadsheets.

- **Knowledge users** These users are analytical and creative. When it comes to applications, they use a lot of graphics and mathematical equations—and then they run multiple applications at a single time. In the Microsoft world, they are also known as *power users.*

The minimum number of processors you need depends on the number of users and types of applications they use. If you have users who run simple data entry applications (clerical users), you can squeeze 50 or more concurrent users on a single processor server. On the other hand, if you have users who are running Office suite applications and a few other special applications (knowledge users), you can put only about 20 concurrent users on a single processor server. Finally, if you have high-end knowledge users who need processor-intensive applications, you might be able to have only 10 concurrent users on a single processor server. Most businesses have a group that includes some of each type of user, and on average, they can get about 25 users per processor.

The type of processor that you use will affect how many users can be supported as well. For example, a Pentium II 450MHz chip will not support as many users as a Pentium III 933MHz. You might be able to fit between 5 percent and 10 percent more users per processor when you invest in faster processors. If you can fit 25 users on a Pentium II 450MHz processor, you could then get as many as 28 users on a Pentium III 933MHz.

Now, let's assume that you need to provide 400 users access to Citrix MetaFrame. Furthermore, 250 of those users will be online simultaneously. Of these 400 total users, 300 are data entry clerical users, 75 are standard knowledge users, and 25 are high-end knowledge users. This is equivalent to 75 percent clerical, 19 percent knowledge, and 6 percent high-end users. You use a test system and discover that on one processor, you can put about 23 clerical users with six knowledge users and one high-end knowledge user (30 total users)—approximating the same percentages of users you expect overall. If you need to have 250 users online simultaneously, you must have a minimum of:

$$\frac{(\text{\# of concurrent users})}{(\text{\# of users on a single processor})} = \text{minimum number of processors}$$

$$250 / 30 = 8.3$$

There is no such thing as a third of a processor, so you need to round that figure up to nine processors as your absolute minimum number of processors.

To figure your minimum number of processors, you need to determine how many processors it will take to support all the knowledge and high-end knowledge users online, with any remaining spots filled by clerical users. If you test and find that you can have 10 high–end users on a single processor, 20 knowledge users on a single pro–cessor, and 55 clerical users on a single processor, you will calculate this formula:

$$\frac{\text{Total \# of high-end users}}{\text{\# of high-end users per processor}} + \frac{\text{Total \# of knowledge users}}{\text{\# of knowledge users per processor}} +$$

$$\frac{\text{Total concurrent users} - (\text{high-end users} + \text{knowledge users})}{\text{\# of clerical users per processor}}$$

$$= \text{upper-limit minimum number of processors}$$

$$\frac{25}{10} + \frac{75}{20} + \frac{250 - (25 + 75)}{55} = 8.977$$

As you can see from this formula, you again need to round up, and you still need only nine processors.

Now your decision is at how to divvy up those nine processors and whether to add processors for growth. You have several options available to you:

1. You can obtain a single DataCenter server with 16 processors. This will pro–vide you the capacity for growth, but it will not provide any redundancy if that one server fails.

2. You can obtain two Advanced Servers with eight processors each. This will provide you the capacity for growth and reasonable redundancy in case of failure. (The redundancy is very good in this scenario because each server is nearly able to handle all the 250 users by itself.)

3. You can obtain one Advanced Server with eight processors and a Windows 2000 Server with between one and four processors. These will provide you small capacity for growth and a small amount of redundancy. (Redundancy here is skewed, however; if the Advanced Server goes down, the standard Windows 2000 server will not be able to provide the processing power required. However, if the Windows 2000 server fails, the Advanced Server can provide the processing power.)

4. You can obtain three Windows 2000 servers with four processors each. This will provide some capacity for growth and a good amount of redundancy. (Redundancy is better here, because if a single server fails, there are still two left, rather than one, as in the other scenarios. In addition, eight processors will be left online if one server fails.)

Options 1 and 4 from the list are depicted in Figure 4.8.

Figure 4.8 Distributing Processors Among Servers Affects Capacity and Redundancy

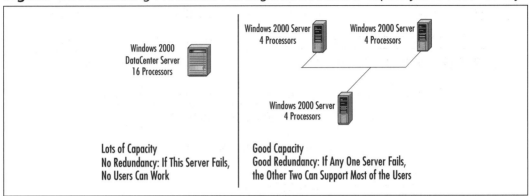

RAM

Windows 2000 Server uses a 32-bit address space. This means that the operating system can address up to 2^{32} bytes of memory can be accessed at any time. 2^{32} is equivalent to 4GB of RAM. This 4GB is divided such that half (2GB) is assigned to each user-mode process and the remaining half (2GB) is assigned to the kernel, handling system data structures. What this means is that the maximum RAM you can have that will affect the way the kernel works is 4GB. With a MetaFrame Server, you will notice when you hit that RAM limit on the kernel because of odd error messages, such as "Out of Paged Memory." If you ever hit this maximum and you have 4GB or more of RAM, your best bet is to scale out by adding more servers to a pool of MetaFrame servers, rather than to scale up the single server with more RAM.

If you need more RAM, you do have options. Windows 2000 Advanced Server supports up to 8GB of RAM on servers that use Intel's Physical Address Extensions (PAEs). Windows 2000 DataCenter Server supports up to 64GB of RAM, but these servers must be built and configured by an original equipment manufacturer (OEM); you can't get the DataCenter Server version off the shelf.

The user-mode process side is interesting. When a user logs on to Citrix MetaFrame and executes an application, if that user is the only user online, the system lets that user have all available RAM. When the second user logs on, the second user uses some RAM, and then there is less available to each user. As more users are added, the available RAM is divided by the number of users and the applications used during each session until all users experience a performance reduction.

The minimum requirements for a Windows 2000 Terminal Services server running Citrix MetaFrame is 64MB, although 128MB minimum is recommended. This 128MB minimum is recommended for the *operating system only.* That's enough to boot up the server and log on without crashing into a variety of blue screen of death (BSOD) errors. However, to actually run Terminal Services for multiple simultaneous users, you need to add RAM.

Clerical users use approximately 4MB of RAM each. Each knowledge user consumes at least 8MB of RAM and probably more, depending on the types of applications he or she uses and whether the user runs several applications simultaneously and will continue to do so on your MetaFrame server. You can run scripts on a test system to simulate how much RAM these applications will use, and with a third-party utility, you can even simulate the same number of users. While executing these tests, you can run Performance Monitor to determine how much RAM is needed for the knowledge user. Or you can estimate at the upper end that each knowledge user should be granted about 20MB of RAM.

You should discover how many of each type of user you intend to have on your system simultaneously. If you have 200 users, but you expect only 40 of them will ever be online at the same time using the Terminal Server, you should estimate enough RAM to accommodate 40 total simultaneous users. Now, if there are 80 knowledge users and 120 clerical users in the original 200, you can estimate that of your 40 simultaneous users, an average of 16 knowledge users and 24 clerical users will be online simultaneously. Then you execute the formula with these simultaneous users and RAM:

((# of knowledge users) × (knowledge RAM)) + ((# of clerical users) × (clerical RAM)) +

(base OS RAM) = lower-limit minimum RAM required

So, given that you have 16 knowledge users who you determine need 20MB RAM, 24 clerical users who need 4MB RAM, and 128MB RAM for the OS, the minimum RAM you need is 544MB.

If you run a system with that 544MB of RAM (hypothetically speaking—there is no way a system can have 544MB) and all 16 knowledge users get online and then all 24 clerical users get online, you will have a system that will perform on the edge of slow. Let's say that you have that system up and running and those users online at once, and all the clerical users log off and are replaced with knowledge users—now you have some trouble. So, you should consider that your upper-limit minimum (for emergency's sake) is:

((# of total simultaneous users) × (knowledge RAM)) +

(base OS RAM)= upper-limit minimum

In our example, the upper-limit minimum is 800MB + 128MB RAM = 928MB RAM. Your next task is to round up the upper limit to the next amount that the system can accept—in this case, 1GB of RAM—and consider that the minimum amount that you will install in the server. You can never have enough RAM, so do add more if you have the budget for it.

WARNING

Growth of the number of users on your system can impact performance significantly. If you have sized a server for 40 users and are then requested to enable 60 simultaneous users, you have a problem. Try to look ahead into the future and determine whether more users will demand access to the Citrix MetaFrame server. You should consider whether your corporate culture promotes adoption of technology at a quick pace and whether your business is experiencing a high growth rate. With this knowledge, you should try predicting whether you will need more hardware to support additional users, or you could simply plan to add more servers.

Storage

Storage on the Citrix MetaFrame server includes the hard drives, diskette drives, CD-ROM drives, and tape backup systems. In some cases, a Citrix MetaFrame server might need access to a storage area network (SAN) for mission-critical data. Some of these storage design decisions are simple. You would most likely purchase a server that already had a diskette drive and a CD-ROM drive. In addition, if you did not place a tape backup system directly on each of your Citrix MetaFrame servers, at least you would have one available on a server somewhere on the network that could back up the MetaFrame server over the network links.

File System

One of the easier tasks that you will perform when you deploy the server is choosing the file system to use. Windows 2000 supports:

- File Allocation Table (FAT)
- 32-bit FAT (FAT32)
- NT File System (NTFS)

FAT is a file system available in many operating systems—DOS, Windows 3.x, Windows 9x, Windows NT, and OS/2, for example. Because it is common to so many operating systems, it is usually selected for multibooting. FAT has a 2GB limitation on partitions.

FAT32 is new to Windows 9x systems. It is not accessible by Windows NT, but Windows 2000 does support it. FAT32 supports partitions larger than 2GB.

NTFS 5.0 is the native file system for Windows 2000. It also supports partitions larger than 2GB. In addition, NTFS 5.0 offers several things that FAT and FAT32 cannot:

- Fault tolerance

- Optimized disk space

- Advanced security

Redundant Array of Inexpensive Disks (RAID) support provides fault tolerance that you must configure. NTFS also includes built-in fault tolerance. Log files help recover files that are changed but not written when a system failure occurs. NTFS also automatically handles bad sectors on the hard drive without displaying error messages.

File compression is one of the ways that NTFS 5.0 optimizes disk space. You can also set disk quotas for individual users to prevent them from storing more than their fair share of files.

Security on Citrix MetaFrame is extremely important because end users are effectively running their applications from the server console. If you don't apply strict security measures, users can obliterate files on the server. NTFS allows an administrator to apply local security on a file-by-file basis. Table 4.1 lists the access control list (ACL) rights that can be assigned.

Table 4.1 NTFS ACL Rights

Right	File or Folder?	Function
None	File and folder	Cannot access the file or folder
Read Data	File	Open and view the file contents
Write Data	File	Change the file contents
Execute Data	File	Run an executable program or batch file
Delete	File	Delete a file
Change Permissions	File and folder	Change the ACL on a file or folder
Take Ownership	File and folder	Become the owner of a file or folder
List Folder	Folder	View the folder contents
Create Files	Folder	Add files or subfolders
Traverse Folder	Folder	Open a subfolder

In Windows NT systems, many people installed FAT for the boot drive because there was no other native way to access the hard drive if the system failed and it was formatted with NTFS. With Windows 2000, however, the Recovery Console enables you to access the NTFS partition and manipulate files on it. The Recovery Console is available by booting the original Windows 2000 CD-ROM, or you can install the Recovery Console to be available on the boot menu by executing **WINNT32 /CMDCONS** from a command prompt any time after the server has been installed.

Because NTFS has so many advantages over both FAT and FAT32, it is the optimal selection for a file system on Citrix MetaFrame.

Redundant Array of Inexpensive Disks

Windows 2000 supports software-based RAID natively. With software-based RAID, if you have enough hard disks installed on the system, you can create a custom RAID configuration without needing to install a special array interface card. The types of software-based RAID that Windows 2000 supports are listed in Table 4.2.

Table 4.2 RAID Types Supported by Windows 2000

RAID Level	Type	Tolerance	Minimum Number of Disks
RAID 0	Disk striping	No tolerance; if a disk fails, the system fails.	3
RAID 1	Disk mirroring	Good tolerance; if a disk fails, the other disk can be configured as the boot disk.	2
RAID 1	Disk duplexing	Good tolerance; if a disk fails or if a disk controller fails, the other disk can be configured as the boot disk.	2
RAID 5	Disk striping with parity	High tolerance; if a disk fails, the array can be rebuilt while the server is running.	3

You should, if possible, implement RAID 5 for fault tolerance. If possible, you should select hardware-based RAID. Hardware-based RAID 5 is superior to software-based RAID 5 because there is no overhead within the operating system or system resources. Aside from that, most hardware-based RAID systems work with hot-swappable disk drives so that if one drive fails within an array, another can replace it without the server being brought offline. Hardware-based RAID, from the OS viewpoint, looks like a single hard disk.

Fibre Channel

The most common storage interface method is Small Computer Systems Interface (SCSI, pronounced *scuzzy*). However, one of the newer technologies is Fibre Channel. Fibre Channel is faster than SCSI and scalable in speed. It also has a Fibre Channel arbitrated loop (FC-AL) that allows multiple devices to be connected on one interface to a single computer.

When you install applications on the local hard disk for a Citrix MetaFrame server, you will probably want the application to load as fast as it can. This will improve performance. When you select your storage system, keep in mind that the faster the access, the better your end users perceive your performance.

Storage Area Networks

SANs use Fibre Channel because of its speed and scalability. Fibre Channel storage systems are attached directly to a storage network, and all the servers on that network are configured to access the data on that storage system. This setup is illustrated in Figure 4.9.

Figure 4.9 SAN Architecture

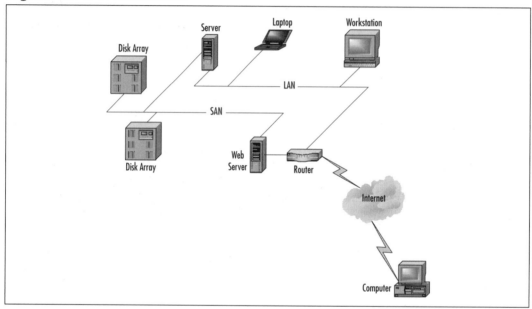

SANs are scalable to terabytes (TB) of information. Local area network (LAN) bandwidth utilization is reduced because a separate conduit is used for data access. SANs are critical to Internet systems due to their scalability. Multiple Internet and intranet servers can all access the same database. In comparison to a traditional storage system, where each server carries the data on its own hard disk, the SAN allows a centrally managed store for data. This translates to not having to consider which file server has a particular file stored on it and not having multiple instances of the same file. Furthermore, both internal users and external Web users enjoy real-time data access.

If you have a SAN implemented in your network, you should consider the type of data access your users need and whether your Citrix MetaFrame server should be directly connected to the SAN. However, since the Citrix MetaFrame server traditionally acts as a client to other servers, it is far more likely that you will not have that server interact directly with the SAN.

Network Interfaces

Some vendors offer server hardware that supports multiple network interface cards (NICs) that can either split up the traffic sent to the server from the same network segment (load balancing) or come online if the main NIC fails (failover redundancy). If you have a server that supports many concurrent users, you might discover that the NIC is a bottleneck. To avoid this, you should select a server that can load balance the traffic between two or more NICs. If you want to avoid the disastrous cost of a NIC failure, you should select a server that supports failover redundancy.

When implementing a Citrix MetaFrame server with more than one NIC, where each NIC is on a separate subnet and separate Internet Protocol (IP) address (a *multihomed server*), you should ensure that the server is not the ICA master browser. When you do install a multihomed MetaFrame server that is an ICA master browser, the ICA browser service can broadcast on one segment, then switch to the other segment, thus causing a muddle with the other Citrix MetaFrame servers. The ICA browser service uses directed packets to communicate with other servers. If you do want to link multiple Citrix servers on two different networks, an ICA gateway that connects two different ICA master browsers is the appropriate configuration.

In order to reconfigure the ICA browser service, open the **Citrix Server Administration** tool. Select the **ICA Browser** tab. Select a **server**, configure the ICA browser to **not attempt to become the master browser**, and click the **Apply** button. Finally, open the **Services** utility in the **Administrative Tools** menu, and stop and restart the ICA browser service.

Modems

One of the business requirements that Citrix MetaFrame can provide is that of remote access to mission-critical applications. If you have this requirement, you face the question of whether to have dialup users call a Citrix MetaFrame server directly or call a Remote Access Services (RAS) server elsewhere on the network.

If you already have a RAS server in place, you might not need to consider modems at all. If you do not or if you feel that your users need to directly access the Citrix MetaFrame, you should select your modems. Citrix MetaFrame should be configured to support the number of concurrent dial-in users you expect. If you need 15 people to dial in and only eight of them will be dialing in concurrently, you need a minimum of eight modems in your modem pool. You should include more than your minimum to be able to handle periods of high demand and for redundancy in case of modem failure. (Not that a modem ever fails…) To handle multiple modems, you can purchase modem cards that support multiple modems or even external modem pools that are rack-mountable.

Up to this point, the word *modem* as we have used it refers to analog modems. In some areas, such as Europe, you might find that you need an Integrated Services Digital Network (ISDN) modem pool. ISDN provides digital access over copper telephone wires. There are two ISDN configurations:

- **Basic Rate Interface (BRI)** A total of 128Kbps bandwidth using one data (D) channel at the rate of 16Kbps and two bearer (B) channels at the rate of 64Kbps. D channels carry overhead traffic; B channels carry voice and data. BRI runs over standard copper telephone cables.

- **Primary Rate Interface (PRI)** A total of 1.472Mbps bandwidth using one D channel at the rate of 64Kbps and 23 B channels at the rate of 64Kbps. PRI uses a T1 leased line and does not run over standard telephone cable.

When your users dial in, they will most likely be using a BRI configuration and in some cases will be using only a single B channel. However, you can have a PRI configuration at your site that allows up to 23 concurrent users dialing into separate B channels. In most cases, this setup requires special hardware—perhaps an ISDN router that accepts the incoming calls separately from the server. If you do purchase an interface card that installs into your server, you will most likely need to add the ISDN card using the manufacturer's provided drivers and the Control Panel's Add/Remove Hardware Wizard, depicted in Figure 4.10.

Figure 4.10 The Add Remove Hardware Wizard

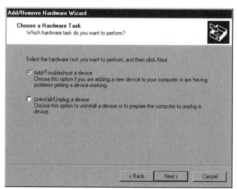

Once that has finished, your next step is to create the connections that will be available to incoming calls. To do so, right-click **My Network Places** and choose **Properties**, then double-click **Make New Connection**. When the wizard appears, select the option to **Accept Incoming Connections**, as shown in Figure 4.11.

Figure 4.11 Adding an Incoming Connection

After clicking **Next**, select the interface on which the calls will dial in. The dialog box depicted in Figure 4.12 enables you to accept virtual private connections through the Internet.

Figure 4.12 Enabling Incoming Virtual Private Connections

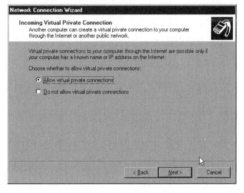

Next, select the users in the Active Directory who can connect. The following screen lets you choose the protocols that are enabled for connecting. On the final dialog box, you can name the connection and click **Finish** to add it.

Availability Planning

Availability planning comes into play when you are trying to ensure that a server is available whenever a person tries to start a session, even if there is a component failure or server failure in the farm. As you might have guessed, a server farm is the ultimate in availability planning. If you have more servers than you need and they are all able to respond to requests, you should always have a session available. In addition to developing a server farm, you should consider having more licenses than you need.

Monitoring the number of sessions used on a daily basis and developing a plan for growth is always a good idea.

Redundant Components

Availability planning on a per-server basis simply involves ensuring that there are redundant components within the server. The main way to ensure that a server is available is to reduce the likelihood that any single component will cause its failure. Not only will redundant components reduce server downtime, but they can increase a server's performance. You should consider the following:

- **Network adapters** Adding multiple network adapters can increase the amount of traffic that a single server can handle as well as ensure that the server can still communicate on the network, even if a network adapter has gone bad.

- **Power supplies** Power supplies do not have very high mean time between failures (MTBF), meaning that they can easily fail. Whenever possible, you should have redundant power supplies in your server.

- **RAM** Some server manufacturers allow you to include a parity memory module or use error-correcting memory. Rather than provide a redundant component, this feature reduces errors that could down the server.

Placing Terminal Services on the Network

Server placement affects the perceived performance of applications on the network. Normally, when you select the placement of a server, you try to keep it as close to the majority of its users as you can in order to manage bandwidth. What is interesting in the Citrix MetaFrame model is that you do not need to consider how close the users are to the Citrix MetaFrame server as long as you verify that there is a path to the server from the users' stations. Instead, your main concern is how easily the Citrix MetaFrame server can access the information that exists on other servers on the network. Therefore, you would place those servers on or near the backbone of the network. This strategy all ties in with network performance.

Before you design the placement of your servers, you should measure your network's performance. An accurate measurement of a network's capacity indicates the network's stability, which is critical to application deployment. To start, you should diagram your network. This diagram should include the following elements:

- Network segments with designated speeds

- Network devices—routers, switches, servers, bridges, firewalls

- Network protocols running on each segment, with applicable address ranges

■ Problem areas in the network where there are multiple errors or the link has reached capacity

Figure 4.13 is an example of this type of logical diagram.

Figure 4.13 A Sample Network Diagram

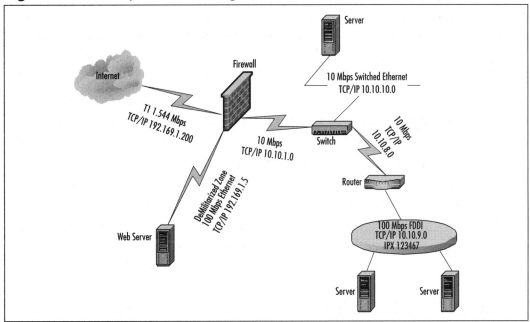

In deciding where to place a Citrix MetaFrame server, whether to use multiple servers, and the types of protocols to implement, you need to consider the aspects of your project listed in Table 4.3. These questions, and their answers, should offer you some guidance in your design decisions.

Table 4.3 Design Questions

Design Question	Purpose
What is the business requirement that the Citrix MetaFrame server will meet? (Remember, the most successful projects use the business requirement to drive the technology configuration.)	This answer tells you to which servers and data the Citrix MetaFrame servers should be placed closest.
How will users connect to Citrix?	This answer tells you the protocols to implement and whether to provide dial-in via RAS or direct connection.

Continued

Table 4.3 Continued

Design Question	Purpose
What applications will be used on the Citrix server?	This answer also tells you the servers that the Citrix MetaFrame servers should be near, as well as the requirements, such as memory requirements for the application, your MetaFrame servers need to be able to support.
What network data or services will the Citrix MetaFrame server need to access as a client?	This answer tells you the configuration your Citrix MetaFrame server will need. For example, if the data that an application needs to access is located on a NetWare server, you need an IPX/SPX-compatible protocol and a NetWare client configured on the Citrix MetaFrame server.
Where do those network servers reside?	If some servers are placed on different segments or even in different buildings, this answer tells you whether to redesign the placement of other servers on the network.
Do any bandwidth utilization problems exist on the links between those servers' and the users' locations?	This answer tells you how to configure the clients as well as indicating some of the bandwidth utilization reduction goals your project can have.
What impact will the Citrix MetaFrame server have on the security policy of the network?	This answer provides you with whether you need to access Internet services through a proxy from the MetaFrame server, whether you need to reconfigure a firewall to enable Transmission Control Protocol (TCP) ports for the ICA protocol, and how to configure user security on the server.
What is the Active Directory design, and which domains contain the data servers that Citrix MetaFrame needs to access?	This answer provides you with the domain in which Citrix MetaFrame should be placed as a member. (Best practices are such that a MetaFrame server should not be a domain controller.)
Are there multiple segments that all need to access the Citrix MetaFrame server but are not connected to each other?	The answer to this question determines whether you need to install a router. You should not multihome a Citrix MetaFrame server, because you can't bind the ICA browser service to a single NIC and you would suffer problems.

Continued

Table 4.3 Continued

Design Question	Purpose
What workstation names or naming conventions are used?	If the names or naming conventions are not unique for all workstations, a new naming convention should be devised and implemented. ICA clients must have unique names in order for printing to function.
What usernames are used?	If usernames are unique, scripts can use the %username% variable to individualize a user's experience. Otherwise, you should consider whether the naming convention will cause a security breach.
Is the user's experience intended to be seamless with a desktop?	The answer to this question guides you to select drive letter assignments that integrate with the user's desktop. Best practices are to remap the server hard drives, starting with M:. However, if there is a conflict, you should select other drive letters, contiguous for each partition on the Citrix MetaFrame server. The client drive will appear as the same drive letter it normally is, so the C: drive is still the C: drive.
Where will user data be stored?	If you maintain user data files on separate servers, application load balancing is more easily implemented, on top of the fact that backup time is reduced for the application server and server performance is increased.
What client hardware and software will be used?	The answer to this question tells you which clients to download from http://download.citrix.com.
How will remote users connect?	The answer to this question determines whether you need to implement direct asynchronous connections or if you can use existing RAS on the network.
What are the users' requirements?	This answer helps decide the applications or services you might need to install that are not part of the initial business required application for which the MetaFrame server was implemented.

Continued

Table 4.3 Continued

Design Question	Purpose
Will some users be given different security requirements than others?	This answer assists in deciding the groups of users and the security to apply to each of the groups. For example, you can prevent one group from printing or copying data but grant those rights to a different group.
Will users need to use their local COM ports or have sound and color enhancements?	This answer helps configure the sessions for users so that they will be able to use their applications in the way with which they are familiar.
What are the users' printing requirements?	Printing is usually a critical aspect of the project, so you should gather detailed information and test printing repeatedly.

Remote Desktop Protocol

Introduced with Windows NT 4.0, Remote Desktop Protocol (RDP) provides the presentation data to create a session on a remote workstation. RDP effectively provides the same basic functions as Citrix's ICA, described later in this chapter. You will discover some differences between the two and that ICA provides features not found in RDP.

What Is RDP?

Under Windows NT 4.0, RDP v4.0 was a new protocol based on the International Telecommunications Union (ITU) T.120 specification. RDP is capable of running on multiple channels and carries keystrokes and mouse clicks and display data between the terminal server and remote workstations. RDP v4.0 supported disconnects and encryption within Terminal Server sessions. This original version worked well over fast LAN connections but did not prove to be all that robust with slower links, such as dialup.

Windows 2000 Server, which includes Terminal Services capabilities, introduced an upgraded RDP v5.0. With improvements that included compression and lower overhead, terminal sessions running RDP v5.0 were able to function over wide area networks (WANs) and slow dialup links. RDP v5.0 has the following features:

- Compression of data stream

- Disk-based bitmap caching, to improve session responsiveness and reduce bitmaps transmitted across the wire

- 56-bit or 128-bit encryption using Rivest Shamir Adleman (RSA) security's RC4 cipher specification

- Clipboard mapping so that users can cut and paste between local applications and the remote session

- Printer redirection for local printing

The way that RDP works on the server is fairly straightforward. Using its own driver, RDP renders graphics (the display from the session) and packetizes the data to send to the RDP clients. The server receives keyboard and mouse clicks from the client through RDP and interprets them into the session.

At the client, RDP passes along that information to the Win32 graphical display interface (GDI) application programming interface (API) so that the graphics can be displayed locally. RDP intercepts the keyboard and mouse clicks to pass them along to the server.

Bandwidth Usage

RDP v5.0 works well over slow links, providing a good response over a 28.8k modem and better over a 56k modem. The key to how RDP uses this bandwidth is based in its use of compressed draw commands to represent graphical data. Since graphics take up the majority of the bandwidth, you should understand how RDP handles them.

If you imagine a 640 x 480 picture, which is the size of a small desktop, there are 307,200 bits, or pixels, that must be assigned a color. Each bit in the picture is located by X and Y numbers. For example, *X1, Y1* is the bit at the upper-left corner, and *X640 Y480* is the bit at the lower-right corner. If you are using 256 colors, you have 78,643,200 options for the entire screen. With a larger screen and more colors, these numbers are enormous! In any case, to draw the screen, a picture that has 307,200 bits of data is the basic amount of data. If you change a single pixel, the entire screen should be retransmitted. At least that's the problem that faced the originators of remote control graphical sessions.

RDP handles this situation using a draw command. Most of the display data on the computer is colored in blocks or lines of the same color. A draw command that says "draw from x1, y1 to x20, y32 with the color blue" creates a blue rectangle on the screen and uses far fewer bits of data than a bitmap stating "x1,y1, blue, x1,y2 blue,…x20,y32 blue."

RDP further reduces bandwidth consumption by sending the data for only the parts of the screen that have changed. If you have a session with Word open and you click the File menu, the only part of the screen that changes is the column on the upper left-hand corner of the screen, where the file menu appears. RDP simply sends the changes for that area rather than transmitting the entire screen. This minimizes the amount of data that is transmitted across the wire. Finally, RDP uses a bulk compression algorithm to further reduce the size of the data transmitted.

Upgrading from RDP 4.0 to RDP 5.0

If you plan to upgrade to Citrix MetaFrame XP for Windows 2000 from an existing Citrix MetaFrame for Windows NT 4.0 Server, Terminal Server Edition, or even an earlier version of Citrix WinFrame, you can do so while conserving the existing user settings and installed applications. The one thing that you should be aware of is that the hardware for older versions of Citrix WinFrame or MetaFrame might not be compatible with Windows 2000 Server. You can check the hardware compatibility on Microsoft's Web site for the HCL, located at www.microsoft.com/hcl/default.asp.

When you are ready to perform your upgrade, you should start with a full backup of the server. The backup should include the registry and all system files.

NOTE

A server recovery plan can save the day if there are problems with your upgrade. You should create an emergency repair disk and have a full backup and original installation disks for all the applications on hand, just in case. Then you should test a rebuild process in the lab and write down the successful steps prior to beginning your upgrade.

After your backup is completed, log off all the users and any disconnected sessions. Then disable connections so that no users are able to connect to the server.

Document all your server requirements:

- Disk-partitioning configuration

- Paging file configuration, if you've specified one

- Protocols to be installed and configured

- Memory requirements, if they've changed

- Special drivers, such as those for NICs that are not included in the base operating system

Obtain all the software installation disks, drivers from the manufacturer, service packs, and hot fixes and have them available during your upgrade procedure.

As with all Windows 2000 installation processes, you should ascertain that the hard disk partition is sufficient for the system files, paging file, and any other applications that need to be installed on that partition. If the partition is not sufficient, you need to repartition the hard disk. You might be able to use a third-party utility such as Disk Image Pro to repartition. If such a program is not available to you, you need to delete the existing partitions as well as all the data and repartition the disk.

If you have sufficient space or if you have successfully repartitioned the disk without losing data, start the installation program. Windows 2000 automatically detects the existing operating system and offers to upgrade. Following the dialog screens and referring to your server requirements document for configuration details, you can complete your upgrade.

If the old partition is retained and it was formatted with FAT, you should convert the file system to NTFS. Once you have converted the drive, you cannot reconvert it. If you have upgraded from a Windows NT 4.0 server and then converted to NTFS v5.0 on Windows 2000, you cannot go back to Windows NT 4.0 without repartitioning the server. Windows NT 4.0 does not understand the new NTFS v5.0 file system included with Windows 2000. This is done with the following command, where you replace *<drive letter>* with the letter of the drive that you are converting at a command prompt window:

```
CONVERT <drive letter>: /FS:NTFS
```

After the upgrade to Windows 2000 Terminal Services, your next task is to install the Citrix MetaFrame XP for Windows 2000 software using its standard installation process.

Requiring TCP/IP

One of the key concepts to keep in mind about RDP is its limitation to a TCP/IP network. Even though many networks use TCP/IP, some have been optimized for other protocol stacks such as Internetwork Packet Exchange/Sequenced Packet Exchange (IPX/SPX). In those networks, using a Windows 2000 Terminal Server with TCP/IP increases the number of protocols and types of traffic traveling across the wire. If a different protocol is required, adding Citrix MetaFrame XP with ICA could be the answer.

Design Impacts of Citrix MetaFrame XP

There are a couple of design impacts when you add Citrix MetaFrame XP on top of Windows 2000 Terminal Services. Citrix MetaFrame XP supports ICA, which means that sessions can run across networks using IPX/SPX or direct dialup methods. Citrix MetaFrame XP also supports farming, which extends the way that applications can be shared. Depending on how you design your network, it can become as straightforward as possible to the users yet still be extremely complex behind the scenes.

Capacity Impacts of Citrix MetaFrame XP

When a Citrix MetaFrame server is deployed, it quickly becomes a mission-critical server on the network. Some users might depend on the server for their entire desktops. Some Internet users could depend on it for delivery of some Web applications. All users depend on it for some form of an application to be delivered to their desktops. Due to the critical nature of the server, you need to reduce the risk of failure. This is done through configuring multiple servers to deliver the same set of applications. This is the process of *scaling out* the servers on the network, in place of *scaling up* an individual server, as illustrated in Figure 4.14.

Figure 4.14 Scaling Out vs. Scaling Up

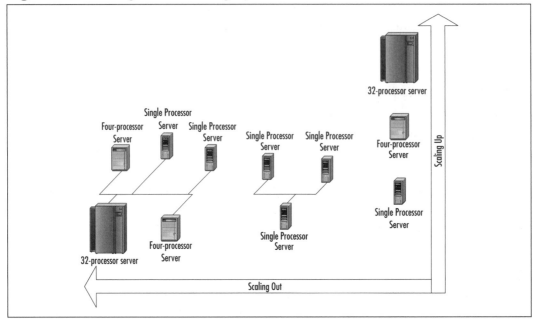

Server Placement on the Network

When there are multiple Citrix MetaFrame servers and they are providing multiple applications, the Citrix MetaFrame servers should be placed close to the backbone, in addition to any data source servers. For example, let's look at a network in which there is a Lotus Notes server in Sarasota, Florida, a SQL server in Boston, Massachusetts, and an Oracle server in Tokyo, Japan. If you deploy three Citrix MetaFrame servers to provide these applications to the network, you have three viable options:

- **Dedicate a Citrix MetaFrame server to providing each application** In this scenario, there would be a Citrix MetaFrame server in Boston to provide the SQL application, a Citrix MetaFrame server in Sarasota to provide the Notes application, and a Citrix MetaFrame server in Tokyo to provide the Oracle application. The advantage to this configuration is optimal performance. The disadvantage is that one server could be maxed out while the others are not being used at all, so there is not a good balance of resources.

- **Place all servers—the SQL, Notes, and Oracle servers as well as the three Citrix MetaFrame servers—on the backbone and load balance the MetaFrame servers** The advantage to this configuration lies in its resource management. The disadvantage is that performance will be driven by the utilization on the backbone.

- **Move all the servers to one location on a single segment and deploy the Citrix MetaFrame servers on that same segment in a load-balancing configuration** This scenario has the advantage of both resource management and optimal performance.

Load Balancing

In general, load balancing distributes the amount of processing that a computer is required to do among two or more similar computers. This distribution results in more work being done in the same amount of time. In essence, load balancing alleviates bottlenecks. It also ensures efficiency and uptime for server farms. The application load-balancing features of Citrix MetaFrame XP through server farming are best implemented with Load Manager, described in Chapter 9, which can balance the capacity of servers to best distribute sessions across the farm.

> **NOTE**
>
> One of the benefits of implementing a load-balancing system is that most such systems include failover capabilities. Because load balancing requires multiple servers all performing the same function, if one server goes offline, the others can automatically take over at the time of the failure. Be aware that load balancing cannot continue a current session from one server to another. In that case, the existing connection is dropped, but when the user reconnects, the application is still available.

There are different types of load balancing: hardware based, software based, and application based. There are several ways to implement standard load balancing. You can install a software application meant for load balancing, send all traffic to that application, and then it will redirect traffic to other servers on the network. This is *software-based load balancing*.

Hardware-based load balancing usually involves a computer, a switch, or a router that redirects traffic to other servers on the network. You can also purchase preconfigured clustered servers that automatically load balance between the servers that are attached to that particular cluster.

Most of these solutions are dependent on network address translation. The traffic is sent to a single network address and then distributed from there. This method does not work well with Citrix MetaFrame servers because it is likely that some servers will provide different applications than others. Citrix MetaFrame depends on a third type of load balancing, called application load balancing.

Application Load Balancing

Application load balancing is a slightly different approach from the other types of load balancing. Citrix developed Citrix Load Balancing Services to be used with multiple WinFrame and MetaFrame servers. This load-balancing process starts when the client requests the use of an application. The server that is contacted by the client determines which servers on the network are configured for that application. Next, that server discovers which MetaFrame server is the least busy. The algorithm used to determine the server that is least busy creates a load factor. The *load factor* consists of the CPU utilization, the measure of the page file utilization, how many users are currently online, plus other system variables. The servers' load factors are compared, and the one with the lowest is selected. Then the Load Balancing Services transparently route that client's session to the least busy server. As an administrator, you can create server affinity so that users will be more likely to connect to a certain server merely by skewing the load factor settings from their default values.

Citrix Load Balancing Services are hardware independent. You can use any hardware platform that will run Windows 2000. The services are also application independent. Any application that can be run on a Citrix MetaFrame server can be load balanced. Any ICA client can connect to a load-balanced application. Load Balancing Services are unlimited. You can configure as many servers as you want into a load-balanced configuration. The services are also network independent. You can configure load balancing across a LAN or a WAN.

> **NOTE**
>
> When you use direct asynchronous connections to a particular server, you will not be able to take advantage of load balancing. The server that accepts a direct asynchronous connection will not be able to move that connection to another server. If you need dialup services, you should provide a dialup RAS server.

The applications are not automatically provided with failover services. However, if a server fails, users can log on to the load-balanced application and begin working again. When you design multiple servers, you should always have user data stored on non-MetaFrame servers so that a single Citrix MetaFrame server failure will not interrupt data access. For example, let's look at a case with two MetaFrame servers—Meta1 and Meta2—that are configured to load balance an application. If a user, Jill, stores her data files on Meta1, and then Meta1 goes down, Jill might be able to connect to the application, but she won't be able to access her data. Even if Meta1 is still online, but Jill connects to Meta2, Jill might not be savvy enough to find her data, or it might be inaccessible because she saved it to a local drive letter on Meta1 rather than to a shared volume.

On the other hand, if data is stored on Data1 and the administrator, JoAnn, has scripted a drive mapping for Jill so that wherever Jill connects to the application, she will always see her data on the J: drive, it doesn't matter if either server fails—Jill will still be able to work on the application and have access to her data files. The only thing that Jill will have lost is her session data. When a server fails, the session vanishes and a new session must be established. In other words, if Jill was working on a file and did not save it, she cannot reconnect to the session to see the changes on that file.

> **NOTE**
>
> When you store data on file servers rather than MetaFrame servers, data integrity is maintained without sacrificing performance. In addition, you will reduce the time it takes to back up the server, thus enabling access to the MetaFrame server for longer periods of time.

License Pooling

License pooling is not the same thing as application load balancing. License pooling does not redirect a client to the least busy server. Instead, when a server is configured with license pooling, it can accept a client connection, even if its own licenses are currently being used but another MetaFrame server in the pool has an available license. When a server is involved in license pooling, it does not need to share out all its licenses. An administrator can reserve some licenses for the server itself and the remaining for the license pool.

For example, let's look at two servers, Pool1 and Pool2, that are configured with license pooling. Say that Pool1 has 20 licenses and Pool2 has 20 licenses, and Pool1 is completely out of sessions. If a client requests access to Pool1, under normal circumstances the client would be denied access. However, in a license pool, Pool1 simply borrows one of Pool2's free licenses and allows the client to connect.

Protocol Expansion

The internetwork impacts the design of client access from various points of entry on the network. The scenarios that follow illustrate how to design the client access given a network model. There are three aspects you should consider:

- LAN
- WAN
- Internet

A LAN Example

The LAN scenario is a single Token Ring network owned by an insurance agency called Finance Advantage. Finance Advantage has 100 people in its agency; 60 of them are agents who work out of home offices. Finance Advantage has a NetWare server and a Windows NT server. They are running both IPX/SPX and NetBIOS on their network. They plan to add a dedicated circuit to an ISP at some point in the next six months, but they have experienced little growth in the size of their company and do not expect to add more than one agent per year over the next three years, so it is not a high priority. They want to implement a Citrix MetaFrame server running on Windows 2000 right away so that their agents can access a new insurance application from telephone lines, and so the administrative staff can access the application over the LAN in the office. The data source for the application will reside on the Windows NT Server that Finance Advantage currently owns. All data files will also be stored there. The new insurance application is a data entry application; with testing, they find that a single processor can handle 45 concurrent users with the application, and each session requires only 4MB of RAM. Figure 4.15 displays the Finance Advantage network.

Figure 4.15 The Finance Advantage Network

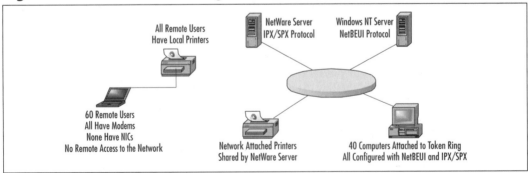

In this LAN environment, you have only one place to put the Citrix MetaFrame server—directly attached to the Token Ring LAN. Although you have the option of installing a router and placing the Citrix MetaFrame server on a different segment, there is no reason to do so. Because the insurance agents are intermittent users, it is likely that of the 100 total users, you would never have more than 60 online simultaneously. This means that you need at least two processors and a minimum of 368MB of

RAM (60 users × 4MB RAM + 128MB base RAM = 368MB RAM), which is rounded up to 512MB of RAM.

Since there is no existing remote access method and because the protocols that are used on the network will eventually change, a direct asynchronous connection for the remote users is preferable. The direct asynchronous method ensures that there is no bandwidth utilization on the LAN consumed by users coming through a RAS server, which means that local printing will not interfere with network performance. This will also ensure that there will never need to be a change on the remote users end when the protocols are switched over, reducing administrative efforts in the future. This means that a single server with two or more processors is the better choice, because that will ensure that the agents only need to dial up one server, since load balancing is not supported with the direct asynchronous method. In using a single server, Finance Advantage selects a 20GB hardware-based RAID array with hot-swap hard disks and dual power supplies, so that there are some redundancy and failover capabilities. They also select a rack-mounted modem pool of 30 modems that connects directly to the Citrix MetaFrame server.

The LAN access method can be through either NetBIOS Extended User Interface (NetBEUI) or IPX/SPX for now, with a change to TCP/IP in the future. Alternatively, the administrative staff can bite the bullet now and deploy the Microsoft TCP/IP client during this project. Finance Advantage decides to use NetBEUI because the Windows NT server that houses the new application also uses NetBEUI. The design for the future Finance Advantage network will resemble Figure 4.16.

Figure 4.16 Finance Advantage Network Design with Citrix MetaFrame

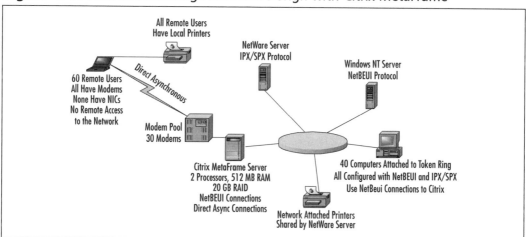

A WAN Example

Affluenz is a banking and credit company with over 60,000 employees worldwide. Corporate headquarters is in New York City, and two other large locations with 5,000 or more users are in Sydney, Australia, and Munich, Germany. Twenty corporate locations throughout the world are connected via various types of links, some satellite, some frame relay, some leased lines. Affluenz uses only TCP/IP across the backbone network since having upgraded their Novell NetWare network to be IP-only. Affluenz has two mainframe computers at its headquarters and 235 Windows 2000 servers across the global network participating as member servers and domain controllers in a two-domain Active Directory forest.

Affluenz has encountered an increased amount of credit card fraud over the past two years and needs a better tracking system. The company purchased a security tracking system that runs on a SQL Server platform; the company has also hired programmers to customize the client for the security department. In each location, between three and 30 security personnel need access to that database. These users might change in number because the security personnel grows at the same rate as Affluenz, which is expecting to double in the next two years. Affluenz has decided to implement Citrix MetaFrame to provide that application without taxing some of the slow links. There are 250 security personnel who will run the application, and an estimated 200 will run it all day long to look at the security alerts that it provides. With the time zone differences globally, the number of concurrent users will be about 175 at high usage periods. The application tested out that 20 users could run simultaneously on the same processor, and 8MB of RAM is required for each session on a Citrix MetaFrame server. No data files will be stored on the server, so the Affluenz standard RAID array with 30GB of space is considered more than acceptable for servers. The new security application will be placed on a database server in the New York headquarters because it will exchange some data with the mainframes located there. Figure 4.17 illustrates Affluenz's current network from a high level.

When we begin designing the Citrix MetaFrame servers for this network, it is apparent that we need nine processors for the concurrent users. The servers will need 8MB RAM × 175 users + 128MB base OS RAM = 1528MB RAM (or 1.5GB). Storage is more than sufficient with a 30GB RAID array. Because Affluenz will be doubling its number of employees over the next two years, we can account for growth by doubling the processing and memory numbers to 18 processors and 3GB RAM. To allow for redundancy and because all users will connect over the network, Affluenz will implement application load balancing with five four-processor servers, each carrying 1GB of RAM. All these servers will be placed on the same segment as the security application SQL database server in New York. Clients will access the server through TCP/IP connections.

Figure 4.17 The Affluenz WAN

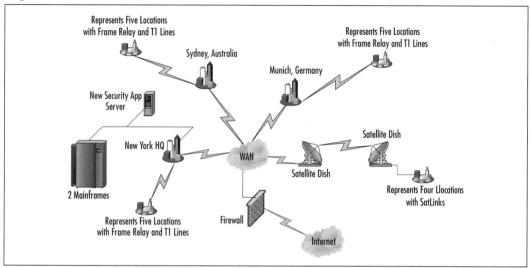

An Internet Example

In this scenario, we have a publishing company called BookMill. BookMill has a single location in Raleigh, North Carolina, with 20 people who work out of that office. BookMill also employs 10 freelance editors and copywriters who work out of their homes across the United States and Canada. In addition, BookMill hires authors to collaborate on book projects from all over the United States and Canada. Although BookMill has over 150 authors who have collaborated on books, only 20 to 30 are working on projects at any one point in time. BookMill sells books on its Internet Web site and uses Internet e-mail to communicate with remote editors, copywriters, and authors. The company is now contemplating deploying Citrix MetaFrame to share out its project application with its editors, copywriters, and authors over its Internet connection.

The BookMill network is an Ethernet LAN connected to the Internet via a T1 line. Two servers provide Web services on the Internet. These servers are placed on a DMZ. The project application is located on a database server on the Ethernet LAN, which uses TCP/IP as its only protocol. The project application has been tested so that 20 users can access it simultaneously on a single-processor server, and it requires 6MB of RAM per user. It is expected that there will be no more than four concurrent users for average usage, but as deadlines approach, there could be as many as 10 concurrent users. BookMill has experienced huge growth over the past three years and might expand into more e-book business during the next two. The company expects to double the number of projects it can support in three years. BookMill wants to make certain that all users can access this application, even if a server fails. The BookMill network is depicted in Figure 4.18.

Figure 4.18 The BookMill Network

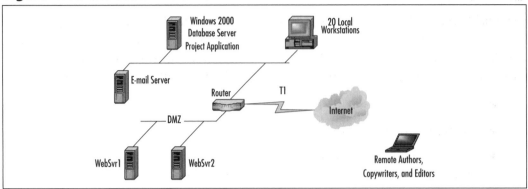

The server will require one processor, even after growth. It will require 20 users (after growth) × 6MB RAM + 128MB base OS RAM = 248MB RAM, which rounds up to 256MB of RAM. The project data will exist on the database server, so a RAID array of 10GB should be sufficient. To support the failover requirement, BookMill needs two servers that meet the one CPU, 256MB RAM, and 10GB storage minimums. These two Citrix MetaFrame servers will be placed on the DMZ. They will be configured to provide the application through an Internet Web page. BookMill's administrator intends to apply security, both at the database server and at the Citrix MetaFrame server, to ensure that only authors, editors, and copywriters currently working on any particular project will be able to access its data. The local workstations will have the application directly installed and will not go through the Citrix MetaFrame server to access the data. The BookMill network design is illustrated in Figure 4.19.

Figure 4.19 BookMill's Network Design

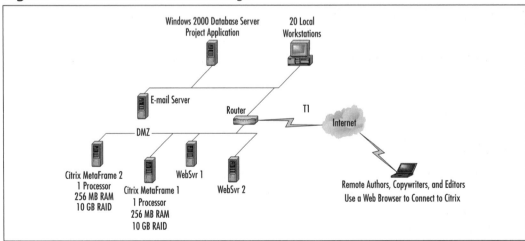

Client Options

Terminal Services offers very few options for clients—32-bit Windows operating systems, in fact. Citrix MetaFrame XP provides a wide ranging group of client options. Since all the clients use the same protocol, Citrix can develop more clients without having to change the server. Citrix MetaFrame XP supports all of the following for clients:

- DOS clients
- 16-bit Windows clients
- 32-bit Windows clients (Windows 95, Windows 98, Windows Me, Windows NT 3.5x, Windows NT 4.0, Windows 2000, Windows XP)
- Windows-based terminals
- Handheld devices (Windows CE, Pocket PC, EPOC)
- Unix (Compaq Tru64, HP-UX, IBM AIX, Linux, SCO, SGI IRIX, Solaris Sparc, Sun)
- Apple Macintosh
- OS/2 Warp
- Web clients (ActiveX, Java, Netscape Plugin)

Since Citrix MetaFrame XP accepts Web clients, sessions can be run from other operating systems besides the ones on this list. The only requirement is that they use a compatible browser with the Web client. This makes Citrix MetaFrame XP an exceptionally flexible application server.

Independent Computing Architecture

Citrix's Independent Computing Architecture (ICA) protocol provides the same types of services as RDP. ICA, however, is much more flexible than RDP. Not only does ICA support a much wider range of client operating systems, but it also runs on multiple types of protocols. This makes Citrix MetaFrame XP an ideal platform for a heterogeneous network.

What Is ICA?

ICA is the protocol that enables the remote control session between the client and the Citrix MetaFrame server. ICA is the only protocol that runs on the direct asynchronous connection. ICA runs over the TCP/IP, IPX/SPX, and NetBEUI protocols for all the other remote control sessions.

ICA is uniquely flexible as a protocol. Although it provides the full protocol stack services on a direct async connection, it provides only the protocol services needed above the protocol that is running. For example, if you create a session over IP, a Network layer protocol (Layer 3), ICA provides the Transport, Session, Presentation, and Application layer services. On the other hand, if you create a session over TCP, a Transport layer protocol (Layer 4), ICA provides the Session, Presentation, and Application layer services. ICA simply fills in the protocol layer gaps for session traffic, as shown in Figure 4.20.

Figure 4.20 ICA Protocol Flexibility

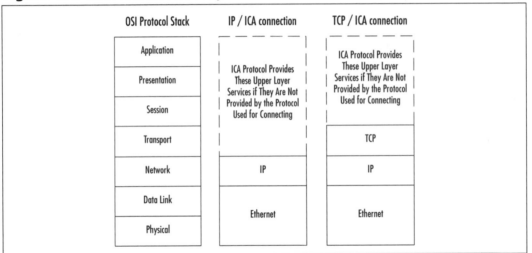

ICA browsing traffic is different from session traffic. Browsing traffic occurs when a client requests a Citrix server for a list of published applications or a list of Citrix servers. When TCP/IP is used, this process is executed over User Datagram Protocol (UDP) port 1604. The session traffic over TCP/IP uses TCP port 1494. When XML is installed on the server and when MetaFrame Feature Release 1 is used, the browsing traffic can be performed over strict TCP/IP instead of UDP.

When you are designing your use of ICA, you should consider your need to reduce bandwidth utilization and enhance user-perceived performance. In order to do so, you can configure the clients to use caching and compression. You should also consider the need for local printing and how that will impact your network and user-perceived performance. Local printing will increase the ICA traffic.

Packet Description

The ICA packet begins with a one-byte command and follows with data, which is optional. To enable the flexibility of being able to run over multiple types of Transport and Network layer protocols, optional preambles are negotiated at connection time. These preambles manage packet transmission.

The ICA frame head is an optional protocol header for stream-oriented transport data. The reliable preamble is used to detect errors. The encryption preamble manages encrypted data. The compression preamble manages compressed data. The ICA command begins the required part of the ICA frame. The ICA command data provides any data that is required by the ICA command and is allowed to be null. The frame tail, which is optional, is used for asynchronous data. Figure 4.21 displays the ICA packet.

Figure 4.21 ICA Frame

Supported Protocols

Specifying the size and number of the servers is only half the job. The other half is specifying how clients will connect to their applications. This boils down to selecting a protocol or method for the ICA client to run on. The types of connections that Citrix MetaFrame supports are:

- Direct asynchronous dial-in

- Internet

- RAS as a remote node

- LAN-connected workstation

- Workstation connected across a WAN

The only type of connection that does not depend on a Network layer protocol is the direct asynchronous connection. This configuration requires that the Citrix MetaFrame server has modems installed that answer ICA-only connections to that particular MetaFrame server. Direct async connections do not provide remote node functionality. Citrix MetaFrame servers also support several protocols.

Transmission Control Protocol/Internet Protocol

TCP/IP is the protocol stack used on the Internet. Most LANs and WANs also use TCP/IP in order to connect to the Internet due to its ability to be routed. TCP/IP supports Point-to-Point Protocol (PPP) as well. The session protocol selection for Citrix MetaFrame allows the administrator to create either TCP or IP connections. TCP connections have the overhead of the TCP header in the packets, whereas in the

IP connections ICA provides connection-oriented services. In fact, of all the methods that you can use to connect to a Citrix MetaFrame server, the only one that cannot use TCP or IP is the direct asynchronous dial-in connection.

Due to TCP/IP's versatility, it is a prime candidate to use as the session protocol. If you intend to connect over the Internet, you must use it.

Internetwork Packet Exchange/ Sequenced Packet Exchange

IPX/SPX is the protocol stack used by Novell NetWare servers. Citrix MetaFrame allows either IPX or SPX connections to be created for sessions. IPX/SPX can be used over PPP connections, so if you have a RAS server that is configured to support it, you can use IPX or SPX connections. However, an IPX or SPX connection is *not* appropriate for use over the Internet.

If you use NetWare servers, you do not have to use IPX/SPX for your connections as long as your workstations support other protocols. For example, if a workstation supports both IPX/SPX and TCP/IP, it can connect to a NetWare server via IPX/SPX and connect to the Citrix MetaFrame server via TCP/IP.

NetBIOS Extended User Interface

NetBEUI is a protocol stack that was used widely on Windows NT servers. The NetBEUI protocol stack is nonroutable and not viable to be used across WANs. NetBEUI also cannot be used across the Internet. However, it can be used on LANs and over PPP remote node connections.

NetBEUI has been slowly weaned out of the Windows NT (and now Windows 2000) line of products. In the Windows NT 3.5x days, NetBEUI was the default protocol. Windows NT 4.x began making TCP/IP the default protocol. With Windows 2000, TCP/IP is required and is no longer just the default protocol if the computer is going to access or otherwise interact with Active Directory.

When you are planning your session protocols, you should avoid adding protocols that you do not already use on your network. If you've already upgraded to Windows 2000, you might have already removed NetBEUI or have had the opportunity to do so. From the perspective of reducing the number of protocols on your network to only those that you need, you should probably avoid using NetBEUI as a connection protocol.

Summary

When you design the Citrix MetaFrame environment, you should start by determining your minimum requirements for the server components:

- Number of processors
- Amount of RAM
- Storage

These requirements are based on the number of concurrent users and the applications used by those users. To ensure that the server requirements will be sufficient for some time going forward, you must adjust these requirements for the growth that the company might experience. Once the minimum requirements are determined, these are then parceled out among one or more servers. Scaling up is preferable when you use direct asynchronous connections; scaling out is preferable for all other situations because of the redundancy it offers.

The Citrix MetaFrame server needs to be placed nearest to the data sources that it will be providing to end users. If multiple servers will be load balanced, all the servers that are providing a single application should be placed on the same network segment as the data source server.

MetaFrame supports multiple protocols for connections as well as direct asynchronous connections. When you design your protocol, you should continue to use the protocols you currently use or plan to use in the near future. For each client that connects, the server needs to have waiting a connection that uses the protocol that the client has installed. Therefore, if a client uses TCP/IP, it cannot connect to an IPX/SPX connection waiting on the server; it would need to find a TCP or IP connection.

Solutions Fast Track

Designing a Three-Tier Solution

- ☑ A thin client server, whether Windows 2000 Terminal Services is installed with or without Citrix MetaFrame XP, provides the middle tier in a three-tiered architecture.

- ☑ When the thin client receives data, it is only receiving presentation data. Business logic takes place on the Citrix MetaFrame XP server.

- ☑ Data storage should separate system files from user-specific configuration and application data files.

☑ Citrix MetaFrame XP servers should be placed as close as possible to the servers with which they will communicate.

Designing and Placing Terminal Servers

☑ Your business requirements should drive your design of the thin client environment.

☑ Capacity planning is based on the number of concurrent users expected and the types of applications used.

☑ Faster processors can handle more sessions. Typically, a Pentium II processor will handle 25 clerical users' concurrent sessions.

☑ Add as much extra RAM as possible to your configuration. It will enhance the users' experience with the thin client system.

☑ NTFS is the optimal choice for a file system. With its extended file properties, you can ensure that files are secured from accidental deletion or corruption.

☑ You can use multiple network adapters to either multihome the server or increase the traffic load that the server can take on a single network segment.

Remote Desktop Protocol

☑ RDP provides the session for Windows 2000 Terminal Services sessions.

☑ RDP is based on ITU's T.120 protocol and has the capability of encryption.

☑ When upgrading from Windows NT 4.0 Terminal Server Edition, you must upgrade from RDP 4.0 to RDP 5.0.

Design Impacts of Citrix MetaFrame XP

☑ When adding Citrix MetaFrame XP, you have more flexibility in designing server farms and application load balancing.

☑ Citrix MetaFrame XP supports multiple protocols and can function on networks with TCP/IP, IPX/SPX, NetBEUI, and direct dialup.

☑ A network designer can choose between scaling up and scaling out the network, improving redundancy and availability of sessions to end users.

Independent Computing Architecture

☑ ICA is the protocol that provides sessions to a Citrix MetaFrame XP server.

☑ Flexible in design, optional preambles for an ICA packet can provide reliability, error detection, compression, and encryption.

☑ ICA clients include all Windows, many UNIX, Macintosh, and OS/2 Warp, and several handheld operating systems.

☑ The ICA Web clients can be used on any compatible browser, even if the operating system is not compatible with a standard ICA client.

Frequently Asked Questions

The following Frequently Asked Questions, answered by the authors of this book, are designed to both measure your understanding of the concepts presented in this chapter and to assist you with real-life implementation of these concepts. To have your questions about this chapter answered by the author, browse to **www.syngress.com/solutions** and click on the **"Ask the Author"** form.

Q: We have been using Windows 2000 Terminal Services in order to remotely manage our servers. We want to add the ability for several end users to run remote sessions at night to access a database application. Will we need to upgrade the server we are going to use?

A: Before deciding if you need to upgrade, you should map out a strategy for your thin client plan. You need to know how many concurrent sessions you will need and how many resources (RAM, storage, CPU cycles) the application will consume. Once you have this information in hand, you can determine whether your current hardware can meet your needs, or if you will need to upgrade.

Q: We have an Oracle application in the New York office that we are planning to implement on Citrix MetaFrame. We also have a PeopleSoft application in Paris, France, that we will use with Citrix MetaFrame. There are 30 users of each application. Both of these applications' users reside in New York and Paris. Where should we place the Citrix MetaFrame server?

A: You should consider deploying two Citrix MetaFrame servers, one in New York to deliver the Oracle application and the other in Paris to deliver the PeopleSoft application. Otherwise, you might want to move one of the servers to the other office on the same segment as the first server and then place a Citrix MetaFrame server on that same network segment.

Q: We don't have the resources to test how many of our users a processor will take on. Most of our users are clerical; about 20 percent of them are knowledge users. How many processors should we put into our server(s) if we have 100 users?

A: If you estimate about 25 users per processor, you will be fairly close to the true number of users per processor. However, you should consider the growth of network use of the Citrix MetaFrame servers, and double up on your resources. By starting with two four-processor servers, you will have more than enough resources for the 100 users, and you can test the number of users your processors will withstand.

Chapter 5

Installing Citrix MetaFrame XP

Solutions in this chapter:

- **Single-Server Installation**

- **Deploying Multiple Servers**

- **Migrating from a MetaFrame 1.8 Farm to MetaFrame XP**

☑ **Summary**

☑ **Solutions Fast Track**

☑ **Frequently Asked Questions**

Introduction

With a design in hand, a network administrator or engineer can prepare for Citrix MetaFrame XP installation. Usually, this process begins with procuring the software and hardware that meet the capacity and availability requirements specified in the design. When the equipment and software have all been obtained, the solution is ready to be installed.

Complex designs could require multiple servers in one or more server farms. Although installing a single server can be done rather easily in a single afternoon, the process of deploying tens or hundreds of servers can become tedious. Servers that participate in a server farm are much easier to manage when they are configured identically. However, manual installations provide too many opportunities for human error. Therefore, when you're faced with a multiserver rollout, a best practice is to deploy an automated installation process.

Automating an installation could be impossible when you're looking at upgrading an existing Citrix MetaFrame 1.8 server farm. The installer should be sensitive to the order of the upgrade process and how to run a mixed farm environment during the installation project. Mixed farms can exist indefinitely. However, a farm that has been fully upgraded to MetaFrame XP can be managed more effectively when it is switched to native mode.

Single-Server Installation

The first step in implementation is installing the Citrix MetaFrame XP server. Beginning with the installation of Windows 2000, several factors can affect performance and reliability of services. The hard disk configuration and logical layout, in addition to redundancy if implemented correctly, can provide performance improvements. Terminal Server is also a critical component; without it, Citrix MetaFrame XP cannot function. Once Terminal Services is installed and configured, you can begin installing Citrix MetaFrame XP.

A Quick Overview of Windows 2000 Installation

The first component of any Citrix MetaFrame XP server is the operating system. When installing Windows 2000 for use with Citrix MetaFrame XP, you must optimize the server. Two key elements related to Windows 2000 are crucial to create an efficient Citrix MetaFrame XP server installation. First, the hard disk configuration affects how the system performs. In addition, the use of Active Directory must be considered to maximize the effectiveness of resources such as Group Policy.

Partitioning the Hard Disk

When you are partitioning the hard disks, you can use one of several configurations. Just about any disk configuration will work, assuming that the disk space requirements are met. The most common configuration is one big array of disks set up as a single logical drive. The operating system, page file, and application program files reside within the same logical disk, as shown in Figure 5.1 Although this works in basic environments, the scalability and redundancy are minimized. For example, if the page file is experiencing performance problems in this scenario, it is possible that the server will be affected overall because the hard disks are over-utilized.

Figure 5.1 Basic Hard Disk Configurations

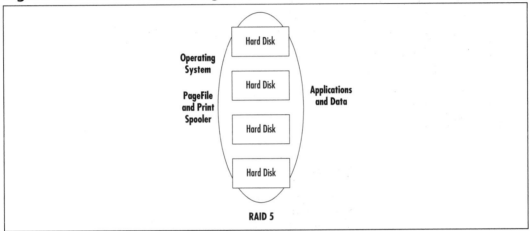

Another common scenario for improving performance on a Citrix MetaFrame XP server is to split apart the resource-intensive functions into separate disks. By separating the operating system, the page file and print spooler, and the application data, you can minimize the impact they have on each other. For example, if the print spooler is separated from the other key components and experiences a problem, the other components are only minimally affected. Figure 5.2 displays an example of an advanced hard disk configuration.

Participation in Active Directory

Active Directory is a significant leap forward for administration, security, desktop control, and versioning of configurations. Group Policy advances well beyond NT 4.0 system policies to integrate security and user configuration into roaming policies that can roam between desktop (fat client) and published application configurations. When designing your MetaFrame environment, it is best to dedicate MetaFrame servers to application serving only. Installing MetaFrame on a domain controller does not allow anonymous access to applications from that server. Furthermore, the overhead induced by a domain controller and/or Active Directory services reduces the number of user sessions that can a MetaFrame server can host. It is also recommended to include all Citrix MetaFrame XP servers within the same organizational unit (OU) for management purposes. This practice allows you to more easily manage servers associated with your farm. Maximize your investment in MetaFrame by taking advantage of Active Directory services and using your MetaFrame servers for application hosting only. An example of the Terminal Services options in Windows 2000 is shown in Figure 5.3.

Figure 5.2 Advanced Hard Disk Configurations

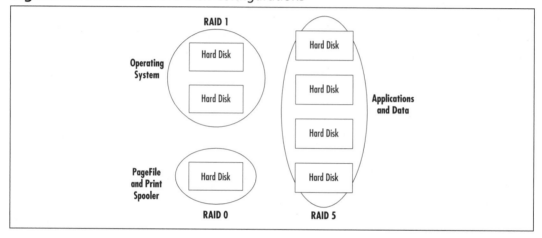

Figure 5.3 Terminal Services User Options

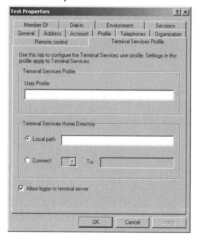

Mixed Mode

Mixed-mode Active Directory is a compromise of features and performance designed for use during a migration to a pure Windows 2000 server environment. Mixed-mode operation is primarily designed to allow Windows 2000 and Windows NT 4 servers and domain controllers to coexist within the same domain. The full features of Active Directory are not available in mixed mode. Group policy and NT 4.0 policies do not work well together. Mixing NT Terminal Services and Windows 2000 MetaFrame servers is possible, but it's difficult to implement roaming profiles, policies, and applications. Because Windows NT 4 does not recognize or cannot take advantage of many new features associated with Windows 2000, you must be careful when trying to use items such as group policies or roaming profiles. For example, suppose you configure Group Policy for users logging in to a Citrix MetaFrame XP server farm consisting of Windows 2000 and Windows NT 4 Terminal Servers. Group Policy will not be properly applied to users logging into the Windows NT 4 Terminal Servers. In many cases, users recognize the performance difference between an NT 4.0 Terminal Services server and Windows 2000 servers, creating a dissatisfying user experience.

Native Mode

Native-mode Active Server can be activated when all domain controllers are running Windows 2000. Native mode allows full implementation of Active Directory features, including Group Policy. Group Policy can be configured to control access (not NTFS security) and roaming profiles that can follow a user from PC to remote session. Native-mode Active Directory provides the most robust set of features for administering back-end functions and creating the most consistent user experience.

If you are using thin client or non-Windows based clients, you will most likely allow your users to run a Windows-style desktop from which they will run various applications. This scenario allows non-Windows 32-bit clients to have the look and feel of a Windows2000-based PC. Unfortunately, it also opens the window of opportunity for users to wreak havoc on your Citrix environment. In the default configuration of a MetaFrame desktop, an end user can shut down the server, thinking he is simply shutting down his workstation, and that could be the least of your worries. An effective Active Directory structure including implementation of Group Policy can eliminate these and other issues, creating a safe and effective environment for end users. You can find a thorough explanation of Active Directory and Group Policy on Microsoft's Web site at www.microsoft.com/windows2000. The site includes a brief discussion of Active Directory features and functions that apply directly to a MetaFrame implementation.

Group Policy-based change and configuration management is designed to centrally manage permissions and presentation of network resources to ensure they are available to users when and where they are needed. Intellimirror is the centralized function that ensures a user configuration is maintained on whatever platform users log on to. This is an evolutionary extension of roaming profiles that permits user files, software, and user-customizable desktop and environment settings are applied to whatever workstation the user logs on to in the enterprise. These features can be used to define policies to restrict user access to areas of the MetaFrame desktop to prevent users from shutting down the server, changing system settings, or otherwise corrupting the configuration you have developed to maximize application performance in your enterprise.

Best practices for implementing a Group Policy for MetaFrame users include:

- Create multiple groups for users who require different desktop access options (e.g., access to a command prompt).

- Create separate access groups for each of your published applications; in some cases, you can nest these to ease administration.

- Use folder redirection to move the default location of My Documents to a separate network share so that user files are not saved within the user profile directory. This can replace the old "H: for Home" drive mapping.

- Remove the shutdown option from the Start menu to minimize options available to end users.

- Remove Control Panel from the Start menu to prevent users from trying to access system components.

- Hide local server drives (M:, N:, and so on, if you remap drives) to restrict access to system files and directories.

- Remove the Run command from the Start menu to prevent users from starting unauthorized applications.

- Remove the MetaFrame management toolbar to prevent users from accessing administrative tools.

- Implement disk quotas to limit user disk use for users.

Additional options used for tightening the environment:

- Prevent right-clicks on the desktop to limit user capabilities and restrict changes to desktop icons.

- Clear the Start menu except for the shutdown (with shutdown server removed) and printers window to provide only the required options for users.

- Do not allow users to install printers; prevent users from adding or deleting printers.

- Allow users to run applications only from icons on the desktop. Then publish applications to add an icon to the user desktop to provide users with only the items required.

- Remove My Computer and My Network Places from the desktop to minimize user access to system and network resources.

Configuring & Implementing...

Windows 2000 with Citrix MetaFrame XP

As described throughout this section, Windows 2000 plays a critical role when you're using Citrix MetaFrame XP. Many of the features and benefits associated with using a Citrix MetaFrame XP server are provided because of the interaction between it and Windows 2000. For example, Group Policy allows a great deal of control over the user experience, allowing administrators to centrally control what users can do. Careful planning must be considered, however, since the same user policies are used within a Terminal Server/Citrix MetaFrame XP environment as on the user's desktop. Computer policies can also be used to specify settings per Citrix MetaFrame XP server. Experiment with the features available in Windows 2000 and how they can be used in cooperation with Citrix MetaFrame XP.

Installing Terminal Services

Once Windows 2000 has been configured, you must set up and configure Terminal Services for use with Citrix MetaFrame XP. Terminal Services provides the multiuser interface on which Citrix MetaFrame XP relies. To install Terminal Services for a Windows 2000 server, the following process must be completed:

1. Start Control Panel by selecting **Start | Settings | Control Panel**.

2. Double-click the **Add/Remove Programs** icon.

3. Select the **Add/Remove Windows Components** icon.

4. Once these steps are completed, scroll down to the **Terminal Services** option and select it, as shown in Figure 5.4. In addition, select **Terminal Service Licensing** if this server will provide that role. Press **Next** to proceed.

Figure 5.4 Enabling Terminal Services

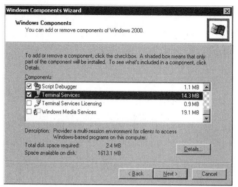

NOTE

Terminal Service Licensing is required to manage licenses for terminal server clients. Client access licenses, or CALs, must be purchased and applied to your Terminal Server Licensing server. This allows any Win32 clients, with the exception of Windows 2000 and Windows XP Professional, to connect to your terminal servers. Windows 2000 and Windows XP Professional have a Terminal Server CAL included with the operating system license. If no licenses are available to Win32 clients, temporary licenses will be created, and they will expire after 90 days. For a more detailed discussion on licensing refer to Chapter 6.

5. Next, select **Application Server** mode, as shown in Figure 5.5, to allow the installation of Citrix MetaFrame XP. Press **Next** to continue. Remote administration mode provides only two available sessions for administrative purposes. Application server mode allows as many connections as the server can handle and is licensed for.

Figure 5.5 Application Server Mode

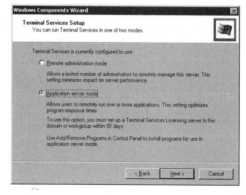

6. Select the option for permissions for application compatibility, as shown in Figure 5.6. Press **Next** to continue. This option is primarily used for compatibility with older applications designed for Windows NT 4 Terminal Server. Only use the **Permissions compatible with Terminal Server 4.0 Users** option if an application requires it to function.

Figure 5.6 Application Compatibility Permissions

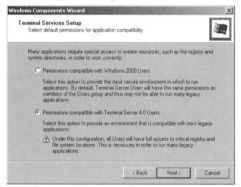

7. Once you're finished, press **Finish** to complete the installation of Terminal Services.

8. If you configured Terminal Server Licensing, you must configure the server to manage CALs.

Designing & Planning...

Terminal Server Licensing Servers

The use of Terminal Server License servers can become problematic when not implemented correctly. Careful placement and configuration of your license server is crucial to the success of your implementation. Furthermore, you must understand what licenses are required from Microsoft. At this writing, all desktop products, with the exception of Windows 2000 and Windows XP Professional, require an individual Terminal Server CAL. More information is available from Microsoft's Web site at http://support.microsoft.com/default .aspx?scid=kb;en-us;Q244749.

Installing Citrix MetaFrame XP

Once Windows 2000 and Terminal Services have been installed and configured, you are ready to commence with the implementation of Citrix MetaFrame XP. Do the following:

1. To begin the installation process for Citrix MetaFrame XP, place the installation CD into the CD-ROM drive. Execute the installation program using the following program: ***<cddrive>*:\autoroot.exe**.

2. Select **I Agree** to accept the End User License Agreement.

3. Select **Next** on the Welcome screen to continue, as shown in Figure 5.7.

Figure 5.7 The MetaFrame XP Welcome Screen

4. Select **Next** to configure Open Database Connectivity (ODBC)-compliant data store options.

5. Choose between **Create a new server farm** or **Join an existing server farm**. Choose the default option to create a new farm, and select **Next**, as shown in Figure 5.8.

Figure 5.8 Creating a New Server Farm

6. Select the **data store** option, as shown in Figure 5.9. This option is available only when you select **Create a new server farm**. Press **Next** to continue.

Figure 5.9 Specifying the Data Store

7. Select the **zone name** to be used, as shown in Figure 5.10. By default, the zone name is the Transmission Control Protocol/Internet Protocol (TCP/IP) network subnet address of the server. Press **Next** to continue.

Figure 5.10 Selecting the Server Zone Name

8. If you selected **Use a local database for the data store** in Step 6, proceed directly to Step 15. Otherwise, continue with the configuration of the third-party database. Select the database driver, as shown in Figure 5.11, and press **Next**.

9. Insert a description and select the server running the SQL or Oracle database, as shown in Figure 5.12. Press **Next** to continue.

10. As shown in Figure 5.13, select the authentication method used for the SQL database. Press **Next** to continue.

Figure 5.11 Selecting a Data Store Source

Figure 5.12 Description and Server Information

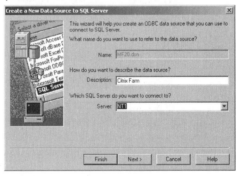

Figure 5.13 SQL Authentication

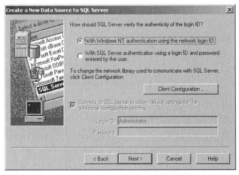

11. Specify the database to use in addition to any database parameters, as shown in Figure 5.14. Select **Next** to continue.

12. Additional SQL parameters can be optimized, as demonstrated in Figure 5.15. Select **Next** to continue.

Figure 5.14 Database Parameters

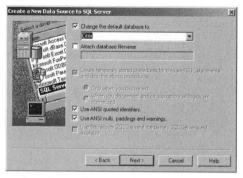

Figure 5.15 Additional Database Parameters

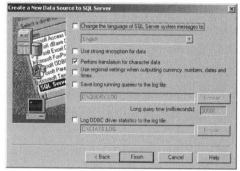

13. Press **OK** to confirm the creation of the ODBC data source to connect to the third-party database.

14. Insert the **username** and **password** for the account used to authenticate to the third-party database, as shown in Figure 5.16. Press **Next** to proceed.

Figure 5.16 Third-Party Database Authentication

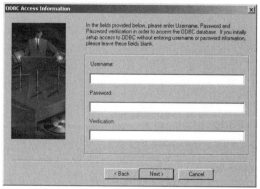

15.   Insert the new **server farm** name and press **Next** to continue, as shown in Figure 5.17.

Figure 5.17 Specifying a Server Farm Name

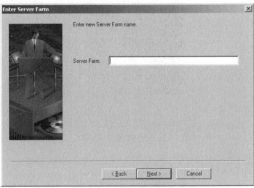

16.   Confirm the server farm name, and press **Next** to continue.

17.   Select interoperability with older versions of Citrix MetaFrame 1.8. Choose to operate in mixed mode only after careful consideration, as discussed later in this chapter. Press **Next** to proceed; see Figure 5.18.

Figure 5.18 Interoperability Mode

18.   Insert the name of an **administrative account** for the Citrix MetaFrame XP server farm. By default, the name of the currently logged-on user is inserted, as shown in Figure 5.19. Press **Next** to continue.

19.   Select the protocols to use in cooperation with Independent Computing Architecture (ICA). TCP/IP will always be selected and is required. Other protocols will be available only if they have already been activated on the server, as shown in Figure 5.20. Select **Next** to continue.

Figure 5.19 Server Farm Administrative User ID

Figure 5.20 Network ICA Connections

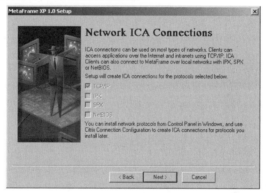

20. Set up any modems for use with RRAS, as shown in Figure 5.21. Press **Next** to proceed.

Figure 5.21 Modem Configuration

21. Press **Next** to configure session shadowing.

22. Select **shadowing options**, as shown in Figure 5.22, and press **Next**. Once selected, these options can be altered only by reinstalling Citrix MetaFrame XP on this server.

Figure 5.22 Shadowing Options

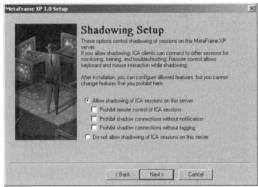

23. Press **Next** to configure server drive mappings.

24. Specify whether to remap server drives during installation, as shown in Figure 5.23. If you select the check box, the drop-down menu allows you to depict the drives after they are remapped. Press **Next** to continue.

Figure 5.23 Server Drive Reassignment

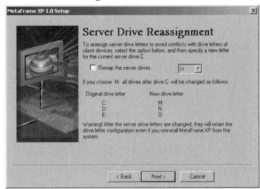

25. Select the **port** used for XML services, as shown in Figure 5.24. By default, the TCP/IP port is shared with Internet Information Services. Press **Next** to continue.

26. Select whether or not **NFuse** should be installed on this server, as illustrated in Figure 5.25. By default, NFuse is installed and set up as the default start page. Select **Next** to continue.

Figure 5.24 Port Used for XML Services

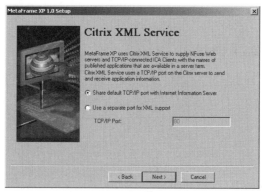

Figure 5.25 NFuse Installation

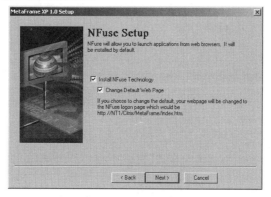

> **NOTE**
>
> Drive remapping can be used to simplify the client environment. When you remap the server drives, a client computer automatically sees its existing hard drive on the local computer as the C: drive within a Citrix MetaFrame XP session. For example, if a user saves a Word document to the C: drive within her Citrix session, it is automatically redirected to the local C: drive on her computer. You should remap server drives before any applications are installed on the local server. Any applications already installed before the server remaps drives will usually not function properly.

27.   Select **Next** to continue installation. The file copy process will begin.

28.   Press **Next** to start the ICA client installation process.

29.   Select the source for the ICA client files. Insert the **network path** or **ICA Client CD** and press **Next**, as shown in Figure 5.26.

Figure 5.26 ICA Client Source Files

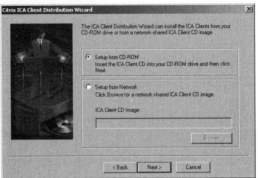

30. Select **Typical** or **Custom** to configure the clients that will be installed on the server. Select **Next** to proceed.

31. Insert your **license** provided by Citrix and press **Add**, as shown in Figure 5.27. A confirmation message will appear. Press **OK** to continue.

Figure 5.27 MetaFrame XP Licensing

32. Accept the product code provided or insert a new one provided by Citrix, as shown in Figure 5.28. Select **Next** to continue.

33. When you're finished, select **Restart** to complete the Citrix MetaFrame XP installation process.

34. Once your machine has restarted, remember to apply any service packs or hot fixes that might be required.

Figure 5.28 Citrix Product Code

Deploying Multiple Servers

When working with larger environments, installing every server manually can become very time consuming. The ability to install multiple servers automatically is not a new concept; therefore, Citrix MetaFrame XP takes into consideration the technologies that already exist. First, you must test your configuration and deploy a pilot to validate that everything meets the desired business goals. Next, you can create unattended installation scripts or clone servers to deploy multiple identical servers efficiently. You must understand the processes involved with server deployment of Citrix MetaFrame XP, including the disadvantages of each methodology.

Testing Configurations and Deploying a Pilot

After you've installed Citrix MetaFrame XP, it is time to get down to the business of testing applications and running a pilot project. The procedures for publishing applications and monitoring performance of your Citrix MetaFrame XP server are covered elsewhere in this book. Use this book to guide your initial installation and configuration, then make changes as necessary to obtain the performance goals and end-user configuration that meets the needs of your environment.

Keys to a successful pilot include:

- **Define success**
    - Define the applications that will be included in your initial rollout.
    - Define the connection types and network access that will be used (TCP/IP, Internetwork Packet Exchange/Sequenced Packet Exchange [IPX/SPX], dialup, broadband, local area network [LAN], wide area network [WAN], etc.).

- Define application performance standards.

- Define cost parameters per user and/or for the project as a whole.

- Define any "show stoppers"—single negative outcomes that jeopardize the entire project.

■ **Establish a testing center**

- Dedicate sufficient hardware to a test environment so that it can be modified and taken offline without negatively impacting your production environment.

- Use sufficient server hardware for three simultaneous users; this should provide sufficient information to determine the effects of users on hardware and scale the production requirements.

- Use a current technology PC with at least 256MB RAM for a test server.

- Try to have client configurations match the variety of clients that will be present in production.

■ **Back up, test, research—and test some more**

- Back up your test server prior to every change, and restore to prechange conditions rather than simply uninstalling or "unconfiguring" changes, especially those that impact the registry.

- Test each application individually prior to testing server load under multiple users and applications.

- When performance standards aren't met, research possible solutions. Listserv archives are excellent for this task.

■ **Define your production environment**

- Define how you will present applications to users, using Program Neighborhood or a desktop session.

- If you're using a desktop, define Active Directory and group policy parameters and test thoroughly to ensure users have sufficient rights to be productive but no permissions that could compromise the environment.

■ **Under-promise, then over-deliver**

- Be conservative in establishing performance standards and reporting benchmark results, especially if users will connect via the Internet and/or a dialup connection.

Once all your applications are running without issue and to the stated performance goals, it is time to scale your production hardware. For MetaFrame servers, the best rule of thumb is buy the fastest of everything you can afford, from disk to CPU, and use your baseline application data to ensure that you have enough RAM. For each application you tested, measure the amount of RAM in use while the application is running. Multiply the amount of RAM each application consumes by the required number of simultaneous users. Total the RAM requirements for each application, plus the amount of server overhead (RAM in use when idle/no connections) and you will have a fairly accurate measure of the requirement to support your production environment. It is recommended that you add 10 percent to the total, as a buffer. Other hardware considerations should include disk configuration and CPU. In configuring hard disks, disk duplexing is the fastest fault-tolerant method for this application. As with all things, budgets could constrain your hardware options; compromise on CPU speed if you must, but never on RAM.

Installing Identical Servers

Once the pilot phase is complete, it is time to deploy your server configurations. To efficiently deploy multiple identical servers, two methods are available to minimize the time spent installing Citrix MetaFrame XP. First, server cloning can be employed using popular software provided by third-party vendors. Unattended installations can also be scripted using a text answer file. Both methods provide advantages and caveats to consider as you determine which meets your needs.

Server Cloning

A common method of deploying multiple, identical servers is through the use of cloning software. This has become an extremely popular alternative to manual installations for servers and workstation operating systems. Several major vendors provide operating system cloning applications. Microsoft has even added cloning capabilities into its latest operating system to ease installation and deployment.

To properly support these environments, Citrix has added support for cloning Citrix MetaFrame XP servers. This does not include the cloning application, only the requirements and capability to use Citrix within this environment. The following steps should be taken prior to creating an image of MetaFrame XP. Once these steps have been completed, the server cloning application can be utilized to create an image to be deployed:

1. A server installed as the first in a farm with an Access database cannot be cloned.

2. Do not use a server with an SSL certificate installed.

3. Select the **default zone name** during installation.

4. Stop the **Independent Management Architecture service** and set it to **manual startup**.

5. Delete the following **registry keys**:

   HKEY_LOCAL_MACHINE\Software\Citrix\IMA\Runtime\HostId

   HKEY_LOCAL_MACHINE\Software\Citrix\IMA\Runtime\ImaPort

   HKEY_LOCAL_MACHINE\Software\Citrix\IMA\Runtime\MasterRanking

   HKEY_LOCAL_MACHINE\Software\Citrix\IMA\Runtime\PSRequired

   HKEY_LOCAL_MACHINE\Software\Citrix\IMA\Runtime\RassPort

   HKEY_LOCAL_MACHINE\Software\Citrix\IMA\Runtime\ZoneName

The following steps should be taken to image a MetaFrame XP server using cloning applications. Once these steps are completed, the server is ready to be utilized by users:

1. The **server name** and **SID** must be changed correctly to support operating system functions and Citrix MetaFrame XP. This is traditionally done by the cloning application.

2. Add the following registry key and set the value to the name of the MetaFrame XP server:

   HKEY_LOCAL_MACHINE\Software\Citrix\IMA\ServerHost

3. Edit the **wfcname.ini file** located on the root of the drive on which Citrix MetaFrame XP is installed, and replace the server name with the desired name of the newly cloned server.

4. Set the **Independent Management Architecture service** to start automatically.

5. Reboot the server to apply the changes and start **MetaFrame XP**.

Unattended Installations

Another option for administrators who are deploying multiple, identical XP servers is the capability to complete an unattended installation. Unattended installations use an answer file to input automated responses during installation of MetaFrame XP. This allows an administrator to install Citrix with minimal involvement while maintaining consistency.

In a process similar to the Microsoft Windows unattended installation, a sample answer file is provided on the MetaFrame XP CD. The unattend.txt file is located in the \W2K\MF and \TSE\MF directories for Windows 2000 and Terminal Server Edition, respectively. Each of the questions that appear during installation can be automated from within this file. A full path to the unattend.txt file must be specified if it is not located in the same directory as the setup executable. To use the answer file during the setup of MetaFrame XP for Windows 2000, the following command must be used:

```
<cdrom>:\W2K\MF\setup.exe /u:answerfile
```

Each section is carefully explained, along with available options and warning messages on using these options. It is critical that once the answer file is configured, proper testing be performed to ensure that the installation is completed as required and successfully. Many of these options require a reinstallation to properly reconfigure a server if they are implemented incorrectly. An example of the Citrix MetaFrame XP answer file is shown in Figure 5.29.

Figure 5.29 An Unattended Answer File

In order to install servers using the unattended installation script, you must first modify the script to meet your requirements. This process can only be completed for servers added to an existing farm. The first server in a Citrix MetaFrame farm must be installed and configured prior to using this procedure. To set up an unattended installation script, you must perform the following steps:

1. Ensure that the server farm to which you are adding servers is reachable and functioning properly.

2. Copy the **installation CD files** for the version you are installing to a network share. For example, Citrix MetaFrame XP for Windows 2000 requires only the \W2K directory for installation.

3. If a direct connection to a Microsoft SQL or Oracle database is required for the data store, the following steps must be completed. Otherwise, go to Step 4.

   a. The **MF20.dsn file** must be copied from the first server in the Citrix farm to a network share. By default, this file is located in the \Program Files\Citrix\Independent Management Architecture directory.

   b. Modify the MF20.dsn file to remove the entry **WSID=MF_Server**.

   c. Save the **MF20.dsn** file to the network share.

4. Modify the **unattend.txt** file to include the Citrix settings you require. Be sure to insert the location of the MF20.dsn file, if applicable. Once this is done, save the **unattend.txt** file to the network share. The following sections should not be modified:

   a. **[Farm Settings]**   This is used only for the first server in a farm.

   b. **[Indirect Connect Settings]**   Not used if direct connections are required.

   c. **[Direct Connect Settings]**   Not used if indirect connections are required.

5. Connect to the **network share** containing your installation files and run **setup.exe** with the **/u:anwserfile** option, as discussed earlier in this chapter.

NOTE

In performing multiple installations simultaneously, no more than 10 servers should be added to a farm at any given time. Due to the bandwidth and database overhead associated with these processes, adding more than 10 servers at a time could adversely affect your server farm performance.

Migrating from a MetaFrame 1.8 Farm to MetaFrame XP

As you prepare to use Citrix MetaFrame XP, you could have older versions that must be migrated. Citrix has provided an upgrade methodology that takes into account the ability to simultaneously run Citrix MetaFrame XP and Citrix MetaFrame 1.8 within the same server farm. Known as Interoperability mode, the ability to migrate servers while minimizing user impact provides for an easier upgrade.

Two modes are associated with a Citrix MetaFrame XP server farm: mixed mode and native mode. By default, all servers operate in native mode, providing all the benefits Citrix MetaFrame XP has to offer. Mixed-mode operation, however, allows for older Citrix MetaFrame 1.8 servers to operate within the same farm. Although this sounds like a great idea, Citrix recommends using Interoperability mode only for a long as necessary. In addition, the company recommends migrating all servers within your farm as quickly as possible once you start. You must understand the benefits and disadvantages of mixed mode and native mode to ensure that user impact is minimized during a migration from Citrix MetaFrame 1.8 to Citrix MetaFrame XP.

Using MetaFrame XP Mixed Mode

To properly support backward compatibility in a MetaFrame 1.8 server farm environment, mixed-mode operation can be enabled. Although recommended only as a migration or temporary option, it does offer additional services and capabilities to administrators. With these features come several stipulations that must be accounted for, however. Within this section, the features and caveats are discussed to properly prepare you for using this capability.

Features provided by mixed-mode operation include these:

- ICA browser compatibility with MetaFrame 1.8 is enabled on every MetaFrame XP server in the farm.

- Program Neighborhood compatibility with MetaFrame 1.8 is enabled on every MetaFrame XP server in the farm.

- MetaFrame 1.8 and MetaFrame XP servers with the same farm name are displayed to clients as a single farm.

- MetaFrame XP servers can respond to legacy UDP client requests.

- Published applications can be load balanced across MetaFrame XP and MetaFrame 1.8 servers with the same farm name.

- License pooling is available between MetaFrame XP and MetaFrame 1.8 servers on the same subnet.

- The MetaFrame XP Citrix Management Console provides intelligence for interoperability with MetaFrame 1.8.

MetaFrame XP servers will always win ICA browser elections, providing more stable data storage. Additional interoperability issues such as license pooling, application migration, and ICA browser elections must be carefully considered.

Citrix Farm Name

To properly support both Citrix MetaFrame 1.8 and MetaFrame XP in the same farm, the name of the server farm must be identical across both server platforms. When installing MetaFrame XP into an existing MetaFrame 1.8 server farm, you must create a new farm during the installation of the first server, using an identical farm name. This allows the data store to be created with the appropriate information and ensures that communication between the two farms will automatically take place. Although they are two separate farms, to the users, applications, and management utilities, they are operating as a single entity.

Application Migration

Based on the nature of Citrix MetaFrame provision of access to applications, clean migration of these applications is critical to the success of any implementation. Within Interoperability mode, MetaFrame XP provides the ability to operate in cooperation with MetaFrame 1.8 to continue providing application services to users. In addition, there are methods for migrating published applications and their associated settings into a MetaFrame XP farm.

It is recommended that you *not* publish applications while operating in a mixed-mode environment. Although this capability exists, it must be performed correctly to accomplish this task. Additionally, when published applications are migrated to MetaFrame XP, a log is maintained in the Winnt\System32 directory. This log can assist in troubleshooting issues that arise.

You must follow several rules when you're dealing with published applications in this type of environment:

- Applications installed prior to MetaFrame XP being added to the farm will upgrade successfully.

- It is recommended that you back up published application settings to help resolve any issues that arise.

- Newly published applications must first be published via Published Application Manager from the MetaFrame XP server. Once this is done, the applications must then be published via the Citrix Management Console. This order must be observed for application publishing to succeed.

- Applications viewed via the MetaFrame 1.8 version of Published Applications Manager can disappear under certain circumstances. Using the MetaFrame XP version of this utility resolves this issue.

- Do not use Published Application Manager to remove MetaFrame XP servers from lists providing this application.

- Applications modified by the MetaFrame XP version of Published Applications Manager cannot be later modified by the version provided with MetaFrame 1.8.

License Pooling

One of the most important features of using mixed-mode operation is the capability to share licenses between MetaFrame 1.8 and MetaFrame XP servers. MetaFrame 1.8 servers with connection licenses installed can share these with all servers located within the mixed-mode server farm. In addition, MetaFrame XP servers can pool connection licenses they maintain to any MetaFrame 1.8 server located on the same subnet within the farm.

Although this feature can help in migrating to MetaFrame XP, you must take note of several caveats. First, MetaFrame XP servers automatically win ICA browser elections. When acting as the master browser, MetaFrame XP converts ICA license gateways to ICA gateways. In addition, if ICA gateways exists prior to the installation of MetaFrame XP into the server farm, licensing updates can take up to 48 hours due to backup ICA browsers. This timing can affect how licensing operates within your farm. In addition, MetaFrame XP servers handle connection licenses differently in mixed mode than in native mode. By default, connection licenses are available to all servers within a farm, in all subnets, in native mode. Within mixed mode, these licenses are statically assigned to server within a particular subnet for a farm. To manually assign licenses where required, administrative intervention is required to ensure that they are delineated properly.

Load Balancing

A new feature available with Citrix MetaFrame includes advanced load-balancing criteria from which to choose. Unfortunately, this capability is not available in a mixed-mode server farm. When you are load-balancing applications across a mixture of MetaFrame versions, only the basic load-balancing parameters in MetaFrame 1.8 are available. In addition, a few rules apply to allow this feature to function properly:

- A MetaFrame XP server must be the master ICA browser.

- Only the default load balanced should be configured for all MetaFrame servers.

- Application publishing rules as described earlier must be considered because they also apply to load-balancing support.

- The QSERVER utility must be used to determine load values across a mixed-mode farm.

Load evaluation occurs differently in a mixed-mode farm. Although this is unusual compared with native environments, it is required to support client requests. The evaluation process is as follows:

1. The ICA client connects to the master ICA browser to determine application availability.

2. MetaFrame XP servers are queried to determine lightest load based on user connections.

3. MetaFrame 1.8 servers are queried to determine lightest load based on user connections.

4. The master browser then chooses between the MetaFrame XP server or the MetaFrame 1.8 server with the least number of connected users. If both servers contain equal values, the MetaFrame XP server is chosen.

ICA Browser Elections

Once MetaFrame XP is operating in mixed mode, the ICA browser service is enabled on all servers in the farm. The master browsers generally maintain and provide information to clients on license usage and application availability. This was a service required in earlier releases of Citrix MetaFrame. MetaFrame XP servers can now participate in "browser elections" with MetaFrame 1.8 servers on the same subnet. Used to determine the server maintaining the master information base about the server farm, this is a critical component when operating MetaFrame 1.8 server farms.

Master browser elections are based on specific criteria. When one of these events occurs, a master browser election is forced to determine which server should maintain this role. If any of the following take place, it will trigger a browser election:

- The Citrix MetaFrame server is started.

- The current master browser does not respond to a request.

- Two master browsers are detected on the same subnet.

Once a browser election is triggered, the server chosen is based on several items. Listed here is the hierarchy of the election process, in order starting with the first rule:

- ICA browser version (higher takes precedence)

- Configured as master browser (with server admin tool or registry)

- Citrix server is Windows 2000 domain controller

- Length of time ICA browser has been running

- Computer name

ICA Gateways

Based on the network architecture of previous MetaFrame versions, broadcast traffic was used to communicate between servers and server farms. To allow servers to communicate across a network, ICA gateways were required. ICA gateways provided virtual links between servers and farms to tunnel all traffic to allow MetaFrame to scale outside a single network. Although MetaFrame XP does not require ICA gateways to perform this function, they are still used for backward compatibility with MetaFrame 1.8.

ICA gateways are currently support in mixed-mode operation to allow master ICA browsers to communicate across subnets. To identify ICA gateways on MetaFrame XP servers, the QSERVER utility must be used. These must be taken into consideration as plans for the upgrade of existing MetaFrame 1.8 servers using ICA gateways are migrated to MetaFrame XP.

License Migration

As part of migrating from an older release of MetaFrame to MetaFrame XP, you must take into account licensing issues. Citrix provides a service know as Subscription Advantage; in this service, clients meeting defined criteria receive free upgrade MetaFrame XP licenses. Additional information related to these licenses can be found at the Citrix Web site.

One important license migration technical note is worth mentioning. When upgrading from MetaFrame 1.8, you must install an existing base license and connection license. If you add a MetaFrame XP upgrade license, it will not function properly if it does not find these original licenses in place.

Citrix Farm and Server Management

To assist with interoperability issues, MetaFrame XP provides an updated version of the Citrix administration utilities used to manage MetaFrame 1.8 servers. It is recommended that you use the updated version of these utilities because they address many of the issues related to interoperability not repaired in the earlier releases. In addition, specific rules apply to using these utilities to avoid causing problems within this environment.

As mentioned earlier, it is recommended that you use the MetaFrame XP version of Published Application Manager to handle any applications across a mixed-mode farm. In addition, the Citrix Administration Utility can be used to manage some settings across both MetaFrame 1.8 and MetaFrame XP servers simultaneously. The use of the MetaFrame XP Citrix Management Console, or CMC, is generally the preferred administration tool.

Using MetaFrame XP Native Mode

As mentioned earlier, MetaFrame XP supports two modes of operation. Native mode provides compatibility within a server farm consisting of Citrix MetaFrame XP 1.0 servers only. A farm containing only MetaFrame XP servers takes full advantage of the new feature set provided in the product, along with several network enhancements. Because the Citrix MetaFrame XP architecture and features are discussed in-depth throughout this book, a limited discussion of how these apply to interoperability is provided here.

Advantages for using native mode include these:

- ICA browser service is disabled on all servers within the farm, limiting the broadcast traffic required on your network. IMA traffic used in its place is not based on broadcast traffic.

- Program Neighborhood services are disabled on all servers within the farm.

- Data collectors are used instead of the ICA browser service. This is a more stable solution.

Summary

The first step to implementing Citrix MetaFrame XP is the installation of the server software. Based on Windows 2000, several factors weigh heavily on performance and reliability of your servers. First, separating the operating system, the page file and print spooler, and the application data should optimize the hard disk configuration. Active Directory can also provide additional advantages to the administrator due to the functionality it offers. Next, Terminal Services must be installed and configured properly. Once that process is completed, the installation of Citrix MetaFrame XP can be started.

Once you have your server configuration laid out, you must deploy a pilot and test the configurations. This allows you to test and validate the configuration options selected. After that, additional tools are available to facilitate the installation of multiple identical servers. Unattended installation scripts and server cloning provide two different methodologies for efficient server installations.

Citrix MetaFrame XP provides backward compatibility with older versions of MetaFrame. Two modes exist within a server farm: native mode and mixed mode. Native mode is the normal state of a server farm consisting of only Citrix MetaFrame XP servers. Mixed mode, or Interoperability mode, allows Citrix MetaFrame XP servers and Citrix MetaFrame 1.8 servers to coexist within the same farm. Several factors must be addressed when you use Interoperability mode: farm name, server and farm management, application migration, license pooling, ICA browser elections, ICA gateways, load balancing, and license migration.

Solutions Fast Track

Single-Server Installation

☑ The operating system, the page file and print spooler, and the application data can be separated within your hard disk configuration to optimize your server for peak performance.

☑ Terminal Services must be activated and configured for application mode to work with Citrix MetaFrame XP.

☑ Active Directory can be used to improve the client experience with features such as Group Policy.

Deploying Multiple Servers

☑ Before implementing your production server farm, you must carefully test and pilot your server configurations.

☑ You can use unattended installation scripts to automate the installation of Citrix MetaFrame XP.

☑ You can use server-cloning software provided by third-party vendors to install multiple servers without following the manual process.

Migrating from a MetaFrame 1.8 Farm to MetaFrame XP

☑ Native mode operates normally with server farms of Citrix MetaFrame XP servers only.

☑ Mixed mode, or Interoperability mode, allows Citrix MetaFrame 1.8 servers to coexist with Citrix MetaFrame XP servers within the same farm.

☑ Several aspects that must be carefully managed when using interoperability mode include farm name, application migration, license pooling, ICA browser elections, ICA gateways, load balancing, license migration, and server and farm management.

Frequently Asked Questions

The following Frequently Asked Questions, answered by the authors of this book, are designed to both measure your understanding of the concepts presented in this chapter and to assist you with real-life implementation of these concepts. To have your questions about this chapter answered by the author, browse to **www.syngress.com/solutions** and click on the **"Ask the Author"** form.

Q: What is the difference between remote administration and application mode with Windows 2000 Terminal Services?

A: Remote administration mode is provided to allow administrators to connect and manage servers. It is limited to two users connected concurrently. Application mode is used for end-user access to applications or services provided by the server. Within this mode, licenses are limited only by the server performance and number of licenses owned.

Q: How can I perform a CD installation for servers using the unattended script file?

A: Once you have completed the steps necessary to create an unattended installation file, you can copy all the files, including the new unattend.txt, to a CD. You can also create a batch file and place it on the CD to call the correct path and unattend.txt file to further minimize the installation process.

Q: When would you typically recommend using Interoperability mode?

A: Citrix recommends against using Interoperability mode but recognizes the need for it. This mode is best used for migrating a Citrix MetaFrame 1.8 server farm without reinstalling the servers. If you use this option, it is recommended that you migrate your servers as quickly as possible to minimize the impact it could have.

Q: What happens to services such as the ICA browser after you turn off Interoperability mode?

A: These services are loaded on Citrix MetaFrame XP servers solely for backward compatibility. Once deactivated, services such as the ICA browser are no longer available because they are no longer required.

Chapter 6

Connecting
Thin Clients

Solutions in this chapter:

- **Client Licensing**

- **Hardware and Software Requirements**

- **Installing RDP Clients**

- **Installing ICA Clients**

- **Automating Installation**

☑ **Summary**

☑ **Solutions Fast Track**

☑ **Frequently Asked Questions**

Introduction

When you're implementing a Citrix MetaFrame XP server farm, one of the toughest planning initiatives is figuring out licensing. Clients can connect to a Citrix MetaFrame XP server in a number of ways. They can connect to shared server drives and printers, requiring a client access license. They can connect via a Remote Desktop Protocol (RDP) Terminal Services session, requiring a Terminal Services client license. They can connect via an ICA session, requiring both a Terminal Services client license and a Citrix MetaFrame XP license. Or they can connect via the Internet and use a different licensing method.

Although the rich variety of client types and connectivity make Citrix MetaFrame XP a versatile solution, it can also be confusing to determine the type of clients to deploy and how to deploy them. For example, a Windows XP machine can run either the RDP client or the ICA client. However, if you're faced with a UNIX or Linux box, the only solution available is ICA.

Once you have selected licenses and determined which clients to deploy to which machines, you need to determine how you will deploy the client software. Via a variety of methods, the client installation can be automated and deployed with little or no user interaction. When there are hundreds or thousands of clients to deploy, automation saves a tremendous amount of time and administrative overhead.

Client Licensing

Designing the Citrix MetaFrame XP server farm does not stop at the hardware level. We need to take into consideration and plan for client licensing so as to provide a good, stable, and legal environment. Licensing ensures that there are always enough sessions available to service your incoming users. Various scenarios are available for licensing; you can either pool licenses across multiple servers, thereby having your servers take advantage of each other's licenses, or you can plan for an exact number of licenses for every server, and as soon as the license count on a particular server is reached, that server stops accepting sessions.

Microsoft Terminal Services licensing is also an imperative step in the design of a MetaFrame XP server environment. To properly plan licensing, you must take into consideration the licensing requirements for Terminal Services and MetaFrame XP. Familiarizing yourself with the following concepts will help you select the best method to use on your servers and will help you determine the number of licenses required to meet your organization's needs:

- **Microsoft Windows 2000 Server CALs** Client access licenses are required if your users will be authenticating to a Windows 2000 server. In many cases, users will also take advantage of file and print services that the Windows 2000 Server family offers. The Windows 2000 Server family has two licensing options, per server or per seat:

- **Per-server mode** Windows 2000 Server CALs are associated with a particular server. Each server needs enough licenses to accommodate users logging on to it. The per-server mode option allows the repeated use of the licenses by various devices. In per-server mode, the CALs aren't assigned to a particular device. A sufficient number of licenses should always be available to accommodate the maximum number of users logging in. For example, if you have 1000 workstations in your organization that sporadically connect to 10 servers with a maximum of 10 connections per server, you need to buy a total of 100 CALs—10 per server. In cases in which devices infrequently access servers, per-server mode is selected.

- **Per-seat mode** In this mode, licenses are assigned on a per-device basis. Each device connecting to a Windows 2000 server requires a CAL. Once a CAL has been assigned to a device, that device can log on or connect to any server in the domain. For example, if you have in your organization 100 workstations that will connect to 200 servers, you need 100 CALs. In cases in which devices frequently access multiple servers, per-seat mode is selected.

You can switch from per-server mode to per-seat mode *once*. This is done by clicking **Start** | **Settings** | **Control Panel** | **Licensing**. See Figure 6.1.

Figure 6.1 The Choose Licensing Mode Dialog Window

- A *license server* is required to track the licenses installed and issued to clients. Terminal servers must have the ability to communicate with the license server before any client is issued a license to access the servers. A License server is activated by Microsoft's clearing house which is a database established by Microsoft to activate License servers and to issue them with client license packs as they request them. One license server is sufficient for multiple terminal servers. A License server must reside on a Domain Controller. The first step is to actually install the Terminal Services Licensing by going to **Control**

Panel | Add/Remove Programs | Add/Remove Windows
Component, check the box by Terminal Services Licensing and click on
Next. After the Installation you will need to activate the license server.
Activate the license server by going to Administrative Tools | Terminal
Services Licensing as seen in Figure 6.2. Right-click the server you want to
make your license server and follow the wizard.

Figure 6.2 Activating a License Server

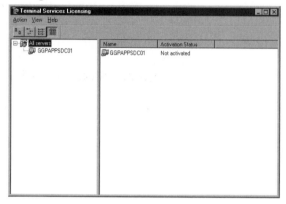

- **Microsoft Windows 2000 Terminal Services client access licenses
  (TS CALs)** When you install Terminal Services, you are prompted to select
  one of two modes: remote administration mode or application server mode.
  (See Figure 6.3.) Your selection determines the licensing requirements you
  will need.

    - *Remote administration mode* does not require any licensing and is provided as
      a remote administration tool, enabling administrators to remotely admin-
      ister their servers using a GUI from Windows-based computers and non-
      Windows-based computers.

NOTE

In remote administration mode, two remote users, usually administrators, can
share a single session for training or assistance purposes.

    - *Application server mode* allows multiple remote clients to simultaneously
      access server applications, thus requiring several different types of licenses.

NOTE

Regardless of the protocol you use to access Terminal Services, whether RDP or ICA, you still need a TS CAL.

Figure 6.3 Terminal Services Mode Selection

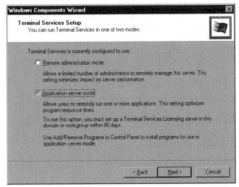

- **Application license** Applications you run on your Terminal Services need to be licensed based on their companies' licensing requirements. For example, if you are running Microsoft Office and your users will use Microsoft Office, you'll need licenses to use the Office application.

- **Citrix connection license** This license is required for ICA clients connecting to a Citrix MetaFrame XP Server in the farm. Each concurrent ICA connection counts as one connection license.

How many licenses will you need? The number of licenses depends on the number of client desktops you are using to access the Terminal Services. Microsoft provides a free Terminal Services license to Windows 2000 Professional and XP Professional desktop OS users. Assuming you have 50 Windows 2000 Professional and 50 Windows XP Professional computers in your organization, you only need 100 Windows 2000 Server CALs. In this scenario, no Terminal Services CALs are needed, since you are using Professional and XP desktops. If the OSs were anything other than Windows 2000 Professional and XP Professional, and assuming that you have 100 machines of mixed Windows 95, 98, and ME, you need a total of 200 licenses, 100 Windows 2000 Server CALs, and 100 TS CALs. In both scenarios, make sure that the applications you are running on the server are properly licensed. If you use ICA as your protocol to access Citrix MetaFrame XP servers, you also need separate Citrix connection licenses. See Table 6.1.

Table 6.1 Licensing Requirements for Various Windows Clients

Client Operating System	TS RDP Licensing	Citrix ICA Licensing	Windows Server CALs
Windows 2000/XP Professional	Free license	Requires license	Requires license
Windows 9.x	Requires license	Requires license	Requires license

RDP Clients

Clients using RDP require the following client licensing:

- **Terminal Services CALs** These clients need TS CALs unless you are using Windows 2000 Professional or Windows XP Professional, in which case you can take advantage of the free license Microsoft offers for users of two operating systems logging on to Terminal Services.

- **Windows 2000 Server CALs** Regardless of the desktop OS you are using, you need a server CAL.

- **Application license** You need to make sure that the application you are running on the terminal server is properly licensed based on the vendor's licensing requirements.

ICA Clients

In order to use ICA, Citrix MetaFrame XP must be installed and running on the server, and a Citrix client for your operating system should be used. Citrix clients are downloadable from www.citrix.com/downloads. Using the ICA protocol requires the following client licensing:

- **Terminal Services CALs** These clients need TS CALs unless you are using Windows 2000 Professional or Windows XP Professional, in which case you can take advantage of the free license Microsoft offers for users of these two OSs logging on to Terminal Services.

- **Windows 2000 Server CALs** Regardless of the desktop OS you are using, you need a server CAL.

- **Application license** You need to make sure the application you are running on the terminal server is properly licensed based on the vendor's licensing requirements.

- **Citrix connection license** Each ICA client connection to a Citrix MetaFrame XP server requires a Citrix *connection license*.

Managing Licensing in a Citrix MetaFrame XP Server Farm

Managing licenses in Citrix MetaFrame XP is accomplished through the Citrix Management Console (CMC). As you might have noticed in reading through this book, the IMA data store is an integral part of Citrix MetaFrame XP, which, in turn is a vital and important role in terms of licensing. The data store stores all licensing information for the Citrix MetaFrame XP server farm. You can use the CMC to complete numerous licensing tasks (described in the next sections):

- Adding licenses
- Activating licenses
- Monitoring product use and connection license count
- Assigning license counts to specific servers in the farm
- Removing license numbers

Adding Licenses

To add a license, you can right-click **Licenses** on the left panel menu and choose **Add License**. Another option is to access the **Actions Menu** and choose **New | License**. When a dialog box appears, enter the **license number** and click **OK**. You will then be prompted to activate the license. If you choose not to activate the license, you'll be given a grace period within which you must activate your license. See Figure 6.4.

Figure 6.4 The Add License Window

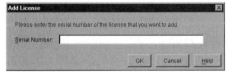

If you don't activate your license before the grace period ends, all the features of MetaFrame XP will cease to function properly. However, you'll still be able to connect to the CMC to add or activate licenses.

Activating Licenses

To activate a license, click **Licenses** in the left-hand menu of the CMC. License information will be displayed in the right panel. Then:

1. Click the **License Numbers Tab** and select the **license** you want to activate.

2. Right-click the **license** and chose **Activate**. A dialog box appears, prompting you to enter an activation code.

3. Open a Web browser and go to www.citrix.com/activate.

4. Use the **Copy to clipboard** option and paste the number on the Citrix activation page when prompted.

5. When you get the activation code from the Citrix Web site, copy and paste it into the **Activation Code text box** and click **OK**. See Figure 6.5.

Figure 6.5 The Activate License Window

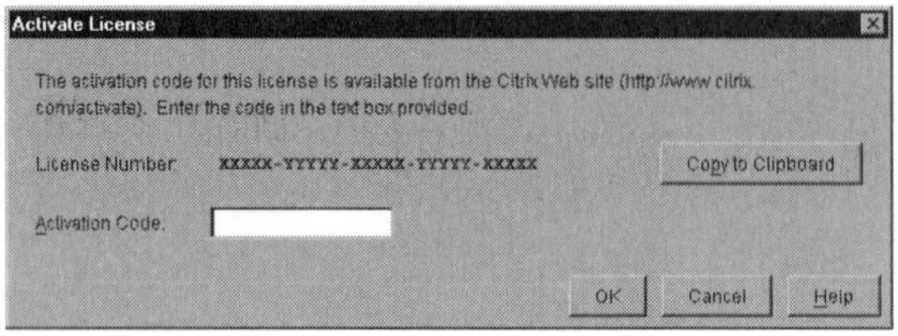

Monitoring Product Usage and Connection Licenses

To monitor usage of product and connection licenses, click **Licenses** on the left-hand menu panel of the CMC (Figure 6.6), then click the **Connection** or **Product** tab to monitor and manage the following:

- **Status** Shows whether the license has been activated, deactivated, expired or is an evaluation license.

- **Description** A short description of the product being licensed (e.g., Feature Release, Connection License Packs, etc.).

- **Count** The total number of connections available for ICA connections.

- **Pooled In Use** The total number of licenses being used.

- **Pooled Available** The total number of remaining licenses not being used.

- **Assigned** The total number of licenses assigned to a server.

- **Assigned In Use** The total number of licenses assigned to a server that are currently in use.

Assigning License Counts to Specific Servers in the Farm

You can assign Citrix licenses in two ways: You can either assign licenses to a single server, or you can assign licenses to a pool. The difference between the two methods is that if you assign licenses to a single server, no other servers in the farm will benefit from these licenses and, in the event that this server goes down, its licenses will not be available until the server comes back online. Using pooled licenses provides for the sharing of licenses among all the servers in the farm; another great advantage is that in the event that a server with pooled licenses should go down, its licenses remain active for 48 hours.

Figure 6.6 Monitoring Licenses

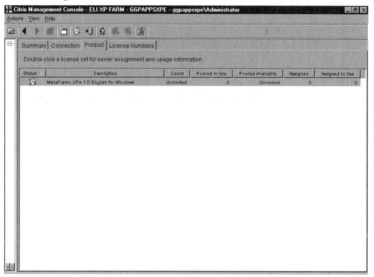

Assigning licensing to a single server also means that you have to buy more licenses for every server individually to accommodate the number of users logging in to that server. License pooling, on the other hand, shares the licenses, thereby saving you money on licensing.

You can assign license counts to specific servers by dedicating a number of licenses to a particular server and removing the specified count of licenses from the pool. Licenses that cannot be assigned include deactivated licenses, demonstration licenses, and evaluation licenses. To assign license counts to a specific server:

1. Right-click **Licenses** in the left-hand menu panel of the CMC and choose **New Assignment**, or click the **Actions** menu option and select **New Assignment**.

2. A wizard appears that will guide you through selecting the server to which you want to assign a license count and will prompt you to enter the number of licenses you want to dedicate to that server.

3. To modify the license assignment for a particular server, click **Servers** from the left pane menu of the CMC and select your server. On the right-hand panel, select the **License** tab and double-click the license you want to modify.

Removing License Numbers

In most cases, the only licenses you should remove are either expired licenses or evaluation licenses. To remove a license:

1. Click **Licenses** in the left pane menu of the CMC and select the appropriate tab on the right pane.

2. Right-click the license you want to remove and click **Remove**.

Licensing Internet Clients

As businesses increasingly rely on the Internet to grow and expand, the need to get business partners and customers closer together has become a necessity. The need to extend your network and make it readily available to clients and partners has prompted companies such as Microsoft, Citrix, and many more to create licensing schemes that would enable these companies to accomplish their tasks with a minimal financial burden when it comes to licensing.

The Internet licensing packages that these companies offer are mostly geared toward the anonymous Internet user. What we mean by *anonymous* in this case is a user who is not an employee of your organization. In other words, we cannot install NFuse, for example, "Webifying" our applications and have our employees log in from anywhere on the Internet for free. This licensing package is usually used for introducing a new product or presenting an idea that you would like your clients to test drive. In this last scenario, the users—even though known—are still anonymous users because they are in no way directly affiliated with your organization.

The following list shows the Internet licensing packages offered by Microsoft and Citrix:

■   **Windows 2000 Server Internet Connector License** This license allows an unlimited number of authentications to Windows 2000 Server via the Internet. This type of licensing replaces Windows 2000 CALs and is used by Web sites that employ server-based authentication. Anonymous users accessing Windows 2000 servers via the Internet do not require CALs.

■   **Windows 2000 Terminal Services Internet Connector License** This license allows up to 200 anonymous CALs to Terminal Services. This method replaces the need for TS CALs and Windows 2000 Server CALs. Windows 2000 Terminal Services Internet Connector License is available through the Microsoft Open, Select, and Enterprise Agreement Volume Licensing programs.

■   **Citrix** This vendor requires a connection license for Web clients connecting to Citrix MetaFrame XP servers. All ICA connections to a Citrix MetaFrame

XP server require a connection license, regardless of how they connect to the Citrix MetaFrame XP servers.

NOTE

An anonymous user is any user connected to the Internet who is not employed by your organization or does not otherwise provide you with any type of goods or services.

Hardware and Software Requirements

Now that we have licensing figured out, we need to shift our attention a bit and focus on making sure our clients are ready to run the software necessary to access those licensed sessions on the MetaFrame XP servers.

Clients have two ways of accessing the servers: either by using Microsoft's RDP, which lacks most of the robust functions and features of ICA, or by using Citrix's ICA protocol, taking full advantage of all the rich and powerful features it offers. The following sections discuss each protocol and its advantages and features; the discussion will help you make a better decision regarding the one you choose to use in your organization.

RDP Clients

Remote Desktop Protocol (RDP) is Microsoft's version of a client protocol that supports and runs only over TCP/IP. RDP is organized at the Presentation layer of the OSI model and controls the transmission and flow of information between the client and the terminal servers. At present, RDP supports only Microsoft Windows-based operating systems. RDP was introduced with Windows NT 4.0 Terminal Server and was known as RDP 4.0. Windows 2000 Terminal Services introduced RDP 5.0, an upgrade to RDP 4.0 with more functionality and new dynamic features.

Let's start our discussion by reviewing the features of RDP 4.0. Then we'll examine the new features available with RDP 5.0.

RDP 4.0 Features

RDP 4.0 first shipped with the Windows NT 4.0 Terminal Server Edition and had a minimal set of features—just enough to run a remote desktop for clients. The following are the most important features RDP 4.0 had to offer:

- **Mouse/keyboard data transmission** Mouse movements and keyboard strokes that the client inputs also need to be transmitted to the server for processing. RDP encodes the movements and strokes and sends them to Terminal Services where they are decoded and processed. After processing, Terminal Services sends an update to the client screen to reflect the actions that were processed.

- **Graphical data transmission** All graphical information needs to be transmitted to the client desktop through a special RDP display driver. Sessions are constructed this way: Every session contains its own Win32 kernel and its separate display driver and has a reserved address in virtual memory. The GDI sends commands to the RDP display driver, which in turn passes them to the Terminal Services device driver for encoding. After encoding, the Terminal Services device driver delivers the data to the transport protocol, which is TCP/IP in this case, for routing and delivery to the client. The client receives the data packets, decodes them, and refreshes the display screen.

- **RDP encryption** The three encryption levels available with RDP are:

    - **Low security** Encryption runs in one direction only, from the client to the server. RDP 5.0 uses 56-bit encryption; RDP 4.0 uses 40-bit encryption.

    - **Medium security** Encryption runs in both directions between the client and the server. Again, depending on the client used, data will either be encrypted at 56 bits (with RDP 5.0) or at 40 bits (with RDP 4.0).

    - **High security** Encryption runs in both directions between the client and the server at 128 bits. It is important to note that 128-bit encryption is available only to users in the United States and Canada.

RDP 5.0 New Features

RDP 5.0, an upgrade of RDP 4.0, has greatly improved RDP in terms of features and has made the user's Terminal Server session much interesting and productive. Here we discuss the many new features that RDP 5.0 offers:

- **Local/remote Clipboard integration** This is one of the great new additions that comes in handy when you're working between your local computer and through a session. This feature allows you to copy and paste information between a locally launched application on your computer and a remote session on a terminal server. For example, if you are browsing the Internet on your local computer and want to run a search on a document open on the terminal server, you can copy the information needed and paste it in the search engine on the remote session.

- **Client printer mapping** With this feature, any locally installed printer that has a matching supported driver installed on the terminal server is automatically mapped and available for your use throughout your session.

- **Session remote control** With this great troubleshooting feature, you no longer have to sit there and guess what the user is trying to tell you. All you do is remotely control the user's session and troubleshoot the problem—or better yet, interact with the user to show them how things are done and what they are doing wrong.

- **Persistent bitmap caching** This useful feature stores persistent or frequently used bitmaps on the local hard drive for faster processing. The bitmaps that are stored locally do not have to be retransmitted, thus improving response time and saving bandwidth.

RDP Hardware Requirements and Recommendations

Table 6.2 illustrates the minimum hardware requirements for each RDP-supported operating system. The table also provides hardware recommendations for every operating system. As you know, one of the main reasons for deploying and using Terminal Services is that the entire load and processing are done on the server side. In other words, if you have enough hardware requirements to run the OS, you should be okay. However, we provide recommendations that we think will improve performance.

Table 6.2 Hardware Requirements and Recommendations

Client Operating System	Hardware Requirements			Hardware Recommendations		
	HDD Space	RAM	CPU	HDD Space	CPU	RAM
Windows 2000 Professional	10MB	32MB	Pentium	20MB	Pentium	64MB
Windows NT 3.51, 4.0 Workstation	4MB	16MB	Pentium	20MB	Pentium	32MB
Windows 95	4MB	16MB	486/33	20MB	Pentium	32MB
Windows 98	4MB	16MB	486/66	20MB	Pentium	32MB
Windows ME	4MB	16MB	Pentium	20MB	Pentium	32MB
Windows for Workgroups 3.11	4MB	16MB	386	20MB	Pentium	32MB

Operating systems that support RDP include the following:

- Windows 2000
- Windows NT 3.51 and 4.0
- Windows 95, 98, and ME
- Windows for Workgroups 3.11
- Windows CE

ICA Clients

ICA clients contain an excellent set of features and functionality. ICA clients are far superior to RDP in terms of functionality and compatibility with other operating systems. Table 6.3 explains the features that ICA offers as they work with each operating system. Here is a list of features that can be found in ICA:

- Local/remote Clipboard integration
- Client device mapping
- Seamless windows
- Session shadowing
- Program Neighborhood
- Application Launching and Embedding (ALE)
- Persistent bitmap caching

Local/Remote Clipboard Integration

The integration of the local and remote Clipboard allows you to copy and paste information between the local computer and your remote session. The operation works exactly as though you were copying and pasting information between applications on the local computer.

Client Device Mapping

Printers, COM ports, and client drives can be mapped in the ICA session. The operation grants the user access to local drives, local printers, and local COM ports on his or her machine through the ICA session. This provides an easy way to exchange files and folders between the remote session and the local computer. Printer remapping also allows the user to print to a local printer so long as the printer driver is installed on the server.

Table 6.3 Program Neighborhood Features Available with Various OSs

	Windows 95, 98, ME, NT, 2000	Windows for Workgroups 3.11	Windows CE	DOS	Mac	Linux	UNIX	Java	Web
Program Neighborhood	✓							✓	✓
Published applications	✓	✓	✓	✓	✓	✓	✓	✓	✓
Seamless windows	✓								
Client device mapping	✓	✓	✓	✓	✓	✓	✓	✓	✓
Audio support	✓	✓	✓	✓	✓	✓	✓		
Encryption	✓	✓	✓	✓	✓	✓	✓	✓	✓
Client auto update	✓	✓	✓	✓	✓	✓	✓		
Clipboard integration	✓	✓	✓	✓	✓	✓	✓		✓
Video	✓								
TAPI modems	✓			✓					
Asynchronous ICA dialup connections	✓	✓	✓		✓	✓	✓		
Business recovery	✓	✓	✓		✓	✓	✓		

Here's an example of how you can map a client's C: drive:

- Open a command prompt and type **net use X: \\client\c$**.

- Alternatively, you can use the **Map Network Drive** option, accessible from the Tools menu in Windows Explorer, or if you are using Windows 2000, right-click either **My Computer** or **My Network Places**, as shown in Figure 6.7.

Figure 6.7 Map Network Drive

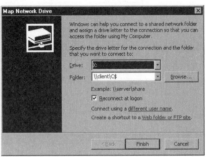

Seamless Window

Seamless window launches applications in a window, just as any other local application would. The purpose is to make the experience as transparent to the user as possible. Links to the application can even be placed on the Start menu; a user can click the link and launch a published application as though it were running locally. The window can be resized, moved around, and closed as a normal locally installed application.

When publishing an application in the CMC, you are presented with two options: You can either publish a desktop or publish an application. If you choose to publish an application, simply configure it to launch without a desktop. If you choose to publish the desktop, you need to launch the application from within that desktop.

You can configure your ICA clients to launch the application in either seamless mode or in remote application mode. When you choose to launch an application in seamless mode, it launches as though it were a locally installed application. See Figure 6.8.

If you choose remote application mode as the application-launching method, it will launch with a desktop behind it; basically, it will be running in a different window, as shown in Figure 6.9.

Figure 6.8 Application Launched in Seamless Mode

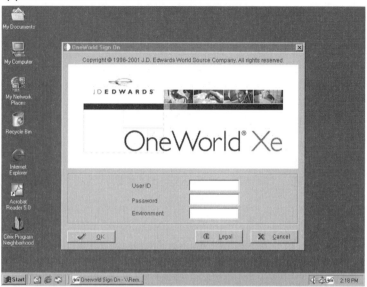

Figure 6.9 Application Launched in Remote Application Mode

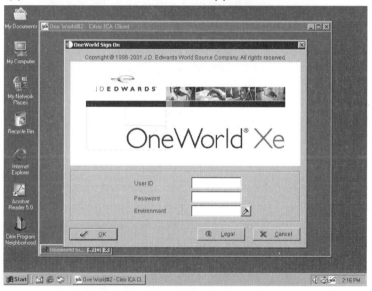

To configure your 32-bit client to launch either a seamless session or a remote desktop session, follow these steps:

1. On the client workstation, double-click **Citrix Program Neighborhood**, which is usually located on your desktop. If the icon has been deleted from

your desktop, the default location in which Setup stores the executable for this file is **%sysmroot%\Program Files\Citrix\ICA Client\pn.exe**.

2. Double-click **Add ICA Connection**.

3. Select the type of connection you will use to access this application.

4. The next screen prompts you to enter a description in the first field. The second field is the transport protocol that will be used to communicate with the Citrix server.

5. In the third field you can select between Server and Published Application. Choose **Published Application** and select the application from the drop-down menu. Then click **Next**. See Figure 6.10.

Figure 6.10 Choosing Between Connecting to a Server or to a Published Application

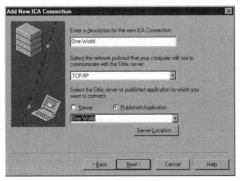

6. This screen prompts you to select how you want to launch your application. Again, your options are either to view it in a seamless window or to view it in a remote desktop window. See Figure 6.11.

Figure 6.11 Choosing Between a Seamless Window and a Remote Desktop Window

7. Follow the wizard until the custom connection is created.

8. After the custom connection is created, double-clicking the name of the connection launches the application in the mode you selected during the Custom ICA Connection creation process.

Session Shadowing

Shadowing is one of the most interesting functions available with the ICA client. Shadowing with ICA is superior to RDP 5.0 in terms of function. Sessions can be shadowed across various servers. The console cannot be shadowed, but you can shadow from the console. For shadowing to complete successfully, your video mode should be the same as or higher than the session you are attempting to shadow. Shadowing is discussed in greater detail in Chapter 7.

Program Neighborhood

Citrix Program Neighborhood allows client PCs to access Citrix MetaFrame servers over the network and connect to application sets. A user makes a connection and is prompted to enter his or her credentials. The credentials are authenticated and, based on the credentials, the user is presented with published applications that he or she can launch and use. Program Neighborhood can be used with Win32 clients or Java clients or through NFuse. Table 6.3 outlines the features available with the various operating systems.

Application Launching and Embedding

ALE is a Citrix technology that allows you to launch an application from a Web browser. The application is launched in a separate window that becomes independent of the Web page that was used to launch it. ALE also allows you to embed the application inside a Web page in a rectangular box, making the application part of the Web browser. In this case, closing the browser closes the application.

Persistent Bitmap Caching

Citrix is always looking for ways to improve the performance of the ICA client over slow communications links such as a dialup connection. Persistent bitmap caching is a feature geared towards improving session performance by storing frequently used bitmaps locally on the client's hard drive, thereby eliminating the need for retransmission with every session.

Bitmap caching works by storing frequently used graphics that the terminal session needs on disk. Therefore, the next time you log in, the server won't need to resend these bitmaps. When connecting the second time, the client basically sends the server a notification that bitmaps are locally stored and there is no need to retransmit them.

As we mentioned earlier, ICA gives you more configuration ability when it comes to bitmap caching, as shown in Figure 6.12. To configure bitmap caching, open **Citrix Program Neighborhood** and click **Tools | ICA Settings**. You can configure the following:

- **Bitmap cache size** The cache size you will allow to be reserved for storing bitmaps on your disk.

- **Bitmap cache directory** The folder or directory location where the cache should be saved to on the client disk.

- **Minimum bitmap size to cache** This option tells the system to cache bitmaps of size 8KB (the default) and larger, which means you can control the size at which the bitmaps can start being stored. You can specify a value between 2KB and 64KB. So if you set this option to 64KB, the system will not cache any bitmaps that are less than 64KB.

Figure 6.12 ICA Bitmap Cache Settings

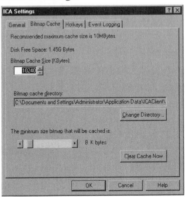

ICA Hardware Requirements and Recommendations

Table 6.4 provides the hardware requirements and recommendations for the Windows operating systems on the Intel platform. We will go into more detail about the other operating systems and platforms in the section, "ICA-Supported Operating Systems."

Table 6.4 Hardware Requirements and Recommendations on the Intel Platform

	Hardware Requirements			Hardware Recommendations		
Client Operating System	HDD Space	RAM	CPU	HDD Space	CPU	RAM
Windows 2000 Professional	10MB	32MB	Pentium	20MB	Pentium	64MB

Continued

Table 6.4 Continued

Client Operating System	Hardware Requirements			Hardware Recommendations		
	HDD Space	RAM	CPU	HDD Space	CPU	RAM
Windows NT 3.51, 4.0 Workstation	4MB	16MB	Pentium	20MB	Pentium	32MB
Windows 95	4MB	16MB	486/33	20MB	Pentium	32MB
Windows 98	4MB	16MB	486/66	20MB	Pentium	32MB
Windows ME	4MB	16MB	Pentium	20MB	Pentium	32MB
Windows for Workgroups 3.11	4MB	16MB	386	20MB	Pentium	32MB

ICA-Supported Operating Systems

ICA truly surpasses RDP in this field by providing support for a wider variety of OSs. ICA has far more clients than RDP and can be installed on OSs such as Linux, Macintosh, and more. This means that clients of these operating systems are able to access Citrix MetaFrame XP servers, whereas RDP users can only be Windows clients. If an IT shop were to choose whether to use a Terminal Services server or Citrix MetaFrame, the biggest decision-making factor would have to be what its client base looks like. If the shop had a mixed environment, there is no guessing—ICA is the product of choice, together with MetaFrame on the server side, of course.

Another reason that you might choose ICA over RDP is that ICA has far more features than RDP, one of which is ICA's ability to dial directly into a MetaFrame XP server—something that is not available with a Terminal Services server. Here are other factors to consider:

- **Windows clients** Check Table 6.4 for all hardware and software requirements and recommendations.

- **DOS** Citrix supports DOS and plans to continue developing new clients and adding more functionality into it. We recommend:

  - DOS version 4.0 or better

  - A 386 processor or better

  - As much conventional memory as you can afford

- **Windows CE** Citrix provides a client for CE, but as you know, the size of the screen makes the experience a little hard to bear. Here are some requirements (note that running the client depends on the device type you are using):

- Device must support 16 colors or more

- Device must have a network card or dialup capabilities with PPP enabled

- Device must be capable of using TCP/IP

- **Macintosh**   The minimum requirements for a Mac system are:

  - A Motorola 68030, 68040, or PowerPC

  - System 7.1 or later

  - A 16 or 256-color display

  - TCP/IP

  - A NIC for network connections to Citrix servers or dialup with PPP software enabled for asynchronous connections

- **UNIX**   SunOS 4.1.4, 5.5.1, or higher; Solaris 1.0, 2.5.1, or higher; DEC HP/UX 10.20 or higher; IBM AIX 4.1.4 or higher; SGI IRIX 6.3 or higher; SCO OpenServer 5, UnixWare 2.1 or 7, Compaq Tru64 or higher.

- **Linux**   Red Hat 5.0 or higher, SuSe 5.3 or higher, Slackware 3.5 or higher, Caldera 1.3 or higher.

- **Web client**   Web clients are offered to enable users to launch applications from within Web browsers. You can use:

  - Internet Explorer 4.0 or higher (ALE ActiveX required)

  - Netscape Navigator 4.01 or higher (ALE Java plugin required)

  - Java applets

Installing RDP Clients

RDP client installation can be done in several ways: either by creating setup diskettes and using them to install the software or by creating a network share, dumping all the required setup files there and running the Setup program. Another way of doing this might be by using a script to deploy RDP as a package or via Group Policy, if you are using Microsoft Active Directory. This section covers manual installation of the 32-bit, 16-bit, and Windows CE clients.

Installation for 32-Bit Windows

Before we can install Windows 32-bit clients, we have to create the setup diskettes. We can do this through a utility in Administrative Tools called the Terminal Services Client Creator. To create Windows 32-bit setup diskettes, follow these steps:

1. Click **Start | Programs | Administrative Tools | Terminal Services Client Creator**.

2. A window pops up, prompting you to select between creating a Windows 16-bit disk or a 32-bit client disk, as shown in Figure 6.13.

   Figure 6.13 The Create Installation Disks Window

3. You will be prompted to install a diskette (referred to as a *floppy*), as shown in Figure 6.14.

   Figure 6.14 The Insert Floppy Prompt

4. During the creation of the diskettes, you will see the copy status window shown in Figure 6.15.

   Figure 6.15 The Copy Status Window

   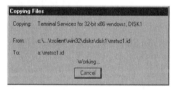

5. After the disk creation process is complete, a screen should pop up, telling you that installation was successful. (See Figure 6.16.)

   Figure 6.16 The Window Informing You That the Operation Was Successful

   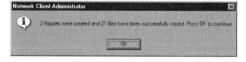

After creating the diskettes, you need to install the software. Follow these steps to do so:

1. Double-click **setup.exe**, located on Disk 1 of the diskettes you just created.

2. You will be presented with the Welcome screen, where you should click **Continue**.

3. Next you will be prompted to enter your name and organization.

4. Then you are presented with the license agreement, which you should accept. (See Figure 6.17.)

Figure 6.17 The License Agreement Window

5. Click the **Setup** button for the installation to start. You can change the folder in which the software will be installed.

6. A window pops up, asking you if you would like this software to be available for all users of this computer or just the user that is currently logged in. Click **Yes** if you want it installed for all users or **No** if you want it installed for only the user currently logged in.

7. Click **OK** to complete the installation.

Installation for 16-Bit Windows

The steps to create 16-bit Windows diskettes are very similar to those we just covered. The only difference is that when you launch the Terminal Services Client Creator, you must select the first option, which is to create a Terminal Services diskette for 16-bit Windows. This operation requires four diskettes instead of two. The remainder of the steps are the same as in the 32-bit Windows creation and installation process outlined in the preceding section.

Installation for Windows CE

The process of installing the Windows CE client is a little different than the previous two processes we covered. The client installation program is not available on the server or through the Terminal Services Client Creator. To get the client installation software, you must download it from Microsoft at the following URL: www.microsoft.com/mobile/downloads/ts.asp. This is a self-extracting file, so all you have to do is double-click the file icon to start the installation. Follow the wizard to install the client.

Installing ICA Clients

A client is available for each of the following operating systems: DOS, 16-bit Windows, 32-bit Windows, Windows CE, Apple Macintosh, OS/2, and UNIX/Linux. The setup files for these clients are available on the ICA Client CD or can be downloaded directly from Citrix at www.citrix.com/download. This section covers details on how to install each client on the various operating systems.

Citrix provides a utility that will create ICA client disks for the following operating systems: DOS and Windows 95, 98, NT, and 3.*x*, as shown in Figure 6.15. To use this utility, go to **Start | Programs | Citrix | MetaFrame XP | ICA Client Creator**. A window like the one shown in Figure 6.18 pops up. Select the operating system for which you want to create installation disks, and follow the wizard.

Figure 6.18 The Citrix ICA Client Creator

Installation for DOS

Citrix still supports DOS and currently offers two versions of the client: a 16-bit version and a 32-bit version. The 16-bit version will no longer be supported or upgraded with any new features, however. Earlier in this chapter, we went over the hardware require-ments for each version of the client; here we review through the installation process:

1. Obtain a copy a of the installation files by going to the Citrix download site or, if you have the ICA Clients CD, you can find the DOS client on it.

2. If you download the file, you need to extract it into a temp directory, then locate the **install.exe** file and run it. If you have the CD, browse to the **\icainst\en\icados32\disks\disk1** directory and run **install.exe** to start the installation process.

3. Installation begins and is very straightforward; simply follow the instructions.

Installation for 16-Bit Windows

Obtain the installation files for this operating system from either the ICA Clients CD or the Citrix download Web site. To install, follow these instructions:

1. If you are installing from CD, browse to the following directory: **\icainst\en\ica16\disks\disk1**. Double-click the **setup.exe** program, which launches the

installation. Follow the wizard, which guides you through the whole process. If you download the client from Citrix, go to Step 2 for more information.

2. Download the file into a temp directory—let's assume it will be **c:\temp**.

3. Either double-click the file or type **filename.exe –d** to extract its contents into the working directory you are in—in this case, **c:\temp**.

4. The extraction usually creates one or more directories that are called disk1, disk2, and so on. Now you have one or more directories in your c:\temp directory.

5. Go into **disk1** and locate the setup.exe file. Run it by typing **setup.exe**.

6. Follow the wizard until setup finishes.

NOTE

The extraction creates two to four directories under the c:\temp directory. If you are using 16-bit Windows, it creates four directories, called disk1, disk2, disk3, and disk4. We recommend that you copy the contents of these directories onto disks so that they can be used on other client machines. To accomplish this task, place a blank formatted diskette in drive A:, then open a command prompt, and type **copy c:\temp\disk1*.* a:**, which will copy the contents of disk1 to the diskette. Do this for all the other disks by simply reissuing the same command and replacing the *1* in *disk1* to match the number of the next directory being copied.

Installation for 32-Bit Windows

The installation files need to be obtained from the Citrix Web site or the ICA Clients CD. If you are using the ICA Client CD, the files are located in **\icainst\en\ica32\disks\disk1**; however, we recommend that you download the latest version from the Citrix Web site. To install the client, follow these steps:

1. If you are installing from CD, find the **setup.exe** file, located in **\icainst\en\ica32\disks\disk1**, and double-click it. Go to Step 4 to continue. If you created setup diskettes, continue to Step 2; if you downloaded the file, go to Step 3.

2. If you created the setup disks using the Citrix Client Creator, insert **disk1** and double-click **setup.exe**.

3. If you downloaded the file, double-click the **ica32.exe** file you downloaded to start the Setup program.

4. Setup begins. The first screen is the Welcome screen. Click **Next**.

5. The next screen is the license agreement screen; read it and then click **Yes**.

6. The next screen prompts you for the location at which the installation files will be created. Accept the default by clicking **Next**.

7. The next screen prompts you for the unique machine name that will be stored in the WFCNAME.INI. Accept the default and click **Next**.

8. The next screen asks you if you want to use the local username and password. Accept the default setting, which is No, and click **Next**. The installation files are copied.

9. When the files are installed, a window pops up to inform you of that fact. Click **OK** to finish setup.

Installation of Windows CE

Windows CE follows the same process in terms of obtaining the installation files. You should go to the Citrix Web site and download the latest files for the Windows CE device to which you are installing. Windows CE has two methods of installation: local installation (the installation program is run from the Windows CE device) or PC installation (the Setup program is run from the PC while the Windows CE device is properly hooked up and communicating with the PC).

To install using the local installation, follow these steps:

1. Copy the **icasetup.*processortype*.cab** file to your Windows CE device.

2. From within the Windows CE device, double-click the downloaded file. You will be prompted to specify a directory where files will be installed.

3. Next, a license agreement window pops up. Click **Accept** to continue with setup.

To use the PC method for installation, follow these steps:

1. Make sure that your Windows CE device is properly connected and able to communicate with your PC.

2. Double-click the ***processortype*icasetup.exe** file and follow the instructions that appear.

3. Setup downloads the necessary files to the Windows CE device.

Installation for Macintosh

As with the other clients, the installation files can either be downloaded from www.citrix.com/download or obtained from the ICA Clients CD. The Macintosh installation is a very straightforward one, as you see from the following steps:

1. To install from CD, browse on your CD to the directory **\icainst\en\ icamac**. If you are downloading from the Citrix Web site, go to Step 3.

2. Copy the file **Macica_sea.hqx** to a temporary drive on your hard drive.

3. Decompress the file with the appropriate utility.

4. Open the **Citrix ICA Client** folder created by the decompression.

5. Double-click the **Installer** icon to start the installation process.

6. Follow the wizard. The installation process is very straightforward.

Installation for OS/2

The OS/2 client needs to be downloaded from the Citrix download site. Follow these steps for more details:

1. Download the **ICAOS2.EXE** self-extracting executable into a temp directory such as **c:\temp**.

2. Open a command prompt and switch to the directory on which you saved the self-extracting download. In our case, we would type **c:\> cd temp**.

3. Type the filename **icaos2.exe** to run it. This extracts all the files in the working directory, which in this case is **c:\temp**.

4. Run the **install.exe** file that was just extracted.

5. Installation will prompt you to select the software you want to install. Select what you want to install and click **Install**.

6. Follow the prompts until the installation completes.

Installation for UNIX/Linux

Download the appropriate software for the flavor of UNIX or Linux you are using and follow these steps:

1. Log on as **root**.

2. Open a **command prompt** window.

3. If you are installing from CD, browse the CD to the **ICAinst/IcaUNIX** directory and select the flavor of the operating system you are using. If you have downloaded the client, you need to "untar" it into a temporary directory.

4. Start the Setup program by typing **./setupwfc** and press **Enter**.

5. A menu appears. Select the **1** option.

6. The installation begins. The first prompt you see is the installation asking you where to install the files. Press **Enter** to install in the default location.

7. Type **y** and press **Enter** to proceed.

8. The license agreement is displayed, and you are prompted to proceed. Type **y** and press **Enter** to continue.

9. After installation completes, the Main menu is displayed again. Select option **3** to exit.

Using Server Auto-Location

Server Auto-Location is a very useful feature that should be enabled by default on the ICA client. For clients to find a Citrix server or published applications on Citrix servers, they need to contact the nearest MetaFrame XP server. This can be done in two ways. The first method is to use Server Auto-Location, which instructs the ICA client to broadcast a packet requesting the IP address of the nearest Citrix server (see Figure 6.19). The first Citrix server that responds is queried for a server list or published applications.

Figure 6.19 ICA Client with Server Auto-Location

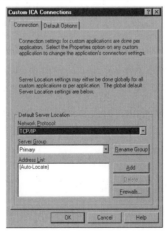

Even though Server Auto-Location is a cool function, it can increase network traffic due to the necessary repeated ICA client broadcasts. To avoid ICA client broadcasts, you should use the TCP/IP + HTTP option for network protocol. The

TCP/IP + HTTP option attempts to resolve the hostname *ica* to a MetaFrame XP server in order to locate it. TCP/IP + HTTP is recommended because it does not increase network traffic at all.

Configuring & Implementing...

DNS Round Robin with ICA Clients

In order to use TCP/IP + HTTP to auto-locate a MetaFrame XP server and avoid any increase in network traffic, DNS should be properly configured. TCP/IP + HTTP relies heavily on DNS, so the proper configuration of DNS is an important step in making this function work. As we mentioned earlier, TCP/IP + HTTP works by attempting to resolve the *ica* hostname to a MetaFrame XP server in order to locate it. The best method to do this is to configure the DNS server with multiple entries for the hostname *ica*; because it associates the *ica* hostname with more than one IP address, this method is called *round robin*.

For example, say that you have three MetaFrame XP servers in your farm; these servers have the following IP addresses: 22.1.1.4, 22.1.1.5, and 22.1.1.6. Assume that your domain name is mydomain.com. You would like ICA clients to be able to auto-locate a MetaFrame XP server. To accomplish this goal, you must add the following to your DNS server:

    ica.mydomain.com IN A 22.1.1.4

    ica.mydomain.com IN A 22.1.1.5

    ica.mydomain.com IN A 22.1.1.6

After you add this information to your DNS server, the Auto-Locate feature in the ICA client is able to locate any of these three servers when it uses TCP/IP + HTTP. Make sure that the MetaFrame XP servers that will be responding to the ICA client auto-locate requests are running the XML service. In this scenario, the three servers are running the XML service.

In the second option, you manually enter the Citrix server's IP addresses in the address list box, as shown in Figure 6.20. The ICA clients can directly query the specified servers for servers or published applications lists. The ICA client will first try to contact each server listed in the Primary group. If no response is returned, requests are then sent to each server listed in the Backup 1 group. If again there is no response, requests are then sent to each server listed in the Backup 2 group. Once a MetaFrame XP server is contacted, a list of all Citrix servers and published applications is provided.

Figure 6.20 Citrix Servers Address Is Manually Entered

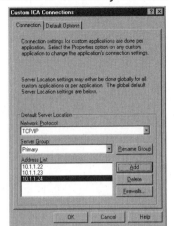

Automating Installation

The most basic and easy way to install the client is manual installation; however, when you are faced with an extraordinary number of clients to deploy (say 1000), manual installation becomes an impossible option. Automation is a great way to handle large client deployments. It might be difficult to configure at first, but once it's up and running, the deployment task becomes a slam-dunk process. Automation can be done in different ways, from using Group Policy's functionality to scripts that will automate installation or deployment servers such as Microsoft SMS.

Deciding When to Automate Installation

The decision to automate installation depends on several different factors relating to your organization. The most important factor that will force you to decide to automate is the *number of client devices* to which you need to deploy the software. If you have a large number, there is no escaping automation. The second factor that might play a role in decision making is the *cost* to automate the installation process. For example, if you are thinking about using Group Policy as your means for deploying applications, you must understand that all the client operating systems need to be either Windows 2000 Professional or Windows XP Professional. Group Policy will work nicely in an environment in which all the client operating systems support and can interact with it; otherwise, it is useless. Deployment servers are another option, but deployment servers cost a great deal of money, and you have to be able to justify their cost, not only for the existing project but for future use. Scripts might also work, but you must be able to write a script that will be able to detect the client operating system before you can deploy the software.

Creating an Automated Client Installation Package

To create a package that is customized with your settings and is ready to be automatically deployed, you have to compile into an MSI package. MSI packages are supported by Group Policy, Citrix's Installation Manager, and deployment server software such as Microsoft Systems Management Server (SMS). To create an MSI package, you can use either Veritas Winstall LE, which ships with Windows 2000 Server, or the package that comes with Citrix's Installation Manager 2.0. The computer on which you intend to create the package must be a clean system with the desired application not installed on it.

To create a package using Veritas Winstall LE, follow these steps:

1. Explore the **Windows 2000 Server CD**. Go into the **VALUADD\ 3RDPARTY\MGMT\WINSTLE** folder.

2. Double-click the **SWIADMLE.MSI** file.

3. The Installation Wizard begins and walks you through the installation.

4. A program group is created under **Start | Programs | Veritas Software**.

5. Take a snapshot of the system prior to the installation of the desired application by going to **Start | Programs | Veritas Software** and click **Veritas Discover**.

6. A wizard is launched and a Welcome screen appears. Click **Next**.

7. Enter a name for the package you are about to compile—for example, **ICAWIN95**.

8. Select a clean directory to which the MSI package should be saved (see Figure 6.21).

Figure 6.21 Package Name and Path

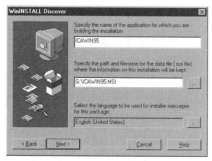

9. Select a drive for the temp files and click **Next**.

10. Select the drive or drives that the Discover program should scan for changes to the system after the application is installed. (See Figure 6.22.)

Figure 6.22 Drives to Scan for Changes the Application Made to the System

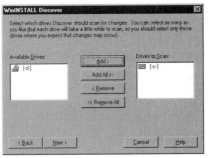

11. The Discover program then starts.

12. Once the program has finished running, a message is displayed, notifying you that the "before" snapshot has been taken. (See Figure 6.23.)

Figure 6.23 The "Before" Snapshot

13. You will be prompted for the setup file of the application from which you intend to make an MSI package. Select the file and click **Open**.

14. The application will install. When it is done, you can open the application and make all the modifications and settings changes you need in order for them to be reflected in the package you are about to create. Make all the changes you need, and when you are ready, close the application.

15. You are now ready to create the "after" snapshot. Click **Start | Programs | Veritas Software** and then click **Veritas Discover**. A window opens, asking you whether you want to take the "after" snapshot or abandon the "before" snapshot. (See Figure 6.24.)

Figure 6.24 The Perform "After" Snapshot Prompt

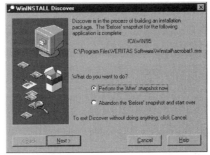

16. Select **Perform the "After" snapshot now** and click **Next**. The check will begin.

17. When the snapshot is done, you will receive a window saying the "after" snapshot is completed and the package has been created. (See Figure 6.25.)

Figure 6.25 The "After" Snapshot Is Completed

Deploying the Package to Multiple Clients

Deploying the package to multiple clients can be done in numerous ways; the right one for you depends on the size of your environment, its diversity, and most important, the method you feel most comfortable utilizing.

Deployment can be done using diskettes and your two feet walking around from client to client and installing the package—or it can be done using a network share, where you would *still* have to walk around but without diskettes. Instead, you would map a drive to the share and install the software. Login scripts are a good method of deploying packages, but they have their disadvantages, as we discuss later in this section. Group Policy is great, unless the clients are not Windows 2000 or XP. Deployment servers remain the ideal method of deployment for large organizations that can justify their cost and put them to good use.

Diskettes

Using diskettes to deploy a package remains an alternative as long as the package is not very big and requires no more than two to four disks. Keep in mind that you will most likely have more than one package to deploy, depending on how many operating systems you are deploying to. Copying the package to diskettes and manually walking around to deploy the package still works well for smaller IT environments.

Scripts

You can use login scripts to automate the installation of client software. Login scripts are processed by any client and can easily be configured to install as soon as the user logs in to the server. However, login scripts get ugly when you have diversified clients in your environment. For example, if you have Windows 32-bit clients and 16-bit clients, you must be able to write the script in a way that detects the kind of operating system used.

Let's take a look at examples of how you can deploy an RDP client and an ICA Win32 client using a login script. For the RDP client:

1. RDP gives you the option to export all the configured connections to a .cns file that can be included in the installation process. During installation, the Setup program checks to see if a CNS file exists, and if it does, it uses the file to populate the installation with the custom connections it retrieves from the file. When this file is included in the installation, the clients not only get the software but also preconfigured connections. To accomplish this goal, follow these steps: Open the **Client Connection Manager**, which can be accessed on any workstation that has Terminal Services Client by going to the **Start | Programs | Terminal Services Client** program group and clicking **Client Connection Manager**.

2. Configure all the connections to the servers that you want users to have.

3. On the File menu, click **File | Export All**.

4. A window pops up, prompting you to enter a filename. Type, for example, **ts.cns** and click **Save**.

5. On a terminal server, create a share directory—for example, **Clients**. Copy to this directory all the clients that will be used in the script. Let's assume we want to install an RDP Win32 client. You would create a directory under the Clients directory called RDPWIN32 and copy all the contents of the RDP Win32 software into it.

6. Copy the file **ts.cns** to the RDPWIN32 directory.

7. Edit your login script to include the following line: **\\servername\clients\ rdpwin32\setup.exe /qt**, where **/qt** tells the script to install in quiet mode with no user interaction at all. The user will not even know the installation is taking place.

For the ICA client:

1. To customize an ICA Win32 client and prepare it for deployment, you must first install the client on a test computer. Configure all the settings and ICA connections you want all your users to have. All the configurations and changes you make are saved in these files: WFCLIENT.INI, MODULE.INI, PN.INI, and APPSRV.INI. The location of these files varies depending on the OS you use and the client you are installing, so we recommend that you run a search on them. To use a login script to deploy Win32 ICA clients, follow these steps: Create a directory called **ICAWIN32** under the Clients directory that we created and shared earlier, and copy the contents of the ICA Win32 client into that directory.

2. Copy the files **WFCLIENT.INI, MODULE.INI, PN.INI,** and **APPSRV.INI** into the ICAWIN32 directory and rename them with the

.SRC extension, replacing the files already there by default. Replacing these files ensures that when the program is installed, it will be installed with the changes you previously made.

3. Edit the login script to include the following line: **\\servername\clients\ icawin32\setup.exe /qt**.

Group Policies

Deploying packages with Group Policy is a very effective method, but one of its main disadvantages is that if the user is not on a desktop that supports Group Policy (such as Windows 2000 Professional or Windows XP Professional), the group policy will be useless. Here we demonstrate how you can deploy and install the package we created earlier in the chapter using Group Policy. The first thing you have to do is create an organizational unit (OU) and group the computers or users that will receive the package. You can use an already existing OU as well.

You can deploy this system using one of two methods: You can deploy it to either the computers in your organization or to the users in your organization. Deploying to the computers in your organization makes the application available on the computers you specify. Deploying the application to the users in your organization installs the application on any computer a user logs in to.

Here we demonstrate how to deploy the application to a select number of computers in your organization. Follow these steps:

1. Open **Active Directory Users and Computers** and right-click the **OU** to which you intend to deploy the application. Click **Properties**.

2. Select the **Group Policy** tab and either edit the policy (if one already exists) or click **New** to create a new policy. Then click **Edit**.

3. In the Group Policy Editor, expand **Computer Configuration** and expand **Software Settings**.

4. Right-click **Software Installation**. Click **New**, and click **Package**.

5. You will be prompted for the MSI package. Browse to it and click **Open**.

6. The Select Deployment Method window pops up (see Figure 6.26). The options are Published, Assigned, or Advanced Published or Assigned. Remember that Published will be installed only if the user manually elects to install it from Add/Remove Programs. The Assigned option is installed as soon as the user clicks the application link that is already in the Start menu.

7. Select the desired option and click **OK**.

8. Your package is added to the Software Installation window in Group Policy, as shown in Figure 6.27.

Figure 6.26 Choosing a Deployment Method

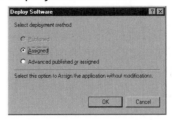

Figure 6.27 The Software Installation Window

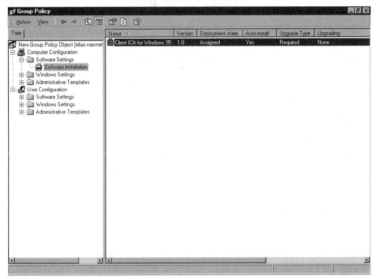

9. You can right-click your package and customize its settings, as shown in Figure 6.28.

Figure 6.28 Customizing the Software Package

Software Deployment Servers

Deployment servers are still the ideal way to deploy software, mainly due to the functionality built into them. Deployment servers such as Microsoft's SMS, for example, provide administrators with the ability to deploy software to numerous clients. Unlike Group Policy, where the clients must be Windows 2000 clients, good deployment server software should free you of this handicap.

Deployment servers also have better bandwidth throttling and load-balancing features, allowing you to phase out a deployment. Deployment server software might also have the ability to detect the type of client it is attaching to and thus deploy the right package for that client. For example, if you have Windows 95 and Windows 2000, some deployment software is able to detect the type of OS and install the appropriate package. Deployment servers might be a little expensive, but their functionality and control pay off in the end, especially if you will be using them constantly in large deployments. In large organizations, deployment servers are the only option to consider.

Summary

When planning the design of your network, you must carefully plan for licensing. Licensing can be costly and complicated, so familiarizing yourself with it can save you money and ensure that you have sufficient licensing to cover the users who intend to use your system.

Citrix MetaFrame XP servers installed on Windows 2000 servers need three main types of licenses. A Windows 2000 server license is always required for authentication purposes and in cases in which you will use file and print services. A Terminal Services license is also required, since you will be accessing a Terminal Services server, and even if you will not use RDP, you still need a TS CAL. Citrix connection licenses are also required for users who will use the ICA protocol to connect to MetaFrame XP servers. Furthermore, any applications that are installed on the Terminal Services server for the purpose of use need licensing accommodations for the users who will work with them.

A Terminal Services server can be installed in either application server mode or remote administration mode. Use application server mode when users will log in to the servers and run applications. Remote administration mode provides for two free licenses and is intended as a remote administration tool for administrators to be able to control their servers and do maintenance from a remote location.

Both RDP and ICA come with tools that allow you to create setup diskettes in order to install the protocol on different clients. Installation can be done the traditional way using diskettes, or it can be done by dumping the setup files on a network share accessible from anywhere on the network. An alternative method could be to package your client software and use automation methods such as scripts or deployment servers to push your package to the various client workstations. In shops where the desktops are Windows 2000 can take advantage of Group Policy, which has a built-in feature that pushes packages to client workstations.

ICA is a more robust and feature-rich protocol that can be installed on various operating systems, from UNIX and Linux to OS/2, DOS, Macintosh, and, of course, Windows. It can also use different transport protocols such as IPX/SPX, NetBEUI, and TCP/IP. RDP, on the other hand, can be used only with the Windows platform and can run only on TCP/IP. RDP is also not as robust or feature rich as ICA.

Solutions Fast Track

Client Licensing

☑ Windows 2000 Server CALs are required, even if you're running Terminal Services. Server CALs are necessary to authenticate users and to use file and print services.

☑ Terminal Services CALs are required for all clients, with the exception of Windows 2000 Professional and Windows XP Professional clients. These operating systems come with a free Terminal Services license.

☑ A Citrix connection license is required for all client devices using the ICA protocol to access MetaFrame XP servers.

Hardware and Software Requirements

☑ RDP is Microsoft's thin client protocol. RDP is limited to the Windows family of operating systems and supports only TCP/IP.

☑ The ICA protocol has an advantage over RDP by supporting far more operating systems and thus more clients. ICA clients are available for Linux, UNIX, Macintosh, OS/2, and, of course, Windows.

☑ The ICA protocol supports more protocols than RDP does, such as IPX/SPX and NetBEUI in addition to TCP/IP, of course.

Installing RDP clients

☑ Windows 2000 servers have an RDP client disk creation tool called Terminal Services Client Creator that is used to create the setup files for installing the RDP client.

☑ RDP clients can only be installed on Windows 16-bit and Windows 32-bit clients.

☑ The installation process is the same on Windows 16-bit clients and Windows 32-bit clients.

Installing ICA Clients

☑ You should always check the Citrix download Web site for the latest ICA Clients. You'll find this Web site at www.citrix.com/download.

☑ Installing the ICA client on Windows CE devices can be done in one of two ways: local installation or PC installation. In local installations, you initiate the setup from the Windows CE device. In PC installations, you install the Setup program on the PC while the CE device is connected to it.

☑ The ICA client can be installed on Linux in its many flavors.

Automating Installation

☑ Diskettes remain the simplest and easiest way to deal with small IT environments.

☑ Login scripts work very well; just make sure that you phase out your installation so as not to drastically increase network traffic and overflow your connection.

☑ Deployment servers such as Microsoft SMS, for example, should be used for large organizations with mixed IT environments.

Frequently Asked Questions

The following Frequently Asked Questions, answered by the authors of this book, are designed to both measure your understanding of the concepts presented in this chapter and to assist you with real-life implementation of these concepts. To have your questions about this chapter answered by the author, browse to **www.syngress.com/solutions** and click on the **"Ask the Author"** form.

Q: We have a global company and will be sharing an HR application around the world. Since half of our users will be asleep at the time the other users are working, do we still need a TS CAL for each user or only for the ones who are online and working?

A: Yes, you still need a TS CAL for every user, because licensing works this way: A license is attached to the client device, so basically every device that logs in consumes a license and hangs on to it. On the other hand, the ICA licenses can be pooled so that you can have half the number of TS CALs for Citrix. That way, when half your users are sleeping on one side of the globe, the other half can take advantage of the licenses. Citrix uses connection licenses and doesn't hang on to them, so it basically releases a license when the user logs out and puts the license back in the license pool for another user to use.

Q: Which clients support Program Neighborhood?

A: Windows 95, 98, ME, NT, and 2000, as well as Java and Web clients, are the only clients that support Program Neighborhood.

Q: I am using Terminal Services. Do I still need a server CAL?

A: Yes, you still need a server CAL for authentication to the server and for any file and print functions you use.

Q: Can I use Group Policy to deploy my client installation packages?

A: Yes, you can, but keep in mind that users of operating systems other than Windows 2000 Professional will not get their packages because Group Policy supports only Windows 2000 and Windows XP.

Q: In which areas is ICA superior to RDP 5.0?

A: ICA supports more operating systems than RDP 5.0, making it a wiser solution for organizations that have diverse environments. ICA also provides richer features and more control over settings than RDP does.

Q: Will I need a license if I am running Terminal Services in remote administration mode?

A: No. Microsoft provides a free license when Terminal Services are configured in remote administration mode. Microsoft offers this license as a service to professionals so that they can control their servers remotely.

Chapter 7

Configuring
the Server

Solutions in this chapter:

- **Configuring Sessions**
- **Configuring Users**
- **Independent Management Architecture**

- ☑ **Summary**
- ☑ **Solutions Fast Track**
- ☑ **Frequently Asked Questions**

Introduction

Implementing Citrix MetaFrame XP in a server farm configuration is a departure from conventional networking. After installation, a server requires further configuration before applications can be launched. Depending on how granular an environment needs to be, you can employ different approaches to configuration.

For Citrix MetaFrame XP, sessions must be created and configured prior to anyone using the new system. The session represents the logical connection that a client makes with the server. A user can invoke multiple sessions, each launching a separate application. Alternatively, a user can invoke a single session that launches an entire desktop. In general, it is best to create sessions with options that meet generic needs, because these sessions are usually available to any user at any time.

Users can have unique session options configured, individualizing how sessions act when users invoke them. You can manage the way printers and drives are mapped and how shadowing works for each person. Configuration is the first step toward managing the server farm.

Configuring Sessions

Part of controlling the user's visual experience and restricting what he or she can do during a session is managed from within the Citrix Connection Configuration tool. This tool also offers more advanced features, all of which we discuss in greater detail in Chapter 8. One of the features that can be enabled or disabled from the Citrix Connection Configuration utility is the ability to allow or deny a connection based on the protocol used. In general, it is recommended that you restrict your users to one protocol, such as Transmission Control Protocol/Internet Protocol (TCP/IP), for example, and reserve one or more connection types strictly for administrator connections. If your users use the Independent Computing Architecture (ICA) protocol over TCP/IP, it is good practice to have Remote Desktop Protocol (RDP) over TCP/IP restricted to administrators only; then if you want to do any maintenance tasks on your server and want to restrict any access to it, you simply disable the ICA protocol and access the server via RDP. Some administrators even install a second network interface card (NIC) in their servers that is dedicated to administrative use or for quick access to the box. Other administrators take this strategy one step further and install a modem as an alternative method of accessing the server in the event of an emergency.

Many of the tools for a "plain" Windows Terminal Server and a MetaFrame server are interchangeable, but the Terminal Services Configuration tool for Windows 2000 and the Connection Configuration tool for MetaFrame have numerous differences and are not interchangeable. We discuss only the MetaFrame version of the tool. In the upcoming sections we discuss the creation and configuration of ICA and RDP sessions using the Citrix Connection Configuration utility.

Creating RDP Sessions

The Remote Desktop Protocol, Microsoft's thin client protocol, is used to access a Windows Terminal Services server. We recommend that you install RDP connections in addition to ICA sessions so that you can dedicate the ICA protocol and all its rich features to your clients and reserve RDP connections for administrative use. Often you will find yourself in a situation in which you want to restrict users' logon to the server in order to install a patch or upgrade an application. To restrict user access, you can disable the ICA protocol and still gain access to the server via RDP. In many cases, this method saves you a trip to the server room.

To create an RDP session, follow these steps:

1. Click **Start | Programs | Citrix | MetaFrame XP | Citrix Connection Configuration**.

2. Click **Connection** and then click **New**.

3. The New RDP Connection window appears, as shown in Figure 7.1. For **Type** you want to select **Microsoft RDP 5.0** from the drop-down menu. Select the transport type you want to use from the **Transport** drop-down menu (for example, **async** for dial-in and modems, **TCP** for NIC cards). Use the tabs at the bottom of the screen to configure your protocol, then click **OK**.

Figure 7.1 New RDP Connection

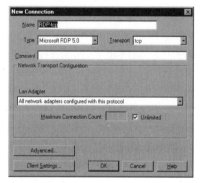

Creating the ICA Sessions

ICA sessions are used in conjunction with MetaFrame XP servers. They offer more features than RDP and greatly enhance a user's session. ICA also supports a wider variety of transport protocols such as IPX/SPX, NetBEUI, and TCP/IP, in addition to direct dial-in using the async protocol for ATAPI devices and modems. To create an ICA session, follow these steps:

1. Choose **Start | Programs | Citrix | MetaFrame XP | Citrix Connection Configuration**.

2. Click **Connection** and click **New**.

3. The New ICA Connection window appears, as shown in Figure 7.2. This time for **Type** we want to select **Citrix ICA 3.0** from the drop-down menu. Select the transport type you want to use from the **Transport** drop-down menu (for example, **async** for dial-in and modems, **TCP** for NIC cards). Use the tabs at the bottom of the screen to configure your protocol as we demonstrate later in the following section, then click **OK**.

Figure 7.2 Creating a New ICA Connection

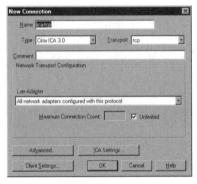

ICA Session Options

The ICA session options are the set of configurable settings that you can set for ICA sessions. The ICA session options consist of three main button categories: the Advanced button, the ICA Settings button, and the Client Settings button, as shown in Figure 7.2. Under each of these buttons lie most if not all the configuration you will ever need to create an ICA session. The Advanced button controls settings such as the session idle timeout, the autologon features, and many more. The ICA Settings button deals with options such as audio quality. Finally, the Client settings enable you to set options such as client printer mappings, drive mappings, clipboard mappings, and more. We discuss these settings in the sections that follow. To begin, follow these steps:

1. Open the Citrix Connection Configuration tool by clicking **Start | Programs | Citrix | MetaFrame XP |Citrix Connection Configuration**. This sequence opens the main configuration window shown in Figure 7.3.

2. In this window, you will see the various connection types available to clients. To modify, we can double-click the selected connection or choose **Edit** from the **Connection** pull-down menu, as shown in Figure 7.4.

Figure 7.3 The Citrix Connection Configuration Window

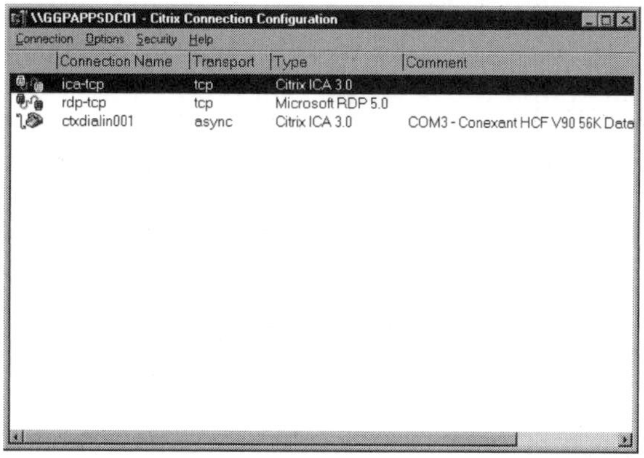

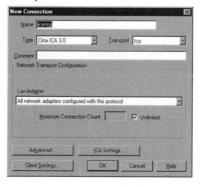

Figure 7.4 Connection Properties

In the Connection Properties window shown in Figure 7.4, the Comments field can be used to identify this connection; for example, you can specify that this connection is Users Connection or Admins Only. The Lan Adapter section allows you to specify which NIC will service this type of connection. This setting can be useful with multihomed computers—for instance, some users on an IPX-only network could connect to the MetaFrame server using IPX on one NIC, whereas other users could connect through a different NIC using TCP/IP only. Some system resources can be recovered by limiting the maximum connection count to the number of licenses you own, which could be a special benefit on small servers that are low on available resources to begin with. We will discuss the other buttons separately.

The Advanced button allows you to enable or disable logons to this connection type altogether or configure an autologon (enabling autologon is considered a high security risk and is not recommended in most environments). You also have the option of setting the timeout settings, initial program settings, shadowing, and reconnect options here or allowing these to be inherited from the client/user configuration settings. If specified here, these settings override the client's or user's settings. A recommended performance enhancement is to disable wallpaper here, which can slow performance noticeably if complex wallpapers are used.

The Advanced button is also where you must set the security requirements for your connection; it also allows you to specify the encryption level for your connection. The default level is Basic encryption, as shown in Figure 7.5. Basic-level encryption is considered weak by today's standards. Stronger encryption levels using the RC5 algorithm are available as an add-on with Citrix SecureICA. The SecureICA product provides 40-, 56-, or 128-bit RC5 encryption. If the server is configured to allow a minimum of 56-bit encryption, the client must connect with either the 56-bit or the 128-bit SecureICA product, or logon will fail. Full 56-bit and 128-bit RC5 encryption capabilities are included as standard fare with the new Feature Release 1 (FR1) server update and version 6.00.910 of the client.

Figure 7.5 Connection Tab Advanced Properties

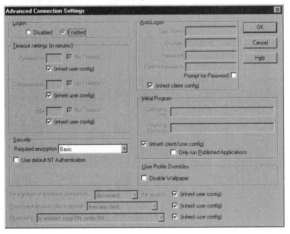

The ICA Sound Settings button (see Figure 7.6) allows you to set the sound quality for ICA connections. (Sound is not supported over RDP 4.0 or 5.0 connections but is supported in RDP 5.1, which will be available with Windows XP or .NET servers.) There are three available settings:

- **Medium** This is the default setting. All waveform data sent to the client is compressed to a maximum of 64Kbps before being transmitted to the client. This can result in a slight decrease in sound quality played on the client machine, but it reduces the CPU utilization on the host machine. This setting is recommended for most local area network (LAN)-based connections and some medium- to high-speed wide area network (WAN) connections.

- **High** This setting plays all waveform data at its native data rate. Sounds at the highest quality level require about 1.3Mbps of bandwidth. This is pretty much equal to the amount of throughput achieved by most T1 connections. You might find that using this level of sound quality impacts performance and consumes bandwidth, especially on networks in which bandwidth resources are small and valuable. We do not recommend the use of this level unless plenty of bandwidth is available and sound quality is of high importance. Don't think about using this option on a WAN connection unless you have greater than T1 bandwidth on both ends or you are going to dedicate the T1 usage exclusively for this traffic. The adage "Don't try this at home" certainly applies here, unless you keep it on your own network, where it can be useful for bandwidth monitoring, load testing, and other purposes. This setting can also increase CPU utilization—not due to the sound processing itself but due to the amount of network traffic being transmitted.

- **Low** This is the recommended setting for modem and most low-bandwidth WAN connections. All waveform data sent to the client is compressed to a maximum of 16Kbps before it is transmitted to the client. This amount of compression results in a severe decrease of the sound quality played back on the client. Applications that use short sound files will not be greatly affected; however, applications that use longer sound files will find that this level provides very poor-quality sound to the point at which not having sound at all sounds better. The lower data rate allows for low-bandwidth connections. This also reduces CPU load on the host, about the same amount as the medium setting, due to the compression used.

Figure 7.6 ICA Sound Settings

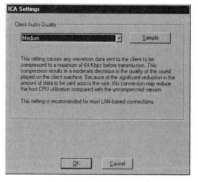

Shadowing

Shadowing one of the most interesting functions available with the ICA protocol. Shadowing with ICA is much superior in terms of function to that offered with RDP

5.0. Sessions can be shadowed across different servers. The console cannot be shadowed, but you can shadow from the console. For shadowing to complete successfully, your video mode should be the same or higher than the session you are attempting to shadow. Shadowing is discussed in greater detail in Chapter 8.

This section concentrates on how to override the settings that were specified when MetaFrame XP was installed. If you recall, during setup of the MetaFrame XP server you were given the option to select some settings for shadowing. Here we demonstrate how you can change these settings. However, one very important point that you need to keep in mind is that if during setup you explicitly selected not to allow any kind of shadowing, this setting cannot be changed unless you reinstall the MetaFrame XP server. This is done as a security measure. The settings you can change control the amount of interaction you can have with the session being shadowed.

The settings that can be modified are the following:

- **Shadowing is enabled: input ON, notify ON** This setting enables shadowing and gives the shadower input; in other words, it gives the user the ability to move stuff around within the shadowee's session and sends a message to the user being shadowed, requesting permission to shadow his or her session.

- **Shadowing is enabled: input OFF, notify ON** This setting enables shadowing and gives the shadower view-only rights to the shadowee's session. This setting also requests permission from the user before you can shadow his or her session.

- **Shadowing is disabled** This setting disables shadowing altogether.

> **NOTE**
>
> As you might have noticed in the first two options, notify is always ON; there is no option for notify OFF. Notify OFF translates to shadowing a user session without the user's permission—it would be like spying on the user. The reason you don't see notify OFF is that when you installed MetaFrame XP, you explicitly selected the option to always request permission before shadowing a user session. Had you selected the option to not notify the user prior to your shadowing a session, the options would be different—you would be given the option of notify OFF in some of these settings.

To modify these settings, you have to open the Citrix Connection Configuration and go into the properties of the protocol you want to modify. Follow these steps to modify the Shadowing settings:

1. Click **Start | Programs | Citrix | MetaFrame XP | Citrix Connection Configuration**.

2. Select the protocol you want to set shadowing permission on and click **Connection**. Then choose **Edit** from the Connection menu.

3. Click the **Advanced** button. The Advanced properties window appears.

4. In the lower-right-hand corner of that screen, **uncheck** the last **inherit user config** check box to allow yourself to modify the shadow settings. See Figure 7.7.

Figure 7.7 The Advanced Button Window Showing Shadowing Settings

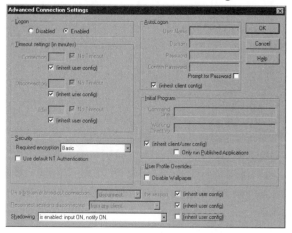

5. From the pull-down menu, select the settings you want to enable or disable and then click **OK**.

Configuring Session Parameters

Configuring session parameters includes the feature to lock down clients' ability to map their local machine clipboards with that of the server, which will result in their inability to copy and paste between their local machines and their ICA sessions. You can also disable a client's printer mappings, therefore preventing the client from printing within his or her session. The following sections discuss how these features are enabled and disabled.

Locking Down Copying and Printing Features

The Client Settings button allows you to configure client mappings to drives, printers, COM ports, LPT ports, clipboard, and audio. These settings override client settings (unless set to **inherit user config**). Logon time can be reduced significantly by disabling mappings that are not being used, especially COM port mappings, and restricting the Other Options setting to connect only the client's main printer. See Figure 7.8.

Figure 7.8 Client Settings and Mappings

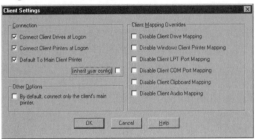

Launching the Entire Desktop or a Single Application

The Advanced button allows you to control what the session does when it is launched. In some cases you might want to be able to just force everyone to use a specific application, maybe you are offering an application in Demo mode and you only want your users to see that application when logging into the server. In other cases you could allow them to launch the desktop when logging in. A third option would be to restrict any kind of access to a particular server unless you are accessing a published application.

The initial Program section controls these parameters, leaving it at the default value of Inherit User Config will not control anything and will allow whatever method the user is using to access the server. If the user is accessing a published application the server will allow the connection. If the user is accessing the desktop of the server it will allow that as well. To configure the server so that it will force the connecting session to work in a particular application only follow these steps:

1. Click **Start | Programs | Citrix | MetaFrame XP | Citrix Connection Configuration**.

2. Double-click the **ICA protocol** and click the **Advanced** button. The Advanced properties window appears.

3. Uncheck the **[inherit client/user config]** check box.

4. In the **Command** box, enter the name of the application executable. For this example, we used **notepad.exe**, as shown in Figure 7.9.

5. In the **Working Directory**, enter the path to that executable again.

6. As soon as the user logs in to the session, Notepad is all the user will be able to work with, as shown in Figure 7.10.

Now assume that you want to enable users to work only with published applications and you don't want to allow any kind of access to the server, so if an experienced user were to create a direct ICA connection to a server in order to gain access to a desktop, he couldn't. To control such activity, check the Only Run Published Applications box in the

Initial Program section of the Advanced button in Citrix Connection Configuration for the ICA protocol. When this box is checked, the next time a user tries a direct connection to the server, he will receive an error message and will not be allowed through. See Figure 7.11 The only way he can gain access to the server is through the use of published applications, so he would have to create an ICA connection to a published application, not directly to the server.

Figure 7.9 The Initial Program Section of the Advanced Button

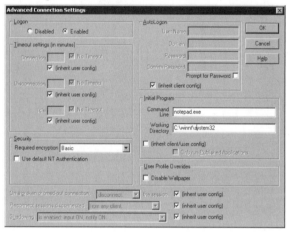

Figure 7.10 Initial Program Launched

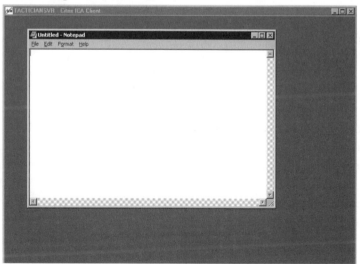

Figure 7.11 Error Message That Appears When the Allow Only Published Applications Setting Is Enabled

Configuring Users

Active Directory plays a key role in configuring and managing the user's computing experience. Many larger companies integrate MetaFrame as member servers into their Windows 2000 Active Directory and let the standard Windows 2000 domain controllers handle the Domain Name System (DNS), replication, and Dynamic Host Configuration Protocol (DHCP) functions. Although MetaFrame running on Windows 2000 will function in a UNIX DNS and DHCP environment, there are less integration effort, more compatibility, and fewer cross-platform security issues when those services are provided on dedicated Windows 2000 domain controllers. Windows 2000 DNS and DHCP servers provide new features and functionality, such as "peering" DNS servers and Dynamic DNS through DHCP, among many others that place them ahead of most similar UNIX-based services in the technology curve. Along with the increased and more granular security controls offered, which some say rival or exceed those in UNIX-based systems, it's safe to say that most shops running MetaFrame Windows products (which are in the majority) also want to use Windows 2000-based domain controllers and DNS. Shops running UNIX-based MetaFrame servers will probably want to stick to their UNIX servers for other tasks as well.

This book does not concentrate heavily on Active Directory design or configuration. Instead, we briefly touch on a few key points that are required or recommended specifically for the tasks we need to accomplish. An in-depth documentation of the *Windows 2000 Server Resource Kit Deployment Planning Guide* (www.microsoft.com/

windows2000/library/resources/reskit/dpg/default.asp) can be very useful; anyone who is serious about Windows 2000 and/or Citrix MetaFrame should have the full retail product close at hand.

> **NOTE**
>
> For more information on Active Directory, refer to other Syngress Publishing titles, including *Windows 2000 Server System Administration Handbook, Mission Critical! Windows 2000 Server Administration,* and especially *Windows 2000 Active Directory, Second Edition*.

Citrix recommends not installing your MetaFrame servers as domain controllers. If you do install a server as a domain controller, dedicate the server to that task and do not serve user applications from the same server. This recommendation is made for performance reasons. If you plan to install a client/server application such as SQL, you should install the SQL server on a separate, non-MetaFrame server and install only the client portion on your MetaFrame servers. If you want to manage your domain controllers remotely, install Terminal Services in Administration mode, which places very little extra load on the server and still allows you to reduce administrative costs by providing the ability to work off-site. MetaFrame can be integrated into your existing or new Active Directory as a member server only, without imposing the system and network performance hit that the Active Directory domain server services require. If you install MetaFrame as a member server, the Active Directory tools won't be installed by default, and you will have to create a custom Microsoft Management Console (MMC) snap-in to manage users and groups from the MetaFrame server.

The User Object property sheet is where all user-specific settings are stored. If you are logged in the console of a domain controller, you get there by clicking **Start | Programs | Administrative Tools | Active Directory Users and Computers**. Expand the Users folder in the left window, then double-click a username, or right-click and choose **Properties**. If you are on a member server or workstation, you need Domain Admin rights and have to browse to the domain controller using a custom MMC. (See the following section for instructions to create a custom MMC for user and computer management.) This is usually the first place you will start customizing what the user can see and do on your server. Citrix MetaFrame works on NT4 domains and Windows 2000 networks without domains, but integrating your server into an Active Directory domain provides a better way to manage and respond to your users' needs. For our configuration guide in this chapter, we use Active Directory Users and Computers from a MetaFrame server also configured as a domain controller. For those who will bring up MetaFrame as a member server, see the section "Using the

MMC Active Directory Users and Computers Snap-In" later in this chapter. Once you're in the Active Directory Users and Groups window, account creation and configuration options are the same.

Many new administrators have had the wits scared out of them or at least skipped a couple of heartbeats after upgrading their first domain controller to Active Directory. Usually, one of the first things you do after upgrading is go into **Computer Management | Local Users and Groups**, shown in Figure 7.12, to see what kind of new cool features you have and start adding your new user accounts, right? Well, what happens when you are greeted with the message shown in the window and you have that big ugly red *X* over your most used utility?

Figure 7.12 The Local Users and Groups Utility

Not to worry—catch your breath, all is still well. The Local Users and Groups utility is disabled after upgrading the server to a domain controller. Remember, domain controllers have no local users or groups any longer; existing accounts are converted to domain accounts.

Using the MMC Active Directory Users and Computers Snap-In

As we discussed, if you have not installed your MetaFrame server as a domain controller, you will not have the Active Directory Users and Computers added to your Programs list automatically. In order for you to manage users and groups, you will have to manually add the snap-in by creating a custom MMC. This is a simple process; once you do it a few times, you will probably find that you use the process quite frequently, since numerous administrative functions can be combined into kind of a "favorites" list of your most often used tools. To begin, follow these simple steps:

1. Click the **Start** button and choose **Run**.

2. Type **mmc** into the **Run** window. This will open a new, blank MMC console window.

3. Next, from the **Console** pull-down, choose **Add/Remove Snap-in**. This step opens an empty Add/Remove Snap-in window.

4. Next, click the **Add** button, and the "Add standalone snap-in" window shown in Figure 7.13 opens and displays the available standalone snap-ins.

Figure 7.13 Adding the Active Directory Snap-In

5. Choose **Active Directory Users and Computers**. Click **OK**.

6. You can now start configuring your Active Directory. You can save this console using a meaningful name, and it will automatically be added to your Administrative Tools program listing.

Creating Users in Active Directory Users and Computers

Now that you have completed the initial steps of creating an MMC console and added the Active Directory Users and Computers snap-in, let's get on with actually creating and configuring a user account. To begin, follow these steps:

1. Click **Start | Programs | Administrative Tools | Active Directory Users and Computers**.

2. Once the Active Directory Users and Computers opens, right-click the **Users** container in the left pane, browse down to **New**, and select **User**.

3. The New User window opens, as shown in Figure 7.14

Figure 7.14 The New User Creation Window

4. Fill in all the necessary information and click **Next**.

5. The next screen prompts you to enter a password and allows you to force the user to change the password on first logon. Click **Next**. See Figure 7.15.

Figure 7.15 The Enter Password Window

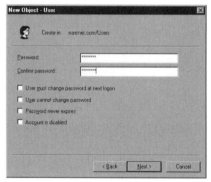

6. This final screen shows you a summary of what you have configured. Click **Finish**. See Figure 7.16.

Customizing User Accounts

After creating the user account, you need to configure it and open the Active Directory Users and Computers again to open a user account. To do this, follow these steps:

Figure 7.16 The Summary Screen Window

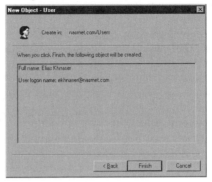

1. Click **Start | Programs | Administrative Tools | Active Directory Users and Computers**.

2. Click the **Users** container in the left pane and double-click the name of the user you just created to bring up the user's property sheet.

3. The user's property sheet opens, and you can configure the settings using the different tabs described in the rest of the section.

The General tab, shown in Figure 7.17, is where you enter the first name, initials, last name, display name, description, office, telephone number, e-mail, and Web page parameters for your user. The "other" buttons allow you to enter additional telephone numbers or Web pages.

Figure 7.17 The General Tab

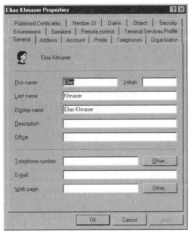

The Address tab, shown in Figure 7.18, is where you enter the street, P.O. box, city, state or province, ZIP code, and country parameters.

Figure 7.18 The Address Tab

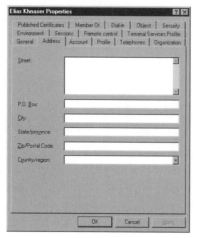

The Account tab is probably the most used tab in the user property sheet. This is where you enter the user logon name, the domain, and the pre-Windows 2000 (NetBIOS) logon name and domain. Pressing the Logon Hours button provides a nice GUI utility to specify the permitted logon. With a few simple mouse clicks and drags, you can easily restrict an employee's working hours from 8:00 to 5:00 Monday through Friday, as shown in Figure 7.19.

Figure 7.19 Restricting User Logon Times

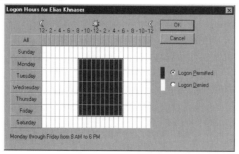

The Log On To button allow you to specify the workstations users can log on to. Just below that is the "Account locked out" check box. Under normal circumstances, this box should appear grayed out. If the box is checked, the account has had more incorrect logon attempts than permitted by your security policy. The user should be contacted immediately, and you should also check your logs to verify whether the user forgot his or her password or instead there has been an unauthorized access attempt. In a secure environment, the account will stay locked until reset by an administrator. In others, it could reset in an hour or other length of time specified in your policy. In the box below "Account locked out" are numerous account options. Forcing the user to change password at next logon is useful if you need to expire an account immediately or you want to give out a default password for new rollouts that then must be changed immediately by the user.

Many companies also use the screen shown in Figure 7.20 to prevent a user from changing a password. This function can be useful if you have a small or restricted environment and want to assign passwords to users to ensure compliance with minimum standards or if you have certain users and services that you don't want changed without notice. This option should always be set on any disabled accounts (such as guest) and for any services that need to log on to function. Several known automated "crack" utilities or unscrupulous people attempting to manually crack your server could attempt to change the password to these services, many of which are already running with Admin access. If these passwords need to be changed, changes are normally made by an administrator logged in to the machine; they are almost never done logged in as the service or disabled user.

Figure 7.20 The Account Tab

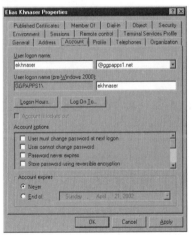

You should not set passwords to never expire. Most companies should have a policy requiring password changes at least every 90 to 120 days. Even every 90 days is not often enough to prevent a brute-force attack if someone can obtain the SAM file from your server or go undetected with an unlimited number of logons. Some programs allow someone to crack any Windows password that is created using normal, single-keystroke methods (alphanumeric and special characters) in a few days or even within hours, depending on the workstation used, if he or she can obtain the encrypted password file.

The main reason for requiring changes is that no matter how much we try to edu-
cate our users and admonish them not to share their passwords, many will still give
their "secret" word out to their close coworkers. What happens when that coworker
leaves the company? With forced change, there is a limited time in which those users
can gain access to your system. Other settings here allow you to disable the account.
Using this feature instead of deleting the account when its inactive allows you to
restore account settings instantly in case you have workers on long absences, contract
workers, and so on. At the very bottom of the Account tab, you can choose a specific
date for an account to expire—a very handy utility. If an administrator knows an
employee's last day of work is September 28, the administrator can set the account to
automatically expire on that day and not worry about forgetting to disable it that day.

The Profile tab shown in Figure 7.21 is used to set the profile path for "normal"
Windows network connections using standard TCP/IP or NetBIOS file and print services. The location of the user's home directory is also set here. These settings do not
affect the RDP and ICA terminal client settings.

Figure 7.21 The Profile Tab

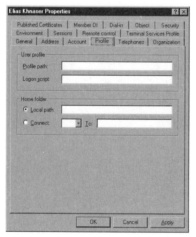

The Telephones tab shown in Figure 7.22 is used to set the user's telephone numbers for home, pager, mobile, fax, and IP phone. It also has a Note field for comments.
Each type also has an "other" button for entering multiple numbers of the same type.

The Organization tab shown in Figure 7.23 has fields for title, department, company, manager, and direct reports. The Manager field has a Change button that allows
you to pick users from Active Directory.

Figure 7.22 The Telephones Tab

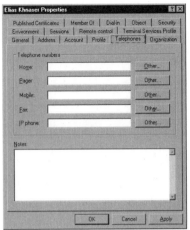

Figure 7.23 The Organization Tab

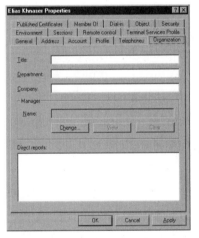

Configuring Remote Control

The Remote Control tab shown in Figure 7.24 is used for Terminal Services-type connections only. It contains a check box to enable or disable remote control (shadowing). This is also where you specify the level of control you want to have—either view only or interactive. Most important, this is where you can remove the requirement to obtain the user's permission before shadowing. By default, user permission is required for shadowing. Think about this before you change the setting; turning off client notification could have undesirable consequences. Viewing a session allows you to remotely watch the monitored session in real time. Interacting allows you to take control of the mouse and directs your keyboard commands to the monitored session.

Figure 7.24 The Remote Control (Shadowing) Tab

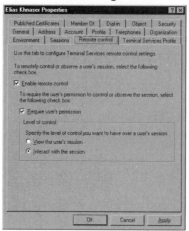

Locking Down the Ability to Copy and Print

Any settings you explicitly specify on a user account take precedence over the general settings that you set up on the protocol level. You might find one setting particularly interesting: You can disable a user's ability to print by not allowing his local printers to be mapped to his session. This can be accomplished by opening the user account in Active Directory Users and Computers and tabbing to the Environment tab. Follow these steps for an easy demonstration of how this is done:

1. Click **Start | Programs | Administrative Tools | Active Directory Users and Computers**.

2. In the left pane, select the **Users** container and double-click the **User** account for which you want to disable printing.

3. The user's property sheet opens. Tab to the **Environment** tab.

4. Uncheck **Connect Client printers at logon** and uncheck **Default to main client printer**. See Figure 7.25.

Mapping Drives

Mapping drives can be accomplished in several different ways, such as using a script to map drives at logon. If you simply want to give your session users one mapped drive, you can easily accomplish that through the Active Directory Users and Computers tool by tabbing to the Terminal Services Profile tab. Follow these simple steps to map a drive in Active Directory Users and Computers:

Figure 7.25 The Environment Tab

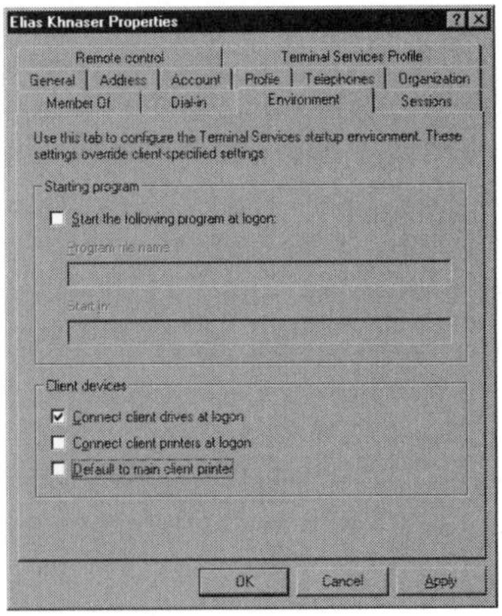

1. Click **Start | Programs | Administrative Tools | Active Directory Users and Computers**.

2. In the left pane, select the **Users** container and double-click the **User** account for which you want to map a drive.

3. The user's property sheet opens. Tab to the **Terminal Services Profile** tab.

4. In the **Terminal Services Home Directory** section, select **Connect**, select a drive letter, and point it to a share location such as \\servername\ usersdirectory\%username%.

5. Click **OK**. The next time your user logs in, he or she will get a drive mapping to the new location.

The alternative method we talked about was scripting. You can map drives using a script. By default, Terminal Services has a file called USRLOGON.CMD, which is located in the %SystemRoot%\System32\ directory. This file is executed automatically at first logon to the server. This script calls another file called USRLOGN1.CMD. However, this file doesn't exist but can be created and used to map drives or to execute any additional commands that need to be executed at logon. To use this file, follow these steps:

1. Open notepad.exe by going to **Start | Run** and typing **notepad**.

2. Notepad opens and maps any drives that need to be mapped using the following command: **net use** *drive letter \\servername\sharename*.

3. When you have written the commands you need to write, click **File | Save As** and name the file **Usrlogn1.cmd**. Browse to %SystemRoot%\System32\ and save the file in this directory.

Connecting Printers

The Environment tab shown in Figure 7.26 is used for Terminal Services connections and allows you to configure the startup environment for your users. In this window, you can specify a starting program for the client to run automatically at logon. If you do so, that will be the only program the user can run, and when the user closes that program, he or she will be logged off the server. You can also specify whether you want to allow the client to connect client drives, connect client printers, and default to a main client printer at logon.

Figure 7.26 The Environment Tab

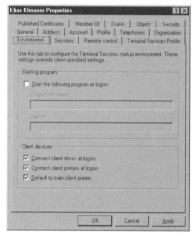

Configuring & Implementing…

Environment Tab Settings

The settings in the Environment tab (see Figure 7.26) override the settings on the Terminal Services RDP or ICA client software. This can be a useful feature if you need to restrict clients from saving files to their client machines' hard drives or from printing sensitive information. Client drive mapping is supported only with ICA connections and is not available for RDP clients at this time. Some add-ons for the Windows 2000 Server Resource Kit (Drmapsrv.exe and Rdpclip.exe) provide enhanced clipboard, file-copying, and client drive-mapping capabilities, but they are not fully supported at this time and do not function using RDP (port 3389) only. They can provide some added functionality for some people. I do *not* recommend testing these tools on a production server. For more information or to download these tools, visit the Microsoft Web site at www.microsoft.com/windows2000/library/resources/reskit/tools/default.asp.

Using Profiles

The Terminal Services Profile tab shown in Figure 7.27 is used to configure the location of profiles for Terminal Services users. A home directory for your Terminal Services users can also be specified and mapped at logon by setting the Connect field and specifying a directory share point. In addition, this tab has a check box to allow or disallow logon to the terminal server.

Figure 7.27 A Terminal Services Profile Tab

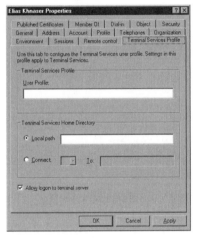

Applying Group Policies

Group Policy is a feature used in Windows 2000 to enhance and control users' desktops and computers. Group Policy is enabled by the Windows 2000 Active Directory Service and can also be used with MetaFrame servers, installed as either domain controllers or member servers. The procedures for using group policies are the same on the either platform, so any procedures we discuss in this section can be used in any configuration of the two.

Group Policy was designed and is used by administrators to help centralize administration of user desktop configurations, reduce user support requirements, and enhance the security of network systems. It handles these tasks by allowing the administrator(s) to customize and control users' access to registry-based settings, security settings, and software installation and maintenance. They can automate many tasks using logon, logoff, startup and shutdown scripts, and OS installation and perform Internet Explorer maintenance. User data files and folders can be redirected from the user's hard drive to network drives, where backups can be performed or preconfigured desktop displays can be pushed to new users. All these options are available, with different levels of access and control being provided to different users and locations, depending on the requirements. This flexibility allows for a developer to have complete (or near-complete) access to their desktops and all kinds of applications while restricting data entry staff, for example, to only the two or three applications they need to perform their job.

The features and controls provided by Group Policy become even more valuable to MetaFrame administrators when you realize that your server becomes the user's desktop machine when they are using a thin client, Terminal Services client, or ICA client connection. How many times have your users broken their desktop machines through ignorance or misuse? We don't really want them doing that to our servers, do we? This is where group policies come into play.

We do not try to go into a detailed discussion of all the finer aspects and programming issues of Group Policy in this chapter. That topic could make up an entire book in itself. Instead we focus on how to get started with Group Policy, how they can improve the user's experience with MetaFrame, and how they can benefit you, the MetaFrame administrator. From there you should be able to develop your own policies and apply them in a manner consistent with your environment.

Let's start off with some of the differences between Active Directory Group Policy and the old-style NT 4 and Win9*x* System Policy Editor. NT 4 allowed you to specify user and computer configurations that were stored in the Registry. While some of the same types of things can be controlled, a look at Table 7.1 shows the newer Group Policy method is the preferred method to use.

Table 7.1 System Policy and Group Policy Features

NT 4 System Policy Features	Active Directory Group Policy Features
NT 4 policies are applied to domains.	AD policies can be associated with sites, domains, and organizational units (OUs).
NT 4 policies can be controlled further by security group membership.	AD policies affect all users and computers in the site, domain, or OU where applied. They can also be controlled by security group membership.
Policies in NT 4 are not secure. Policies can be changed by a user with the Registry editor (Regedit.exe).	AD policies are secure. Only an administrator can change the settings. Updates can be pushed to clients on scheduled basis.
The settings are persistent (sometimes longer than intended). Settings persist until the policy setting is reversed or until a user manually edits the Registry. Often this is not the desired behavior.	AD policies are removed and rewritten whenever policy changes. They are removed when a policy no longer applies. This prevents a "burn," or a permanent change to the client machine registry.
NT 4 policies are limited to mandated desktop behavior based on the Registry changes applied by the administrator.	AD policies can enhance the user's computing environment by allowing more finely tuned desktop control.

Configuring & Implementing...

Windows 2000 Group Policy

Like NT 4, Windows 2000 uses administrative templates as part of its policy structure. Some policies in NT 4, if mistakenly enabled, could require you to visit each desktop to restore to the setting you want. Windows 2000 policies act like a filter applied over the Registry rather than a brute-force overwrite as with NT 4 and can easily be removed from your server configuration in seconds. Windows 2000 accomplishes this goal partly by implementing a new administrative template style.

By default, three .adm files are installed in the Group Policy console: System.adm, Inetres.adm, and Conf.adm. Conf.adm is not loaded by default and contains settings for Microsoft NetMeeting. Inetres.adm contains settings for Internet Explorer. System.adm contains settings for a variety of other features. This new-style .adm file still allows you to edit the template file and add to the existing 450 settings if you need to. However, any additional registry settings should be placed in \Software\Policies or \Software\Microsoft\Windows\CurrentVersion\Policies to avoid those unwanted persistent Registry modifications. Also for this reason, you should *not* attempt to use any old NT 4-style .adm files with Windows 2000. If you're looking for more information about .adm files, the Windows 2000 Resource Kit CD-ROM contains a searchable reference file, GP.chm, which has many details about the administrative template settings.

Understanding Group Policy and Active Directory

Understanding how group policies function is a key factor in designing your Active Directory structure. It is strongly suggested that you seek professional help, either to assist in designing your Active Directory structure or by attending certified training programs in Active Directory *before* you implement or upgrade an existing network infrastructure. Small details in the way you design and implement Active Directory now could save considerable time and effort in the future or be the source of a large overhaul project sooner than desired.

One of the most important design issues is groups, groups, and more groups. Try to adjust your thinking and divide everything into groups. The more ways to group and types of groups you can come up with, the more finely grained your control will become. Now think of these groups as *containers*. Active Directory users store objects in containers.

There are two types of Group Policy objects: local and nonlocal. Every Windows 2000-based computer has only one local Group Policy object. In the following section, we discuss nonlocal group policies and how to configure them in a domain environment.

Group Policies can be applied (linked) to OU, Domain, and Site containers in Active Directory. They are applied in the following order:

1. Local

2. Site

3. Domain

4. OU

The order in which policies are applied is important to remember because by default, policy applied later overwrites policy applied earlier if the setting was either marked as Enabled or Disabled. Settings that are marked Not Configured are skipped, and the setting applied earlier is allowed to persist. OU profiles have the highest precedence and are applied beginning at the highest OU (in the Active Directory tree) containing the user or computer account and ending with the one closest to the user or computer object. If multiple policies are applied at an OU level, they are applied in the order specified by the administrator.

A Group Policy object linked to a site applies to all domains at the site. A Group Policy object linked to a domain applies directly to all users and computers in the domain and by inheritance to all users and computers in any OUs below the domain. A Group Policy object linked to an OU applies directly to all users and computers in that OU and by inheritance to all users and computers in any OUs below that OU.

NOTE

This section describes the default behavior of policy inheritance. There are, of course, ways to either force group policies to or prevent group policies from affecting certain groups of users or computers. The No Override and Enforce Policy Inheritance settings are powerful tools, but their excessive use can be confusing to administrators and should be avoided when possible. Sometimes, however, using these tools can be the most effective solution. As you should with any custom settings that might not be readily apparent to other administrators, be sure to document use of these tools and develop a policy or set a standard procedure stating when they will be used.

Several of the settings available under the Security portion of Group Policy will be ignored if linked at the OU level. To be effective, all the settings under the Security section should be applied to the domain. This includes settings for password policy, audit policy, user rights, event log, and security options.

It is not possible to link a Group Policy object to a "generic" container. These are generally considered the "built-in" containers. If you look at the folders in the Active Directory window, you'll see that the generic folder icons look like "plain" folders. The icon for an OU looks almost the same, but there is a small book on the folder. This means you cannot place a Group Policy directly on the built-in Users or Computers containers. These containers will, however, inherit a policy that is applied to the domain they are under.

Computer policy processing is completed before the **Ctrl + Alt + Del** logon box is displayed. User policies are completed before the shell is active and available for the user to interact with. Windows 2000 group policies are processed every 90 minutes by default, so if a user changes something that is mandated by domain policy, it will be set back to the domain policy within the 90-minute time frame. This function can be changed under Computer Configuration | Administrative Templates | System | Group Policy | Group Policy Refresh Interval for Computers. There is a time limit of 60 minutes for all the client-side extensions to finish processing policy. A client-side extension that is not finished after 60 minutes will be stopped and the policy settings will not be processed. There is no policy setting to change the client timeout setting.

Creating a Custom MMC for Group Policy

In order for you to manage group policies, you must manually add the snap-in by creating a custom MMC. This is a simple process; once you do it a few times, you will probably find that you use the process quite frequently. Numerous administrative functions can be combined into kind of a "favorites" list of your most often used tools. To begin, click the **Start** button and choose **Run**. Then type **mmc** into the **Open** window. This action opens a new, blank MMC window. Next, from the Console pull-down, choose **Add/Remove Snap-in**. This step opens an empty Add/Remove Snap-in window. Next, click the **Add** button, and the Add Standalone Snap-In window shown in Figure 7.28 opens and displays the available standalone snap-ins.

Figure 7.28 Adding the Group Policy Snap-In

Choose **Group Policy**. Click **OK** and you can now choose the **Local Computer** policy object, or you can click the **Browse** button to browse local domains for their policy, then pick from the available policies (see Figure 7.29).

Figure 7.29 Browsing the Domain Policies

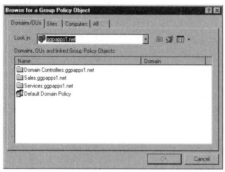

You can save this console using a meaningful name, and it will automatically be added to your **Administrative Tools** program listing. Click **OK** to open the Group Policy snap-in you just created and you can start configuring your user environment (see Figure 7.30).

Figure 7.30 Group Policy Snap-In

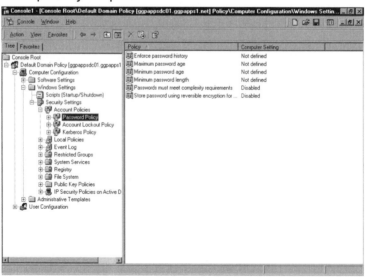

Notice that by default, all the computer settings are "Not defined." This means that when the policy is applied, it will be ignored. Simply double-click an entry to modify and then link your policy to the container you want to apply it to. The best way to learn about group policies is by working with them. Remember, it's a lot more forgiving than the old NT 4 system policies. If a policy doesn't work the way you thought it would or it breaks something, simply remove it and no harm's done. Group Policy might seem difficult and as though it involves a lot to learn, but if you take it a little bit at a time, you will find that it will save you hours of workstation configuration time.

We discussed earlier how policies could be applied either locally or nonlocally. In the next example we add three snap-ins to our Group Policy MMC. We use the Local Computer Policy, the GGPAPPS1 Domain Policy (created as a new policy object for the ggpapps1.net domain instead of using the Default Domain Policy), and the Active Directory Users and Computers snap-ins to demonstrate how inheritance works and how you can view the "effective" policy settings for a computer. In the right-hand window in Figure 7.31, we see three columns. The "Policy" column defines the policy for us. In this example, we are looking specifically at the Password Policy setting. The "Local Setting" column displays the default policy settings for the local machine's password history (0), maximum age (0), minimum age (0), minimum password length (0), and complexity requirements (disabled).

Figure 7.31 Local Group Policy Settings

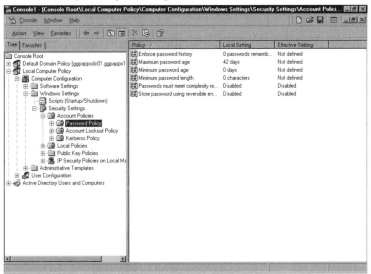

In the example in Figure 7.32, we see what happens after we apply a policy to the domain with different settings for the Password Policy. The Local Settings remain the same, but the Effective Settings have now changed to the values we applied to the domain. In all cases (other than the exceptions noted previously), domain policies take precedence over local machine policies.

This allows administrators to have certain settings become mandatory throughout the domain. These same features can be applied to services, Registry settings, file and folder permissions, and virtually every aspect of all the domain's servers and computers. Extreme care should be taken when you disable services; ensure that they are not required by other specialty servers or workstations or that policy inheritance is blocked for those special requirements. This is where grouping and proper Active Directory design and forethought can really pay off for you.

Figure 7.32 Effective Group Policy Settings

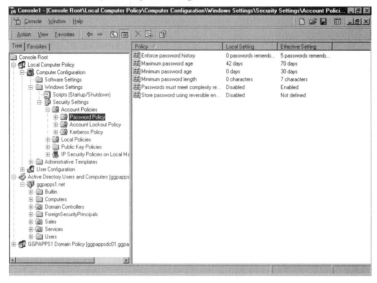

WARNING

Although **Run only allowed Windows applications** is a good security setting to begin with, it does not provide ironclad security by itself. This setting only restricts users from running applications started from Windows Explorer. It does not prevent them from running processes that are started from other processes, such as Task Manager. It also does not prevent them from running "nonallowed" applications if they are started from a command prompt. If you use this setting, in most cases you should also use the **Disable the command prompt** setting. We even go so far as to check the permissions of all sensitive .exe files on the server and remove user permissions from the files themselves when it is deemed appropriate to do so.

To get into more detail with policy settings, let's look at some of the user settings. In Figure 7.33, if we go to **User Configuration | Administrative Templates | Windows Components | System**, we have the option to **Run only allowed Windows applications**. This is a recommended setting to help secure your system, especially if you have one group of clients connecting to your server from the Internet or an "outside" corporate link.

Figure 7.33 Restricting Users to "Run Only Allowed Windows Applications"

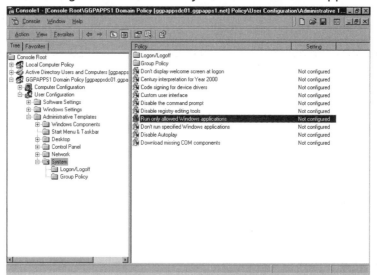

Most "outside" clients need access to only a few applications; it would probably be an unnecessary security risk to give them full desktop access. To restrict these users, you need only add the applications you want them to run and then apply this policy to their group containers. Your corporate users will still enjoy the full desktop or whatever other applications you have granted them access to while your server and data will be protected from would-be intruders. There are many more such nice restrictions, some of which you might want to apply to your corporate or "inside" users as well, such as removing the Run command, displaying a logoff choice, or even disabling the ability to change users' home pages. Figure 7.34 shows a few more choices. It would be impossible to list them all here without starting another book. Look around and you will be quite pleased at what you find.

As the last example of user policies, let's look at the location for the logon warning. If you go to **Windows Settings | Security Settings | Local Policies | Security Options** (shown in the right-hand window of Figure 7.35), you will see "Message text for Users attempting to Log on" and "Message title for Users attempting to Log on."

If you put text in these values, the text will be displayed to the user as a popup window at logon. This is a great place for No Trespass, Security, and Privacy warnings. Once the system is configured and enabled, every user must click **OK** on the popup window in acknowledgment of your warning before being allowed to continue and being asked for a username and password. If your message is worded correctly, it should meet most legal requirements for monitoring and notification of trespass to unauthorized users.

Figure 7.34 Additional User Policy Restrictions

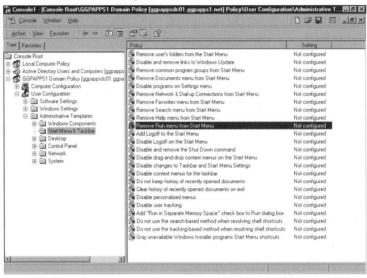

Figure 7.35 System Logon Warning Text

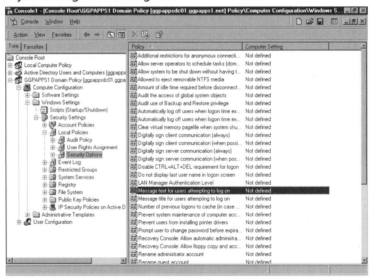

> **NOTE**
>
> It is always a good idea to group your MetaFrame servers in a separate OU. That way you can set a separate Group Policy that will be implemented only on these particular servers. So, if you have different servers in your environment, they will not be affected by the settings you specify for these servers. It is also worthy to

note that within the Group Policy hierarchy, the Computer Configuration node is the node that will affect the servers. The User Configuration node mostly deals with settings for the users logging in to the server.

Independent Management Architecture

Independent Management Architecture (IMA) is the foundation upon which Citrix MetaFrame XP builds in order to provide scalability. IMA is an architectural model that greatly enhances and simplifies management and administration. It is a server-to-server communications protocol that uses User Datagram Protocol (UDP) port 2512 to gather and store information about published applications, license pooling, and load-balancing information. IMA is a major advancement and a great improvement in Citrix products. Some of the features of the IMA are:

- The Citrix Management Console (CMC) is dedicated to providing a centralized location for administering all aspects of the Citrix servers, from printer drivers and license information to published applications.

- Simple Network Management Protocol (SNMP) support is a great new feature that allows you to set up traps that most monitoring software will be able to tap into and send back alerts regarding several components of the server. The server going down or the print spooler hanging are examples of alerts you can configure using SNMP.

- Auditing and logging comprise another feature that has been greatly improved. You now have the ability to audit and log session shadowing and administrative actions.

- Citrix configuration information is now stored in one central location.

- UDP broadcasts are no longer used by ICA clients to find Citrix servers and published applications.

Zones

Zones are groupings of Citrix servers, regardless of geographic location into logical collections. Using zones, Citrix server farms can now span multiple geographic locations. Each zone has its own data collector server, thereby limiting data collection WAN traffic by keeping all information relevant to the servers in that zone local on a Citrix server that is part of the zone. By default, a zone consists of all the Citrix servers on a subnet. The data collector has inherited the role of the master browser that was available with MetaFrame 1.8, but the data collector is much more stable and reliable and was built to play this role. It is necessary to note that even though each zone has only one data collector, all MetaFrame XP servers have enough information to assume this role in the event of a failure.

Configuring servers and grouping them in different zones is a very straightforward task. Simply open the properties of the farm from the CMC by right-clicking the farm and choosing **Properties**. Select the **Zones** tab from the window that pops up, as shown in Figure 7.36. In this window, you can either create a new zone by clicking **New Zone**, or you can add or remove servers within zones. You can also delete zones from this window.

Figure 7.36 The Zones Configuration Tab

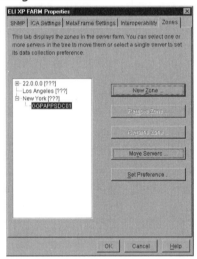

Data Store

The *data store* is created when you install your first Citrix MetaFrame XP server. It serves as a method of storing server configuration data, license data, printer drivers, and Citrix farm administrators. The data store uses a database engine to store its data, such as Microsoft Access for small environments or Microsoft SQL server or Oracle for environments of any size. See Table 7.2 for more details. The data store concept is the foundation that ensures stability and allows for scalability. Data store connections can be made in two ways: direct or indirect connections.

Direct connections utilize an Open Database Connectivity (ODBC) driver and require that one be properly installed and configured so that the server can communicate directly with the database. *Indirect connections* use a Citrix XP server to make a connection to the database. This method eliminates the need to install and configure an ODBC driver on every server. However, one disadvantage of using this method is that it creates a single point of failure for the server that is passing through the connections to the database.

Table 7.2 Database Versions Compatible with XP Servers

Database Type	Versions Supported
Microsoft Access	Terminal Server and Windows 2000, including compatible drivers
Microsoft SQL	Microsoft SQL Server 7 SP 2 and SQL 2000; Terminal Server requires MDAC 2.6
Oracle	Oracle 8i, version 8.1.6 Oracle 7, version 7.3.4 Oracle 8, version 8.0.6

Data Collector Local Host Cache

The data collector found in MetaFrame XP servers is the inheritor of the LATE ICA master browser in previous versions, which we all hated because of its instability and its tendency to hang all the time. The data collector is an enhanced version that is far more reliable and far superior to the ICA master browser. Like its predecessor, the data collector maintains a list of all the servers and their published applications. It maintains the servers' IP addresses as well. XP servers use TCP/IP for server-to-server communications, ridding us completely of the use of UDP, used with older versions.

One data collector is available per zone and is chosen via elections, much like the elections that were used to choose the ICA master browser. When a new a server joins the farm or if the data collector is down or unavailable, an election is held for a new data collector. Four levels of preferences exist for selecting the new data collector, as shown in Figure 7.37.

By default, all servers are set to the default preference levels, except the first server that was installed in the farm; that one holds the level of most preferred. These preferences are set in the Zones tab of the farm properties. The election process selects the server with the highest preference; if no server with most preferred status is selected, the data collector goes down the list until as a last resort it selects a server from the "not preferred" list.

Figure 7.37 Data Collector Preferences

The local host cache is actually one of the coolest new features of XP. It is a cache a version of the data store database locally on every server in an Access database. It accomplishes an enhancement in performance; because the server does not have to continually contact the data store for farm information, it has a locally cached version of it, so response time is improved. The local host cache also maintains enough information that will allow the server to fully function for 48 hours in the event that the data store goes down for any reason. During this time, the server will continuously attempt to contact the data store server. If within 48 hours the data store is not contacted, the server stops accepting connections and the license is terminated.

The local host cache might get out of sync with the data store if the IMA misses a synch or change event. If this happens, you can issue the following command from a command prompt:

```
dsmaint refreshlhc
```

The local host cache maintains the following information:

- Information on all servers in the farm
- Information specific to itself
- Information on Windows domain trust relationships in the farm
- Published applications names within the farm

Summary

In this chapter, we looked at many different ways you can customize and enhance the user experience using Citrix MetaFrame. You can use group policies, not just to save you configuration time, but also for providing different levels of permissions to different users. You can use shadowing to provide user assistance and distance learning.

Consider the following network design (see Figure 7.38). Here a company is able to use MetaFrame servers located in its publicly accessible DMZ to securely provide access to several external, DMZ, and even internal sensitive database servers to users located on its internal corporate network, dialup users, and even clients remotely on the Internet, all from the same load-balanced MetaFrame server farm. Using group policies, you can restrict remote noncorporate Internet users to connecting to the MetaFrame server and seeing only one or two applications provided by the corporation. The MetaFrame servers could then connect users to Web pages or read-only copies of internal databases housed in the public DMZ. At the same time, a corporate user can log on to the same MetaFrame server and be provided with a full suite of applications—even be granted secure access to the internal database systems.

Figure 7.38 Secure Extranet Design with MetaFrame

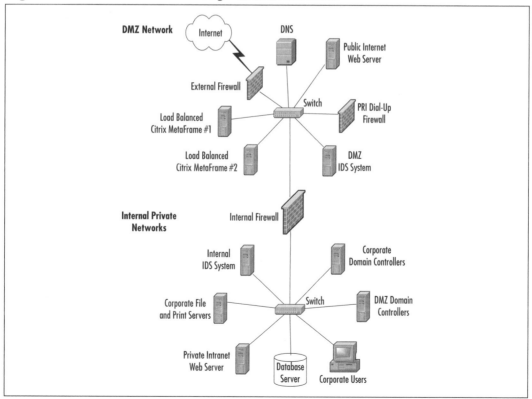

Let's discuss in more detail exactly how this is done and how it meets today's security needs. For more details on this design, let's assume that the Internet firewall is correctly configured, with all ports blocked from the Internet other than those needed for essential services into the public demilitarized zone (DMZ). There is also a firewall in place that restricts the dialup user access to the public DMZ and the private corporate network. As a failproof line of defense, they also have an additional firewall between the public DMZ and their private internal network. Intrusion detection systems are installed in both the public DMZ and the private internal network.

In a configuration like this, corporate workers can access the extranet MetaFrame DMZ servers and any other internal or external resources directly from their desktop machines. The private corporate network machines are inaccessible directly from the Internet and can be accessed only by passing through the MetaFrame server, which acts as an application proxy. The corporate workers could then go home or traveling on the road and access the network from the Internet, or from a direct analog/ISDN dialup into the DMZ and be presented with exactly the same desktop view, applications, and access to resources that he had from his desk at the office. All this could be provided securely using the latest RC5 128-bit encryption. If they desired, they could even use single sign-on, so when the user logs in to the public DMZ MetaFrame server, he is authenticated by an internal protected domain controller. Users love not having to remember multiple passwords and don't even seem to complain as much about complexity when they can cut the number of them substantially. Furthermore, in this example, the company could provide secure access to highly sensitive intranet servers that are protected on the private network and, although directly inaccessible from the Internet, can be accessed by their corporate users having the proper credentials and policies by passing through the MetaFrame servers.

At the end of the chapter, we went over Independent Management Architecture (IMA) and explained its features and benefits and how it helps scalability and promotes stability in the Citrix farm. We discussed zones and their benefits. We covered the data store and its primary use and function. We also covered the data collector and the local host cache—how they are used and how they benefit the Citrix farm.

Solutions Fast Track

Configuring Sessions

☑ Creating ICA and RDP sessions can be done from within the Citrix Connection Configuration tool. Modifying session options and settings can also be accomplished with this tool.

☑ The Advanced button in the properties of a selected protocol can help you set settings such as how long a session can remain idle before it is disconnected. You can set up shadowing options from this button as well.

☑ You can easily lock down the ability to copy and print by opening the properties of a particular protocol and then clicking the Client button. There you can disable the client clipboard mapping and the client printer mappings.

Configuring Users

☑ You can create user accounts using the Active Directory Users and Computers MMC snap-in. From within this tool, you can modify the various user account parameters.

☑ Understanding and familiarizing yourself with Group Policy can greatly help you administer your environment.

☑ Profiles can be used to force a set of specific settings on users connecting to your terminal server. Profiles can be mandatory, therefore preventing any user from making any changes you explicitly set.

Independent Management Architecture

☑ The IMA is an architectural model on which Citrix MetaFrame XP builds in order to provide scalability.

☑ Zones are the grouping of MetaFrame XP servers into logical collections, regardless of geographical location.

☑ The data store is the database that is created with the installation of the first MetaFrame XP server in your farm. It will store all the information required for your farm to operate properly.

Frequently Asked Questions

The following Frequently Asked Questions, answered by the authors of this book, are designed to both measure your understanding of the concepts presented in this chapter and to assist you with real-life implementation of these concepts. To have your questions about this chapter answered by the author, browse to **www.syngress.com/solutions** and click on the **"Ask the Author"** form.

Q: I don't seem to have the Active Directory Users and Computers tool on my Programs list under Administrative Tools. How can I manage domain user accounts?

A: The machine you are on is not a domain controller. The Active Directory Users and Computers choice is available only in the Programs list of domain controllers. You can still manage Active Directory by either using RDP or ICA to run a remote session and using the tools on the domain controller, or you can create a custom MMC to manage Active Directory from a member workstation or server (which requires Admin privileges). See the section on "Creating a Custom MMC" in this chapter.

Q: I tried to set the password policy for our Developers group to use complex passwords of seven characters, but it doesn't seem to work.

A: The password policy is located in the Security section of Group Policy. For the Security portion of the policy to be effective, it must be linked to the domain. If it is linked to an OU, it will be ignored.

Q: I want to edit some group policies, but I can't find the Group Policy administration tool.

A: Group policies must be edited using the MMC, either as a standalone console or from within the Properties of an Active Directory container object. See the section, "Creating a Custom MMC."

Q: We rolled out a new application and it seems to bring down our T1 whenever users connect to it.

A: Check the settings for client audio and make sure that they are not set to High (1.3Mbps). Medium (64Kbps) or Low (16Kbps) settings should be used for most WAN connections.

Q: Which UDP port does the IMA use?

A: IMA uses UDP port 2512.

Q: I have an environment that has 25 Citrix MetaFrame XP servers and is expected to grow another 10 in the next year. Which database software is recommended for this environment?

A: The ideal database software in this situation is Microsoft Access, since Access is recommended for environments of up to 50 servers. This means that your current and future growth is taken into account. However, if your organization already has an implementation of SQL Server or Oracle, creating an additional database for the IMA using these database servers is also a good idea, since you already have the application set up. The IMA database is not a disk-intensive one and will always be small in terms of disk space.

Chapter 8

Citrix MetaFrame XP Management

Solutions in this chapter:

- Using the Citrix Management Console
- Using the Citrix Installation Manager
- Using the Citrix Server Administration Tool
- Using the Citrix Connection Configuration
- Configuring the SpeedScreen Latency Reduction Manager

☑ Summary

☑ Solutions Fast Track

☑ Frequently Asked Questions

Introduction

Managing a server farm requires some method of pulling all the server data together. The data must be stored, and, as changes are made to each server, the data must be updated. Simply gathering, storing, and updating data about the servers is not enough. You must have a way to access the data and make changes to it so that you can manage the members of your server farm. All these needs are provided by the *Citrix Management Console* (CMC).

Administrators have other needs in managing server farms. They must manage how applications are deployed to each server. They need to configure printer drivers. Finally, they need to have a central view into the connections that are running in the farm.

Citrix MetaFrame XP comes in three versions. The versions do not all have the same utilities. This chapter reviews the server farm management utilities and with which version of Citrix MetaFrame XP each can be used.

Using the Citrix Management Console

The CMC is a helpful new tool introduced with MetaFrame XP. It centralizes the management and administration process of the entire MetaFrame farm. The CMC is divided into two main panes: the left pane and the right pane. The left pane is organized in a tree-like view starting with the farm name, followed by all the various tools that manage attributes of the farm. The right pane displays information about the current selection in the left pane. Sometimes tabs are displayed in the right pane, allowing you further flexibility and management options. See Figure 8.1 for a snapshot of what the CMC looks like.

The CMC is like a one-stop shop where you can do all your usual management tasks and much more. For example, you can handle the following:

- **MetaFrame farm administration** Right-clicking the farm name in the left pane of the CMC allows you to modify global settings that affect the server farm.

- **Load evaluators** This node allows you to monitor the performance of various components on your server, such as CPU utilization, memory usage, and page faults. You can think of it as Citrix's version of Performance Monitor, available with Windows NT and 2000 Servers.

- **MetaFrame XP Server administration** This tool was a standalone tool in earlier versions of MetaFrame; it can still be run independently for backward-compatibility reasons. From within this node in the CMC you can administer users, sessions, processes, licenses, Load Manager Monitor, printers, and print drivers. Expanding the Servers node in the left pane of the CMC and selecting a server enables these tabs in the right pane and displays the relevant information.

- **Published application management** This node allows you to install and administer published applications. You can publish an application to one server or multiple servers in your farm.

- **License administration** This node provides a centralized location for administering your licenses. You can assign and reserve licenses or add and remove licenses from this node. Here you can do everything related to licensing.

- **Printer management** One of the best enhancements in MetaFrame XP is the robust printer and print driver management. From within this node, all printer management is accomplished. Print driver replication is also done through this node, and here you can enable the Citrix Universal Print Driver.

Figure 8.1 The Citrix Management Console, or CMC

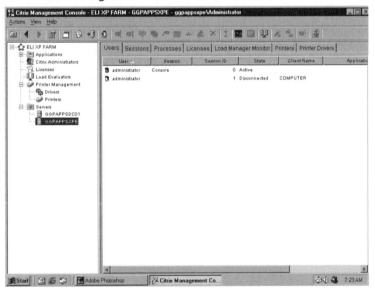

NOTE

Citrix MetaFrame XP relies heavily on the CMC; therefore, any add-on product that you install will be manageable from within the CMC. For example, if you install the Citrix Installation Manager, a node will be created for it in the left pane of the CMC and you can manage it from there.

The nice thing about the CMC is that it's a standalone tool that can also be installed on your desktop, eliminating the need to log on to a MetaFrame server to do maintenance tasks. Later in this chapter we discuss the requirements for installing the CMC on a desktop.

A good example of what can be administered from within the CMC is the Servers node. The Servers node replaces the Citrix Server Administrator tool that was available with earlier versions of MetaFrame. When you select the Servers node in the left pane of the CMC, you are presented with three tabs in the right pane. These three tabs are Contents, Users, and Printer Bandwidth. The Contents tab lists the servers available in the farm. The Users tab displays all the users connected on all the servers in your farm. Finally, the Printer Bandwidth tab lists the servers and how much bandwidth is allocated for each.

Expanding the Servers node in the left pane and selecting a server from the list allows you to manage different tasks. For example you can view the users connected to that particular server by clicking the **Users** tab in the right pane. This will provide you with a list of users and their current connection status, such as whether they are connected or disconnected, how long they have been logged in, their session IDs, the client names, the applications they are using, and their idle time. By right-clicking any of your users' names, you can do administrative tasks such as resetting them, logging them off, disconnecting them, shadowing them, and sending them a message. We discuss the functions of the Citrix Administration tool later in this chapter.

Minimum Requirements

As we mentioned earlier, the CMC is a standalone tool that can be installed on a desktop, eliminating the need to launch an Independent Computing Architecture (ICA) session to manage your MetaFrame XP servers. It is important to note that launching the CMC inside an ICA session adds an extra load on the server, consuming memory and CPU resources that we would rather save for other sessions. Therefore, installing the CMC on a desktop and launching it from there saves you valuable resources.

Table 8.1 displays the software and hardware requirements for the CMC. The operating systems that can run the CMC are Microsoft Windows NT 4.0 Workstation, Windows NT 4.0 Server, Windows 2000 Professional, and all server versions. Since the CMC is a Java-based program, Sun Java Runtime Environment (JRE) version 1.3 is required and is automatically installed with the CMC.

Table 8.1 CMC Minimum Installation Requirements

Hardware Requirements	Software Requirements
Pentium processor or better	
64MB RAM	Sun JRE version 1.3
25MB disk space	Windows NT 4.0 Workstation and Server and Windows 2000 Professional and all server versions

Establishing Connectivity with the Data Store

Every MetaFrame XP server farm has one central data repository, known as the *data store,* which stores configuration information about the various published applications, licensing, printers, servers, and the like. The data store can be an Access database, a SQL database, or an Oracle database. Access databases are used for small to medium-sized environments; SQL and Oracle can be used for any size farms and are easily scalable. Connectivity to the data store can either be a direct connection or an indirect connection, as illustrated in Figure 8.2.

Figure 8.2 Direct and Indirect ODBC Connections to the Data Store

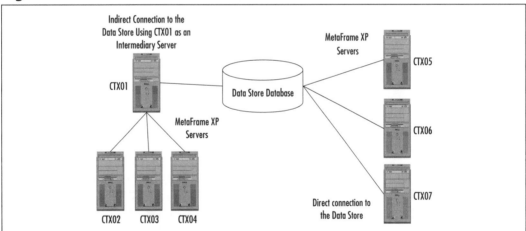

MetaFrame XP servers can make a direct connection to the data store via TCP on port 2513. A direct connection requires that you have the proper ODBC drivers installed prior to your connection to the data store database. ODBC drivers vary depending on the type of database you are using, whether Access, SQL, or Oracle.

The other method of connecting to the data store is indirect access, which uses one MetaFrame server as the point server that receives the requests from the other MetaFrame servers and passes them through to the data store using a direct connection. In this case, ODBC drivers need only be installed on the server that is acting as the point server, eliminating the need to install it on every server. MetaFrame XP servers communicate between each other on TCP port 2512.

WARNING

To prevent bottlenecks and degradation of performance, do not use Microsoft SQL Server and Oracle in indirect mode. When you use Microsoft Access in indirect mode, your user load should stay light in order to prevent performance degradation.

When you use Access as your database, it is good to note that both Windows NT 4.0 Terminal Server Edition and Windows 2000 have the proper ODBC driver installed, so your system is ready for a direct connection to the data store. If the database you have chosen is SQL or Oracle, you must install the appropriate ODBC driver.

Configuring a Direct ODBC Connection to a SQL Server Database

All MetaFrame XP servers in the farm that will directly connect to a SQL server that homes the data store database must configure an ODBC connection to the database. To configure a direct ODBC connection to a SQL server database, follow these steps:

1. Log in to your Windows 2000 MetaFrame XP server as an Administrator or user with sufficient privileges.

2. Click **Start | Programs | Administrative Tools | Data Sources (ODBC)**.

3. The ODBC Data Source Administrator window opens. Select the **System DSN** tab, as shown in Figure 8.3.

Figure 8.3 The ODBC Data Source Administrator Window

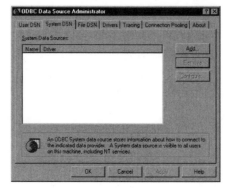

4. Click **Add...** The Create New Data Source window appears. Scroll all the way to the bottom and select **SQL Server**, as shown in Figure 8.4, and click **Finish**.

Figure 8.4 The Create New Data Source Window

5. The Create a New Data Source to SQL Server window opens. Enter a name to refer to the data source in the Name field. You can type a short description in the Description field. From the drop-down menu, select the SQL server on which the database is located, or you can type in the server name or IP address, as shown in Figure 8.5. If DNS is properly configured, you should be able to see a list of SQL servers. Click **Next** to continue.

Figure 8.5 The Create a New Data Source to SQL Server Window

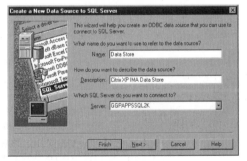

6. The next window deals with authentication. The default authentication method is Windows NT authentication, which is also Citrix's recommendation for high-security environments. Select **With Windows NT authentication using the network login ID**, as shown in Figure 8.6. Click **Next** to continue.

7. This screen allows you to select the correct database on the SQL server. Check the "Change the default database to" check box and select the appropriate database from the drop-down menu. The drop-down menu lists all available databases on the SQL server. See Figure 8.7. Click **Next** to continue.

Figure 8.6 Data Source SQL Server Authentication

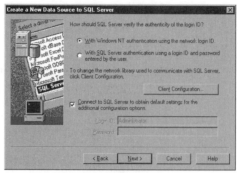

Figure 8.7 Selecting the Appropriate Database on the SQL Server

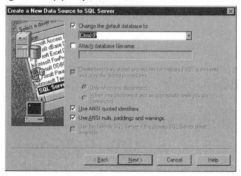

8. This screen has many configurable options, such as which language SQL server messages should appear in, the level of encryption, and more. Unless you need to change them, these settings can be left at the default settings shown in Figure 8.8. Click **Finish** to continue.

Figure 8.8 The Data Source Settings Miscellaneous Settings Window

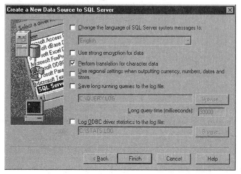

9. The summary screen listing all the settings that were entered throughout these steps, as shown in Figure 8.9, appears. This screen provides you with a method to test your ODBC connection to the SQL server. Click the **Test Data Source** button to test the connection.

Figure 8.9 The ODBC Connection Summary Window

10. If all goes well, you should see a message that reads "TESTS COMPLETED SUCCESSFULLY!" as shown in Figure 8.10. Click **OK**.

Figure 8.10 The ODBC Connection Test Results Window

11. Finally, you should see your system data source in the ODBC Data Source Administrator window, as shown in Figure 8.11.

NOTE

When using Microsoft SQL Server as your database server for the data store, it is always a good idea to install the latest Microsoft Data Access Components (MDAC) drivers. These drivers and other valuable utilities such as the MDAC component checker tool, which identifies the installed version of MDAC, can all be downloaded from www.microsoft.com/data/download.htm.

Figure 8.11 System DSN Shown in the ODBC Data Source Administrator Window

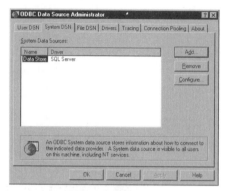

Configuring & Implementing…

Changing the TCP Port Used for Indirect Connection to the Data Store

If port 2512, which is used for indirect connections to the database, is inconvenient, you can change the port number by editing the Registry. Make sure that you back up the Registry before making any changes to it.

On the server holding the data store, edit the following Registry key and change its value to the number you want:

```
HKLM\Software\Citrix\IMA\ImaPort
```

On all the other MetaFrame XP servers, change the value of the Registry key to match the one you entered:

```
HKLM\Software\Citrix\IMA\PsServerPort
```

Configuring Automatic Data Refresh

The CMC is a dynamic tool that updates and displays information promptly as it receives notification of events occurring on the MetaFrame XP servers. However, to provide this level of service, the CMC is constantly and frequently utilizing the network to communicate with the servers, thereby increasing network traffic. For the sake of reducing network traffic, some events are not automatically refreshed by default. These events include a server that comes online or an ICA session that is starting.

Automatic Data Refresh is a feature that you can set to automatically refresh data based on a predefined interval of 10, 30, 60, or 90 seconds. There are two ways of updating data in the CMC. One, you can configure Automatic Data Refresh and thus control how frequently your information is updated. Two, you can simply press the F5 key on your keyboard and force a data refresh. This latter method is efficient and can preserve bandwidth.

We recommend that you always initiate a manual refresh prior to making any changes. That way, you are sure to be viewing the most recent information. For example, even if Automatic Data Refresh is enabled and set, it is always a good idea to manually refresh licenses.

The Automatic Data Refresh window has two tabs, one for user data and one for license data, as shown in Figures 8.12 and 8.13.

Figure 8.12 The Automatic Data Refresh Window

Figure 8.13 The License Data Tab in the Automatic Data Refresh Window

To configure Automatic Data Refresh settings, follow these simple steps:

1. Open the **CMC**.

2. Click the **View** menu and select **Preferences**.

3. The Preferences window pops up. Select the type of data for which you want to set autorefresh settings by selecting one of the two tabs available. In this example, make sure that you are in the **User Data** tab, as shown in Figure 8.12.

4. You can configure autorefresh for three options: servers, server folders, and applications. Once you select one of them, the drop-down menu enables you to set an interval of 10, 30, 60, or 90 seconds.

5. Click **OK**.

Organizing Server and Application Folders

The server and application folders in the CMC provide a location where you can place servers and applications. Even though servers and applications can be installed directly under these two parent folders, some administrators might want to further organize their servers and applications, thereby easing manageability. This can be achieved by creating child folders and logically grouping servers and applications.

To create subfolders under the servers or applications folder in the CMC, follow these steps:

1. Open the **CMC**.

2. Highlight either the applications folder or the servers folder as shown in Figure 8.14.

Figure 8.14 Right-Clicking in the Application Folder

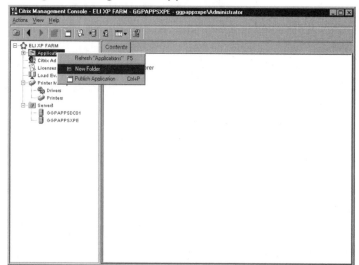

3. Right-click the highlighted folder and click **New Folder** from the menu that pops up.

4. Once the subfolder has been created you can simply drag and drop servers or applications to it.

Using the Citrix Installation Manager

The *Citrix Installation Manager (CIM)* is an advanced deployment tool available for use with MetaFrame XPe. It facilitates the quick deployment of applications to one or more servers in the farm. Applications or packages can also be deployed across a WAN. Packages that were installed using CIM can also be uninstalled using the tool, making it an imperative addition to your set of favorite administrative tools. You can use the CIM to automate the installation of applications, service packs, patches, hotfixes, and even Registry changes. Some of the features of CIM 2.1 include:

- A Packager capable of creating Application Deployment File (ADF) packages

- An Installer capable of installing ADF and MSI (Windows Installer files) packages; MSI packages must be created by third-party software but can be deployed using the Installer

- Scheduling the ADF or MSI application deployment package

- Installation of ADF packages created with MetaFrame 1.8 Installation Management Services 1.0

- Multiple application package deployment

- Status of installed jobs viewed from the console

Configuring & Implementing...

Installing Citrix Installation Manager 2.1 After FR1 Installation

If you install CIM 2.1 after MetaFrame XP Feature Release 1 (FR1) was installed, you need to reinstall FR1 before all the features of CIM will work. You might get the following error message: "Unknown Error Occurred Loading imsmgr.jar. Error Code 44C." Consult Citrix Document ID: CTX467868 for more information. You can search for the Citrix Document ID number at the Citrix Solution Knowledge Base located at http://knowledgebase.citrix.com/cgi-bin/webcgi.exe?New,KB=CitrixKB.

CIM 2.1 is three-component software that includes the Packager, the Citrix Installation Manager 2.1 plug-in for the CIM console, and the Installer. A proper implementation of CIM requires the following:

- A workstation or server that has the Citrix Management Console installed on it

- A network share where the ADF and MSI deployment packages can be stored

- MetaFrame XPe servers that are part of an IMA server farm that will be receiving the packages

- An application packager machine that will be used to create the packages

Configuring the Packager Utility

The Citrix Packager utility is used to create ADF packages; we recommend that you dedicate a server or a workstation that will be used solely for the purpose of building packages. The reason to dedicate a machine for building packages is that the machine will be clean and the software freshly installed and unused, therefore producing error-free packages.

It is important to note that different operating systems require different packages. It is also worth noting that in some cases the target computer receiving the package must be at a certain level with the software installed on it, especially when dealing with Windows NT 4.0 packages. Sometimes, for example, the target computer should be at a certain service pack level, or maybe Internet Explorer needs to be version 4.0 or 4.01.

To build a package using the Packager utility, follow these steps:

1. Click **Start | Programs | Citrix | Citrix Installation Manager | Citrix Packager**.

2. The first screen you see is the Project Wizard, as shown in Figure 8.15. Select **Create a new project using project wizard** and click **Next**.

Figure 8.15 The New Project Window

3. The next screen asks you to select a Project Wizard. Select **Package an Installation Recording** (shown in Figure 8.16) and click **Next**.

Figure 8.16 The Project Wizard Selection Window

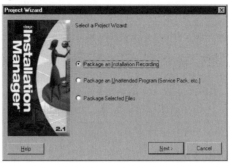

4. Step 1 of the wizard (shown in Figure 8.17) prompts you for a project name and a location where you want to place the package files and the package itself. A network share is recommended, even though in this scenario you have to browse to the actual directory.

Figure 8.17 The Project Name and Location Window

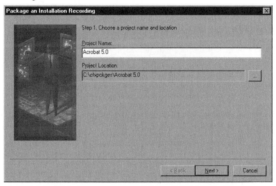

5. Step 2 of the wizard prompts you for the actual executable that will install the program and any command-line parameters that you would like to add to customize your setup. See Figure 8.18.

Figure 8.18 The Installation Program Window

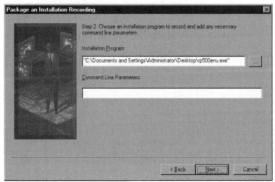

6. Step 3 of the wizard prompts you to either specify a compatibility script or leave it at no compatibility script, as shown in Figure 8.19.

Figure 8.19 The Compatibility Script Window

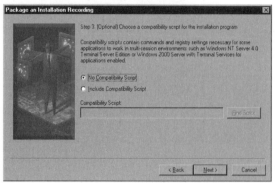

7. Step 4 of the wizard prompts you for a location where the package will be built. It usually defaults to the location you specified in Step 1. See Figure 8.20.

Figure 8.20 The Package Storage Location

8. This final screen shows you the results of the information you entered in the different prompts. Review it, and click **Finish** when ready. See Figure 8.21.

9. The recording starts and the installation of the application proceeds as it would normally. The recording will indicate when it is done, and the project will then be ready to build the package. See Figure 8.22.

10. Click **Project** from the File menu and click **Build Package**. The process begins posting (see Figure 8.23).

11. The package builds and is stored in the shared location under its project name.

Figure 8.21 The Summary Screen

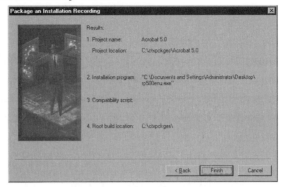

Figure 8.22 The Project Overview Window

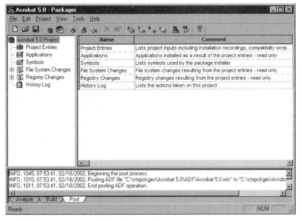

Figure 8.23 The Build Package Window

Setting Up the Installer Utility

The *Installation Manager Installer* must be installed on every MetaFrame XPe server in the farm that will receive ADF or MSI packages. The Installer consists of three components:

- **ADF Installer** Used to install ADF packages.
- **MSI Installer** Used to install MSI packages.

■ **Independent Management Architecture (IMA)** Used as a means to send and receive data such as scheduling and configuration information to the ADF installer.

Before the Installation Manager Installer can properly function it needs a user account with enough rights to the network share where the packages are stored, and enough rights to install applications on the MetaFrame XPe servers in the server farm. To set up this user account, follow these steps:

1. Open the **CMC**.

2. Right-click the **Installation Manager** node in the left pane of the CMC and select **Properties**. The Installation Manager Properties window appears. See Figure 8.24.

Figure 8.24 The Installation Manager Properties Window

3. Click **Browse** and select the proper user account. Click **Add**, then click **OK** and enter the user's password. See Figure 8.25.

Figure 8.25 The Add User Account Window

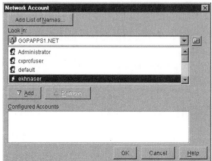

Using the CIM Plug-In for the CMC

Now that we have built a package, let's use the CIM plug-in for the CMC to deploy this package to the servers in the server farm. The following steps demonstrate how to do this:

1. Open the **CMC**.

2. Expand the **Installation Manager** node and right-click **Packages**.

3. Select **Add Package**.

4. A window pops up, prompting you for the package name and its location, as shown in Figure 8.26. The package can be of .wfs or .msi extensions.

Figure 8.26 The Package Name and Location Window

5. A window pops up asking if you would like to add any transform command-line switches. You have the option to select **Yes** or **No** depending on whether your application needs further switches for proper installation. *You will be prompted for this option only if you are deploying an MSI package.*

6. Your package is now displayed under the Packages node and is ready to be installed. Right-click **Packages** and move down the menu to **Install Package** and click it.

7. The first screen that you see prompts you to select the servers you would like to receive the package (see Figure 8.27). Highlight the server and click **Add**. You are also given the option to filter the operating system for which this package is destined.

8. The next screen is for scheduling (see Figure 8.28). You can click **Edit** and schedule the time when your package should be deployed. Click **Finish**.

Uninstalling Packages

When you're uninstalling packages or applications, it is very important to keep in mind how these packages or applications were originally installed. Applications that were installed using the normal setup program that comes with the software can be removed the traditional way by choosing **Add/Remove Programs** in the Control Panel. Packages or applications that were deployed and installed using the CIM need to be uninstalled using the CIM and *not* Add/Remove Programs.

Figure 8.27 The Servers Receiving Package Window

Figure 8.28 The Scheduling Window

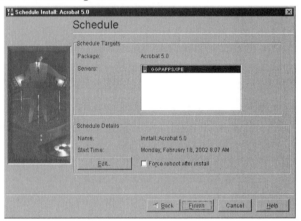

The CIM keeps a log of all the packages that were installed using its utilities; to uninstall a package, follow these steps:

1. Open the **CMC**.

2. Expand the **Installation Manager** node and highlight **Packages**.

3. On the right pane, select the **Installations** tab. A list of all installed packages on all the MetaFrame servers is displayed.

4. Right-click the server holding the package to be uninstalled and select **Uninstall Package**.

Using the Citrix Server Administration Tool

Citrix Server Administration still ships with MetaFrame XP as a standalone tool for the simple purpose of aiding administrators working in a mixed-mode environment. It should be used in the transition period while migrating to a native-mode MetaFrame XP server farm. The CMC has effectively replaced the Citrix Server Administration tool and absorbed all its features and functions for managing users and servers in the farm. Some of the features of the Server Administration tool include:

- Viewing server information
- Viewing session information
- Viewing users
- Viewing processes on a server
- Viewing published applications
- Shadowing users
- Sending a message to users
- Resetting sessions
- Ending processes
- Logging off users

Citrix Server Administration is divided into two panes: the left-hand pane, known as the *context pane*, and the right-hand pane, known as the *detail pane*. The context pane has three tabs that each offer a configuration option (see Figure 8.29):

- **Servers** Selecting this tab displays a list of all the available Citrix and terminal servers.

- **Published Applications** This tab displays a list of all published applications. Published applications that are not part of a server farm are listed as Unassociated Applications.

- **Video Servers** This tab displays a list of VideoFrame servers and information about their video streams.

Figure 8.29 The Citrix Server Administration Tool

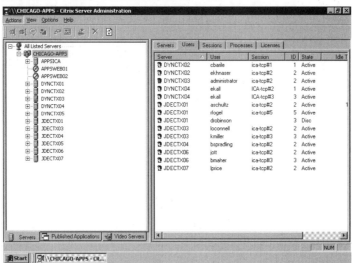

Managing Servers

The context pane of the Server Administration tool displays a list of servers; highlighting any of these servers displays in the detail pane several tabs that enable you to view different configurable options for the servers (see Figure 8.30):

- **Users** This tab lists currently connected users on the selected server; right-clicking any of these users provides you with a menu of management options.

- **Sessions** This tab displays a list of active and idle sessions for the selected server and gives you the ability to do some management tasks by right-clicking the selected session.

- **Processes** This tab provides you with a list of processes running on the selected server and gives you the ability to end a process by right-clicking it and selecting the appropriate option from the drop-down menu.

- **License** This tab provides licensing information for the selected server.

- **ICA Browser** This tab gives you numerous configuration options regarding the ICA browser settings or the selected server.

- **Information** This tab provides information regarding the operating system, any installed service packs, and hotfixes installed on the selected server.

Figure 8.30 Server Tabs

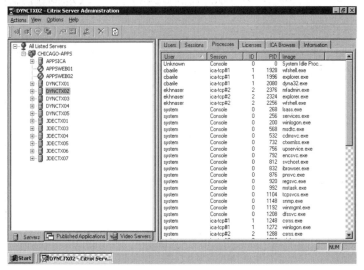

Managing Users and Sessions

The Citrix Server Administration tool provides you with a way to manage users and sessions. By right-clicking a user or session name, you get a menu with the following options:

- **Connect** Allows you to connect to a different ICA session or reconnect a disconnected session.

- **Disconnect** Allows you to disconnect a session without ending it. The session continues to run on the server and can be reconnected at a later time as needed.

- **Send Message** Sends one or more users a message. You can hold down the Shift key and click additional users, then right-click and send them all a message at the same time.

- **Shadow** Allows you to shadow a user's session. You can either interact with the session or view what is going on in order to pinpoint a problem or troubleshoot an issue. This is a great help desk function.

- **Reset** Immediately terminates a user's sessions with no notice or any grace period to close any open files or applications.

- **Status** This option allows you to view bytes and frames and to easily see if data is flowing back and forth. This too is a good troubleshooting mechanism.

- **Logoff** This option is a little more merciful on the user and gives the user a grace period to close applications and open files before it terminates his or her session.

Let's consider an example of how you would use these tools. Assume that a user is working on a very important document and is suddenly disconnected from the server. He tries to reconnect but doesn't seem to be able to log back into his session, so he gives you a call. You can check the CSA and find his username. In most cases his session will have the Disc status. You right-click that session and click **Connect**. You are then connected to that session and are able to save his document to a shared location so that he can access and retrieve his document.

Look at another example of how to use these options. Assume that a server is behaving erratically and requires a reboot. The server has 15 users connected to it. You can select all the users by holding down the **Ctrl** key on the keyboard and clicking the names of the users one at a time until they are all selected. At this point you can right-click any one of them and click **Send Message**. You send a message asking the users to log off and log back in. In the meantime, you can right-click that particular server and click **Disable New Logons** so that when the users reconnect, they will attach to another server. This way you free the server of its sessions and disturb your users as little as possible.

Shadowing

The Citrix shadowing utility provides the ability to remotely control, monitor, and interact with another user's session. During a shadow session, the session being monitored is displayed in the shadower's session window. The monitored session can be viewed only, or the shadower can interact with the monitored session, depending on the configuration. When the session is placed in interactive mode, all keyboard and mouse strokes are passed to the monitored session.

Shadowing is one of the most powerful tools available on the MetaFrame server; as is always the case with such tools, it has the potential for misuse. The power of these tools lies in their ability to spy on users without their permission, which can be considered an intrusion of privacy and could have legal consequences. For these reasons, you should make careful selection of the user base that will be given Shadowing rights, and you should configure shadowing according to your company policy.

Microsoft Windows 2000 Terminal Services supports one-to-one shadowing (remote control) using RDP 5. Like the Microsoft product, a Citrix MetaFrame server also allows for one-to-one shadowing using RDP from within the Citrix Server Administration tool. Using the ICA protocol, MetaFrame supports one-to-one, one-to-many, and many-to-one shadowing using the Shadow taskbar. In previous versions, you could not establish shadow sessions from the console without installing the client and running a virtual session to the client from which to initiate the shadow session. The MetaFrame taskbar now provides the ability to shadow user sessions from the console. The many-to-one shadow sessions provide a fantastic remote learning tool. Several students (or remote clients) can shadow one instructor, who can teach from the comfort of her own office or training facility. Think of the savings that could result for companies that frequently have to fly clients or users across the country for software training and then pay for meals and lodging, too.

> ## WARNING
>
> By default, a user who is being shadowed is prompted with a popup window telling them that \\server\user is requesting to control their session remotely and giving them the option to allow or refuse the shadow session. This notification can be disabled in the connection profiles or in the individual user profile. Before disabling this notification, be sure that you have the authority to do so and have obtained the necessary waiver(s) from your users. Many companies now require, at every initial server logon, a popup with some type of legal disclaimer and privacy waiver. This could also suffice for monitoring purposes, depending on the wording. Consult with your attorney before attempting to conduct any "covert" monitoring. Failure to do so could have serious legal ramifications. For all these reasons, many companies have decided not to allow any sort of shadowing.

Specifying Shadow Permissions to a Connection Profile

By default, normal users do not have permissions to shadow other users. Shadowing is an advanced feature normally reserved for administrators only. Under some circumstances, however, you might find it necessary to grant shadow permissions to other users, perhaps temporarily or long term, such as with a distance learning program or corporate training over a WAN. Obviously, it would not be wise to give remote users and probably not even your own users full administrative rights over your server just so they can shadow. It might not be wise to leave these permissions on all the time or long term, since you can't control whom users can shadow. If you do need to grant users shadowing rights, you might have to place special configurations and restrictions on the server or the domain. The steps to grant shadow permissions are simple, but they can be hard to locate and remember:

1. Create a new group and call it something like **shadow group**.

2. Next, add any users you want to have shadow rights to the shadow group you just created.

3. Now all you have to do is assign the users the permissions.

4. While you're still in the Citrix Connection Configuration utility, highlight the connection type you want to configure and choose the **Security | Permissions** pull-down menu from the main Connection Configuration screen. You should see the ICA users and permissions window shown in Figure 8.31.

Figure 8.31 Assigning Shadow Users

5. Click the **Add** button and add your **shadow group** from the user list. By default, it will be given **Guest Access**.

6. Check the box to grant **User Access** as well.

7. Click the **Advanced** button to bring up the Advanced User Permissions window.

8. Highlight your shadow group and click the **View/Edit** button, as shown in Figure 8.32.

9. After you click the **View/Edit** button, you will see a permission page with **Query**, **Logon**, **Message**, and **Connect** selected. Here is where you also want to select **Shadow**, as shown in Figure 8.33.

10. That's it! Click **OK** until you return to the connection configuration screen. Your new shadow group is ready to start watching.

Be sure to instruct the users on proper shadowing methods. You might also want to configure shadowing for viewing only if your application requirements allow it; this will keep the shadowers from inadvertently interacting with the monitored sessions.

Figure 8.32 Advanced User Permissions

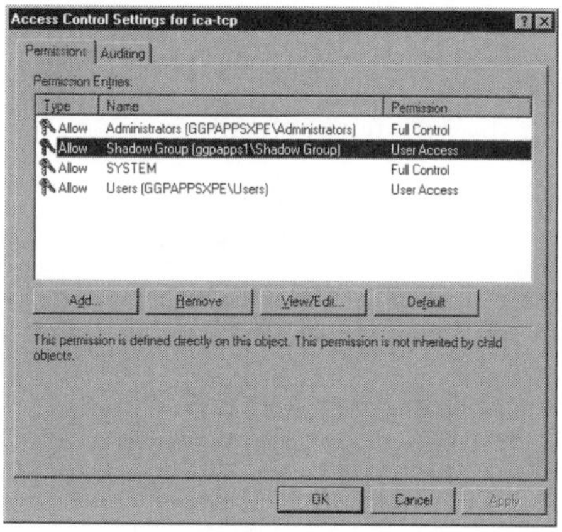

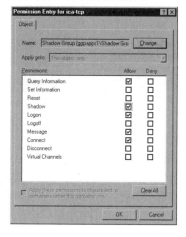

Figure 8.33 Granting the Shadow Permission

Establishing a Shadowing Session

There are two methods to establish shadow sessions on Citrix MetaFrame. The first uses the ICA Shadow taskbar; the second is accessed from within the Citrix Server Administration tool. The preferred method is the first, using the Shadow taskbar, since it has the most features and the most flexibility.

Establishing a Shadow Session Using the Shadow Taskbar

Let's first establish a shadow session using the Shadow taskbar:

1. Click **Start | Programs | Citrix | MetaFrame XP Tools | Shadow Taskbar**, or simply click the **Shadow Taskbar** icon at the bottom of the

MetaFrame toolbar. The Shadow taskbar opens and a new toolbar should appear at the top of your screen.

3. Click the **Shadow** button. You will be presented with the Shadow Session option screen shown in Figure 8.34.

Figure 8.34 The Shadow Taskbar

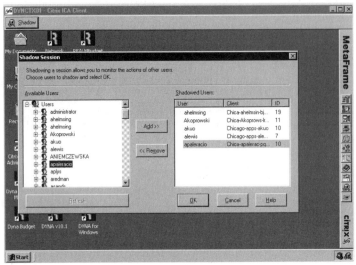

3. Expand the **Users** folder in the left window and highlight the name of the user you want to shadow. It might take a few seconds to enumerate the users and applications.

4. Click the **Add** button. Repeat Steps 3 and 4 until all the users you want to shadow appear in the right window.

5. Click the **OK** button to begin shadowing.

6. By default, the users will be presented with a popup window, asking for permission to shadow them. (See the preceding Warning sidebar.)

7. If the users accept the shadow session or if notification has been disabled, you are now able to view and/or interact with their sessions. You will also have a button added to the Shadow taskbar for each session you are monitoring. You can switch between sessions by clicking the respective button on the taskbar.

8. To log out of the shadow session, use the hotkey **Ctrl + ★** (default) or the hotkey you configured for the session. You can also right-click the session button on the taskbar and click **Stop Shadow**.

Establishing a Shadow Session Using the Citrix Server Administration Tool

Now let's establish a shadow session using the Citrix Server Administration Tool:

1. Click **Start| Programs | Citrix | MetaFrame XP Tools | Citrix Server Administration**. This sequence starts the Citrix Server Administration tool in a new window. It might take a few seconds to enumerate the users and applications. See Figure 8.35.

Figure 8.35 The Citrix Server Administration Tool

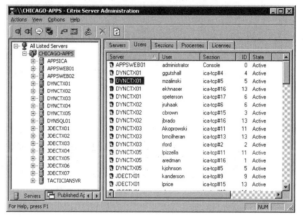

2. Right-click the name of the user you want to shadow, then choose **Shadow**, or select the user you want to monitor and choose **Shadow** from the **Action** pull-down menu.

3. By default, the users are presented with a popup window asking for permission to shadow. (See the preceding Warning sidebar.)

4. If the users accept the shadow session or if notification has been disabled, you are now able to view and/or interact with their sessions.

5. To log out of the shadow session, use the hotkey **Ctrl + *** (default) or the hotkey you configured for the session.

Desveloping & Deploying...

Expert Shadowing Tips

Shadowing is a great tool (and fun to play with), but it does have its limitations. The Console session itself cannot be shadowed (a good thing). Here are some of the capabilities and limitations you need to know in order to make the best use of the shadow feature.

- Sessions started using Citrix Server Administration are capable of only one-to-one sessions.

- Sessions can also be started and function the same using Terminal Services Manager (referred to as *remote control* instead of *shadowing*).

- You cannot shadow or enumerate RDP users with the Shadow taskbar, only ICA clients.

- Since the Shadow taskbar cannot enumerate RDP users, you cannot shadow RDP users from the console, nor can RDP support many-to-one or one-to-many sessions.

- If a user refuses the shadow session by answering "No" or fails to respond "Yes" to grant permission within approximately 30 seconds, the request will time out and, in either case, return an error message #7044 stating that "The request to control another session was denied."

- You may start a shadow session only from the same protocol—for example, RDP to RDP, ICA to ICA.

- You cannot shadow an ICA session from a RDP session, or vice versa.

- Even though you can only shadow a user who is using the same protocol, such as ICA to ICA or RDP to RDP, you are still free to select the Transport protocol you like. An ICA session running over TCP can shadow another ICA session running over IPX, for example.

- The shadowing session must be capable of an equal or greater video resolution than the session being monitored, or the shadowing operation will fail.

- Be sure you have the hardware required for the task. Running multiple shadow sessions can use a large amount of server memory and system resources. Many companies that need numerous shadow sessions usually dedicate one or more servers to the task. Load balancing can be extremely helpful in this situation.

Continued

- Only administrators have the permissions to shadow other users by default. To grant other users shadow rights, create a special group, then assign that group shadow permissions in the Advanced Security tab of Connection Profiles. See the sidebar titled "Specifying Shadow Permissions" in the "Connection Profiles" section for a detailed explanation.

- When you shadow another user's session, your performance drops by half. Let's say that you have a connection of 28.8kbps and you shadow another user. Your connection performance as the shadower is reduced to half, or 14.4kbps in this example.

Using the Citrix Connection Configuration Tool

The Citrix Connection Configuration tool is used to configure and manage network protocols and to allow incoming connections to a Citrix server. Connections range from ICA, RDP, or async connections for dial-in users via modem or AT Attached Packet Interface (ATAPI) devices. From within this tool, you can set security on the various protocols as well as configure their options. Upon the installation of MetaFrame on top of Terminal Server, an ICA and an RDP connection are automatically created— although configuring them is a task that you have to accomplish. RDP is Microsoft's version of a thin client protocol used to access Terminal Server and remotely establish sessions on those servers.

NOTE

A benefit to having both RDP and ICA configured on your servers is that should you want to prohibit users from logging in while you perform maintenance tasks on your servers, you can disable the ICA protocol and use RDP for your access. You can do so by opening the Citrix Connection Configuration tool, right-clicking the protocol you want to disable, and clicking **Disable**. Obviously, the only way this works is if you have deployed only ICA clients to your users. If you have Windows XP on your network, note that it comes with a native RDP client via which users can access the server, so keep an eye on that as well.

RDP, however, lacks many of the features that are available with ICA. For example, RDP is limited to supporting only TCP/IP, whereas ICA can support a larger number of protocols, including TCP/IP, IPX, Sequenced Packet Exchange (SPX), and NetBIOS. The ICA client is also readily available for virtually any kind of operating system, whereas RDP is strictly limited to Microsoft operating systems. See Figure 8.36 for a snapshot of the Citrix Connection Configuration tool.

Figure 8.36 The Citrix Connection Configuration Tool

To add a new connection to the Citrix Connection Configuration tool, follow these steps:

1. Open the Citrix Connection Configuration tool by going to **Start | Programs | Citrix | MetaFrame XP | Citrix Connection Configuration**.

2. From the **Connection** menu, choose **New Connection**. The new connection window appears. See Figure 8.37.

Figure 8.37 The New Connection Window

3. Give the connection a name. From the **Type** drop-down menu, select either **Citrix ICA 3.0** or **Microsoft RDP 5.0**.

4. From the **Transport** drop-down menu, select the transport method, **TCP** or **Async**.

5. Click **OK**.

Now that you have created a connection, you have to customize it using the various options available through the properties of each connection. Right-clicking any of the connections and going to Properties opens the Properties window, where you can configure three options:

- **Advanced** These are the advanced options available for a selected connection. This setting allows administrators to configure security for incoming connections (see Figure 8.38).

Figure 8.38 The Advanced Window

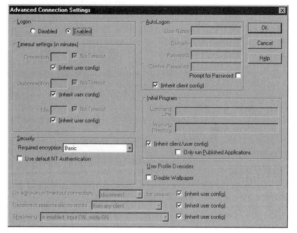

> **NOTE**
>
> We strongly recommend that you configure a timeout setting, which will terminate connected, disconnected, or idle sessions after a specified amount of time. This setting preserves resources on the server by not allowing a user to remain idle for more than a defined time period—one hour, for example. This can also help prevent the ICA browser from crashing in older versions of MetaFrame.

- **ICA Settings** This button allows administrators to configure the level of audio settings the client receives; the options are low, medium, or high. The higher you put this setting, the more bandwidth it will require. See Figure 8.39.

- **Client Settings** This button gives you the ability to configure many client options, such as printer mappings, drive mappings, and many other user-level settings. See Figure 8.40.

Figure 8.39 The ICA Settings Window

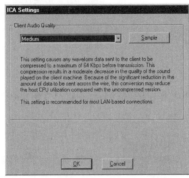

Figure 8.40 The Client Settings Window

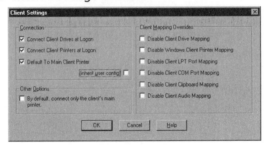

NOTE

Unless it's absolutely necessary to keep it enabled, we recommend that you disable the client audio mapping. This frees resources on the server, makes the client session run more smoothly and with lesser latency, and can preserve bandwidth.

So, how can we use all these functions to our advantage when administering these servers? Let's assume that you are in an environment where your users are in the habit of logging in to a MetaFrame server in the morning and staying connected all day. In the middle of the day, you see a list of users with idle times of six or seven hours. These idle times represent unnecessary resources being consumed on the server. To prevent users from connecting and staying connected forever, you can set a timeout setting for idle sessions or even disconnected sessions. The cleaner your server, the better it will run. To accomplish this task, you can open the **Citrix Connection Configuration** tool, double-click the protocol on which you want to set these settings, and click the **Advanced** button. In the Timeout Settings section, you can configure it to drop connections that have been connected for a certain amount of time. Disconnected sessions can also be dropped based on a similar preconfigured interval. The interval is set in minutes.

Let's look at another scenario. Say that you are in an environment where you don't care to give your users sound. You can disable client audio mapping. This is a great way to enhance the quality and the speed of user sessions. To disable client audio mapping, open the **Citrix Connection Configuration** tool, double-click the protocol on which you want to disable this setting, and click **Client Settings**. Check the box by **Disable Client Audio Mapping**. This choice ensures that no sound is transmitted in your users' sessions.

Configuring the SpeedScreen Latency Reduction Manager

The *SpeedScreen Latency Reduction Manager* was especially developed to help reduce bandwidth load on the incoming session, thereby speeding up the connection and the client's interaction with the server. This feature was mainly created for slow connections such as dialup or slow network connections. The user might notice a latency when typing a word, for example, where he does not see the result of what he is typing until a few seconds later, or maybe he double-clicks the mouse or selects something that doesn't seem to take effect until a few seconds later. This sort of behavior frustrates users. Citrix has developed SpeedScreen specifically to address these issues.

The two main features of the SpeedScreen Latency Reduction Manager are:

- **Local text echo** This feature ensures that whatever the user is typing instantly appears on his or her screen. See Figure 8.41.

Figure 8.41 The Local Echo and Mouse Click Window

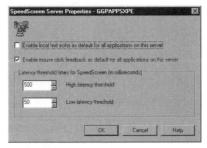

- **Mouse click feedback** This feature acknowledges the clicks the user makes and changes the mouse pointer to an hourglass, informing the user that it is performing the command and that no further clicks are necessary.

To configure SpeedScreen, follow these steps:

1. Open the SpeedScreen Latency Reduction Manager by choosing **Start | Programs | Citrix | MetaFrame XP | SpeedScreen Latency Reduction Manager**. See Figure 8.42.

Figure 8.42 The SpeedScreen Latency Reduction Manager

2. Right-click the Citrix server on which you want to configure SpeedScreen. Click **Server Properties**. The SpeedScreen Latency Reduction Server Properties window appears.

3. From this window you can enable or disable local text echo or mouse click feedback. You can also set thresholds for SpeedScreen refresh times.

You can also configure a specific application to take advantage of SpeedScreen Latency Reduction. This can be accomplished by following these simple steps:

1. Open the SpeedScreen Latency Reduction Manager by choosing **Start | Programs | Citrix | MetaFrame XP | SpeedScreen Latency Reduction Manager**.

2. Right-click the server the application is installed on and click **Add New Application**.

3. A wizard starts and guides you through selecting the application. Next you will be asked to browse to the application executable.

4. After clicking **Next**, you come to a screen that prompts you to either check or uncheck **Local text echo** for this application.

5. The next screen prompts you to select between applying these settings to only this installation of the application or to all installations of this application.

6. Click **Finish**.

7. After the wizard completes, the application is added to the list under its respective server. From this point you can right-click that application and go to **Application Properties**. See Figures 8.43 and 8.44.

Figure 8.43 Application in SpeedScreen Latency Manager

Figure 8.44 The Application Settings Window

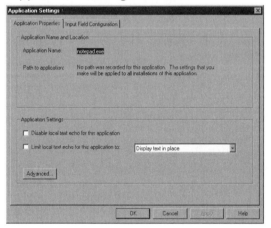

8. This window offers two tabs, **Application Properties** and **Input Field Configuration**, both of which offer further options that you can configure to tweak SpeedScreen into providing better performance.

When would you use SpeedScreen Latency Reduction Manager? Should you use it over any connection or in specific instances? The purpose behind the creation of SpeedScreen Latency Reduction Manager is to speed up and improve sessions that run over slow communication links. SpeedScreen Latency Reduction Manager need not be implemented on a LAN, because the communications lines are very stable. It is a great idea to implement this technology when your connection is wireless and prone to error or instability. Satellite links and dialup services are also candidates that benefit from this feature.

Summary

In this chapter we have covered several important features that make the overall management of Citrix MetaFrame XP servers easier. We started off by talking about the Citrix Management Console (CMC) and how it centralizes management of servers, users, and published applications. The CMC provides for a centralized point for managing licenses and print drivers and adding Citrix administrators. Some advantages of using the CMC are that it can be installed on a desktop running a supported operating system such as Windows NT 4.0 or Windows 2000. In addition, you can install Citrix Installation Manager (CIM), which adds a plug-in to the CMC, enabling you to install packages from within the CMC. Farm properties can also be managed from the CMC.

The CIM is a three-component package that includes the Packager, the Citrix Installation Manager 2.1 plug-in for the Citrix Management Console, and the Installer. The Packager creates ADF packages. The Installer installs ADF and MSI packages and needs to be installed on every MetaFrame XP server in the farm that will receive these packages. The CIM plug-in for the CMC, which is used to schedule package deployment, determines how many packages will be installed and allows you to view the status of packages being deployed. You can also uninstall packages that were installed with CIM from within the CMC.

Citrix Server Administration is a tool used to manage users, servers, published applications, and video servers. This tool has been replaced by the CMC, but it still exists and can be useful in migrations or in environments where previous versions of MetaFrame and WinFrame still exist.

Citrix Connection Configuration is a tool designed to create and administer the type of connections that can be made to a Citrix MetaFrame XP server. You can create a new connection and configure and modify the various features and settings available through the Citrix Connection Configuration.

The SpeedScreen Latency Reduction Manager enhances slow connections such as dialup and slow network connections. Its features include a *local text echo*, which ensures that the user gets a prompt response and can see the results of what he or she is typing, and a *mouse click echo*, which acknowledges to the user the fact that he or she has clicked on something by turning the mouse pointer into an hourglass until the command is executed. These features prevent the user from continuously clicking and overclocking the CPU.

Solutions Fast Track

Using the Citrix Management Console

☑ The Citrix Management Console is a great new tool that centralizes the administration of your server farm, giving you all the tools you need to properly administer the farm.

☑ Direct connections to the IMA occur when a MetaFrame server establishes a direct connection to the IMA database. Indirect connections occur when one MetaFrame server acts as an intermediary for the other servers, linking them to the IMA.

☑ Data can be set to autorefresh; however, this function is disabled by default because it requires extra bandwidth. Manually refreshing data using the F5 key is recommended.

Using the Citrix Installation Manager

☑ The Packager is a tool that ships with Citrix Installation Manager and is used to create ADF packages. It is recommended that you dedicate a computer for machine builds.

☑ The Citrix Management Console plug-in adds a snap-in to the CMC, allowing you to administer CIM packages and features from one central location.

☑ The Installer is composed of three components: the DF installer, the MSI installer, and the IMA, which is used as a means of communication with the ADF installer.

Using the Citrix Server Administration Tool

☑ Citrix Server Administration is a tool used for administering older versions of MetaFrame, WinFrame, and Terminal Servers. Citrix recommends using the CMC for any administration needs but offers this utility for backward compatibility.

☑ Managing servers is easily accomplished using the Citrix Server Administration tool; you can view users connected to the servers, sessions, processes, licenses, and information regarding the operating system and the hotfixes and services packs installed on it.

☑ Managing users is another function administrators cope with on a daily basis. The Citrix Server Administration tool provides you with the ability to connect, disconnect, shadow, send a message, reset, or log off users.

Using the Citrix Connection Configuration Tool

☑ Citrix Connection Configuration is a utility used to create and configure connections such as an ICA Connection; you can configure its client, advanced, and ICA settings.

☑ RDP is Microsoft's version of a thin client protocol. However, it is not as robust or feature rich as ICA.

☑ Async connections are used with ATAPI devices, mainly modems, to allow direct dial-in connections to the server.

Configuring the SpeedScreen Latency Reduction Manager

☑ Local text echo is a feature of SpeedScreen latency that will not allow a delay to occur between the time when the user types and the time when the results are actually seen on the monitor.

☑ Mouse click echo is a function that changes the mouse pointer when a click command is issued. The pointer changes to an hourglass, indicating to the user that it is processing the command.

☑ You can configure SpeedScreen Latency Reduction by application to provide latency reduction and management, even to certain fields within an application.

Frequently Asked Questions

The following Frequently Asked Questions, answered by the authors of this book, are designed to both measure your understanding of the concepts presented in this chapter and to assist you with real-life implementation of these concepts. To have your questions about this chapter answered by the author, browse to **www.syngress.com/solutions** and click on the **"Ask the Author"** form.

Q: On which TCP port are direct connections established to the IMA database?

A: Direct connections to the IMA database are established on TCP port 2513.

Q: We are a very security-oriented company and usually like to scramble the default ports used by the products we use. On which TCP port are indirect connections established to the IMA database? Can this be changed?

A: Indirect connections to the IMA database are established on TCP port 2512. This port *can* be changed, by editing two Registry keys as follows:

- On the server holding the data store, edit the following Registry key and change its value to the number you want:
  HKLM\Software\Citrix\IMA\ImaPort

- On all the other MetaFrame XP servers, change the value of the Registry key to match the one you entered:
  HKLM\Software\Citrix\IMA\PsServerPort

Q: I noticed that Automatic Data Refresh disabled by default. Why? I am thinking about enabling it and setting its refresh interval to 10 seconds. Are there any considerations I have to account for?

A: Yes. Automatic Data Refresh is disabled by default because of the extra network traffic it generates. Enabling the Automatic Data Refresh should be done when its use doesn't affect network performance. If your network suffers from traffic and slowness, it is a bad idea to enable this feature. The alternative method of data refresh is the old-fashioned method: using the F5 key on your keyboard. However, if you are happy with your network performance, you can enable Automatic Data Refresh. Because the setting of 10 seconds will generate a great deal of unnecessary traffic, I recommend you chose a higher setting.

Q: Our published applications require at least 16-bit colors to run properly. We would also like to offer our users some sound. Which connection type, ICA or RDP, would meet these requirements?

A: The protocol that should be used in this case is most definitely ICA. RDP doesn't provide for colors greater than 256 and cannot offer sound, so the obvious choice is ICA, which can provide colors of up to 24 bits as well as sound and is a far more advanced and feature-rich protocol.

Q: How does SpeedScreen enhance a user's overall session experience? Should I use it over any connection type?

A: By invoking features such as local text echo and mouse click echo, the user will not be frustrated when typing and not seeing the results of his actions or when using the mouse and not seeing a prompt response to his mouse action. With SpeedScreen, these issues are addressed, and thus the overall experience over slow links is greatly improved. The purpose of the SpeedScreen Latency Reduction Manager is to enhance user sessions over slow links, so it should be used only over slow communication lines such as wireless, satellite, and dialup.

Q: I have a server farm that counts 15 servers centralized on a LAN. Which database can I use for the data store? What type of ODBC connection should I make to the data store?

A: In this scenario, your choice should be Microsoft Access. Access is very fast and can service a farm that has up to 50 servers without degrading performance. Your farm is also centralized on a LAN, so you do not need database replication. Microsoft Access accepts only indirect ODBC connections.

Q: We have a large MetaFrame XP server farm and we are wondering which database engine to use, Microsoft SQL or Oracle. How should we configure ODBC connections?

A: Citrix claims that both Microsoft SQL and Oracle database servers performed equally well when tested on large farms and over WAN links, so in this case you can chose the database application that your IT staff or you are more comfortable operating and administering. ODBC should be configured for direct connection. Direct connection eliminates the unnecessary step of using an intermediary server to connect to the database. Direct-mode connections minimize the IMA service start time.

Chapter 9

Installing and Publishing Applications

Solutions in this chapter:

- Selecting Compatible Applications
- Installing Applications
- Optimizing Application Performance
- Publishing Applications
- Program Neighborhood

☑ Summary

☑ Solutions Fast Track

☑ Frequently Asked Questions

Introduction

Applications are the entire reason for deploying a thin client solution. Without an application, the only thing a user sees when she connects is an operating system desktop—a mere shell of what she really needs.

A multitude of applications can be used on Citrix MetaFrame XP. Many applications cannot be used, however. Some run fine on the server locally, but due to their intense graphics or video, they do not perform well over a slow link. You can use variety of methods to enable compatibility and optimize performance; these methods are discussed in this chapter.

Once an application is installed, it can be published for use. Users can access the application through Program Neighborhood or NFuse. Both users and administrators should become familiar with Program Neighborhood and the ICA toolbar.

Selecting Compatible Applications

Citrix MetaFrame XP for Windows servers support the use of 16-bit and 32-bit Windows-based applications in addition to DOS applications. Careful consideration must be given to all applications that are to be installed on any Citrix MetaFrame XP server. A single application that performs poorly on a Citrix MetaFrame XP server might affect not only the user running the application but all other users connected to the same server. This poor performance could be exhibited by excessive CPU-generated tasks or excessive bandwidth. These behaviors from this single application can create an undue burden on the server, causing all other connected users to contend with this poorly performing application. Applications installed on a MetaFrame server do not necessarily need to be compatible with the client platform—a major benefit to running applications from a MetaFrame environment.

An ideal application for a MetaFrame environment is one that is 32-bit, makes proper use of the registry to store per-user and global information about the program, and is bandwidth and graphically efficient. Most newly written programs exhibit these traits, especially those written for Windows 2000 and that are certified. It is almost impossible, however, to create and maintain a MetaFrame environment without at least a single application that requires some form of manipulation in order for it to work correctly. A Microsoft white paper outlines some suggestions aimed toward application developers for optimizing their applications in a multiuser environment. Some of the documented items include these:

- **Correctly separating per-user information** This task is achieved by storing user information in the HKEY_CURRENT USER (HKCU) hive and by storing global application information in the HKEY_LOCAL_ MACHINE (HKLM) registry hive. By keeping per-user information in the

HKCU hive, users can save personal settings within a program without affecting the personal settings of another user. For example, consider a spell-check option within a program. User A can disable spell-check within her application while not affecting the personal settings of User B, who has the spell-check feature enabled. Global information, such as the path to an application or the components installed, can be installed to the HKLM hive.

- **Minimizing splash screen use** Splash screens can introduce unnecessary bandwidth consumption and force the user to wait to access the application.

- **Do not assume that a single IP address or computer name equates to a single user** This can be particularly troubling within a MetaFrame environment. For example, to keep network drives within reasonable size limits, disk quota software monitors all network shares to make sure that they stay within their limits. To alert users that their network share is nearing capacity, it sends a message to the IP address of all users attached to the network share. In the case of a user working from a MetaFrame server, this message is directed to the server's IP address, but instead of a single user receiving the capacity alert, all users attached to the server receive the alert, whether they share the same network drive or not. As can be expected, this message can make for some confused users.

To read the entire contents of the Microsoft document, refer to the following link: www.microsoft.com/WINDOWS2000/techinfo/planning/terminal/tsappdev.asp.

Citrix MetaFrame servers can also run 16-bit applications, but they are run through a process called Windows on Windows (WOW) that translates the 16-bit applications into enhanced mode. Because of WOW, these 16-bit applications require more server resources in the form of processor utilization and memory consumption. On average, a server running 16-bit applications can reduce the number of users per processor by 40 percent and cause the memory required per user to increase 50 percent. For these reasons, every attempt should be made to run 32-bit applications whenever possible.

Some of the more common problems with 16-bit and MS-DOS-based applications are these:

- **MS-DOS-based applications poll for device input** Certain MS-DOS-based applications poll for certain activities such as keyboard, mouse, or other hardware device inputs. This is especially true in keyboard polling. Many MS-DOS-based applications "poll," or query, the keyboard, waiting for some form of input. This polling is often too CPU-intensive to run effectively on a Citrix MetaFrame XP server.

- **Fox Pro-based MS-DOS databases tend to be CPU interrupt-intensive** This can over-utilize CPU resources, causing resources to be taken away from all other user sessions.

- **Problems with legacy Windows applications** Legacy Windows-based applications that directly access .ini files instead of using standard functions might not work correctly if multiple users simultaneously access the same .ini file.

Another issue with running DOS windows on Citrix MetaFrame XP servers is that the DOS applications run at odd screen sizes or in full-size screens only at unexpected times, which can be frustrating to users. Batch files can be used to start a DOS window in a more controlled manner. The use of batch files to start a DOS application and set specific environment controls is an ancient art and not often used to launch individual applications today. However, an administrator should investigate using batch files when DOS applications are required. Not having the right environment results in an inconsistent or unstable application, which is easily fixed by a batch file or system tweaking. These are a few of the problems associated with older, legacy applications. The following Microsoft MSDN site has more details on this subject: http://msdn.microsoft.com/library/default.asp?url=/library/en-us/termserv/tsovr_9cok.asp.

To summarize, when at all possible, use 32-bit applications. For the 16-bit and MS-DOS-based applications on which users currently depend that you are considering migrating into a MetaFrame environment, investigate upgrades or 32-bit alternatives whenever possible.

Preparing the Environment

Take the time to plan the environment you'll build if you're in the preproduction stages. Insufficient planning at this stage could cause problems later when you're managing the environment. Take the time to document the following:

1. Generate a list of all the applications that are to be installed within the Citrix MetaFrame XP environment. This includes all the standard applications in addition to any helper applications such as Adobe Acrobat.

2. Generate a list of all the system components required by the list of standard applications. An example is an application that requires the Microsoft Oracle ODBC Driver version 2.5.

3. Outline any additional software that might be needed to install the applications onto the servers. For example, installing Microsoft Office 2000 requires the use of a transform file. You can customize a transform file using the Custom Installation Wizard included in the Microsoft Office 2000 Resource Kit.

4. Design a matrix of all potential users of these applications, delineating groups that will use each application. Refer to Table 9.1 for an example.

Table 9.1 A Matrix of Applications and Potential Users

	Microsoft Office 2000	FTP Voyager	Personal Communications	Adobe PageMaker
Accounting	X		X	
Advertising	X		X	X
Executive	X			
Human resources	X		X	
Information technology	X	X	X	

5. Create a list of users who will be responsible for testing the applications and determining whether or not the applications work to their satisfaction.

By preparing this information in advance, you can minimize your chance of running into surprises during the server setup. Ensure that the users who have been chosen to help test an application understand the responsibility of their task and that they will be working in a test environment. Make it clear that their input is very important in helping to work out all the bugs in the environment before the server is put into a production state.

Installing Applications

Installing any application on a Citrix MetaFrame server in a correct and repeatable fashion is as important as any other administrative function performed within a MetaFrame environment. If the applications are installed while missing key components or are installed differently across server farms, it does not matter how well the servers scale or how users to access the applications. Here are some steps to perform before the installation process:

1. Read any documentation regarding the application's installation and the minimum hardware and software requirements. It is a waste of time to attempt to install an application if the operating environment does not meet the application's minimum requirements.

2. Install the software on a workstation before installing it on a Citrix MetaFrame server. This step allows an administrator to understand the kind of application installation options that can be expected, in addition to the complexity and knowledge required to install the application. In circumstances in which people within the company have working knowledge of how the

application has been installed in the past, it is best to have them advise or monitor the installation process.

Once these steps have been completed, the application may be installed on a Citrix MetaFrame server. Here are the basic procedures for installing an application onto a Citrix MetaFrame server (a more detailed example of the steps follows):

1. Log on to the console of the MetaFrame server with a user who is a member of the local Administrator group.

2. Ensure that no users are logged on to the server. This can be done by using the Citrix Management Console.

3. Enter **install mode** before installing the application via the **Add/Remove Programs** applet within **Control Panel** or from the command prompt by typing **change user /install**.

4. Install the application.

5. Document the entire process to duplicate later.

6. Enter execute mode once the application installation has ended by typing **change user / execute** at the command prompt.

7. Perform any additional installation modifications that might be required, such as exploiting installation mode to make global changes (which we discuss later) or running an application compatibility script.

8. Reboot the server, if necessary, and begin testing the application.

NOTE

Before attempting an application installation, you can run a baseline against the server. Select a base number of users, such as 30. Run Performance Monitor to check the type of resources—CPU, memory, disk I/O—that are being used and save the chart. Then, after the application has been installed, run Performance Monitor again and compare the new application chart against the old.

To demonstrate, here is an example of how to install Adobe Acrobat 5.05 from start to finish:

1. Log on to the console of the Citrix MetaFrame Server using the local Administrator account.

2. From the **Citrix MetaFrame XP toolbar**, open the **Citrix Management Console** and highlight the server from the Servers node (see Figure 9.1). Ensure that no other users are logged on to the server.

Figure 9.1 The Citrix Management Console Showing Active Sessions

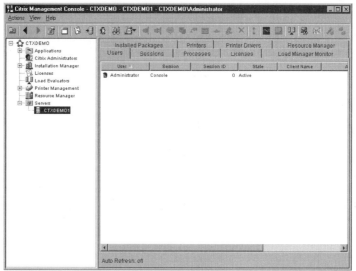

3. Close the **Citrix Management Console**.

4. From the desktop, select **Start | Settings | Control Panel**.

5. Within the Control Panel, double-click the **Add/Remove Programs** applet.

6. From the Add/Remove Programs window, click the **Add New Programs** button. (See Figure 9.2.)

Figure 9.2 The Add/Remove Programs Applet

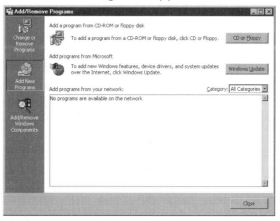

7. Select the **CD or Floppy** button.

8. At the Install Program From Floppy Disk or CD-ROM screen, select **Next**. (See Figure 9.3.)

Figure 9.3 Entering Install Mode

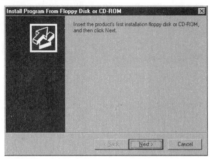

9. At the Run Installation Program message, either browse to or enter the path to the Adobe Acrobat 5.05 installation executable. (See Figure 9.4.)

Figure 9.4 Entering the Application Installation Executable Path

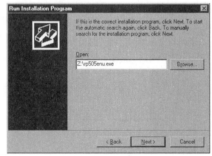

10. Once you've entered the path, select **Next**. This will place the server in install mode. The Adobe Acrobat Reader 5.0.5 Setup will begin.

11. At the Adobe Reader 5.0.5 Setup screen, select **Next**. (See Figure 9.5.)

Figure 9.5 Beginning the Acrobat Reader Installation

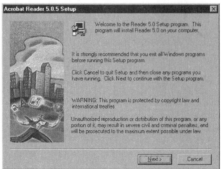

12. At the Choose Destination Location screen, enter the desired destination folder and select **Next**. (See Figure 9.6.)

   Figure 9.6 Choosing the Destination Location for Acrobat Reader

13. The Setup program installs the program. At the Information dialog box, select **OK**.

14. At the After Installation screen, select **Next**. (See Figure 9.7.)

   Figure 9.7 Ending the Installation

15. The Finish Admin Install screen appears, as shown in Figure 9.8. Select **Finish**. The server will exit install mode and resume execute mode.

   Figure 9.8 Entering Execute Mode

   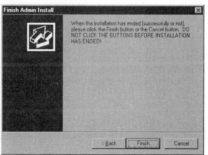

16. At this point, the installation is complete and users are ready to execute the program, once published. Now we can take advantage of any changes that would be beneficial to all users. To illustrate this point, from the desktop, select **Start | Run** and type **cmd** in the Open: text field. Select **OK**.

17. From the command prompt, type **change user /install**. (See Figure 9.9.)

Figure 9.9 Entering Install Mode from the Command Prompt

18. From the desktop, select **Start | Programs | Acrobat Reader 5.0**.

19. Once Acrobat Reader opens, from the **Edit** menu, select **Preferences**.

20. Select the **Comments** menu from the left. On the right, change the **Font** type from **Arial** to **Tahoma** and select **OK**. (See Figure 9.10.)

Figure 9.10 Changing the Comments Font

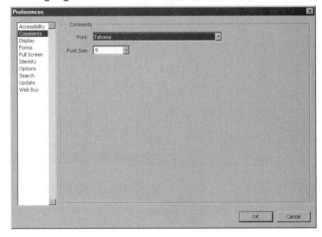

21. Close Adobe Acrobat.

22. Return to the command prompt and type **change user /execute**. (See Figure 9.11.)

Figure 9.11 Entering Execute Mode from the Command Prompt

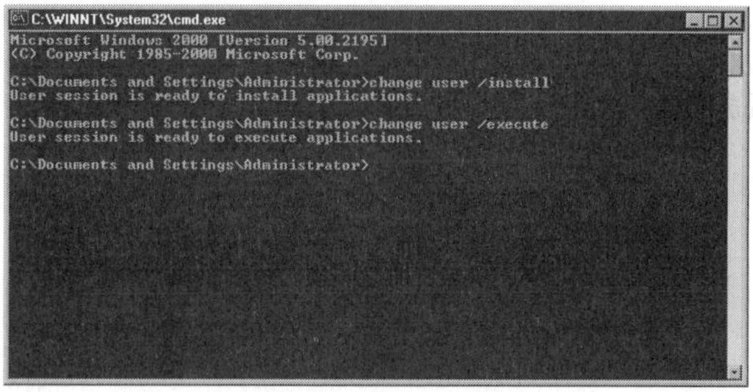

23.   Type **exit** at the command prompt to close.

This is an example install of a typical 32-bit application from start to finish. The last few steps take advantage of the install mode feature to pass along application preferences to all users. This could be done, for example, after installing Microsoft Word to enable the spell-check feature for everyone by default.

Designing & Planning...

Research Applications Before Installing Them

You can avoid headaches if you do proper research on an application before installing it in a Citrix MetaFrame environment. Here are four simple things you can do prior to installing an application or promising that an application will work within a MetaFrame environment:

- **Read the documentation provided by the vendor** This might sound obvious, but it's often not done. By reading the documentation, an administrator can get an idea of the resources the application requires and how the application works.

- **Call the vendor to ask if they know of any customers running the application within a Citrix MetaFrame environment** Citrix MetaFrame is run in 100 percent of the Fortune 100 companies and 90 percent of the Fortune 500 firms, which means that many different applications are used within a Citrix MetaFrame environment. The vendor might be able to provide support for the product within the environment or give you a contact person to call to ask questions.

Continued

> ■ **Research the application on several different online forums geared toward helping professionals in their day-to-day administration of a Citrix MetaFrame environment** Two great places to look for help or information are Citrix's Solution Forums, located at www.citrix.com/support, and The Thin Net at http://thethin.net.

Using the Correct Installation Mode

Citrix MetaFrame XP servers support two basic modes of operation: execute mode and install mode. Choosing the correct mode for an installation is a critical component in deploying an application. What happens during these two modes is explained in detail in the "Shadow Registry" section later in this chapter.

Execute mode is the default operating mode for a Citrix MetaFrame XP server; the server boots into this mode and runs in it until placed in install mode. Execute mode allows the server to operate in a nonglobal fashion. If an application were to be installed while the server is in execute mode, the changes the application makes to the server, such as registry and .ini file changes, would be stored only for that user. In a rare circumstance, these would be the desired conditions for installing an application. Not only would administrators need to log in to the server as each user who needed the application installed, they would also need to do the same every time the application required an upgrade. Performing installations in this manner will quickly reduce the implementation's ROI.

Install mode is the preferred method for installing applications because it allows the server to operate in a global fashion. This method specifically monitors the server for application installations. Install mode allows the application to install in a way that allows each user to launch, customize, and utilize the application so that when one user launches the application, his settings are kept completely separate from those of the next user.

There are two ways to enter install mode. The first is by opening a command prompt and typing:

```
change user /install
```

Once you've done that, perform the install as normal. Once the install has completed, type from the command prompt:

```
change user /execute
```

Refer to Figure 9.11 for an example of entering and exiting install mode. Reentering execute mode informs the server that the installation is complete and places its mode of operations back into a nonglobal fashion. If the program needs to reboot the server and allows the option of performing the reboot now or later, always select later. The system might not record the necessary changes to the registry if execution mode is not entered before the reboot.

The second method for placing the server into install mode is via the Add/Remove Programs applet in Control Panel. This method automatically begins and ends install mode for the installer.

Shadow Registry

As previously mentioned, most 32-bit applications written today use the HKEY_CUR-RENT_USER (HKCU) registry hive to store per-user information. During install mode, the server tracks registry and .ini file changes. These changes are copied, or *shadowed*, into a special place in the registry called the *shadow registry*. Figures 9.12 and 9.13 show the HKCU\Software and its mirrored shadow registry hive.

Figure 9.12 The HKCU\Software Registry Hive

Figure 9.13 The Shadow Registry

When a server is placed into install mode, several functions are performed:

1. The server monitors all entries made to the registry within HKCU\Software and proliferates these changes to HKLM\Software\Microsoft\Windows

NT\CurrentVersion\Terminal Server\Install, also known as the shadow registry. All .ini file changes made within the %systemroot% or %systemroot%\system are placed into HKLM\Software\Microsoft\Windows NT\CurrentVersion\Compatibility\IniFiles.

2. The server registers the time that the registry and .ini files were last updated and are stored under HKLM\Software\Microsoft\Windows NT\CurrentVersion\Terminal Server\Install\IniFile Times. The values of these keys are stored as the number of seconds that have passed since January 1, 1971.

3. Any changes to .ini files are written to the appropriate .ini files in the %systemroot% directory.

When a server is placed into execute mode, the following functions are executed:

1. The server monitors applications that make calls to the HKCU\Software registry hive. If the registry key the application is looking for does not exist, the server references the shadow registry. Should the key exist within the shadow registry, this key and any subkeys are copied to the appropriate location within HCKU\Software.

2. The server redirects references to .ini files within the %systemroot% to the user's personal Windows directory. If the .ini file does not exist within the user's Windows directory but does within the %systemroot%, the .ini file from the %systemroot% is copied to the user's Windows directory.

3. When a user logs into the server, userinit.exe compares the last update time of the registry and .ini files with the user's last registry sync time. The user's last synch time is stored as HKCU\Software\Microsoft\Windows NT\CurrentVersion\Terminal Server\LastUserIniSyncTime. The user's last update time on .ini files is stored as the file INIFILE.UPD within her personal Windows directory. If any of the current user's registry or .ini files are older than that of the servers, they are updated. By default, the registry keys updated are first deleted from HKCU and then copied. .Ini files are either merged with or completely replaced by the newer versions and old copies are then renamed to .ctx.

The Windows Installer

Windows Installer is a component of the Windows 2000 operating system that allows you to simplify the application installation process. By applying a set of defined rules during the installation process, Windows Installer can manage the installation and uninstallation of applications. The Windows Installer technology is made up of mainly three components: the Windows Installer service, the application package (in the form of an

.msi file), and a transform file, which is able to modify the way the application is installed (in the form of an .mst file).

A great example of this technology is Microsoft Office 2000. With the Microsoft Office 2000 CD and the Office 2000 Resource Kit, an administrator can completely customize Microsoft Office 2000 installation components. In fact, an administrator cannot install Office 2000 without the use of a transform file on a server running Terminal Services in application server mode. The reason is that some of the default settings of a typical Office 2000 install are inappropriate for a Windows 2000 server running in application server mode. One such example is the Install on First Use feature, which installs a component of Office 2000 only when the feature is first needed. This behavior might be fine for a workstation installation, but it's inappropriate on a Terminal Server where users have access to neither the server nor the Office 2000 CD-ROM to install the feature. Another example of a component inappropriate for a Terminal Server is the animated Office Assistant. These animations take up unnecessary server resources, especially when run by multiple users. The Office 2000 Resource Kit comes with a preconfigured transform file, called TERMSRVR.MST, which customizes an appropriate Terminal Server installation of Office 2000.

To illustrate the power of transform files over a Windows Installer application installation, let's look at an example of a typical Office 2000 installation. In order to complete this exercise, an administrator must have the Office 2000 Resource Kit installed. The kit can be found at www.microsoft.com/office/ork/2000/download/ORKTools.exe. Here's how the installation goes:

1. Providing that the typical installation was used to install the Office 2000 Resource Kit, from the desktop, select **Start | Programs | Microsoft Office Tools | Microsoft Office 2000 Resource Kit Tools | Custom Installation Wizard**.

2. Insert the Microsoft Office 2000 CD.

3. At the Custom Installation Wizard screen, select **Next**.

4. At the Open the MSI File screen, browse to or enter the path to the **Data1.MSI** file located on the Microsoft Office 2000 CD-ROM and select **Next**.

5. At the Open the MST File screen, select the **Open an existing MST file** radio button and enter the path to **TERMSRVR.MST** located within the Office 2000 Resource Kit folder. Select **Next**.

6. At the Select the MST File to Save screen, enter the path and name of the MST file to be saved with the customizations and select **Next**. In this example, the path and name of the transform file is **D:\Office.MST**.

7. At the Specify Default Path and Organization screen, enter the default installation path and organization name and select **Next**.

8. At the Remove Previous Versions screen, ensure the **Default Setup behavior** radio button is selected and select **Next**.

9. At the Set Feature Installation States screen, customize the installation as necessary. When you're finished, select **Next**.

10. At the Customize Default Application Settings screen, ensure that the **Do not customize; use Microsoft default values** radio button is selected and select **Next**.

11. At the Add Files to the Installation screen, select **Next**.

12. At the Add Registry Entries screen, select **Next**.

13. At the Add, Modify, or Remove Shortcuts screen, select **Next**.

14. At the Identify Additional Server screen, select **Next**.

15. At the Add Installations and Run Programs screen, select **Next**.

16. At the Customize Outlook Installation Options screen, select the **Do not customize Outlook profile and account information** radio button and select **Next**.

17. At the Customize IE 5 Installation Options screen, select the **Do not install Internet Explorer 5** radio button and select **Next**.

18. At the Internet Explorer 5 Recommended dialog box, select **Yes**.

19. At the Modify Setup Properties screen, select **Next**.

20. At the Save Changes screen, select **Finish**.

21. At the Custom Installation Wizard screen, the Custom Installation Wizard provides an example command to run to install Office 2000. The command in this example is **setup.exe TRANSFORMS=D:\Office.MST /qn+**.

Deploying Applications to a Server Farm

Since a single server has limitations on the number of users it can handle before performance degradation becomes a noticeable issue for users, running the same application on multiple servers allows a server farm to combine the computing power of multiple single servers. To allow for this practice, Citrix has provided administrators two tools to help achieve this goal: Installation Manager and Load Manager.

Installation Manager

Installation Manager, or IM, is an add-on tool included with Citrix MetaFrame XPe that allows an administrator to install an application across the entire server farm simultaneously, regardless of physical location, network connection type, or individual server specifications. When an administrator publishes an application that has been scheduled for installation, each of the servers targeted for deployment downloads and installs the package at a predetermined time. In addition to installing applications, IM can also install service packs, upgrades, and other such files. Packages that can be used with IM are Application Deployment File (ADF) and Microsoft Installer (MSI) packages. ADF packages can be created with the Citrix Packager; MSI packages are usually precompiled and cannot be edited without the use of a tool such as InstallShield.

IM provides the following basic operations:

- The ability to package an application into an ADF file

- Adding packages and their contents into the IM database using either the Packager or CMC

- Scheduling packages for deployment to specified servers

- Viewing the status of scheduled package deployments.

Installation Manager includes the following three components:

- **Citrix Installation Manager plug-in** The Installation Manager plug-in for the Citrix Management Console is an administration tool based on the IMA that adds existing packages (ADF or MSI) to the IM database and schedules the package for installation on Citrix servers in the server farm. This component needs to be installed only on servers that add, schedule, and install packages on target servers.

- **Citrix Installer service** The Installer service is a background service that executes scheduled requests from CMC to install applications. This component needs to be installed on all servers that will receive packages.

- **Citrix Packager** The Citrix Packager is a program that is used to create ADF packages for installation on target servers. The Packager monitors the application installation process, records the changes as installation commands in a script, and packages the installation files for remote deployment. This component should be installed only on servers dedicated to creating ADF packages.

The following set of steps is an example of the application packaging process as well as the delivery of the package to multiple servers within the server farm. The application packaged in this example is SecureCRT version 3.4:

1. From the desktop of the dedicated Citrix Packager, select **Start | Programs | Citrix | Citrix Installation Manager | Citrix Packager**.

2. At the Project screen, select the **Create a new project using project wizard** radio button and select **Next**. (See Figure 9.14.)

Figure 9.14 Creating a New Project

3. At the Project Wizard screen, ensure that the **Package an Installation Recording** radio button is selected and select **Next**. (See Figure 9.15.)

Figure 9.15 Creating an Installation Recording

4. At the Package an Installation Recording screen, enter **SecureCRT** in the "Project Name:" text field and select **Next**. (See Figure 9.16.)

NOTE

Three packaging options are available with the Project Wizard: *Package an Installation Recording* is used for most typical application installations. *Package an Unattended Program* is used for programs that are silent installs (no user intervention). *Package Selected Files* simply builds a list of files and/or folders to be packaged and deployed.

Figure 9.16 Defining a Project Name

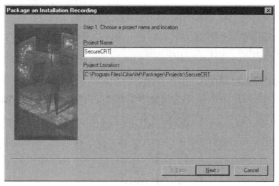

5. At the Package an Installation Recording screen, enter the path to the installation program and select **Next**. (See Figure 9.17.)

Figure 9.17 Specifying the Installation Program

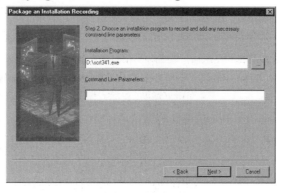

6. At the Package and Installation Recording screen, ensure that the **No Compatibility Script** radio button is selected and select **Next**. (See Figure 9.18.)

Figure 9.18 Declining to Add an Application Compatibility Script

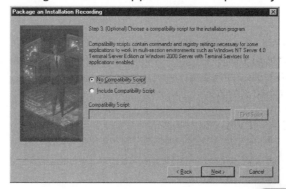

NOTE

If the program has an application compatibility script, ensure that it is included. By selecting the Include Compatibility Script radio button, an administrator has the opportunity to add an application compatibility script to be deployed along with the installation of the application. The Packager includes a list of application compatibility scripts that can be used.

7. At the Package and Installation Recording screen, enter the path where the build files should be located. This location does not need to be local, and users do not need to have access to these files. In this example, select drive **D:** as the Root Build Location and select **Next**. (See Figure 9.19.)

Figure 9.19 Selecting the Root Build Location

8. At the Package an Installation Recording screen, select **Finish**. (See Figure 9.20.)

Figure 9.20 Verifying Package Options

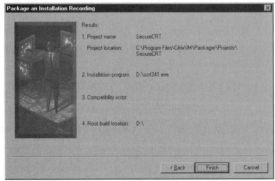

9.   At the SecureCRT License Agreement screen, select **I Agree**.

> **NOTE**
>
> Please note that different applications have different options and that the directions provided in this example might vary from environment to environment.

10.   At the Welcome! screen, select **Next**.

11.   At the Install Changes screen, select **Next**.

12.   At the Select Directory screen, enter **D:\Program Files\SecureCRT 3.0** and select **Next**.

13.   At the Select Profile Options screen, select **Next**.

14.   At the Choose Protocols screen, select **Next**.

15.   At the Ready to Install! screen, select **Finish**.

16.   At the Success! screen, deselect the **View Readme now?** check box and select **OK**.

17.   At the Recording Completed screen, select **Done**. (See Figure 9.21.)

Figure 9.21 Recording Completed

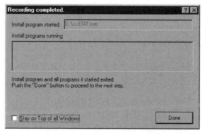

18.   At the Installation Packager dialog box, select **OK**.

19.   Close the Packager.

20.   Launch the Citrix Management Console by selecting **Start | Programs | Citrix | Citrix Management Console**. CMC is used to add and distribute applications for a Citrix MetaFrame XP server farm.

21.   From the Installation Manager node, right-click **Packages** and select **Add Package**. (See Figure 9.22.)

Figure 9.22 Adding a New Package to the IM Database

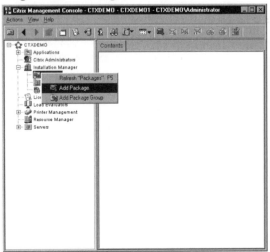

22. At the Add Package screen, enter **SecureCRT** as the package name, then enter the path to the .wfs file and select **OK**. Installation Manager responds that the package was successfully added.

23. Right-click the **SecureCRT** package and select **Install Package**.

24. At the Servers screen, assign the servers to receive the package and select **Next**. (See Figure 9.23.)

Figure 9.23 Selecting the Servers to Receive the Package

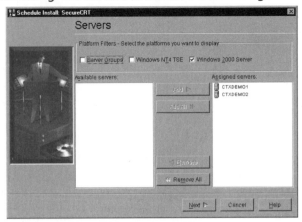

25. At the Schedule screen, select **Finish**.

26. From the Installation Manager node, highlight the **Summary node** and select the **All Jobs** tab.

27.   Ensure that the status of the job is a success. (See Figure 9.24.)

Figure 9.24 Ensuring Package Installation Success

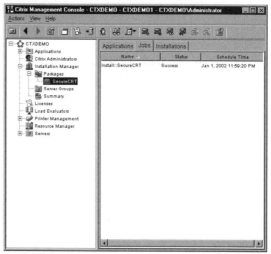

28.   To finish, publish the application as you normally would.

Load Manager

Load Manager, a tool built into Citrix MetaFrame versions XPa and XPe, allows an administrator the ability to set up, monitor, and adjust a server and published application loads in a server farm, giving users the ability to run their applications more efficiently and effectively. Load Manager offers an administrator the following features concerning published applications:

■   Balance published application loads across multiple Citrix servers in a server farm.

■   Monitor application loads across the server farm.

Load Manager works by calculating server load based on rules and routing users to published applications on servers with the lightest loads. In effect, when a user launches an application from an application set, the data collector for the zone determines which servers host the application and, of those, which server is the least busy. The data collector routes the user to this server to allow the best possible user experience at the time of launch.

Load Manager contains two important components: rules and load evaluators. *Rules* are small modules of executable code that query specific conditions and performance metrics for both servers and published applications. Each rule contains a set of parameters that can be customized. Many of these parameters specify a full load or no load on a server. For example, the rule Server User Load allows an administrator to specify the maximum number of users the server will handle. Once this number is reached, the server reports a full load and no longer accepts connections. Figure 9.25 shows the Server User Load rule.

Figure 9.25 The Server User Load Rule

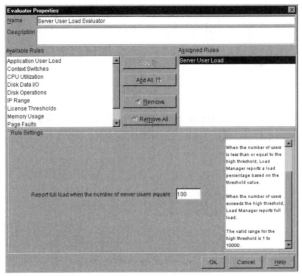

The following are the rules that Load Manager includes:

- Application User Load
- Context Switches
- CPU Utilization
- Disk Data I/O
- Disk Operations
- IP Range
- License Threshold
- Memory Usage
- Page Fault
- Page Swap
- Scheduling
- Server User Load

A *load evaluator* is a set of one or more rules. A single load evaluator can be attached to both servers and applications. Server load is determined by the rule with the highest load value. The Default load evaluator, which is applied to all Load Managed servers by default, uses the Server User Load rule. The Server User Load rule reports a full load when 100 users are logged on to that server. The following set of steps is an example of how to create a new load evaluator and attach this evaluator to a server:

1. Launch the Citrix Management Console by selecting **Start | Programs | Citrix | Citrix Management Console**.

2. Right-click the **Load Evaluators** node and select **New Load Evaluator**. (See Figure 9.26.)

Figure 9.26 Creating a New Load Evaluator

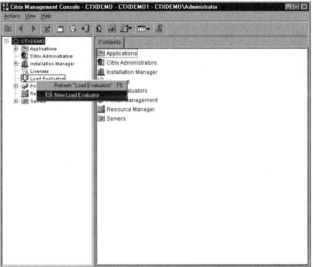

3. At the New Evaluator screen, enter a name and description for the new load evaluator.

4. From the Available Rules List, select and assign the following rules: **IP Range**, **License Thresholds**, and **Memory Usage**.

5. Configure the thresholds in each of the rules. Use Table 9.2 to refer to a description of each of the rules. See Figure 9.27 for an example.

Table 9.2 Selected Load Evaluator Rules and Their Descriptions

Rule	Description
IP Range	This rule allows your load evaluator to enable or disable access to a published application based on whether or not the IP addresses of the ICA clients are within the specified IP address ranges. This rule should be used in conjunction with another rule. This rule will not load balance connections by itself.
License Thresholds	This rule allows your load evaluator to calculate a load based on the number of assigned or pooled connection licenses used on each server.
Memory Usage	This rule allows your load evaluator to calculate a load based on memory utilization.

Figure 9.27 Load Evaluator Rules

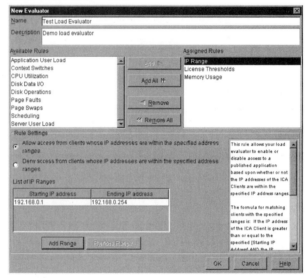

6. Select **OK** once finished.

7. To attach the load evaluator to a server within CMC, right-click the server and select **Load Manage Server**. (See Figure 9.28.)

8. From the Load Manage Server window, highlight the newly created load evaluator and select **OK**. The load evaluator has been successfully attached to the server.

Figure 9.28 Load Managing a Server

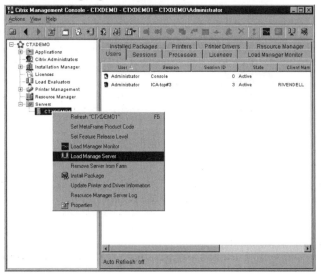

NOTE

In a Citrix MetaFrame XP server farm environment in which the servers don't all have the same hardware, the servers will not be able to handle the same number of users. Some of the servers might have more memory or more processors and thus are able to handle more users. In situations like these, use rules such as CPU Utilization and/or Memory Usage to effectively balance the load. Remember, not all rule combinations make sense in all environments. Take into careful consideration the various aspects of the environment before load balancing the servers. As long as a load evaluator is attached to a server, applications can be published across servers. When you're publishing an application, during the Specify Servers portion, select from the list of available servers the ones that will load balance the particular application. (See Figure 9.29.)

Figure 9.29 Specifying Multiple Servers to Load Balance an Application

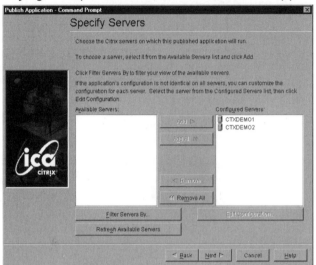

Removing Applications

Removing or uninstalling an application is a process that depends on two items: how the application was installed and the installation package type. Installation package types come in a wide variety of installation methods. They can be as simple as a self-extracting executable that simply extracts files to the file system without relying on advanced programming techniques. They can also be as robust as an MSI package that contains complete uninstallation information so that when the application needs to be installed, it can be installed without leaving any remnants behind. If an application was installed via a package such as Installation Management or a Windows Script Host (WSH), the application can be undone by simply reversing the installation process. The following are some key concepts related to removing applications:

- Applications that install themselves via self-extracting executables that do not use API functions are often simple to remove, provided that you know what files are within the package. Simply removing the extracted files safely removes the application.

- Programs that were installed via the Add/Remove Programs applet in Control Panel can often be uninstalled the same way. However, uninstalling through this method does not always remove all files. Files in use during the uninstallation process, such as .dll files in the %systemroot%\system32 folder, might not be removed. Generally, Windows informs the uninstaller of files that it could not remove so that they can be removed manually.

- Programs installed through Installation Manager can be removed by simply uninstalling the application through the IM database.

- WSH installations can be "rewound" by creating a version that backs out of all the changes that were made during the installation.

- With imaging software such as Ghost, you can create images for servers before you install an application. This way, if the application needed to be uninstalled, the image created last can be restored, placing the server in the preapplication installation state.

- A file called instaler.exe, located in the Windows 2000 Server Resource Kit, tracks changes made during an application install and can be used in conjunction with a program called uninst.exe to reverse the changes made during installation.

Optimizing Application Performance

Poor application performance can leave users with a bad impression of the application's response time on the Citrix MetaFrame XP server. Poor performance can be a result of anything from an incorrectly configured application to unnecessary video graphics being displayed or wasted bandwidth on unneeded audio. An administrator can perform some general tasks to remedy some of these situations. Among these tasks are using application compatibility scripts (ACSs) to remedy specific application problems running in a multiuser environment, disabling unneeded audio and video.

Using Application Compatibility Scripts

Many applications written to date are not multiuser aware, meaning that the application developers envisioned only a single user running the application. This does not mean that the application is poorly written or that it will not run well within a Citrix MetaFrame environment. ACSs were devised specifically to combat some of the more common problems with programs such as these. These ACSs are nothing more than intricate batch files. Microsoft includes several ACSs, located within the %systemroot%\Application Compatibility Scripts folder. Keep in mind that these ACSs are examples and will run in a majority of environments, but they might need to be modified slightly to enable them to work in a particular environment. Table 9.3 lists applications that require either an ACS or a transform file for it to work correctly within a Terminal Server environment. All these scripts, with the exception of the Microsoft Office 2000 transform file, are included with Windows 2000.

Table 9.3 Application Compatibility Scripts

Program	Script
Corel Office 7	Coffice7.cmd
Corel Office 8	Not supported
Eudora Pro 4.0	Eudora4.cmd
Lotus Notes 4.x	Lnote4u.cmd
Lotus Smart Suite 9	Ssuite9.cmd
Lotus Smart Suite 97	Ssuite97.cmd
Microsoft Access 2.0	Office43.cmd
Microsoft Access 7.0	Office95.cmd
Microsoft Access 97	Office97.cmd
Microsoft Excel 5.0	Office43.cmd
Microsoft Excel 7.0	Office95.cmd
Microsoft Excel 97	Office97.cmd
Microsoft Excel 97 (stand-alone installation)	Msexcl97.cmd
Microsoft Exchange 5.0 and higher	Winmsg.cmd
Microsoft ODBC	ODBC.cmd
Microsoft Office 4.3	Office43.cmd
Microsoft Office 95	Office95.cmd
Microsoft Office 97	Office97.cmd
Microsoft Office 2000	Requires Transform file
Microsoft Outlook 97	Outlk98.cmd
Microsoft Outlook 98	Outlk98.cmd
Microsoft Outlook Express	Outlk98.cmd
Microsoft PowerPoint 4.0	Office43.cmd
Microsoft PowerPoint 7.0	Office95.cmd
Microsoft PowerPoint 97	Office97.cmd
Microsoft Project 95	Msproj95.cmd
Microsoft Project 98	Msproj98.cmd
Microsoft Schedule+ 7.0	Office95.cmd
Microsoft SNA Client 4.0	Sna40cli.cmd
Microsoft SNA Server 3.0	Mssna30.cmd
Microsoft SNA Server 4.0	Sna40srv.cmd
Microsoft Visual Studio 6.0	MSVS6.cmd
Microsoft Word 6.0	Office43.cmd

Continued

Table 9.3 Continued

Program	Script
Microsoft Word 7.0	Office95.cmd
Microsoft Word 97	Office97.cmd
Microsoft Word 97 (standalone installation)	Msword97.cmd
Netscape Communicator 4.0x	Netcom40.cmd
Netscape Communicator 4.5x	Netcom40.cmd
Netscape Communicator 4.6x	Netcom40.cmd
Netscape Navigator 3.x	Netnav30.cmd
Peachtree Complete Accounting 6.0	PchTree6.cmd
PowerBuilder 6.0	PwrBldr6.cmd
Visio 5.0	Visio5.cmd

Table 9.4 presents a list of the scripts that make up the ACS environment.

Table 9.4 The Components of the ACS Environment

Script	Description	Path
ChkRoot.cmd	This script is referenced by several ACSs that rely on the %*rootdrive*% variable. If Rootdrv2.cmd does not exist, this script creates it and opens Notepad so that the %*rootdrive*% variable can be specified.	%systemroot%\ Application Compatibility Scripts
SetPaths.cmd	This script is called by Usrlogon.cmd and is used to extract paths into environment variables, allowing other scripts to run without needing hardcoded system path strings.	%systemroot%\ Application Compatibility Scripts
Rootdrv.cmd	This script is called by Usrlogon.cmd and simply calls Rootdrv2.cmd, if it exists.	%systemroot%\ Application Compatibility Scripts
Rootdrv2.cmd	This script is called by Rootdrv.cmd and contains the drive letter specified.	%systemroot%\ Application Compatibility Scripts
Usrlogn1.cmd	This script is called by Usrlogon.cmd and is first created by an ACS that does not require the %*rootdrive*% variable.	%systemroot%\system32

Continued

Table 9.4 Continued

Script	Description	Path
Usrlogn2.cmd	This script is called by Usrlogon.cmd and is first created by an ACS that does require the *%rootdrive%* variable.	%systemroot%\system32
Usrlogon.cmd	This is the central file for the ACS environment and is called every time a user logs in. This script performs the following, in order: Calls setpaths.cmd, usrlogn1.cmd, sets the *%rootdrive%* variable, and calls usrlogn2.cmd.	%systemroot%\system32

Usrlogon.cmd is the central script for the ACS environment. Figure 9.30 lists the contents of the Usrlogon.cmd file.

Figure 9.30 The Contents of the Usrlogon.cmd File

```
@Echo Off

Call "%SystemRoot%\Application Compatibility Scripts\SetPaths.Cmd"
If "%_SETPATHS%" == "FAIL" Goto Done

Rem
Rem This is for those scripts that don't need the RootDrive.
Rem

If Not Exist "%SystemRoot%\System32\Usrlogn1.cmd" Goto cont0
Cd /d "%SystemRoot%\Application Compatibility Scripts\Logon"
Call "%SystemRoot%\System32\Usrlogn1.cmd"

:cont0

Rem
Rem Determine the user's home directory drive letter. If this isn't
Rem set, exit.
Rem

Cd /d %SystemRoot%\"Application Compatibility Scripts"
Call RootDrv.Cmd
```

Continued

Figure 9.30 Continued

```
If "A%RootDrive%A" == "AA" End.Cmd


Rem
Rem Map the User's Home Directory to a Drive Letter
Rem


Net Use %RootDrive% /D >NUL: 2>&1
Subst %RootDrive% "%HomeDrive%%HomePath%"
if ERRORLEVEL 1 goto SubstErr
goto AfterSubst
:SubstErr
Subst %RootDrive% /d >NUL: 2>&1
Subst %RootDrive% "%HomeDrive%%HomePath%"
:AfterSubst


Rem
Rem Invoke each Application Script. Application Scripts are automatically
Rem added to UsrLogn2.Cmd when the Installation script is run.
Rem


If Not Exist %SystemRoot%\System32\UsrLogn2.Cmd Goto Cont1


Cd Logon
Call %SystemRoot%\System32\UsrLogn2.Cmd


:Cont1


:Done
```

The *rootdrive* variable was devised to compensate for the shortcoming of Windows NT being unable to map the root directory of a drive letter beyond the share point. This is a feature inherent in both Novell NetWare and Windows 2000. Both Windows 2000 and Windows NT have *%homedrive%* and *%homepath%* variables. Windows 2000 also supports another variable called *%homeshare%*, which points directly to the share point of the home directory. Using Figure 9.31 as an example, refer to Table 9.5 for the values derived for the variables under Windows 2000 and Windows NT.

Figure 9.31 The Terminal Services Profile Tab

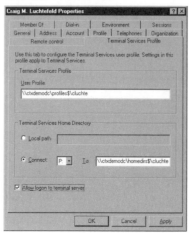

Table 9.5 Windows 2000 and Windows NT Variables

Variable	Windows 2000 Path	Windows NT Path
%homedrive%	P:	P:
%homepath%	\	\cluchte
%homeshare%	\\ctxdemodc\homedirs$\cluchte	N/A

In this example, were the user to go to his P: drive in Windows 2000, he would be at the root of his home directory. In Windows NT, however, he would actually be one level up, at the homedirs$ folder. So, for the Windows NT user, the path to his home directory would be P:\%username%. This presents a problem for the Windows NT 4.0 administrator, who must install an application but cannot specify P:\%username% as a path during the installation. In addition to this problem, take for example two users within a Windows 2000 domain who log on to a Citrix MetaFrame XP server. User A has drive P: specified as her home directory; User B has drive U: specified as his home directory. As an administrator, what drive must be specified to allow personal information to be stored in both users' home directories without installing the application for each user?

The *%rootdrive%* variable was created to accommodate the first problem and inadvertently fixes the second problem as well. The *%rootdrive%* variable is a drive letter separate from the Windows 2000 or Windows NT *%homedrive%* variable. This drive letter must be something universal that everyone who logs on to a Citrix MetaFrame server can share. During user logon, Usrlogon.cmd runs the following command to specify the *%rootdrive%* variable to equal *%homedrive%%homepath%*:

```
Subst %RootDrive% "%HomeDrive%%HomePath%"
```

Subst is a command used to associate a path with a drive letter. To understand this point, consider the following two examples:

- **Example 1** UserA logs in to an NT 4.0 Terminal Server Edition server with a %homedrive% variable specified as P: and a %homepath% variable specified as \UserA. When UserA logs in, Usrlogon.cmd substitutes drive X: as P:\UserA. Now an administrator who needs to install an application for all users can specify drive X: because everyone who logs in to the server will be mapped to the root of their home directories through the %rootdrive%.

- **Example 2** UserB and UserC both log in to a Windows 2000 Citrix MetaFrame server. UserB has %homedrive% specified as P: with a %homeshare% specified as \. UserC has %homedrive% specified as U: with a %homeshare% specified as \. When UserB logs in to the server, drive X:\ is substituted for P:\. When UserC logs in to the same server, drive X:\ is substituted for U:\.

The %rootdrive% variable is created the first time someone runs an ACS that requires %rootdrive% to function. These ACSs call the ChkRoot.cmd, which in turn looks for the Rootdrv2.cmd file that specifies the drive letter to use for the %rootdrive%.

You can create the %rootdrive% any time, if it doesn't already exist, by running the ChkRoot.cmd script. This will open Notepad editing the Rootdrv2.cmd file, asking for a drive letter to be specified. Once you're specified the drive letter, save the file and close Notepad. (See Figure 9.32.)

Figure 9.32 Specifying the Rootdrive

Disabling and Enabling Sound

By default, sounds are enabled within a Citrix MetaFrame XP environment, whether those sounds can be heard or not. These sounds include the Windows logon sound, critical stops, exclamations, and many more. Imagine the overhead on the server to process these sounds in addition to everything else going on behind the scenes for 30 or more users.

To disable sounds for all users, from the desktop select **Start | Settings | Control Panel** and select the **Sounds and Multimedia** applet. Within the **Scheme** section, select the **drop-down box**, select **No Sounds**, and click **OK** (see Figure 9.33). This will disable all sound events within Windows, NetMeeting, Windows Explorer, Media Player, Power Configurator, and Sound Recorder.

Figure 9.33 Disabling Sound in Windows 2000

You can also enable sounds by default in applications that are installed on the server. Try exploiting the install mode feature to disable sounds for all users within the application. To disable the audio virtual channel completely to optimize the ICA protocol:

1. From the ICA toolbar, launch **Citrix Connection Configuration**.

2. Double-click the **ica-tcp** protocol.

3. From the Edit Connection screen, select the **Client Settings** button.

4. From the Client Settings screen, within the Client Mapping Overrides section, check the **Disable Client Audio Mapping** check box and select **OK**. (See Figure 9.34.)

Figure 9.34 Disabling the Audio Virtual Channel

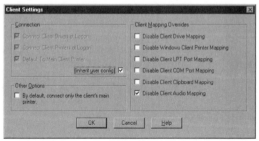

Handling Video

Intensive video-streaming applications such as Macromedia Flash, Microsoft NetMeeting, and Windows Media Player are examples of applications that can have extremely poor effects on a Citrix MetaFrame server. The best ways to handle these sorts of applications are to either disallow their use or remove them altogether. The following are several examples of actions you can perform to disallow some of these affects:

- By publishing applications, users have less chance of running some of these applications. Video files such as .avi and Macromedia Flash might still be accessible if they're accessed through applications such as Internet Explorer or Windows Explorer. If users are running a workstation platform, make every effort to run these sorts of applications locally, if they are needed.

- NetMeeting is installed by default on a Windows 2000 server, but it can be disabled through NTFS permissions. Disallow user access to the following file: %ProgramFiles%\NetMeeting\conf.exe. Certain components of NetMeeting can also be disabled through Windows 2000 Group Policy.

- Macromedia Flash can also exhibit poor performance on a Citrix MetaFrame server. In addition, some Flash applications poll the keyboard the same way some DOS applications poll for keyboard input. A single instance of an application like this can take up 100 percent of a single processor. If installed, Macromedia Flash can be disabled through NTFS permissions by disallowing user access to the file %systemroot%\system32\macromed\flash\swflash.ocx.

Always test graphics-intensive applications before deploying them. When these applications are needed, limit their use as much as possible.

Setting Graphics Levels to Optimize Performance

By optimizing the ICA protocol to discard unneeded virtual channels, placing a few registry overrides, running the latest ICA client, and a couple of miscellaneous settings, you can realize some bandwidth and performance gains with little work. This section lists a few suggested tweaks that can help keep a MetaFrame environment lean and mean.

Several important changes can be made to the registry to help improve response time for users. Table 9.6 lists the keys that can be created and how they help.

Table 9.6 Registry Keys to Help Optimize Performance

Description	Key Name
Stabilizes profiles	HKLM\CurrentControlSet\Control\Terminal Server\ WinStations\ICA-tcp\UserOverride\Control Panel\Desktop\ AutoEndTasks="1"

Continued

Table 9.6 Continued

Description	Key Name
Reduces network traffic	HKLM\CurrentControlSet\Control\Terminal Server\ WinStations\ICA-tcp\UserOverride\Control Panel\ Desktop CursorBlinkRate="-1"
Improves Explorer interface response	HKLM\CurrentControlSet\Control\Terminal Server\ WinStations\ICA-tcp\UserOverride\Control Panel\ Desktop DragFullWindows="0"
Improves user interface responsiveness	HKLM\CurrentControlSet\Control\Terminal Server\ WinStations\ICA-tcp\UserOverride\Control Panel\ Desktop MenuShowDelay="10"
Stabilizes profiles	HKLM\CurrentControlSet\Control\Terminal Server\ WinStations\ICA-tcp\UserOverride\Control Panel\ Desktop WaitToKillAppTimeout="20000"
Improves Explorer interface response	HKLM\CurrentControlSet\Control\Terminal Server\ WinStations\ICA-tcp\UserOverride\Control Panel\ Desktop SmoothScrol=dword:"00000000"
Disables the use of wallpapers	HKLM\CurrentControlSet\Control\Terminal Server\ WinStations\ICA-tcp\UserOverride\Control Panel\ Desktop Wallpaper="(none)"
Improves Explorer interface response	HLKM\SYSTEM\CurrentControlSet\Control\Terminal Server\ WinStations\ICA-tcp\UserOverride\Control Panel\ Desktop\WindowMetrics\MinAnimate="0"

In addition to modifying the registry, you can make several changes within the Windows GUI and some of the Citrix management tools to help optimize performance. Here are some examples:

- Disable Active Desktop. From the desktop, select **Start | Programs | Administrative Tools | Terminal Services Configuration**. Highlight the **Server Settings** folder and double-click the **Active Desktop** key. Select the **Disable Active Desktop** check box.

- Disable any virtual channels not being used in Citrix Connection Configuration, such as audio, to cut down on the size of the ICA protocol.

- Run applications with the minimum color level needed. Notepad does not need 24-bit color to run effectively.

- Within the Citrix Management Console, select the properties of the server farm and highlight the **ICA Settings** tab. Enable the **Discard redundant graphics operations** for bandwidth savings. Disable for a performance increase.

Lastly, several changes within the ICA client can help improve performance. The following are several modifications that can be made to the Default Options within an application set, as shown in Figure 9.35:

- **Use data compression** Data compression reduces the amount of data that needs to be transferred but requires additional processor resources to compress and decompress the data. If the connection is limited in terms of bandwidth, enabling data compression increases performance.

- **Use disk cache for bitmaps** Bitmap caching to disk stores commonly used graphical objects such as bitmaps in a local cache on the client's hard disk space. If the connection is bandwidth limited, enabling disk caching increases performance.

- **Queue mouse movements and keystrokes** Queuing causes the client to send mouse and keyboard updates to the Citrix server less frequently. Check this option to reduce the number of network packets sent from the ICA client to the Citrix server. Leaving this option unchecked makes the session more responsive to keyboard and mouse movements.

- **Enable SpeedScreen Latency Reduction** SpeedScreen Latency Reduction is a collective term used to describe the functionality that helps enhance user experience on slower network connections. Latency reduction is available only if you're connecting to a server that is configured and licensed for latency reduction.

Figure 9.35 Optimizing the Citrix ICA Client

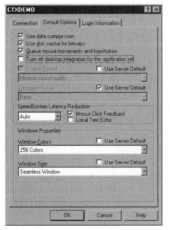

> **NOTE**
>
> A great resource for application and server optimizations can be found at http://groups.yahoo.com/group/citrixnw/. Rick Dehlinger of Citrix Systems maintains a document, currently 41 pages, of every sort of application, server, and miscellaneous optimizations.

Monitoring Applications

Monitoring applications is an important function that Citrix MetaFrame administrators must do from time to time. Before an application is put into production, it should be tested to make sure it won't bring any surprises as far as performance. Benchmarking an application to the what kind of processor and memory utilization it will require is a good way to help determine whether or not the servers in the environment will be able to handle a typical user load. In addition, not all applications work on the first install, and not all have an ACS readily available to fix the problem. In circumstances like these, an administrator needs access to tools that will help troubleshoot the application problem or problems.

Performance Monitor is a wonderful tool for determining the processor requirements for a typical application. This tool is included with Windows 2000 and can be started by running **perfmon.exe** from the command prompt. You can perform a simple test to monitor processor utilization by running the following steps:

1. Launch **Performance Monitor**.

2. Either from a Citrix session or from the console, launch the application to be tested.

3. From the toolbar, select the **Add** button.

4. Under Performance Object, select **Process**. Highlight **% Processor Time** from the counters list. Highlight the application executable from the instances list and select **Add**. When you're finished, select **Close**. (See Figure 9.36.)

Figure 9.36 Adding Counters to Performance Monitor

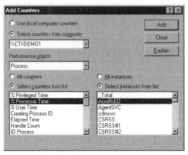

5. Run the application as it would run in production. By glancing back and forth from Performance Monitor to the application, an administrator can get an idea of how certain functions within the application affect the server. (See Figure 9.37.)

Figure 9.37 Performance Monitor in Action

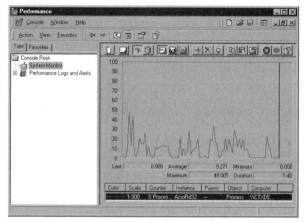

In addition to Performance Monitor, Task Manager is a quick and easy tool to use to determine how much memory is being used by a specific process. To launch Task Manager, right-click the **taskbar** and select **Task Manager.**

To monitor the registry, Registry Monitor, or regmon, from Sysinternals is a helpful tool for troubleshooting and tracking down what is happening behind the scenes when applications make calls to the registry. Figure 9.38 shows an example of regmon in action.

Figure 9.38 A Sample Screen from Registry Monitor

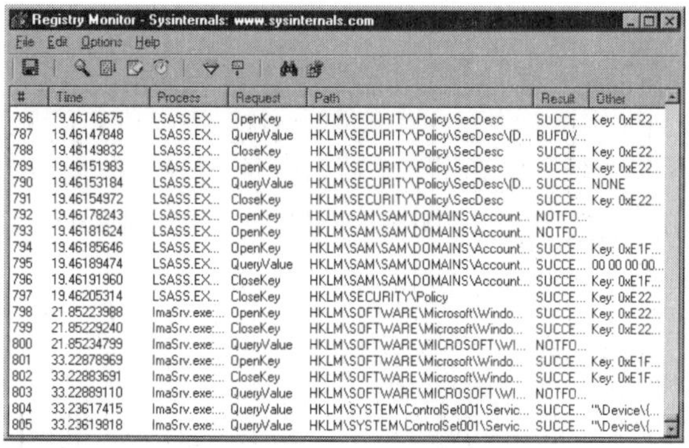

Sysinternals has another utility called File Monitor, or filemon, that is similar to regmon. Filemon is a great utility to track where programs query for file data, what .dll files it may call, or troubleshooting NTFS security permission problems. Figure 9.39 shows some output from filemon.

Figure 9.39 Filemon in Action

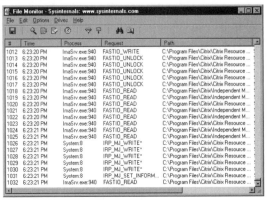

In addition to these tools, Sysinternals has many other useful utilities for download at www.sysinternals.com.

Publishing Applications

Publishing applications is a process that allows users to easily access applications located within a Citrix MetaFrame server farm. This is an important feature in moving to an application-centric computing environment. These applications can then be distributed to the users based on user or group membership, without regard to the server on which the application resides. These applications make up what is called an *application set*. Citrix MetaFrame environments that publish applications gain the following three benefits:

- Increased control over application deployments
- Increased security because users no longer have access to a Citrix MetaFrame server desktop
- A simplified environment from which users can access their applications

The Citrix Management Console is the tool responsible for the creation of published applications. Publishing an application does not need to be done from the console of the server or servers hosting the application. Here are the steps to create a new published application:

1. Open the **Citrix Management Console** and log on with an account that has **Read-Write privileges**.

2. Right-click the **Applications** node and select **Publish Application**. (See Figure 9.40.)

Figure 9.40 Creating a New Published Application

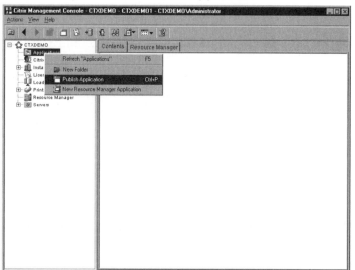

3. From the Welcome to the Application Publishing Wizard screen, enter the name and description of the application that is to be published (see Figure 9.41) and select **Next**.

Figure 9.41 Defining the Display Name and Description

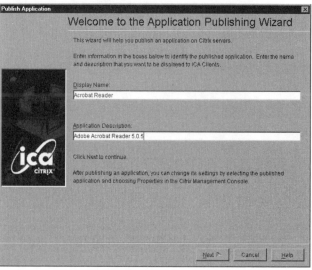

4. From the Specify What to Publish screen, ensure that the **Application** radio button is selected. Enter the path to the application executable and working directory and select **Next**. (See Figure 9.42.)

Figure 9.42 Defining the Executable and Path

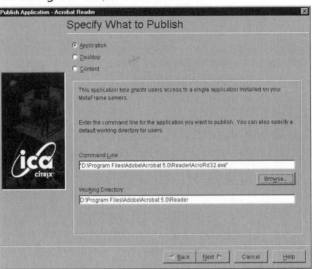

5. From the Program Neighborhood Settings screen, define how the application will be presented to the end user. Figure 9.43 shows a representation of the default settings. Select **Next** when you're finished.

Figure 9.43 Identifying How the Application Will Be Presented

6. From the Specify Application Appearance screen, define the published application appearance parameters and select **Next**. (See Figure 9.44.)

Figure 9.44 Selecting the Published Application Appearance Parameters

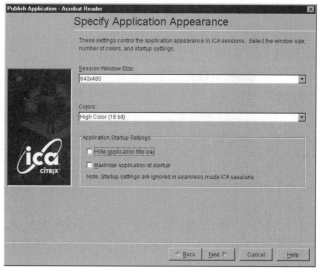

7. From the Specify ICA Client Requirements screen, define the **default settings** for a published application and possible minimum requirements. Figure 9.45 deviates from the default settings and turns audio off in this example.

Figure 9.45 Specifying ICA Client Default and Minimum Requirement Settings

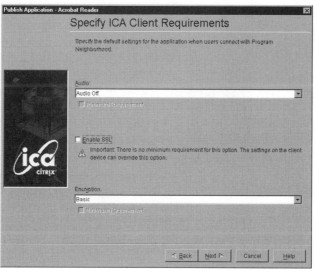

8. From the Specify Application Limits screen, determine any limits you want to be placed on the application. (See Figure 9.46.)

Figure 9.46 Specifying Application Limits

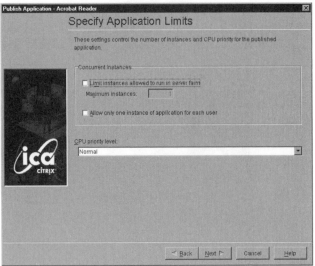

9. At the Specify Servers screen, determine which servers should host this application. (See Figure 9.47.)

Figure 9.47 Determining the Server to Host the Application

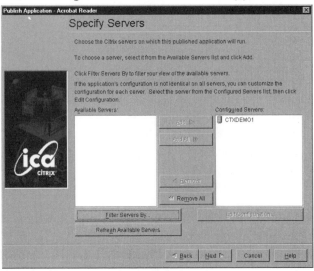

10. From the Specify Users screen, enter the names of the groups and/or users that will have access to this published application. (See Figure 9.48.) Select **Finish** to complete the published application process.

Figure 9.48 Specifying the Users Who Will Have Access

Configuring & Implementing...

Creating Groups for Published Applications

When creating published applications, an idea to think about is creating a group for each of the applications to which users will need access. This provides an easy way to configure each published application, because administrators do not have to enter each user into each published application they need to access. Common groups can be created for items such as Microsoft Office or applications that everyone will receive, such as Windows Explorer or Internet Explorer. For each application, add the group created for the application and a Citrix administrators group so that you don't have to place all your Citrix administrators in each of your application groups.

No additional work is needed for this application to appear in Program Neighborhood if the application set has already been established. (Figure 9.49 illustrates the new published application within Program Neighborhood.) Additionally, if the published application resides on a server that is participating in NFuse, no additional work is needed for the application to appear.

Figure 9.49 The Published Application Within Program Neighborhood

Program Neighborhood

Program Neighborhood is the ICA client interface that allows a user to access his or her particular application set. When you perform a single authentication to the server farm, a user is presented with the applications she has access to. The Program Neighborhood interface not only allows a user to view her application set, but she can change some of the application set properties such as audio and encryption as well. Figure 9.50 shows the Program Neighborhood Application Set interface; Figure 9.51 shows the corresponding published applications created within the Citrix Management Console.

Figure 9.50 Citrix Program Neighborhood Application Set

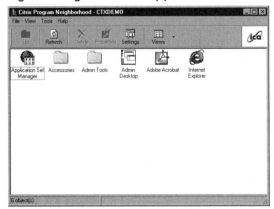

Using the ICA Toolbar

The ICA Administrator toolbar is a configurable toolbar that resides on the desktop. You can use the ICA toolbar to launch Citrix MetaFrame management tools in addition to any other type of program or content. Following the reboot of the installation of MetaFrame XP on a server, the toolbar appears to those who have administrative access to the local machine. Located on the ICA toolbar by default are all the Citrix MetaFrame XP management tools. Simply click an icon from the toolbar to launch the associated management tool. (See Figure 9.52.)

Figure 9.51 The Citrix Management Console Displaying Published Applications

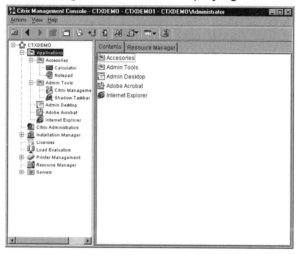

Figure 9.52 The ICA Toolbar

To launch the toolbar if it is not already displayed, from the desktop select **Start | Run**, type **icabar.exe**, and select **OK**. Table 9.7 lists the programs listed on the ICA toolbar by default

Table 9.7 ICA Toolbar Programs and Descriptions

Program	Description
ICA Client Creator	Use this utility to create diskettes or disk images for installing ICA client software.
ICA Client Update Configuration	Use this tool to manage the Client Update Database on a MetaFrame XP server. The database contains current ICA client software for each supported client platform and can be used to install ICA clients when users log on to the server.
Shadow Taskbar	Shadowing allows administrators to view and control ICA client sessions remotely. You can use the Shadow taskbar to shadow sessions and switch among multiple shadowed sessions.

Continued

Table 9.7 Continued

Program	Description
Citrix Connection Configuration	Use this utility to configure the connections that ICA clients use to link to MetaFrame servers.
SpeedScreen Latency Reduction Manager	Use this tool to configure local text echo and other features that improve the user experience on slow networks.
ICA Client Distribution Wizard	Use the ICA Client Distribution Wizard to create or update the ICA Client Update Database.
Documentation	This is a link to the %ProgramFiles%\Citrix\Documentation folder, which hosts several important Citrix MetaFrame documents.
Citrix SSL Relay Configuration Tool	Use this utility to secure communication between an NFuse-enabled Web server and your MetaFrame server farm.
Citrix Management Console	Use this centralized administration tool to monitor and manage many aspects of MetaFrame XP operation, from single servers to multiple server farms.

In addition to being able to run the ICA toolbar from Citrix MetaFrame servers, you can also publish it as an application to be accessible via a workstation. To publish the ICA toolbar, specify the location of the application as %systemroot%\system32\icabar.exe.

Summary

Citrix MetaFrame XP servers running within Windows 2000 provide a robust platform from which to publish applications. These servers support 32-bit, 16-bit, and MS-DOS-based applications. However, careful choices must be made in selecting these applications. A single application that performs badly can affect all users on a server.

Installing these applications onto a server must be done carefully and with some previous thought. It is important to remember to place the server in the correct mode, usually install mode, before installing an application, so the server knows to watch for an application install. The changes made during an application install while the server is in install mode are placed into a special location in the registry called the shadow registry. The shadow registry is a repository for registry entries and files that the system uses as users need them.

Take advantage, when possible, of the powerful features found in Installation Manager and Load Manager. Installation Manager helps an administrator install an application across multiple servers within a server farm; Load Manager can publish that application across those multiple servers.

Application compatibility scripts, or ACSs, are intricate batch files designed to fix some problems with applications that were not designed to be multiuser compatible. ACSs allow an administrator to provide unique settings and constructs for applications at runtime. This facility enables an administrator to configure a great many settings as a user starts a session.

Optimizing applications and the Citrix MetaFrame server allows for a better end-user experience when you're running applications within the environment. Disabling sound and intensive video-based applications can help free resources for other applications. In addition, a multitude of settings can be modified in the registry, on the server, and within the ICA client to help give the user a better overall experience.

Publishing applications enables a move beyond the traditional paradigm of client-to-server connections to move to an application-centric archetype of client-application connections. By defining an application as an object, administrators can define a user's experience vai application permissions rather than file permissions.

Program Neighborhood is the 32-bit client that allows a user to access these published applications through a simplified environment. Users can customize their application sets to allow certain features such as encryption or audio, if needed. The ICA toolbar is the interface administrators use to provide access to the most common Citrix management tools.

Solutions Fast Track

Selecting Compatible Applications

☑ Whenever possible, use 32-bit applications that will work well within a Citrix MetaFrame environment.

☑ When you're developing an application for use in a multiuser environment, follow Microsoft's suggested guidelines for optimum application performance and compatibility.

☑ Before placing the environment in production, gather a list of all the applications that need to be installed as well as the groups that will need access to certain applications.

Installing Applications

☑ Make sure to use the correct installation mode when you install applications. The application might not work as intended or at all if this step is not followed.

☑ Installation Manager and Load Manager allow an administrator to install and publish an application across multiple servers within a server farm, quickly and effectively.

☑ Take special care when you're uninstalling applications. Remnants of an application left behind can cause problems with other programs or future application installations.

Optimizing Application Performance

☑ Application compatibility scripts are sets of intricate batch files that fix some of the more common problems with applications that were not specifically written for multiuser environments.

☑ Many items can be modified within a Citrix MetaFrame environment to can enhance a user's experience running applications.

☑ An administrator must have knowledge of the more common tools needed to monitor and troubleshoot applications.

Publishing Applications

☑ By publishing applications, users can access their application sets in a simplified environment.

☑ The Citrix Management Console is the tool responsible for publishing applications.

☑ Administrators can set default properties for applications and even force minimum requirements before a user is allowed to launch an application.

Program Neighborhood

☑ Program Neighborhood allows users to access an application set based on their credentials.

☑ The ICA toolbar allows an administrator easy access to the most common Citrix management tools.

Frequently Asked Questions

The following Frequently Asked Questions, answered by the authors of this book, are designed to both measure your understanding of the concepts presented in this chapter and to assist you with real-life implementation of these concepts. To have your questions about this chapter answered by the author, browse to **www.syngress.com/solutions** and click on the **"Ask the Author"** form.

Q: Within my environment I have 25 different applications that I want to publish. Do I have to walk through the wizard for every single application?

A: No. Walk through the wizard for the first application. When you're finished, right-click the application within the Citrix Management Console and select **Copy Published Application**. From there, simply rename the new application and edit the properties of the application to change the path to the executable and icon display.

Q: How can I publish a copy of Explorer? When I do this now, it brings up a full desktop.

A: Create a new folder wherever it is that you install your applications, and name it **Explorer**. Copy **explorer.exe** from the %systemroot% to the new folder and rename the executable to something else. Publish this renamed executable.

Q: The application that I just installed runs only for administrators. When a regular user tries to run it, it fails. What is the problem?

A: More often that not, in a situation like this, an NTFS permission somewhere is holding up the regular user. Try running a utility such as File Monitor from Sysinternals or using the auditing features of Windows to track down the problem.

Q: I have a command-line variable that I need to pass to my application. Is this possible with published applications?

A: Yes. Within the published application, in the **Application Location** tab, enter the command-line variable after the path to the executable. This is frequently seen with Internet Explorer to open the first page to the company Web site. An example command line is:

```
C:\Program Files\Internet Explorer\iexplore.exe
http://www.syngress.com
```

Q: I have published all these applications, but no one except me can see them. What am I doing wrong?

A: Make sure that in the properties of the published application, all the users or groups that need access to the application have been specified under the Users tab. Users authenticating to the server farm through Program Neighborhood will see only the applications to which they have access.

Chapter 10

Security and Load Management

Introduction

Whenever you're connecting a computer to the Internet, that computer is open to sabotage. Worms and viruses can destroy entire systems, from the operating system right down to the hardware. Intruders can access servers on the Internet and obtain the passwords for administrative functions, using them later to wreak havoc on the system. Bored or unskilled programming students, also known as *script kiddies*, can download complex scripts from a hacker's Web site and test it on any vulnerable server just to see what happens.

Among many of the destructive attacks that can take place is the theft of confidential data. This activity is especially sensitive in the areas of e-commerce and financial systems; the theft of confidential data can destroy a company's competitive edge. Even a Citrix MetaFrame XP server, whose traffic consists mainly of graphics transmitted to clients and keyboard and mouse clicks received from clients, can be preyed upon by a saboteur.

Keeping the server farm running well across all servers is partly a matter of managing loads in addition to ensuring that data is kept safe. If a server farm is scaled up over time, it is likely that some servers will be more powerful than others. Some will have more processors or more powerful processors. Some will have more memory. As such, some servers will be capable of supporting more sessions than others. Ensuring equitable load management can optimize a farm.

Security Strategies for a Citrix MetaFrame XP Server Farm

To protect vital information from unauthorized intruders, it is vital that you secure your network and computer assets. As computer and network systems have become more common, the need for security has grown exponentially. As an administrator, you must give careful consideration to ensure that you take into account every option that can assist in securing the computing environment. Although Citrix MetaFrame XP provides several methods to ensure security of vital information, other products and solutions are used to protect data throughout a computing environment. Options such as virus protection, intrusion detection, and firewalls are among the most common solutions used today.

Virus Protection

By definition, a *virus* is a piece of computer code that produces unwanted results; it has the unique ability to replicate itself. A virus can perform an amazing array of damage, ranging from annoying messages and extensive resource utilization to destroying files and systems and causing massive outages. In addition, virus-like programs known as *worms* have become more prevalent due to their potential impact. The ability to protect computers against these types of attacks has become more a necessity than a luxury.

When considering antivirus software in your Citrix MetaFrame XP server farm, you must take into account several factors. First, you must evaluate the various products along with feature sets to provide a solution to meet your organization's needs. It's very important to ensure that the software you select is supported in a Terminal Server and Citrix MetaFrame XP server environment. This could have been difficult a short time ago, but many of the major antivirus software vendors now provide supported solutions.

In addition to using antivirus software on your Citrix MetaFrame XP servers, you can use various products throughout the network to protect other resources available to a Citrix MetaFrame XP client, such as file servers, electronic mail, and Internet Web filtering. Limiting your users' capability to surf the Web or use e-mail can also reduce the risk of virus infection. When you use antivirus software on your Citrix MetaFrame XP server, you must carefully configure the application to minimize the impact to end users. Most antivirus solutions provide real-time scanning of file access, but you must carefully consider its impact to server performance. Carefully test how this software impacts the overall client experience to ensure that it's not causing more damage than good. In addition, active scanning can be performed to search the entire system for any virus. Although this is an effective tool, it is recommended that you use it after hours because it can cause severe performance degradation and interfere with your users.

Last, antivirus software use signatures to identify virus patterns while scanning. To ensure you are monitoring for the latest virus infections, you must periodically update the signatures from the manufacturer. Most software solutions available today offer scheduled automatic updates. In addition, you can manually update the signature files if needed. It is recommended that you determine an acceptable interval for updating your antivirus signatures. You should check for new signatures at least once a week and install updates only after hours, to minimize user impact. In addition, if you become aware of any new virus infections, immediately check the manufacturer's Web site for signature updates and information about the infection.

One of the most common threats today, virus attacks produce an astounding impact on organizations. With estimated damages being reported in the billions of dollars by various news sources, virus protection is a critical component to ensure that your networking environment is secure. Antivirus programs created by third-party software developers have become a huge part of any organization's security program.

Intrusion Detection

Another security measure you must consider is monitoring for network intrusion. As hackers become more prevalent and savvy, you need additional tools to help protect your network environment. Intrusion detection is a strategy that any organization must at least consider in connecting the organization's computers to any public network.

Intrusion detection can be defined as the ability to monitor and react to computer misuse. Many hardware and software products on the market today provide various levels of intrusion detection. Some solutions use signatures to monitor for known attacks. Some platforms provide network monitoring; others are host-based systems. Some solutions react to particular alerts, such as shutting down services; others use a more passive approach. You must carefully select an intrusion detection strategy to ensure that your network resources remain secure from unwanted trespassers.

Similar to virus protection, various locations and methods are appropriate to using intrusion detection. The most common use is to install an intrusion detection solution to monitor the access points from the Internet or outside world into your private networks. For example, you might want to monitor for intruders on your Web servers. There are two main types of solutions: network-based and host-based. *Network-based intrusion detection* monitors network traffic for particular signs if malicious behavior. For example, if a user is continually trying to access a port known to be used with worms or Trojans, that could trigger an alert. *Host-based intrusion detection* programs are software products that are installed on your servers to monitor for suspicious behavior. This solution watches for virus-like activity to prevent it before it infects anything. It is critical to determine where you should monitor for intrusion and provide the appropriate solution to achieve these goals.

Firewalls

When connecting your computing resource to other networks such as the Internet, you must consider how you control access between your network and the others. In addition, some resources within your organization (such as human resources department computers that hold confidential personal information) need to be secured from internal intruders. A *firewall* is a common technique used to meet these requirements.

A firewall is traditionally used to secure one set of network resource from another network. The most common implementation of firewalls today is organizations connecting their internal private networks to the Internet. A firewall allows administrators to restrict outside individuals' access to internal resources. Although many firewall products are on the market, a firewall is more a security strategy than a single product. The solution to fit your needs might be available in a single product, but many times multiple devices are required to completely secure a network. For example, many firewall implementations include items discussed earlier in this chapter, such as intrusion detection and virus scanning. As an administrator, you must select the options and product that best suit your environment's requirements.

In order to utilize Citrix MetaFrame XP with firewalls, you must carefully consider who and what resources need to be available to external users. For example, if you want NFuse to be accessible to home users, you must allow the appropriate services to traverse the firewall.

For example, connecting to your NFuse Web site using HTTP requires TCP port 80. For users to access this service, port 80 must be allowed to traverse your network to the server hosting the NFuse pages. If you have elected to use SSL services to protect your NFuse Web pages, TCP port 443 must be opened instead of port 80. In addition, TCP port 1494 is used to establish ICA client sessions directly with Citrix MetaFrame XP servers. Figure 10.1 displays a common scenario for allowing traffic for Citrix MetaFrame XP to pass through a firewall. Table 10.1 displays the most common ports associated with Citrix MetaFrame XP services.

Figure 10.1 An Example of Firewall Use for Citrix MetaFrame XP

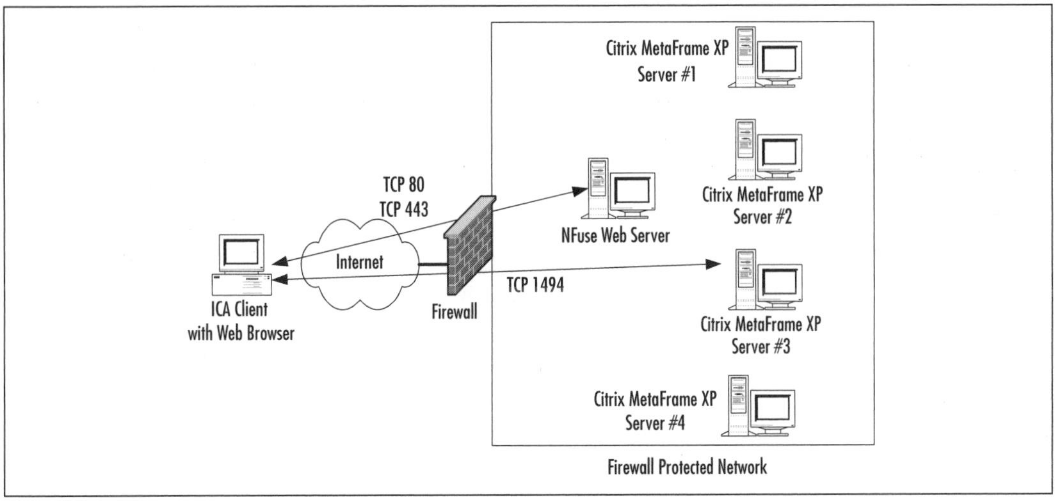

Table 10.1 Services Associated with Citrix MetaFrame XP

Port	Description
TCP Port 80	HTTP Web pages; used with NFuse servers.
TCP Port 443	HTTPS Web pages; used with NFuse servers using SSL technology for security or with the SSL Relay service.
TCP Port 1494	ICA session traffic; used for connecting to Citrix MetaFrame XP server farms.
UDP Port 1604	ICA Browser Services; used with older clients for browsing for Citrix MetaFrame server farms.
TCP Port 2512	IMA Service; used for server-to-server communication.
TCP Port 2513	Citrix Management Console; used for console communication to server farms.

Encrypting Citrix MetaFrame XP

In addition to the numerous security solutions and products available on the market today, Citrix MetaFrame XP provides built-in capability to help secure server and client communications from intruders. Using a standard technology known as *encryption*, server-to-server and client/server communication can be protected against intruders. Understanding how encryption works and where to apply it is important to ensure proper implementation of a secure server farm. Once you understand how encryption is used, you can properly set up the products and add-ons provided for Citrix MetaFrame XP.

Understanding Encryption

Encryption is the process of converting data into nonreadable text, also referred to as *ciphertext*. Ciphertext is used for transmitting confidential data. Once the data has arrived at its destination, it is then reconverted into the original data through a process known as *decryption*.

Various types of data encryption are available on the market today. Each type provides both benefits and disadvantages, including categories such as strength of security, ease of use, and standardization. The effectiveness of any security algorithm is found in its strength and the keys used to secure it. Weaker security algorithms are more easily cracked; however, if implemented properly, these system can still provide very effective solutions.

Encryption techniques are based on using keys similar to keys for your home or car. Using a key to open your car door is a method that identifies you as someone authorized to use the car. Whomever has possession of this key is able to access the car. Based on mathematical algorithms, encryption keys work the same way. If you have the correct key, you can encrypt or decrypt the data from ciphertext.

Symmetric Key Encryption

Primarily two forms of encryption are in use today. The most common form of encryption uses the *symmetric algorithm*. This method requires that each individual or device that accesses this encrypted data possess a copy of the key. Commonly referred to as *shared-key encryption* because it uses a single key for encryption and decryption, this is a relatively simple encryption technology to implement, but it might not provide the best security.

One common issue with symmetric encryption algorithms is the way the keys are transported to other users. If this type of key is obtained by an unauthorized user (such as during the encryption setup process), that unauthorized user can then easily decrypt that data, resulting in loss of data integrity. Most solutions that use symmetric keys to encrypt data also provide additional secure methods by which to negotiate and transport these keys to ensure that they are secured.

Another issue associated with symmetric keys is managing multiple identities. If you want to communicate securely using symmetric keys without all users having access to all data, you must maintain multiple keys. For example, Jane at Company A wants to send data to Bill at Company B. Jane must configure communications to Bill using Key 1, and Bill must use the same key. Now Jane also wants to communicate with Bob at Company X. To communicate with Bob, Jane must use a different key; therefore, Key 2 is created. As the number of companies or individuals grows, so does the number of keys required to maintain communications among them. Now imagine using this technology on an enterprise scale.

The most common implementation used today is the Digital Encryption Standard, or DES. Based on a fixed 56-bit symmetric key, this algorithm creates a single key based on a binary number used to encrypt and decrypt data. Using a block cipher methodology, it uses 64-byte blocks to randomly populate a key. Currently in use by organizations such as the National Security Agency (NSA), DES offers 72 quadrillion possible encryption keys at this point. In addition, developers have created a stronger version of DES, known as Triple DES, or 3DES, because it applies the DES key three times in a row when encrypting data. Figure 10.2 displays an example of symmetric key processing.

Figure 10.2 Symmetric Keys

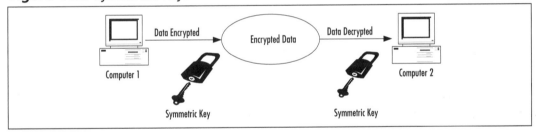

Asymmetric Key Encryption

The second method of encryption uses an asymmetrical algorithm and is commonly known as *public key encryption*. Although similar to the symmetric algorithm, this technology uses two keys to encrypt data. The first key is held privately in a secure location for the receiver to decrypt data sent to him. This validates that the receiver is authentic. The second key is freely published, is used to encrypt the data, and is commonly posted in public locations. This allows anyone to send the data, but only the holder of the private key is authorized to receive and decrypt the data. Even the public key originally used to encrypt the message cannot be used to decrypt it. This encryption technique allows you to send the public key over insecure channels and still maintain the integrity of encrypted data.

Therefore, if Tom wants to send encrypted data to Jim, he uses Jim's public key to encrypt it. Once the data is transferred to Jim, he uses his private key to decrypt the data. This system ensures that only Jim can access the data.

Created by and named for Ron Rivest, Adi Shamir, and Leonard Adleman, the *Rivest-Shamir-Adleman* (RSA) data encryption standard is the most commonly used asymmetric algorithm. It uses prime numbers to randomly generate public and private keys. A common application using RSA encryption includes Pretty Good Privacy (PGP) and Novell NetWare for a secure client-to-server communications channel. Similar to RSA, *Diffie-Hellman* is another common algorithm. Primarily used to transfer symmetric keys securely, Diffie-Hellman provides another form of asymmetric keys. A common example of asymmetric key encryption is using PGP to digitally sign e-mail communications. If you use a PGP signature, recipients of your messages can ensure that your e-mails are authentic. Figure 10.3 displays an example of how asymmetric keys work.

Figure 10.3 Asymmetric Keys

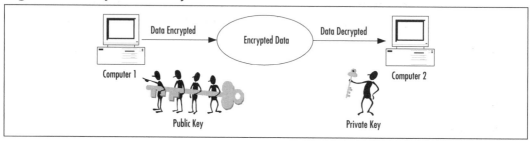

Secure Sockets Layer

Secure Sockets Layer (SSL) was created to encrypt data transmitted between a client computer and a Web server. Traditionally, Web traffic is transmitted in cleartext, potentially providing network intruders with sensitive data. Netscape developed SSL to provide a secure communications method by which to converse across the Internet. Based on RSA public/private key technology using digital certificates, SSL has become the standard for secure communication across the World Wide Web and can be used to complement your security strategy for your Citrix MetaFrame XP server farm.

SSL is used to confirm the identity of a server or a client machine and then encrypt all traffic between the two devices. For example, when you process a credit card transaction through a Web site, you want to ensure the identity of the receiver. SSL allows digital signatures to be used and are verified by a trusted *certificate authority* (CA). When you connect to a Web site using SSL, a certificate is processed, validating that the Web site is authentic. If it isn't, an error is issued, allowing you to determine whether to continue or not. As the process is completed, all traffic between your client and the Web site is encrypted to ensure that someone else cannot monitor the data flow.

SSL can be very useful when you're trying to secure a Citrix MetaFrame XP NFuse server. Using SSL with NFuse allows you to first confirm that your Web site is authentic to users. In addition, traffic such as authentication will not be sent cleartext, increasing your security risk. In order to use SSL with Web sites, you connect using Secure Hypertext Transfer Protocol (HTTPS) instead of HTTP. Once this is configured, you no long need to use standard HTTP services—you can rely solely on HTTPS to ensure that your site is secured.

Encryption Strength Options

Another important factor in implementing encryption strategies is defining the strength of your solution. In addition to the encryption techniques used, the key length is a major factor in determining the strength of any algorithm. For example, 16 bits in a key provide 65,536 possible key combinations. As the number of bits increases, so do the number of key variations. When you factor the computing power of today's computers, the ability to try every combination of larger keys, such as 128 bits, can take quite a few years to complete. Citrix MetaFrame has five encryption levels from which to select:

- Basic
- 128-bit login only
- 40-bit
- 56-bit
- 128-bit

NOTE

The 128-bit encryption method has been banned for export to several countries. Originally, it was difficult to export 128-bit products outside the United States, but the U.S. government has relaxed this requirement, and only countries affected by a U.S. trade embargo are affected. This includes countries such as Afghanistan, Iraq, Iran, Libya, Syria, Cuba, North Korea, or Sudan.

Each option provides 128-bit encryption for the logon process, and then the selected key strength is used to secure the remainder of ICA traffic throughout the session. Once a session has been established, all traffic, with the exception of a small encryption header, will be secured. This traffic includes items such as:

- Keystrokes
- GUI information

- Mouse data
- Client drive data
- Client printer data

Where Can You Use Encryption

Using a combination of symmetric and asymmetric key technologies, Citrix MetaFrame XP provides a comprehensive encryption solution to ensure secure communications. First, Citrix MetaFrame XP uses RC5, a fast block cipher developed for RSA security, as the symmetric key technology to encrypt all ICA traffic between clients and servers. To exchange these keys securely, Citrix has implemented the Diffie-Hellman asymmetric key algorithm. When an ICA client session is initiated, a unique public/private key pair is generated and passed through the communications channel. Once communication is established, these key pairs are used to arrive at the same RC5 symmetric key. Using a 1024-bit symmetric key, the client then begins processing ICA traffic and logon information.

Figure 10.4 displays how each of the encryption technologies is used to provide a complete solution. The communications path for initiating a connection through NFuse to a Citrix MetaFrame XP server farm is shown.

Figure 10.4 Encryption Technologies at Work

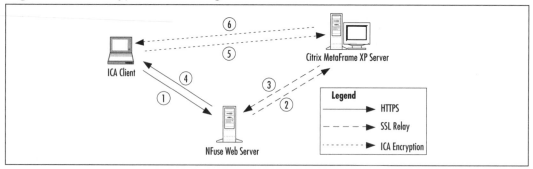

1. Client connects to a secured Web page using HTTPS.
2. The NFuse server validates the user and requests available applications using SSL Relay service to encrypt traffic.
3. Citrix MetaFrame XP server returns published applications available for this user.
4. The NFuse server provides a Web page using HTTPS with available applications.

5. ICA client connects directly to the Citrix MetaFrame XP server providing published applications.

6. A communications channel is opened using ICA encryption, and the client session begins.

Encrypting Server, Published Application, and Client Communications

The most commonly configured options for encryption with Citrix MetaFrame XP are used to encrypt traditional ICA client-to-server communications. There are several ways to accomplish this task:

- Encrypting traffic at the server level

- Setting encryption for each published application

- Setting encryption on an individual client basis

You must understand how each option affects the overall environment and how the options can be used together successfully.

The first option is encrypting traffic for all connections coming into the server. When you select this option, all ICA sessions initiated to the configured server encrypt data to the specified strength. This option mandates that each server must be configured independently, requiring administrators to touch each server any time this setting must be modified. For larger server farms, this requirement can be very prohibitive. The advantage to this approach is that all ICA connections communicating with this configuration are encrypted, whether through any published application or a custom ICA connection.

The next option involves setting encryption options per published application. The primary advantage of using this methodology is that it applies to all servers using the published application. Any user connecting through this application will use the specified encryption level across all servers in the Citrix MetaFrame XP server farm. Another advantage is that you can specify different levels of encryption for each published application. For example, if a user connects to a financial application, you might require him to use 128-bit encryption. At the same time, other users connect to a word processing tool over slow network links. For these connections, you may opt to force users to use only 40-bit encryption. If the settings were managed at the server level, as described in the last section, you would have to separate the user connections by server or configure each client independently to allow this to work. By configuring encryption for each published application, you can easily manage multiple encryption levels simultaneously, without the users knowing the difference.

The third option involves specifying an encryption level for the ICA client device. By default, the ICA client attempts to use whatever encryption strength is requested by the server. You can configure the ICA client to use different encryption strengths if the server or published application allows it. For example, if the server connection encryption strength is set to 56-bit, the ICA client cannot connect unless it is using 56-bit or higher. If you're connecting as an administrator to your Citrix MetaFrame XP server farm across the Internet, you might prefer to use 128-bit encryption to ensure that traffic is secured.

Using HTTPS

Encrypting the ICA client traffic secures the session information, but you must also consider accessing an NFuse Web site. By default, client devices accessing an NFuse Web site transmit data in cleartext. If you want to ensure that your communications are completely secure, you must consider using SSL on the Web server providing NFuse services. When you install a server certificate, the Web site can digitally sign and encrypt packets as they are sent between the client device and the Web server.

Using the SSL Relay Service

Another security issue to consider is the way that traffic is passed between the NFuse server and the XML service on Citrix MetaFrame XP servers. In a process that is similar to standard Web traffic, data is transmitted in cleartext. Although the password is slightly encrypted, it does not provide a secure alternative to the encryption methods discussed in this chapter. To assist you with this problem, Citrix has developed the SSL Relay service. This service allows you to configure all traffic passing between NFuse Web servers and a Citrix MetaFrame XP server to use SSL encryption.

NOTE

Although encryption is available using the pass-through authentication technology for Citrix MetaFrame XP, it is highly recommended that you disable this feature. Serious security flaws have been identified with this technology, potentially providing the username, password, and domain information in cleartext. For more information, download the *Advanced Concepts for MetaFrame XP* guide from www.citrix.com.

Clients That Can Support Encryption

In order to utilize encryption technologies, the ICA client software must be able to negotiate encrypted sessions. To accomplish this task, you must run a minimum version of 6.01 of the Citrix ICA client software. In addition, Feature Release 1 for Citrix MetaFrame XP provides some additional enhancements related to security. To utilize these new features, a minimum of version 6.20 of the ICA client software must be installed. Utilizing the client upgrade database can relieve the administrative overhead of managing client versions, because the database can be used to deploy the version you want to use. For more information about the client upgrade database, go to www.citrix.com.

Configuring Encryption on Citrix MetaFrame XP

Now that you have an understanding of what encryption technology can do and when to use it, the next step is to secure your Citrix MetaFrame XP server farm. Several products and techniques ensure that your environment is secured. The first step to configuring encryption options is to understand the various techniques and how they apply to your environment. For example, configuring encryption on ICA connections affects all client communication to a server; setting encryption on a single client applies only to itself. Encryption can be applied to the server, particular published applications, or even to a single client connection. In addition, traffic using Web technologies such as NFuse servers can be encrypted using solutions such as HTTPS and the SSL Relay.

Configuring & Implementing...

Determining the Encryption Strength to Use

When you are implementing encryption within your Citrix MetaFrame XP server farm, it is critical to correctly identify the encryption strength to use and where it will be configured. All encryption strengths, with the exception of basic, utilize 128-bit strength for the logon process. Afterward, they revert to the selected option, such as 56-bit. You might ask, "Why not just use 128-bit encryption if it's the best?" Unfortunately, the stronger the encryption algorithm, the more performance overhead is required on the server and client communications. For example, 128-bit encryption will not function properly when you use a 33.6Kbps modem connection to access a Citrix MetaFrame XP server. In the same manner, client performance degrades faster over inconsistent network links when you use higher-strength encryption algorithms. Carefully test each option that might suit your environment; it can have a major impact on the performance of your server farm.

Configuring Server Encryption

The most common method for encryption data is configuring each server to request the encryption strength. Each server has the ability to specify particular connection settings for all ICA communications, including encryption strength. Configuration is done this way:

1. Open the **Citrix Connection Configuration utility** by selecting **Start | Programs | Citrix | MetaFrame XP | Citrix Connection Configuration**.

2. Right-click **ICA–TCP** and select **Edit**, as shown in Figure 10.5.

   Figure 10.5 Selecting the Protocol to Configure

3. Select the **LAN Adapter** to configure. By default, all LAN adapters are chosen. Next, select the **Advanced** button to configure encryption options, as shown in Figure 10.6.

   Figure 10.6 Selecting the Advanced Button

4. In the Security section, select the encryption strength to use, as shown in Figure 10.7. By default, **Basic** is the encryption strength selected.

5. Once this process is completed, select **OK** to complete this configuration. Close the Citrix Connection Configuration utility.

Figure 10.7 Selecting the Encryption Strength

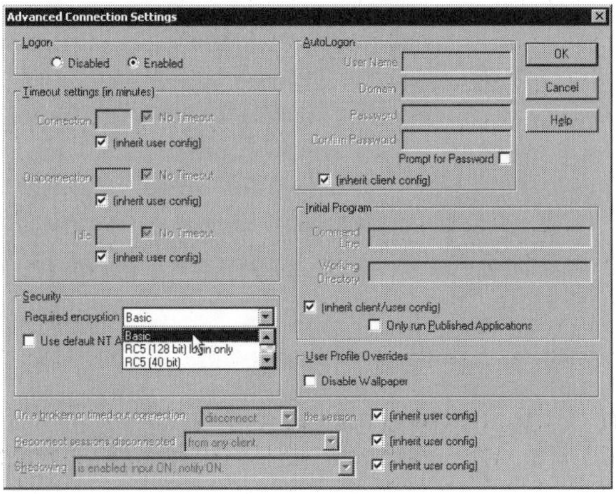

> **NOTE**
>
> The encryption settings defined in the Citrix Connection Configuration utility are server specific. Therefore, you must configure this option on each server in your farm to apply it to all users and connections.

Configuring Published Application Encryption

In addition to configuring encryption strength at the server level, you can also set it up per published application. This method allows you to further control the applications that are encrypted and specify different levels for each, if needed. To specify the encryption level, you can select the encryption strength used for the published application when you create it, as shown in Figure 10.8. In addition, you can choose a minimum requirement that forces clients to connect at the specified encryption level or higher or the connection will be refused.

Once the published application is set up, you can go back and alter the encryption level as needed. Unlike the server connection encryption, when you specify the encryption for the published application, all users connecting to this application use the encryption requirements on all servers. You do not have to change this setting more than once.

As shown in Figure 10.9, you can modify the properties of a published application from within CMC. As with the setup process for published applications, you can also specify the minimum required connection strength.

Figure 10.8 Specifying the Encryption Level During Published Application Setup

Figure 10.9 Encryption Properties of a Published Application

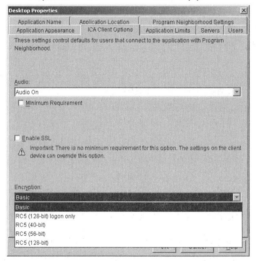

Configuring Client Encryption

In addition to configuring encryption strengths for server connections and published applications, the ICA client computer can specify encryption options. When you create custom ICA connections, the option to modify the encryption strength is offered. As shown in Figure 10.10, the ability to configure encryption options is consistent throughout the Citrix MetaFrame XP environment.

Figure 10.10 Configuring Encryption for Custom ICA Connections

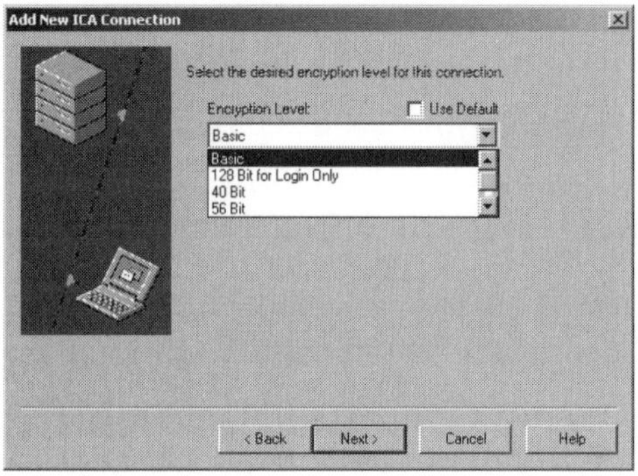

> **NOTE**
>
> In configuring encryption, if anything beyond basic is selected, automatic logon will no longer be allowed.

Disabling Pass-Through Authentication on Win32 ICA Clients

Another security factor to consider is known security vulnerabilities associated with using the pass-through authentication technology. Issues have been encountered that can present a security problem; well-documented procedures can provide the username, password, and domain name to malicious users. Therefore, Citrix recommends disabling this technology. Use the following process to disable pass-through authentication on a Win32 ICA client:

1. In the Win32 ICA client, select **Tools | ICA Settings**.

2. Remove the check for **Pass-Through Authentication**.

3. Delete the following files from the ICA client to prevent the feature from being enabled again: **Ssoncom.exe**, **Ssonstub.dll**, and **Ssonsvr.exe**.

Using HTTPS with NFuse

The next option available is used to secure the NFuse Web interface. When users connect to the NFuse home page, HTTPS can be set up and configured to secure all traffic that passes between the NFuse Web site and the ICA client. Using SSL technology, you must first request a server certificate from a trusted CA. Once this process is completed, use the Internet Services Manager administrative tool to configure your Web site to use

HTTPS. By setting the properties on the Web server, you can manage the way HTTPS is utilized. For example, you can specify that only SSL connections via HTTPS can be used. You can also force 128-bit encryption, as shown in Figure 10.11. Once HTTPS has been configured, type the name of your NFuse server into the Web browser using the prefix of *https*. An example of a secured Web site is https://nfuseserver.mycompany.com.

To configure an IIS Web server to use SSL technology, the following steps must be completed:

1. Obtain a digital certificate from a trusted CA such as www.verisign.com.

2. Start the IIS administrator tool by selecting **Start | Programs | Administrative Tools | Internet Services Manager**.

3. Select the Web server and highlight the NFuse Web site. The default Web site is used initially.

4. Right-click the Web site and select **Properties**.

5. Select the **Directory Security** tab to configure digital certificates.

6. Select the **Server Certificates** button to initiate the wizard to configure a server certificate.

7. Complete the Web Server Certificate Wizard to assign the certificate you obtained from the CA.

8. Once the wizard has completed, select the **Edit** button, as shown in Figure 10.11, to require the use of SSL for this Web site. Select **OK** once you have finished.

Figure 10.11 Requiring SSL Services

Configuring the Citrix SSL Relay

As explained earlier in this chapter, communication between an NFuse Web server and the Citrix MetaFrame XP server farm is not encrypted. In addition, the SSL TCP port can be used for client-to-server communication instead of TCP port 1494 to pass through a firewall. The SSL Relay service has been designed to address both these issues. To use the SSL Relay service, you must first obtain a server certificate from a trusted authority such as www.verisign.com. The same certificate used for HTTPS with NFuse, as described earlier, can also be used for the SSL Relay service. Once you receive the certificate, copy it into the key storage located at %SYSTEMROOT%\ SSLRelay\Keystore\certs.

To configure the SSL Relay service, complete the following tasks:

1. Open the Citrix SSL Relay Configuration Tool by selecting **Start | Programs | Citrix | MetaFrame XP | Citrix SSL Relay Configuration Tool**.

2. Verify that a certificate is displayed, as shown in Figure 10.12. This should be the certificate copied into the %SYSTEMROOT%\SSLRelay\Keystore\certs folder.

Figure 10.12 Configuring Relay Credentials

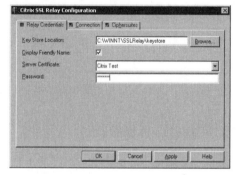

3. Type the password set up for this server certificate, if needed.

4. Next, Select the **Connection** tab, as shown in Figure 10.13. Insert the TCP/IP address of each Citrix MetaFrame XP server to which this server will communicate. Specify the port for each server on which the XML service is running.

5. Select the **Ciphersuites** tab to configure the algorithms to accept from the Web server, as shown in Figure 10.14. This allows you to further define the encryption methodologies used with the SSL Relay service.

6. When that's done, select **Apply** and **OK** to finish configuring the SSL Relay service.

Figure 10.13 Configuring SSL Relay Connections

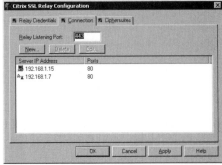

Figure 10.14 Configuring the Ciphersuites

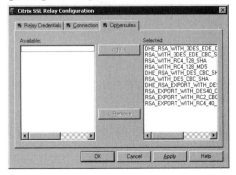

Using Load Manager

Security is an important aspect of ensuring availability, so resource management can quickly become a nightmare if it's not properly administered. The ability to dynamically direct client sessions to servers based on set requirements can greatly enhance not only the availability of application servers but also the performance impact on a client session. As server resources become more heavily taxed, Citrix MetaFrame XP can direct client sessions to other servers to minimize the impact to users.

Load Manager is included in Citrix MetaFrame XPa and XPe and is installed automatically during the Citrix MetaFrame XP installation process. This product allows you to set up and monitor load balancing between multiple Citrix MetaFrame XP servers within a single farm based on resource usage. For example, if a server is experiencing a large amount of processor usage, new client sessions can be directed to log on to another server that is less utilized. Although processor usage is a common criterion to use with Load Manager, there are quite a few other parameters to select from, including memory usage, page file usage, disk activity, and number of users.

Managing Load-Balanced Applications

To appreciate how Load Manager can benefit you within a Citrix MetaFrame XP server farm, you must first understand how this product works. Once a user has chosen to connect to a Citrix MetaFrame XP load-balanced farm, the client first contacts the MetaFrame "data collector" to obtain a list of available servers. The data collector maintains a list of servers available for each published application and each server's current load values as determined by load evaluators. Each server is responsible for maintaining its own load values and reporting them to the data collector.

The data collector uses the lowest load value to determine to which server the client is directed. In this example, clients accessing the Notepad application will be directed to server NT1. After the data collector selects a server, this information is passed back to the ICA client. The ICA client then initiates a direct connection to the published application running on the designated server. If a server is currently exceeding an assigned load value, it reports itself with a load of 9999 and thereby restricts new client sessions from being initiated. Once a client connects to the designated Citrix MetaFrame XP server, load management no longer affects a user session. Load Manager handles only incoming client sessions and will not redirect existing client connections. For example, if a user logs in to a Citrix MetaFrame load-balanced published application and the server fails, the client session must reinitiate the connection process all over again.

Designing & Planning...

Developing Load Management Strategies

When you use Load Manager, you must give careful consideration to the load evaluators used and how they are implemented. The first step is to identify the key bottlenecks you must monitor. Common items such as CPU or processor utilization might be required, or you might want to stipulate a specific range of clients. You must understand what it is you need to monitor before you implement load management. The next process involves measuring the rule values to use within your environment. You must be aware of what the thresholds need to be set up to enable adequate usage. In addition to these items, here are a few recommendations for using Load Manager:

1. Start by using one of the provided evaluators to familiarize your-self with how they function. Once you require more customization, try copying an evaluator and modifying the rules to meet your needs.

Continued

2. Profile the server to understand what normal utilization should be. This allows you to more clearly define effective thresholds for use with load management.

3. Try to minimize the number of evaluators used on your servers. Although it might be necessary to use multiple evaluators, it is recommended that you keep the evaluators from becoming too complex.

4. Never set a load evaluator rule threshold the maximum value a server can process. Leave the server some extra power in case it is needed.

Load Evaluators

Another item to discuss relating to Load Manager is *load evaluators*. Load evaluators are designed to allow administrators to manage the aspects by which a load is established. In older versions of Citrix MetaFrame, load balancing was severely limited by the capabilities of managing how load values were determined. Load Manager is the utility developed for Citrix MetaFrame XP that allows you to determine what variables to use.

Load evaluators consist of a set of rules that are used as criteria to express load values. The combination of the defined rules allows administrators more flexibility to ensure that servers are managing client sessions properly. New load evaluators can be created and customized to meet the needs based on the rules Citrix provides. They can also be assigned to published applications and/or servers as required. Default values are provided for each rule but can be modified to meet application or server needs. After an evaluator has been assigned, loads for servers are calculated using the evaluator with the highest load values.

Citrix also provides two basic evaluators, default and advanced, to get you started. The *default evaluator* consists of one rule: Server User Load. This evaluator uses the default values for this rule of 100 users maximum and provides a starting point for administrators. The *advanced evaluator* is designed to calculate three different rules: CPU utilization, memory usage, and page swap. This option is designed to more closely monitor server utilization and provides a superior solution to start with. The default and advanced evaluators can be copied, but they cannot be altered or deleted.

Load Evaluator Rules

As described earlier in this chapter, rules are used within load evaluators to dictate load values. An integral part of the load management process, rules provide the basics for statistically evaluating server performance based on preset values and thresholds. Each rule works independent of other rules and monitors a particular aspect of the Citrix

MetaFrame XP server. For example, the CPU utilization rule can be used to monitor overall CPU utilization on the server. With the default values of a maximum load of 90 percent and a minimum load of 10 percent, CPU activity can be the basis for evaluator load calculations.

Within this example, two servers exist: one with a load of 55 percent and another with a load of 35 percent. When a user accesses the Citrix server farm, the data collector looks at the load from both servers with this rule and sends the new client session to the server with 35 percent. As the ICA client logs in to the server and accesses applications, the CPU resources can rise. If they rise above 55 percent, new client sessions will be redirected to the other server. If the CPU utilization rises above 90 percent, no more new client sessions will be allowed until the CPU utilization drops below 90 percent again.

Each rule can be modified to a value defined by the administrator. Most rules allow for minimum and maximum thresholds, such as CPU utilization. When load reaches the maximum threshold configured, that server is no longer available for new client sessions until the threshold is no longer met. The minimum threshold defines the point at which a server reports no load. For example, by default the memory utilization rule does not report any load if utilization is below 10 percent. This allows for greater flexibility in configuring load evaluator rules.

Other rules, such as the scheduling, license threshold, and IP range rules, are used to enforce restrictions. Administrators can use these rules to logically allow or disable access based on a common set of criteria. For example, you could restrict users' ability to access an application after 10:00 P.M. to prevent access during backup intervals using the scheduling rule. You could also restrict certain remote clients to specific servers if requirements are dictated using the IP range rule. Table 10.2 describes each rule and provides threshold values where appropriate.

NOTE

Once load management is installed, Citrix MetaFrame XP automatically assigns the default load evaluator to each server.

Table10.2 Load Evaluator Rules

Rule	Description	Load Values
Application User Load	Rule specifying the number of users available to use a specified published application on a specific server.	Default value of 100. Value range of 1–10,000.

Continued

Table10.2 Continued

Rule	Description	Load Values
Context Switches	Server load is calculated based on CPU context switches per second. This helps to identify CPU process switching.	By default, CPU is loaded at 16,000 context switches. No load is reported at 900.
CPU Utilization	Server load is calculated based on CPU utilization.	By default, a full load is reported at 90% utilization. No load is reported at 10%.
Disk Data I/O	Server load is calculated by monitoring disk data I/O in kilobytes per second. This helps monitor disk performance issues.	By default, a full load is 32,767.
Disk Operations	Server load is calculated by monitoring disk operations.	By default, a full load is reported when exceeding 100 disk read/writes per second.
IP Range	This rule monitors the Citrix client's TCP/IP address.	An address range can be defined to allow or disallow specific clients.
License Threshold	Monitors license usage for sessions on each server.	By default, a full load is reached at 50%. No load is reported at 10%.
Memory Usage	Monitors overall memory utilization on a server.	By default, a full load is reported at 90% utilization. No load is reported at 10%.
Page Fault	Monitors number of page faults per second.	By default, a full load is reported at 2000 per second.
Page Swap	Monitors number of page swaps per second.	By default, a full load is reported at 100 per second.
Scheduling	Creates a schedule of allowed or disallowed times to for client access to a server or published application.	Any times can be specified.

Continued

Table10.2 Continued

Rule	Description	Load Values
Server User Load	Rule specifying numbers of sessions allowed per server.	Default value of 100. Value range of 1–10,000.

> **NOTE**
>
> It is important to understand the difference between the Server User Load evaluator and the Application User Load evaluator. Both provide similar functionality; however, the Server User Load evaluator monitors all sessions on the server. If this server is providing multiple published applications, the number of users assigned may be larger than for a single application. The Application User Load evaluator monitors only the number of users on a server running the specified application.

Creating and Assigning a Load Evaluator

Follow these steps to create and assign a load evaluator:

1. Select **Load Evaluators** from within the Citrix Management Console. Right-click and select **New Load Evaluator**, as shown in Figure 10.15.

   Figure 10.15 Creating a New Load Evaluator

2. Next, insert a name and description to be used for this evaluator. Select from the various load evaluators from the left panel and press **Add**. As shown in Figure 10.16, modify the default values if required for each evaluator chosen, and press **OK** to continue.

Figure 10.16 Designating Load Evaluator Properties

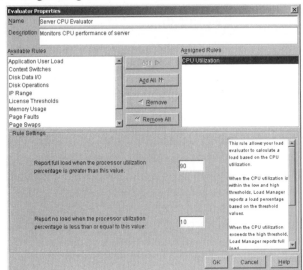

3. Once completed, the load evaluator can be assigned to a published application. Select the published application, as shown in Figure 10.17, to which to assign the load evaluator. Right-click the item and select **Load Manage Application**.

Figure 10.17 Assigning Load Evaluators to Applications

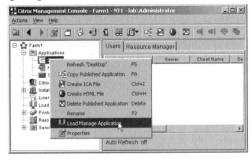

4. Finally, select the server(s) to assign the evaluator, and press **Add**. Highlight the appropriate evaluator, and press **OK** to complete this task, as shown in Figure 10.18.

Once load evaluators have been created and assigned to a particular server or published application, you need a method of tracking them. Within the Citrix Management Console, the load evaluator option offers the ability to identify which evaluators are assigned to applications or servers. As shown in Figure 10.19, a report is available to show evaluator assignees and can be specified by server, application, or evaluator. For example, Figure 10.19 identifies that the default evaluator has been assigned to the Notepad application located on servers NT1 and NT2.

Figure 10.18 Specifying Load Evaluators

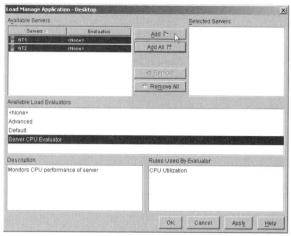

Figure 10.19 Usage Report for Load Evaluators

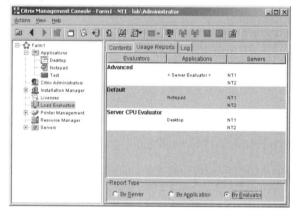

Calculating Load Values

Now that you have created load evaluators, assigned rules, and specified thresholds specified, you must gain an understanding of how the Citrix MetaFrame XP server monitors and reports these values. This understanding is critical to maintaining your server farm. You have learned how to monitor evaluators and rules assigned to specific applications and servers, but how do you tell the current load based on these rules?

Citrix MetaFrame XP uses load evaluators and thresholds that are defined to calculate the overall load for a server or application. As explained earlier in this chapter, within each rule are specified maximum and minimum thresholds. These values are used to help determine load calculations for each rule. By modifying these values, you can determine how loads are calculated and reported for user sessions.

Servers report load values to the data collector in four-digit integers ranging from 0000 to 9999. Altering the maximum and minimum load thresholds is one method of adjusting the outcome of the load values reported. The load value is calculated using the following formula:

$$\frac{\text{Current rule value}}{\text{(maximum threshold – minimum threshold)}}$$

Each rule must follow this calculation. The end results will vary depending on the rules defined and the threshold values. For example, two servers are load managed within a single farm and use the default evaluator. Note that the default evaluator measures only user connections. Using the calculation, we can measure what the load of a particular server is based on the number of users currently connected.

Using the default values provided with this evaluator, use the preceding formula to calculate the load based on six users connected to the server:

1. Apply the default and current values to the load formula:

$$\frac{\text{Current rule value (6)}}{\text{(maximum threshold (15) – minimum threshold (0))}}$$

2. Subtract the minimum threshold from the maximum threshold:

$$\frac{\text{Current rule value (6)}}{\text{(maximum threshold – minimum threshold = 15)}}$$

3. Divide the combined threshold value by the current value:

$$6 / 15 = 0.4 \ (40\%)$$

4. Using the method by which servers report values to the data collector, calculate 40% of 10,000. Remember that servers report values ranging from 0000–9999.

$$10000 \times 0.4 \ (40\%) = 4000$$

The load value reported to the data collector from this exercise is 4000.

Monitoring Load-Balanced Applications

Once an application has been set up with Load Manager, careful monitoring must be performed to ensure evaluators have been properly defined. Various utilities are available to facilitate this task, but the most common tool is Load Manager Monitor. As shown in Figure 10.20, Load Manager Monitor provides the ability to actively monitor load evaluator behavior and current status by graphing activity. Each rule is listed independently while also measuring the overall evaluator load based on all rules configured. This utility is available from within the Citrix Management Console.

Figure 10.20 Using the Load Manager Monitor

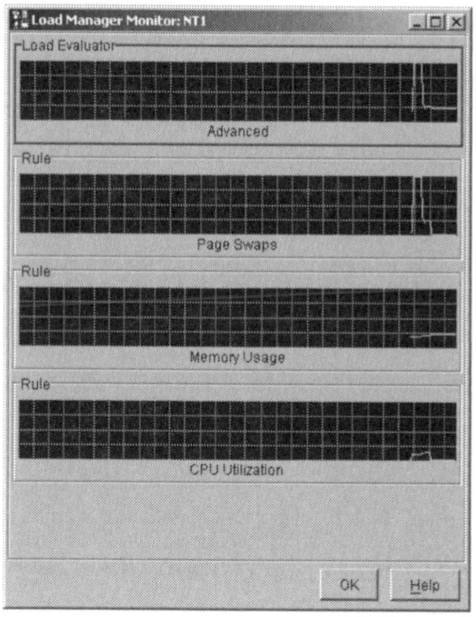

An additional utility that provides more granular detail is QFARM.exe. Installed by default with Citrix MetaFrame XP, the QFARM command-line utility allows you to monitor load evaluators in more detail than the graphical user interface. For example, load values can be displayed for each server, by application, or both simultaneously. In addition to reporting load values, this single utility can display other items, including the current zone data collector, license information, and server membership. As shown in Figure 10.21, QFARM can be a powerful utility for administering and troubleshooting load management.

Figure 10.21 An Example of Current Load Values for Published Applications and Servers Using QFARM

NOTE

When multiple rules are defined within a load evaluator, the rule with the greatest load is reported.

Summary

The first step in securing any computing environment is developing a comprehensive security strategy. Although Citrix MetaFrame XP provides some built-in capabilities, it might not cover every aspect of your requirements. To resolve this dilemma, you can use some common third-party solutions. The most common solution is virus protection. Used to protect against malicious computer code, virus protection is almost a requirement these days. To monitor your network resources from outside trespassers, intrusion detection software is recommended. This software monitors for unauthorized probing or use of your computing resources. Firewall software is another key component of your security strategy; it provides the gateway to other networks. To protect your internal network, a firewall is generally placed between secured resources and public networks such as the Internet.

One of the primary security mechanisms employed by Citrix MetaFrame XP is encryption technology. Based on industry-standard mathematical algorithms, encryption is used to scramble data as it is transmitted across the network to prevent unauthorized users from accessing it. Using several different technologies, including symmetric keys, asymmetric keys, and Secure Sockets Layer (SSL), Citrix MetaFrame XP works to completely secure the entire server farm. When you use Citrix MetaFrame XP, you choose from among five different encryption strengths: basic, 128-bit logon only, 40-bit, 56-bit, and 128-bit encryption. Once your system is configured properly, all traffic traversing the server farm is encrypted, with the exception of a small encryption header. This includes items such as keystrokes, mouse data, graphical data, client data, and client printing. Using a series of solutions, Citrix MetaFrame covers all the bases.

The most common configuration includes Independent Computing Architecture (ICA) encryption for server connections, published applications, and ICA client. In addition, SSL can be used via Secure Hypertext Transfer Protocol (HTTPS) for NFuse Web servers and the SSL Relay services for communication between Web servers and server farms. To support encryption technology, the ICA client device must be installed with a minimum of version 6.01 of the client software. To take advantage of Feature Release 1 options, the client device must be installed with client software of 6.20 or higher.

Once you comprehend encryption technologies, you next need to learn how to configure them properly. Various tools are provided to configure encryption, such as the Citrix Management Console, the Citrix Connection Configuration tool, and the SSL Relay Server Configuration tool. Understanding how each is used will allow you to effectively implement your encryption strategy. In addition, you must understand your Web servers' configuration tool to properly configure HTTPS services for your NFuse pages. This configuration forces client connections to the NFuse server to process only encrypted pages.

Another critical component in ensuring uptime of your Citrix MetaFrame XP server farm is the Load Manager product. With the ability to manage resources across servers to ensure availability, Load Manager is a handy tool. Based on "load evaluators," Load Manager uses rules you define to process incoming ICA client connections. The load evaluators you create continually monitor server usage and report load values to a central data collector so that client connections can be routed to the server with the least load. Rules used in load evaluators consist of items such as processor utilization, memory utilization, license usage, and memory usage, to name a few. Using the Citrix Management Console, you can use the provided default load evaluators or create your own custom evaluator. You must then apply these evaluators to the servers and/or published applications for which you want to monitor. After you apply the rules, use the Load Monitor utility to monitor overall usage to ensure that you are getting the maximum use of your servers without overloading them. Using a predefined formula, you can monitor exact usage and monitor usage through the server farm via command-line utilities.

Solutions Fast Track

Security Strategies for a Citrix MetaFrame XP Server Farm

- ☑ Virus protection is required to protect against malicious computer code and worms. Virus protection is implemented by installing third-party software on computers in danger of getting infected.

- ☑ Intrusion detection software is utilized to monitor and react to network intruders. A variety of solutions exist, from active to passive, network-based and host-based, and signature versus anomaly monitoring.

- ☑ Firewalls are used to protect private networks from public resources. Firewalls are most commonly used to protect your internal network when it connects to the Internet.

Encrypting Citrix

- ☑ Citrix MetaFrame XP uses industry-standard encryption algorithms based on symmetric keys, asymmetric keys, and Secure Sockets Layer (SSL).

- ☑ Five RC5 encryption strengths are available: basic, 128-bit logon only, 40-bit, 56-bit, and 128-bit. When you set RC5 encryption, all client connections use 128-bit encryption for logon and then begin using the defined encryption strength for the remainder of the connection.

☑ To secure the entire Citrix MetaFrame XP solution, several encryption technologies are used. Symmetric and asymmetric keys are used in the form of RC5 encryption and Diffie-Hellman public/private keys to secure Independent Computing Architecture (ICA) traffic. SSL is used in the form of Secure Hypertext Transfer Protocol (HTTPS) for client-to-NFuse-Web-server traffic, and the SSL Relay service is used to encrypt traffic between NFuse Web servers and Citrix MetaFrame XP servers.

Configuring Encryption

☑ To configure encryption technologies, different tools are required based on how you want to implement encryption. Citrix Management Console is used to configure published application encryption settings. Citrix Connection Configuration utility is used to configure server connection encryption. The ICA client software must be used to configure client-specific connections.

☑ To configure HTTPS, you retrieve a server certificate from a certificate authority (CA) and apply it to your Web server. When clients connect to your Web server, they must use the prefix *https* instead of *http*.

☑ To configure the SSL Relay service, you must apply a server certificate from a CA. Once completed, you must configure the server connections that will be used along with the Transmission Control Protocol (TCP) port. By default, TCP port 443 is used.

Using Load Manager

☑ Load Manager provides the capability to assign incoming ICA client connections to servers based on the least load. This allows you to ensure that servers are not over-utilized.

☑ To use Load Manager, you must decide on a load evaluator, assign rules to each evaluator, and configure the thresholds for each rule. Once that's done, you assign the load evaluator to published applications or servers as required.

☑ Using the Load Manager Monitor and command-line utilities, you monitor load usage across your Citrix MetaFrame XP server farm.

Frequently Asked Questions

The following Frequently Asked Questions, answered by the authors of this book, are designed to both measure your understanding of the concepts presented in this chapter and to assist you with real-life implementation of these concepts. To have your questions about this chapter answered by the author, browse to **www.syngress.com/solutions** and click on the **"Ask the Author"** form.

Q: If 128-bit encryption is the strongest solution, why would I use anything else?

A: With the strong encryption technology comes additional server and ICA client overhead. Although most network connections will not be affected, inconsistent WAN connections or slow dialup networking connections can be affected by the encryption strength used.

Q: Do I need to use a firewall, intrusion detection, and virus protection simultaneously?

A: Your requirements depend on how your environment is designed. You might require none of these or all three. For example, if outside computer code can be inserted into your computers via electronic mail, diskette, or another method, you might want to consider using virus protection. If your network is connected to other resources such as the Internet, you might want to consider using a firewall. The need for any of these products must be evaluated on a case-by-case basis.

Q: Why are there so many different ways to configure encryption within Citrix MetaFrame XP?

A: In order to meet organizations' varied requirements, Citrix has tried to provide a great deal of flexibility in how and what can be configured relating to encryption technologies. Because so many different variables are involved in using these features, you must truly understand how they all work and the overall affect to take complete advantage of the technology.

Q: What advantage does Load Manager offer when I can point users to individual servers to separate the load between them?

A: Load Manager allows client connections to be dynamically allocated to servers in real time. This capability helps ease your administrative burden in managing all these connections. In addition, you can add and remove servers seamlessly, without having to recreate user connections.

Q: Why are rules such as IP Range and License Threshold used in Load Manager to determine how heavily used a server is?

A: Citrix MetaFrame XP provides the flexibility to monitor not only server resource utilization but also things such as license usage and source network location. For example, if you want all incoming connections from a particular network to use a particular set of servers, the IP range provides this ability.

Q: To encrypt all traffic passing through the entire Citrix MetaFrame XP solution, why do you have to configure multiple items?

A: Several of the technologies involved, such as Web services, are not controlled or maintained by Citrix. Using other third-party solutions such as Netscape Web server or Internet Information Services as a Web server requires its own method to secure them. Fortunately, industry-standard products such as SSL provide an easily implemented technology that can be used to complete these tasks.

Chapter 11

Extending Citrix MetaFrame XP Over the Internet

Solutions in this chapter:

- Business Reasons for Providing Applications Over the Internet

- Deploying Applications with NFuse

- Using VPNs with Citrix MetaFrame XP Clients

- Deploying Applications to Launch from a Browser

☑ Summary

☑ Solutions Fast Track

☑ Frequently Asked Questions

Introduction

The Internet truly revolutionized computing for businesses. Instead of thinking in terms of connecting one office to another for sharing information and applications, we are connecting everyone to the Internet cloud. With this paradigm shift, telecommunications and computing no longer have geographical barriers. The global marketplace is available to everyone to use for e-commerce and e-business—even as an extension of their internal networks.

Citrix NFuse was developed to provide an Internet portal to applications. Using NFuse, a company can personalize the way that applications appear to users who launch them from a Web browser.

NFuse is not the only way that applications can be used across the Internet. Virtual private networking (VPN) enables the native ICA client to function across the Internet. A Windows 2000 Terminal Services server without Citrix MetaFrame XP can provide browser-launched applications with the Terminal Services Advanced Client.

Business Reasons for Providing Applications Across the Internet

Since its inception, the World Wide Web has exploded in popularity as both a research instrument and a business communications tool. Web technologies have become a major driver for businesses due to their simplicity and availability to such a large user base. Using Web technologies—not only across the Internet but also for internal business applications such as intranet sites—provides a way to access resources efficiently. The ability to provide application availability over the Internet has become commonplace among businesses for a variety of reasons. Using VPN technology with Citrix MetaFrame XP provides remote access for users who work while traveling or from home. Providing applications via intranet sites offers administrators the ability to implement a new software package without ever touching a single desktop. Software demonstrations can be performed remotely through ICA sessions, without the need for special installation setups or high bandwidth requirements. Providing other vendors access to business applications is another way that Web-based technologies extend the business outside traditional boundaries.

Using Citrix MetaFrame XP with VPN for Telecommuters

As the need for application-hosting technology has steadily grown, so has the need for accessing these applications over public networks. Once of the most common techniques used today is VPN. As users travel around the globe or work from home, the need increases to securely access company resources remotely. Using VPN technology, users can connect securely over the Internet and access resources as though they were on the local network.

Using Web-based technologies such as NFuse in cooperation with VPN provides a simple solution using technology that any computer user can handle. Because it's based on using Web browsers such as Internet Explorer and Netscape Navigator, any user who can surf the Web can access a server farm from home or a remote location. In addition, using Web-based technology allows administrators to centrally manage application deployment. Instead of trying to install and upgrade applications for remote users, one change can be made centrally to the server farm and propagated to all users automatically.

Another benefit of using Web-based technologies for telecommuters via Citrix MetaFrame XP is the resulting bandwidth efficiency. Using normal applications over the Internet can require large amounts of bandwidth and provide extremely sluggish performance. Using Citrix technologies with VPN, a standard 56kbps dialup connection can support the most grueling applications. For example, an accounting package in use can require 250–300kbps to function properly across a standard network connection. For users dialing into your network or connecting across the Internet, bandwidth to support this application might not be available. Users would typically be unable to connect, or they could experience extremely poor performance. With Citrix MetaFrame XP technology, remote users can connect and run their applications as though they were on the LAN while requiring only 10–20kbps of bandwidth.

Integrating Applications into Intranets

Another advantage to Web-based technologies is the ability to integrate any application right into an intranet Web site. Intranets have become popular for providing a centralized source of information for employees or various business divisions within a company. The ability to provide application functionality within a Web page can truly streamline the dissemination of resources. Using Citrix Web-based technologies such as NFuse, you can—without touching a desktop—create Web site portals that include applications available to a large number of users.

For example, let's say that your organization wants to implement new employee time-tracking software but doesn't want to install it on every personal computer. Using Citrix MetaFrame XP and NFuse, you can post a link to your intranet page to the application. As users are informed of the software's existence, they connect to the Web site, click a URL for the application, and the application starts. If a PC does not have the ICA client software, it is automatically downloaded and installed.

Providing Software-Based Demos

Software products steadily grow in magnitude along with the requirements to utilize them. With the addition of new features and functionality, an application package is consistently changing in size. Traditionally, remote software demonstrations were rarely successful, due to setup issues and bandwidth constraints. With application hosting via Citrix MetaFrame XP, remote software demonstrations have become much easier to offer. Using Web technologies to facilitate demonstrations provides an easy way to allow potential customers to view your application.

For example, say that a user wants to evaluate an accounting package. The vendor has a Citrix MetaFrame XP server with NFuse configured to allow the potential customer to connect and evaluate the application. The user connects via the Internet to the accounting software vendor's Web site and initiates an ICA session. The customer can seamlessly and efficiently browse through a copy of the accounting software that has been set up and configured correctly by the vendor. This allows the potential client to evaluate the software on its merits and not be distracted by problems trying to run it across the Internet. In addition, the application does not have to be distributed, allowing organizations to maintain tighter control over who has copies. This allows you to manage who has access to your application and ensure that only licensed users receive the functionality your software provides.

Extending Applications Between Businesses

As organizations have grown, the need to share information and applications among business vendors and customers has become more prevalent. Providing up-to-date information for customers can represent the difference between maintaining them and losing them to a competitor. The process of using Citrix MetaFrame XP along with Web-enabled technologies such as NFuse to provide access to the most challenging applications via the Internet is greatly simplified.

For example, car manufacturers work with thousands of distributors throughout the world to make their products. The ability to efficiently communicate and share information is critical, not only to the manufacturer, but to the distributors, to ensure that their customers remain happy. Assume that a car manufacturer wants to see schematics for a new engine component. The overall amount and magnitude of the information associated with this component could amount to gigabytes of data. A part distributor could provide Citrix MetaFrame XP to allow customers (i.e., car manufacturers) to log in to its network and view engineering schematics. This system allows customers to effectively search and find the information they need, without the distributor having to package and send them large amounts of data.

Deploying Applications with NFuse

Because of the increased usage and availability of Web-enabled applications described earlier in this chapter, Citrix MetaFrame XP includes Web-based solutions to access published applications from a server farm. Using standard technologies such as Java and HTML pages, solutions have been created to provide Web-based programs, with no application modifications required.

NFuse 1.6 works by providing a Web interface to the Program Neighborhood services provided by Citrix MetaFrame XP. NFuse is used to create Web sites that can be integrated into your organization's Internet or intranet sites. As users connect and authenticate themselves, they receive a list of published applications, based on their credentials. Once a user selects an application, an ICA session is opened to a Citrix MetaFrame XP server farm. NFuse provides administrators the ability to dynamically provide connection details for user sessions, thereby minimizing the administrative overhead of using published applications.

Figure 11.1 displays how NFuse communication works with each of the required components. Here's how it works, step by step:

Figure 11.1 The NFuse Communication Process

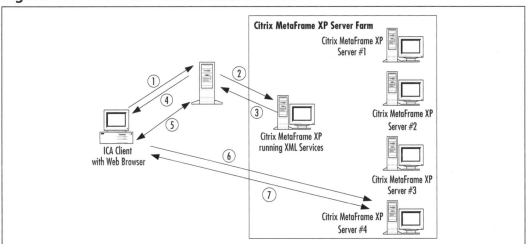

1. The user opens a Web browser and connects to the NFuse Web pages on the Web server. Using HTTP, the user access the NFuse login pages and enters their login, password, and domain information.

2. Using NFuse Java objects, the Web server contacts the designated server running Extensible Markup Language (XML) services. This server provides the communications link between the Web server and the Citrix MetaFrame XP server farm.

3. Using XML services, the Citrix MetaFrame XP server returns a list of published applications available based on the user credentials. The NFuse Java objects are used to communicate via XML and provide this list to the Web server.

4. Using Java objects, an HTML page is generated, with links to each published applications consisting of ICA files based on a standard populated template file. ICA files are discussed in further detail later in this chapter. An HTML Web page is provided to the user via her Web browser; it contains a list of available published applications.

5. Next, the user selects the link to a published application. The link is used to download the ICA file for the particular application and executes on the ICA client device.

6. The ICA client initiates a session with the Citrix MetaFrame XP server designated in the ICA file.

7. The ICA session is established, and the published application is ready for use.

Citrix Web Components

When implementing NFuse into your Citrix MetaFrame XP environment, you must consider three primary components. Each component plays a key role in using NFuse. Understanding each component and how it fits into the NFuse solution is critical to properly implementing and maintaining this environment. The Citrix server farm provides published applications for user access. The Web server handles NFuse Web pages and communicates directly with the Citrix MetaFrame XP server farm. The ICA client connects to the NFuse Web site to enumerate the available published applications. Once selected, the published application starts, and communication begins between the ICA client and the Citrix MetaFrame XP server farm.

Citrix MetaFrame XP Server Farm

The Citrix MetaFrame XP server farm is the backbone of application publishing within NFuse. The server farm is a collection of Citrix MetaFrame XP servers working together to provide centralized application use to ICA clients. In addition to Citrix MetaFrame XP servers, Citrix MetaFrame for UNIX servers and Citrix MetaFrame for Windows 1.8 servers can also coexist within the same farm and utilize NFuse.

Application publishing provides a mechanism by which to offer particular applications based on a user's logon credentials. Using a traditional ICA client, the Program Neighborhood is used to provide application publishing down to the desktop. Once a user selects the application to use, an ICA session is established with the Citrix

MetaFrame XP server farm and the application is made available to the user. The list of applications provided to each user is known as the *application set*.

The NFuse Web server provides a Web-based solution for Program Neighborhood. Using standard Web pages, Java objects, and XML, NFuse provides an application set to user via a standard customizable Web page. NFuse communicates with the Citrix MetaFrame server farm using XML services installed on a specific Citrix MetaFrame XP server. Although the XML service defaults to TCP port 80, any TCP port can be specified. A common scenario for modifying the XML service port assignment occurs when other sites are in use on the server hosting acting as the XML host for the Citrix MetaFrame XP server farm. Because port 80 is used for Web services by default, XML services benefit from using a different port.

By default, the XML service is installed and configured during the initial installation of Citrix MetaFrame XP. As shown in Figure 11.2, the XML service is enabled by default and set to share port 80 with Internet Information Services. If a separate port is specified, the NFuse server must also be modified to recognize this change.

Figure 11.2 XML Service Configuration During Citrix MetaFrame XP Server Installation

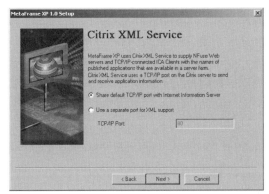

> **NOTE**
>
> Once the Citrix MetaFrame XP server installation is complete, you might need to install or modify the XML service. The Citrix Management Console allows you to change this option by modifying the server properties using the MetaFrame Settings tab. Citrix also provides a command-line utility installed with Citrix MetaFrame XP to perform these tasks. The utility, ctxxmlss.exe, is located in %SYSTEMROOT%/system32.

In addition to the XML services, NFuse is enabled and installed by default during the initial installation of Citrix MetaFrame XP. As shown in Figure 11.3, NFuse is selected by default, and the default Web page is altered to the NFuse logon page.

Figure 11.3 NFuse Installation Options During Citrix MetaFrame XP Server Installation

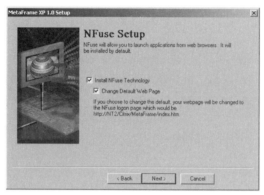

Web Server

The second component of NFuse is the Web server. The Web server provides the Web interface to the user and acts as the liaison between the Citrix MetaFrame XP server farm and the ICA client. As NFuse provides application publishing via a Web-enabled Program Neighborhood, the Web server handles the HTTP pages provided to the user. Using a series of Java objects, extensions installed onto the Web server allow communication directly to the server farm to occur. The Java objects serve three primary functions:

- User authentication to the Citrix MetaFrame XP server farm

- Retrieving application sets based on user credentials

- Providing administrators the ability to modify the user experience without intervention

During installation of NFuse services, a series of files, including Java objects, sample Web pages, and configuration files, are loaded onto the Web server. Using configuration files such as %SYSTEMROOT%\java\trustlib\nfuse.conf, administrators can customize the user experience and provide support for a variety of network configurations, including issues such as NAT, SSL, and Novell NDS login authentication.

Once ICA clients have logged in to the server farm via an NFuse Web page, ICA files are provided via hyperlinks. NFuse uses a template ICA file and populates the various fields dynamically for each hyperlink. By customizing this template file, you can control user behavior and available options. An example of an ICA template file is shown in Figure 11.4.

Figure 11.4 A Template ICA File Used with NFuse

In addition to managing NFuse configuration options, Citrix has provided a utility that creates a customized Web site based on options you determine are needed. Specifying many of the options included in the NFuse.conf configuration file, this wizard also allows you to manage the overall look using one of several Web site designs provided by Citrix.

Creating a Customized NFuse Web Site

To create a customized site using previous versions of NFuse, follow these steps:

1. Download and execute the **NFuseWizard.exe** file to being installation. Follow the prompts to complete the installation process.

2. Start the Web Site Wizard by selecting **Start | Programs | Citrix | NFuse | Web Site Wizard**.

3. Press **Next** to begin the Web site customization.

4. As shown in Figure 11.5, check the **Override Default Citrix Server** option and insert the server and port names if you want to modify which server NFuse communicates with. Select **Enable SSL** and insert the relay server and relay port if you're using SSL Relay service. Once all that is done, select **Next** to continue.

5. Select a Web site layout design from the options provided, as shown in Figure 11.6. Press **Next** to proceed.

6. Select the type of Web site and NFuse setup you prefer. By default, **HTML for IIS** is selected. After you've made your selection, press **Next** to continue, as shown in Figure 11.7.

Figure 11.5 Configuring XML Services and SSL Relay Services

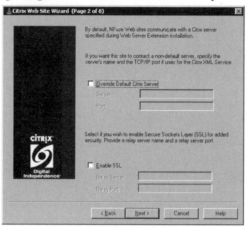

Figure 11.6 Sample Web Page Layout Designs for Use with NFuse

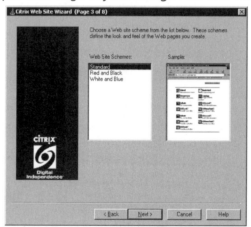

Figure 11.7 Determining Web Server Platform Operation for NFuse

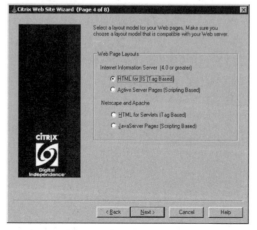

7. Next, choose how published applications will be provided to users via NFuse, as shown in Figure 11.8. Based on your organization's needs, you can choose separate windows or seamless connections inside a Web page. Enable ticketing can also be selected to increase security with NFuse. Once you've made your selection, press **Next**.

Figure 11.8 Selecting Published Application Behavior

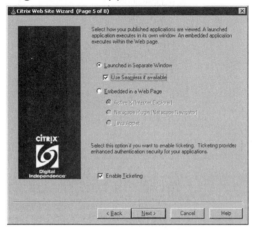

8. You can define additional properties for published applications, such as Show Icon or Show Name. Select the options you want for published applications and press **Next**, as shown in Figure 11.9.

Figure 11.9 Additional Published Application Properties

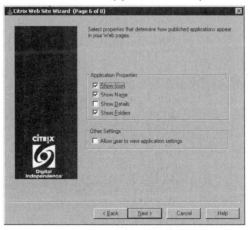

9. As shown in Figure 11.10, select user authentication properties to define how users log on to NFuse and the Citrix MetaFrame XP server farm.

Figure 11.10 User Authentication Properties for NFuse

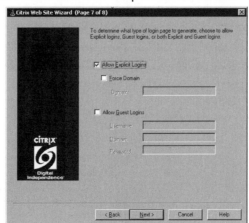

10. Validate your selections for the NFuse Web site and enter the file location to save the generated files. By default, files are saved to you user profile location. When you're done, press **Finish**.

11. After the wizard has completed, press **OK** to close the utility.

12. Finally, copy the files that were created into the Web site root directory. Users can begin accessing your NFuse Web site.

ICA Client

The third component you'll encounter when you work with NFuse is the ICA client. The ICA client in reference to NFuse represents any device that can run a Web browser capable of connecting to NFuse servers and the Citrix ICA client software. An ICA client may consist of:

- A networked personal computer
- A thin client device
- A handheld device running Windows CE

Working together, the Web browser and the ICA client software are used to contact the NFuse server, log on to the Citrix MetaFrame server farm via NFuse, and open published applications.

When a user first connects to an NFuse Web server, he is sent to a logon page to authenticate his identity. If the computer does not have the ICA client software, the NFuse Web server offers to install the client software immediately using the Web-based ICA client installation. It is important to note that ICA client software is not maintained in a Client Update Database as it is on a conventional Citrix MetaFrame XP server. To update the ICA client software, you must copy the new files to the \Citrix\ICAWEB\ directory located in the Web server root directory for the Web site. A variety of ICA client devices are supported, as we discuss later in this chapter.

Once authenticated, the NFuse Web server provides links to published applications. The ICA client device can use these links to initiate ICA sessions directly with the Citrix MetaFrame XP server providing the application. After the user is done with the application, the ICA session closes automatically.

NOTE

NFuse can detect a preexisting version of the ICA client only for 16-bit and 32-bit Windows computers. All other clients are offered for installation each time a user connects to the NFuse Web server.

Installing NFuse

Now that you have an understanding of NFuse and the various components required, the next step to using NFuse is the implementation. First, you must meet the basic requirements for NFuse. Check that the Citrix MetaFrame XP server farms are running the correct service pack and feature release level. In addition, the Web server must meet platform specifications to be compatible with NFuse. Furthermore, the ICA client devices must posses a Web browser capable of connecting to and initiating an NFuse session.

Once the minimum requirements have been satisfied, the next step is installation. Following the correct installation process will keep you from having to deal with unnecessary administrative headaches. In addition, you might want to further customize NFuse to better suit your customers' needs.

Minimum Requirements for Installing NFuse

To install NFuse services, you must ensure that your systems meet the minimum requirements. Tested to provide maximum stability, the most common products found in networking environments today are included in the list. What's most important is to ensure that version levels of the various products meet the minimum requirements.

The first item to access is the Citrix MetaFrame XP server farm. In addition to Citrix MetaFrame XP servers, older versions of Citrix MetaFrame for Windows and Citrix MetaFrame for UNIX can be used. The following are compatible versions of Citrix MetaFrame that can be used with NFuse:

- Citrix MetaFrame XP for Windows 1.0

- Citrix MetaFrame 1.8 for Windows, Service Pack 2 or 3 with Feature Release 1
- Citrix MetaFrame for UNIX 1.1 with Feature Release 1 and XML services

In addition to these platform requirements, the server farm must meet some general requirements, including:

- Citrix MetaFrame servers must be members of a server farm.
- Published applications must be set up and available for users.
- If you're using Citrix MetaFrame 1.8, published applications must be set up using the server farm management scope.
- If you're using Citrix MetaFrame for UNIX, published applications must be configured for use with NFuse using XML services.

NOTE

The Citrix server farm is backward compatible with older versions of NFuse. Any farm consisting of Citrix MetaFrame XP 1.0 and Citrix MetaFrame 1.8 servers can work with NFuse versions 1.0, 1.5, 1.51, and 1.6. Farms consisting of Citrix MetaFrame for UNIX servers can function only with NFuse 1.5, 1.51, and 1.6.

The next item to consider is the Web server. Because Citrix does not provide Web server software, the most common third-party products are supported for use with NFuse. Table 11.1 displays the supported Web server platforms and requirements. Although other Web server platforms using Java servlets and Java pages may run NFuse, this listing represents the tested and supported platforms by Citrix.

Table 11.1 Supported Web Server Platforms for NFuse

Web Server	Operating Systems	Servlet Engine	Java Developers Kit (JDK)
Internet Information Server 4.0	Windows NT 4.0 Server	Java Virtual Machine (included in Internet Explorer)	N/A
Internet Information Server 5.0	Windows 2000 Server	Java Virtual Machine (included in Internet Explorer)	N/A
Apache 1.3.20	Red Hat 6.2 and 7.1 Solaris 7 & 8	Jserv 1.22 * GNU 1.01 Tomcat 3.2.2	Sun 1.3.1
Netscape iPlanet 4.1	Solaris 7 & 8	iPlanet 4.1	Sun 1.3.1

Continued

Table 11.1 Continued

Web Server	Operating Systems	Servlet Engine	Java Developers Kit (JDK)
Tomcat 3.2.2	Red Hat 6.2 and 7.1 Solaris 7 & 8	Tomcat 3.2.2	Sun 1.3.1
IBM HTTP 1.3.12.2	Solaris 7 & 8	WebSphere 3.5.2	Sun 1.2.2

The final component within the NFuse architecture is the ICA client, which is just as critical as the two other components. NFuse supports a wide variety of ICA clients to meet the need of most organizations, including most Windows versions. As described in Table 11.2, most other common operating systems are also supported. The only ICA client software that is not NFuse compatible is for DOS clients. ICA client software is provided with Citrix MetaFrame XP Server and can be downloaded from the Citrix Web site at www.citrix.com.

Table 11.2 Supported ICA Client Versions for NFuse

Operating Platform	Supported Web Browsers	ICA Client version
Win32	Internet Explorer 4.01 and above Netscape Communicator 4.77 and above Netscape Navigator 6.01 and above	6.1.963 and above
Win16	Internet Explorer 4.01 and above Netscape Navigator 4.08 and above	6.1.961 and above
Java	Internet Explorer 4.01 and above Netscape Communicator 4.77 and above Netscape Navigator 6.01 and above	6.0.1146 and above
Tru64 UNIX, HP/UX, IBM AIX, and UNIX for SGI	Netscape Communicator 4.77 and above Netscape Navigator 6.01 and above	3.0.42 and above
Linux/ARM	Netscape Communicator 4.77 and above Netscape Navigator 6.01 and above	3.0.86 and above
Solaris/Sparc	Netscape Communicator 4.77 and above Netscape Navigator 6.01 and above	6.0.915 and above
Solaris/Intel	Netscape Communicator 4.77 and above Netscape Navigator 6.01 and above	3.0.35 and above
SCO UNIX	Netscape Communicator 4.77 and above Netscape Navigator 6.01 and above	3.0.36 and above
Macintosh	Internet Explorer 4.01 and above Netscape Communicator 4.77 and above Netscape Navigator 6.01 and above	6.0.66 and above

Installation Process

In the process of installing Citrix MetaFrame XP server, NFuse is installed on the server by default. If you elected not to install NFuse or want to install it on a separate Web server, you must use the installation program provided for NFuse. Two different installation programs are provided with NFuse, depending on the platform you are using:

- Windows version for Internet Information Server
- UNIX version for Apache, iPlanet, Tomcat, and IBM solutions

Because Internet Information Server is the most commonly deployed platform, we discuss its installation process here. To install the IIS Web server extensions:

1. Verify that the XML service is operational on the Citrix MetaFrame XP server farm.

2. Execute the **NFuseWebExtSetup-IIS.exe** file to begin installation.

3. Click **Next** to continue the installation process.

4. Select **Yes** to accept the end-user license agreement.

5. Select **Yes** to stop the Internet Information Server Web services to complete the installation, as shown in Figure 11.11.

Figure 11.11 Stopping Web Services to Continue Installation

6. Select **Next** to use the default location for uninstall information for the Web extensions. Selecting **Browse** allows you to modify the file location as needed.

7. Next, insert the name of the Citrix MetaFrame XP server running the XML services, as shown in Figure 11.12. You can also specify the port used by XML services on this server. When you're done, press **Next**.

8. Identify the location of the root URL location for the Web server, as shown in Figure 11.13. This specifies where NFuse files will be installed for user access. By default, **c:\inetpub\wwwroot** is selected. When you're done, press **Next** to continue.

9. Insert the Citrix ICA Clients CD into the CD-ROM drive and provide the path to the Web clients, as illustrated in Figure 11.14. This allows the Web clients to be placed on the Web server for installation via the NFuse Web site. When you're done, select **Next**.

Figure 11.12 Identifying the Server Running XML Services

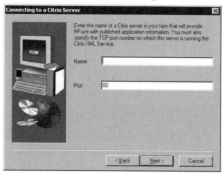

Figure 11.13 Specifying the Root Location for Web Services

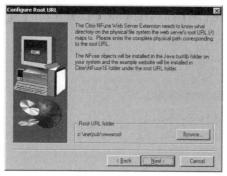

Figure 11.14 Installing the Web Clients onto the NFuse Server

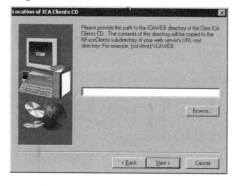

10. A final review of the options you selected is offered. Review the items listed and press **Next** to continue the installation process. An example is shown in Figure 11.15.

11. Once you're done, the file copy process begins, and the Web services are restarted.

Figure 11.15 Reviewing Items Chosen for Installation

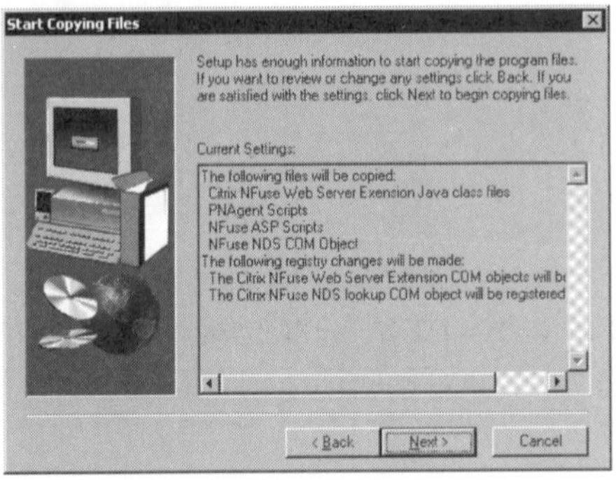

12. Finally, select **Finish** to complete the Web extensions installation.

Customizing NFuse

Once installation is completed, NFuse is ready for user connections. The default NFuse setup offers a complete solution requiring no modifications out of the box. If you want to modify the behavior of NFuse, such as how it looks or the application appearance, you must understand what options are available for configuration. There are several methods by which to customize NFuse. Depending on the options you want modified, you use configuration files or wizards to achieve your goals.

Configuring & Implementing...

NFuse Project Columbia

With the help of various Citrix engineers, an initiative to reduce the administrative overhead for customizing NFuse, known as Project Columbia, was begun. Project Columbia consists of template files placed on the Web server, offering simplified administration in addition to several advanced features such as backup XML server designation, multiple server farm access, and advanced security features. For more information on Project Columbia, see the Citrix Developers Network located at www.citrix.com/cdn.

NFuse uses several different configuration files to control how user sessions are managed in addition to Web server-to-server farm communication. Stored in %SYSTEMROOT%\java\trustlib, two of the most critical of these configuration files used are NFuse.properties and NFuse.conf. NFuse.properties has the task of managing actions such as encoding method and path for the NFuse.conf file. The NFuse.conf file provides a text-based configuration file for managing the various features available with NFuse, such as NAT usage, NFuse feature usage, and ICA client downloads. Once this file has been modified, the Web services on the server must be stopped and restarted for the changes to take effect. An example of the NFuse.conf file is shown in Figure 11.16.

Figure 11.16 Customizing the NFuse Server Using NFuse.conf

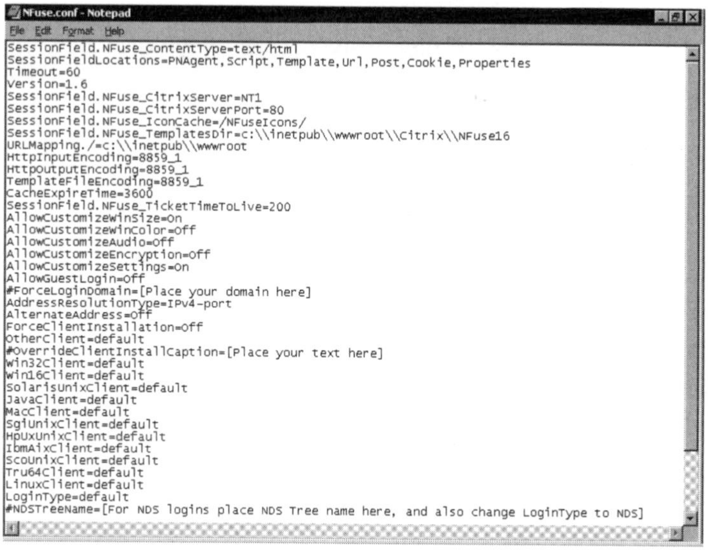


```
SessionField.NFuse_ContentType=text/html
SessionFieldLocations=PNAgent,Script,Template,Url,Post,Cookie,Properties
Timeout=60
Version=1.6
SessionField.NFuse_CitrixServer=NT1
SessionField.NFuse_CitrixServerPort=80
SessionField.NFuse_IconCache=/NFuseIcons/
SessionField.NFuse_TemplatesDir=c:\\inetpub\\wwwroot\\Citrix\\NFuse16
URLMapping./=c:\\inetpub\\wwwroot
HttpInputEncoding=8859_1
HttpOutputEncoding=8859_1
TemplateFileEncoding=8859_1
CacheExpireTime=3600
SessionField.NFuse_TicketTimeToLive=200
AllowCustomizeWinSize=On
AllowCustomizeWinColor=Off
AllowCustomizeAudio=Off
AllowCustomizeEncryption=Off
AllowCustomizeSettings=On
AllowGuestLogin=Off
#ForceLoginDomain=[Place your domain here]
AddressResolutionType=IPv4-port
AlternateAddress=Off
ForceClientInstallation=Off
OtherClient=default
#OverrideClientInstallCaption=[Place your text here]
Win32Client=default
Win16Client=default
SolarisUnixClient=default
JavaClient=default
MacClient=default
SgiUnixClient=default
HpUxUnixClient=default
IbmAixClient=default
ScoUnixClient=default
Tru64Client=default
LinuxClient=default
LoginType=default
#NDSTreeName=[For NDS logins place NDS Tree name here, and also change LoginType to NDS]
```

Java Objects

Another component of NFuse Web services is the Java object. Java objects are used to allow server scripts or custom-written Java applets to perform Citrix MetaFrame XP-related tasks. Nine objects can be used; each has a different method of defining its use. When you use the Web Site Wizard, the finished product includes usage examples of Java objects. Java objects perform a variety of tasks:

- Authenticating users to the Citrix MetaFrame XP server farm
- Retrieving available applications for each user
- Modifying applications as required before users access them
- Using template files to provide ICA and HTML files to users as required

Table 11.3 lists the Java objects available for use with NFuse.

Table 11.3 Java Objects Used with NFuse

Java Object	Description
CitrixWireGateway	Used for communication between the Citrix MetaFrame XP server farm and the Web server running NFuse services.
ClearTextCredentials	Handles user authentication, with the server farm providing the application set.
GroupCredentials	Used for application retrieval by domain user groups. When published applications are set up by group membership, this Java object facilitates determining the groups to which the user belongs.
AppEnumerator	Displays applications available for the authenticated user.
App	Represents application objects containing the properties for a single application.
AppSettings	Maintains application properties for modification.
AppDataList	Maintains a listing of app objects for quick lookups of application data.
AppListCache	Contains a cache of AppDataList so that constant communication is not required between the Web server and the Citrix MetaFrame XP server farm.
TemplateParser	Used on text files to handle tag substitution. This Java object allows you to use template HTML and ICA files and populate the data for each user.

Using VPNs with Citrix MetaFrame XP Clients

Another popular method of using the Internet to connect to Citrix MetaFrame XP server farms is via VPN. VPN solutions have become popular for remote access because they provide high levels of security while allowing users to access private resource across public networks such as the Internet. Organizations are using VPNs to provide secure links for user access from home and remote offices while minimizing the costs associated with expensive dedicated leased lines.

VPN solutions work by having a source computer initiate a secure session with a remote computer. Once a connection is established, all traffic is encrypted using technologies such Internet Protocol Security (IPSec) to ensure that data is kept out of the hands of would-be intruders. If someone were trying to eavesdrop on the data transmission, it would be unreadable.

Two types of configurations can be established via VPNs. The first allows a remote user to directly connect to a private network. Using a client component, a single computer creates a session with a remote VPN server. Once the session has been established, the user can access any remote resources available.

The second method involves creating a "tunnel" between two networks. Routers or gateway computers initiate a session with the remote network. Once connection is established, traffic can be routed through the VPN tunnel for as many users as the connection can support. This is a common scenario for a single remote site connecting over public networks that involve multiple users. For example, a branch office connecting to a headquarters facility over the Internet could use a VPN tunnel to facilitate communication securely. VPN tunnels minimize the administrative overhead of having multiple clients connect via VPN through the same channel. Figure 11.17 displays an example.

Figure 11.17 Example VPN Scenarios

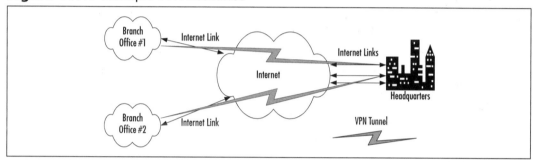

There are three main aspects to a VPN session. First, the VPN server represents the device accepting connections. This device could be a VPN concentrator, another personal computer, or a VPN server. The VPN client represents the device initiating the connection. This could be a Windows client PC, another VPN server, or a gateway set up to establish a tunnel between networks. The last aspect is the security protocols used to communicate between the VPN devices. Including protocols such as Layer 2 Tunneling Protocol (L2TP) and Point-to-Point Tunneling Protocol (PPTP), the security protocol is usually requested by the VPN client device and agreed on by the VPN server.

Using VPN solutions with Citrix MetaFrame XP has become a commonplace method of accessing applications. In conjunction with VPN technology built into the Microsoft operating systems, everything needed to set up and configure VPN sessions is already in place. With Windows 2000 server, Microsoft has provided a VPN server solution using Routing and Remote Access Services (RRAS). Using L2TP or PPTP, Windows-based clients can create VPN connections across any network or dialup networking connection to attach to a Citrix MetaFrame XP server farm.

Let's imagine that Joe needs to connect to a financial application hosted on his company's Citrix server farm. Using a VPN session, he wants to connect from home and work as needed. Joe first creates a VPN connection using L2TP as the transport protocol. Using parameters provided by the administrator, such as TCP/IP address and user credentials, Joe is able to complete the setup of his VPN client. Joe then uses a cable modem to connect to the Internet from home. He initiates the VPN session he created earlier. The VPN client crosses the Internet back to the corporate office and contacts the VPN server. The VPN server authenticates his request, and the communications channel is opened between the VPN server and the VPN client.

Using the Citrix ICA client software, Joe connects to the Citrix MetaFrame XP server farm as though he were on the local network. All traffic passes through the VPN session he initiated, and the data is encrypted. Once he has completed his tasks, Joe closes the ICA session with the Citrix MetaFrame XP server farm. He then closes the VPN connection to finish working with the corporate office. Now Joe has secure access to all his applications available through Citrix using VPN technologies.

Deploying Applications to Launch from a Browser

As discussed earlier in this chapter, Citrix provides a Web-enabled Program Neighborhood to allow application-publishing capabilities via a Web site. Administrators can take advantage of application-publishing technology in addition to centralized management, while users only have to know how to use a common Web browser. NFuse offers an excellent solution, but Citrix offers another, simpler technology that works well in many environments, such as demonstration sites.

Designing & Planning...

Using NFuse versus ALE or the Terminal Services Advanced Client

As Citrix MetaFrame XP has matured, so have the Web-based technologies included with it. ALE was designed to allow users to connect to static applications over the Web. It still is in use today but has been primarily replaced by NFuse due to the latter's advanced feature sets and dynamic nature. The Terminal Services Advanced Client is provided by Microsoft and primarily used to connect to a remote desktop via RDP or in environments in which Citrix MetaFrame XP is not used. All three products offer excellent solutions, depending on your organization's requirements, but NFuse has quickly become the dominant product.

Based on the same Web-enabled technology, a simpler methodology for publishing applications is known as *Application Launching and Embedding,* or *ALE.* The predecessor to NFuse, ALE creates a static ICA file used to pass session information to ICA clients. Whereas NFuse dynamically allocates ICA files on demand, ALE requires that an administrator manually update the file each time a change is needed. In addition to creating ICA files, an HTML page can be created, including the ICA client file links to publish to users as needed.

In addition to ALE, Microsoft offers a Web-based solution that provides limited functionality via Terminal Services. This solution, known as the Terminal Services Advanced Client, provides a Web-based solution for users who don't have Citrix MetaFrame.

ICA Files

The most important aspect of Web-enabled Citrix technologies is the ICA file, used to provide ICA session information to client computers. ICA connections cannot be completed without the required information. For example, without knowing the server network address, the ICA client does not know how to locate the Citrix MetaFrame XP server. With NFuse, the ICA file is dynamically propagated using template files. With ALE technologies, ICA files are statically configured using the Citrix Management Console.

Creating an ICA File for a Published Application

The following exercise walks you through the process of creating an ICA file for a published application:

1. Publish an application such as Microsoft Office or Notepad using the Citrix Management Console.

2. Within the Citrix Management Console, highlight the published application you created. Right-click the application and select **Create ICA File**.

3. Select how much information about the creation process you want. If you to choose **Minimize explanation required**, all the following options will be provided on two pages for configuration, without any explanation. For this exercise, select the default of **Explain each setting** and press **Next** to continue, as shown in Figure 11.18.

4. Next, select the application appearance for user sessions. Screen size and color depth are among the options to select, as shown in Figure 11.19. Press **Next**.

Figure 11.18 Processing the ICA File Creation Wizard

Figure 11.19 Application Appearance Settings

5. Select the encryption strength to use for this session and press **Next**, as shown in Figure 11.20.

6. Choose whether ICA traffic is compressed, as shown in Figure 11.21. Press **Next** to continue.

Figure 11.20 Selecting Encryption Strength for the ICA Connection

Figure 11.21 ICA Compression Options

7. Next, select audio settings, as shown in Figure 11.22.

8. Select whether to use TCP/IP+HTTP browsing, as shown in Figure 11.23. When you connect to Citrix MetaFrame XP server farms using this technology, the Web services port 80 is chosen by default, instead of the typical connection method.

Figure 11.22 Audio Settings

Figure 11.23 TCP/IP HTTP Browsing Options

9. Enter the name and file location to save the ICA file you are creating and press **Next** to continue.

10. You are prompted to create an HTML template Web page for this ICA connection. Select **Yes** or **No** and press **Next** to proceed, as shown in Figure 11.24.

Figure 11.24 Creating an HTML Web Page for the ICA Connection

11.   Finally, you are prompted to review your configuration settings. Once you've done that, press **Finish** to complete the wizard.

Server Parameters

In order to understand how ICA files function, you must take a look at the file itself. Similar to a Windows .ini file, an ICA file is a text-only configuration tool to customize session operation. Inside these files, as shown in Figure 11.25, variables are defined with assigned values. Variables are used to define items such as server network address, application appearance, encryption strengths requested, and logon authentication. Table 11.4 displays several common server parameters with a brief explanation.

Table 11.4 Common ICA Server Parameters

Server Parameter	Default Value	Description
Address	none	Defines the network address and port to connect to a Citrix MetaFrame XP server. Normally, the server TCP/IP address is listed with a port of 1494.
ClientAudio	Off	Defines whether client audio is enabled or disabled.
AutoLogonAllowed	Off	Specifies whether the autologon capabilities can be used, if available.

Continued

Table 11.4 Continued

Server Parameter	Default Value	Description
EncryptLevelSession	1	Specifies encryption level to use: 1 = Basic 2 = RC5 128-bit logon only 3 = 40-bit 4 = 56-bit 5 = 128-bit
NetBIOSBrowserAddress	none	Specifies the TCP/IP address for the Citrix farm master browser.
TransportDriver	none	Determines the network protocol driver, such as TCP/IP or IPX, to use in connecting.
UseAlternateAddress	0	Determines if the Citrix MetaFrame server farm is accessible across a network using NAT. Used in conjunction with the ALTADDR command-line utility: 0 = No 1 = Yes

Figure 11.25 An Example of an ICA File

Using the Terminal Services Advanced Client

Another component to consider when you're evaluating Web-based solutions is the Microsoft Terminal Services Advanced Client, or TSAC. Solving similar issues as NFuse, TSAC is a Windows 32-bit Active-X control used to run a Terminal Services session from within a Web browser. Although you cannot use published applications with this solution, custom Web page development allows you to take advantage of Terminal Services features and deploy applications using Internet Explorer.

Similar to the ALE technologies discussed earlier, TSAC offers limited capabilities compared with Citrix Web technologies. First, only Internet Explorer can be used to connect using TSAC. This limits the number of clients and desktop platforms that can connect. Many of the advanced features available with Citrix technologies, such as load-balanced applications, published applications, and advanced client features, are not available with TSAC. As you can see, TSAC is only meant to provide a very basic solution to Web-based Terminal Services.

In order to install these Web services, you must download and set up the TSAC Web package available from www.microsoft.com/windows2000/technologies/terminal/default.asp. The package does not have to be installed on a Terminal Server. It must be applied to a Windows NT 4.0 or Windows 2000 server running Internet Information Services 4.0 or later. Once you've downloaded the package, extract the files into the TSWEB directory under the root of your Web site. For example, c:\inetpub\wwwroot\tsweb would be used by default. Once you've extracted the files, users can connect to the Web site using the TSWEB directory. Figure 11.26 shows an example of a user connecting to the TSWEB Web server.

Figure 11.26 Example of the TSAC Web Services

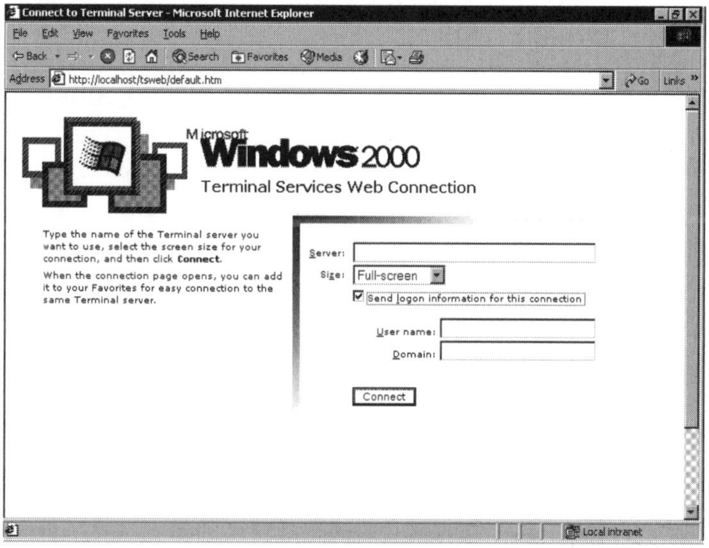

Summary

The Internet has created a new way of doing business and communicating using Web-based technologies. With Web-based Citrix technologies such as NFuse, accessing remote applications for telecommuters via virtual private network (VPN) connections is dramatically decreased in terms of cost. In addition, Web technologies, in cooperation with Citrix MetaFrame XP, allow for the implementation of applications via internal intranet sites, reducing the costs of deploying or upgrading applications. Web-enabled technologies also provide a medium for software-based demonstration and business-to business applications.

Citrix has created a portal technology capable of providing access to published applications via a Web browser. NFuse consists of three main components: Citrix MetaFrame server farm, a Web server, and the ICA client. With software capable of using the most popular Web server and ICA client devices, access to NFuse services is available to the majority of users. By default, NFuse is installed with Citrix MetaFrame XP. If needed, utilities are available to install NFuse on standalone Web servers or other Citrix MetaFrame XP servers located in the server farm. Using configuration files and wizards, NFuse can be customized to meet the needs of your user community. Another key component of NFuse, the Java object, is used for communication between the server farm and the Web server.

The use of VPN as a remote access solution has become a popular method for access Citrix MetaFrame XP server farms. Three main components are used with a VPN solution: VPN server, VPN client, and security protocol such as Layer 2 Tunneling Protocol (L2TP) or Point-to-Point Tunneling Protocol (PPTP). Although there are various solutions on the market, Microsoft provides built-in server and client components in its operating systems, allowing ease of implementation.

In addition to NFuse, you can use Application Launching and Embedding (ALE) to Web-enable applications. Using ICA files, ALE technology uses parameters identified by the administrator to provide a URL to an ICA file for remote applications, minimizing the configuration required for ICA clients. Microsoft also offers a Web-based client for its own Terminal Services using the Terminal Services Advanced Client (TSAC).

Solutions Fast Track

Business Reasons for Providing Applications Across the Internet

☑ Using Citrix Web-based technologies, applications can be easily deployed through Internet or intranet Web sites.

☑ Using Citrix MetaFrame XP and NFuse with VPNs, remote access can be provided for applications that traditionally require large amounts of bandwidth.

☑ Business-to-business models that use Citrix MetaFrame XP and Web-based technologies have been adopted, allowing vendor transactions to occur seamlessly.

Deploying Applications with NFuse

☑ NFuse requires three key components: a Citrix MetaFrame XP server farm, a Web server, and the ICA client.

☑ NFuse is installed by default during the Citrix MetaFrame XP server installation process. Utilities are available to install NFuse services on other servers for Internet Information Server and various UNIX flavors.

☑ Once NFuse is installed, several tools are available to customize NFuse operation, including the NFuse.conf file, the NFuse.properties file, and the Web site creation wizard.

Using VPNs with Citrix MetaFrame XP Clients

☑ VPNs provide a secure, encrypted connection to private resources over public networks such as the Internet.

☑ There are three main components to a VPN solution: a VPN server, VPN clients, and tunneling protocols such as L2TP or PPTP.

☑ Microsoft provides built-in tools for server and client support, such as Routing and Remote Access for server service and L2TP and PPTP client support.

Deploying Applications to Launch from a Browser

☑ Citrix Web-enabled technologies use ICA files to provide configuration data to the ICA client.

☑ ICA files contain server parameters with variables defined to specify items such as server network address, application appearance, and encryption strengths.

☑ Microsoft offers a Web-based technology for Terminal Services, known as the Terminal Services Advanced Client (TSAC). Providing minimal functionality compared with Citrix technologies, TSAC represents a simpler alternative for Web-based terminal server users with Citrix MetaFrame XP.

Frequently Asked Questions

The following Frequently Asked Questions, answered by the authors of this book, are designed to both measure your understanding of the concepts presented in this chapter and to assist you with real-life implementation of these concepts. To have your questions about this chapter answered by the author, browse to **www.syngress.com/solutions** and click on the **"Ask the Author"** form.

Q: How do I know what the ICA server parameters should be set to when I'm looking at the file?

A: The *Configuration Guide for ICA Win32 Clients* provides a reference. The guide is located on the Citrix Web site at www.citrix.com; it explains the various parameters and their values.

Q: Where are the NFuse files located on my Web server?

A: They are primarily found in the Citrix directory under the root of the default Web site. The remainder of the files are located in the %SYSTEMROOT%\java\trustlib directory.

Q: How do I change the port used for XML services on a MetaFrame XP server?

A: The primary method is using the Citrix Management Console. Select the server and open its properties. Located on the MetaFrame settings page, the XML service port setting can be specified.

Q: Can I install NFuse on Web servers other than what's listed in the minimum requirements?

A: Any server capable of running Java servlets can potentially run NFuse. However, it might not be supported by Citrix if you have issues.

Q: Why does Citrix offer Application Launching and Embedding *and* NFuse? Doesn't NFuse do everything that ALE does and more?

A: ALE technology was released before NFuse to Web-enable applications. NFuse is a portal technology that allows greater flexibility than the ALE technology. Because ALE is still used in many environments, though, Citrix has chosen to support both concurrently.

Chapter 12

Printing

Solutions in this chapter:

- **Creating Client Printers**
- **Printing in a Server Farm Environment**
- **Troubleshooting Printing Problems**

- ☑ **Summary**
- ☑ **Solutions Fast Track**
- ☑ **Frequently Asked Questions**

Introduction

Even if everything else works perfectly, a user will not be happy if printing fails. Printing is one of the few outputs that a computer provides. It gives users valuable hardcopy versions of the work they produce. As such, the printing function is extremely important to users.

In the three-tier architecture of a Citrix MetaFrame XP solution, printing is a complex process. Local printers are connected to the client; some printers are connected to the server; others are available on the network. In addition, the user's session must recognize the printer before its applications can print.

Understanding printing is your first step toward being able to successfully configure and troubleshoot the printing process. Even though an administrator configures printing when first deploying Citrix MetaFrame, you need to constantly manage the print environment, ranging from updating print drivers to managing the print queue.

Defining Printer Terminology

We must define printer terminology before we can get into more details about configuring your printing environment in MetaFrame XP. Printer terminology is often confusing because of the repeated use of the word *print*—thus using a term to define it. Here is a list that will help you brush up on printing terminology:

Printer Many people confuse the term *printer* with the physical print device. The term *printer* doesn't mean the physical print device; rather, it is a logical reference to a print device. The printer is actually the icon you see when you open the Printers folder in Control Panel. Think of this icon as the virtual representation of the physical print device.

Print device The print device is the actual physical printing equipment attached to a serial or parallel communications port on your computer. It is an output device that takes information from your computer in a format it understands and outputs it to hard copy.

Print driver The print driver is the software that is installed on the operating system that acts as the translator between the various applications and the physical print device. The driver translates the print commands into language the printer understands in order to output the print job. Print drivers also enable special printer features and advanced functionality.

Print job A print job is the term given to any document that has not been output to hard copy yet or has not yet appeared on the physical print device. Any document submitted for printing is called a print job. A print job can consist of one or more documents.

Print queue The print queue is a staging area where submitted print jobs are lined up in the order in which they were received by the physical print device. A print queue is like a waiting line for print jobs. Print queues are usually located on print servers and are accessed via a printer share. On a Windows system you can view you print queue by going to **Start | Settings | Control Panel | Printers** and double-clicking the name of a printer in the window that pops up; this list of names is the printer queue, as shown in Figure 12.1. It is important to note that more than one print queue can exist for the same print device. In this situation, you can have a second print queue that expedites certain print jobs, processing them first. This is a service you would offer your company's executives, for example. Two or more printers can also service one print queue, thereby processing jobs faster.

Figure 12.1 A Print Queue Window

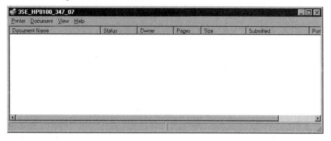

Print server A print server is usually a server dedicated to several printers that are accessed by users over a network. The server's main duty is to route print jobs among computers and the physical printers attached to the print server. The print server also provides a centralized location from which you can manage print queues. Usually every printer is associated with only one print queue, so if you have three printers, you also have three queues to manage and administer on your print server. However, more than one print queue can exist for a single print device.

Printer share A printer share is a logical printer, usually on a Windows server, that is shared and that allows multiple users to connect and print to the physical print device. A printer share can be made available on a Windows workstation and even Windows 9x. It can exist in any environment in which the printer can be shared and is able to provide printing services to users.

Network printers Network printers are print devices that are accessible from any location on the network. Network printers usually reside on a print server. A network printer can also be a client's local printer that is shared on the network. A network printer can be attached to a MetaFrame XP server that is not part of a farm. It is basically any printer that can be shared and accessed from any point on a network.

Local printers A local printer is a printer that is directly connected to a computer via cable or port. It cannot be accessed from the network and is available only to users of that particular computer. Local printers can be attached to MetaFrame XP servers in a farm. They can basically be attached to any computer that accepts a serial or parallel cable.

Creating Client Printers

One of the most useful MetaFrame features is its ability to make local client printers available to the user during an ICA session. This means that you can launch your ICA session and run your applications within that session, and when you are ready to print, you can print to your locally attached printer as though you were working locally on your computer. This capability is very convenient for users because they are no longer bound to use only the network printers that an administrator installs but can take full advantage of their own local printers as well.

Autocreating Printers

As we discussed in the previous section, the ICA protocol gives you the ability to make locally attached printers available for use within an ICA session. This feature, known as *autocreated client printers*, is available with 16-bit and 32-bit ICA clients. For autocreated client printers to work, several steps need to be properly addressed:

1. The print driver installed on the Citrix MetaFrame XP servers must match the print driver installed on the client computer.

2. The name of the print driver must be identical between the Citrix MetaFrame XP servers and the client computer. The next section on the impact of print driver names provides more information.

3. The driver must then be replicated to all Citrix MetaFrame XP servers so that the user can use the driver, regardless of which Citrix MetaFrame XP server he or she is connected to.

The autocreated client printer now automatically makes available the client's locally attached printer the next time he or she logs in to the MetaFrame XP servers. A user is able to identify his or her printer by the unique name that the server assigns. This name is in the following format: *clientname#\printername* (see Figure 12.2), whereby *clientname* is the name of the client workstation on Windows 32-bit client platforms and *printername* is the logical name of the printer as it appears in the Printers folder in Control Panel on the client's workstation.

Figure 12.2 The Autocreated Client Printer Properties Window

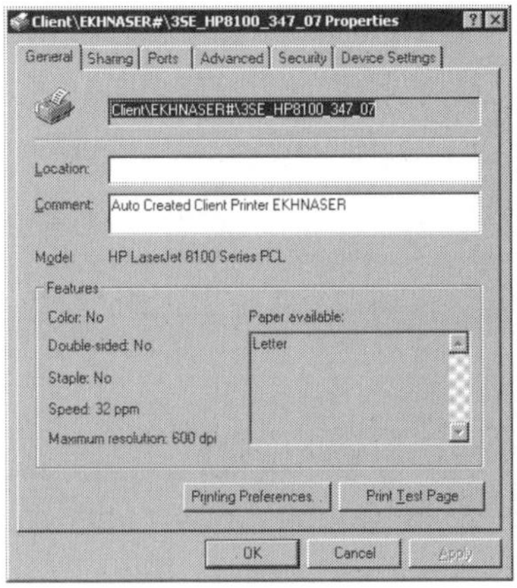

The autocreated client printer should automatically disconnect when the user logs off, but in some cases in which print jobs are stuck in the print queue, a printer will remain visible until either the server is recycled or the print spooler directory is cleaned. For users who don't log off but rather put their session in disconnect mode, the autocreated printer is not deleted nor disconnected; it remains mapped and ready to service the user when he reconnects to his or her session. In this case, the printer remains until the session is completely logged off the server. In some cases, users disconnect their sessions and move to other workstations to reconnect to the same session they were in before, but the autocreated printer will not work because *clientname* has changed.

Configuring & Implementing…

Creating a Script to Clean Up the Spooler Directory

It is recommended that you clear out the print spooler files in the spooler directory using a script. This task can be automated and scheduled to run prior to the nightly reboot of the Citrix servers, for example. As you probably know by now, it is strongly recommended that you reboot Citrix servers daily due to the many instances of user mode that the Terminal Server creates, which can lead to memory leaks and cause problems. You can take advantage of this reboot cycle to do some maintenance tasks, such as clearing print spool files.

Follow these steps to create the script for clearing the print spool files and scheduling this job to run daily:

1. Open Notepad by going to **Start | Run** and typing **notepad**.

Continued

2. When Notepad opens, type the following text:

```
change logon /disable
net stop spooler
del %windir%\system32\spool\printers\*.* /q
```

3. Click **File** in the File menu and choose **Save As**.

4. Name the file (for example, **spoolerscript.bat**). Make sure that the file's extension is *.bat* and not *.txt*.

5. Click **Save**.

6. Go to **Start | Settings | Control Panel** and select **Scheduled Tasks**.

7. Double click **Add Scheduled Task**.

8. Click **Next** on the first screen that appears.

9. The second screen prompts you to browse to the location where you saved the spoolerscript.bat file. Select the file and click **Next**.

10. Follow the wizard, configuring how often you would like this script to run and when it should run.

It is usually good to have this script run about five minutes prior to the daily server reboot schedule.

NOTE

During a user's session, her autocreated client printer is available exclusively to that user, with the exception of administrators, of course. No other user will have access to the autocreated client printer.

Impact of Print Driver Names

Print driver names play a big role in the success or failure of an autocreated printer. The print driver name installed on the Citrix MetaFrame XP servers must exactly match the name of the print driver installed on the client workstation; otherwise, no autocreation will occur.

In the event that the names don't match, you can manually create a mapping (described in the next section), specifically telling the server that this client print driver name should be associated with a particular server print driver. This needs to be done when you're dealing with Windows 9x print drivers; the naming process is usually different from naming Windows NT or 2000 drivers.

Later in this chapter, we discuss the ability to use the Citrix Universal Print Driver that is available with Feature Release 1.

Mapping Print Driver Names

We have been discussing the autocreation feature available with MetaFrame XP and how sensitive it is—to the point that the slightest mismatch in print driver names can cause the process to fail. For autocreation to work, the name of the print driver installed on the client machine must match exactly that name installed on the server. This is fine and dandy when you're dealing with Windows NT 4.0, Windows 2000, and Windows XP drivers because print driver names are almost always identical, but the difference is clear when you deal with Windows 9x print drivers.

For example, a Windows 9x print driver might be named HP LaserJet 5Si/Mx, whereas the Windows NT 4.0 or Windows 2000 print driver name might be HP LaserJet 5Si. In this scenario, the autocreation process will fail simply because the names don't match.

Another problem occurs when the client is using the manufacturer's print drivers versus those available from Microsoft. The print driver names are almost always different between the native Microsoft naming conventions and those used by the manufacturer. Here is where *mapping* comes in.

Mapping print driver names basically tells the server to associate the HP LaserJet 5Si/Mx client driver with the HP LaserJet 5Si server driver in our example, thereby allowing autocreation to complete and printing to occur.

To create a print driver name mapping, follow these steps:

1. Open the **Citrix Management Console** (CMC).

2. In the left menu console, expand the **Printer Management** node.

3. Right-click the **Drivers** subnode and click **Mapping**.

4. The Mapping window appears. Click **Add**. See Figure 12.3.

   Figure 12.3 The Add Mappings Window

5. Type the client name and match it with a driver name installed on the server. Click **OK**.

6. The mapping is shown in the Mapping window (see Figure 12.4). Click **OK**.

Figure 12.4 Viewing the Driver Mapping

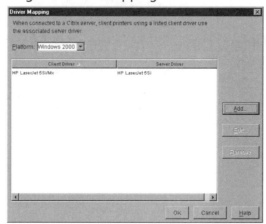

At this point, we have mapped the HP LaserJet 5Si/Mx driver to the HP LaserJet 5Si driver, so basically any Windows 9x client that has the 5Si/Mx driver will be able to print in the ICA session because the server will automatically map that driver to the server-installed driver of 5Si.

Using Network Printers

Clients logging on to Citrix MetaFrame XP servers can take full advantage of network printers and print to them directly from within their sessions, as would any other Windows clients on the network. Users can add these servers in one of two ways: either by choosing **Start | Settings | Printers** and double-clicking **Add Printer** or using the **net use** command from a command prompt to map that network printer to their LPT ports. This process, however, is dependent on how the user's environment is configured; in some environments in which only published applications are available, the user doesn't have the option of mapping the printer or even adding one. In some other environments in which the user is presented with a desktop, that function might be locked down, either by the use of Group Policy or by simply giving the user a mandatory profile that doesn't include access to the print folder or to a command prompt.

We recommend that an administrator add these network printers in CMC and enable them to autocreate based on the user's group membership. A user from the accounting group, for example, would be preconfigured to use the accounting printer, and so on. To configure a network printer in CMC, follow these steps:

1. Open the **CMC**.
2. Expand the **Printer Management** node in the left pane of the screen.
3. Select the **Printers** subfolder. A list of printers should appear on the right.

4. Right-click a printer and click **Auto-Creation**. See Figure 12.5.

Figure 12.5 The Autocreation Option When Right-Clicking a Printer

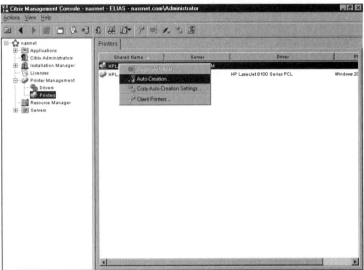

5. The Auto-Creation Settings window appears, prompting you for a user or a group with which to associate the autocreation.

6. Select your group, or if you want to select a specific user, check the box that says **Show Users**, select your users, and click **OK**. See Figure 12.6.

Figure 12.6 The Auto-Creation Settings Window

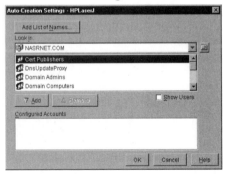

You have just configured a printer to autocreate for a specific group or user. The next time a member of that group or a specified user logs in to the MetaFrame XP servers, they will have the option to print to this printer, and it will autocreate for them without having to do anything at all.

Using Local Printers

Local printers are used in MetaFrame XP, just as in any other Windows NT/2000 server or workstation. Local printers are printers that are locally attached to the MetaFrame XP server through a parallel or serial communications port. Everything is done using the Printers folder, which is accessible by going to **Start | Settings | Printers** or to **Control Panel | Printers** and manually adding the printer. After you add the local printer, its name should automatically appear in the Printers subnode of the Printer Management node in Citrix Management Console.

To install a local printer on a MetaFrame XP server, follow these steps:

1. Log on to a MetaFrame XP server as an Administrator or using an account with sufficient privileges.

2. Click **Start | Settings | Printers** and double-click **Add Printer**.

3. Click **Next**.

4. Make sure **Local printer** is selected, and uncheck the **Automatically detect and install my Plug and Play printer** check box.

5. Select the communications port to which the printer is attached (LPT1 or COM1, for example) and click **Next**.

6. Select the appropriate print driver for the device being installed and click **Next**.

7. Assign the printer a name and click **Next**.

8. The next window asks you whether you would like to share this printer. Select **Share as** and assign it a share name such as **localprinter**. Click **Next**.

9. Follow the wizard until setup is complete.

10. Open the CMC and make sure that the newly added printer shows up in the Printers subnode of Printer Management. See Figure 12.7.

Printing in a Server Farm Environment

Citrix has greatly improved printing with MetaFrame XP and has provided a set of tools to make the installation and management of printers and print drivers even easier. As with most other administration and management tools, Citrix has centralized Printer Management as a node in CMC, so all administrative tasks are accomplished from within the CMC. You now have the ability to import an entire print server from the network and make its drivers available in your MetaFrame XP server. Replication of the print drivers from one server to all the servers in the farm is another great feature of MetaFrame XP. You can automate replication can also be automated so that as soon as a new server joins the farm, replication occurs to install the supported print drivers.

Figure 12.7 The Newly Added Local Printer Appears in the CMC

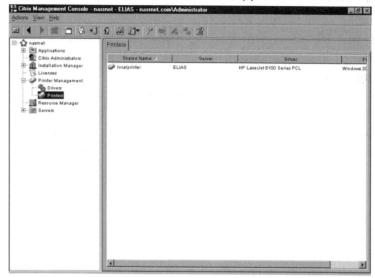

Replicating Print Drivers

Replicating print drivers across all MetaFrame XP servers in the farm is an imperative step that must be accomplished before a user can log on and use a particular printer. Before Citrix introduced driver replication, an administrator had to manually log on to every server in the farm and install the necessary drivers. You can imagine how much of an administrative inconvenience this was, in addition to lacking any method of keeping track of what you have installed where.

What Citrix recommends you do for print driver replication is dedicate a server in the farm where you would always install new drivers; you would then initiate replication from that server to the rest of the farm. IMA provides a replication function that allows an administrator to replicate a print driver to all servers in the farm or to select servers only. Autoreplication lists can be saved in the IMA for future use, these lists offer a way to install all the drivers necessary on newly added servers, thereby quickly bringing these servers to the same level as the others in the farm.

To replicate a print driver, follow these steps:

1. Open the **CMC**.

2. Expand the **Printer management** node.

3. Select the **Drivers** subnode.

4. In the right control pane, use the server pull-down menu to select the server from which you will replicate the drivers to the rest of the server.

5. Right-click the driver you want to replicate and select **Replicate Driver**. A warning message pops up, as shown in Figure 12.8.

Figure 12.8 Replication Driver Warning Message

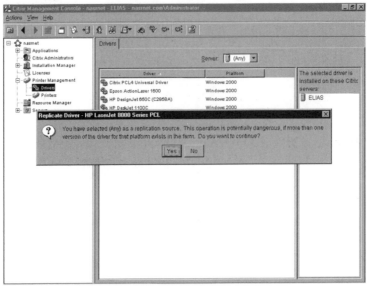

6. The Replicate Driver dialog box appears; either choose to replicate to all Citrix servers, or select one or more servers to replicate to. See Figure 12.9.

Figure 12.9 The Replicate Driver Window

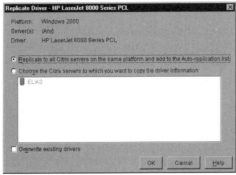

7. View the **Drivers** subnode in CMC to make sure that the driver has been replicated to all servers in the farm.

Importing Print Servers

A great new feature available through MetaFrame XP that administrators might be interested in is the ability to import a print server from the network and make its printers readily available for use by users logging in to MetaFrame XP servers. As you know, the network printers that are not installed or mapped on a MetaFrame XP server are not available for use by the ICA clients. Importing the network print server provides for an easy and fast way to make network printers available to ICA clients.

To import a print server, follow these steps:

1. Open the **CMC**.

2. Right-click the **Printer Management** node and select **Import Print Server**.

3. You will be prompted to enter the print server's name and a user account with sufficient privileges to access these printers. See Figure 12.10.

Figure 12.10 The Import Network Print Server Window

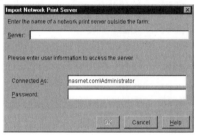

7. Once the network print server has been imported, it should be listed in the **Printer Management** node in the **Network Print Servers** tab. See Figure 12.11. Make sure that you verify that all its printers were also properly imported by expanding the Printers subnode and making sure the printers are all there.

Figure 12.11 The Imported Network Print Server

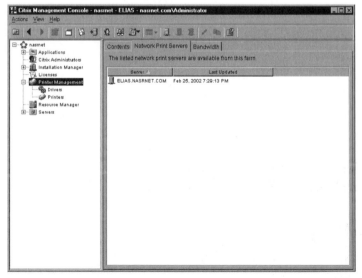

NOTE

Once a network print server has been imported into the MetaFrame XP farm, it cannot be reimported. Its information is also not dynamically updated; therefore, if any changes occur on the print server, a manual refresh or update must be initiated in order to update the print server. Any change in the printer's properties or any newly added printers or deleted printers require an update or refresh before they take effect on the farm. To refresh or update the print server, simply right-click the server in the CMC and select **Update Print Server**.

Managing Print Drivers

Print drivers are a very sensitive issue, especially in a MetaFrame environment. Using the wrong print driver or an incompatible print driver results in the server having symptoms that can range from a simple print spooler hang to the infamous Blue Screen of Death.

Citrix has designed a new feature called *driver compatibility* that allows you to create two sorts of lists. The options are to either allow only drivers in this list (only the drivers listed will be deemed compatible and thus used). The second option is to allow all drivers except those in the list (all drivers are deemed compatible except the ones listed).

This tool can be an interesting one for creating compatible or incompatible drivers for use with the servers. All these tools are geared toward making your life as an administrator as easy as possible and offering you different tools that will ensure a stable printing environment at all times.

To create these driver compatibility or incompatibility lists, follow these steps:

1. Open the **CMC**.

2. In the left pane, expand the **Printer Management** node.

3. Right-click the **Drivers** subnode and select **Compatibility**. The driver compatibility window appears.

4. Select the kind of list you intend to create. Your options are to either **Allow only drivers in the list** or **Allow all drivers except those in the list**.

5. Click **Add**.

6. Select a driver from the drop-down menu and click **OK**. The driver appears in the driver compatibility window. See Figure 12.12.

7. Repeat these steps until you have created a satisfactory list.

8. Click **OK**.

Figure 12.12 Viewing the Driver Compatibility Window

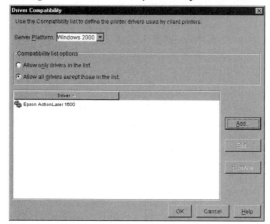

Updating Print Drivers in the XP Data Store

The IMA on every MetaFrame XP server regularly scans the print registry keys and compares its information against that available in the data store. In the event that the IMA should discover a new driver, for example, that driver's information is written to the data store.

So how do we install a print driver? That depends on the operating system you are using. If you are using Windows NT, there is one way of doing it; if you are using Windows 2000, there are two ways.

On Windows NT 4.0 Terminal Server Edition and Windows 2000, you can do the following:

1. Click **Start | Settings | Printers**.

2. Double-click **Add Printer** and go through the regular installation of the printer.

3. When you're done and a printer icon is created for that printer, delete the **printer icon**. This deletes the icon but preserves the files that were installed.

On Windows 2000 servers, you have an alternative and easier way of updating print drivers by following these steps:

1. Click **Start | Settings | Printers**.

2. On the File menu, click **File | Server Properties**.

3. The **Print Server Properties** open, as shown in Figure 12.13. From this window you can add, remove, update, or view driver properties.

Figure 12.13 Print Server Properties

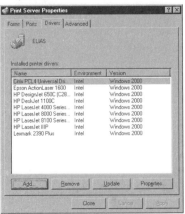

This latter method is easier and more convenient, since we don't have to go through the steps of installing the printer and sharing and assigning a name for it, and then deleting its logical representation. Simply install the driver's files. Once the print driver has been installed, open the **CMC**, expand **Printer Management**, and select **Drivers**. The driver should appear in the list to the right. If the driver does not appear, wait a few minutes before refreshing the list by right-clicking the **Drivers** node and selecting **Refresh Drivers**.

Configuring & Implementing...

Citrix Universal Print Driver

Citrix MetaFrame XP Feature Release 1 introduces the Citrix Universal Print Driver, a very generic PCL4 print driver stripped of any features. The driver is a new feature that frees you from the hassle of installing print drivers for different devices on the MetaFrame XP servers. This driver generates the print jobs in PCL4 format and passes the jobs to the local machine for processing. The local machine uses its locally installed print driver to output the print job.

The Universal Print Driver can be used with almost any printer. If you can print to your local printer outside the ICA session, you should be able to print to it using the Citrix Universal Print Driver. This is a wonderful capability, especially when you don't support all kinds of devices; now you can tell your users that almost any printer they can print to locally, they can print to from their ICA session.

Continued

Home users with DeskJet printers that usually are not supported by administrators can now print to their DeskJets. Users who use those Xerox printers that are also usually not supported now find themselves printing.
To configure the Universal Print Driver follow these steps:

1. Open the **CMC**.

2. Right-click **Printer Management** and click **Properties**. The Properties window pops up.

3. Under the Print drivers section, select **Universal Driver Only**. See Figure 12.14.

Figure 12.14 Printer Management Properties Window

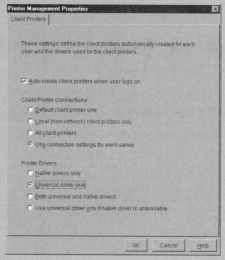

4. Click **OK**.

If you are still using MetaFrame 1.8 and are interested in implementing something similar to the Universal Print Driver, check out UniPrint from FutureLink Canada at www.uniprint.net. UniPrint can also be used with Citrix MetaFrame XP and offers many of the features that the Citrix Universal Print Driver lacks, such as the ability to print on both sides, and it supports color.

Troubleshooting Printing Problems

Printing problems can occur in your farm. Your ability to analyze and quickly troubleshoot problems is an essential part of your administrative duties. Printing has been impressively improved in Citrix MetaFrame XP, especially with the introduction of the Universal Print Driver, available in Feature Release 1. When troubleshooting printers, you must always remember that the problem is not always related to MetaFrame XP. The problem can lie in the operating system on which MetaFrame XP was installed, whether Windows NT or Windows 2000. The problem can lie in the print drivers installed on the local client machines; if they become corrupted, printing might not occur at all or the computer might output garbage from the printer. When you're troubleshooting printing issues, you can check a few things that might resolve your problems quickly:

- Check the print queue for any jobs that are stuck. If you find any, delete them, then stop and restart the print spooler service by clicking **Start | Programs | Administrative Tools | Services**, locating the **Print Spooler** service, right-clicking it, and selecting **Restart**.

- Check the physical connectivity to the printer, whether Ethernet cable if it is a network printer or a serial or parallel cable if it is a local printer.

- Another issue you want to consider when troubleshooting printer issues is verifying that the ICA client machine name is unique. To do this, view and, if necessary, edit the WFCNAME.INI file in the root of C:. This name is used as part of the printer name and is also used for redirecting print jobs back to the local printer.

- The Application log in the Event Viewer is a valuable tool for discovering and in many cases resolving errors that are logged by MetaFrame XP servers.

These issues are common ones that you should monitor and check when you face a printing problem. When installing a new print driver on the Windows NT or 2000 MetaFrame XP server, you should be certain that the driver is compatible with Terminal Services and that it will not "blue screen" your server. The print driver manufacturer will most likely mention whether or not this driver has been approved for use with Terminal Services. In Table 12.1 you can find a list of printing problems, their causes, and how to resolve them.

Table 12.1 Printing Problems, Causes, and Resolutions

Problem	Cause	Resolution
My server "blue screens" on printing.	Server blue screens can occur when you're using a print driver that's not supported for use on Terminal Services.	To resolve this issue, make a note of the DLL filename that appears on the blue screen, restart the server, and search for that file. When you locate it, right-click it and choose **Properties**. Try to identify the print driver with which this file is associated. After you identify the bad print driver, click **Start	Settings	Printers**, click **File	Server Properties**, select the driver, and remove it.
Users are having problems printing large files via MetaFrame. How can I optimize the process of printing large files?		Adjust the module.ini file with the following settings: [ICA 3.0] Bufferlength=8192 [ClientPrinter] Windowsize=2048 MaxWindowsize=8192 See www.thethin.net for reference.
Users are reporting that their printouts are unreadable or that the printer is printing garbage.	Bad cable to the printer or print drivers have become corrupted.	Check the physical cable to the printer and then reinstall the print drivers.
Users are reporting that they can print at times, but at other times they can't.		The first thing you should check is to make sure that the client print driver is installed on all the MetaFrame XP servers in the farm, thereby ensuring that the driver is readily available for use, regardless of which server the ICA client attaches to. Without this driver installed, the autocreation process will not work properly.

Continued

www.syngress.com

Table 12.1 Continued

Problem	Cause	Resolution
Users are reporting that they aren't getting their local printers mapped when they log in to the MetaFrame XP servers.		Verify that the installed client print driver name matches exactly that installed on the server. If the name doesn't match exactly, no autocreation will occur. You can use a mapping to associate a client print driver with a specific server printer.
The print queue is full, but printing is stalled.	The print server serves more than one physical print device. If a document is jammed or corrupted and stuck in any of the queues, printing will stall for all the physical print devices attached to the print server.	Delete the problematic print job and then stop and start the print spooler service on the print server. Users should resubmit any deleted jobs.
Users are complaining that none of their print jobs are being output.	Several things might cause this problem: an unplugged physical cable to the print device; a stuck print spooler; the printer is out of paper or out of toner; or something has physically happened to the print device.	Make sure that the actual print device isn't reporting any device errors about things such as toner, paper, or any manufacturer malfunctions. Check the print cable. Finally, check the print spooler and make sure it is not stuck. Stop and start it if necessary.

Local Client Printers Failing to Autocreate in ICA Sessions

Local client printers failing to autocreate is probably one of the most frequently occurring issues within a Citrix MetaFrame environment. We will examine some basic troubleshooting steps that you should follow and double-check when faced with this kind of issue:

- Open the Citrix Connection Configuration tool on the MetaFrame XP server by choosing **Start | Programs | Citrix | MetaFrame XP | Citrix Connection Configuration**. Double-click the **ICA protocol**. Click the **Client Settings** button and verify that **Connect client printers at Logon** and **Default to main client printer** are both checked.

- In the **Client Settings** in Citrix Connection Configuration, also verify that the following are *not* checked:

  - Disable Windows Client Printer Mapping

  - Disable Client LPT Mapping

- Verify that the needed print drivers are installed on both the client workstation and on all the Citrix MetaFrame XP servers in the farm.

- Verify that the print driver names match exactly on both the client workstation and on the MetaFrame XP servers.

- Verify that *clientname* is unique.

- In the event that administrators are the only ones who can autocreate printers and regular users cannot, make sure that the users have at least READ, WRITE, and EXECUTE permissions to the following:

  - %SYSTEMROOT%\system32\spool

  - %SYSTEMROOT%\system32\printer.inf

Creating a Printer Pool

A *printer pool* offers you the ability to connect one logical or virtual printer to several physical print devices through multiple ports. Let's assume that you have three HP LaserJet 8100 physical print devices across which you would like to create a printer pool to facilitate and speed up the output of users' print jobs. When users submit print jobs, the jobs are divided among these three physical print devices. The print jobs are processed via the available port and are therefore output faster, since three physical print devices are servicing these jobs.

Some benefits of using a printer pool include:

- A printer pool speeds up the printing process, thereby decreasing the time in which print jobs are queued.

- A printer pool is very convenient for users; because they have to print to only one printer, the output is determined by the printer pool. Of course, the administrator would set up the printers in the printer pool to be very close to each other so as not to confuse users or make them chase around the office looking for their documents.

- A printer pool increases printing performance in a high-volume printing environment.

- Management is easier in a printer pool. In the event that a printer in the pool should fail or be taken down for maintenance, users are still able to print without being affected by the defunct printer.

NOTE

In a printer pool, all the physical print devices participating in the pool should be identical in order for proper printing to occur.

To set up a printer pool follow these stepson the print server or wherever the printers are installed or are administered from:

1. Click Start | Settings | Printers.

2. Add the printer with the correct driver and share the printer.

3. Once the printer is installed, right-click it and go to **Properties**.

4. Select the **Ports** tab and check the **Enable printer pooling** check box, as shown in Figure 12.15.

Figure 12.15 Enabling the Printer Pooling Option

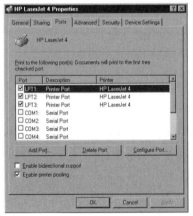

5. Select the various ports associated with the physical print devices participating in the pool. For example, if LPT1 was the original port on which the first print device was installed, select LPT2 or the port associated with another physical print device. Figure 12.15 also shows three ports selected for a single print device.

6. When you're done, click **OK** to exit the Properties window.

Creating an Expedited Print Queue

In any environment, the need often arises for granting a group of users priority over others in terms of printing. This priority group of users could be the CEO of the company and the board of directors, for example. Expediting their print jobs and giving them priority could become a necessity. It is possible to create a second print queue to a single physical print device and giving it priority printing over the other queue.

Before you create the priority queue, make sure that you have already created a group in Active Directory Users and Computers and have added the users who will be granted priority printing access to this queue. For the purpose of the example, let's assume that you have created a group named group2 and have added all the right users to it.

To create a second priority print queue and grant group1 users exclusive right to print to it, follow these steps:

1. Click **Start | Settings | Printers**.

2. Right-click the printer you want to set priority for and click **Properties**.

3. Click the **Advanced** tab in the Properties window.

4. In the Priority section, use the Up and Down Arrow keys to set a priority. Priority is 1–99, with 1 being the lowest and 99 the highest. Set the priority level for the first printer to **1**.

5. Click the **Security** tab and make sure that the **Everyone** group has rights to print to this printer.

6. Create the second logical printer that points to the same print device and give it a different name (the same name cannot be given to more than one logical or virtual printer). (To add another logical printer, double-click the **Add Printer** icon and follow the wizard.)

7. Right-click this newly added logical printer and go to **Properties**.

8. Click the **Advanced** tab in the Properties window.

9. In the Priority section, use the Up and Down Arrow keys to set priority to **2**. Note that the priority given to this printer is higher than that given to the first printer; therefore, print jobs sent to this print queue will take precedence. See Figure 12.16.

10. Click the **Security** tab and remove the **Everyone** group that was added by default and add group2, which you created earlier, and add the selected group of users who will have access to print to this print device. See Figure 12.17.

11. Click **OK** to apply the settings and close the window.

Figure 12.16 The Printer Properties Advanced Tab Window

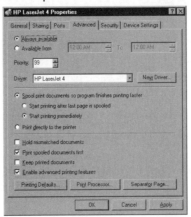

Figure 12.17 The Printer Properties Security Tab Window

Summary

Printing in a MetaFrame XP environment can seem a little complicated for a new administrator until you familiarize yourself with the various tools and features at your disposal. The autocreation feature is one of the most sought-after features in MetaFrame XP and enables a user in an ICA session to print to various printers without having to even install these printers. They are simply autocreated for the user.

Network printers can be used on MetaFrame XP servers as well, and an administrator can set the users and groups for whom printers are autocreated when they log in. Local printers are another option available to an administrator; they are installed on MetaFrame XP servers just as they would be installed on any other Windows 2000 server.

Gone are the days where you had to log in to every server in your farm and install the same driver so you would have consistency across all servers. With MetaFrame XP, you have the option of replicating print drivers across all servers in the farm with one simple mouse click. In the event that there is a print server on your network, you can import all its installed printers instead of having to reinstall and configure all these printers all over again.

Finally, one of the greatest new features available with MetaFrame XP Feature Release 1 is the Citrix Universal Print Driver, a generic PCL4 print driver that can be used on almost any print device of any make and model.

Solutions Fast Track

Creating Client Printers

☑ The autocreated printer feature automatically makes the client's local machine available for the user to print to from within an ICA session. The user doesn't need to install anything the printer autocreates if a set of criteria is met.

☑ Network printers can be made available for users to print to from within their ICA sessions. Network printers can be added in the CMC, and permissions can be set to which groups or users get these printers autocreated for them when they log on to a MetaFrame XP server.

☑ Local printers can be installed and attached directly to a MetaFrame XP server just as you would install and attach them to any Windows 2000 server.

Printing in a Server Farm Environment

☑ Print driver replication needs to occur in order to standardize the list of supported print drivers across all MetaFrame XP servers so that regardless of which server a user connects to, the same set of drivers is available to service the user's printing needs.

☑ Importing a print server from your network can save you time installing network printers. After importing the print server, you need to periodically update it to make sure that it is still current with regard to newly added printers or even deleted printers.

☑ The Citrix Universal Print Driver is a very simple and featureless PCL4 driver that is so generic it can work with almost any print device and can be used as an alternative method to installing and replicating drivers—one driver for all devices.

Troubleshooting Printing Problems

☑ Make sure that you always check to see if the name of the print driver installed on the client matches exactly that of the print driver installed on the server.

☑ If driver replication doesn't occur after the installation of new drivers, you could experience an issue when your user logs on to a MetaFrame server that doesn't have the right drivers installed. That user will be able to print to some servers and not print to other servers. Always make sure that printer replication occurs.

☑ Windows 2000 Event Viewer can be your friend in some cases for troubleshooting printer issues. Always keep an eye on the Application log within Event Viewer for any errors or error codes.

Frequently Asked Questions

The following Frequently Asked Questions, answered by the authors of this book, are designed to both measure your understanding of the concepts presented in this chapter and to assist you with real-life implementation of these concepts. To have your questions about this chapter answered by the author, browse to **www.syngress.com/solutions** and click on the **"Ask the Author"** form.

Q: We have a print server on the network with many printers already installed on it. Is there an easy way to import these printers without having to actually reinstall all the printers?

A: Yes. You can use a feature within CMC called Import Print Server. Using this tool, you can specify the name of the print server in your network, and a wizard automatically installs the printers. You must manually reinstall the print drivers, though.

Q: What do I need to do in order for autocreated printers to work?

A: The first thing you need to do is install the print driver on all the MetaFrame XP servers in your farm. The second thing is to make sure that the print driver installed on the local client machine matches in name that which is installed on the server. Third, make sure that your client machine name is unique, and check that you can open the WFCNAME.INI file located in the root of C:.

Q: Where are the print driver and replication information stored in the server farm?

A: The IMA stores the print driver and replication information.

Q: How can I view the installed print drivers on Windows 2000 MetaFrame XP servers?

A: You can view a list of the drivers installed on the server by choosing **Start | Settings Printers**. On the File menu, click **File | Server Properties** and select the **Drivers** tab. From this window, you can view, add, or delete any driver installed.

Q: Why should I consider using the Citrix Universal Print Driver that's available with Feature Release 1?

A: The Universal Print Driver can eliminate the need to install print drivers for your various print devices. It is also a great idea to use the Universal Print Driver to give broader support to your client base, enabling users to print on devices from virtually any printer manufacturer and any model.

Q: Is it a good idea to clean the files in the spool directory? If yes, how often?

A: It is definitely recommended that you clear the spooler directory on a regular basis. We recommend that you implement a script that runs a few minutes prior to the regular server reboot. This way, you ensure that when the server comes back up, there are no files in the spooler directory that could cause unstable printing services.

Q: The default number of print jobs that can be sent to the spooler is 10. Is there any way I can increase this number so that the print spooler can accept more than 10 jobs?

A: Yes, you can. Use the Citrix CltPrint.exe Utility to increase the number jobs of the print spooler can accept. You can execute the utility by opening a command prompt and typing **CltPrint /pipes:nn**. Pipes are the number of jobs the spooler can accept. You can also run the command with the **/q** syntax, which will display the current number of configured pipes.

Q: We are considering using the Citrix Universal Print Driver in our Citrix environment. Are there any disadvantages to doing so that we should be aware of?

A: The Citrix Universal Print Driver, like any other technology, has its pros and cons. Some disadvantages of using the Citrix Universal Print Driver are that you could lose the ability to print in color and you will not be able to print full duplex, which means on both sides of the paper. However, the pros related to the Citrix Universal Print Driver make it a technology worth exploring. With the Universal Print Driver, you can use one print driver for almost any type of printing device, thereby offering your users the freedom to print to any piece of equipment. It frees you from the hassle of installing print drivers and making sure that you don't crash your server doing it. If you don't want to lose these features but still want to take advantage of the technology, check out UniPrint from FutureLink Canada. UniPrint prints in color and in full duplex.

Chapter 13

Wireless and Mobile Solutions

Solutions in this chapter:

- Business Drivers for Wireless Solutions

- Planning a Wireless Solution

- Designing a Wireless Solution Using a Public Wireless Network

- Designing a Private Wireless Network

☑ Summary

☑ Solutions Fast Track

☑ Frequently Asked Questions

Introduction

The mobile Internet is a trend that is growing. People want to access the Internet from any location, using any device and without needing any wires. Once users are connected to the Internet, it is not a far leap to want to access and run applications.

There are a couple challenges with the mobile Internet. First, wireless communication does not provide an extensive amount of bandwidth. Applications cannot consume much before overwhelming a wireless link. Second, mobile devices do not have much in the way of processing power and memory. Applications must be simplified if they are to run natively on the mobile device.

Citrix MetaFrame provides a solution that overcomes these limitations. Because applications run on the Citrix MetaFrame server and processing is limited on the ICA client, a rich application environment can be delivered to mobile devices. ICA clients also consume extremely low bandwidth, which works well in a wireless network. This chapter discusses the ways to design a wireless solution powered by Citrix MetaFrame.

Business Drivers for Wireless Solutions

As the world continues to move further through the information age, businesses are turning more to technology to gain a competitive advantage in their respective industries. Every day, businesses make strategic decisions based on information that is as up to date as they can obtain. It follows that the ability of an organization to send and receive information and thus act on that information faster than its competitors gives it a distinct advantage over competition. Until now, no one has been able to collect and act on information in a real-time manner.

Vendors like Citrix have been working hard to create a fast, reliable solution for information delivery in as close to real time as possible with today's current technologies. The Citrix MetaFrame XP family of products is one of the first implementations of server-based computing to integrate the convenience of wireless technology into a solution that makes information available to the business user anywhere, anytime. Citrix MetaFrame technology is being used to provide secure and manageable access to most Windows-based applications to mobile users over whatever wireless WAN connections are available. Users are enjoying wireless access via laptops, handheld computers, and personal digital assistants (PDAs) as well as PDA phones.

As businesses implement wireless solutions, IT organizations within those businesses face a basic issue: the need to use resources in a wireless environment now. If this goal can be accomplished without special technical enablement or code rewrites, IT can save considerable work, and the organization can avoid frustrating delays and unwanted expense.

Citrix reinforces its ability to provide solutions that include three main benefits. First, it offers a consistent user experience—in other words, users will not notice a difference in performance, environment, or functionality, whether they are using wire-less access or conventional wired access. Second, it adds simplicity for IT workers who have to provide consistent, powerful, effortless business access for mobile users. Third, it offers a cost-effective transition to the Web-centric environment for organizations that implement the Citrix solution.

Citrix provides an end-to-end solution, including the following features:

- Access
- Low bandwidth
- Web deployment
- High security
- Application server farms.

There are only two requirements for creating a Citrix-based wireless connection: a device capable of running the Citrix ICA client and a wireless connection to the Citrix MetaFrame server.

The Need for Mobility

Business is not a static entity. As a result, information must be made available to the professional on the go whenever and wherever needed. Today in business, intellectual capacity is a far greater asset than an employee's physical capabilities. Many employees are housebound or live in geographically remote locations. Organizations employ mobile sales professionals who need to be able to contact the corporate network for resources to perform their work duties, such as contact management, record keeping, communication, and product presentation. Mobile communications provide all these resources to professionals, anywhere they go.

Portable computers and cell phones provide business with some measure of connectivity to their corporate information stores. This capability is pretty much standard now and no longer offers much competitive advantage to professionals who need to access and send information on the fly. Time is wasted every time a traditional mobile computer user has to find a phone line to dial in to the corporate network or the Internet. Even with broadband services such as DSL, a mobile user is still locked at a location and enjoys no real freedom of movement.

The growth of the Internet has allowed many organizations to extend their reach to parts of the world that would have been fiscally unfeasible to venture into before. As new applications that require increased network bandwidth emerge, 56K modems are becoming obsolete. Remote users are becoming increasingly unable to effectively function within the confinements of traditional wired access methods. Few conventional client/server applications can function adequately on as low bandwidth as is provided by modems at times. There is no way to predict the quality of a connection. The cost associated with providing remote users with hardware that can support all the necessary applications over these connections is falling, but still greater return on investment can be realized.

Network-based solutions such as Citrix MetaFrame XP have been bridging the gap in the cases in which money and bandwidth have not been able to provide the needed services. In a server-based environment, all the resources are housed where they can be best supported—at the corporate or enterprise network. Clients simply connect and control the services from remote locations. More business can be done by a sales professional who has near-instantaneous connectivity to corporate resources that can be provided to a prospect on site rather than having the do call-backs or send paper correspondence to prospects after a meeting.

For example, employees of a large Dutch bank use the Citrix ICA client over wireless links daily to provide onsite mortgage offers to customers. This tool creates enormous advantage for this organization over its competitors. Usually, mortgage officers must physically take a prospect's information back to the office to prequalify them for a mortgage. The Citrix solution allows the officer to contact the office instantaneously, check the customer's credit rating, get preapproval, and retrieve loan rates and terms for the prospect in the time it takes most of their competitors to get back to the office. This process results in an increased number of mortgage accounts and higher customer satisfaction because the customer can see first-hand what is being done to get them the mortgage.

The following sections discuss more of the benefits of server-based computing and how Citrix MetaFrame XP brings these benefits to an organization.

Selecting Citrix for Rich Applications over Low Wireless Bandwidth

Most of the developed world enjoys coverage via one or more wireless service providers. Current and future developments in wireless technology promise greater bandwidth, and with it, support for advanced applications. Citrix MetaFrame and the ICA client provide support for a variety of applications over the bandwidth levels available on current provider networks. All that is needed on a client machine—whether a PC, laptop, or handheld computer—is the ICA client.

Having only to install a software client for connectivity has a huge effect on return on investment for corporations, because all applications are actually run on servers in the corporate office and not on the client device. The ICA client only sends and receives keyboard input, screen refreshes, and audio over its connection. This has been demonstrated to be possible over bandwidth as low as is provided by Global System for Mobile Communication, or GSM (9.6kbps). The Citrix ICA client can allow a mobile professional to send and receive e-mail, read and write documents, and the like as it supports all of today's leading productivity applications, such as Microsoft Office. The added benefit is that corporate information stays where it belongs, on the corporate network, and work can be done wherever a cell phone connection can be made. This opens up the possibility for all types of applications that were heretofore bound to the corporate LAN to be used remotely with ease.

The architecture of the Citrix MetaFrame XP wireless solution is built on the proven server-based computing ICA architecture on which all MetaFrame's services run. Citrix has pinpointed the most viable wireless technologies and is continuously working to further optimize the ICA protocol to provide even better performance in the future.

Citrix has identified the three main challenges facing wireless WAN (WWAN) MetaFrame customers:

- **High connection latency** The time it takes for input from the client to travel to the server and results to travel back to the client is too great to be feasible.

- **High variable connection latency** The latency described in the first point frequently varies during the connection from good quality to poor quality.

- **Restricted bandwidth** The bandwidth of modem or wireless connections is often not high enough to support acceptable application performance.

The addition of Citrix SpeedScreen3 and NFuse technologies addresses these challenges even further than previous Citrix implementations. By further lessening the bandwidth overhead for running applications via the ICA client, even faster screen refreshes and passing of client input than before are possible. This has been proven even at the minimum functional bandwidth provided by popular wireless technologies such as GSM, Cellular Digital Packet Data (CDPD), and General Packet Radio Service (GPRS).

How Citrix Provides Higher Functionality on PDAs

PDAs are designed to be light and nonprocessor-intensive devices. However, with the growth of the wireless industry, PDAs and handheld computers are now being used as more than just address books and electronic memo pads. In wireless networks, the main concern is latency. Thin clients rely on the quality of the connection in order to operate and access server resources effectively. High latency as is experienced using the current convergent wireless technology can be overcome using Citrix MetaFrame XP technology. Any PDA that runs the Windows CE or Pocket Windows operating system is capable of the productivity of a laptop or desktop machine through the application of the Citrix MetaFrame XP wireless solution. The Citrix ICA client allows the PDA to connect to the corporate network and send and read e-mail, create and edit documents, and give video presentations. This is possible because none of the actual data that the mobile worker is manipulating comes across the connection to the PDA. Only the keyboard strokes and screen refreshes travel across the link. Current wireless technology can guarantee, at best, bandwidth of about 46kbps. This is more than enough bandwidth to provide excellent performance using the ICA client.

For connections of low or poor bandwidth, Citrix enhancements such as SpeedScreen3 effectively reduce bandwidth requirements and improve application performance for the client. The Citrix SpeedScreen3 component reduces bandwidth requirements by reducing the bandwidth that the ICA protocol uses.

Higher functionality on devices such as PDAs is achieved by employing Citrix's proprietary SpeedScreen Latency Reduction (SLR) technology. SLR consists of two subcomponents: local text echo and mouse click feedback. *Local text echo* maintains acceptable response and performance levels over wireless connections on PDAs by affecting a best-effort screen painting of the application display and transferring via the ICA protocol to the client. The actual display usually follows the simulation. The simulation is able to travel faster than the actual data display because it is actually on the client. The actual display that follows is almost always identical to the best guess. The display is repainted so rapidly that end users rarely notice the change.

In cases of low-bandwidth connections, the SLR local text echo client component intercepts user input and displays the results of the input on the client screen. The local text echo component also sends the input via the ICA protocol to the SLR component on the server. The SLR component on the server also provides information on fonts and other display features concerning the running application to the SLR client. This is done via querying the application and supplying the information to the client via the ICA protocol. The SLR components can be configured to compensate for latency via the ICA settings on the client and the SLR Manager on the server.

The *mouse click feedback* component works to influence customer input by displaying an hourglass mouse pointer whenever a user makes a mouse click over a high-latency link. The hourglass pointer reverts to normal when the process invoked by the mouse click is complete. This lets the end user know that his input is being processed. Figure 13.1 illustrates the SLR Properties screen, where latency handling is configured.

Figure 13.1 SpeedScreen Latency Manager Properties

Installing Citrix ICA Client on a Windows CE Device

The installation of the Citrix ICA client on a Windows CE device such as a PDA is very similar to installation on a Windows computer. There are two installation types: local installation and installation from a PC. The following steps guide you through the procedures for local installation:

1. Double-click the **icasetup** icon.
2. Specify the directory in which you want to install the client. Click **OK**.
3. Click **Accept** when the license agreement appears. Installation will complete.

The following are the steps for PC installation:

1. Connect the **Windows CE** device to your **PC** via whatever cable type you use.
2. Double-click the **icasetup** icon on your PC.
3. Follow the instructions to download the ICA client files to your device.

Configuring the ICA Client

The ICA client allows you to make two types of ICA connections: a connection to a specific MetaFrame server or a connection to a published application. The following steps show how:

1. Click **Start | Programs | ICA CE Client | Remote Application Manager**.
2. Click **New** on the **Entry** menu.
3. Select the type of connection you need to make on the **Specify Connection Type** dialog box.
4. Select either a Citrix server or a published application, depending on the type of connection you want to make.
5. Select a title for the connection. Check the box to create a shortcut on your desktop if you want.
6. Click **Finish**.

Planning a Wireless Solution

For years, countless network design and consulting engineers have struggled to streamline the design and implementation process. Millions of dollars are spent defining and developing the steps in the design process in order to make more effective and efficient use of time.

For the network recipient or end user, the cost of designing the network can sometimes outweigh the benefit of its use. As a result, it is vital that wireless network designers and implementers pay close attention to the details associated with designing a wireless network in order to avoid costly mistakes and forego undue processes. This section introduces you to the six phases that a sound design methodology encompasses. The phases are as follows:

- Performing an analysis of the existing network environment

- Conducting a preliminary investigation regarding the necessary changes

- Creating a design

- Finalizing the design

- Implementing that design

- Creating the necessary documentation that will act as a crucial tool as you troubleshoot

The section features a discussion of integrating the Citrix MetaFrame XP wireless solution to provide application services to corporate customers.

Creating a Private Wireless LAN

There are obvious benefits to creating private wireless LANs (WLANs) in both the home and corporate environments. The first readily visible benefit is the absence of hardwired connections and the expense associated with conventional copper-cabled office space. The absence of wires also eliminates the physical limitations of hardwired connections to some extent, because wires do not have to be pulled for every station on a LAN.

Wireless networks are designed along the same guidelines as hardwired networks. Designers of wireless networks must perform the same tasks to ensure a design that fits the intended use and the expected performance levels as wired networks. However, wireless networks also bring their own set of difficulties to the design process. You must consider the presence of other devices that could generate signals that can cause interference. The effective range of the signal in the building that houses the network and thus the number and placement of access points is another important element. Security must also be considered. These elements should all be carefully planned in the beginning phases of the network design.

Implementing MetaFrame does not add to the complexity of the WLAN design because users and applications are configured the same way as with wired connections.

Required Wireless Infrastructure Equipment

The equipment required for a wireless infrastructure closely resembles that needed for a wired LAN. The only additions to the infrastructure are wireless access points and wireless network cards. In fact, a wireless infrastructure can be constructed on top of a wired infrastructure and then tap the resources of the wired LAN (see Figure 13.2).

Figure 13.2 A Typical Hybrid Wired/Wireless Network

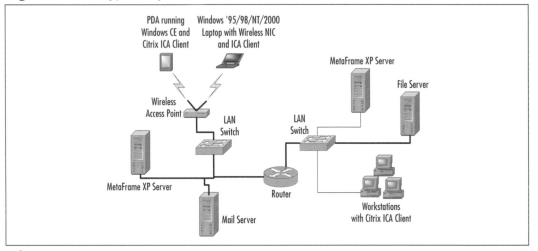

Designing & Planning...

Don't Go Totally Wireless

Wireless LANs do provide a great deal of freedom of movement in an office and facilitate collaborative work. However, the benefits of wireless networking don't make it the be-all and end-all solution in an organization. Latency might not be a critical factor in most client-side applications, but server performance relies heavily on network bandwidth and throughput. That is why the wired networking segment has nothing to fear from the recent spike in wireless technology. In a totally wireless office, servers would soon grind to a halt as a result of the 11Mbps bottleneck. Build your wireless network to *complement* your wired network infrastructure, and you can then reap the benefits of wireless technology.

IEEE 802.11

Prior to the adoption of the 802.11 standard, wireless data-networking vendors made equipment that was based on proprietary technology. Wary of being locked into a relationship with a specific vendor, potential wireless customers instead turned to more standards-based wired technologies. As a result, deployment of wireless networks did not happen on a large scale and remained a luxury item for large companies with large budgets.

The only way WLANs will be generally accepted will be if the wireless hardware involved has a low cost and has become a commodity items like routers and switches. Recognizing that the only way for this to happen would be if there were a wireless data-networking standard, the Institute of Electrical and Electronics Engineers' (IEEE's) 802 Group took on their eleventh challenge. Since many of the members of the 802.11 Working Group were employees of vendors making wireless technologies, there were many pushes to include certain functions in the final specification. Although this level of interest slowed the progress of finalizing 802.11, it also provided momentum for delivery of a feature-rich standard left open for future expansion.

On June 26, 1997, the IEEE announced the ratification of the 802.11 standard for wireless LANs. Since that time, costs associated with deploying an 802.11-based network have dropped, and WLANs are rapidly being deployed in schools, businesses, and homes.

In this section, we discuss the evolution of the standard in terms of bandwidth and services. We also discuss WLAN standards that are offshoots of the 802.11 standard.

As in all 802.x standards, the 802.11 specification covers the operation of the media access control (MAC) and physical layers. As shown in Figure 13.3, 802.11 defines a MAC sublayer, MAC services and protocols, and three physical layers.

Figure 13.3 802.11 Physical and Data Link Layer Protocols

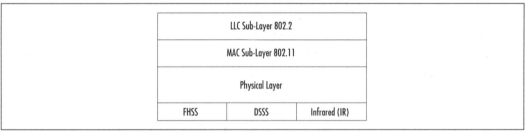

The three physical layer options for 802.11 are infrared (IR) baseband and two radio frequency (RF) options. Due to line-of-sight limitations, very little development has occurred with the IR option. The RF physical layer is composed of Frequency Hopping Spread Spectrum (FHSS) and Direct Sequence Spread Spectrum (DSSS) in the 2.4GHz band. All three physical layers operate at either 1Mbps or 2Mbps. The majority of 802.11 implementations utilize the DSSS method.

FHSS works by sending bursts of data over numerous frequencies. As the name implies, it hops between frequencies. Typically, the devices send information on up to four frequencies simultaneously and only for a short period of time before hopping to new frequencies. The devices using FHSS agree on the frequencies being used. In fact, due to the short time period of frequency use and device agreement of these frequencies, many autonomous networks can coexist in the same physical space.

DSSS functions by dividing the data into several pieces and simultaneously sending the pieces on as many different frequencies as possible—unlike FHSS, which sends on a limited number of frequencies. The DSSS process allows for greater transmission rates than FHSS but is vulnerable to greater occurrences of interference. This is because the data spans a larger portion of the spectrum at any given time than FHSS. In essence, DHSS floods the spectrum all at one time, whereas FHSS selectively transmits over certain frequencies.

As mentioned earlier, the primary reason WLANs were not widely accepted earlier was the lack of standardization. It is logical to question whether vendors would accept a nonproprietary operating standard, since vendors compete to make unique and distinguishing products. Although 802.11 standardized the physical layer, MAC, the frequencies on which to send and receive, transmission rates, and more, it did not absolutely guarantee that differing vendors' products would be 100-percent compatible. In fact, some vendors built backward-compatibility features into their 802.11 products in order to support their legacy customers. Other vendors have introduced proprietary extensions (for example, bit-rate adaptation and stronger encryption) to their 802.11 offerings.

To ensure that consumers can build interoperable 802.11 wireless networks, an organization called the Wireless Ethernet Compatibility Alliance (WECA) tests and certifies 802.11 devices. The WECA's symbol of approval means that the consumer can be assured that the particular device has passed a thorough test of interoperations with devices from other vendors. This reassurance is important when you're considering devices to be implemented into your existing network, because if the devices cannot communicate, it complicates the management of the network—in fact, you will essentially have to deal with two autonomous networks. It is also important when you're building a new network because you might be limited to a single vendor.

Since the first 802.11 standard was approved in 1997, there have been several initiatives to make improvements. As you will see in the following sections, an evolution is unfolding with the 802.11 standard. The introduction of the standard came with 802.11b. Then along came 802.11a, which provides up to five times the bandwidth capacity of 802.11b. Now, accompanying the ever-growing demand for multimedia services, is the development of 802.11e. Each task group, outlined here, is endeavoring to speed up the 802.11 standard, making it globally accessible while not having to reinvent the MAC layer of 802.11:

- **The 802.11d Working Group** This group is concentrating on the development of 802.11 WLAN equipment to operate in markets not served by the current standard. (The current 802.11 standard defines WLAN operation in only a few countries.)

- **The 802.11f Working Group** This group is developing an *Inter-Access Point Protocol* due to the current limitation prohibiting roaming between access points made by different vendors. This protocol would allow wireless devices to roam across access points made by competing vendors.

- **The 802.11g Working Group** This group is working on furthering higher data rates in the 2.4GHz radio band.

- **The 802.11h Working Group** This group is busy developing spectrum and power management extensions for the IEEE 802.11a standard for use in Europe.

802.11b

Ignoring the FHSS and IR physical media, the 802.11b physical layer uses DSSS to broadcast in any one of 14 center-frequency channels in the 2.4GHz industrial, scientific, and medical (ISM) radio band. As Table 13.1 shows, North America allows 11 channels; Europe allows 13, the most channels allowed. Japan has only one channel reserved for 802.11, at 2.483GHz.

Table 13.1 Frequencies and the Countries in Which They Are Used

Channel Number	Frequency (GHz)	North America	Europe	Spain	France	Japan
1	2.412	X	X			
2	2.417	X	X			
3	2.422	X	X			
4	2.427	X	X			
5	2.432	X	X			
6	2.437	X	X			
7	2.442	X	X			
8	2.447	X	X			
9	2.452	X	X			
10	2.457	X	X	X	X	
11	2.462	X	X	X	X	
12	2.467		X		X	
13	2.472		X		X	
14	2.483					X

Many devices compete for airspace in the 2.4GHz radio spectrum. Unfortunately, most of the devices that cause interference, such as microwaves and cordless phones, are especially common in the home environment. As you can imagine, the viability of an 802.11b network depends on how many of these products are near the network devices.

One of the more significant competitors of 802.11b comes in the form of the emerging Bluetooth wireless specification. Though designed for short-range transmissions, Bluetooth-compatible devices utilize FHSS to communicate with each other. Cycling through thousands of frequencies a second, this technology looks as though it poses the greatest chance of creating interference for 802.11. Further research will determine exactly what—if any—interference Bluetooth will cause to 802.11b networks. Many companies are concerned about oversaturating the 2.4GHz spectrum and are taking steps to ensure that their devices "play nicely" with others in this arena. Members of a consortium known as the Bluetooth Special Interest Group are responsible for developing and enhancing Bluetooth technology.

These forms of interference will directly impact the home user who wants to set up a wireless LAN, especially if neighbors operate interfering devices. Only time will tell if 802.11b will be able to stand up against these adversaries and hold onto its lead in the marketplace.

802.11a

Due to the overwhelming demand for more bandwidth and the growing number of technologies operating in the 2.4GHz band, the 802.11a standard was created for WLAN use in North America as an upgrade from the 802.11b standard. The 802.11a standard provides 25Mbps to 54Mbps bandwidth in the 5GHz spectrum (the unlicensed national information infrastructure [U–NII] spectrum). Since the 5GHz band is currently mostly clear, chance of interference is reduced. However, that could change, since it is still an unlicensed portion of the spectrum. The 802.11a standard is designed mainly for the enterprise, providing Ethernet capability.

The 802.11a standard is one of the physical layer extensions to the 802.11 standard. Abandoning spread spectrum completely, 802.11a uses an encoding technique called Orthogonal Frequency Division Multiplexing (OFDM). Although this encoding technique is similar to the European 5GHz HiperLAN physical layer specification, which is explained in greater detail later in the chapter, 802.11a is currently specific to the United States.

As shown in Table 13.2, three 5GHz spectrums have been defined for use with 802.11a. Each of these three center-frequency bands covers 100MHz.

Table 13.2 802.11a Frequencies and Channels

Regulatory Area	Frequency Band	Channel Number	Center Frequencies
USA	U-NII Lower Band 5.15–5.25GHz	36	5.180GHz
		40	5.200GHz
		44	5.220GHz
		48	5.240GHz
USA	U-NII Middle Band 5.25–5.35GHz	52	5.260GHz
		56	5.280GHz
		60	5.300GHz
		64	5.320GHz
USA	U-NII Upper Band 5.725–5.825GHz	149	5.745GHz
		153	5.765GHz
		157	5.785GHz
		161	5.805GHz

802.11e

The IEEE 802.11e is providing enhancements to the 802.11 standard while retaining compatibility with 802.11b and 802.11a. The enhancements include multimedia capability made possible with the adoption of quality of service (QoS) functionality as well as security improvements. What does this mean for a service provider? It means the ability to offer video on demand, audio on demand, high-speed Internet access, and voice-over-IP (VoIP) services. What does this mean for the home or business user? It allows high-fidelity multimedia in the form of MPEG2 video and CD quality sound and redefinition of the traditional phone use with VoIP.

QoS is the key to the added functionality of 802.11e. It provides the functionality required to accommodate time-sensitive applications such as video and audio. QoS includes queuing, traffic-shaping tools, and scheduling. These characteristics allow priority of traffic. For example, data traffic is not time sensitive and therefore has a lower priority than applications such as streaming video. With these enhancements, wireless networking has evolved to meet the demands of today's users.

The 802.11 architecture can best be described as a series of interconnected cells. It consists of the following: the wireless device or station, the access point (AP), the wireless medium, the distribution system (DS), the Basic Service Set (BSS), the Extended Service Set (ESS), and station and distribution services. All of these components, working together, provide a seamless mesh to give wireless devices the ability to roam around the WLAN, looking for all intents and purposes like wired devices.

The Basic Service Set

The core of the IEEE 802.11 standard is the *Basic Service Set*. As you can see in Figure 13.4, this model is made up of one or more wireless devices communicating with a single access point in a single radio cell. If there are no connections back to a wired network, this is called an *independent BSS*.

Figure 13.4 A Basic Service Set (One Cell)

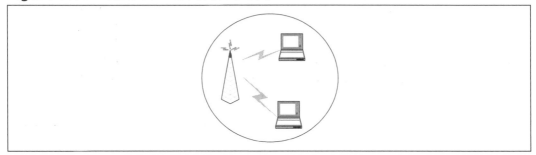

If there is no AP in the wireless network, it is referred to as an *ad hoc network*. This means that all wireless communication occurs directly between the members of the ad hoc network. On a wired network, we refer to this as *peer-to-peer communication*. In wireless terms, *ad hoc* means that new users can join this network by simply turning on a wireless device within the range of the network. This capability poses considerable security risk because no standard system polices this type of network. The IEEE 802.10 committee responsible for developing a security standard that would include wireless networks is in hibernation and has not yet introduced anything feasible. Figure 13.5 describes a basic ad hoc network.

Figure 13.5 A Simple Ad Hoc Network

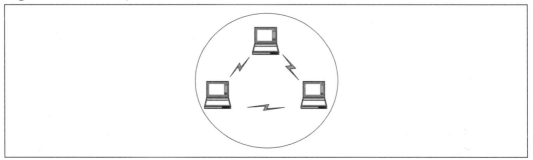

When the BSS has a connection to the wired network via an AP, it is called an *infrastructure BSS*. As you can see in the model shown in Figure 13.6, the AP bridges the gap between the wireless device and the wired network. As shown in the diagram, an AP is basically a hub or bridge from a wireless network to a wired network. An AP sits on a wired network, just like any other network device. APs are usually configured with a network address so that they can communicate with the wired network. An infrastructure BSS network has advantages over a simple ad hoc network in much the same way that a server-based network has advantages over a peer-to-peer network. Infrastructure networks provide more resources to wireless clients because wireless clients can access the resources of the wired network. There is a greater measure of security than in an ad hoc network, at least at the file level; for example, infrastructure network file and directory access permissions can be imposed on the wireless clients as well. The one shortfall is in terms of physical security. Wireless networking devices are by nature portable and as a result must be physically secured.

Figure 13.6 802.11 LAN Infrastructure Architecture Showing Overlapping Wireless Coverage Zones

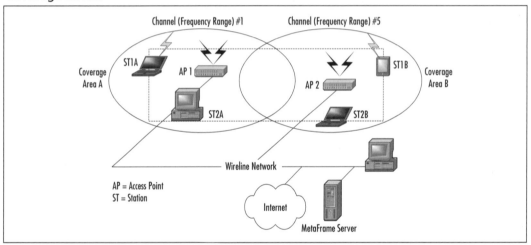

Since multiple APs exist in this model, the wireless devices no longer communicate in a peer-to-peer fashion. Instead, all traffic from one device destined for another device is relayed through the AP. Even though it might look as though this system would double the amount of traffic on the WLAN, it also provides for traffic buffering on the AP when a device is operating in a low-power mode.

The Extended Service Set

The compelling force behind WLAN deployment is the fact that with 802.11, users are free to move about without having to worry about switching network connections manually. If we were operating with a single infrastructure BSS, this moving about would be limited to the signal range of our one AP. Through the *Extended Service Set*, the IEEE 802.11 architecture allows users to move between multiple infrastructure BSSs. In an ESS, the APs talk among themselves, forwarding traffic from one BSS to another as well as switching the roaming devices from one BSS to another. They do this using a medium called the *distribution system* (DS). The distribution system forms the spine of the WLAN, making the decisions whether to forward traffic from one BSS to the wired network or back out to another AP or BSS.

What makes the WLAN so unique, though, are the invisible interactions between the various parts of the ESS. Pieces of equipment on the wired network have no idea that they are communicating with a mobile WLAN device, nor do they see the switching that occurs when the wireless device changes from one AP to another. All the wired network sees is a consistent MAC address to talk to, just as though the MAC were another node on the wire.

Services to the 802.11 Architecture

Nine different services provide behind-the-scenes support to the 802.11 architecture. Of these nine, four belong to the *station services* group and the remaining five to the *distribution services* group.

Station Services

The four station services (*authentication, deauthentication, data delivery*, and *privacy*) provide functionality equal to that of standard 802.3 wired networks.

The authentication service defines the identity of the wireless device. Without this distinct identity, the device is not allowed access to the WLAN. Authentication can also be made against a list of MACs allowed to use the network. This list of allowable MAC addresses may be on the AP or on a database somewhere on the wired network. A wireless device can authenticate itself to more than one AP at a time. This sort of "pre-authentication" allows the device to prepare other APs for its entry into their airspace.

The deauthentication service is used to destroy a previously known station identity. Once the deauthentication service has been started, the wireless device can no longer access the WLAN. This service is invoked when a wireless device shuts down or when it is roaming out of the range of the AP. This frees up resources on the AP for other devices.

Just like its wired counterparts, the 802.11 standard specifies a data delivery service to ensure that data frames are transferred reliably from one MAC to another. This data delivery is discussed in greater detail in the following sections.

The privacy service is used to protect the data as it crosses the WLAN. Even though the service utilizes an RC4-based encryption scheme, it is not intended for end-to-end encryption or as a sole method of securing data. Its design is intended to provide a level of protection equivalent to that provided on a wired network—hence its moniker, Wired Equivalent Protocol (WEP).

Distribution Services

Between the Logical Link Control (LLC) sublayer and the MAC, five distribution services make the decisions as to where the 802.11 data frames should be sent. As we will see, these distribution services make the roaming handoffs when the wireless device is in motion. The five services are *association*, *reassociation*, *disassociation*, *integration*, and *distribution*.

The wireless device uses the association service as soon as it connects to an AP. This service establishes a logical connection between the devices and determines the path the distribution system needs to take in order to reach the wireless device. If the wireless device does not have an association made with an AP, the DS will not know where that device is or how to get data frames to it. As you can see in Figure 13.7, the wireless device can be authenticated to more than one AP at a time, but it will never be associated with more than one AP.

Figure 13.7 Wireless Authentication Through the Association Service

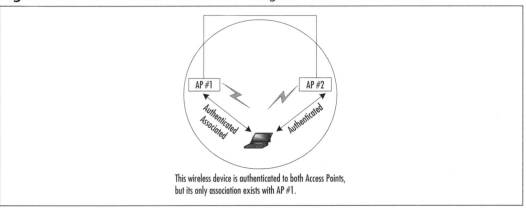

This wireless device is authenticated to both Access Points, but its only association exists with AP #1.

As we will see in later sections dealing with roaming and low-power situations, sometimes the wireless device will not be linked continuously to the same AP. To keep from losing whatever network session information the wireless device has, the reassociation service is used. This service is similar to the association service but includes current information about the wireless device. In the case of roaming, this information tells the current AP what the last AP was. This information allows the current AP to contact the previous AP to pick up any data frames waiting for the wireless device and forward them to their destination.

The disassociation service is used to tear down the association between the AP and the wireless device. This could be necessary because the device is roaming out of the AP's area, the AP is shutting down, or any one of a number of other reasons. To keep communicating to the network, the wireless device has to use the association service to find a new AP.

The distribution service is used by APs to determine whether to send the data frame to another AP and possibly another wireless device or if the frame is destined to head out of the WLAN into the wired network.

The integration service resides on the APs as well. This service does the data translation from the 802.11 frame format into the framing format of the wired network. It also does the reverse—taking data destined for the WLAN and framing it within the 802.11 frame format.

The CSMA-CA Mechanism

The basic access mechanism for 802.11 is carrier sense multiple access collision avoidance (CSMA-CA) with binary exponential backoff. This is very similar to the carrier sense multiple access collision detection (CSMA-CD) that we are familiar with when dealing with standard 802.3 (Ethernet) but with a couple of major differences.

Unlike Ethernet, which sends out a signal until a collision is detected, CSMA-CA takes great care to not transmit unless it has the attention of the receiving unit and no other unit is talking. This is called *listening before talking* (LBT).

Before a packet is transmitted, the wireless device listens to hear if any other device is transmitting. If a transmission is occurring, the device waits for a randomly determined period of time and then listens again. If no one else is using the medium, the device begins transmitting. Otherwise, it waits again for a random time before listening once more.

The RTS/CTS Mechanism

To minimize the risk of the wireless device transmitting at the same time as another wireless device (and thus causing a collision), the designers of 802.11 employed a mechanism called *Request to Send/Clear to Send* (RTS/CTS).

For example, if data arrived at the AP destined for a wireless node, the AP would send a RTS frame to the wireless node requesting a certain amount of time to deliver data to it. The wireless node would respond with a CTS frame saying that it would hold off any other communications until the AP was done sending the data. Other wireless nodes would hear the transaction taking place and delay their transmissions for that period of time as well. In this manner, data is passed between nodes, with a minimal possibility of a device causing a collision on the medium.

This process also solves a well-documented WLAN issue called the *hidden node*. In a network with multiple devices, the possibility exists that one wireless node might not know all the other nodes that are out on the WLAN. Thanks to RST/CTS, each node hears the requests to transmit data to the other nodes and thus learns what other devices are operating in that BSS.

Acknowledging the Data

When sending data across a radio signal with the inherent risk of interference, the odds of a packet getting lost between the transmitting radio and the destination unit are much greater than in a wired network model. To make sure that data transmissions would not get lost in the ether, *acknowledgment* (ACK) was introduced. The acknowledgement portion of CSMA-CA means that when a destination host receives a packet, it sends back a notification to the sending unit. If the sender does not receive an ACK, it knows that this packet was not received and transmits it again.

All this activity takes place at the MAC layer. Noticing that an ACK has not been received, the sending unit is able to grab the radio medium before any other unit can, and it resends the packet. This system allows recovery from interference without the end user being aware that a communications error has occurred.

Configuring Fragmentation

In an environment prone to interference, the possibility exists that one or more bits in a packet will become corrupted during transmission. No matter the number of corrupted bits, the packet will need to be resent.

When operating in an area where interference is not merely a possibility but a reality, it makes sense to transmit smaller packets than those traditionally found in wired networks. Smaller packets allow for a faster packet retransmission.

The disadvantage to doing this is that if there are no corrupted packets, the cost of sending many short packets is greater than the cost of sending the same information in a couple of large packets. Thankfully, the 802.11 standard has made this a configurable feature. This way, a network administrator can specify short packets in some areas and longer packets in more open areas where interference is low.

Using Power Management Options

Because the whole premise of wireless LANs is mobility, having sufficient battery power to power the communications channel is of prime concern. The IEEE recognized this and included a power management service that allows the mobile client to go into a sleep mode to save power without losing connectivity to the wireless infrastructure.

Utilizing a 20-byte Power Save Poll (PS-Poll) frame, the wireless device sends a message to its AP letting it know that is going into power-save mode and that the AP needs to buffer all packets destined for the device until it comes back online. Periodically, the wireless device will wake up and see if there are any packets waiting for it on the AP. If there aren't, another PS-Poll frame is sent, and the unit goes into a sleep mode again. The real benefit here is that the mobile user is able to use the WLAN for longer periods of time without severely impacting the device's battery life.

Multicell Roaming

Another benefit to wireless LANs is being able to move from wireless cell to cell as you go around the office, campus, or home, without the need to modify your network services. Roaming between APs in your ESS is a very important portion of the 802.11 standard. Roaming is based on the wireless device's ability to determine the quality of the wireless signal to any AP within reach and decide to switch communications to a different AP if it has a stronger or cleaner signal. This decision is based primarily on an entity called the *signal-to-noise* (S/N) *ratio*. In order for wireless devices to determine the S/N ratio for each AP in the network, APs send out *beacon* messages that contain information about the AP as well as link measurement data. The wireless device listens to these beacons and determines which AP has the clearest and cleanest signal. After making this determination, the wireless device sends authentication information and attempts to reassociate with the new AP. The reassociation process tells the new AP which AP the device just came from. The new AP picks up whatever data frames that might be left at the old AP and notifies the old AP that it no longer needs to accept messages for that wireless device. This frees up resources on the old AP for its other clients.

Even though the 802.11 standard covers the concepts behind the communication between the AP and the DS, it doesn't define exactly how this communication should take place. This is because there are many different ways this communication can be implemented. Although this system gives a vendor a good deal of flexibility in AP/DS design, there could be situations in which APs from different vendors might not be able to interoperate across a distribution system due to the differences in how those vendors implemented the AP/DS interaction. Currently, an 802.11 Working Group (802.11f) is developing an Inter-Access Point Protocol. This protocol will be of great help in the future, allowing companies that have invested in one vendor's products to integrate APs and devices from other vendors into their ESSs.

Security in the WLAN

One of the biggest concerns facing network administrators in implementing a WLAN is data security. In a wired environment, the lack of access to the physical wire can prevent someone from wandering into your building and connecting to your internal network. In a WLAN scenario, it is impossible for the AP to know if the person operating the wireless device is sitting inside your building, passing time in your lobby, or seated in a parked car just outside your office. Acknowledging that passing data across an unreliable radio link could lead to possible snooping, the IEEE 802.11 standard provides three ways to set a greater amount of security for the data that travels over the WLAN. Adopting any (or all three) of these mechanisms will decrease the likelihood of an accidental security exposure.

The first method uses the 802.11 Service Set Identifier (SSID). This SSID can be associated with one or more APs to create multiple WLAN segments within the infrastructure BSS. These segments can be related to floors of a building, business units, or other data-definition sets. Since the SSID is presented during the authentication process, it acts as a crude password. Because most end users set up their wireless devices, these SSIDs could be shared among users, thus limiting their effectiveness. Another downside to using SSIDs as a sole form of authentication is that if the SSID were to be changed (due to an employee termination or other event), all wireless devices and APs would have to reflect this change. On a medium-sized WLAN, rotating SSIDs on even a biannual basis could prove to be a daunting and time-consuming task.

As mentioned earlier, in the station services section, the AP also can authenticate a wireless device against a list of MAC addresses. This list could reside locally on the AP, or the authentication could be checked against a database of allowed MACs located on the wired network. This typically provides a good level of security and is best used with small WLAN networks. With larger WLAN networks, administering the list of allowable MAC addresses requires some back-end services to reduce the amount of time needed to make an addition or subtraction from the list.

The third mechanism 802.11 offers to protect data traversing the WLAN was also mentioned earlier, in the section on station services. The *privacy service* uses an RC-4-based encryption scheme to encapsulate the payload of the 802.11 data frames, called WEP. WEP specifies a 40-bit encryption key, although some vendors have implemented a 104-bit key. As mentioned previously, WEP is not meant to be an end-to-end encryption solution. WEP keys on the APs and wireless devices can be rotated, but since the 802.11 standard does not specify a key-management protocol, all key rotation must be done manually. As with the SSID, rotating the WEP key would affect all APs and wireless users and take significant effort on the part of the network administrator.

Some network designers consider WLANs to be in the same crowd as RAS devices; they claim the best protection is to place the WLAN architecture behind a firewall or VPN device. Such a setup would make the wireless client authenticate to the VPN or firewall using third-party software (on top of WEP). The benefit here is that the bulk of the authenticating would be up to a non-WLAN device and would not require additional AP maintenance.

The uses of 802.11 networks can range from homes to public areas such as schools and libraries as well as businesses and corporate campuses. The ability to deploy a low-cost network without the need to have wires everywhere allows wireless networks to spring up in areas where wired networks would be cost prohibitive. The 802.11 services allow the wireless device the same kind of functionality as a wired network yet give the user the ability to roam throughout the WLAN.

Using a Public Wireless Network

The use of public wireless networks to provide services to end users is coming into its own with the evolution of the second-generation (2G) technologies and the coming of the third-generation (3G) technologies. New wireless service providers are beginning to appear. More conventional service providers have also begun to develop and offer wireless services. Carriers such as AT&T and Verizon are currently offering wireless service to the home and business consumer.

The rebirth of the Ricochet network in February 2002 promised improved service levels for customers choosing to leverage the already existing public wireless infrastructure to provide service. The major aspect of employing public wireless networks for communication is coverage area. Even the largest providers offer only limited regional coverage. The coupling of the current and future access methods with Citrix technology as well as VPN technology can go a long way toward the user's dream of being always connected, everywhere.

Connecting Via Cellular Modems to the Internet

Currently, wireless connections to public network can be effected through the use of cellular modems. Citrix MetaFrame supports wireless connections via cellular modems employing any of the available cellular access methods. Almost all these technologies are available for general use in the United States. Many vendors have capitalized on the availability of service and market modems that are capable of connecting to the Internet via cellular ports that plug right into a cell phone. This method is almost identical to using a conventional wire modem line and dialing an ISP modem except that data is being transmitted over the service provider's wireless infrastructure instead of the PSTN.

The performance of the Citrix ICA client over the cellular carrier is often minimal at best because it is difficult to guarantee bandwidth above 9.6Kbps, depending on your geographic location and the range of the cellular coverage zones. Usually if a digital cell phone is out of its coverage area, it switches to analog and disrupts cellular modem service.

Public Wireless Protocols

As we mentioned in the beginning of this section, more traditional service providers are developing wireless service offerings that can enable laptop and handheld computer users to access the Internet and their corporate networks on the go. Citrix is poised to take advantage of this growth explosion in the wireless market and has developed MetaFrame XP with that goal in mind. Whatever method is used to access the Internet, Citrix technologies are able to function over it and bring superior performance to the end user. The following sections discuss the most promising public wireless network technologies to date.

Ricochet

The Ricochet wireless system employs a modified FHSS technology called *microcellular packet-switched FHSS*. Metricom Inc., Ricochet's previous owner, was able to consistently provide average bandwidth of 175kbps with bursts of up to 400kbps in 21 major metropolitan cities in the United States. Unfortunately, Metricom Inc. filed for bankruptcy in mid-2001 and shut down the Ricochet network, seemingly indefinitely. However, new broadband service provider Aeirie Networks Inc. purchased the Ricochet network at the end of 2001. In 2001, before news of the Ricochet network shutdown was made public, Citrix gave very favorable ratings to the Ricochet wireless service for use with MetaFrame and the ICA client. Aeirie means to reactivate the Ricochet network and began testing in its home city of Denver, Colorado, in February 2002.

Global System for Mobile Communications

GSM is an international standard for voice and data transmission over a wireless phone. Utilizing three separate components of the GSM network, this type of communication is truly portable. A user can place an identification card called a *subscriber identity module* (SIM) in the wireless device, and the device will take on that user's personal configurations and information. This includes telephone number, home system, and billing information. Although the United States has migrated toward the PCS mode of wireless communication, in large part the rest of the world uses GSM.

The architecture used by GSM consists of three main components: a *mobile station*, a *base station subsystem*, and a *network subsystem*. These components work in tandem to allow a user to travel seamlessly without service interruption, while offering the flexibility of allowing any device to be used permanently or temporarily by any user.

The mobile station has two components: mobile equipment and a SIM. The SIM, as mentioned, is a small removable card that contains identification and connection information; the mobile equipment is the GSM wireless device. The SIM is the component within the mobile station that provides the ultimate in mobility. This is achieved because you can insert the SIM into any GSM-compatible device and, using the identification information it contains, you can make and receive calls and use other subscriber services. This means that if you travel from one country to another with a SIM, and you place the SIM into a rented mobile equipment device, the SIM will provide the subscriber intelligence back to the network via the mobile GSM-compatible device. All services to which you have subscribed will continue through this new device, based on the information contained on the SIM. For security and billing purposes, the SIM and the terminal each have internationally unique identification numbers for independence and identification on the network. The SIM's identifier is called the International Mobile Subscriber Identity (IMSI). The mobile unit has what is called an International Mobile Equipment Identifier (IMEI). In this way a user's identity is matched with the

SIM via the IMSI, and the position of the mobile unit is matched with the IMEI. This system offers some security in that a suspected stolen SIM card can be identified and flagged within a database for services to be stopped and to prevent charges by unauthorized individuals.

The base station subsystem, like the mobile station, has two components: the base transceiver station and the base station controller. The base transceiver station contains the necessary components that define a cell and the protocols associated with the communication to the mobile units. The base station controller is the part of the base station subsystem that manages resources for the transceiver units as well as the communication with the mobile switching center (MSC). These two components integrate to provide service from the mobile station to the MSC.

The network subsystem is, in effect, the networking component of the mobile communications portion of the GSM network. It acts as a typical Class 5 switching central office. It combines the switching services of the core network with added functionality and services as requested by the customer. The main component of this subsystem is the MSC. The MSC coordinates the access to the POTS network and acts similarly to any other switching node on a POTS network. It has the added ability to support authentication and user registration. It coordinates call handoff with the base station controller, call routing, and coordination with other subscribed services. It utilizes Signaling System 7 (SS7) network architecture to take advantage of the efficient switching methods. There are other components to the network subsystem, called *registers*: the visitor location register (VLR) and the home location register (HLR). Each of these registers handles call routing and services for mobility when a mobile customer is in her local or roaming calling state. The VLR is a database consisting of visitor devices in a given system's area of operation. The HLR is the database of registered users of the home network system.

Other Public Wireless Protocols

Other wireless technologies are not widely used by the public today but are worth mentioning, simply because they complement the previously discussed solutions and could be available as alternatives in situations that would preclude the implementation of the more familiar protocols. Let's look at some of these technologies and their uses.

Wireless Application Protocol

The *Wireless Application Protocol* (WAP) has been implemented by many carriers today as the specification for wireless content delivery. WAP is an open specification that offers a standard method to access Internet-based content and services from wireless devices such as mobile phones and PDAs. Just like the OSI reference model, WAP is nonproprietary. This means that anyone with a WAP-capable device can utilize this specification to access Internet content and services. WAP is also not dependent on the network, meaning that WAP works with current network architectures as well as future ones.

WAP, as it is known today, is based on the work of several companies that got together in 1997 to research wireless content delivery: Nokia, Ericsson, Phone.com, and Motorola. It was their belief at that time that the success of the wireless Web relied on such a standard. Today, the WAP Forum consists of a vast number of members, including handset manufacturers and software developers.

WAP uses a model of Internet access that is very similar in nature to the standard desktop PC using Internet Explorer. In WAP, a browser is embedded in the software of the mobile unit. When the mobile device wants to access the Internet, it first needs to access a WAP gateway. This gateway, which is actually a piece of software and not a physical device, optimizes the content for wireless applications. In the desktop model, the browser makes requests from Web servers; it is the same in wireless. The Web servers respond to URLs, just like the desktop model, but the difference is in the formatting of the content. Because Internet-enabled phones have limited bandwidth and processing power, it makes sense to scale down the resource-hungry applications to more manageable ones. This is achieved using the Wireless Markup Language (WML). A WML script is used for client-side intelligence.

Multichannel Multipoint Distribution Service

Allocated by the Federal Communications Commission (FCC) in 1983 and enhanced with two-way capabilities in 1998, *Multichannel Multipoint Distribution Service* (MMDS) is a licensed spectrum technology operating in the 2.5GHz to 2.7GHz range, giving it 200MHz of spectrum to construct cell clusters. Service providers consider MMDS a complementary technology to their existing DSL and cable modem offerings because it provides access to customers not reachable via these wireline technologies. See Figure 13.8 for an example of a service provider MMDS architecture.

MMDS provides from 1Mbps to 2Mbps of throughput and has a relative range of 35 miles from the radio port controller (RPC) based on signal power levels. It generally requires a clear line of sight between the radio port (RP) antenna and the customer premises antenna, although several vendors are working on MMDS offerings that don't require a clear line of sight. The *fresnel* zone of the signal (the zone around the signal path that must be clear of reflective surfaces) must be clear from obstruction so as to avoid absorption and reduction of the signal energy. MMDS is also susceptible to a condition known as *multipath reflection*. Multipath reflection or interference happens when radio signals reflect off surfaces such as water or buildings in the fresnel zone, creating a condition in which the same signal arrives at different times. Figure 13.9 depicts the fresnel zone and the concept of absorption and multipath interference.

Figure 13.8 MMDS Architecture

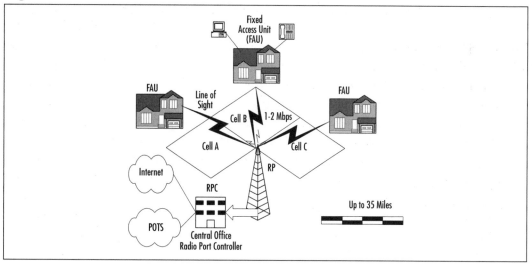

Figure 13.9 The Fresnel Zone

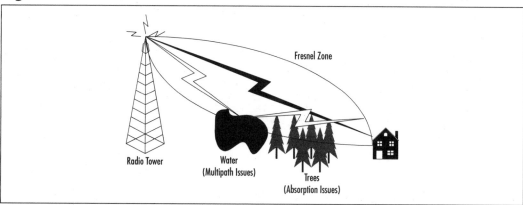

Local Multipoint Distribution Service

Local Multipoint Distribution Service (LMDS) is a broadband wireless point-to-multipoint microwave communication system operating above 20GHz (28–31GHz in the United States). LMDS is similar in its architecture to MMDS, with a couple of exceptions. LMDS provides very high-speed bandwidth (upward of 500Mbps) but is currently limited to a relative maximum range of 3 to 5 miles of coverage. It has the same line-of-sight issues that MMDS experiences and can be affected by weather conditions, as is common among line-of-sight technologies.

LMDS is ideal for short-range campus environments requiring large amounts of bandwidth or highly concentrated urban centers with large data/voice/video bandwidth requirements in a relatively small area. LMDS provides a complementary wireless architecture for the wireless service providers to use for markets that are not suited for MMDS deployments. Figure 13.10 illustrates a generic LMDS architecture.

Figure 13.10 LMDS Architecture

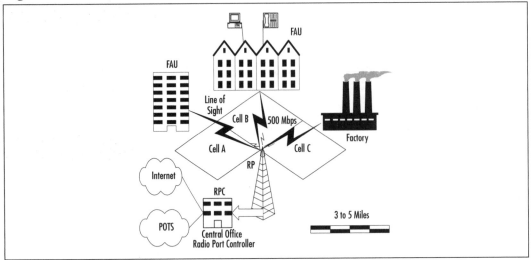

Wireless Local Loop

Wireless Local Loop (WLL) refers to a fixed wireless class of technology aimed at providing last-mile services normally provided by the local service provider over a wireless medium. This includes POTS as well as broadband offerings such as DSL. As stated earlier, this technology provides service without the laying of cable or use of an incumbent local exchange carrier (ILEC), which in layman's terms is the Southwestern Bells of the world.

The generic layout involves a point-to-multipoint architecture with a central radio or RPC located at the local exchange (LE). The RPC connects to a series of base stations RPs via fixed access back to the LE. The RPs are mounted on antennas and arranged to create coverage areas or sectored cells. The radio located at the customer premises, or fixed access unit (FAU), connects to an external antenna optimized to transmit and receive voice and data from the RPs. The coverage areas and bandwidth provided vary depending on the technology used, and coverage areas can be extended through the use of repeaters between the FAU and the RPs. Figure 13.11 provides a generic depiction of a wireless local loop architecture.

Point-to-Point Microwave

Point-to-Point (PTP) Microwave is a line-of-sight technology that is affected by multipath and absorption, much like MMDS and LMDS. PTP Microwave falls into two categories: licensed and unlicensed, or spread spectrum. The FCC issues licenses for individuals to use specific frequencies for the licensed version. The advantage of the licensed

PTP Microwave is that the chance of interference or noise sources in the frequency range is remote. This is critical if the integrity of the traffic on that link needs to be maintained. In addition, if the link is going to span a long distance or is in a heavily populated area, the licensed version is a much safer bet, since the probability of interference is greater in those cases. The drawback to licensed PTP Microwave is that it could take a considerable amount of time for the FCC to issue the licenses, and fees are associated with those licenses. Unlicensed PTP Microwave links can be used when a licensed PTP Microwave is not necessary and expediency is an issue.

Figure 13.11 Wireless Local Loop Architecture

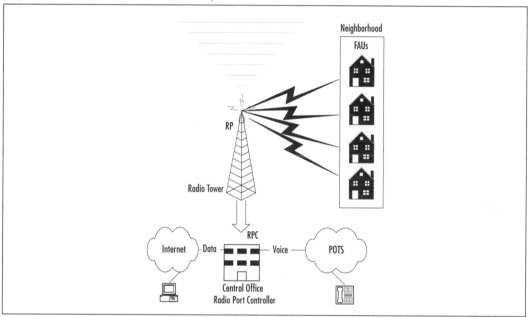

Since PTP can span long distances, determined mostly by the power of the transmitter and the sensitivity of the receiver as well as by traditional weather conditions, many aspects must be considered in designing a PTP Microwave link. First, a site survey and path analysis need to be conducted. Obstructions and curvature of the earth (for links over six miles) determine the height of the towers or the building required to build the link in a line-of-sight environment. As stated earlier, the fresnel zone must be clear of obstructions and reflective surfaces to avoid absorption and multipath issues. Predominant weather conditions can limit the distance of the PTP Microwave link because the signal is susceptible to a condition called *rain fade*. The designers must factor the predicted amount of signal degradation in a projected area into the design based on reliability requirements for the PTP Microwave link. Figure 13.12 gives a basic depiction of a PTP Microwave link.

Figure 13.12 Point-to-Point Microwave Architecture

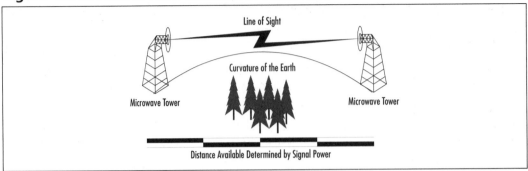

Designing a Wireless Solution Using a Public Wireless Network

One of the first factors that you need to consider when designing a wireless solution using a public wireless network is the device that will be used. Compatibility of devices is essential for the success of interoperable 802.11 wireless networks. A wireless solution that employs one of the public wireless networks provides service to the mobile professional over a large geographic region. A service provider must be chosen based on quality of service versus cost, adherence to standards, and area of coverage. The solution provides a foundation on which the end user can access basic Internet services such as Web browsing and Web-based email. The addition of other components such as VPN technology affords the end user the ability to communicate with a corporate network and work as though in the office, to some degree. A consideration of the constraints discussed in the preceding sections assists in making design decisions for service. Let's look at a hypothetical example of a public wireless network-based solution.

ABC Widgets has been a valve and widget maker in the shipbuilding industry for the past 20 years. The CEO, Lou Franklin, wants to enhance the company's marketing operations. He believes that his sales force should be better able to showcase their products by giving dynamic, graphical presentations. His marketing staff creates wonderful presentations for all their products and services. However, there is a problem. The presentations consume too much memory and disk space on the salespeople's laptops.

Lou is about to decide to order 15 new more powerful laptops for his sales staff when David Brown, the IT manager, proposes that they keep the current laptops and instead invest in a new server and MetaFrame. David proposes that they also purchase wireless Internet service from the local telecom provider, since their salespeople often give presentations to managers on shop floors or at shipbuilding sites, away from any wired Internet access. Lou agrees and the server is purchased. After a few weeks of testing the reliability of the wireless access and support training for the IT staff, ABC's sales force is now able give presentations on the fly, anywhere within the coverage area of their wireless service provider.

Selecting Clients

The clients of a public wireless network probably cover the gamut of computer hardware capable of Internet access. Everything from desktop machines and laptops to PDAs, all equipped with wireless modem cards or cellular modems that are able to connect to the provider's network, can access wireless services. The clients selected are also based on the operating systems of the devices they will run on. Citrix supports a flavor of the ICA client for every major operating system. There is a client for Windows, Windows CE, and Pocket Windows and Macintosh as well as UNIX and Linux. In ABC's case, the clients are all laptops running Windows 98.

Server and Infrastructure Design

As with any deployment of servers in the creation of a high-performance server-based solution, the placement of servers and services is an essential factor. Infrastructures that render services easily accessible yet highly secure require appropriate server hardware design as well as appropriate location of the servers within the infrastructure. In the case of public networks, this is the concern of the service provider. Important servers in a service provider's public network include Web servers, authentication servers, and mail servers. The infrastructure must put a premium on security, because this is a public network.

Citrix MetaFrame XP Access over the Internet

NFuse makes applications more available by creating custom portals for use by individuals or groups that contain the specific applications and data sources they need. Using NFuse, administrators are able to publish custom Program Neighborhoods for specific groups or individuals based on their responsibilities and job functions on a server that clients can access via the Internet. Figure 13.13 illustrates the NFuse architecture that ABC would employ for serving applications over the Web. Web sessions typically use even less bandwidth than conventional ICA sessions. This allows the end user to leverage the additional bandwidth into greater performance and response from the application he is using. All the processing still occurs on the server; however, the connection is even lighter because now the some of the burden of user input is being handled by a Web interface on a server much closer to the MetaFrame application server.

Figure 13.13 Citrix NFuse Used to Serve Applications over the Web

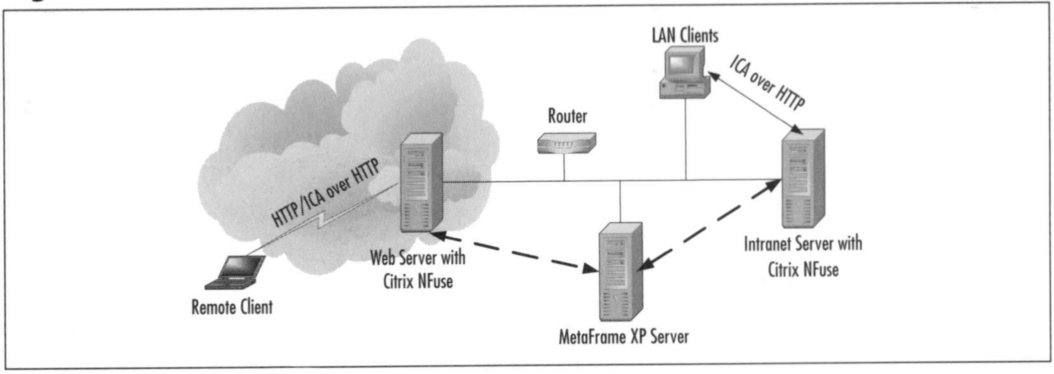

Using VPNs

The use of a VPN suggests that the end user needs to connect to and interact with a private network. In most cases, this private network is a corporate LAN. Use of VPN hardware or software provides a highly secure method for information exchange between a mobile professional and her corporate office. Many VPN solutions available on the market today provide very good support of remote access to corporate networks. Citrix Extranet is one solution to the problem of remote connectivity. Citrix Extranet, like all of Citrix's products, is designed to integrate seamlessly into a MetaFrame environment and provide secure remote access to MetaFrame-hosted applications. ABC's sales force can use Extranet to create secure connections through ABC's corporate firewall to the MetaFrame server.

Configuration Considerations

Since the main area of concern is latency when it comes to the Citrix ICA client and more so when operating over a public wireless network, the focus of our ABC configuration will be to lessen latency or at least to create more continuity of service for end users. SpeedScreen3, as we have already discussed, can be configured to reduce perceived latency during an ICA session. The ICA clients themselves can also be adjusted to handle latency through the SLR component that is installed as part of the client.

Designing a Private Wireless Network

Designing a private wireless network (see Figure 13.14) is much the same as designing a solution based on a public network; the only difference is that service also must be provided for by the design engineer. Again, standardization of equipment and protocols would be appropriate. The engineer or the administrator would have greater control over equipment standards on both the client and the server sides.

Figure 13.14 Private Wireless LAN Infrastructure

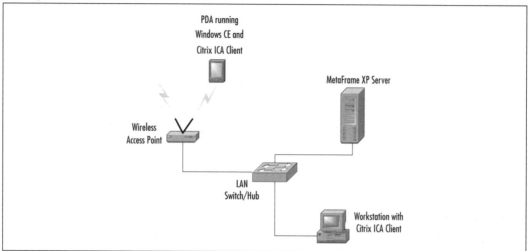

Selecting Clients

The selection of wireless network clients for a private network goes along the same lines as a public network. Both solutions rely on the same 802.11 standard, so the same clients can be used in either situation. The choice simply depends on the desired function of the client and the operating system environment in which it is intended to perform.

Server and Infrastructure Design

You must pay closer attention to server and infrastructure design because this area of the design is not done for you by a service provider. Server placement is the key here. As with a wired network, the placement of a server on an area of the network that is designed to handle high numbers of connections and serve clients with a high level of performance is the ideal recourse. In routed environments, it might be wise to place a MetaFrame server on each network segment that you want to serve.

Although throughout this chapter we have preached the benefits of wireless technology, it must be made clear that in almost every case, in order to provide a reliable high level of service to wireless clients, it is recommended that the servers they access use a wired connection. This is acceptable for two main reasons. First, wired network connections offer far better speeds than wireless network connections for communication between servers. Second, wired network connections are easier to secure by denying physical access to the servers where all the data and applications reside in the thin client/server computing model.

Design Steps for a Private Wireless Network

There are a few different schools of thought as to how to go about designing a private wireless network. The reality of the situation is that your design depends on the desired goals for the particular network that needs to be designed. We follow a five-phase design model, which still encompasses the six areas discussed in the design of a public wireless network. The model we employ includes the vision phase, the design phase, the testing and development phase, the pilot phase, and the production phase. We discuss these phases in detail and see how they are employed in our hypothetical scenario.

ABC Widgets has impressed its clients with the technology that its sales staff is using to deliver sales presentations. One of ABC's clients, Steadfast Inc., an anchor maker, is thinking about installing a private wireless network in its corporate headquarters. Steadfast's CIO, Hank Carter, inquires about the process of implementing ABC's wireless solution, and David Brown refers him to the solutions provider that designed and implemented ABC's wireless solution.

Hank meets with the provider consultants to discuss a solution for Steadfast. The following is an outline of the implementation that resulted in a new private wireless network for Steadfast:

1. During the vision phase, the requirements for the network are gathered and feasibility studies are conducted. The overall concept of what services the network should provide is developed, and expectations are set for the eventual outcome. In our example, the consultants took a tour of Steadfast's facilities, and possible access point locations were identified. Depending on the size of the infrastructure, this process can take hours to weeks to complete.

2. The design phase involves mapping out the infrastructure. This is usually done in drawings and models of the proposed network. This process gives the engineer a good idea of how much hardware is needed, because during this phase, real dimensions and capacities are used. Diagrams of Steadfast's current and proposed infrastructure are created.

3. In the testing and development phase, a lab simulating network conditions at the proposed site is created, and reliability, scalability, and latency are evaluated. The engineers simulate traffic in the test network identical to traffic that runs over Steadfast's network. Modification can be made as a fit for the proposed solution. Protocols could even be eliminated or added (e.g., the addition of the ICA protocol that Citrix clients and servers use to communicate and run applications).

4. The pilot phase involves setting up the infrastructure, either in part or entirely, and testing it with a few clients. Steadfast's IT department are outfitted with wireless network cards for their laptops; they test the network for four weeks by trying to complete administrative tasks from different locations in the facility.

5. Once Hank and his staff are satisfied with the results, Steadfast enters into the implementation phase and rolls out wireless network cards to all laptop users in the company. Employees are able to view, edit, and create documents via ICA connections to two MetaFrame servers running all the company's productivity applications, no matter where the users are located in the facility. This system allows shop-floor managers in Steadfast's warehouse to update inventory and shipping databases on the fly.

Summary

This chapter introduced wireless network technology and how it can enhance business. We discussed what might drive businesses to turn to wireless solutions and how Citrix wireless solutions can provide superior performance to wireless clients because of ICA's scalability and functionality. The three items of concern for wireless WAN (WWAN) links were identified. We discussed how MetaFrame XP provides superior wireless service for clients on low-bandwidth, high-latency connections using the capabilities of SpeedScreen to reduce latency.

We defined the standards associated with 802.11 and gave examples of how it may be used. We delved into the technologies associated with public and private wireless networks such as Multichannel Multipoint Distribution Service (MMDS), Wireless Application Protocol (WAP), Point-to-Point (PTP) Microwave, and Global System for Mobile Communication (GSM). We discussed their strengths, weaknesses, and the situations in which they are used.

We examined the process of designing wireless public and private networks and identified their components. We introduced the steps involved in designing and implementing wireless solutions using both public and private wireless networks, which includes client selection, server configuration, and other hardware infrastructure considerations. We also discussed flaws and security concerns associated with these technologies. We then showed how Citrix MetaFrame XP fits into these scenarios and enhances the services offered.

Solutions Fast Track

Business Drivers for Wireless Solutions

- ☑ Citrix solutions provide three main benefits: a consistent user experience; simplicity for IT workers who have to provide a consistent, powerful, effortless business access for business users; and a cost-effective transition to the Web-centric environment for organizations that implement the Citrix solution.

- ☑ The ICA client only sends and receives keyboard input, screen refreshes, and audio over its connection. This has been demonstrated to be possible over bandwidth as low as is provided by GSM (9.6kbps). The Citrix ICA client can allow a mobile professional to send and receive e-mail, read and write documents, and the like.

☑ The three main challenges facing wireless WAN (WWAN) MetaFrame customers are high connection latency, high variable connection latency, and restricted bandwidth.

Planning a Wireless Solution

☑ The phases of a sound network design methodology are performing an analysis of the existing network environment, conducting a preliminary investigation regarding the necessary changes, creating a design, finalizing the design, implementing the design, and creating the necessary documentation that will act as a crucial tool as you troubleshoot.

☑ The 802.11 architecture can best be described as a series of interconnected cells consisting of the wireless device or station, the Access Point (AP), the wireless medium, the distribution system, the Basic Service Set (BSS), the Extended Service Set (ESS), and station and distribution services.

☑ Nine different services provide behind-the-scenes support to the 802.11 architecture. Authentication, deauthentication, data delivery, and privacy are station services. The remaining five services are distribution services—they are association, reassociation, disassociation, integration, and distribution.

Designing a Wireless Solution
Using a Public Wireless Network

☑ The Global System for Mobile Communication (GSM) is an international standard for voice and data transmission over a wireless phone. The architecture used by GSM consists of three main components: a mobile station, a base station subsystem, and a network subsystem. All three components work in tandem to allow a user to travel seamlessly without service interruptions.

☑ Wireless Application Protocol (WAP) is an open specification that offers a standard method to access Internet-based content and services from wireless devices. In WAP, a Web browser is embedded in the software of the mobile unit.

☑ Point-to-Point (PTP) Microwave is a line-of-sight technology that is affected by multipath and absorption, much like Multichannel Multipoint Distribution Service (MMDS) and Local Multipoint Distribution Service (LMDS). PTP Microwave falls into two categories: licensed and unlicensed.

Designing a Private Wireless Network

☑ The major difference between a public network and a private network is that the private network does not rely on an external service provider for connectivity service.

☑ Wireless client selection depends on the operating system and the hardware platform. Standardization of client and server platforms is easier to control.

☑ On larger routed wireless private networks, service may be enhanced by placing a MetaFrame server on each subnet.

Frequently Asked Questions

The following Frequently Asked Questions, answered by the authors of this book, are designed to both measure your understanding of the concepts presented in this chapter and to assist you with real-life implementation of these concepts. To have your questions about this chapter answered by the author, browse to **www.syngress.com/solutions** and click on the **"Ask the Author"** form.

Q: What are the requirements for creating a Citrix-based wireless connection?

A: The only two requirements for creating a Citrix-based wireless connection are a device capable of running the Citrix ICA client and a wireless connection to the Citrix MetaFrame server.

Q: Does the addition of Citrix SpeedScreen3 better the Citrix solution?

A: Yes. SpeedScreen3 effectively reduces bandwidth requirements and makes applications easier to access on the server side. Citrix SpeedScreen3 reduces bandwidth requirements by reducing the bandwidth that the ICA protocol uses.

Q: As part of the 802.11 architecture, what function does the authentication service provide, and why is this function needed?

A: The authentication service defines the identity of the wireless device. Without this distinct identity, the device is not allowed access to the WLAN. Additionally, authentication can be made against a list of MACs allowed to use the network.

Q: What benefit would NFuse bring to my Citrix MetaFrame solution?

A: NFuse creates a portal to the MetaFrame server published applications over the Web by creating a customizable Web site that features only the applications that a particular user or group needs.

Building a Portal

Introduction

On the Internet, users prefer Web sites that are presented with some personalization. It is said that a person's favorite word is his or her own name. Therefore, Web sites that personalize the user experience are more likely to keep users coming back.

A variety of systems must be in place in order to personalize a site. First, the user must be identified. Second, the user must be authenticated. Finally, the user must be linked to personal data and presented with the results.

This chapter describes how to configure a portal using NFuse for providing information on the Internet to authenticated users. In addition, this chapter discusses Citrix XPS and the use of Extensible Markup Language (XML) to create Web services and use them in a portal solution.

Introducing Portals

A *portal* is a centralized point of access for users connecting to your site from the Internet. Think of a portal as a gateway or entry point into the Internet. The concept of portals has recently been brought to the forefront because of the fast growth of the information superhighway, the Internet.

The Internet is a large virtual "place" where information on almost anything is available on one Web site or another. The idea behind portals is to organize a visitor's particular interests in one virtual location, thereby attracting that visitor time and again to this Web site. The information that a portal can offer a visitor is almost infinite, ranging from news, sports, and stock quotes to Web-based e-mail and much more. The idea is to centralize and personalize the surfer's virtual experience and keep him or her coming back to this portal. More visitors means more traffic, and more traffic means more money; the more surfers your portal can attract, the easier you can sell advertising on your site. Two types of portals exist:

- **Public portals** These include commercial portals that offer a wide variety of free or fee-based services. Free services portals include those that offer customized and personalized information such as news and stock quotes. Fee-based services include application leasing, whereby you can use a certain application—Microsoft Word, for example—for a fee. The service buyer logs in to the portal and launches the application to use it; when the user is done, she closes the application. This is helpful when an application is expensive to buy and you only need to use it for a certain project.

- **Private portals** Often known as *virtual offices,* companies offer their employees Web-based access to company information, their own personal files, and access to run familiar office applications through these portals. Corporate portals become a mobile virtual office whereby an employee has the ability and the tools to make important business decisions, no matter where he or she might be. All they need is an Internet connection and a Web browser.

A common denominator with almost all portals is personalization. All portals personalize a user's Web pages and deliver only the content the user needs. A great example of a public free portal is My Yahoo!, which allows a user to customize the type of content that is displayed and how it is presented on the user's own dynamically created Web page. Refer to Figure 14.1 for an example of my personal Yahoo! portal.

The great thing about portals is that they are dynamic and constantly changing, so you're not the one changing the information. For example, take a closer look at My Yahoo!. When Reuters updates its news, My Yahoo! Is automatically updated because it links to Reuters to get its news information. The same thing goes for sports and stock quotes. Almost every section of the portal is linked to another Web site from which it gets its data. Portals like My Yahoo! aim to create a sense of the enormous virtual community. It goes without saying that when you sign on to the Internet, you start at the portal. There you check your e-mail, read Reuters news, check the sports from ESPN, and make sure your stock prices are going up with CNNfn, for example. After checking all of that, you move on to doing your business. For a consumer, it's as much a daily eye-opener as having a cup of coffee with your newspaper of choice in the morning before you start your day.

Figure 14.1 My Yahoo! Personalized Portal

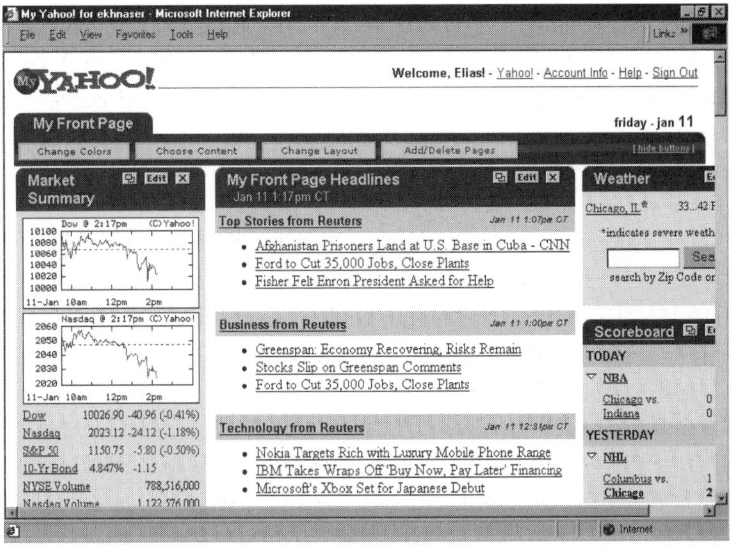

How can you use a portal in your organization? A private portal comes into play and becomes a necessity for your organization when you have several databases that your employees access. For example, say that you have a database that stores employee information, salary information, information on days off, and other similar data. This database can be accessed at employees.mycompany.com. You might offer Web mail access as well through another Web page, at webmail.mycompany.com. You might have a third page for NFuse, located at nfuse.mycompany.com. In this scenario, you have three different Web sites that employees have to remember and access to acquire information or applications they need to complete their work. A portal centralizes these three databases, so your users need to access only myportal.mycompany.com, for example—one login, one set of credentials to remember. What they will find inside is three sections of the Web page, each dedicated to one of these databases. One section will tell users how many days off they have and salary information. Another section will offer them access to their Web mail. A third section displays their NFuse applications or "Webified" applications. Many more sections may be added to the portal, such as corporate news and stock quotes.

This is a small example. Most companies have more than three databases or three Web pages that employees need to access. At some point, it becomes inconvenient and time consuming for users to keep accessing different pages to get the information they need. This is where portals come into play; they centralize all these databases and sites and allow users to personalize and customize what they see, making the portal a one-stop Web page for everything they need to do, no matter where they are. On a single page, you can see your e-mail inbox, you can see your published applications and other specific information.

For example, an employee opens his Web browser, types **myportal.mycompany .com**, authenticates his identity by providing his username and password, and is greeted by name and sees a page displayed with his personalized content. A sample portal is shown in Figure 14.2.

Citrix NFuse Application Portal

Citrix NFuse application portal software extends MetaFrame's power and functions into the virtual workplace by "Webifying" applications already installed on the MetaFrame server. NFuse is a three-tiered solution that includes a Citrix server, a supported Web server, and an ICA-enabled client device using a supported Web browser. NFuse utilizes published applications to the fullest and takes them to the next level by making any published application available and accessible via the Web. An application such as Microsoft Word can be launched and used from a Web browser without sacrificing any features and without writing a single line of code. The application runs, fully featured, without any modification or feature depletion.

In addition to Webifying any application that can be installed on Terminal Server, NFuse enables you to publish a desktop, giving your users the same feel and look as though they were sitting at their workstations at work. When users connect to your NFuse Web page, they are prompted to log in and, based on their credentials, a dynamic Web page is instantly created for them, giving them access to their familiar Windows, UNIX, and Java applications. NFuse supports Microsoft Active Directory Authentication and Novell Directory Services (NDS), making user authentication simple. Users can use their Microsoft Windows or Novell NDS credentials, eliminating the need to log in twice.

Figure 14.2 A Personalized Portal with Published Applications

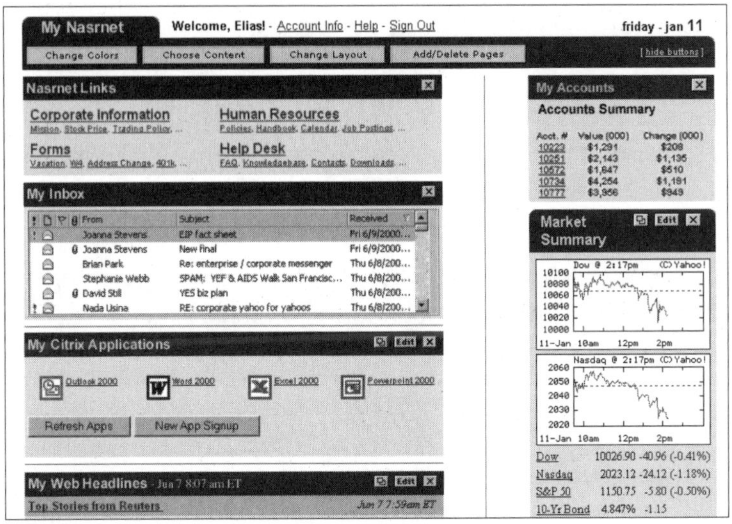

Personalizing Data Presentation

The key feature that portals build on to sell or offer their services is personalizing data presentation. Portals usually have business relationships with other Web sites and offer their information in the portal. For example, a portal could have an agreement with CNN that all portal news will be fetched from CNN. Another agreement might be with ESPN with regard to sports, the *Wall Street Journal* for stock quotes, and so on. These categories are then offered to the user. Portals are usually divided into sections, and the user is given the freedom to choose which section is placed where on his or her personalized page. For example, the user may choose to place his news in the top-left corner and the sports section in the lower-left corner, with stock quotes in the middle. The user is also given the freedom to customize the color scheme within the portal. All of this is done from a Web interface.

Citrix NFuse in turn offers some user personalization by allowing you to customize the NFuse Web page color settings from 16 colors to True Color 24 bit, as well as the way an application is launched (seamless, full screen), audio and encryption mappings, and the way applications are displayed in the portal (with or without icons, text, or description) The NFuse Web page is also a great way to make important system announcements, such as whether the Exchange mail server or the Lotus Notes server is down and for how long. It is a great way to provide technical support for users who are away from the office or working at a late hour, when tech support is not available.

You can enable your users to have control over certain settings within the NFuse Web page by making the following modifications to the Nfuse.conf file found in %SYSTEMROOT%\java\trustlib\NFuse.conf (see Figure 14.3):

- **AllowCustomizeWinSize=On** A value of ON here makes the Window Size drop-down menu visible in order to allow the user to customize the window size in which an application is launched.

- **AllowCustomizeWinColor=On** A value of ON here makes the Window Color drop-down menu visible in order to allow the user to change the color settings.

- **AllowCustomizeAudio=Off** A value of ON here makes the Client Audio drop-down menu visible in the Settings window. A Value of OFF completely disables and removes the drop-down menu from the Settings window.

- **AllowCustomizeEncryption=Off** A value of On here allows the user to view the Encryption drop-down menu in the Settings window. A value of OFF completely hides this section.

- **AllowCustomizeSettings=On** This parameter controls all the others. If a value of OFF is set here, nobody will be able to get access to the Settings window to make any modifications. If a value of ON is set, users can modify the settings through the Tools icon in the NFuse application list window.

Figure 14.3 The Settings Window with Audio and Encryption Disabled

It is a good idea to give your users some control over some of these settings, such as window size. Some users might like to have the application launch in full screen, whereas others might prefer to have the application launch in seamless mode. As an administrator, you really shouldn't care which is their preferred method, as long as the users are happy and comfortable with the settings. The same goes for the ability to change colors. The only two settings over which we recommend you *do not* give any control to users are the audio and encryption settings. Audio settings should be off-limits because you might have bandwidth considerations of which the user is unaware, and audio settings have an effect on performance, so you should always be the one to control them. Encryption settings should always be in compliance with your security policies; therefore, they should be locked down as well. Encryption settings should always conform with the specific encryption level you specify.

By clicking the **Settings** icon (see Figure 14.4), your users can modify the following settings:

- **Remember Folder Location** If this option is selected, the system will "remember" the default folder location for the user currently logged in. For example, if a user previously logged in and launched an application for a certain folder, the next time that user logs in, the system will default her back to that location, saving her the extra step of actually double-clicking or browsing down through the folders to get to the application she intends to launch.

- **Application Detail Display** This option allows the user to select whether he wants to enable icons, names, and descriptions. The selections the user makes here are reflected in the application display. Selecting the Icon check box, for example, displays an icon next to the application; checking the Name box displays the application's name; finally, checking the Description box displays the description you specified for this application. All the settings are the ones you set when you published the application in the Citrix Management Console. Whatever icon you specified for that application, the CMC will show up next to the application here. The same goes for name and description—whatever you specified in the CMC is reflected here.

- **Window Size** This setting controls how the applications are launched—seamless window, full screen, or other settings. When users log in to NFuse, they are presented with their customized list of applications. When a user clicks an application, it will launch based on the settings entered here.

- **Window Color** This option specifies colors. The options available are 16 colors, 256 colors, high-color 16 bit, and True Color 24 bit. When applications are launched, the depth of colors applied is taken from the settings the user specifies here. The more graphic-intensive the application, the higher the color scheme the user can set for it.

- **Client Audio Setting** This option defines audio settings. The choices are off, low quality, medium quality, or high quality. This setting controls the quality of the sound that the user hears. The higher the sound quality, the more bandwidth it consumes.

- **Encryption** This setting defines encryption levels. The options are basic, 128-bit SecureICA for login, 40-bit SecureICA, 56-bit SecureICA, 128-bit SecureICA, or SSL.

Figure 14.4 The Settings Window

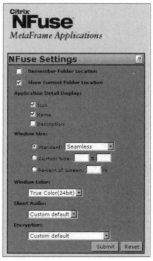

Managing Portals from a Single Point

Managing the portal content and browser appearance depends on the tools your programmers have created for you to manage the portal. Most portal deployment software has Web management interfaces that enable you to manage the portal. Citrix XPS, for example, offers the Portal Management Console (PMC). The PMC allows you to install, configure, and manage the portal from a single location. Yahoo! Portal Builder 3.0 also provides a Web interface to manage the entire portal.

Managing an NFuse application portal is done through the CMC and the NFuse.conf file. Applications are managed through the CMC, and configuration is done through the NFuse.conf file. When you modify your application settings within the CMC, the changes are immediately reflected in NFuse. There is no need to make any additional modifications to your applications. Here lies the beauty and power of NFuse. Any changes you make to your applications within the Citrix farm are reflected in

NFuse seamlessly, without any additional steps or tasks. The NFuse.conf file also presents administrators with a central location to configure important NFuse settings. To manage the applications in the portal:

1. Open the **CMC**.

2. On the left menu pane, expand the **Applications** node. Right-click the application you want to manage and click **Properties**. A window appears where you can make changes to the application.

You can select the **Servers** tab and choose additional servers that support this application, thereby load-balancing the application. You can choose the users who can access the application by selecting the **Users** tab and adding the users or groups. NFuse checks to see which users or groups have rights to this application and then creates the dynamic page with the appropriate applications on it. This step is imperative, because this is how you tell NFuse which applications to provide to which users. As we said, managing an application in NFuse is the same as managing an application in the server farm. The process is the same, and any modifications made in the CMC for the farm are automatically and instantly reflected in NFuse. (Refer to Chapters 2 and 9 of this book for more information on how to manage applications in the server farm.)

Building a Portal with NFuse

Building the NFuse application portal is a straightforward process. You can get the portal up and running with the Citrix defaults in minutes. The customization might take extra time. The beauty of NFuse is that you can Webify all the applications you want—whether Windows, UNIX, Java, or maybe a mixture of them all—without writing a single line of code. However, you need to familiarize yourself with some important concepts prior to building the NFuse portal. NFuse relies on Citrix's Application Launching and Embedding (ALE) technology plus Citrix Program Neighborhood. Let's define these two concepts.

NFuse Webified applications have two methods of running; they are either launched in a separate window or embedded in a Web browser window, where the application runs as part of a Web browser window. This technology is known as *Application Launching and Embedding* (ALE). For this technology to work, an ActiveX control is needed for users of Internet Explorer, a plug-in for Netscape Navigator, or a Java applet for any Java-enabled device. The two components of ALE are as follows:

- **Application launching** Application launching occurs when you access a portal and click the desired application, which launches in a totally separate and new window that is not tied in any way to the Web browser window used to launch the application. As soon as the application launches in the separate window, you can close all the other windows without affecting the launched application.

- **Application embedding** In application embedding, you access the portal and click the desired application that is embedded in the Web browser, and the application becomes part of the browser window. The application runs inside a box in the Web browser window, so closing that window closes the application.

You might be faced with a situation where users of both launched and embedded applications get into the habit of using the *X* in the top-right corner to close their application or Web browser window. This method of logging off doesn't really log them off; rather, it disconnects their session. A disconnected session still consumes a good deal of server resources; for this reason, you should always instruct your users on the proper way of logging off. You have several options: configuring a timeout setting or setting a timeout limit on disconnected sessions.

You can configure a timeout setting in the Citrix Connection Configuration tool that will clear a disconnected session from the server after a certain period of time. To accomplish this task, follow these steps:

1. Click **Start | Programs | Citrix | MetaFrame XP | Citrix Connection Configuration**.

2. Double-click the ICA protocol and click the **Advanced** button.

3. At the very bottom of the screen, uncheck the **On a broken or timed-out connection** check box and select **reset** from the drop-down menu. See Figure 14.5.

Figure 14.5 The Advanced Connection Settings Window

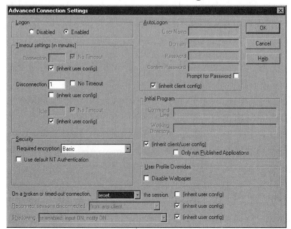

As soon as a disconnected session occurs, this setting resets the connection immediately, thereby clearing the server form disconnected sessions and freeing the resources that session holds up on the server.

Another option is to set a timeout limit on disconnected sessions. Here you allow a disconnected session to remain on the server for a certain amount of time. The idea behind disconnected sessions is, if the user needs to log off for a half hour, for example, but doesn't want to log off the server yet, the user can disconnect the session for a short period of time and then reconnect when he is ready to work again. A disconnected session doesn't consume as many resources as a fully connected session; however, because most users don't know how to use this feature or don't even know it exists, they disconnect their sessions but they usually really mean to log off. In environments where you have a mixture of experienced and inexperienced users and you can't completely use the function we just discussed, you can set a timeout feature by doing the following:

1. Click **Start | Programs | Citrix | MetaFrame XP | Citrix Connection Configuration**.

2. Double-click the ICA protocol and click the **Advanced** button.

3. Uncheck the second **inherit user config** box in the Timeout settings (in minutes) section.

4. Uncheck the **No Timeout** check box. See Figure 14.5.

5. Enter a value in minutes for when a session that is in disconnect status should be reset or logged off.

Citrix *Program Neighborhood* allows client PCs to access Citrix MetaFrame servers over the network and connect to application sets. You can publish applications and assign them to users without modifying each user's desktop. The newly published applications will appear the next time the Program Neighborhood window refreshes. Program Neighborhood is available only to Windows 32-bit, Java, and Web clients. All other clients must use the pass-through feature to be able to access Program Neighborhood features and functions.

Building a fully functional NFuse application portal requires the installation and configuration of the following:

- A Citrix MetaFrame XP server
- A supported Web server
- Customizing NFuse using the NFuse.conf file
- Customizing the Web page look

Citrix MetaFrame XP Server

NFuse needs to query a Citrix MetaFrame XP server that is member of a farm for application set information. All the applications you intend to offer through the NFuse portal should already be installed, published, and configured using the Citrix Management Console. NFuse simply queries that server for all its published applications, automatically Webifies them, and makes them available for access in the portal. For information on how to install, configure, and publish applications using the CMC, refer to Chapters 8 and 9 of this book.

A Supported Web Server

You can use NFuse on the following Windows/Web server combinations:

- Internet Information Server 4.0 on Windows NT 4.0 Server and Windows NT 4.0 Server, Terminal Server Edition
- Internet Information Server 5.0 on the Windows 2000 Server family

You can use NFuse on the following UNIX Web server/operating system/ servlet engine/JDK combinations shown in Table 14.1

Table 14.1 Supported UNIX Web Servers

Web Server	Operating System
Apache 1.3.20	Red Hat 6.2
	Red Hat 7.1
	Solaris 7
	Solaris 8
iPlanet 4.1	Solaris 7
	Solaris 8
Tomcat 3.2.2	Red Hat 6.2
	Red Hat 7.1
	Solaris 7
	Solaris 8
IBM HTTP 1.3.12.2	Solaris 7
	Solaris 8

NOTE

We strongly recommend that you dedicate a separate server to act as your IIS Web server. Installing IIS on a MetaFrame XP server consumes a great deal of valuable server resources.

Installing the Web Server Extensions on the Internet Information Server

The server you decide to dedicate as your Web server or the server you intend to use as your Web server needs to have Web Server Extensions installed on it. This server may be a Windows server or a UNIX server. Web Server Extensions install all the files needed to run NFuse properly. To install the Web Server Extensions on a Windows 2000 IIS 5.0 Web server, follow these steps:

1. Log in as **Administrator** or an account with administrative rights.

2. Browse to and double-click the file **NFuseWebExtSetup-IIS.exe**. The Web Server Extensions can be downloaded for free from the Citrix Web site at www.citrix.com/download/.

3. A wizard will guide you through the installation.

4. You will be prompted to enter the name of a Citrix MetaFrame XP server on which the XML service is running and to specify the port it is running on. To find out the port number on MetaFrame XP servers, right-click the server name in the CMC and select **Properties**. Select the **MetaFrame Settings** tab to view the port being used, as shown in Figure 14.6.

Figure 14.6 The XML Server That Will Provide Published Applications

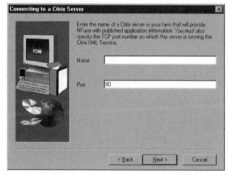

NOTE

The XML service works as a contact point between NFuse and the Citrix servers. The XML service provides published application information to ICA clients and NFuse via TCP/IP. We recommend that you install the service on all Citrix servers in the farm and configure NFuse to have more than one Citrix server to contact for redundancy.

Configuring & Implementing...

IIS Port Sharing Can Cause an NFuse Error

If you intend to install NFuse on a system that already has Internet Information Server 5.0 (IIS) and Citrix MetaFrame XP on the same machine, you could experience problems when you upgrade to MetaFrame XP SP1/FR1. NFuse users might receive the following error when they launch published applications:

```
Error: Citrix XML service or Program Neighborhood service may be
down or temporarily overloaded. [503 temporarily overloaded].
```

To resolve this issue, follow these steps:

1. Copy the file **wpnbr.dll** from the directory \InetPub\Scripts\ to the %SYSTEMROOT%\system32\, replacing the file in this directory. (If you receive a sharing violation error while copying the file, restart the computer and try again.)

2. Make sure that the file you are copying has a timestamp of **August 9, 2001**.

3. Stop and start the **IMA service**.

For more information, consult Citrix Document ID: CTX200573; you'll find it by visiting the Citrix Knowledge Base at knowledgebase.citrix.com.

Customizing NFuse Using the NFuse.conf File

NFuse 1.6 has eliminated the use of the famous Web Site Wizard that accompanied previous versions to configure and customize NFuse. Instead, NFuse 1.6 has centralized the configuration into a single file, NFuse.conf, which is located in %SYSTEMROOT%\ java\trustlib\NFuse.conf. Here we demonstrate some of the functionality that can be accomplished by editing the NFuse.conf file.

Configuring Multiple XML Servers

As we mentioned earlier in this chapter, NFuse needs to query a Citrix server that is running the XML service in order to return an application set that it can display on the portal Web page. When you're installing NFuse, you are prompted to provide the name of a Citrix server and the port number where the XML service is configured to run. What if that server that you configured during setup goes down for any reason? At this point you have no redundancy—no additional servers that might fill this role and keep the portal up. The result is that NFuse will be unable to return an application set, and therefore users will be unable to work.

To prevent this situation, you can configure NFuse to query additional MetaFrame XP servers in the farm. In the event that the initially specified server goes down, NFuse queries the second server assigned to this role. To accomplish this configuration, you can add redundant servers by extending the following parameters in the NFuse.conf file (see Figure 14.7):

- **SessionField.NFuse_CitrixServer=** You can add servers NFuse can query for application set information in this parameter. Separate your server names with commas.

- **SessionField.NFuse_CitrixServerPort=** The default port number for the XML service is 80, unless you have changed it. The value of 80 should be fine. However, in the event that the XML service port number is different between servers—for example, if one server is running the XML service on the default port 80 and the other server is running the XML service on port 8080—here is where you can specify these ports. Again, separate the ports with commas.

Figure 14.7 Configuring Additional Servers That NFuse Can Query for Applications

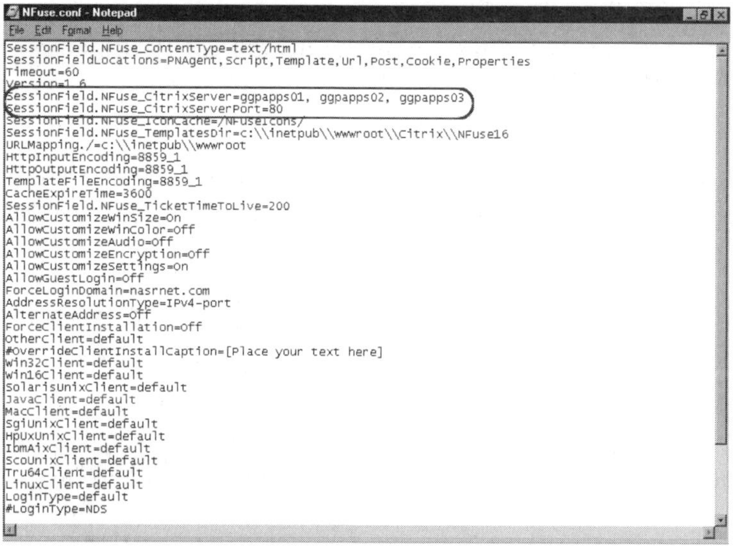

Guest Login

You can enable guest logins by editing the NFuse.conf file and changing the value of the following parameter to ON:

- **AllowGuestLogin=on** Changing this value to ON causes NFuse to display a Guest User option to appear on the NFuse login page, as shown in Figure 14.8.

Figure 14.8 Guest Login

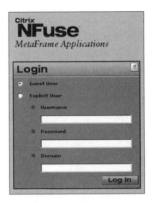

Guest users use one of the 15 AnonXXX (anonymous) user accounts that MetaFrame XP installs on the local server during setup. Guest users can run only published applications that have been enabled for anonymous user connections. To enable an application for anonymous user connections, follow these steps:

1. Log in to the **CMC**.

2. Expand the **Applications** node in the left pane.

3. Right-click the desired application and click **Properties**.

4. Select the **Users** tab and check the **Allow Anonymous Connections** check box. See Figure 14.9.

Figure 14.9 The Users Tab in Application Properties

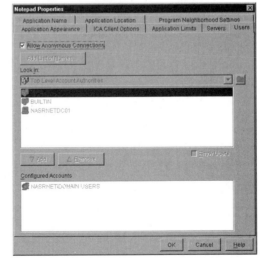

> **NOTE**
>
> If you set the AllowGuestLogin parameter to ONLY, you disable the Login/Logout feature on the portal whereby any anonymous user that accesses the portal will be taken immediately to the application set. Enabling this feature disables any kind of logins to the portal, so anyone can launch the applications.

Specifying a Default Domain

Forcing a default domain has always been a favorite value, because it eliminates another step for users to remember. It also spares an administrator or the helpdesk the torture of explaining it or reminding users that they need to enter it. To specify a default domain, edit the NFuse.conf file and change the value of the following parameter to reflect your domain name:

- **ForceLoginDomain=mydomain.com**   If the value is set, the users are not prompted to enter the domain name. If value is left blank, Active Directory users have to log in using their user principal names (user@domain.com). Specifying a domain name causes NFuse to react as illustrated in Figure 14.10.

Figure 14.10 Domain Set by Default in NFuse.conf

> **NOTE**
>
> If you have users authenticating to different domains, this parameter should never be set. It should remain blank so that a user can specify to which domain he or she is authenticating.

> **NOTE**
>
> An important thing to remember is that after making any changes to the NFuse.conf file, you have to stop and restart the IIS Admin Service in Windows before the changes take effect.

Customizing the Web Page Look

After you successfully install the Web Server Extensions, a directory is created in \Intepub\wwwroot\citrix\nfuse16 that contains the NFuse Active Server Pages (ASP) files. An ASP programmer should have no problem working with the existing ASP pages and modifying them to meet company guidelines and appearance.

For the hardcore programmers who simply want to build the pages from scratch and then apply the NFuse code to them, they can refer to the "Customizing NFuse" PDF documentation available on the NFuse CD. In that document you will find all the tags and parameters needed to add the NFuse code.

Providing Windows Applications in the Portal

To provide for Windows applications in the portal, you need to first properly install the application on all Terminal Servers that will be supporting it. After you install the application, you need to publish it. The following steps guide you through the process of publishing an application:

1. Log on to a Citrix MetaFrame XP server as **Administrator**.

2. Open the **CMC**.

3. On the left menu pane, right-click **Applications** and then select **Publish Application**.

4. A wizard will guide you through the process of publishing the application.

To publish the desktop, follow the same steps. As soon as the wizard launches, it prompts you for a name and description. Enter, for example, **Desktop** for name and describe it, for example, as **Company desktop**. Click **Next**. The second window allows you to select between publishing an application or publishing the desktop, as shown in Figure 14.11. Select **Desktop** and click **Next** and follow the wizard. For more information on how to publish applications or a desktop, refer to Chapter 9 of this book.

Figure 14.11 The Publish Application Desktop Window

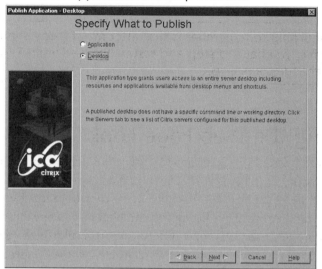

Providing UNIX and Java Applications in the Portal

To provide UNIX applications in the portal, you need to install the application on the server or servers that will support it. After you install the application, you need to publish it. The following steps guide you through the process of publishing an application on the UNIX OS:

1. Log on to a Citrix MetaFrame server for UNIX as a Citrix **Administrator**.

2. At the command prompt, type **ctxappscfg**. The following prompt will appear: **App Config**.

3. At the App Config prompt, type **add**. You need to provide the following information:

    -   **Name** The name of the published application.

    -   **Command Line** The command line required to run the application.

    -   **Working Directory** The default working directory.

    -   **Anonymous [yes | no]** Entering **y** configures the application for anonymous users. Entering **n** configures the application for explicit users.

5. At the App Config prompt, type **exit**.

To publish the desktop, follow the same steps, except keep the command-line value blank, thereby specifying that you are publishing a desktop.

> **NOTE**
>
> The XML service needs to be installed and enabled for the published applica-
> tions to appear in NFuse. The option to install version 1.6 of the Citrix XML ser-
> vice is available when you install Feature Release 1 for MetaFrame for UNIX.

Using SSL Encryption

Secure Socket Layer (SSL) was originally developed by Netscape. SSL has become a standard accepted worldwide for authenticating and encrypting communications on the Web
between clients and servers. SSL runs on top of TCP/IP, which is used by higher-level
protocols such as HTTP or FTP to route and transport data on the Internet. SSL allows
the client to identify the server as trustworthy by verifying that its certificate and public
key were issued by a certificate authority (CA) listed in the client's list of trusted CAs.

You can use SSL with NFuse 1.6 to make sure that your data is exchanged in a
totally secure environment between your client device and the servers you interact
with. You need to secure the following three lines of communication:

- Communication between the client device and the NFuse Web server

- Communication between the NFuse Web server and the Citrix server

- Communication between the client device and the Citrix server

Securing Communication Between the
Client Device and the NFuse Web Server

NFuse uses a Web browser to interact with the Web server, prompting administrators to
secure this line of communication, given that critical data is exchanged insecurely
through this channel. NFuse submits a user's username to the Web server as cleartext
and uses basic encryption to secure the user's password and domain name. This poses a
security concern that warrants the implementation of SSL to provide tighter security.
To use SSL, you need to use a Web server and Web browser that support SSL. You must
obtain a server certificate from a CA.

The CA verifies who you are to the client. It basically tells the client that you are
who you say you are and thus can be trusted. You can go to companies such as VeriSign
or Baltimore to obtain certificates that your browser will accept as trusted. You can also
issue your own certificates; however, the disadvantage of issuing your own certificates is
that you would have to train your users to accept the certificate, whereas certificates
from the mentioned companies are trusted and are installed by default in users'
browsers. If you issue your own certificates, your users will get a message that your

certificate is not trusted, which usually scares users unless they are properly instructed and notified. For more information about this topic, refer to the book *Configuring Windows 2000 Server Security* (ISBN 1-928994-02-4) from Syngress Publishing.

Securing Communication Between the NFuse Web Server and the Citrix Server

NFuse uses a Java object to pass the user's credentials to the Citrix MetaFrame server's XML service and return application set information to the NFuse Web server, therefore warranting secure communication. Citrix SSL Relay must be installed in order to implement SSL between the NFuse Web server and the Citrix server. Citrix SSL Relay secures communications among ICA clients, NFuse Web servers, and Citrix MetaFrame XP servers. By default, Citrix SSL Relay listens on port 443. To configure SSL Relay, do the following:

1. Obtain a server certificate from a CA.

2. Install the SSL certificate on the SSL Relay server.

3. Configure NFuse to use SSL.

Obtain a Server Certificate from a Certificate Authority

There are two ways of obtaining a server certificate. You can either buy one from a commercial CA such as VeriSign Inc. or Baltimore Technologies, or you can issue your own server certificate by installing, for example, Microsoft certificate services. The advantage of buying a commercial server certificate is that NFuse and the ICA clients have built-in support for server certificates issued by VeriSign and Baltimore. If you issue your own certificate, it will be equally safe, but you will have to endure the burden of installing the root certificate to your client devices.

Install the SSL Certificate on the SSL Relay Server

SSL Relay requires certificates to be in Personal Electronic Mail (PEM) format. Do the following:

1. Copy the file to the **\certs** subdirectory of the keystore directory (%SystemRoot%\sslrelay\keystore, by default).

2. Choose **Start | Programs | Citrix | MetaFrame XP | Citrix SSL Relay Configuration Tool**.

3. On the **Relay Credentials** tab, select your server certificate from the **Server Certificate** list and enter the certificate password in the **Password** box.

4. Click **OK** to save changes and close the Citrix SSL Relay Configuration tool.

If your certificate is in Microsoft Internet Information Server (IIS) version 4 or 5 format, you need to export the certificate and then convert it to PEM. To export a Microsoft Internet Information Server certificate, follow these steps:

1. To run the Microsoft Management Console (MMC), click **Start | Run**, type **mmc**, and then click **OK**.

2. Click the **Console menu** and then choose **Add/Remove Snap-in**.

3. Click **Add**.

4. Select **Certificates** and click **Add**. The Certificates snap-in dialog box appears.

5. Click **Computer account** and then click **Next**. The Select Computer dialog box appears.

6. Verify that **Local computer** is selected and then click **Finish**.

7. Click **Close** to close the Add Standalone Snap-in dialog box.

8. Click **OK** to close the Add/Remove Snap-in dialog box.

9. In the left menu pane of the console, click the **plus sign** for **Certificates (Local Computer)** to expand the folder.

10. In the left menu pane of the console, click the **plus sign** for **Personal** and then click **Certificates**.

11. In the right menu pane of the console, right-click the certificate to export, and then select **All Tasks | Export | Certificate Export Wizard**.

To convert a Microsoft Internet Information Server Key Storage file or personal information exchange (.pfx) protocol file to PEM format, use the Citrix keytopem utility. At a command prompt, switch to the %SystemRoot%\sslrelay\ directory and type **keytopem input-file output-file**. *Input-file* represents the file exported from IIS; *output-file* represents the file that you are creating. Make sure the file is in .PEM format.

Configure NFuse to Use SSL

You need to add the following parameters and their corresponding values in the NFuse.conf file:

■ **SessionField.NFuse_RelayServer=citrix.companu.com** Enter the name of a MetaFrame XP server running SSL Relay.

■ **SessionField.NFuse_RelayServerPort=443** Make sure the value here matches the port number of the SSL Relay server specified in **SessionField.NFuse_RelayServer**.

- **SessionField.NFuse_Transport=SSL**

- **SslKeystore=C:\\WINNT\\keystore\\cacerts**

Communication Between the Client Device and the Citrix Server

Citrix recommends that you use SSL or SecureICA encryption to secure a line of communication between the ICA client devices and the Citrix servers. SSL and SecureICA support 128-bit encryption; however, one advantage SSL has over SecureICA is that SSL verifies the identification of the MetaFrame XP servers. Feature Release 1 for both MetaFrame XP and MetaFrame for UNIX has support for SecureICA. A different ICA client is required if you use SecureICA.

Synchronizing Application Status

Citrix has recently introduced the ICA Win32 Program Neighborhood Agent, which is a client that works with NFuse 1.6 to provide application links not only to Web pages but also to win32 desktops. The applications can be deployed on the desktop, in the Start menu, or in the Windows system tray. The applications appear as though they were installed locally, and the experience is virtually seamless to the user. Use this type of client in environments where you are deploying NFuse 1.6 but are not allowing your users access to a Web browser. To configure or change the defaults of your ICA Win32 Program Neighborhood Agent, you need to edit the Config.xml file located in the \Inetpub\wwwroot\Citrix\PNAgent directory on the NFuse Web server. Table 14.2 displays the parameters that can be edited or added to the Config.xml file.

Table 14.2 Parameters in the Config.xml File

Parameter	Default Value	Description
FolderDisplay/StartMenuDisplay/ RootFolder	true	Adds links to applications in user's Start menu.
FolderDisplay/StartMenuDisplay/ RootFolder	programs	Specifies the name of the folder to group the application links into on the Start menu.
FolderDisplay/DesktopDisplay/ Enabled	false	Specifies the name of the folder to group applications into on the desktop.
FolderDisplay/DesktopDisplay/ Icon/Name	Citrix Program Neighborhood	The name of the folder on the Windows desktop.

Continued

Table 14.2 Continued

Parameter	Default Value	Description
FolderDisplay/ SystemTrayMenuDisplay/Enabled	true	Displays published applications in the Program Neighborhood Agent system tray.
ConfigurationFile/Location	http://servername/ Citrix/PNAgent/ config.xml	URL to get configuration information.
Request/Enumeration/Refresh/ OnApplicationStart	true	Refreshes published application data when Program Neighborhood Agent is run.
Request/Enumeration/Refresh/ OnResourceRequest	false	Refreshes published application data when a published application is run.
Request/Enumeration/Refresh/ Poll/Enabled	true	Refreshes enumeration on a timed interval.
Request/Enumeration/Refresh/ Poll/Period	6	If Request/Enumeration/ Refresh/Poll/Enabled is true, this parameter specifies the interval, in hours, at which published application data is refreshed.

Synchronizing an application's status across the farm is easily done with Citrix MetaFrame XP. If you wanted to take an application down for maintenance or upgrade, assuming this application is supported by more than one server, you can disable that application and run the maintenance or upgrade required and then reenable it. To accomplish this goal, follow these steps:

1. Open the **CMC**.

2. Expand **Applications**.

3. Right-click the application you intend to run maintenance on and click **Properties**.

4. On the **Application Name** tab, you are given the option to disable the application. See Figure 14.12. You can check the status of the application you have just disabled on the servers by expanding **Servers** in the left menu pane of the CMC, right-clicking the name of the server you want to check, and clicking **Properties**. Select the **Published Applications** tab (see Figure 14.13). A window opens that lists all the published applications and their current status. You should see Disabled for the application we just brought offline.

Figure 14.12 The Application Name Tab

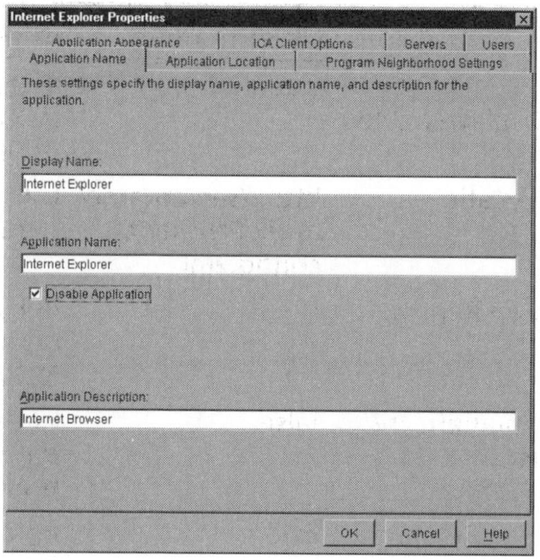

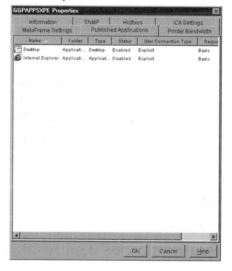

Figure 14.13 The Server Properties Window

Using Authentication in a Portal

Authentication has been greatly improved with the introduction of NFuse 1.6. Novell users, for example, can now log in to Citrix MetaFrame XP servers via NFuse using their Novell Directory Services (NDS) credentials, eliminating the need to authenticate twice. NFuse also supports Microsoft Active Directory authentication, which is the default authentication method.

Active Directory

Microsoft Active Directory is the default method of authentication in NFuse. The following parameters in NFuse.conf relate to Active Directory authentication:

- **LoginType=default** Tells NFuse that you will be using Active Directory authentication.

- **ForceLoginDomain=** As we stated earlier in the chapter, entering a value for this parameter automatically authenticates users to the specified domain. This saves the user the extra step of entering a domain name and saves you a phone call from users asking what their domain is. This is a good parameter to set when all your users are members of the same domain. This feature should *not* be used, however, when you have users authenticating to multiple domains.

- **AllowGuestLogin=** This parameter was discussed in detail in the "Configuring NFuse Using the NFuse.conf File" section earlier in this chapter.

Novell Directory Services

To use NDS authentication in NFuse, you need to change the values of three parameters in NFuse.conf. These parameters are:

- **LoginType=NDS** Tells NFuse to use Novell for authentication.

- **NDSTreeName=** If LoginType is set to NDS, you need to specify an NDS tree name.

- **SearchContextList=** You will want to make the appropriate changes here as well to accommodate Context.

Configuring & Implementing...

Deploying an ICA Web Client via the NFuse Portal

Part of configuring the NFuse environment is working out a way to deploy ICA clients to users who don't have NFuse installed. An excellent way of doing that is to use the NFuse Web portal to push an ICA Web client version to the connecting users. As soon as your users browse to the NFuse Web page, the page detects whether or not they have the Web client. If they do, the page doesn't prompt them to install it. If they don't have the client, the page prompts them

Continued

to install it. To configure the portal to push the ICA Web client to the user base, follow these steps:

1. Obtain the latest copy of the ICA Web client from www.citrix.com/download.

2. Copy the **Wficat.cab** file to the \InetPub\wwwroot\ directory.

3. Copy the following HTML code into the body of the main HTML page, usually default.asp or Blank.htm:

```
<OBJECT classid="clsid:238f6f83-b8b4-11cf-8771-00a024541ee3"

CODEBASE="/wficat.cab#Version=6,1,963,0"

width=0 height=0><BR>

</OBJECT>
```

For more information, visit www.thethin.net.

Making these changes in the NFuse.conf file results in NFuse switching authentication to Novell NDS, as shown in Figure 14.14.

Figure 14.14 NDS Authentication

Customizing NFuse with Project Columbia

Project Columbia version 6.36 for NFuse 1.6 is a Citrix technical support-customized NFuse Web page. It builds on the technology available with NFuse 1.6 and extends its features and functions to address common configuration issues. The features available with Project Columbia are customized Web scripts that are not available with the standard installation of NFuse 1.6.

Some of the features included with Project Columbia version 6.36 for NFuse 1.6 are the ability to:

- Query multiple server farms for published applications and merge them in one portal page.

- Choose from a menu of domains during logon.

- Use Port Address Translation to route users to more than one internal MetaFrame server through a single external IP address.

- Specify multiple servers running the XML service per server farm for fault tolerance and load balancing.

- Override the Web server's default server farm address.

- Allow users to change expired Windows NT 4 or Active Directory domain passwords.

- Use NAT to service internal and external users connecting from the same Web site.

- Use client-side SOCKS proxy servers to route ICA client sessions.

- Push the installation of ICA clients to Windows users who do not already have ICA clients installed.

- Hide applications or folders by name.

- Change the size and layout of icons.

To install and use Project Columbia, access www.citrix.com/cdn and follow these steps:

1. NFuse 1.6 should be installed and fully functioning prior to installing Project Columbia version 6.36.

2. Download the Project Columbia zip file to your Web server's hard drive.

3. Unzip the contents of the file into a directory under \Inetpub\wwwroot on the Web server.

4. Stop and start the IIS Web server.

5. Project Columbia is now installed.

After you install Project Columbia, take a closer look at how you can configure it. Project Columbia is configured from a single text file, Config.txt. This file contains all the configuration settings and parameters that control the behavior and functionality of Project Columbia. To configure this file, follow these steps:

1. Browse to the location where you copied the Columbia files on the Web server—for example: \Intepub\wwwroot\columbia.

2. Double-click the folder **Config** and open the file **Config.txt**, which looks like Figure 14.15.

Figure 14.15 The Config.txt File

3. Configure all your settings and refer to the help document available in the Config directory to help you configure the various sections of the file.

4. When you are done configuring, stop and start the IIS Web server for the changes to take effect.

Building a Redundant NFuse Portal

The Web server that hosts the NFuse application portal software is probably the weakest link or component in the entire network design, especially if your user base is completely reliant on NFuse to get access to published applications. The Citrix server farm in most cases has more than one server and can afford to lose a server for a few hours, maybe days, because other MetaFrame XP servers in the farm can continue to offer the published applications the user needs to get work done.

Consider a situation in which your user base is completely dependent on NFuse. In such a case, your users have no means of accessing any sort of published applications except through the NFuse portal; therefore, if the NFuse server goes down, production is brought to its knees. To avoid this undesirable situation, you should take the necessary steps to ensure that the NFuse portal is up and running at all times—what better way of doing this but to utilize the Network Load Balancing feature that comes built into Windows 2000 Advanced Server. The idea is to bind two or more servers together, creating a third *virtual* server. It is this virtual server that your user base accesses. This virtual server is supported by two or more actual servers, so if one server goes down, the other server keeps the virtual server running and offering services. See Figure 14.16.

Figure 14.16 Network Load Balancing an NFuse Portal

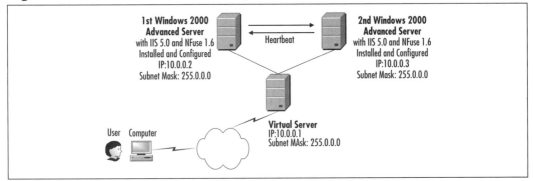

The servers supporting the virtual server use what is known as a *heartbeat* to continue telling each other they are up and functioning. When one server goes down, it stops responding to heartbeats. Within 5 seconds the other server acknowledges this fact and starts supporting the virtual server solely or divides the load among the other servers (if more than two servers were configured to support the virtual server).

To build this redundant system, make sure that you have the following requirements:

1. Two servers with Windows 2000 Advanced Server installed and configured as follows:

   ■ Make sure Internet Information Server 5.0 (IIS) is installed with the default options.

   ■ Make sure Terminal Services is installed. (Remote Administration mode is sufficient, since we will not be providing any applications.)

   ■ Make sure the local Users group has the Log on Locally right defined and configured in Group Policy.

2. Install Citrix NFuse Application Portal software with the default settings on both servers.

After meeting these requirements, you need to configure the Network Load Balancing properties. To do so, follow these steps:

1. Click **Start | Settings | Network and Dial-Up Connections**.

2. Right-click **Local Area Connection** and click **Properties**.

3. Check the **Network Load Balancing** check box and click **Properties**. See Figure 14.17.

Figure 14.17 Network Load Balancing Properties

4. Enter the IP address you have reserved for your virtual server in the Primary IP address field.

5. Enter a subnet mask in the appropriate field.

6. In the full Internet name box, enter the DNS name you want to give your cluster. Make sure this DNS name points to the IP address you gave the virtual server in Step 4.

7. Click the **Host Parameters** tab to obtain the screen shown in Figure 14.18.

Figure 14.18 The NLB Host Parameters Tab

8. The Priority section is used to set the unique host ID, which means every server that will actually participate in the network load-balancing process needs to be assigned a unique ID. The first server is ID 1, and then you can increment them by clicking the Up or Down Arrow keys.

9. The **Initial cluster state** check box is self-explanatory. If you check the box, the specified server is active in the load-balancing process.

10. The **Dedicated IP address** field is where you enter the same IP address as the one specified in the TCP/IP properties of the NIC.

11. Enter the appropriate subnet mask.

12. Click the **Port Rules** tab to get to the screen shown in Figure 14.19.

Figure 14.19 The NLB Port Rules Tab

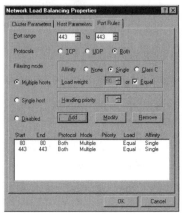

13. Set the Port range 80 to 80 for HTTP connections. You can also set an additional range of 443 to 443 for HTTPS SSL traffic.

14. The **Protocols** section should be set to **Both** to allow the previously configured port ranges to use TCP and UDP traffic.

15. In the **Affinity** section, select **Single** for optimal session state.

16. Make sure **Multiple Hosts** is selected in the **Filtering mode** section.

17. Click **OK**.

Repeat these steps on the second server with a slight modification in Steps 9 and 10. In Step 9, select a unique ID, and specify the proper IP address in Step 10.

Now that you have created the virtual server, you must direct users to it. The first thing you need to do is create a friendly name or address for the NFuse portal—for example, nfuse.mycompany.com—and point it to the virtual server's IP address. This is done in DNS by creating an alias. The alias would be nfuse.mycompany.com, with an

IP address of 10.0.0.1 in the example. When your users access this address, they are accessing the virtual server and will not even notice the difference in the event that any server goes down. The only time service will be interrupted is when there is a problem with the virtual server.

Designing & Planning…

Citrix XPS and NFuse Elite, Code-Named Project South Beach

Citrix XPS is an XML-based portal builder package that focuses on information and content delivery services. With the help of content delivery agents, Citrix XPS can plug into many Web sites and fetch information to be displayed in a specified section on the portal. You can plug into sites such as CNN or Reuters for the latest news, or you can plug into ESPN for the latest sports, E*trade for a market update, and so on.

User-level personalization can be achieved by allowing users to completely customize the portal. A graphical Theme Designer empowers your users with the ability to change the look and feel of the portal. The alternative to designing your own theme using the graphical Theme Designer is the availability of templates. XPS offers various templates that you can choose from to customize the way the Web page looks.

You can manage the entire portal using the Portal Management Console, or PMC, which centralizes all the administrative tasks into one control panel for the entire portal.

The next generation of Citrix XPS will be NFuse Elite, code-named Project South Beach. Project South Beach promises to integrate all the power and dynamics offered by NFuse application portal software and Citrix XPS's information and content delivery engine, creating a one-stop shop that will offer everything you need to get a portal up and running, including published applications. The product will offer all this without requiring you to write a single line of code. Project South Beach was still in beta testing when this book was written, but we do have a list of some of the features Citrix promises the product will include. *Content Delivery Agents* (CDAs) are Web-based applications that will be able to deliver internal and external content to the portal. CDAs will have the following features:

- Alert Broadcaster
- Database Viewer
- Embedded Citrix

Continued

- Independent Computing
- Architecture (ICA)
- Instant Messaging
- Interactive Poll
- Internal Search
- Internet E-mail
- Internet Search
- Message Center
- News Viewer
- Citrix NFuse
- Online Auctions
- Personnel Locator
- Shared Documents
- Shopping Center
- Stock Tracker
- Travel Planner
- Weather Snapshot
- Web Favorites
- Website Viewer
- World Clock
- All the features of an NFuse Application portal

Summary

Portals are intended to be a user's entry point into the endless virtual world of the Internet. Portals offer their visitors everything they can to keep users coming back. The building block of portals is user personalization. Portal creators try to personalize and give the user as much control over the layout, colors, and display of the information as possible, creating the feeling of a virtual community.

There are two types of portal. First, public or commercial portals offer free and fee-based services ranging from news and stock quotes to application leasing. Second, private portals, also known as virtual offices, offer employees access to corporate information and news, their files, and familiar office applications such as Word, Excel, and Outlook. Most portal software offers centralized management tools. NFuse, for example, utilizes the Citrix Management Console to manage a portal.

NFuse uses a file called NFuse.conf to customize all configuration settings for a portal. Any changes you make in the NFuse.conf file will not take effect until you stop and start the IIS Admin service. The ability to use SSL in a portal offers an extra level of securing communications between the ICA client device and the NFuse Web server.

NFuse 1.6 offers Microsoft Active Directory and Novell NDS authentication support, thereby eliminating users' need to log in twice. Now you can use your Novell NDS credentials to authenticate on the portal and use its features. Setting the authentication type is also done in the NFuse.conf file.

Project Columbia is a customized sample NFuse Web page that Citrix tech support staff created to address some common configuration issues. With Project Columbia, you have the ability to fetch application sets from multiple domains and merge them into one portal. You can also specify more than one MetaFrame XP server to run the XML service for redundancy. Project Columbia also offers a centralized location, the Config.txt file, to set all these configuration parameters.

NFuse Web servers are the weakest component in a Citrix network design. For that reason, some form of redundancy is unavoidable, especially in environments where the only method of accessing published applications is through NFuse. Utilizing one of the most powerful features available with Windows 2000 Advanced Server solves this problem. The feature, called Network Load Balancing, allows you to link two or more servers to create a virtual server that your users access. This virtual server is supported by these physical servers, which communicate between each other through a technology known as a *heartbeat*. The heartbeat continuously pings the servers; if at any time within 5 seconds a server doesn't receive a reply, it automatically assumes the other server is down and either takes on the responsibility of keeping the virtual server up or divides the load among the remaining servers.

Solutions Fast Track

Introducing Portals

☑ A portal is a user entry point to the Internet. A portal centralizes and personalizes user data and offers services such as news, stock quotes, and, in corporate portals, office applications.

☑ Personalization is the basis and the building block of portals. All portals advertise personalization in one form or the other, offering the visitor the sense of a "home" on the Web. By personalizing the user's information and greeting her when she enters the portal, portal creator's message is, "This is your virtual home." Most portal software offers centralized management in one way or another. The Citrix Management Console provides most of the management functions of NFuse.

Building a Portal with NFuse

☑ NFuse is a three-tiered technology that includes a Citrix server, a supported Web server, and an ICA client device.

☑ The NFuse.conf file provides a central location to configure the various settings that control NFuse behavior. SSL can be used to secure the communication of data between the Web server and the ICA client device via port 443.

Using Authentication in a Portal

☑ When you edit the NFuse.conf file, the parameter LoginType= defines the authentication method to use in the portal.

☑ NFuse 1.6 supports Active Directory authentication and offers the ability to force a specific domain, eliminating a step for your users by setting the default domain in the NFuse.conf file.

☑ One of the newest features of NFuse 1.6 is its supports of Novell NDS authentication. This is also set in the NFuse.conf file.

Customizing NFuse with Project Columbia

☑ Two or more Windows 2000 Advanced Servers with IIS 5.0 can be installed and configured to offer fault tolerance and redundancy to NFuse.

☑ Network Load Balancing creates a virtual server to which your user base connects to in order to access NFuse.

☑ Project Columbia is a Citrix tech support-customized NFuse Web site that offers many common configuration needs.

Building a Redundant NFuse Portal

☑ Users might have no means of accessing any sort of published applications except through the NFuse portal; to avoid this dependence, it is desirable to use the Network Load Balancing feature of Windows 2000 Advanced Server to bind two or more servers together, creating a third virtual server for the user base to access.

Frequently Asked Questions

The following Frequently Asked Questions, answered by the authors of this book, are designed to both measure your understanding of the concepts presented in this chapter and to assist you with real-life implementation of these concepts. To have your questions about this chapter answered by the author, browse to **www.syngress.com/solutions** and click on the **"Ask the Author"** form.

Q: What is a portal, and why would my organization need one?

A: A portal is your central point of Internet access for information and applications needed for your day-to-day business. An organization would want to install a portal to give its employees access to all the information they need and all the tools they need to get their job done, regardless of where they are.

Q: Can you have Windows and UNIX applications in the same portal?

A: Yes. With NFuse 1.6, you can provide both Windows and UNIX applications. Java applications are also supported.

Q: We are a Novell shop. I would like to know if support has been added for Novell NDS with NFuse 1.6?

A: Yes. With the introduction of NFuse 1.6, Novell NDS support has been added, eliminating users' need to authenticate twice.

Q: What do I need to personalize my portal to provide customized information and content and Webified legacy applications?

A: You need a portal builder like Citrix XPS or Project South Beach, or you can buy Yahoo!'s Portal Builder. These products allow you to customize the user experience and give users the ability to personalize the portal. They also provide customized and diversified access to information. Of course, you need NFuse to Webify your applications in the portal.

Q: We are running two applications in our company. We have dedicated a set of servers to each application and have divided these servers into two different farms. Each application has its own farm and its own set of servers supporting it. We want to use NFuse. Is there any way we can merge these two applications into one portal instead of having two portals and two locations where the user logs in?

A: Absolutely. If you use Project Columbia, you will find that all your concerns are addressed. With Project Columbia you can merge applications from several different farms into one central portal Web page, eliminating the need to log in twice from different portals.

Q: I have already set up an NFuse 1.5 portal, which is up and running. Will I be able to upgrade to NFuse 1.6?

A: Yes, you can. However, you will be missing out on all the newer features available with NFuse 1.6.

Chapter 15

Monitoring and Maintenance

Solutions in this chapter:

- **Establishing Baseline Performance**
- **Citrix Network Manager**
- **Network Monitor**
- **Resource Manager**
- **Backup and Recovery**

☑ **Summary**

☑ **Solutions Fast Track**

☑ **Frequently Asked Questions**

Introduction

When it comes to servers, what goes up, must come down. Servers cannot operate continuously forever. Even when running for extended periods of time, a server will suffer performance issues.

Applications are not created equally as far as a server is concerned. Some applications do not return server resources to the system when they've been used and then closed. Some applications leak memory. Some are simply unstable. When you run an application server, these problems increase dramatically.

Managing a server includes watching performance and being able to troubleshoot and resolve problems that occur. A variety of utilities can be used to manage individual servers and entire server farms.

Of all the server management strategies, the most important could be the backup and recovery strategy. Backing up servers is considered a best practice. It is hoped that you will never need to execute a server recovery, but the recovery strategy is even more important than the backup process.

Minimizing and Troubleshooting Server Problems

Most systems administrators would agree that monitoring and troubleshooting are the most important tasks a sys admin performs. Building and configuring a server or server farm require a certain level of knowledge and expertise, but the process can be as easy as following a recipe. Step 1, install the operating system; Step 2, install the programs; Step 3, add users. Most rookies can do it. The ability to track down and resolve issues particular to your environment, on the other hand, takes a pro. Developing and maintaining these skills can ensure your continued employment or help you secure a more favorable position. Overall, a server or server farm that performs in a consistent and well-oiled manner creates content users, happy managers, and a productive environment. All those things equate to fewer headaches for the administrator as well.

So, how do we attain this administrative bliss? Each environment and each server is unique, with a unique set of applications and users. No book can describe everything to watch out for or everything that can go wrong, and certainly no one can tell you how to correct every situation you encounter. Problems can result from hardware failures, corrupted drivers, incompatible software or configuration settings, user actions, policies, and myriad other scenarios. What can you do to minimize the number of problems you face? How should you proceed when you encounter problems? The very best advice we can give is to suggest that you find out, preferably in advance, what resources are available to you; learn as much as you can about them, and then employ them on a regular basis. It is essential to become adept at monitoring and troubleshooting your server or server farm. This, more than anything else, will set you apart from other administrators and ensure that you remain a necessary commodity.

In the sections that follow, we describe a few of the tools included with Microsoft Windows 2000 or Citrix MetaFrame XPe that you can use in monitoring and trouble-shooting your servers.

Establishing Baseline Performance

How do you know what is "normal" for your server? If a user complains that the server is "running really slow," what can you do to discover what, if anything, is wrong? If you have a performance baseline, you could run a few tests, compare the results to your baseline, and clearly see if there is a performance problem. If you do not have a base-line, you could be in for a long day. The process of establishing a baseline can be time consuming, but it's well worth it in the long run. Once completed, a baseline will pro-vide a standard by which you can easily measure your server performance in the future.

What can a performance baseline tell you? A baseline can tell you if the server is actually experiencing a slowdown or if there is something else going on. It is not unusual for a Citrix MetaFrame server to be blamed for problems associated with LAN or WAN saturation or other problems users experience. This is especially true in envi-ronments where thin client machines are used instead of PCs. It is especially important to keep servers running smoothly when users' computers have no hard drives and all applications are run from the servers.

A baseline can also help you determine whether or not the tuning tweaks you have been applying actually work. As mentioned, each environment is different, so it would be unrealistic to assume that all tuning techniques will work in all environments. The majority of tuning tweaks are meant for servers that run the usual collection of applica-tions, such as Microsoft Office, Microsoft Internet Explorer, and Microsoft Outlook. If your environment utilizes a different mix, the tweaks could work against you. Establishing a baseline, then retesting your server afterward could show you the real story.

Collecting Baseline Data

So, how does one establish a baseline? There are a few variations, but all suggest one thing: Test the server *before* and *after* placing it in production. This is particularly impor-tant in a server-based environment. If the server crashes or slows to a crawl, users might as well go home. This scenario, in addition to being very frustrating for the adminis-trator, can spell the end of server-based computing for your environment. In other words, it is critical that you take or make the time to test your servers. Test the hard-ware, the operating system, and applications.

If the system is new, test the hardware first. Although most vendors run burn-in tests prior to delivering the system, you should verify that all the server's pieces and parts are functioning as they should. It is not unusual for RAM, cables, or other com-ponents to become loose during shipment. Open the hood and make sure that all components are seated securely before you power up the server for the first time. If you add processors, RAM, hard drives, or other components, test after each addition to make sure each functions as it should. If you have access to hardware-testing software, run the servers for at least 24 hours before installing the operating system. Shut the system down and restart several times to make sure there are no problems.

Next, install the operating system and apply service packs and patches. This time, run performance tests against the operating system and I/O. Again, shut down and restart the system to make sure it does not hang. Record your observations, and run the tests again for good measure. Do not forget that consistency in testing will help eliminate the risk of invalid data. Although this process is sometimes tedious, it can save you time and embarrassment if problems arise later on.

The third step is to install the applications. In large companies, where administrators move from one environment, operating system, or version to another, it can be difficult to remember all the rules all the time. So, at the risk of being redundant:

- Always install your applications using Add/Remove Programs.

- Always install applications from the console.

- Always disable logons and make sure that no users are connected to the server.

- Always turn off antivirus or other unneeded services.

Merely remembering these simple rules can vastly reduce the amount of pain associated with managing your Citrix MetaFrame servers.

Once you have the applications installed, test and document the server again. It is not unusual to see a slight drop in performance compared with the tests run on the operating system alone. This is normal. What you are looking for is the normal performance level at each stage.

The next step is to test the fully loaded system. You might want to keep a number of users on "retainer" for just such purposes. Select the users based on their computing level (both power users and typical users) and the applications they tend to use.

NOTE

If you would rather not use live "guinea pigs," you can buy applications to simulate the effect of users on the system. We prefer to use the real thing because only then can we be reasonably sure that the test environment closely reflects that of the production environment.

The goal is to have a group of users who realistically tax the server. This group should use the server exclusively until you are satisfied that all applications have been thoroughly tested and you have collected enough performance data for your baseline.

Designing & Planning…

Load-Testing Your Server

This is also a great time to perform *load testing* on your server. Load testing looks at the resources, such as processor and RAM, consumed by the applications. Because all the applications will run from the server, not from the individual workstations, it is important to know which applications and the number of instances of the applications that can be run before server performance is impacted. Load testing can be performed using live test users or automated testing software that simulates high-usage scenarios.

After you have installed the operating system, service packs, and patches, install the core set of applications that represent what typical users run on a daily basis. Next, have your test users log in, one at a time, and test the system by performing common tasks while you monitor the server's performance. During the monitoring, you should note any changes in memory or processor utilization.

As you increase the user load, you should see the resource consumption increase in a linear fashion. A drastic change might indicate a problematic application. Unfortunately, we must often run applications on our servers that do not behave well, so it is up to us to make the proper adjustments in user load to compensate. Theoretically, you should be able to support 25 users on a server, but you may have to drop that number down to 20 or fewer, depending on the applications used.

As with collecting data for your baseline, run the tests several times, using typical and power users. Look for changes that might impact server performance and the user experience. Load-testing the network I/O is also important. The server might be in peak condition, but if the network is slow, users will not know the difference. Even though the ICA protocol consumes very little network bandwidth, other applications, such as streaming video, audio, and database connections, can cause the network to lag, creating performance problems. Some older database client connections fail to disconnect once the application is closed and require scripts and/or Registry changes to release. This type of problem might be overlooked if real users were not employed for testing.

Make sure that you know the peak times for your environment. Data must be collected during peak times during each day and month, such as first thing in the morning, after shift changes, and during accounting cycles. Once you have collected sufficient data and you feel comfortable that the data is valid, compare and record the data and store it in a safe place where you can access it when needed. Data should then be collected on a regular basis and compared with your baseline. Changes in performance can signal problems or potential problems, such as an application leaking memory, and you'll need to make the necessary adjustments. If you have several identical servers in your server farm, you might also want to compare the performance baselines against the other servers. This is a valid test only if the hardware, operating system, patches, and applications are identical.

As mentioned, you can use a number of tools to manage and monitor your server or farm. Several are included with the operating system, others with Citrix MetaFrame XPe, and still others via third-party vendors. The tools you choose are a matter of personal preference and budget. If you or your company can afford some of the fancier third-party tools or Citrix MetaFrame XPe, we recommend giving them a try; they can make your job much easier. The following sections describe some of the tools that can be used to create your baseline and for continued monitoring and server management.

Examining the Event Viewer

If you have much experience with Microsoft operating systems, you are most likely familiar with the Event Viewer, which is included with both Windows NT 4.0 and Windows 2000. The Event Viewer is installed by default under Administrative Tools on both operating systems. The Event Viewer is a front-end utility used to display the actual logs located in the %systemroot%\system32\config folder. Both the NT4.0 and Windows 2000 versions include the following logs:

- The System log contains events related to system components such as services, drivers, or hardware.

- The Security log contains events related to logons, logon attempts, and resource usage. Auditing must be turned on before events are recorded in the log.

- The Application log contains events logged by applications or programs.

If your Windows 2000 server's role is that of a domain controller, the Event Viewer contains three additional logs:

- The Directory Service log contains events related to Directory Services, Global Catalog, and Active Directory.

- The Domain Name System (DNS) Server log contains DNS information and errors.

- The File Replication Service log contains events related to replication to other servers.

Since it is not advisable to run Terminal Services or Citrix MetaFrame on a domain controller, we limit our discussion to the System, Security, and Application logs.

The Event Viewer, although underrated, is often the first stop in monitoring and troubleshooting servers. For many administrators, a typical workday begins with a quick inspection of the Event Logs. If there have been any application errors, problems with services, or system-related events, they will be recorded in the System and Application logs. A quick look at the Security log allows you to check on audited events such as file access or failed logon attempts. Remote servers and workstations can also be monitored from your local Event Viewer, providing that they have accounts in the domain or in a trusted domain and are connected to the network. To view the logs of a remote computer, right-click **Event Viewer** (local) and, from the **context** menu, and select **Connect to Another Computer**.

Although the event information provided is not always self-explanatory, it's a good starting place. The Event Viewer allows you to monitor events that take place on your servers and workstations and detect activities that require your attention. Analyzing the events can help you resolve issues related to security, resource allocation, applications, and system problems. In addition, by archiving the logs, you create a historical reference that you can refer to in the future. If you are unfamiliar with the interface, take a look at Figure 15.1. This example is from a Windows 2000 server, but the Event Viewer provided with Windows NT 4.0 is very similar. As you can see, the left pane allows you to select the log you want to view, and the right pane shows the actual events recorded in that log.

Information is recorded in the logs for any significant event that occurs to the operating system or within an application. For critical events that require immediate attention, you can also be alerted by a popup message on the console monitor. The information and format of the event vary, depending on the type of event, but the event ID and description usually provide enough detail for you to figure out what happened. However, there are exceptions. We have run across a few that left us baffled as to their meaning. For entries that do not immediately convey clear meaning, check the Citrix and Microsoft Knowledge Bases for clarification. If you are still unable to locate the information you need, you can consult a number of free resources available on the Internet. We've listed a few in the section, "Handling Events."

Making Sense of Events

Three event types are generated in the System and Application logs and two additional for the Security log. The events recorded in the System and Application logs are automatic; no intervention is necessary to begin the logging. For events to be recorded in the Security log, however, auditing must be turned on. It is important for you to understand the type of events that occur in each log and what they might be telling you about your server, applications, or security. Table 15.1 provides descriptions and examples of common events.

Figure 15.1 The Windows 2000 Event Viewer

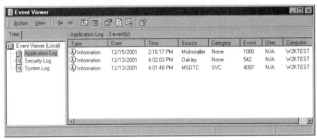

Table 15.1 Log Event Types

Type	Description	Example
Error	Indicates a significant condition has occurred in the system or an application.	System shutdown, a failed driver, duplicate IP address, malfunctioning hardware, or loss of data.
Warning	Warns of potential system and application problems that could cause trouble in the future.	Low disk space, unconfigured drivers, a lost network link, or a timed-out request to another server.
Information	Provides status and information about the system and applications.	Successful operation of drivers and services; information about application errors when popup messages have been turned off; print job status and Save Dump information.
Success Audit	Tracks successful security access. Auditing must be turned on for security events to be logged. Success Audit events can be found only in the Security log.	Successful logons; file and object access.
Failure Audit	Tracks failed security access. Auditing must be turned on for security events to be logged. Again, you will see this type of event only in the Security Log.	Failed logons; file and object access.

Each event in the log also contains an event header that contains specific information regarding:

- The type of event, whether an Error, Warning, Information, Success, or Failure audit event.

- The date and time the event occurred.

- The source driver, service, or application that reported the event.

- The category, if applicable; this is a number used internally by the component that reported the event.

- The event ID number by which the event is referenced by Microsoft.

- The name of the computer on which the event occurred.

- The name, if applicable, of the user who received the report.

To learn more about an event, double-click on the event to open its Properties sheet, as shown in Figure 15.2. The Properties sheet reiterates the information in the preceding list and provides binary information that can be assessed by programmers or support personnel. Often the event ID and description are referenced in the Microsoft and/or Citrix Knowledge Base.

Figure 15.2 Event Properties

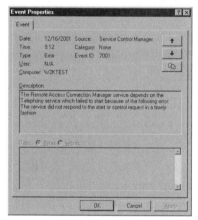

Managing the Event Viewer

The event logs record information daily and, if left unmanaged, could become enormous. Microsoft, of course, took care to set defaults that prevent this from happening, but you can adjust those defaults to suit your own needs. In addition, each log's properties can be set individually. Figure 15.3 shows the Properties sheet associated with the Application log on a Windows 2000 system. To open an Application log Properties sheet in Windows 2000, open the **Event Viewer**, select a **Log**, click **Action**, and select **Properties**.

The Log Properties sheet in Windows 2000 has two tabs: the General tab and the Filter tab. The General tab provides information about the log such as its physical location; its current size; the dates on which it was created, last accessed, and modified, and the configurable properties of Maximum Log Size and what to do once the log has reached its maximum size. You are also given the option to reset the defaults and clear the log. The default log size is set at 512KB, but for a Citrix MetaFrame application server, this is much too small. Citrix recommends setting the log to 1024KB and to overwrite as needed, but in some cases, you might want to archive the logs or keep them active for a longer period of time. The important thing to remember is that if the logs fill up, the server could halt. If you decide to keep the logs small, be sure to set them to overwrite as needed or be *very* sure to save and clear the logs on a regular basis. In some scenarios, the logs may be set up to 4096KB; although this setting certainly provides room for growth, it might require moving the logs from their default locations to another with more room. This can be accomplished by editing the Registry; of course, all the usual caveats apply. Remember to back up your Registry, and before you begin, be sure you know how to restore the Registry.

Figure 15.3 Event Log Properties

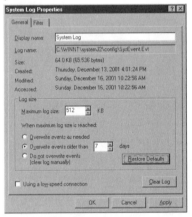

Configuring & Implementing...

Backing Up and Restoring the Registry

Perhaps you have noticed that every time you read something about modifying the Registry, it is followed by a warning that states that modifying the Registry could cause serious problems or irreparably damage your system. The warning is legitimate. You could actually end up rebuilding the system from scratch. For this reason, it is extremely important to back up the Registry before you change it in any way. In fact, it is also a good idea to back up the Registry before you make any changes to your server, including installing or removing applications. There are a number of ways to back up the Registry, but the safest way is to use Windows 2000 Backup. To use the Windows 2000 Backup utility to back up the Registry:

Continued

1. Go to **Start | Programs | Accessories | System Tools | Backup**.
2. Click the **Backup** tab (see Figure 15.4).

Figure 15.4 Windows 2000 Backup Utility

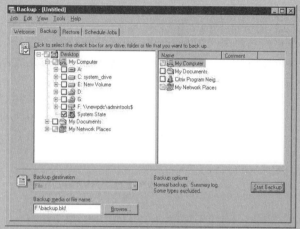

3. Expand **My Computer** and check **System State Backup**.
4. Select the media and a filename and path where you will store the backup, then click **Start Backup**.
5. Next, click the **Advanced** button and uncheck **Automatically Backup System Protected Files with the System State**. Click **OK**.
6. Click **Start Backup**.

To restore the Registry from backup:

1. From the Backup utility, click the **Restore** tab.
2. Locate the media and location where you stored the backup and check the backup you want to restore.
3. Make sure that you are restoring to the proper location. The default is to restore to the original location.
4. Click **Start Restore**.

To modify the location of the Event Viewer logs:

1. Go to **Start | Run** and type **Regedt32**, then click **OK**.

2. Select **HKEY_LOCAL_MACHINE**, then double-click to expand the System hive.

3. Navigate down to the **\CURRENTCONTROLSET\SERVICES\ EVENTLOG** folder.

4. For each log you want to move, open the corresponding folder and double-click the **File** value, as shown in Figure 15.5.

Figure 15.5 Changing the Location of the Event Logs

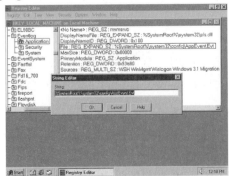

5. Change the string value to the new drive and path, then click **OK**.

6. After you have made the changes, quit the Registry editor and restart the server.

Filtering and Searching for Events

Use the Filter tab to select the events that are displayed in the Event Viewer window. By default, the Event Viewer displays all events in a log, sorted by the most recent date. The Filter options provide a way to customize your view of the displayed events. As shown in Figure 15.6, events can be filtered by date, specific event types, event source or category, event ID, user, computer, or description.

Figure 15.6 The Event Viewer Filter Properties

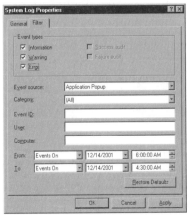

A similar feature provided in Windows 2000 and NT 4.0 is the Event Viewer Find utility, located under View. With Find, you can specify search criteria and locate specific events without making Event Viewer your default view. This feature is extremely helpful if you are concentrating on a particular event and need to find all occurrences of that event.

Configuring & Implementing...

Event Viewer Tips

The following points will help you in your work with Event Viewer:

- When configuring your server, be sure to set the Event Viewer's log size to one appropriate for your environment. If you opt to keep your logs for historical reference, do not forget to save and clear the logs on a regular basis, because a full log might cause the server to hang and require a reboot.

- Citrix recommends setting the logs to 1024KB and to overwrite as needed.

- If disk space is an issue, you can move the logs to a location other than the default by editing the Registry.

- Be especially careful when security auditing is enabled, because logs tend to fill up quickly.

Handling Events

The events recorded in the event logs are seldom easy to decipher. Even when the message appears to be straightforward, it might not be, and although it is too much to hope that you will never see a warning or error message in your server's logs, there is help if you do. A number of resources are available to assist you in deciphering the events in your logs. Both Microsoft and Citrix provide several support options, including:

- Phone support
- Knowledge bases
- User forums
- White papers
- Subscription services

The knowledge bases are a good starting place. Your choice of Microsoft or Citrix will depend on the nature of the warning or error message. If it is clearly Microsoft related, search the Microsoft Knowledge Base. If the event clearly points to Citrix, begin there. Each site contains information referencing the other, and if you begin on the wrong site, it could point you in the right direction. To search the Microsoft Knowledge Base, go to http://support.microsoft.com. To check the Citrix Knowledge Base, go to www.citrix.com/support.

To locate the knowledge base article that relates to an event, you need the information from the event's Properties sheet. In particular, take note of the event ID, the source, and the description of the event. Try searching the knowledge base for the event ID first; if that does not return the information you need, search on keywords from the description. Be sure to use the correct spelling, and keep your query short but specific. Figure 15.7 shows the Citrix support Web site Knowledge Base search utility.

Figure 15.7 Citrix Solutions Knowledge Base

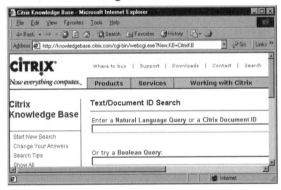

Even though the knowledge bases contain a wealth of information, there are times when the information you seek cannot be found in a knowledge base, because the event is too new, because the event is too specific to your environment, or because you have not hit on the correct sequence of keywords. If you find yourself in this position, you can turn to a number of other resources:

- **Microsoft Online TechNet** This free site devoted to the IT professional provides quick access to troubleshooting tools, information about known issues, service packs, patches, and driver downloads. The Online TechNet can be found at www.microsoft.com/technet.

- **Microsoft TechNet subscription** Monthly TechNet subscriptions can be purchased through Microsoft. The subscription provides monthly CD-ROM updates containing Knowledge Base articles, information, utilities, service packs, and patches. Single-user licenses start at $299 or $499 for TechNet Plus, which includes Microsoft software betas.

- **Citrix Solution Tools Plus** Citrix provides quarterly subscriptions that include Citrix Knowledge Base articles, information, and best practices on CD-ROM. In addition to the CDs, Citrix sends out a monthly *Solution News* online newsletter and *Solution Flash* to notify users of updates to Citrix products and Knowledge Base articles.

- **Phone support** If you are unable to locate the information pertaining to a particular warning or error, you might need to contact Microsoft or Citrix support. Both provide fee-based support services to fit various organizations or needs.

- **User forums and newsgroups** Both Microsoft and Citrix provide links to their user forums and newsgroups. The forums are active discussion areas where administrators can interact with peers and support technicians. Forums and newsgroups can be extremely helpful when you cannot locate a knowledge base article or have specific questions about third-party applications.

The Internet can be one of your most valuable tools. Many Web sites are devoted to IT professionals, and a growing number are focused on server-based computing. Like the Microsoft and Citrix forums and newsgroups, these sites offer a place to give and receive free advice. Here are a few of our favorites:

- www.dabcc.com
- www.thinclient.net
- www.winnetmag.com/forums
- http://groups.yahoo.com/group/citrix
- The alt.os.citrix newsgroup

Each site includes information about the latest bugs, service packs, patches, and links to other sites. If you are unable to locate the information in a knowledge base and do not need immediate support, the forums are a great way to find and share information with your peers. Be sure to read and conform to each site's protocols, and search the site for answers to your question prior to posting a question.

With any luck, you will locate a knowledge base article or reference to the event in question on one of the sites. Many times the problem's resolution will include a service pack, hotfix, or Registry change. Just remember that all systems and environments are unique, and an action that corrects one problem could create another. If at all possible, try the fix on a test server before putting it on a production one. If that is not possible, be sure to back up your server and Registry contents before applying the fix or making the change. Also keep in mind that service packs, patches, and hotfixes must be installed as though they were normal applications unless otherwise noted.

Using the System Information Tool

Have you ever wished there was one place you look and find all the configuration information about not only the local system but remote systems as well? If so, your wish has been granted. Windows 2000 has centralized most of the system management tools within the Microsoft Management Console, or MMC. Microsoft has long included a similar utility in the Microsoft Diagnostics (MSD) tool and the later version, WinMSD, found in NT 4.0, but it lacked some functionality and was rarely thought of. The Windows 2000 equivalent has a few updated features and actually comes in quite handy. The System Information tool provides current, vital information about your system, in a read-only format. It cannot be used to test or change settings on your system, only to view and monitor your existing hardware and software configurations. To run the System Information tool, go to **Start | Programs | Administrative Tools | Computer Management**. Figure 15.8 shows the MMC and the System Information tool.

Figure 15.8 The Windows 2000 System Information Tool

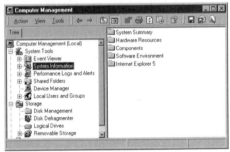

NOTE

You can access the System Information tool by typing **winmsd** from the command prompt or from **Start | Run**.

There are three main sections within the MMC: System Tools, Storage, and Services and Applications. The System Information tool is appropriately located within System Tools. Beneath System Information, there are five additional subfolders that provide information about your system. They are:

- System Summary
- Hardware Resources
- Components

- Software Environment
- Internet Explorer

The System Summary folder displays a list of the system's basic configuration. Here you will find the version and build of the operating system, the BIOS version, the amount of installed and available memory, virtual memory, available virtual memory, and pagefile size. This is a great place to look if you are unfamiliar with a system and its resources. You might also be asked to look here if you call a vendor for support.

The Hardware Resources folder contains several files containing information about the system's hardware. Again, you cannot change, enable, disable, or test settings here. If you need to make changes or test a component, go to Device Manager. What you can do is quickly check for hardware conflicts or sharing. Table 15.2 provides details on the subfolders and the information they contain.

Table 15.2 Hardware Resources

Resource	Description
Conflicts/Sharing	Lists the system components that are sharing an IRQ and/or those that are in conflict.
DMA	If you have any Direct Memory Access devices installed in your system, you will find them listed here. DMAs have the ability to move data from a device to RAM without involving the processor and are rarely seen in newer systems.
Forced Hardware	Hardware that is not supported by Plug-and-Play will be listed here.
I/O	The Input/Output folder contains the I/O components and the areas of virtual memory used by them.
IRQs	System interrupt requests (IRQs) are shown here. If any are shared or in conflict, you will also see them in the Conflicts/Sharing folder.
Memory	Provides information regarding virtual memory areas used by system devices. The information is similar to that displayed in the I/O folder.

Even if you have not already used this resource, you will grow to depend on it, especially if you frequently add to or upgrade the hardware on your systems. The information provided in the Hardware Resources folder is some of the most valuable found in the System Information tool. If you have ever installed new hardware only to find either that it will not work or another device has stopped working as a result, check the Hardware Resource folder. Look under Conflicts/Sharing or IRQs to find out if there are hardware components battling over memory or if IRQs exist.

The third folder under Hardware Resources is the Components folder. This is another resource you will most likely grow to appreciate. The information is similar to that displayed in Conflicts/Sharing but from a different prospective. Components provides a list of hardware devices and the system resources they are using. Not all the devices listed are installed on your system. If the device is actually installed on your system, right-click the device to view its Properties sheet. The Properties sheets provide details relevant to the device, including driver versions, I/O, and IRQs that it uses. Beneath the Components folder, 11 subfolders represent the classes of components that may be installed on your system. They are:

- **Multimedia** Audio and visual codecs, CD-ROMs, and sound devices.

- **Display** Adapter information such as name, type of display, resolution, and pixels.

- **Infrared** Properties of infrared devices installed on the system.

- **Input** Keyboard and pointing device information.

- **Modem** Information pertaining to installed modems.

- **Network** Includes adapters, protocols, and Winsock information.

- **Ports** Information about serial and parallel ports.

- **Storage** Information about storage devices and their associated drivers.

- **Printing** Installed print drivers.

- **USB** Information about installed USB devices.

- **Problem Devices** Information about any device that might not be functioning as they should or devices that have been removed incorrectly.

The fourth folder beneath Hardware Resources is Software Environment. It also contains subfolders that deal with the software running on your system, as well as files and services in use by the software. Table 15.3 lists the subfolders and describes the information contained within each.

Table 15.3 Software Environment Folder Subfolders

Folder	Description
Drivers	Lists all the drivers, their type (kernel or file system), state (stopped or running), and a brief description of what the driver does.
Environmental Variables	Includes path information for the system, location of temporary folders and files, processor identification, and operating system version.

Continued

Table 15.3 Software Environment Folder Subfolders

Folder	Description
Jobs	Contains a subfolder for each type of job running on the system.
Network Connections	Shows all network connections and their associated drive letters.
Running Tasks	Contains a list of executables currently run by the services. File version, date, and file size are also displayed.
Loaded Modules	Dynamic Link Libraries (DLLs) currently running on the system, their version, date, manufacturer, and path.
Services	A listing of all the nonsystem services available on the system, running or not, and the start mode (manual, automatic, or disabled.)
Program Groups	Displays Terminal Services profile associations and all the groups available in the Start menu.
Startup Programs	Displays all programs configured to run at startup.
OLE Registration	Contains Object Linking and Embedding associations.

The remaining folder, Internet Explorer 5, contains the settings unique to IE 5. The information provided includes:

- **Summary** Displays version, build, path, cipher strength, content advisor, and Internet Explorer Administration Kit settings (IEAK).

- **File Versions** Information about all IE files, versions, dates, and vendors.

- **Connectivity** Dialup, LAN and/or proxy connection settings.

- **Cache** Displays a summary of objects in the cache, temporary Internet files, and refresh settings.

- **Content** Displays a summary of personal and other certificates.

- **Security** Information regarding the security-level settings, including trusted sites, intranet, and restricted sites.

In addition to providing real-time information about your system, the System Information tool allows you to print and save the information within the folders as either a text (.txt) or information (.inf) file. To save the information within a folder to a file, right-click the folder you want to save and select **Save As**, then choose the file type.

Configuring & Implementing...

Saving System Information to a File

Occasionally, you might need to send a support technician files that contain information about the system you have called about. Technicians frequently request the System Summary because it contains details about your system's vendor, operating system and build, BIOS, RAM, and virtual memory. In order to send the information via e-mail to the technician, you must first save the information in a file. To save the System Summary:

1. Log on to your system as **Administrator**.

2. Right-click **My Computer** and select **Manage**.

3. Expand System Information by clicking the **+**.

4. Right-click **System Summary**. This will bring up a menu that allows you to save the System Summary information as a text file or as an information file, search for information using Find, print, refresh, or get help.

5. Select **Save As Text File** and provide a path and name. Figure 15.9 is an example of a System Summary saved as a text file.

Figure 15.9 A System Summary Report

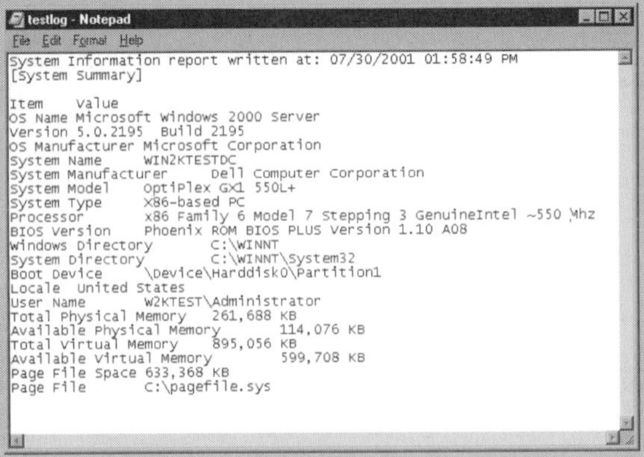

Monitoring System Performance

Another tool you might already be familiar with is the Performance Monitor, or PerfMon. This graphical performance-monitoring utility is available in both Windows NT 4.0 and Windows 2000. In Windows NT 4.0, look under Administrative Tools. In Windows 2000, it is incorporated into the MMC, under Performance Logs and Alerts, as depicted in Figure 15.10. If you prefer the older interface, you can find it on the Windows 2000 Server Resource Kit.

Figure 15.10 Performance Logs and Alerts

NOTE

You can also type **Perfmon** into **Start | Run**. This opens the System Monitor with the Performance Monitor screen active.

PerfMon provides a way to gather and examine information about server activity and resource usage either in real time or over a period of time. The tools described earlier in this chapter are important for monitoring the health of a system, but PerfMon is Window's primary tool used to collect data for creating a baseline, sizing the server, and locating server bottlenecks. It is important to understand the relationships between the server resources and server performance. By monitoring each resource, one at a time, you will begin to understand what is happening in your server behind the scenes.

Understanding Objects and Counters

PerfMon gathers and examines information by monitoring performance counters within systems and applications. Counters are sets of measurable properties that each component (referred to as an *object*) has related to it. Some of the more common objects are:

- Server
- Processors
- Memory
- Physical and logical disks
- Users
- Connections

Objects that represent individual processes, sections of shared memory, and physical devices are defined. Each object has associated with it a series of counters that represent the measurable characteristics of the object. An example is the Processor object, which includes the *%Processor Time* and *%User Time* counters. Some objects exist on all Windows systems; others are associated with specific applications. PerfMon is extensible, which allows software vendors to make changes by adding objects and their subsequent counters associated with their products.

Each object can have several instances. An *instance* shows how many of the particular objects are available in the system. For example, a server with multiple processors will have multiple instances of the Processor object. Another example is hard disks; if your system has several hard disks, there will be several instances of the associated objects. Other objects such as Memory and Server do not have instances.

Adding Performance Monitor Counters

To view objects and counters that can be used to monitor your system, choose **Start | Programs | Administrative Tools | Performance**, or open the MMC and go to **Performance Logs and Alerts**. To add counters, highlight **System Monitor** in the left pane and click the **+** sign on the button bar on the right. You can also right-click a blank area of the Performance Monitor and select **Add Counters** from the **context** menu. Until now, the monitor portion of the screen has been blank. All objects, counters, and instances must be selected and added. From the Add Counters dialog box, select the objects and one or more related counters to add to the display, as shown in Figure 15.11.

Figure 15.11 The Performance Monitor Add Counters Dialog Box

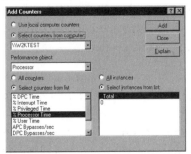

From the Add Counters dialog box, you also have the option of selecting counters from either the local computer or a remote computer. This capability can prove helpful if you have multiple servers running the same applications. If one server appears to be slowing down, you can compare it to other servers on the same graph. Another helpful feature found on the Add Counters dialog box is the Explain button. If you have questions about a counter, highlight the particular counter and click **Explain** for information. Once you have added the objects and the counters, they will be displayed as a graph. Each counter will have a color associated with it, and a color key will be displayed at the bottom of the screen, as shown in Figure 15.12.

Figure 15.12 The Performance Monitor Display

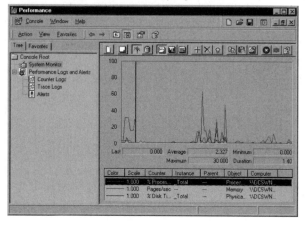

Using Performance Counters

Now that we have seen how to add the counters, let's take a look at some of the counters you might want to chart for your baseline or load testing. For the most part, these are generic counters that you might monitor on any Windows NT 4.0 or Windows 2000 system.

Processors

Process threads require processor cycles to run. If the demand exceeds the supply, long processor queues develop and system response time degrades. Three counters that can help you monitor the overall processor load are:

- **% Processor Time** If processor utilization is over 75 percent, on average, the processor is working fairly hard. You might consider increasing the number or the speed of existing processors in the server. To determine processor utilization, monitor the **%Processor Time** counter under the **Processor** object. %Processor Time shows the percentage of elapsed time that a processor is busy executing non-idle threads. If the %Processor Time counter consistently registers at or near 75 percent, the processors might be slowing the system response time.

- **Processor Queue Length** A sustained queue length of 2 or more generally means that the server has reached its user load capacity. This counter measures the number of current threads waiting in the queue for processing time. It is an instantaneous reading, not an average of readings over a period of time. To produce a "normal" reading for your baseline, monitor this counter frequently and manually record the data.

- **Interrupts/sec** Common causes of excessive interrupts are defective device adapters or badly designed device drivers. Interrupts degrade system performance because most of the processor time is spent handling them. A moderately busy server (32-bit hard disk adapter, network card, and about 12 users) experiences an average of 100 interrupts per second. If the number of interrupts per second increases noticeably without a corresponding increase in system activity, it could indicate a hardware problem or a faulty driver.

> **NOTE**
>
> When you monitor processor queue length from a remote server, the values could appear higher than when you monitor them locally. This occurs because the Processor Queue Length counter is an instantaneous counter that counts all the ready threads in that instant. If the system is handling a remote procedure call (RPC), the ready thread count can increase. This is only a temporary situation and resolves itself as soon as the RPC is completed.

Memory

Server memory takes the biggest hit on a Windows 2000 system. As we all know, every new version of the operating system and each new version of an application require more and more memory. If you do not have sufficient memory on your system, you will definitely feel the pain—and so will your users. Table 15.4 lists a few important memory counters that you should keep an eye on.

Table 15.4 Performance Monitor Memory Counters

Counter	Description	Explanation
Available Bytes	Displays the size of the virtual memory available for applications.	There should always be at least 4MB available. If there's not, you might not have enough memory, or you could have an application experiencing a memory leak.
Pages/sec	Displays the current rate at which pages are read from disk back into physical memory because of page faults or written to the disk to free RAM.	More than 20 pages per second indicate excessive paging and could suggest that your system needs more memory.
Commit Limit	Displays the amount of memory that can be committed without making the pagefile larger.	The pagefile should be at least 2.5 times the size of your system's RAM but can be increased if the required space is available.

Continued

Table 15.4 Continued

Counter	Description	Explanation
Committed Bytes	Displays the amount of memory committed to processes currently running on the system.	This is the amount of memory that is in use and not available to other processes.

Physical and Logical Disks

Disk problems on Citrix MetaFrame XP servers are usually related to paging due to the memory load the applications place on the server. When the physical memory is maxed out by the load of applications and users, the server begins using the hard disks to support virtual memory. Two counters that should be monitored on both physical and logical disks to measure performance are:

- **% Disk Time** Displays the percentage of the physical disk that is busy. If the disk is busy more than 90% percent of the time, you should probably add another disk.

- **Current Disk Queue Length** Displays the current number of data transfers waiting in queue. If you are averaging more than 2, you will notice the degradation. Keep this number as small as possible.

Configuring & Implementing...

Performance Monitoring Tips

Here are a few tips that will help you get the most out of your system performance monitoring:

- Before starting System Monitor, turn off screen savers and disable nonessential services.
- Increase the size of your pagefile by at least 100MB.
- Set monitoring of counters to run at regular intervals of at least 10 to 15 minutes apart.
- Save and store the logs for historical reference, trend analysis, and capacity planning.

Tracking "Leaky" Applications with PerfMon

Exactly what constitutes a "leaky" application, and what causes it? Simply put, an application is referred to as *leaky* when it refuses to release system resources or continues to consume resources such as RAM, pagefile, or CPU time. Frequently, buggy applications are to blame for memory leaks, but unanswered popup messages and print dialog boxes can cause similar problems with CPU usage because they wait for user interaction. A problem of this nature can cause the system to perform sluggishly and could eventually cause the server to hang, requiring a reboot.

What can be done to track down and put a stop to such resource theft? You can use a couple tricks to track down the applications that are consuming more than their fair share of resources, but it's a good idea to disable popup messages, including Dr. Watson and printer dialog boxes, on your MetaFrame servers. Printer notification is disabled by default on Windows 2000, but old Dr. Watson is still alive and kicking. Disabling popups requires modifying the Registry, so remember to back up the Registry before you make any changes. To disable Dr. Watson (see Figure 15.13):

1. Go to **Start | Run** and type **Regedt32**, then click **OK**.

2. Select **HKEY_LOCAL_MACHINE** then double-click to expand the **System** hive.

3. Navigate down to **\Software\Microsoft\Windows NT\CurrentVersion\ AeDebug**.

4. Clear the contents of **Debugger:REG_SZ:**.

Figure 15.13 Disabling Dr. Watson

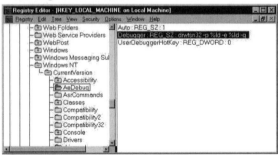

To track down those leaky applications, you need to generate a PerfMon log. If you created a performance baseline for your server, it will come in handy later for comparison. Try this exercise to get the feel of using Performance Monitor. To begin your search for the leaky application:

1. Go to **Start | Programs | Administrative Tools | Performance**.

2. Click the **+** sign to add a new counter.

3. From the **Processor Object** drop-down menu, select **Process**.

4. Select the following counters and click **Add**:

   - Pool Non-Paged Bytes

   - Pool Paged Bytes

   - Private Bytes

   - Handle Count

5. From the **Performance Object** drop-down menu, select **Memory**.

6. Select the **Available Bytes** counter and click **Add**.

Watch for counters that consistently increase or decrease. For instance, if you notice that your available number of bytes continues to drop while the number of private bytes rises, you most likely have an application leaking memory. This means that some process is consuming the available memory. To narrow it down and determine which application is the culprit, begin a new log, adding only the counters you noted. If you noticed that private bytes consistently increased while the available bytes decreased, add only those two counters. Add individual instances of those counters until it is clear which application is causing the problem.

What should you do when you have discovered a leaky application? Perform the following steps:

1. If there are services related to the application, stop them and any that are dependent on or interact with them.

2. Check the respective knowledge bases for known issues and fixes. Most software manufacturers have Web sites and knowledge bases. If there is a hotfix or service pack, install it on a test server first to make sure the fix doesn't break something else. If everything goes well, install the fix on the production server.

3. If you do not find a fix, try contacting the vendor's support staff. The issue might be new, or they might still be developing the fix. You might be able to obtain a beta version of the fix to test on your test server.

4. In the worst-case scenario, the software could be proprietary or legacy and you will be unable to find a fix. If this is the case, you might want to find an alternate application or locate a programmer who can rewrite or update the code.

Although MetaFrame XP does not require regular server reboots, it is a good practice to do so. If any applications or processes leak or hog memory, rebooting the server will free that memory. If you make server reboots a part of your server farm maintenance, Citrix recommends cycle booting. Cycle booting is simply periodically shutting down and restarting the servers. Furthermore, recommendations include rebooting the servers in groups with no more than 50 servers per group and with at least 10 minutes between groups. The reasoning behind cycle booting is that the IMA service starts after the reboot and establishes a connection to the data store to update the host cache.

Designing & Planning…

My Leaky Application

If you have discovered no leaky applications running on your server, you can consider yourself very lucky, but if you would like to get a feel for what you would see and how your server would behave if there were leaky applications, you can use a Windows 2000 Resource Kit utility to simulate a memory leak. Look under **Performance Tools** for **LeakyApp.exe**. A word of caution, however: Do not run this tool on a production server. If you have a test server, run Performance Monitor, adding the **Memory | Available Bytes** and **Processor | Private Bytes** counters. Next, run **LeakyApp.exe** and watch what happens. You should see the Memory | Available Bytes drop while the Processor | Private Bytes counter sits at 100 percent, as shown in Figure 15.14. When you click **Stop**, you should see the counters return to their normal state.

Figure 15.14 Performance Monitor Showing the LeakyApp Simulation

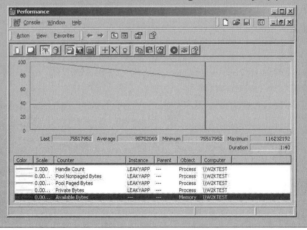

The amount of data transferred and the time it takes to complete the transfer depend on the size and configuration of your server farm. Rebooting in groups will help reduce the amount of time it takes for the IMA service to start and will reduce the load on the data store. For larger server farms, it could take 6 minutes or more to restart the IMA service. If the service has not started within 6 minutes, you will receive a message stating that the IMA service could not be started. Wait a little while longer before you panic. The Service Control Manager has a timeout of 6 minutes. If you have a larger farm, it could take more than 6 minutes for the IMA service to start.

Citrix Network Manager

Citrix Network Manager works with third-party Simple Network Management Protocol (SNMP) consoles to provide systems management capabilities to Citrix MetaFrame XPe servers. The Network Manager consists of an SNMP agent and plug-ins that support HP OpenView and Tivoli NetView. With the SNMP console, it is possible to remotely manage your Citrix MetaFrame XPe servers using the same network management package that might be in use elsewhere on your network. With Network Manager and your third-party SNMP console of choice, you can:

- Terminate processes on Citrix MetaFrame XPe servers
- Shut down and restart Citrix MetaFrame XPe servers
- Disconnect, log off, and send messages to active sessions and processes

If these all sound like things you can accomplish with Citrix MetaFrame XPe, you're right! Citrix MetaFrame XPe can perform many of the same tasks as third-party Network Management solutions, but only for Citrix MetaFrame servers. If your environment requires a solution that will work for all the various servers in the network, Citrix Network Manager could be the right one for you.

NOTE

Citrix Network Manager is available only with Citrix MetaFrame XPe. It is not packaged with the base Citrix MetaFrame XP or XPa products.

System Requirements

Citrix Network Manager comes only with Citrix MetaFrame XPe. It does not come with the base Citrix MetaFrame XP or XPs license and it cannot be purchased separately. The requirements for Network Manager are the same as those for Citrix MetaFrame XPe, with the addition of:

- Microsoft SNMP services
- Tivoli NetView 5.1.2 or later
- HP OpenView Network Node Manager 6.1 or later

Installing Network Manager

As mentioned, Microsoft SNMP services must be installed prior to installing Network Manager. The SNMP services are not installed by default on either Windows NT 4.0 or Windows 2000. To install SNMP:

1. Exit all open applications.

2. Open **Control Panel** and select **Add/Remove Programs**.

3. Select **Add/Remove Windows Components**.

4. Click **Management and Monitoring Tools** and then click **Details**.

5. Select **Simple Network Management Protocol** and then click **OK**.

6. Restart the server.

7. Reapply any installed service packs.

After SNMP has been installed, you are ready to install the Citrix Network Manager plug-ins. To install the plug-ins:

1. Exit all applications.

2. Load the **Network Manager CD-ROM**. If your CD-ROM drive supports autorun, the Network Manager splash screen will appear; if not, choose **Start | Run** and type **d:\autorun.exe** to start the installation.

3. Once the splash screen has appeared, select the plug-in you want to install, either HP OpenView or Tivoli NetView.

4. Follow the on-screen prompts to complete the installation.

Designing & Planning...

The Citrix Management Console

If you are running the SNMP management console on a computer other than the Citrix MetaFrame XPe server, it is a good idea to install the Citrix Management Console on that computer as well because it provides other management capabilities not found in Network Manager.

To secure your servers and prevent unauthorized users from performing potentially dangerous tasks, you should configure the SNMP service to accept only packets from known SNMP management consoles or remove the Read/Write access permissions from all SNMP communities and use the Citrix Management Console to perform all management tasks.

SECURITY ALERT!

On Windows 2000 systems, the default SNMP permissions are Read Only; on Windows NT 4.0 Terminal Server Edition, the default permissions are Read/Write. To use the remote management capabilities on a Windows 2000 server using the Network Manager plug-in, you must change the SNMP community permissions to Read/Write. However, if the Citrix SNMP agent is enabled, this can allow users to remotely perform administrative tasks such as:

- Logging off or disconnecting users
- Sending messages to users
- Terminating processes
- Rebooting the server

Enabling the SNMP Agent

Before you can begin using Network Manager, you must enable the SNMP agent and configure the traps. SNMP support is not enabled by default on Citrix MetaFrame XPe; you must manually enable the SNMP agent and configure the trap settings using the Citrix Management Console. To enable and configure the SNMP agent from the Citrix Management Console:

1. Log on to the **CMC** as **Administrator**.

2. Select the server or server farm from the console tree.

3. Go to the **Actions** menu and select **Properties**.

4. From the Properties dialog box, click the **SNMP** tab.

5. If you're enabling the agent for a server farm, select **Enable SNMP Agent On All Servers**; if enabling the agent for one server only, clear the **Use Farm Settings** check box.

6. Configure the SNMP agent and traps settings.

A Citrix MetaFrame XPe server with the SNMP agent enabled can send 11 status traps, as shown in Table 15.5. The traps and their associated thresholds can be set in the Citrix Management Console for a server farm or for a single server.

Table 15.5 Available Traps

Trap Name	Trap Number	Trigger	SNMP Console Reaction
trapSessionLogon	2	User logon.	
trapSessionLogoff	1	User logoff.	
trapSessionDisc	3	User disconnect.	
trapSessionThreshold	4	Number of sessions on the server has exceeded the configured limit.	Session Information icon turns red.
trapSessionsThesholdNormal	9	Number of concurrent sessions has fallen below the configured limit.	Session Information icon turns green.
TrapMfAgentUp	8	Citrix SNMP agent started on server.	
TrapLicLowTheshold	5	Number of available licenses has fallen below warning threshold.	License information icon turns yellow.
TrapLicLowThresholdNormal	10	Number of available licenses has increased above reset threshold.	License information icon turns green.
TrapLicOut	6	All licenses have been used.	License information icon turns red.
TrapLicOutNormal	11	Licenses that were completely allocated are now available.	License information icon turns yellow.
TrapLicDenied	7	Not used.	

The configured traps can be monitored from the SNMP management console by any of the following methods:

- **The Citrix MetaFrame icon colors** A spot check of the icon colors is the quickest way to get a general idea of the Citrix MetaFrame servers in the network.

- **Event Viewer** All traps received by the SNMP console are logged to the Event Viewer logs.

- **The Citrix TrapDialog monitor** Popup messages are displayed when status change traps are received.

- **Notification actions** You can configure notification actions to send an e-mail or page to administrators when traps are triggered for serious events.

Network Monitoring

Network Monitor, or NetMon, is a network diagnostic tool that is bundled with Windows NT and Windows 2000. The version that ships with NT and Windows 2000 is the "lite" version; the full version is a component of Microsoft Systems Management Server (SMS). Network Monitor is used to monitor network traffic and troubleshoot network-related events such as a server that is sending or receiving an inordinate amount of traffic or poorly configured workstations, printers, and servers. Although it is not as easy to use or as feature-rich as the hardware-based network monitors (commonly called *sniffers*), NetMon can help you determine if slowdowns are due to network traffic or problems on your servers.

NOTE

Microsoft Operations Manager (MOM), a recent standalone offering from Microsoft, is now the system-monitoring package of choice. SMS and MOM two products are similar in that they both automatically deploy agents in order to monitor systems, but whereas SMS focuses on hardware and software inventory and deployment, MOM's primary duty is to monitor the health of your systems and to let you know when something is amiss. MOM can be used to monitor Windows 2000, NT, Novell, UNIX, and Lotus Notes servers.

NetMon provides a graphical display of LAN statistics such as:

- The source address of the computer sending the packet

- The destination address of the computer receiving the packet

- The protocols used to send the packets

- A portion of the data being sent

Network Monitor is able to do all this by collecting or capturing data on the frames going across the network. The data is then stored in a capture buffer, which is a reserved area of memory. Once the data has been captured, it can be saved to a text or capture file for later analysis. Network Monitor collects and displays several pieces of information, including:

- The source address of the computer sending the frame

- The destination address of the computer that received the frame

- The protocol used

- The data or portion of the data sent

> **NOTE**
>
> It's a good idea to check your capture buffer before you capture data. The default maximum size for Windows 2000 is 1GB. NT's default maximum is 8MB less than the total amount of RAM installed on the system. To check or set the buffer size, choose the **Capture** menu and select **Buffer Settings**.

If you know the type of frame you are looking for, Network Monitor can filter the frames and collect information on the type you have specified. If you were interested in seeing only data about a particular protocol, you could enable filtering and capture only that specified data. A real-life situation might be to locate any workstations that have unnecessary protocols installed or to look at the amount of ICA traffic on the network.

System Requirements

Network Monitor requires a NIC that supports promiscuous mode. If you are running Network Monitor on a remote computer, the local machine's network card does not need to support promiscuous mode. Network Monitor is not installed by default. To install Network Monitor:

1. Exit all open applications.
2. Open **Control Panel** and select **Add/Remove Programs**.
3. Select **Add/Remove Windows Components**.
4. Click **Management and Monitoring Tools** and then click **Details**.
5. Select **Network Monitor** and then click **OK**.
6. Restart the server.

Capturing Traffic

To start Network Monitor, choose **Start | Programs | Administrative Tools | Network Monitor**. If you have more than one network card installed on your machine, you need to select a network to enable the Capture menu. If you have only one network card installed, the Capture menu is already enabled. To begin capturing network data, select **Start** from the **Capture** drop-down menu. Network Monitor immediately begins capturing frames and will continue until you stop the capture or the capture buffer fills up. To stop the capture, select **Stop** from the **Capture** menu. Figure 15.15 shows the Network Monitor interface. To save the captured data, click **File | Save As**.

Figure 15.15 Microsoft Network Monitor

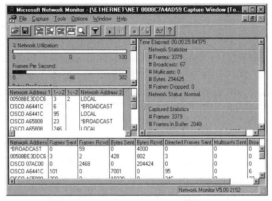

Resource Manager

Resource Manager is a monitoring utility created specifically for the MetaFrame XP server-based environment. Other, less server-based utilities often do not give accurate readings because they are not in tune with the server-based environment. They do not take into account that the server is performing 100 percent of the processing and that multiple users are running sessions, sometimes multiple sessions, from the server at one time.

Resource Manager allows you to collect, display, and analyze information about your server or farm and capture real-time performance data and produce reports. It can show you the applications that are running, how many instances of those applications are running, and who is running them. You can track the resources consumed by each user, user group, and application. You can use Resource Manager to:

- Manage resources
- Monitor and analyze system performance, application usage, and user behavior
- Identify and diagnose potential problems
- Gather statistical data
- Create reports
- Gauge and justify future resource needs

- Plan and scale servers and server farms

- Monitor or ignore processes

- Automatically reboot servers

During installation, Resource Manager automatically creates a set of default "metrics" that represent a variety of system and/or network processes and events. If the value of a metric falls outside the normal range, Resource Manager can inform the system administrator in a number of ways. During installation, Resource Manager automatically creates a default set of metrics and assigns upper and lower limits to define the normal operating range of each.

System Requirements

Citrix Resource Manager is *not* included with the base Citrix MetaFrame XP license and is not available in MetaFrame XP or MetaFrame XPa. Resource Manager is part of the Citrix Advanced Management Features bundled with Citrix MetaFrame XPe.

Citrix Resource Manager can be installed on Microsoft Windows NT 4.0 Terminal Server Edition, Service Pack 5 or later, or on the Windows 2000 Server family. If it's installed on Terminal Server Edition, the Microsoft Data Access Component (MDAC) version 2.51, Service Pack 1 or later must be installed prior to installing Citrix MetaFrame XPe and Resource Manager. You must also be sure that all servers running Resource Manager can connect to the MetaFrame XP data store and that the data store is currently running. Resource Manager uses the data store to hold configuration information about the servers, applications, and users.

Installing Resource Manager

Installing Resource Manager is fairly simple. One you have installed the operating system and Citrix MetaFrame XP, you are ready to install Resource Manager.

NOTE

Do not forget to activate your MetaFrame XPe licenses. Valid, activated licenses are required before you can use many of Resource Manager's features.

To install Citrix Resource Manager:

1. Make sure your system has adequate resources to run Resource Manager. If you have met or exceeded the requirements for the operating system, Terminal Services, and MetaFrame XP, this should not be a problem.

2. If you're installing on Microsoft Windows NT 4.0 Terminal Services Edition, install **MDAC 2.51**, **SP1** or later.

3. Make sure there are no users logged in to the system and that logons are disabled.

4. Place the **Citrix Resource Manager CD-ROM** into a drive that supports autoplay, and the splash screen should appear within seconds. If it does not, type: **d:\autorun.exe** to start the application (where *d:* is the CD-ROM drive letter).

5. Click **Citrix Resource Manager Setup** *once*.

6. If prompted, restart the server after installation has completed.

Configuring & Implementing...

Citrix MetaFrame Farm Metric Server

The first server you install Citrix Resource Manager on becomes the *farm metric server*. This means that this server will interpret metrics applying to the server farm. Citrix recommends that the farm metric server be configured as a Citrix MetaFrame XP data collector and carry only a light load of applications and users.

The Citrix Resource Manager is installed as part of the CMC. The CMC, like the MMC, centralizes the management utilities that you can use to manage and monitor your server or farm. During installation, Resource Manager is integrated into the CMC. To open the CMC, click **Start | Programs | Citrix | Citrix Management Console**. When the console starts, you must provide a server name, user account, and password. Unlike Microsoft's Administrative Tools, you must have administrative rights to use the CMC.

The CMC view is divided into two panes. The left pane displays a list of components within the server farm; the right pane displays information about the selected component, as shown in Figure 15.16.

Figure 15.16 The Citrix Management Console

Configuring & Implementing...

Using Remote Connections to Resource Manager Servers

If you prefer to view Resource Manager data from a remote server or non-MetaFrame workstations, you need only to install the CMC from the Citrix MetaFrame XP Server CD-ROM.

Using Citrix Resource Manager

To access real-time information about the servers in a farm, click **Servers** in the left pane, then select the server you want to monitor. In the right pane, click the **Resource Manager** tab to display the current status of all the servers currently monitored (see Figure 15.17). You can also display a real-time list of all the components currently in an alarm state by clicking **Watcher Window**. The Watcher window can remain visible on the desktop while the CMC is open to notify you of any problems. Components that are running normally will not be shown in the Watcher window. To view the Resource Manager Server log, right-click a server name and select **Resource Manager Server Log** or press **Ctrl+Alt+B**.

Figure 15.17 The Citrix Resource Manager Real-Time Monitor

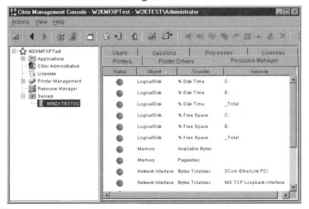

If you have applications with limited licenses, you might want to configure Resource Manager to monitor them. You can add limits to the count metric that will warn if a defined number of instances is approaching or generate an alarm if the limit number has been exceeded. To add applications for Resource Manager to monitor:

1. Right-click the **Applications** folder in the CMC.

2. From the menu, select **New Resource Manager Application** (see Figure 15.18). The Resource Manager Application Wizard guides you through adding the application. Your application is now listed under the Application folder in the left pane.

Figure 15.18 Adding Applications to Resource Manager

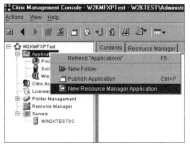

3. Highlight the **Application** folder in the left pane, and then double-click the application in the right pane. You should see only the application in question under the Resource Manager tab.

4. Right-click the application and select **Add/Remove Metrics**.

5. The next screen allows you to select **Count** as the metric and gives you the option to remove all metrics or apply to other applications. If you have added other applications, you can add the metric to them at this time. Click **OK** to finish. Now that you have added the metric, you should see it listed under the Counter column.

6. To set the number of applications allowed to run, right-click the application again and select **Properties**. From this screen you can set limits for the number of instances of the application running at the same time. Settings can be configured for yellow, red, and what the system should do once the limit has been reached, such as e-mailing the administrator. This screen also allows you to apply these settings to other applications being monitored. Click **OK** to finish.

Once you have configured the applications, click the **Applications** folder in the left pane and select **Resource Manager** in the right pane. Your applications should now be listed with a colored indicator next to them. If an application's instances exceed the limits you placed on them, the indicators will change colors (see Figure 15.19).

Figure 15.19 Application Status

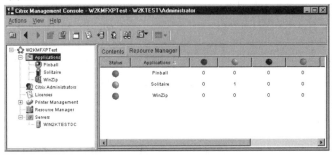

Resource Manager uses *metrics*, or conditions that relate to each component and application running on your server or within your farm. The metrics have threshold variables, and when the threshold for a given component has been reached, Resource Manager produces an alert and can even notify the administrator. Colored indicators are used to display the status of each monitored component. The status indicator colors are shown in Table 15.6.

Table 15.6 Status Indicators

Indicator Color	Meaning
Green	Indicates normal operation.
Yellow	Indicates a potential problem that might need further analysis. Indicates an alarm state.
Red	Indicates a problem that requires attention. Indicates an alarm state.
Blue	The metric is inactive and needs to be configured.
Black	The metric is set to "sleep" (an indefinite pause) and is not currently being monitored.
Gray	The metric is set to "snooze" (a timed pause) and is not currently being monitored.

Metrics

Resource Manager defines a default set of metrics that are specific to your server and operating system. Alarm thresholds are also defined for the metrics; they alert you to potential problems. There are default metrics for Microsoft Windows NT Terminal Server Edition and for the Windows 2000 Server family. This is all very similar to the terminology used for Windows Performance Monitor. The metrics can be fine-tuned, changed, added, or removed to better fit your environment. Once you become accustomed to what is normal for your server farm, you can adjust the metrics as needed.

Within a server farm, one server acts as the farm metric server and interprets the metrics for the entire farm. The farm metric server is the first server on which Resource Manager was installed but can be changed to any other server in the farm that has Resource Manager installed. If for some reason the farm metric server is not available, a backup server takes its place until it is operational again.

A metric consists of objects, instances, and counters. As we learned in the preceding section, objects are server components that possess a set of measurable properties; they are physical or logical server resources. The default set of metrics for a Windows 2000 Server and their associated counters are:

- Network Interface
- Processors
- Memory
- Logical Disks
- System
- Page File
- Terminal Services

It's a good idea to keep an eye on these metrics and know the norm for your server or farm. For managers and users to buy into server-based computing, they must feel as though they are running their applications from their own desktop machines. Be sure that you know the default metrics, what they monitor, and what they could be telling you about your servers:

- The default metric for Network Interface is Bytes Total/sec. This metric monitors the network traffic coming into and from the server. A high metric counter can mean that more user sessions are connected than the NIC can handle.

- There are two metrics for Processor: %Interrupt Time and %Processor Time. A high count for %Interrupt Time means that your system is spending an inordinate amount of time processing interrupts rather than processing requests. This can be indicative of hardware problems or a very busy server. If the %Processor Time count is high, it could also mean that your server is too busy, or it could be a runaway or hung program. To find out if it is a program or process causing the problem, use the Current Process report.

- Memory has one default metric: Available Bytes. A high reading here can mean that your system is short on memory and accessing the pagefile too often. This condition is called *thrashing*. If this is the case, disk usage and paging counters will also be high. It could also mean that the system is overloaded, too many applications that consume large amounts of memory are running, or an application or process is as fault.

- The metrics for Logical Disk are %Disk Time and %Free Space. %Disk Time monitors disk usage and indicates how busy a disk is. This could be the result of too little physical memory or an application or process that makes frequent and extensive use of the disk. A value of 100% could indicate that the disk is too slow to support the number of requests it receives. If the server is running out of disk space, the %Free Space counter will be high. This value usually indicates that larger or additional disks are required.

- The System metric monitors Context Switches/sec. A high reading means that too many processes are competing for processor time. To resolve this issue, you might consider adding more or faster processors.

- The Page File metric is %Usage. A high reading usually indicates that the pagefile is too small.

- The Terminal Services metric monitors Active and Inactive sessions and can indicate that there are too many users either logged in using resources or disconnected and using resources. Even though a session is disconnected, it is still consuming server resources. It's a good idea to limit the time a session can be in the disconnected state.

WARNING

Disk thrashing is an indication that there is not enough physical memory and the pagefile is being accessed frequently. The metric to watch is Memory/ Available Bytes.

Generating Resource Manager Reports

Resource Manager provides a variety reports that can be used to examine the data reported by your server or farm. As shown in Figure 15.20, reports can be based on real-time system information or snapshots, current processes, and current users. The information can be used as historical reference, baselines, usage billing, justification for future resource purchases, or any number of other instances.

The System Snapshot allows you to pinpoint a moment in time and examine the status of the server at that moment. This feature can prove extremely useful for troubleshooting problems that occurred at a time when you were not available. Say, for instance, that you are in a meeting when a problem occurs on the server. The junior administrator manages to handle the situation but has no idea what caused the problem. You can use the System Snapshot to run a report for the time the problem occurred and use that report to diagnose the problem. Data is gathered and stored every 15 seconds by default and kept for 48 hours. The arrow buttons under "Time of current view" allow you to scroll backward and forward in time in 15-second intervals (see Figure 15.21).

Figure 15.20 Resource Manager Reports

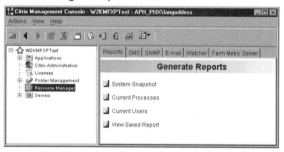

Figure 15.21 A System Snapshot Report

Current Process can produce reports based on the applications and processes running on servers within the farm. You might use this report if a process currently running has entered an alarm state, for example.

Current Users produces reports on user and application activity. A user activity report can be helpful in determining how many sessions a user has open and which applications are being run by the user. The report also provides information on when users' sessions began, how long the sessions have been established, the number of processes running, and the number of instances of each.

The last option on the Reports screen is View Saved Report. This option allows you to retrieve and view saved reports.

Creating a Report

To create a report within Resource Manager:

1. Log in as **Administrator**.

2. Open the **CMC**.

3. Log in as a **Citrix MetaFrame XP administrator**.

4. From the CMC, click **Resource Manager** in the left pane. In the right pane, make sure the **Reports** tab is highlighted.

5. Select **Current Users** (for this example).

6. Select the server to monitor.

7. Click **Generate**.

The report will be generated using an HTML form and will display the following information:

- Server name

- Date and time the report was run

- The number of open sessions

- The number of active processes

- The number of users currently logged in

- The session name

- The protocol being used

- The session's start date and time

- The duration of the session

- The process count for each user

- The active process and instances of each process for each user

From within the report itself, you are given the option to save the report either as HTML or CSV that can be imported into a spreadsheet or database.

Sending Alerts

Resource Manager can be configured to send alert messages to designated administrators when the status of the monitored component changes, either to an alarm state or back to normal operating status. Each monitored component can be individually configured to trigger an alert and notify the appropriate person. The alerts can be sent in the following ways:

- Short Message Service (SMS) text messages to cell phones or pagers
- SNMP messaging
- E-mail messages

To configure the alerts, highlight Resource Manager from within the Citrix Management Console and select the type of alert you want to configure from the right pane.

Backup and Recovery

No matter how careful you are, things can and will go wrong. It's just a matter of time. All you can do is take every precaution possible and have an arsenal of tools ready to combat whatever problems occur. Backing up your servers, including the Registries and data stores, on a regular basis can be your saving grace in the event of a disaster. However, a few other tools are available that can definitely make your life easier. Windows 2000 includes a few new or improved features, and there are several third-party utilities that can help as well. We start by discussing the various backup strategies, then move on to a few other tools that would make great additions to your administration tool kit.

Backup Strategies for Standalone Servers

System backups can be a real lifesaver, especially when you are backing up a file server. Where data is concerned, backing up and restoring is usually a breeze. Application servers, however, are a different matter. Not only must you be sure to back up the system, you must back up the Registry and update your backups every time you make changes to the server. If you are lucky, your server will not change much once you have installed the applications. There are the occasional service packs, hotfixes, and patches, but these do not happen every day.

Restoring an entire application server and all the applications from backup is another story. It is not fun, it is not easy, and it is often problematic. For application servers, including Citrix MetaFrame servers, you might want to consider an alternative backup strategy. Think about this: A good implementation of Citrix MetaFrame will be on a standalone or member server, so there will be no Active Directory, DNS, Security Accounts Manager (SAM), user profiles, or data residing on it. What you will have, besides the operating system, are applications, patches, hotfixes, and service packs. Again, these do not change that frequently. A backup strategy that creates an image of the entire system and that could be updated when needed would be a great solution.

Luckily, this can be done and is being done via third-party utilities. One such utility, System Guardian/XC by DuoCor (www.duocor.com), allows you to image the entire system onto separate disks, somewhat like a mirror set. Unlike a mirror set, however, you can control updates to the mirror, keeping the image pristine until you are ready to update it. If disaster strikes, you simply remove the original disk set, replace it with the mirrored set, and reboot. Furthermore, if your hardware is all the same, you can install and configure one server, create the disk image, and move it to the next server. You will need to change the server name, IP address, and security identifier (SID) afterward.

If third-party utilities are not possible or if you prefer a good old backup, Microsoft has improved the backup utility incorporated in Windows 2000. The new backup utility, located under System Tools in the Accessories folder, allows you to back up not only onto tape, but also onto disks, CDs, and network-accessible volumes. A System State backup backs up the Registry, Component Services Class Registration database, system startup files, and Certificate Services database on a nondomain controller. Figure 15.22 shows the new Windows 2000 backup utility. From this interface, you can create backups, restore from backup, schedule jobs, and create emergency repair disks.

Figure 15.22 Windows 2000 Backup and Recovery Tools

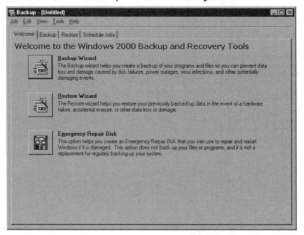

Windows 2000 Backup Procedures

To create a backup using the Windows 2000 Backup utility, select Backup Wizard from the Backup utility main screen. This choice starts the wizard and walks you through the process of backing up your server. The next screen, shown in Figure 15.23, asks you to specify what you want to backup. The options are:

- Backup everything on my computer
- Backup selected files, drives, or network data
- Only backup the System State data

The first two options are fairly self-explanatory. If you select the first option, you will back up the entire contents of the server. If you select the second option, you will be given the choice to back up selected files, drives, or network data. The third option, to back up the System State data, allows you to back up the Registry, system boot files, and COM+ class registration database. This is the information you need to restore your server if you reinstall it versus restoring it all from a backup. On a domain controller, the System State backup also includes a copy of Active Directory and the SYSVOL directory.

Figure 15.23 The Windows Backup Wizard

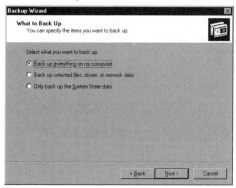

After selecting the type of backup you want, the next screen prompts you to choose where you want to place the backup and to give a filename. Once you have done this, a summary screen is displayed and you are prompted to either finish or go on to advanced options. The advanced options allow you to specify how to back up your server and when. Table 15.7 lists the available advanced backup options.

Table 15.7 Advanced Backup Options

Option	Explanation
Type of backup	Choices are Normal, Copy, Incremental, Differential, or Daily backups. The default option is Normal.
Verify data?	Verifying the data compares the backup with the original or source. This adds additional time to your backup but is a good practice. The default is No.
Use hardware compression?	This option is available only if you're backing up to tape. It increases the storage capacity of the tape. The default is No.
Append of replace existing backup sets?	This option gives you the choice of appending data to an existing backup or overwriting it with the new backup. The default is Append.

Continued

Table 15.7 Continued

Option	Explanation
Restrict access?	This option allows you to restrict access to others creating backups. The default is No.
Name of backup and media	This option allows you to provide a name for the backup and name the media it will be backed up on. The default is the time and date the backup was created.
When should the backup be run?	This option allows you to schedule your backups to run at a convenient time. The default is Now.
Back up migrated remote storage data?	This feature allows you to back up and move seldom used files to a remote storage location.

Backup Types

When accessing the advanced backup options, you are prompted to define the type of backup to perform. The choices, as shown in Figure 15.24, are:

- **Normal (full)** A normal, or full, backup backs up all selected files, with the exception of the Registry. After each file is backed up, the archive bit is reset or turned off. A full backup consumes more time but is easier to restore. Typically, full backups are run on a regular basis and supplemented with incremental or differential backups.

- **Copy** A copy backs up all selected files but does not reset the archive bit. A copy is typically used when a backup of all files is needed, regardless of the archive bit settings.

- **Incremental** An incremental backup is normally run between full backups, usually on a daily basis when data files are concerned. An incremental backup backs up only files with the archive bit turned on—in other words, files that have changed since the last backup, whether full or incremental. This type of backup is usually the quickest but takes the longest to restore. When restoring from incrementals, you must first restore the most recent full backup, then each incremental run thereafter.

- **Differential** A differential backup also supplements a full backup and is generally run on a daily basis. It too backs up only files with the archive bit turned on, but instead of resetting the bit when finished, it leaves it turned on. This causes all files that have changed to be backed up each time the differential backup is run, until the next full backup is run. This takes a while longer to back up but is quicker and easier to restore than an incremental backup.

When restoring from differentials, you must first restore the most recent full backup, then only the last differential run since.

- **Daily** The daily backup is similar to the differential in that it backs up all files with the archive bit turned on and does not reset the archive bit. However, it only backs up files changed during the current day. Restoring from daily backups requires the most current full backup plus every daily backup since.

Figure 15.24 Backup Types

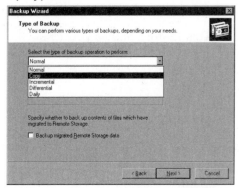

Choosing What and How to Backup Your Servers

As stated earlier, Citrix MetaFrame servers are, under normal circumstances, fairly static. Once you have a full system backup, you should not need to perform additional backups unless you add or upgrade applications or apply service packs or patches. It is still a good idea, however, to perform regular backups, even if you do not change a thing. As stated earlier, if something can go wrong, it will. It is best to be prepared. There is always a chance that the backup will become corrupted, get lost, or be erased. You do not want to put all your faith into one tape.

If you do not have access to third-party products such as those described earlier or if you prefer to do things the traditional way, you can use the Windows Backup utility. Deciding what you back up, what media to back it up onto, and how often to back up are personal choices, but to provide the most coverage, a normal (full) backup should be run on a regular basis and either incremental or differential backups run after any changes are made to the system. Be sure to back up the Registry and your Resource Manager's data store if it is located on a Citrix MetaFrame server. As for media, tape backups are the most practical due to the size of a full backup. A good policy is to store the tapes offsite for a period of time or at least until another full backup has been run.

NOTE

The Windows Backup utility does not have the capability to backup open files. To make sure that you have backed up the entire system, schedule a regular day and time to perform the backups. Make sure that no users are logged in to the system, and disable logons. Stop the server service to make sure that no files are in use, and remember to perform a System State backup to cover the Registry. Afterward, enable logons and start the server service. The entire process can be automated by employing scripts.

Restoring Data from a Backup

The Windows Backup utility also provides for file restores via the Restore Wizard or manually by selecting the Restore tab. The wizard walks you through the restore, just as it did the backup process.

First you are prompted to select the media and location where the backup resides. Next you are given the option to select individual files or folders or the entire backup. You are also given the opportunity to specify advanced options. They are:

- Select a location for the files to be restored to. This can be the original location, an alternate location, or a single folder.

- Next, you are prompted to specify how to restore files that already exist on the disk. Your options, as shown in Figure 15.25, are to not replace the file, replace the file only if it is older than the backup copy, and always replace the file.

Figure 15.25 Restoring Files

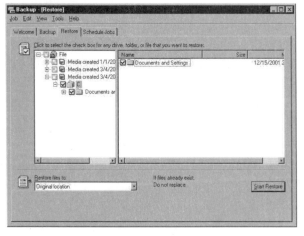

- The next option allows you to restore security or special system files. The options, as shown in Figure 15.26, are to restore security, restore the removable storage database, and restore junction points, not in the folders and file data they reference. The options you choose here depend on the file system the original file resided on. If you backed up the data from an NTFS drive and are restoring it to an NTFS drive, you are given the option to restore security settings on the files. If you backed up and are restoring to a FAT file system, you are given the option to restore the removable storage database. This one applies only if you have removable storage devices. You need to worry about restoring junction points only if you have mounted drives. *Junction points* are physical locations on a mounted NTFS volume that point to another area of disk or to another disk.

Figure 15.26 Advanced Restore Options

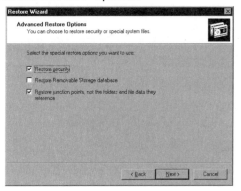

After providing this information, you are shown a summary screen with the options you chose. If you have missed something, you can go back at this point and correct it, or you can click **Finish** to begin the restore.

Backup Strategies for Server Farms

Developing and implementing a backup strategy is of huge importance in an enterprise environment where there may be hundreds of servers as well as different operating systems and various server roles. Downtime and/or loss of data can spell the end of an up-and-coming business or could cost established businesses substantial losses. Backing up and properly maintaining your MetaFrame server farm is extremely important, especially when users depend on the servers for their entire desktop or other critical applications. Do not wait until a disaster occurs before developing a backup strategy for your farm. In the next section, we discuss some of the routine and periodic tasks you might encounter while administering a MetaFrame XP server farm.

Maintaining MetaFrame XP Server Farms

Along with the usual server and operating system maintenance, other tasks specific to MetaFrame servers need to be carried out to keep your server farm running smoothly and to prevent disasters from occurring. Some of the tasks you will be faced with are:

- Backing up and restoring the IMA data store

- Migrating the data store

- Replacing MetaFrame servers

- Changing farm membership

- Recovering an unresponsive server

- IMA service troubleshooting

Backing Up the IMA Data Store

Maintaining the IMA data store for your server farm is a must. Because the data store contains all the configuration information for the server farm, including license information, you cannot afford to lose it. As you might recall from prior chapters, every server farm has one IMA data store residing on an Access, Microsoft SQL, or Oracle database. It contains not only the MetaFrame licensing information but configuration settings and information about the servers in the farm, published applications, trust relationships, and permissions. If the data store is corrupted or the server it resides on goes down, the rest of the servers in the farm will pull their information from their local cache—for 48 hours. After that, no more licenses will be issued, and users will not be able to log on.

That scenario should provide an excellent motivation for paying close attention to your data store. Citrix recommends backing up your data store every day. The methods used will depend on the database employed. If you are using Microsoft SQL or Oracle, you either need to have some experience with the product or should consult the product documentation. For Access data stores, you need to use the **dsmaint backup** command-line utility provided by Citrix. As you will learn, the **dsmaint** command has several uses, including migrating, reconfiguring, failover, and compacting the data store.

To back up and restore or move an Access data store to a new server:

1. Run **dsmaint backup**.

2. Copy the **mf20.mdb** file from the %Program Files\Citrix\Independent Management Architecture folder to the corresponding folder on the new host server.

3. Create a new data source name (DSN) file on the new host that points to the local database.

4. Run **dsmaint failover** on all servers in the farm to point them to the new host server.

5. Make sure that the IMA service is running, then execute **dsmaint config** and point to the new DSN. Use the default user account and password: **citrix/citrix**.

6. Change the old server's role to that of indirect server. The new server will now hold that data store and all other servers will access it indirectly. To change the server's role, you must modify the Registry. Don't forget to back up the Registry before making any changes. Once you have backed up the Registry, modify the following key: **HKLM/SOFTWARE/Citrix/IMA/ Database Driver**.

7. Change **imaaccess** to **imaodbc**.

8. Stop and restart the IMA service on the new host server.

9. Once the new host server's IMA service has started, stop and start the IMA service on all the other servers in the farm.

As mentioned earlier, you cannot use **dsmaint backup** to back up an Oracle or MS SQL data store. Backups must be executed according to the documentation for the database used. If you have moved the data store to a new server, you must reconfigure the servers in the server farm so that they can locate it. Once you have restored the database on the new host server:

1. Create a new DSN that points to the new database.

2. Run the **dsmaint config** command to reconfigure the servers to point to the new database. The syntax for the command is: **dsmaint config /user:username /pwd:password /dsn:dsnfilename**.

3. Stop and restart the IMA service.

4. Check the Registry to make sure the new settings were successful. The pointer to the DSN is located in the HKEY_LOCAL_MACHINE\ SOFTWARE\Citrix\IMA\DataSourceName Registry key.

After you have verified that the correct DSN is being used and the IMA service has started, copy your newly created DSN file to the other servers in the server farm, leaving the data collector for last for performance reasons. Run the **dsmaint config** command on all servers, then stop and restart the IMA service.

Migrating an Access Data Store to Oracle or MS SQL

An Access database might work for a small server farm's data store, but as the farm's size increases, you will want to migrate the data store to a more scalable and stable platform. The command **dsmaint migrate** is the same for migrations from Access to both MS SQL and Oracle. Afterward, you must use the **dsmaint config** command to reconfigure the other servers in the farm.

Unlike other operations on MetaFrame servers, you can migrate the data store during operating hours with users logged in to the farm. Users who are currently logged in will not be affected, but until the IMA service is restarted, no new sessions can connect. Citrix does suggest that you restart the server's IMA services in groups of 10 or fewer or risk a bottleneck at the database server, resulting in delays. To migrate an Access data store to an MS SQL or Oracle database:

1. Create a new database on the new host server. Again, if you are not familiar with the database platform, make sure you consult the database documentation prior to beginning the migration.

2. Create a new DSN file that points to the new database.

3. On the new host server, execute the **dsmaint migrate** command. The syntax is **dsmaint migrate /scrdsn:dsnfilename /srcuser:username /srcpwd:password /dstdsn:dsnfilename /dstsuer:username /dstpassword:password**. That's a long one! The parameters for both the source and destination are as follows: *Dsnfilename* = the full path to the DSN file. If the path has spaces in it, enclose the path in quotation marks. *Username* = the username for the database, and *password* = the password for the database.

4. Once you have migrated the database, run the **dsmaint config** command (as shown previously) on the source server to reconfigure it to point to the new host and data store.

5. Stop and restart the IMA service on the new host server.

6. Copy the newly created DSN file to the other servers in the server farm and run the **dsmaint config** command to establish a direct connection to the new database.

7. Stop and restart the IMA service on all the other servers in the server farm.

At some point you might also encounter the need to migrate your data store from MS SQL to Oracle. This can be done and requires the same steps as migrating from Access to MS SQL or Oracle. However, after you have stopped and restarted the IMA service on the new host, you might want to check the Registry to be sure that the changes have been made. When you are sure the correct drive and DSN are in place, copy the DSN to the remaining servers, then stop and restart their IMA services.

NOTE

MDAC 2.5 must be installed prior to migrating to an MS SQL database. Microsoft Windows 2000 Server ships with MDAC 2.5 and is upgraded to version 2.5, SP2, with Windows 2000 SP2. If you are unsure of the version you are running, you can download a MDAC Component Checker utility from www.microsoft.com/data/download.htm#Ccinfo.

Replacing MetaFrame Servers

For a variety of reasons, you might need to replace a server. Perhaps the server has inadequate resources, needs maintenance, or as frequently happens, the lease has expired. In any case, it is not too difficult to replace a server, especially if it does not host the data store. The most time-consuming part of replacing a server is installing the OS, MetaFrame, licenses, and applications. If you are lucky and the hardware is identical, you can clone the original server and restore the image on the new server. Several products on the market, such as Symantec Ghost (www.symantec.com), do this quite well. The drawback to using a such a utility to clone your servers is that you need storage space for the clone image and, depending on the size of the drives, it could take a while to restore. Another product that's not as well known but is gaining a following is DuoCor's XactCopy (www.duocor.com). The only caveat to using XactCopy is that you need an extra drive or array of drives that match those with the OS and applications. These are used for an exact duplicate of the first drive or array. The duplicate drives can then be removed and either used to create a new server (after changing the server name, IP, and SID) or be set aside (or sent offsite) as a backup. The trick is to pick the best option for your environment.

Once you have a replacement server with OS and MetaFrame installed, you can shut down the original server and boot the new server. As long as the server has the same name and IP address, the data store will never notice the difference, because it does not track serial numbers or SIDs. Since all the configuration settings are stored in the data store, there is no need to reconfigure MetaFrame settings, but if your server is not an exact duplicate of the first, you need to run **dsmaint config** to point the new server to the data store and stop, then start, the IMA service. The last step is to run **qfarm** to make sure that the right IP address is associated with the new server.

Changing Farm Memberships

Many organizations today are in flux, constantly growing or consolidating their resources, including data centers. In this context, MetaFrame servers are no exception. You might find yourself moving existing servers to other departments or sites and adding them to existing farms at those locations. Or perhaps you need to create a new farm and prefer to use an existing server for the first server in the farm. The problem with simply moving the server to the new location or farm is that all the configuration information is stored in the data store, and each server in the farm has a local host cache. If the server cannot contact the data store, it will use its local cache for 48 hours, then refuse logons. For this reason, the local host cache and all references to the data store must be removed from the server. The server then must be redirected to the new data store and a new local cache created.

This all can be done using a utility called *chfarm,* located on the MetaFrame XP CD-ROM in the \W2K\MF\MF folder. Chfarm is simple to use, but like so many other utilities, it must be used with caution. If you don't use chfarm correctly, you run the risk of corrupting your data store. It would be wise to make a backup copy of your data store prior to running chfarm. Unlike the **dsmaint** command, chfarm is a GUI application that guides you through the process of removing the server from the farm and adding it to the new farm. The process must be run from the CD-ROM or from a network image; chfarm requires the MetaFrame XP installation files because it actually reruns the installation, beginning with the farm membership questions.

Once you have executed chfarm, it performs the following tasks to remove the server from its current server farm:

- Stops the server's IMA service
- Uninstalls the IMA service and all the local IMA settings

Next, chfarm begins the process of adding the server to the new server farm or creating an entirely new farm by launching the IMA configuration component of the installation program. This portion of the setup gathers configuration information and provides the options to create a new server farm or join an existing server farm. Depending on your selection, you will be asked for configuration information for a new server farm, or if you are joining an existing farm, you will be asked for the name of the farm, the type of connection, and the zone. Then chfarm:

- Installs the IMA service
- Starts the IMA service
- Reinitializes the license database

If all went as planned, your server should now either be a member of a new server farm or the first member of a new farm. There are, however, some caveats. As stated earlier, the chfarm utility must be used with caution, because it could corrupt your data store. Here are a few details you should know before using chfarm:

- Do not cancel the installation process—not even if you receive error messages while you're performing the IMA setup. Canceling the process leaves your server only partially installed and with no option to uninstall in Add/Remove Programs. If you do receive errors, you need to follow the procedures for recovering an unresponsive server given in the next section.

- Chfarm was intended for use on functioning servers only. Do not use chfarm on a server that has been removed from a server farm with either the CMC or chfarm.

- Remember to close any open CMC connections before beginning the process. If all connections are not closed, the connections will be dropped when the IMA service is stopped.

- If your server farm uses an Access database hosted on a member of the farm, run chfarm on that server only after all other members have been moved to the new farm. To properly execute, chfram requires connectivity to the farm's data store. If chfarm deletes the data store, the other servers will be rendered unresponsive.

- Chfarm does not migrate published application information or settings. You need to manually configure published applications.

Recovering an Unresponsive Server

An unresponsive server is one that does not respond to IMA requests. As stated previously, canceling the chfarm process or running chfarm on the server hosting the data store *before* moving the other servers to the new farm can leave you with unresponsive servers.

> **NOTE**
>
> This process is intended only for servers that have become unresponsive due to problems changing farm membership or as a last resort for servers experiencing IMA problems. For IMA service problems, Citrix recommends working through the troubleshooting process before attempting the recovery process. Once you've performed the recovery process, you cannot back out of it.

Once you have determined that the recovery process is your only option, begin the recovery process by following these steps:

1. Use the **rmvica** utility to completely uninstall MetaFrame from the unresponsive server. The syntax for rmvica is **rmvica /nods /u**. The parameters

prevent rmvica from attempting to contact the data store; the command performs an unattended uninstall that removes MetaFrame XP documentation and the CMC then restarts the server.

2. Use the **CMC** to remove the server from the farm. Right-click the server and select **Remove Farm**.

3. Reinstall MetaFrame and rejoin the farm.

If you don't correctly remove the server by first uninstalling MetaFrame, the server will still show up in the CMC and you will be unable to remove it by right-clicking and selecting Remove Farm. In order to remove the server, you must edit the host file found in **%systemroot%\winnt\system32\drivers\etc** and add an entry for the server. Once you've made and saved the entry, use the CMC to remove the server.

Configuring & Implementing...

Troubleshooting the IMA Service

Here are a few things to try if the IMA service fails to start and the issue is unrelated to using chfarm:

- Check the Registry. If the value for the HKLM/Software/Citrix/IMA/Runtime/CurrentlyLoadingPlugin Registry key is blank, either the local cache is missing or the IMA service could not connect to the data store.

- For direct connections, make sure that the ODBC connections to the database exist and are configured correctly.

- For indirect connections, make sure that the IMA service is running on the host server.

- Make sure that the Spooler service is run by System and not a user.

- If an error code of 2147583649 is reported on boot, the local system account temp directory could be missing. Try starting the service as the local administrator. If this works, check for the missing temp folder. Make sure that the server's environmental paths are correct for both Temp and Tmp files.

- If the IMA service fails to stop, check to see if the SMS NetMon2 client is installed on the server. If it is, uninstall it and attempt to stop the IMA service again. The SMS NetMon2 client is not supported on MetaFrame servers.

How should you plan your backup strategy? Ultimately, your strategy depends on your environment and its policies, but here are a few things to consider as you plan:

- Remember that it is not advisable to run Terminal Services and Citrix MetaFrame on a domain controller or to use the server as a file server.

- Create user home directories on separate file servers. Point all user personal files, such as My Documents, Favorites, Outlook .pst, custom dictionary files, and the like, to this location.

- Remember to back up your data store. Do not forget how important this database is to your server farm. If you're using an Access database, use **dsmaint backup**; if you're using an MS SQL or Oracle database, consult the database documentation.

- Create and store Resource Manager's data store on a file server that is backed up on a regular basis.

- Schedule regular and frequent backups of the file server using a combination of full and incremental or differential backups.

- Schedule regular and frequent backups of your domain controllers. Do not forget to back up the Registries and Active Directory.

- Evaluate enterprise storage solutions, hardware, software, and media. Become familiar with the technology so that you can be sure you have selected the right combination for your environment and capacity. Tape drives and tape media are the most commonly used, and there are many types and brands to choose from. Make sure the backup software you use has the ability to back up open files and the Registry and schedule automatic backups.

- Store your backup tapes offsite. Many vendors now offer this service as well as pickup and delivery of the tapes.

- Decide who will perform the backups and allow them appropriate permissions.

- If you have a large server farm, consider purchasing third-party solutions such as System Guardian. Not only can you clone your servers, provided that you have the same hardware, but these solutions provide redundancy. If the original disk set becomes corrupt, you can have the server back up and running on the mirror set within minutes as opposed to the hours it would take to restore your server from backups.

Recovery and Business Continuity

With so much of today's business dependent on computers, applications, and networks, it is no wonder that terms such as *high availability, disaster recovery,* and *business continuity* have become the catchphrases of the day. E-businesses cannot afford interruptions or downtime when they are competing against bricks-and-mortar companies, nor can traditional businesses afford to have their workforce disabled due to system outages. Fortunately, there are a number of ways you can ensure that your business will go on, even in the event of physical disaster such as fire that destroys a data center. The best plan for you and your environment depends on the size of your installation and the amount of funds available for disaster recovery processes.

Disaster recovery is a broad topic; it would be difficult to address all the options here, but we hope to give you some ideas and a head start on planning your own disaster recovery strategy. Let's begin on a small scale. What sort of things can be done relatively quickly and inexpensively to improve your chances of recovering from a disaster? Does the size of the disaster matter? If your users or customers are unable to access your servers and data, that constitutes as a disaster because it could cause loss of business and loss of income. Take a look around at your environment. Are there single points of failure? Redundancy is relatively easy to accomplish. Here are a few suggestions on how to create redundancy and provide disaster recovery in your environment:

- Configure your servers with redundant drives. As mentioned earlier, some third-party utilities make this fairly easy to accomplish. If that is not possible, there is always good old Microsoft disk mirroring. For servers that are not running Citrix MetaFrame or Terminal Services, you can also rely on RAID 5 and hot-swappable drives, although it doesn't hurt to have a backup set of imaged disks sitting on the shelf just in case.

- Keep current backups and store them offsite to protect your data.

- If you have the resources, configure a hot-swap server that can be placed in production if a key server fails or needs maintenance.

- Make sure that you have sufficient power to keep your servers running in the event of a power outage. Many uninterruptible power supplies (UPS) are available, and if your data center needs to be highly available and you can afford it, look into generators as well. Do not forget redundancy. If you have the resources and the need, have backup power supplies as well.

- Do not forget network redundancy. Unless your site is so small it does not need to communicate with the outside world, you might want to implement dual WAN links.

- Set up alerts to page administrative personnel in the event of power outages, air-conditioning problems, or other problems that could take down the system.

- Dual data centers are another option—again, if your data center size and needs warrant it and you have the resources. Create two data centers, each servicing 50 percent of your users on a regular basis and able to handle the other 50 percent in the event of a disaster. The alternative is to run only one data center and use the other as a "hot site."

- Outsourcing is another alternative. Many companies provide redundant data centers for their customers. This option could even save you money, because businesses that provide this service often share the building with several clients. They provide the security, electricity, redundant systems, liability insurance, and staff, and the costs are divided among the customers.

Business Continuity and Citrix MetaFrame XPe

Businesses that require high availability and have the financial resources to afford a redundant site should consider MetaFrame XPe to deliver applications and services to their users. MetaFrame XPe, as you might recall from earlier chapters, includes Citrix NFuse. NFuse is an application portal that provides for application publishing within Web pages. The applications can be accessed from any client as long as the client has a standard Web browser. If the client is used as a single point of access, applications can be run from multiple server farms, locations, and platforms. When NFuse is combined with a disaster recovery plan that includes a dual site, users can continue to access required applications from other offices, home, or anywhere else they can access a computer with a Web browser.

The numbers of alternatives for disaster recovery and redundant systems are growing. You should make the discussion of and planning part of the planning stage for a new data center or server farm and constantly reevaluate those that are already in service. Establishing regular checkpoints to discuss and evaluate your options is a good practice. Be on a constant lookout for those single points of failure, and implement redundancy whenever possible. Set up a testing schedule for your redundant equipment, UPS, generators, or other hardware. Review vendor service agreements, and make sure that you have the support level you need for critical systems. Do not forget the small but obvious: Document all adds, moves, and changes to your systems and provide physical security for them.

Summary

Some of the most important and most difficult aspects of systems administration include monitoring and troubleshooting. It is typically a skill learned (or earned) with time and experience. No one book can detail all the problems that might occur or all the situations you might find yourself in as an administrator. The best you can do is explore your resources, learn, and utilize all that you can. Not all ideas will appeal to you, and not all will be applicable to your environment. However, all are worthy of a trial run, a test to see what they can do for you. Have you ever thought of what tools you would want to have with you if you were shipwrecked on a deserted island? If you ended up with even a nail file, you might consider yourself lucky! There could be times in your career that having some of the basic tools and knowing how to use them will come in almost as handy. Which would you choose? What tools will be in your administrator's tool kit?

Event Viewer is a must-have. It is basic, simple, and easy to use. It can tell you if there are problems such as services that failed to start, or it can inform you that someone has been attempting to break into your network. It can even provide documentation and historical reference for your servers.

What about the System Information tool? It is an updated version of the old Microsoft MSD. It provides read-only information about your server and can also provide documentation. If you have multiple servers in your farm, this might be another tool you choose to keep because it can be used to quickly access information about each server in your farm.

Performance Monitor is a definite must-have. It is the best tool, bundled with Windows NT and 2000, to help you create your performance baseline. Since it is incorporated in the operating system, there is nothing more to install. You can begin monitoring your server using Performance Monitor immediately after installing the operating system. It can also be used when installing and testing new applications by providing information about resource usage.

Microsoft's Network Monitor, even though the "lite" version, is another valuable resource. Since it is provided free with Windows NT 4.0 and Windows 2000, why not use it? Even if there is a router or t-com person in your environment, you might want to do a little exploring on your own. It is always a good feeling to have uncovered the root of a problem, without needing to interrupt someone else. Learning how to use the lite version also gives you a head start on learning and growing adept at using the full-fledged version bundled with Microsoft SMS.

Citrix Network Manager is a great tool if you have or will be using HP OpenView or Tivoli NetView to manage your servers. Network Manager allows you to manage and monitor your Citrix MetaFrame XPe servers using the same network management tools you use for the rest of your servers.

Resource Manager builds on the functionality of Microsoft's Performance Monitor by adding components specific to server-based computing. Although it is not included with the base MetaFrame XP license, it is well worth the additional expense.

Backing up your servers and data is one of the most important tasks a network administrator performs. Simply creating and running server backups does not always protect your servers or your business. You must know what to back up and how to properly do it. This knowledge requires careful analysis of your environment—operating systems, databases, and applications. Get to know what steps you must take to create reliable backups and know how to restore them. Don't wait until a problem arises to learn how to handle the situation.

Creating and implementing a disaster recovery plan is essential if your business depends on a network, servers, and clients. Downtime, in most cases, equates to lost revenue. Research the methods available and implement those within your business budget. Test the implementation to make sure it works before disaster strikes! Document the process and make sure that all concerned parties are aware of their roles and what must be done.

Solutions Fast Track

Establishing Baseline Performance

- ☑ A performance baseline tells you the normal performance level for your server.

- ☑ Performance tests should be run before and after making changes to your system and the results documented and compared with the previous data.

- ☑ Run performance tests during peak times in your environment to discover the maximum workload on your servers.

Citrix Network Manager

- ☑ Citrix Network Manager works with third-party SNMP consoles to extend network management capabilities to MetaFrame XPe servers.

- ☑ Citrix Network Manager comes bundled with Citrix MetaFrame XPe only.

- ☑ Tivoli NetView 5.1.2 or later, HP OpenView Network Node Manager 6.1 or later, and SNMP are required to use Citrix Network Manager.

Network Monitor

- ☑ Network Monitor is packaged with the Windows 2000 Server family and is a "lite" version of the utility found in Microsoft SMS.

- ☑ Network Monitor is used to monitor network traffic and troubleshoot network events. It can help you discover if the problem is related to the server, a NIC, a router port, or a congested network.

- ☑ Network Monitor collects data by capturing packets off the network. The source and destination computer, protocol used, and portions of the data can be displayed.

Resource Manager

- ☑ Resource Manager comes bundled with Citrix MetaFrame XPe only.

- ☑ Resource Manager is a resource-monitoring utility created specifically for the server-based environment.

- ☑ Resource Manager provides a variety of reports that can be used to examine the data reported by your server or farm.

Backup and Recovery

- ☑ Backups are extremely important, especially where data is concerned. It is a good practice to perform regular backups on all your servers, including the Registry.

- ☑ Third-party utilities can create exact images of your Citrix MetaFrame servers. These images can be updated manually after changes have been made, or you can revert to a clean copy in the event of corruption.

- ☑ Running a full (or normal) backup on a regular basis and differential backups daily provides for the quickest restores.

- ☑ Use **dsmaint backup** to back up your Access data store and **dsmaint failover** to point the other servers in the farm to the new host server.

Frequently Asked Questions

The following Frequently Asked Questions, answered by the authors of this book, are designed to both measure your understanding of the concepts presented in this chapter and to assist you with real-life implementation of these concepts. To have your questions about this chapter answered by the author, browse to **www.syngress.com/solutions** and click on the **"Ask the Author"** form.

Q: What tools can I use to create a performance baseline for my Windows 2000/Citrix MetaFrame servers?

A: A variety of tools included with Windows 2000 and MetaFrame XPe that can provide the information needed to create a performance baseline. Performance Monitor is a good place to start. It is bundled with both Windows NT 4.0 and Windows 2000 and can be used soon after installing the OS. Citrix Resource Manager is another tool that was specifically designed for a server-based environment. It can provide about the system, applications, sessions, and users.

Q: I have noticed some error messages in my system's Event Viewer, but I have been unable to locate a Microsoft Knowledge Base article that pertains to it. How can I find the information I need without paying for a support call?

A: Try using the Microsoft newsgroups or Citrix User Forums. Most errors are not isolated to just one environment. If you are seeing an error or having problems with certain applications, you can bet others are experiencing problems as well. Someone might have already found the information you seek and could be willing to share it.

Q: I suspect that one of our users has been downloading MP3s while at work. I have not been able to catch him, but I have noticed that the server slows down noticeably when he comes on shift. Is there a way I can track down the culprit without bothering our t-com person?

A: Try using Network Monitor. It is not installed by default, so you might need to install it. Network Monitor can provide information on data frames traversing the network, the source computer, and the destination computer. If your guy is creating network traffic, you should be able to trace it with NetMon.

Q: We have purchased Citrix MetaFrame XPe, but when I attempt to install Citrix Network Manager, I am told that I do not have the required programs on my server. What am I lacking?

A: Citrix Network Manager works with third-party network management utilities to provide system management capabilities to Citrix MetaFrame XPe servers. This means that you can manage your Citrix MetaFrame XPe servers using the same network management programs you use to manage the other servers in your environment. Unfortunately, at this time, Citrix Network Manager works only with Tivoli NetView and HP OpenView. If you do not currently use one of these in your environment, you can't use Citrix Network Manager.

Q: My company is interested in finding an application that can monitor and produce reports on resource usage, application usage, and session and user count on our Citrix MetaFrame XPe servers. Is there a product on the market that provides these features?

A: Yes! Citrix Resource Monitor is bundled with Citrix MetaFrame XPe and provides the functionality you mention and more. With Citrix Resource Monitor, you can monitor your server or server farm, applications, users, and sessions.

Q: We are just beginning to think about disaster recovery and business continuation strategies. We have had a few discussions but cannot seem to locate a good starting place. Can you suggest one?

A: Yes. Take a look at your environment and note any single points of failure. If a critical server goes down, is there one to take over? What about power outages? Anyplace you can find a single point of failure is vulnerable and should be considered high risk.

Q: What type of events should I expect to see in my event logs under normal circumstances?

A: That depends on how your system is configured, the applications you are running, whether or not you have enabled security auditing, and if you have customized any of the Event Viewer settings. Typically, you will see information events that inform you of services loading, applications starting up, print jobs running, and the like.

Q: What if I do not want to see print job events in the event log?

A: Windows adds an information event in the application log every time a print job leaves the spooler. You can disable this function by making a change to the Registry. Be careful, however—the usual caveats apply. To disable this notation, change the **Dword** value to **0** as shown here:

```
[HKEY_LOCAL_MACHINE\SYSTEM\CurrnetControlSet\Control\Print\Providers]
Value Name: Event Log
```

```
Data Type: REG_DWORD (DWORD Value)
Value Data: (0 = disable)
```

Q: Can I set up Performance Monitor to run at a scheduled time, then save to a file?

A: Yes. To create a new schedule, from within **Performance Monitor Logs and Alerts**, right-click **Counter Logs** and select **New Log Settings**. Give your log a name, and click **OK**. This will bring up the log's Properties sheet. The Properties sheet has three tabs: General, Log Files, and Schedule. From the General tab, you can add the counters you want to monitor and provide an interval of time to sample. From Log Files, you can choose a location to save the log to, select the type of log file (binary, CSV, or TSV), and set the log file size limit. From Schedule, you can set the start and stop time and date and specify what to do once the log file closes—either start a new log file or run a command.

Q: Can a performance log graph be displayed in HTML format?

A: Yes. To save your graph as an HTML file, right-click your displayed graph and selected **Save As**. In the **Save As** dialog box, type the filename and path, then select the file type **Web Page (*.htm)** from the drop-down list.

Q: Is there a way to have the system notify me when a counter reaches a certain limit?

A: Yes. You can have the system notify you by creating a new alert in Performance Logs and Alerts. To create a new alert, right-click **Alerts** and select **New Alert Setting**. Provide a name for your alert and click **OK**. This opens up a Properties sheet with three tabs: General, Action, and Schedule. From the **General** tab, click **Add** to add the counters to monitor. Specify when to send the alert by selecting either **Under** or **Over** and a value for **Limit**, then set the sampling interval and unit of time. You can also provide an identifying comment on the General page. From the **Action** tab, select what you want to occur when the alert has been triggered. The choices are to log an event in the application event log, send a network message to a specific user account, start a performance log, or run a program. On the **Schedule** tab, set a time and date to start and stop scanning for the triggered alerts.

Q: What types of things can Resource Manager monitor?

A: Resource Manager can monitor hard disks, logical disks, processors, memory, network interfaces, Terminal Services, user sessions, application usage, pagefile usage, and the system.

Q: Why would you need to monitor specific applications?

A: Applications can be added to Resource Manager with a metric for Count enabled. You might do this if you were interested in tracking the number of instances of an application that are run on a regular basis. This might help justify keeping or replacing certain applications based on usage.

Q: What is the difference between Microsoft Performance Monitor and Citrix Resource Manager, and do I need both?

A: The major difference between Performance Monitor and Resource Manager is that Resource Manager provides tools to help you monitor Citrix MetaFrame XP servers that run 100 percent of the applications from the server and multiple instances of the applications. Performance Monitor does not incorporate those tools. Whether or not you use both is a personal decision.

Q: How many metrics can be monitored at one time?

A: Citrix recommends limiting the total number to less than 50.

Q: What does it mean when metrics are reported as negative numbers?

A: These values should be ignored.

Q: How do I back up my Access data store?

A: Use the **dsmaint backup** command. For SQL and Oracle databases, use the process recommended by the application.

Q: When I rebooted my server, I received an error message stating that the IMA service failed to start with an error code of 2147483649. What does this mean?

A: Typically, this means that the system account is missing its temp folder. Try starting the IMA service with the local administrator account. If that works, track down the missing temp folder and change the account back to system.

Q: While I was moving a MetaFrame server to a new server farm using the **chfarm command**, the process was interrupted and did not complete. Now the server is unresponsive. What should I do to repair the server?

A: You need to use the recovery process to join the server to the new server farm. This entails uninstalling MetaFrame using the **rmvica** utility, removing the server from the farm from the CMC, and then reinstalling MetaFrame.

Index

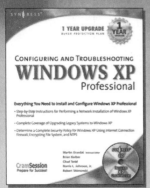